Statistics

SYSTAT® 7.0 for Windows®

For more information about SYSTAT® software products, please visit our WWW site at *http://www.spss.com* or contact

Marketing Department
SPSS Inc.
444 North Michigan Avenue
Chicago, IL 60611
Tel: (312) 329-2400
Fax: (312) 329-3668

SYSTAT is a registered trademark and the other product names are the trademarks of SPSS Inc. for its proprietary computer software. No material describing such software may be produced or distributed without the written permission of the owners of the trademark and license rights in the software and the copyrights in the published materials.

The SOFTWARE and documentation are provided with RESTRICTED RIGHTS. Use, duplication, or disclosure by the Government is subject to restrictions as set forth in subdivision (c)(1)(ii) of The Rights in Technical Data and Computer Software clause at 52.227-7013. Contractor/manufacturer is SPSS Inc., 444 N. Michigan Avenue, Chicago, IL, 60611.

General notice: Other product names mentioned herein are used for identification purposes only and may be trademarks of their respective companies.

ImageStream® Graphics & Presentation Filters, copyright © 1991-1997 by INSO Corporation. All Rights Reserved.

ImageStream Graphics Filters is a registered trademark and ImageStream is a trademark of INSO Corporation.

SYSTAT® 7.0: Statistics

Preface

Release 7.0 is the most comprehensive expansion of SYSTAT in its entire history. The core of this expansion is the incorporation of the supplements that used to be sold separately in DOS versions (LOGIT, PROBIT, SETCOR, SURVIVAL, TESTAT, SIGNAL, and TSLS). These modules were rewritten and adapted to a Windows environment, given *quick graphs*, and revised to be more consistent with the other SYSTAT modules. The other part of this expansion is a number of routines that I have been waiting until Release 7.0 to include in the main package (POSAC, TREES, CONJOINT, CORAN, and PERMAP). Like some of the other routines in earlier versions of SYSTAT, I wrote these for fun rather than for anticipated markets. These new procedures are documented in *SYSTAT: New Statistics.*

The other major development is the addition of bootstrapping to almost every SYSTAT module. We have implemented this capability with a one-pass algorithm that does not require extra data sets to be made. Bootstrapping and related computer-intensive methods are receiving a lot of attention among statisticians. For many technical reasons, bootstrapping has been late in coming to comprehensive statistics packages. I hope that its introduction in SYSTAT will make bootstrapping more widely available to researchers.

It is a huge step from writing a statistical or graphical routine to implementing it in its final form. These modules would never have appeared without the careful design, interface programming, editorial support, and general project management of the SYSTAT team and others at SPSS. I wrote in the preface to Release 6.0 that I was excited about the future of SYSTAT at SPSS. I never imagined, however, how much would happen in a year. SPSS has expanded enormously this last year and has created a scientific division to develop and market scientific products. This has given SYSTAT more resources and has created more excitement for all of us at SPSS.

Leland Wilkinson
Sr. Vice President, SYSTAT Products
SPSS Inc.

Contents

Contents

Contents

Contents

Contents

Contents

Contents

Contents

Introduction to Statistics

Leland Wilkinson

Statistics and *state* have the same root. Statistics are the numbers of the state. More generally, they are any numbers or symbols that formally summarize our observations of the world. As we all know, summaries can mislead or elucidate. Statistics also refers to the introductory course we all seem to hate in college. When taught well, however, it is this course that teaches us how to use numbers to elucidate rather than to mislead.

Statisticians specialize in many areas—probability, exploratory data analysis, modeling, social policy, decision making, and others. While they may philosophically disagree, statisticians nevertheless recognize at least two fundamental tasks: description and inference. Description involves characterizing a batch of data in simple but informative ways. Inference involves generalizing from a sample of data to a larger population of possible data. Descriptive statistics help us to observe more acutely, and inferential statistics help us to formulate and test hypotheses.

Any distinctions, such as this one between descriptive and inferential statistics, are potentially misleading. Let's look at some examples, however, to see some differences between these approaches.

Descriptive Statistics

Know your batch

Sum, mean, and standard deviation

Stem-and-leaf plots

The median

Sorting

Standardizing

Inferential Statistics

What is a population?

Picking a simple random sample

Specifying a model

Estimating a model

Confidence intervals

Hypothesis testing

Checking assumptions

Introduction to Statistics

Descriptive Statistics

Descriptive statistics may be single numerical summaries of a batch, such as an average. Or, they may be more complex tables and graphs. What distinguishes descriptive statistics is their reference to a given batch of data rather than to a more general population or class. While there are exceptions, we usually examine descriptive statistics to understand the structure of a batch. A closely related field is called exploratory data analysis. Both exploratory and descriptive methods may lead us to formulate laws or test hypotheses, but their focus is on the data at hand.

Consider, for example, the following batch. These are numbers of arrests by sex in 1985 for selected crimes in the United States. The source is the *FBI Uniform Crime Reports*. What can we say about differences between the patterns of arrests of men and women in the United States in 1985?

CRIME	MALES	FEMALES
murder	12904	1815
rape	28865	303
robbery	105401	8639
assault	211228	32926
burglary	326959	26753
larceny	744423	334053
auto	97835	10093
arson	13129	2003
battery	416735	75937
forgery	46286	23181
fraud	151773	111825
embezzle	5624	3184
vandal	181600	20192
weapons	134210	10970
vice	29584	67592
sex	74602	6108
drugs	562754	90038
gambling	21995	3879
family	35553	5086
dui	1208416	157131
drunk	726214	70573
disorderly	435198	99252
vagrancy	24592	3001
runaway	53808	72473

Know your batch

First, we must be careful in characterizing the batch. These statistics do not cover the gamut of U.S. crimes. We left out curfew and loitering violations, for example. Not all reported crimes are included in these statistics. Some false arrests may be included. State laws vary on the definitions of some of these crimes. Agencies may modify arrest statistics for political purposes. Know where your batch came from before you use it.

Sum, mean, and standard deviation

Were there more male than female arrests for these crimes in 1985? The following output shows us the answer. Males were arrested for 5,649,688 crimes (not 5,649,688 males—some may have been arrested more than once). Females were arrested 1,237,007 times.

```
                      MALES        FEMALES
N of cases               24             24
Minimum            5624.000        303.000
Maximum         1208416.000  334053.000
Sum             5649688.000 1237007.000
Mean             235403.667     51541.958
Standard Dev     305947.056     74220.864
```

How about the average (*mean*) number of arrests for a crime? For males, this was 235,403 and for females, 51,542. Does the mean make any sense to you as a summary statistic? Another statistic in the table, the *standard deviation,* measures how much these numbers vary around the average. The standard deviation is the square root of the average squared deviation of the observations from their mean. It, too, has problems in this instance. First of all, both the mean and standard deviation should represent what you could observe in your batch, on average: the mean number of fish in a pond, the mean number of children in a classroom, the mean number of red blood cells per cubic millimeter. Here, we would have to say, "the mean *murder-rape-robbery-...-runaway* type of crime." Second, even if the mean made sense descriptively, we might question its use as a typical crime-arrest statistic. To see why, we need to examine the shape of these numbers.

Stem-and-leaf plots

Let's look at a display that compresses these data a little less drastically. The stem-and-leaf plot is like a tally. We pick a most significant digit or digits and tally the next digit to the right. By using trailing digits instead of tally marks, we preserve extra digits in the data. You can read more about this display in *SYSTAT: Graphics,* but for now, notice the shape of notice the shape of the tally. There are mostly smaller numbers of arrests, and a few crimes (such as larceny and driving under the influence of alcohol) with larger numbers of arrests. Another way of saying this is that the data are *positively skewed* toward larger numbers for both males and females.

```
Stem and Leaf Plot of variable:        MALES, N = 24
      Minimum:        5624.000
      Lower hinge:      29224.500
      Median:       101618.000
      Upper hinge:     371847.000
      Maximum:    1208416.000

         0 H 011222234579
         1 M 0358
         2   1
         3 H 2
         4   13
         5   6
         6
         7   24
       * * * Outside Values * * *
            12   0

Stem and Leaf Plot of variable:        FEMALES, N = 24
      Minimum:         303.000
      Lower hinge:       4482.500
      Median:        21686.500
      Upper hinge:      74205.000
      Maximum:     334053.000

         0 H 00000000011
         0 M 2223
         0
         0 H 6777
         0   99
         1   1
         1
         1   5
       * * * Outside Values * * *
             3   3
```

The median

When data are skewed like this, the mean gets pulled from the center of the majority of numbers toward the extreme with the few. A statistic that is not as sensitive to extreme values is the *median*. The median is the value above which half the data fall. More precisely, if you sort the data, the median is the middle value or the average of the two middle values. Notice that for males the median is 101,618, and for females, 21,686. Both are considerably smaller than the means and more typical of the majority of the numbers. This is why the median is often used for representing skewed data, such as incomes, populations, or reaction times.

We still have the same representativeness problem that we had with the mean, however. Even if the medians corresponded to real data values in this batch (which they don't, since there is an even number of observations), it would be hard to characterize what they would represent.

Sorting   Most people think of means, standard deviations, and medians as the primary descriptive statistics. They are useful summary quantities when the observations represent values of a single variable. We purposely chose an example where they are less appropriate, however, even when they are easily computable. There are better ways to reveal the patterns in these data. Let's look at sorting as a way of uncovering structure.

I was talking once with an FBI agent who had helped to uncover the Chicago machine's voting fraud scandal some years ago. He was a statistician, so I was curious what statistical methods he used to prove the fraud. He replied, "We sorted the voter registration tape alphabetically by last name. Then we looked for duplicate names and addresses." Sorting is one of the most basic and powerful data analysis techniques. The stem-and-leaf plot, for example, is a sorted display.

We can sort on any numerical or character variable. It depends on our goal. We began this chapter with a question: are there differences between the patterns of arrests of men and women in the United States in 1985? How about sorting the male and female arrests separately? If we do this, we will get a list of crimes in order of decreasing frequency within sex.

MALES	FEMALES
dui	larceny
larceny	dui
drunk	fraud
drugs	disorderly
disorderly	drugs
battery	battery
burglary	runaway
assault	drunk
vandal	vice
fraud	assault
weapons	burglary
robbery	forgery
auto	vandal
sex	weapons
runaway	auto
forgery	robbery
family	sex
vice	family
rape	gambling
vagrancy	embezzle
gambling	vagrancy
arson	arson
murder	murder
embezzle	rape

You might want to connect similar crimes with lines. The number of crossings would indicate differences in ranks.

Standardizing

This ranking is influenced by prevalence. The most frequent crimes occur at the top of the list in both groups. Comparisons within crimes are obscured by this influence. Men committed almost 100 times as many rapes as women, for example, yet rape is near the bottom of both lists. If we are interested in contrasting the sexes on *patterns* of crime while holding prevalence constant, we must *standardize* the data. There are several ways to do this. You may have heard of standardized test scores for aptitude tests. These are usually produced by subtracting means and then dividing by standard deviations. Another method is simply to divide by row or column totals. For the crime data, we will divide by totals within rows (each crime). Doing so gives us the proportion of each arresting crime committed by men or women. The total of these two proportions will thus be 1.

Now, a contrast between men and women on this standardized value should reveal variations in arrest patterns within crime type. By subtracting the female proportion from the male, we will highlight primarily male crimes with positive values and female crimes with negative. Next, sort these differences and plot them in a simple graph. The result is shown below:

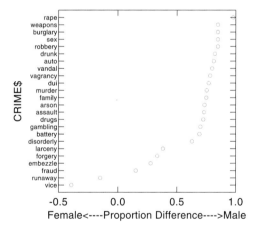

Now we can see clear contrasts between males and females in arrest patterns. The predominantly aggressive crimes appear at the top of the list. Rape now appears where it belongs—an aggressive, rather than sexual, crime. A few crimes dominated by females are at the bottom.

Inferential Statistics

We often want to do more than describe a particular sample. In order to generalize, formulate a policy, or test a *hypothesis*, we need to make an *inference*. Making an inference implies that we think a model describes a more general *population* from which our data have been randomly *sampled*. Sometimes it is difficult to imagine a population from which you have gathered data. A population can be "all possible voters," "all possible replications of this experiment," or "all possible moviegoers." When you make inferences, you should have a population in mind.

What is a population?

We are going to use inferential methods to estimate the mean age of the unusual population contained in the 1980 edition of *Who's Who in America*. We could enter all 73,500 ages into a SYSTAT file and compute the mean age exactly. If it were practical, this would be the preferred method. Sometimes, however, a sampling estimate can be more accurate than an entire census. For example, biases are introduced into large censuses from refusals to comply, keypunch or coding errors, and other sources. In these cases, a carefully constructed random sample can yield less-biased information about the population.

This an unusual population because it is contained in a book and is therefore finite. We are not about to estimate the mean age of the rich and famous. After all, *Spy* magazine used to have a regular feature listing all the famous people who are not in *Who's Who*. And bogus listings may escape the careful fact checking of the *Who's Who* research staff. When we get our estimate, we might be tempted to generalize beyond the book, but we would be wrong to do so. For example, if a psychologist measures opinions in a random sample from a class of college sophomores, her conclusions should begin with the statement, "College sophomores at my university think…" If the word "people" is substituted for "college sophomores," it is the experimenter's responsibility to make clear that the sample is representative of the larger group on all attributes that might affect the results.

Picking a simple random sample

That our population is finite should cause us no problems as long as our sample is much smaller than the population. Otherwise, we would have to use special techniques to adjust for the bias it would cause. How do we choose a *simple random sample* from a population? We use a method that ensures that every possible sample of a given size has an equal chance of being chosen. The following methods are *not* random:

– Pick the first name on every tenth page (some names have no chance of being chosen).
– Close your eyes, flip the pages of the book, and point to a name (Tversky and others have done research that shows that humans cannot behave randomly).

– Randomly pick the first letter of the last name and randomly choose from the names beginning with that letter (there are more names beginning with C, for example, than with I).

The way to pick randomly from a book, file, or any finite population, is to assign a number to each name or case and then pick a sample of numbers randomly. You can use SYSTAT to generate a random number between 1 and 73,500, for example, with the expression:

```
1 + INT(73500*URN)
```

There are too many pages in *Who's Who* to use this method, however. As a short cut, I randomly generated a page number and picked a name from the page using the random number generator. This method should work well provided that each page has approximately the same number of names (between 19 and 21 in this case). The sample is shown below:

AGE	SEX
60	male
74	male
39	female
78	male
66	male
63	male
45	male
56	male
65	male
51	male
52	male
59	male
67	male
48	male
36	female
34	female
68	male

AGE	SEX
50	male
51	male
47	male
81	male
56	male
49	male
58	male
58	male
38	female
44	male
49	male
62	male
76	female
51	male
51	male
75	male
65	female
41	male
67	male
50	male
55	male
45	male
49	male
58	male
47	male
55	male
67	male
58	male
76	male
70	male
69	male
46	male
60	male

Specifying a model

To make an inference about age, we need to construct a model for our population:

$$a = \mu + \varepsilon$$

This model says that the age (a) of someone we pick from the book can be described by an overall mean age (μ) plus an amount of error (ε) specific to that person and due to random factors that are too numerous and insignificant to describe systematically. Notice that we use Greek letters to denote things that we cannot observe directly and Roman letters for those that we do observe. Of the unobservables in the model, μ is called a parameter, and ε, a random variable. A parameter is a constant that helps to describe a population. Parameters indicate how a model is an instance of a family of models for similar populations. A random variable varies like the tossing of a coin.

There are two more parameters associated with the random variable ε but not appearing in the model equation. One is its mean (μ_ε), which we have rigged to be 0, and the other is its standard deviation (σ_ε or simply σ). Because a is simply the sum of μ (a constant) and ε (a random variable), its standard deviation is also σ.

In specifying this model, we assume the following:

- The model is true for every member of the population.
- The error, plus or minus, that helps determine one population member's age is independent of (not predictable from) the error for other members.
- The errors in predicting all the ages come from the same random distribution with a mean of 0 and a standard deviation of σ.

Estimating a model

Because we have not sampled the entire population, we cannot compute the parameter values directly from the data. We have only a small sample from a much larger population, so we can estimate the parameter values only by using some statistical method on our sample data. When our three assumptions are appropriate, the sample mean will be a good estimate of the population mean. Without going into all the details, the sample estimate will be, on average, close to the values of the mean in the population.

We can use various methods in SYSTAT to estimate the mean. One way is to specify our model using **Linear Regression**. Select *AGE* and add it to the **Dependent** list. With commands:

```
REGRESSION
MODEL AGE=CONSTANT
```

This model says that *AGE* is a function of a constant value (μ). The rest is error (ε). Another method is to compute the mean from the **Basic Statistics** routines. The result is shown below:

```
                     AGE
N OF CASES            50
MEAN              56.700
STANDARD DEV      11.620
STD. ERROR         1.643
```

Our best estimate of the mean age of people in *Who's Who* is 56.7 years.

Confidence intervals

Our estimate seems reasonable, but it is not exactly correct. If we took more samples of size 50 and computed estimates, how much would we expect them to vary? First, it should be plain without any mathematics to see that the larger our sample, the closer will be our sample estimate to the true value of μ in the population. After all, if we could sample the entire population, the estimates would be the true values. Even so, the variation in sample estimates is a function only of the sample size and the variation of the ages in the population. It does not depend on the size of the population (number of people in the book). Specifically, the standard deviation of the sample mean is the standard deviation of the population divided by the *square root* of the sample size. This *standard error of the mean* is listed on the output above as 1.643. On average, we would expect our sample estimates of the mean age to vary by plus or minus a little more than one and a half years, assuming samples of size 50.

If we knew the *shape* of the sampling distribution of mean age, we would be able to complete our description of the accuracy of our estimate. There is an approximation that works quite well, however. If the sample size is reasonably large (say, greater than 25), then the mean of a simple random sample is approximately *normally distributed*. This is true even if the population distribution is not normal, provided the sample size is large.

We now have enough information from our sample to construct a normal approximation of the distribution of our sample mean. The following figure shows this approximation to be centered at the sample estimate of 56.7 years. Its standard deviation is taken from the standard error of the mean, 1.643 years.

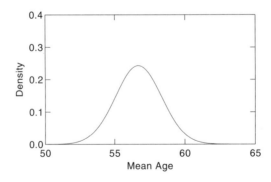

We have drawn the graph so that the central area comprises 95% of all the area under the curve (from about 53.4 to 59). From this normal approximation, we have built a 95% symmetric confidence interval that gives us a specific idea of the variability of our estimate. If we did this entire procedure again—sample 50 names, compute the mean and its standard error, and construct a 95% confidence interval using the normal approximation—then we would expect that 95 intervals out of a hundred so constructed would cover the real population mean age. Remember, population mean age is not necessarily at the center of the interval that we just constructed, but we do expect the interval to be close to it.

Hypothesis testing

From the sample mean and its standard error, we can also construct *hypothesis tests* on the mean. Suppose that someone believed that the average age of those listed in *Who's Who* is 61 years. After all, we might have picked an unusual sample just through the luck of the draw. Let's say, for argument, that the population mean age *is* 61 and the standard deviation is 11.62. How likely would it be to find a sample mean age of 56.7? If it is very unlikely, then we would reject this *null hypothesis* that the population mean is 61. Otherwise, we would fail to reject it.

There are several ways to represent an alternative hypothesis against this null hypothesis. We could make a *simple alternative* value of 56.7 years. Usually, however, we make the alternative *composite*—that is, it represents a range of possibilities that do not include the value 61. Here is how it would look:

H_0: $\mu = 61$ (null hypothesis)

H_A: $\mu \neq 61$ (alternative hypothesis)

We would reject the null hypothesis if our sample value for the mean were outside of a set of values that a population value of 61 could plausibly generate. In this context, "plausible" means more probable than a conventionally agreed upon *critical level* for our test. This value is usually 0.05. A result that would be expected to occur fewer than five times in a hundred samples is considered significant and would be a basis for rejecting our null hypothesis.

Constructing this hypothesis test is mathematically equivalent to sliding the normal distribution in the above figure to center over 61. We then look at the sample value 56.7 to see if it is outside of the shaded area. If so, we reject the null hypothesis. The following *t* test output shows a *p* value (probability) of 0.012 for this test. Because this value is lower than

0.05, we would reject the null hypothesis that the mean age is 61. This is equivalent to saying that the value of 61 does not appear in the 95% confidence interval.

```
One-sample t test of AGE with 50 cases;   Ho: Mean =      61.000

     Mean =        56.700           95.00% CI  =     53.398 to     60.002
     SD  =         11.620                                t =        -2.590
                                     DF  =     49   Prob =            0.013
```

The mathematical duality between confidence intervals and hypothesis testing may lead you to wonder which is more useful. The answer is that it depends on the context. Scientific journals usually follow a hypothesis testing model because their null hypothesis value for an experiment is usually 0 and the scientist is attempting to reject the hypothesis that nothing happened in the experiment. Any rejection is usually taken to be interesting, even when the sample size is so large that even tiny differences from 0 will be detected.

Those involved in making decisions—epidemiologists, business people, engineers—are often more interested in confidence intervals. They focus on the size and credibility of an effect and care less whether it can be distinguished from 0. Some statisticians, called Bayesians, go a step further and consider statistical decisions as a form of betting. They use sample information to modify prior hypotheses. See Box and Tiao (1973) or Berger (1985) for further information on Bayesian statistics.

Checking assumptions

Now that we have finished our analyses, we should check some of the assumptions we made in doing them. First, we should examine whether the data look normally distributed. Although sample means will tend to be normally distributed even when the population isn't, it helps to have a normally distributed population, especially when we do not know the population standard deviation. The stem-and-leaf plot gives us a quick idea:

```
          Stem and leaf plot of variable:     AGE    , N =    50

Minimum:            34.000
Lower hinge:        49.000
Median:             56.000
Upper hinge:        66.000
Maximum:            81.000

                3    4
                3    689
                4    14
                4  H 556778999
                5    0011112
                5  M 556688889
                6    0023
                6  H 55677789
                7    04
                7    5668
                8    1
```

There is another plot, called a dot histogram (dit) plot which looks like a stem-and-leaf plot. We can use different symbols to denote males and females in this plot, however, to see if there are differences in these subgroups. Although there are not enough females in the sample to be sure of a difference, it is nevertheless a good idea to examine it. The dot histogram reveals four of the six females to be younger than everyone else.

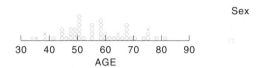

A better test of normality is to plot the sorted age values against the corresponding values of a mathematical normal distribution. This is called a *normal probability plot*. If the data are normally distributed, then the plotted values should fall approximately on a straight line. Our data plot fairly straight. Again, different symbols are used for the males and females. The four young females appear in the bottom left corner of the plot.

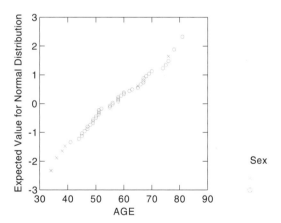

Does this possible difference in ages by gender invalidate our results? No, but it suggests that we might want to examine the gender differences further to see whether or not they are significant.

References

Berger, J.O. 1985. *Statistical decision theory and Bayesian analysis.* 2nd ed. New York: Springer Verlag.

Box, G.E.P., and Tiao, G.C. 1973. *Bayesian inference in statistical analysis.* Reading, Mass.: Addison-Wesley.

Making Frequency Tables

Leland Wilkinson and Laszlo Engelman

When variables are categorical, frequency tables (crosstabulations) provide useful summaries. For a report, you may need only the number or percentage of cases falling in specified categories or cross-classifications. At times, you may require a test of independence or a measure of association between two categorical variables. Or, you may want to model relationships among two or more categorical variables by fitting a loglinear model to the cell frequencies. This chapter concentrates on the first task, describing how to use **Crosstabs** and **Loglinear Model** to form one-way, two-way, and multiway tables. Tests and measures for two-way tables are discussed in Chapter 3, and loglinear models are discussed in Chapter 15.

Both **Crosstabs** and **Loglinear Model** can make, analyze, and save frequency tables that are formed by categorical variables (or table factors). The values of the factors can be character or numeric. Both procedures form tables using data read from a cases-by-variables rectangular file or data recorded as frequencies (for example, from a table in a report) with cell indices. In **Crosstabs**, you can request percentages of row totals, column totals, or the total sample size.

Making Frequency Tables

Overview

One-way and Two-way Tables

Multiway Tables

Summary

Overview

There are many formats for displaying tabular data. This chapter examines layouts for counts and percentages and also describes how to save tables as frequencies with cell indices.

Crosstabs on the **Stats** menu provides:

One-way	Frequency counts, percentages, tests, etc., for single table factors or categorical variables
Two-way	Frequency counts, percentages, tests, etc., for the crosstabulation of two factors
Multiway	Frequency counts and percentages for series of two-way tables stratified by all combinations of values of a third, fourth, and so on, table factor

Loglinear Model provides TABULATE for forming two-way and multiway tables.

Organizing your data

There are two ways to organize data for tables:

— The usual cases-by-variables rectangular data file
— Cell counts with cell identifiers

For example, you may want to analyze the following table about applicants to business schools:

		Status	
		admit	deny
Sex	male	420	90
	female	150	25

Following are two ways that the data might look for the cases-by-variables method:

PERSON	SEX$	STATUS$	...
1	female	admit	...
2	male	deny	
3	male	admit	
⋮			
684	female	deny	
685	male	admit	

PERSON	SEX	STATUS	...
1	2	1	...
2	1	2	
3	1	1	
⋮			
684	2	2	
685	1	1	

In the table on the left, the categories are identified by characters; in the table on the right, the categories are identified by numbers.

Instead of entering one case for each of the 685 applicants, you could use the second method to enter four cases:

SEX$	STATUS$	COUNT
male	admit	420
male	deny	90
female	admit	150
female	deny	25

For this method, the cell counts in the third column are identified by selecting **Data⟶Frequency**. With commands:

```
FREQUENCY = count
```

Getting started

For one-way tables, use **Stats⟶Crosstabs⟶One-way**:

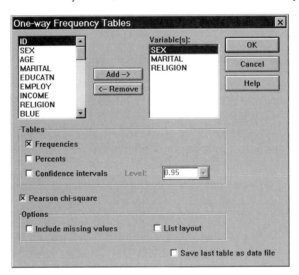

For two-way tables, use **Stats**➡**Crosstabs**➡**Two-way**:

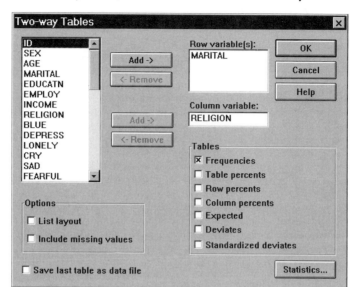

For a multiway table (a series of two-way tables stratified by one or more factors), use **Stats**➡**Crosstabs**➡**Multiway**:

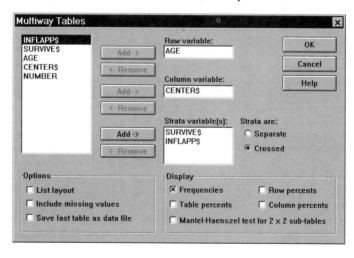

To form a table in **Loglinear Model**, use **Stats➧Loglinear Model**, and type the following:

```
LOGLIN
  USE filename
  TABULATE var1 * var2 * … * rowvar * colvar
```

Then click **OK.**

Using commands

For one-way tables in XTAB, specify:

```
XTAB
  USE filename
  PRINT / options
  TABULATE varlist / options
```

For two-way tables, specify:

```
XTAB
  USE filename
  PRINT / options
  TABULATE rowvar * colvar / options
```

For multiway tables, specify:

```
XTAB
  USE filename
  PRINT / options
  TABULATE varlist * rowvar * colvar / options
```

To form a table in LOGLIN, specify:

```
LOGLIN
  USE filename
  TABULATE var1 * var2 * … * rowvar * colvar
```

One-way and Two-way Tables

Crosstabs prints one-way, two-way, and multiway tables. For each, there is a standard layout and a **List layout**.

This section presents five examples. Even if one of the later examples parallels your problem, you may want to scan the earlier examples for options and features that apply.

2.1 One-way tables

This example uses questionnaire data from a community survey (Afifi and Clark, 1984). The *SURVEY2* data file includes a record (case) for each of the 256 subjects in the sample. Use **Stats**➧**Crosstabs**➧**One-way** to request frequencies for gender, marital status, and religion. The values of these variables are numbers, so use **Data**➧**Label** to add character identifiers for the categories. If the words *male* and *female* were stored in the variable *SEX$*, you would omit **Label** and tabulate *SEX$* directly. If you omit **Label** and specify *SEX*, the numbers would label the output.

```
XTAB
    USE survey2
    LABEL sex       / 1='Male',  2='Female'
    LABEL marital   / 1='Never', 2='Married',
                      3='Divorced', 4='Separated'
    LABEL religion  / 1='Protestant', 2='Catholic',
                      3='Jewish', 4='None', 6='Other'
    TABULATE sex marital religion
```

> ***Note:*** *When using the **Label** dialog box, you can omit quotes around category names. With commands, you can omit them if the name has no embedded blanks or symbols (the name, however, is displayed in capital letters).*

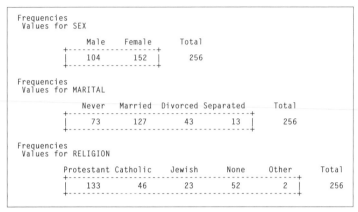

```
Frequencies
  Values for SEX

                Male    Female      Total
        +--------------------+
        |    104      152    |        256
        +--------------------+

Frequencies
  Values for MARITAL

              Never   Married  Divorced Separated      Total
        +-------------------------------------+
        |     73       127        43       13 |        256
        +-------------------------------------+

Frequencies
  Values for RELIGION

        Protestant Catholic   Jewish     None     Other    Total
        +------------------------------------------------+
        |    133        46       23       52        2 |     256
        +------------------------------------------------+
```

In this sample of 256 subjects, 152 are females, 127 are married, and 133 are Protestants. We deleted portions of the output that report chi-square statistics for testing the equality of cell counts. If you want your output to appear as shown, enter the command

```
PRINT NONE / FREQ
```

before the **TABULATE** command.

List layout

Selecting **List layout** produces an alternative layout for the same information. Percentages and cumulative percentages are part of the display.

```
PRINT NONE / LIST
TABULATE sex marital religion
PRINT
```

```
           Cum           Cum
  Count   Count   Pct    Pct SEX
    104     104  40.6   40.6 Male
    152     256  59.4  100.0 Female

           Cum           Cum
  Count   Count   Pct    Pct MARITAL
     73      73  28.5   28.5 Never
    127     200  49.6   78.1 Married
     43     243  16.8   94.9 Divorced
     13     256   5.1  100.0 Separated

           Cum           Cum
  Count   Count   Pct    Pct RELIGION
    133     133  52.0   52.0 Protestant
     46     179  18.0   69.9 Catholic
     23     202   9.0   78.9 Jewish
     52     254  20.3   99.2 None
      2     256    .8  100.0 Other
```

Almost 60% (59.4) are female, approximately 50% (49.6) are married, and more than half (52%) are Protestants. **List layout** is discussed in more detail in Chapter 4. You can also use TABULATE *varlist*/ LIST as an alternative to PRINT NONE / LIST.

2.2 Two-way tables

This example continues with the data from the last example, using **Stats**➠**Crosstabs**➠**Two-way** to crosstabulate marital status against religion.

```
XTAB
    USE survey2
    LABEL marital  / 1='Never', 2='Married',
                     3='Divorced', 4='Separated'
    LABEL religion / 1='Protestant', 2='Catholic',
                     3='Jewish', 4='None', 6='Other'
    TABULATE marital * religion
```

❶ Frequencies
   MARITAL (rows) by RELIGION (columns)

	Protestant	Catholic	Jewish	None	Other	Total
Never	29	16	8	20	0	73
Married	75	21	11	19	1	127
Divorced	21	6	3	13	0	43
Separate	8	3	1	0	1	13
Total	133	46	23	52	2	256

❷ WARNING: More than one-fifth of fitted cells are sparse (frequency < 5).
   The following significance tests are suspect.

Test statistic	Value	DF	Prob
Pearson Chi-square	22.718	12.000	0.030

The highlighted numbers below correspond to those in the output:

❶ In the sample of 256 people, 73 never married. Of the people that have never married, 29 are Protestants (the cell in the upper left corner), and none are in the *Other* category (their religion is not among the first four categories). The *Totals* (or marginals) along the bottom row and down the far right column are the same values displayed for one-way tables above.

❷ By default, **Crosstabs** prints the *Pearson chi-square* statistic for testing the independence of marital status and religious preference. To omit this information, specify

```
PRINT NONE / FREQ
```

before requesting tables. You will be warned that the expected values are too small to believe the probabilities printed with the statistic. Tests for two-way tables are discussed in Chapter 3.

Omitting sparse categories

There are only two counts in the last column, and the counts in the last row are fairly sparse. It is easy to omit rows and/or columns. You can:

- Omit the category codes from the **Data➠Label** request

  or

- Use **Data➠Select cases** to indicate which cases to use

Note that **Label** and **Select cases** remain in effect until you turn them off. If you request several different tables, use **Select cases** to ensure that the same cases are used in all tables. The subset of cases selected via **Label** applies only to those tables that use the variables specified with **Label**. To turn off the **Label** specification for *RELIGION*, for example, specify:

```
LABEL religion
```

We continue from the last table, eliminating the last category codes for *MARTIAL* and *RELIGION*:

```
SELECT marital <> 4 AND religion <> 6
TABULATE marital * religion
SELECT
```

With commands, remember that you can press the F9 key to retrieve previous commands and edit them.

```
           Protestant  Catholic   Jewish     None     Total
          +-------------------------------------------+
Never     |     29        16         8         20     |     73
Married   |     75        21        11         19     |    126
Divorced  |     21         6         3         13     |     43
          +-------------------------------------------+
Total           125        43        22         52         242

Test statistic                        Value         DF         Prob
   Pearson Chi-square                 10.368      6.000        0.110
```

A LOGLIN table

LOGLIN displays the same table as shown below. Note that you can exclude the sparse categories by omitting them from the LABEL specification.

```
LOGLIN
    USE survey2
    LABEL marital  / 1='Never', 2='Married',
                     3='Divorced'
    LABEL religion / 1='Protestant', 2='Catholic',
                     3='Jewish', 4='None'
    TABULATE marital * religion
```

```
Number of cells (product of levels):   12
                        Total count:  242

Observed Frequencies
====================

MARITAL    |              RELIGION
           | Protestant  Catholic   Jewish      None
-----------+---------------------------------------------
Never      |        29        16        8          20
Married    |        75        21       11          19
Divorced   |        21         6        3          13
-----------+---------------------------------------------
```

List layout

The **List layout** specification introduced in Example 2.1 is also available for two-way and multiway tables in **Crosstabs**. Following is the panel for marital status crossed with religious preference:

```
XTAB
    USE survey2
    LABEL marital  / 1='Never', 2='Married',
                     3='Divorced'
    LABEL religion / 1='Protestant', 2='Catholic',
                     3='Jewish', 4='None'

    PRINT NONE / LIST
    TABULATE marital * religion
    PRINT
```

```
           Cum           Cum
  Count   Count   Pct    Pct  MARITAL    RELIGION
     29      29  12.0   12.0  Never      Protestant
     16      45   6.6   18.6  Never      Catholic
      8      53   3.3   21.9  Never      Jewish
     20      73   8.3   30.2  Never      None
     75     148  31.0   61.2  Married    Protestant
     21     169   8.7   69.8  Married    Catholic
     11     180   4.5   74.4  Married    Jewish
     19     199   7.9   82.2  Married    None
     21     220   8.7   90.9  Divorced   Protestant
      6     226   2.5   93.4  Divorced   Catholic
      3     229   1.2   94.6  Divorced   Jewish
     13     242   5.4  100.0  Divorced   None
```

After requesting the table, you can specify PRINT without an argument to return to the default mode for PRINT. Alternatively, you can use TABULATE ... / LIST.

2.3
Inputting
cell
frequencies

Crosstabs, like other SYSTAT procedures, reads cases-by-variables data from a SYSTAT file. However, if you want to analyze a table from a report or a journal article, you can enter the cell counts directly. This example uses counts from a four-way table of a breast cancer study of 764 women. The data are from Morrison et al. (1973), cited in Bishop, Fienberg, and Holland (1975). There is one record for each of the 72 cells in the table, with the count (*NUMBER*) of women in the cell and codes or category names to identify their age group (under 50, 50 to 69, and 70 or over), treatment center (Tokyo, Boston, or Glamorgan), survival status (dead, alive), and tumor diagnosis (minimal inflammation and benign, maximum inflammation and benign, minimal inflammation and malignant, maximum inflammation and malignant). For the full table, see Example 2.6 and Example 2.7. This example illustrates how to form a two-way table of *AGE* by *CENTER$*.

To read a file containing counts with a cell identifier, use
Data➧Frequency to identify the variable containing the cell counts.

```
XTAB
    USE cancer
    FREQ = number
    LABEL age / 50='Under 50', 60='50 to 69',
                70='70 & Over'
    TABULATE center$ * age
```

```
Frequencies
  CENTER$ (rows) by AGE (columns)

             Under 50   50 to 69  70 & Over      Total
           +-----------------------------------+
   Boston  |     58        122         73       |    253
           |                                    |
   Glamorgn|     71        109         41       |    221
           |                                    |
   Tokyo   |    151        120         19       |    290
           +-----------------------------------+
   Total        280        351        133           764

  Test statistic                      Value        DF       Prob
    Pearson Chi-square                74.039     4.000      0.000
```

Of the 764 women studied, 290 were treated in Tokyo, 151 were in the youngest age group, and 19 were in the 70 or over age group.

A two-way
LOGLIN
table

LOGLIN displays the same table as shown below:

```
LOGLIN
    USE cancer
    FREQ = number
    LABEL age / 50='Under 50', 60='50 to 69',
                70='70 & Over'
    TABULATE center$ * age
```

```
Number of cells (product of levels):    9
                       Total count:   764

Observed Frequencies
====================
CENTER$            AGE
          | Under 50    50 to 69    70 & Over
----------+----------------------------------
Boston    |       58         122           73
Glamorgn  |       71         109           41
Tokyo     |      151         120           19
----------+----------------------------------
```

Extended results for Crosstabs

Crosstabs provides three modes, or categories, of output: **Short**, **Medium**, and **Long**. Each has statistics or features associated with it. Use **Edit⟶Options** to specify the mode (see **Length** under **Output Results**). With commands, SHORT, MEDIUM, LONG, and NONE are arguments of the PRINT command.

Short is assumed unless you already specified a different category in the current run. For **Short**, **Crosstabs** prints the frequency table and the Pearson chi-square statistic (see Example 2.2).

```
PRINT SHORT / FREQ  CHISQ
```

To omit the chi-square statistic, specify:

```
PRINT NONE / FREQ
```

This mode remains in effect until you change it or quit.

By specifying **Medium**, you get the frequencies and statistics provided by **Short** and, for a two-way table, all of the statistics applicable to the table. With **Long**, you get the statistics listed for **Short** and **Medium** and other statistics appropriate for assessing test results.

List
layout

With commands, the alternative **List layout** in Example 2.1 and Example 2.2 is requested as follows:

```
PRINT argument / LIST
```

Percentages

It is often helpful to view tabulated data as proportions of a total rather than as raw frequencies. **Crosstabs** provides three options for percentages:

Table percents   Replace each cell frequency with its percentage of the total table count

Row percents   Replace each cell frequency with its percentage of the row total

Column percents   Replace each cell frequency with its percentage of the column total

See Example 2.5 and Example 2.7.

Defining, labeling, and ordering categories

In your data, values of category codes can be numbers or characters. Use **Data**➠**Label** to select codes, reorder codes, group codes, and/or label your output. For example, if data values are as follows:

MARITAL   1, 2, 3, 4

EDUCATN   1, 2, 3, 4, 5, 6, 7

GNP$ D, U, and a blank for missing

TUMOR$ MaxMalig, MinBengn, MinMalig, MaxBengn

valid specifications are:

```
LABEL marital / 1=Never, 2=Married,
                3=Divorced, 4=Separated
LABEL marital / 2=Married, 3=Divorced, 1=Never

LABEL educatn / 1,2='Dropout', 3='HS grad',
                4,5='College', 6,7='Degree +'

LABEL gnp$    / 'D'=Developed, 'U'=Emerging
LABEL gnp$    / ' '=Missing, 'D'=Developed,
                'U'=Emerging
```

In the second **Label** specification for *MARITAL*, we have deleted the separated people and reordered the categories. For *EDUCATN*, we grouped the seven data values into four categories. In the second request for *GNP$*, we added a category for missing codes.

Note: *When using the **Label** dialog box, you can omit quotes around category names. With commands, you can omit them if the name has no embedded blanks or symbols (the name, however, is displayed in capital letters).*

Ordering categories

SYSTAT automatically sorts the categories of each table factor:

 – Numerically for numeric variables
 – Alphanumerically for string variables

You can use **Data⟶Label** to reorder categories, as shown above for *MARITAL*, or you can use **Data⟶Order**. If you want categories to be listed in the same order as they first appear in the data file, specify, for example,

```
ORDER center$ tumor$ / SORT=NONE
```

To list them in a specific order, specify:

```
ORDER tumor$ / SORT='MinBengn', 'MaxBengn',
                     'MinMalig', 'MaxMalig'
```

To list categories alphabetically in ascending or descending order, specify:

```
SORT=ASC or SORT=DESC
```

Defining intervals

Sometimes, to form categories, you may need to define intervals along a continuous variable. For example, if *AGE* is a numeric variable in your data, specify

```
LABEL age /    .. 12=child, 13 .. 19=teen,
                     20 ..    =adult
```

to group the subjects into three age groups. Alternatively, use **Data⟶Transform⟶Let**. Under **Function Types**, choose **Groups and Intervals**. Use the **Cut** function to form a new variable named, for example, *AGEGROUP* with values 1, 2, and 3 and then use **Data⟶Label** to name the categories. With commands:

```
LET agegroup = CUT(age, 12, 19)
LABEL agegroup / 1=child, 2=teen, 3=adult
```

That is, the value of *AGEGROUP* for every subject of age 12 or less is 1, the value for anyone of age 12.00001 through 19 is 2, and the value for anyone older than 19.0 is 3.

2.4 Missing category codes

You can choose whether or not to include a separate category for missing codes. For example, if some subjects did not check "male" or "female" on a form, there would be three categories for *SEX$*: male, female, and blank (missing). By default, when values of a table factor are missing, SYSTAT does not include a category for missing.

To include an additional category for the missing codes, use the **Include missing values** option on the **One-way**, **Two-way**, or **Multiway** dialog boxes; use the **Missing values** option from **Data➠Order**; or add a blank code for SYSTAT's code for missing character data (' ') or a period for missing numeric values.

```
LABEL sex /   .=Missing, 1=Male, 2=Female
LABEL sex$ / ' '=Missing, M=Male, F=Female
```

In the *OURWORLD* data file, some countries did not report the GNP to the United Nations. In this example, we selected **Include missing values** from **Stats➠Crosstabs➠Two-way** for a table that crosstabulates *GNP$* with *GROUP$*, and we followed this request with a **Data➠Label** statement that omits the category for missing.

```
XTAB
    USE ourworld
    TABULATE group$ * gnp$ / MISS

    LABEL gnp$ / 'D'='Developed', 'U'='Emerging'
    TABULATE group$ * gnp$
```

```
Frequencies
  GROUP$ (rows) by GNP$ (columns)

                      D       U    Total
          +-----------------------+
Europe    |    3      17      0   |   20
Islamic   |    2       4     10   |   16
NewWorld  |    1      15      5   |   21
          +-----------------------+
Total          6      36     15       57
```

```
Frequencies
  GROUP$ (rows) by GNP$ (columns)

              Developed  Emerging    Total
          +-----------------------+
Europe    |     17         0      |    17
Islamic   |      4        10      |    14
NewWorld  |     15         5      |    20
          +-----------------------+
Total           36        15           51
```

List layout

List layout displays the same data as shown below:

```
PRINT / LIST
TAB group$ * gnp$
PRINT
```

```
            Cum         Cum
   Count   Count   Pct   Pct GROUP$      GNP$
      17      17  33.3  33.3 Europe      Developed
       4      21   7.8  41.2 Islamic     Developed
      10      31  19.6  60.8 Islamic     Emerging
      15      46  29.4  90.2 NewWorld    Developed
       5      51   9.8 100.0 NewWorld    Emerging
```

Note that there is no entry for the empty cell.

2.5 Percentages

Percentages are helpful for describing categorical variables and interpreting relations between table factors. **Crosstabs** prints tables of percentages in the same layout as described for frequency counts. That is, each frequency count is replaced by the percentage. The percentages are:

- The total frequency in its row
- The total frequency in its column
- The total table frequency (or sample size)

To request one or more of these percentages, use **Stats⇒Crosstabs⇒ Two-way** and select **Row percents, Column percents**, and/or **Table percents**. With commands, insert PRINT before TABULATE:

```
PRINT argument / ROWP COLP PERC
```

Here we request these percentages for the second table in Example 2.4:

```
XTAB
    USE ourworld
    LABEL gnp$ / 'D'='Developed', 'U'='Emerging'
    PRINT NONE / ROWP  COLP  PERCENT
    TAB group$ * gnp$
```

```
Percents of total count
  GROUP$ (rows) by GNP$ (columns)

           Developed  Emerging      Total       N
          +--------------------+
  Europe  |   33.33       .00  |    33.33      17
  Islamic |    7.84     19.61  |    27.45      14
  NewWorld|   29.41      9.80  |    39.22      20
          +--------------------+
  Total       70.59     29.41      100.00
     N           36        15                  51
```

```
Row percents
 GROUP$ (rows) by GNP$ (columns)

           Developed  Emerging      Total       N
          +--------------------+
 Europe   | 100.00       .00   |   100.00      17
 Islamic  |  28.57     71.43   |   100.00      14
 NewWorld |  75.00     25.00   |   100.00      20
          +--------------------+
 Total      70.59     29.41       100.00
    N          36        15                   51

Column percents
 GROUP$ (rows) by GNP$ (columns)

           Developed  Emerging      Total       N
          +--------------------+
 Europe   |  47.22       .00   |    33.33      17
 Islamic  |  11.11     66.67   |    27.45      14
 NewWorld |  41.67     33.33   |    39.22      22
          +--------------------+
 Total     100.00    100.00       100.00
    N          36        15                   15
```

Notice how the row percentages change when we include a category for the missing *GNP$*:

```
PRINT NONE / ROWP
LABEL gnp$ / ' '=Missing, 'D'='Developed',
             'U'='Emerging'
TAB group$ * gnp$
PRINT
```

```
Row percents
 GROUP$ (rows) by GNP$ (columns)

          Missing Developed  Emerging    Total      N
         +------------------------------+
 Europe  |  15.00    85.00       .00    | 100.00    20
 Islamic |  12.50    25.00     62.50    | 100.00    16
 NewWorld|   4.76    71.43     23.81    | 100.00    21
         +------------------------------+
 Total     10.53    63.16     26.32       100.00
    N          6        36        15                57
```

Here we see that 62.5% of the Islamic nations are classified as *Emerging*. However, from the earlier table of *Row percents*, it might be better to say that among the Islamic nations reporting the GNP, 71.43% are *Emerging*.

Saving tables

Use **Save last table as data file** on the **One-way**, **Two-way**, or **Multiway** dialog box to save your current table in a SYSTAT file. Later, you can request tables using the new file of frequency counts. With commands:

```
SAVE filename
```

For two-way tables, SYSTAT also saves expected values, deviates, and standardized deviates (see Chapter 3).

Multiway Tables

Loglinear Model and Crosstabs provide different layouts for multiway tables. The **Loglinear Model** layout is more compact and easy to read. **Crosstabs** forms a series of two-way tables stratified by all combinations of values for the third, fourth, and so on, table factors and displays marginal totals for each stratum. As with two-way tables, **Crosstabs** also provides percentages of rows, columns, and the total sample size. The input for both procedures can be the usual cases-by-variables data file or cell counts with numeric or character identifiers.

2.6
A four-way
LOGLIN table

For this example, we use data from the cancer study described in Example 2.3. Here we use LOGLIN to display counts for a $3 \times 3 \times 2 \times 4$ table (72 cells) in two dozen lines. In the next example, we display column percentages for each survival-by-tumor status (*TUMOR$*) stratum.

Use **Data➠Label** to assign names to the *AGE* categories (they are coded 50, 60, and 70), and use **Data➠Order** to order the categories for *CENTER$* as they first appear in the data file. Use **Data➠Order** to list the categories for benign tumors before those for malignant tumors. The order of the factors in the table below is the same as that in the TABULATE instruction.

```
LOGLIN
    USE cancer
    FREQ = number
    LABEL age / 50='Under 50', 60='59 to 69',
                70='70 & Over'
    LABEL center$ / SORT=NONE
    ORDER tumor$  / SORT ='MinBengn', 'MaxBengn',
                          'MinMalig', 'MaxMalig'

    TABULATE age * center$ * survive$ * tumor$
```

```
Number of cells (product of levels):   72
                       Total count:  764

Observed Frequencies
========================================
AGE         CENTER$   SURVIVE$ |              TUMOR$
                               | MinBengn   MaxBengn   MinMalig   MaxMalig
------------+---------+--------+-------------------------------------------
Under 50  Tokyo     Alive      |      68         9         26         25
                    Dead       |       7         3          9          4
                               +
          Boston    Alive      |      24         0         11          4
                    Dead       |       7         0          6          6
                               +
          Glamorgn  Alive      |      20         1         16          8
                    Dead       |       7         0         16          3
------------+---------+--------+-------------------------------------------
50 to 69  Tokyo     Alive      |      46         5         20         18
                    Dead       |       9         2          9         11
                               +
          Boston    Alive      |      58         3         18         10
                    Dead       |      20         2          8          3
                               +
          Glamorgn  Alive      |      39         4         27         10
                    Dead       |      12         0         14          3
------------+---------+--------+-------------------------------------------
70 & Over Tokyo     Alive      |       6         1          1          5
                    Dead       |       3         0          2          1
                               +
          Boston    Alive      |      26         1         15          1
                    Dead       |      18         0          9          3
                               +
          Glamorgn  Alive      |      11         1         12          4
                    Dead       |       7         0          3          3
------------+---------+--------+-------------------------------------------
```

2.7
A four-way
XTAB table

When you have three or more table factors, **Stats▸Crosstabs▸Multiway** forms a series of two-way tables stratified by all combinations of values of the third, fourth, and so on, table factors. The order in which you choose the table factors determines the layout. Your input can be the usual cases-by-variables data file or the cellwise counts with category values.

For this example, we display the same frequency counts as in Example 2.6 but organize them differently:

```
XTAB
   USE cancer
   FREQ = number
   LABEL age      /    50='Under 50', 60='50 to 69',
                       70='70 & Over'
   ORDER center$ / SORT=none
   ORDER tumor$ / SORT='MinBengn', 'MaxBengn',
                       'MinMalig', 'MaxMalig'
   TABULATE survive$ * tumor$ * center$ * age
```

The last two factors selected (*CENTER$* and *AGE*) define two-way tables. The levels of the first two factors define the strata. The **Data▸Label** and **Data▸Order** instructions are the same as those in Example 2.6. After the table is run, we edited the output and moved the four tables for *SURVIVE$* = *Dead* next to those for *Alive*.

```
Frequencies
  CENTER$ (rows) by AGE (columns)
          SURVIVE$    = Alive                        SURVIVE$    = Dead
          TUMOR$      = MinBengn                     TUMOR$      = MinBengn

          Under 50 50 to 69 70 & Over   Total        Under 50 50 to 69 70 & Over   Total
         +---------------------------+               +---------------------------+
Tokyo    |   68       46        6     |    120  Tokyo |    7        9        3     |    19
Boston   |   24       58       26     |    108  Boston|    7       20       18     |    45
Glamorgn |   20       39       11     |     70  Glamorgn|  7       12        7     |    26
         +---------------------------+               +---------------------------+
Total        112      143       43         298  Total     21       41       28         90

          SURVIVE$    = Alive                        SURVIVE$    = Dead
          TUMOR$      = MaxBengn                     TUMOR$      = MaxBengn

          Under 50 50 to 69 70 & Over   Total        Under 50 50 to 69 70 & Over   Total
         +---------------------------+               +---------------------------+
Tokyo    |    9        5        1     |     15  Tokyo |    3        2        0     |     5
Boston   |    0        3        1     |      4  Boston|    0        2        0     |     2
Glamorgn |    1        4        1     |      6  Glamorgn|  0        0        0     |     0
         +---------------------------+               +---------------------------+
Total         10       12        3          25  Total      3        4        0          7

          SURVIVE$    = Alive                        SURVIVE$    = Dead
          TUMOR$      = MinMalig                     TUMOR$      = MinMalig

          Under 50 50 to 69 70 & Over   Total        Under 50 50 to 69 70 & Over   Total
         +---------------------------+               +---------------------------+
Tokyo    |   26       20        1     |     47  Tokyo |    9        9        2     |    20
Boston   |   11       18       15     |     44  Boston|    6        8        9     |    23
Glamorgn |   16       27       12     |     55  Glamorgn| 16       14        3     |    33
         +---------------------------+               +---------------------------+
Total         53       65       28         146  Total     31       31       14          76

          SURVIVE$    = Alive                        SURVIVE$    = Dead
          TUMOR$      = MaxMalig                     TUMOR$      = MaxMalig

          Under 50 50 to 69 70 & Over   Total        Under 50 50 to 69 70 & Over   Total
         +---------------------------+               +---------------------------+
Tokyo    |   25       18        5     |     48  Tokyo |    4       11        1     |    16
Boston   |    4       10        1     |     15  Boston|    6        3        3     |    12
Glamorgn |    8       10        4     |     22  Glamorgn|  3        3        3     |     9
         +---------------------------+               +---------------------------+
Total         37       38       10          85  Total     13       17        7          37
```

List layout

The **List layout** specification is available on the **Stats➦Multiway** dialog box. With commands:

```
PRINT / LIST
TAB survive$ * center$ * age * tumor$
```

Count	Cum Count	Pct	Cum Pct	SURVIVE$	CENTER$	AGE	TUMOR$
68	68	8.9	8.9	Alive	Tokyo	Under 50	MinBengn
9	77	1.2	10.1	Alive	Tokyo	Under 50	MaxBengn
26	103	3.4	13.5	Alive	Tokyo	Under 50	MinMalig
25	128	3.3	16.8	Alive	Tokyo	Under 50	MaxMalig
46	174	6.0	22.8	Alive	Tokyo	50 to 69	MinBengn
5	179	.7	23.4	Alive	Tokyo	50 to 69	MaxBengn
20	199	2.6	26.0	Alive	Tokyo	50 to 69	MinMalig
18	217	2.4	28.4	Alive	Tokyo	50 to 69	MaxMali
6	223	.8	29.2	Alive	Tokyo	70 & Over	MinBeng
1	224	.1	29.3	Alive	Tokyo	70 & Over	MaxBengn
1	225	.1	29.5	Alive	Tokyo	70 & Over	MinMali
5	230	.7	30.1	Alive	Tokyo	70 & Over	MaxMalig
24	254	3.1	33.2	Alive	Boston	Under 50	MinBeng
11	265	1.4	34.7	Alive	Boston	Under 50	MinMali
4	269	.5	35.2	Alive	Boston	Under 50	MaxMali
58	327	7.6	42.8	Alive	Boston	50 to 69	MinBeng
3	330	.4	43.2	Alive	Boston	50 to 69	MaxBeng
18	348	2.4	45.5	Alive	Boston	50 to 69	MinMali
10	358	1.3	46.9	Alive	Boston	50 to 69	MaxMalig
26	384	3.4	50.3	Alive	Boston	70 & Over	MinBengn
1	385	.1	50.4	Alive	Boston	70 & Over	MaxBengn
15	400	2.0	52.4	Alive	Boston	70 & Over	MinMali
1	401	.1	52.5	Alive	Boston	70 & Over	MaxMali
20	421	2.6	55.1	Alive	Glamorgn	Under 50	MinBengn
1	422	.1	55.2	Alive	Glamorgn	Under 50	MaxBeng
16	438	2.1	57.3	Alive	Glamorgn	Under 50	MinMali
8	446	1.0	58.4	Alive	Glamorgn	Under 50	MaxMali
39	485	5.1	63.5	Alive	Glamorgn	50 to 69	MinBengn
4	489	.5	64.0	Alive	Glamorgn	50 to 69	MaxBengn
27	516	3.5	67.5	Alive	Glamorgn	50 to 69	MinMali
10	526	1.3	68.8	Alive	Glamorgn	50 to 69	MaxMalig
11	537	1.4	70.3	Alive	Glamorgn	70 & Over	MinBeng
1	538	.1	70.4	Alive	Glamorgn	70 & Over	MaxBengn
12	550	1.6	72.0	Alive	Glamorgn	70 & Over	MinMalig
4	554	.5	72.5	Alive	Glamorgn	70 & Over	MaxMali
7	561	.9	73.4	Dead	Tokyo	Under 50	MinBengn
3	564	.4	73.8	Dead	Tokyo	Under 50	MaxBengn
9	573	1.2	75.0	Dead	Tokyo	Under 50	MinMali
4	577	.5	75.5	Dead	Tokyo	Under 50	MaxMali
9	586	1.2	76.7	Dead	Tokyo	50 to 69	MinBeng
2	588	.3	77.0	Dead	Tokyo	50 to 69	MaxBeng
9	597	1.2	78.1	Dead	Tokyo	50 to 69	MinMali
11	608	1.4	79.6	Dead	Tokyo	50 to 69	MaxMali
3	611	.4	80.0	Dead	Tokyo	70 & Over	MinBengn
2	613	.3	80.2	Dead	Tokyo	70 & Over	MinMali
1	614	.1	80.4	Dead	Tokyo	70 & Over	MaxMali
7	621	.9	81.3	Dead	Boston	Under 50	MinBeng
6	627	.8	82.1	Dead	Boston	Under 50	MinMali
6	633	.8	82.9	Dead	Boston	Under 50	MaxMali
20	653	2.6	85.5	Dead	Boston	50 to 69	MinBeng
2	655	.3	85.7	Dead	Boston	50 to 69	MaxBeng
8	663	1.0	86.8	Dead	Boston	50 to 69	MinMali
3	666	.4	87.2	Dead	Boston	50 to 69	MaxMali
18	684	2.4	89.5	Dead	Boston	70 & Over	MinBeng
9	693	1.2	90.7	Dead	Boston	70 & Over	MinMali
3	696	.4	91.1	Dead	Boston	70 & Over	MaxMalig
7	703	.9	92.0	Dead	Glamorgn	Under 50	MinBengn
16	719	2.1	94.1	Dead	Glamorgn	Under 50	MinMali
3	722	.4	94.5	Dead	Glamorgn	Under 50	MaxMali
12	734	1.6	96.1	Dead	Glamorgn	50 to 69	MinBeng
14	748	1.8	97.9	Dead	Glamorgn	50 to 69	MinMali
3	751	.4	98.3	Dead	Glamorgn	50 to 69	MaxMali
7	758	.9	99.2	Dead	Glamorgn	70 & Over	MinBeng
3	761	.4	99.6	Dead	Glamorgn	70 & Over	MinMali
3	764	.4	100.0	Dead	Glamorgn	70 & Over	MaxMali

The 35 cells for the women who survived are listed first (the cell for Boston women under 50 years old with *MaxBengn* tumors is empty). From the *Cum Pct* column, we see that these women make up 72.5% of the sample. Thus, 27.5% did not survive. With commands:

```
PRINT argument / LIST
TABULATE var1 * var2 * var3…
```

Percentages

While **List layout** provides percentages of the total table count, you might want others. Here we select **Column percent** in **Crosstabs** to print the percentage surviving within each age-by-center stratum shown in Example 2.6.

```
PRINT NONE / COLPCT
TABULATE age * center$ * survive$ * tumor$
PRINT
```

```
Column percents
 SURVIVE$ (rows) by TUMOR$ (columns)
            AGE        = Under 50
            CENTER$    = Tokyo

            MinBengn  MaxBengn  MinMalig  MaxMalig     Total      N
           +----------------------------------------+
Alive      |  90.67     75.00     74.29     86.21   |   84.77    128
Dead       |   9.33     25.00     25.71     13.79   |   15.23     23
           +----------------------------------------+
Total       100.00    100.00    100.00    100.00      100.00
   N            75        12        35        29                 151

            AGE        = Under 50
            CENTER$    = Boston

            MinBengn  MaxBengn  MinMalig  MaxMalig     Total      N
           +----------------------------------------+
Alive      |  77.42       .00     64.71     40.00   |   67.24     39
Dead       |  22.58       .00     35.29     60.00   |   32.76     19
           +----------------------------------------+
Total       100.00    100.00    100.00    100.00      100.00
   N            31         0        17        10                  58

            AGE        = Under 50
            CENTER$    = Glamorgn

            MinBengn  MaxBengn  MinMalig  MaxMalig     Total      N
           +----------------------------------------+
Alive      |  74.07    100.00     50.00     72.73   |   63.38     45
Dead       |  25.93       .00     50.00     27.27   |   36.62     26
           +----------------------------------------+
Total       100.00    100.00    100.00    100.00      100.00
   N            27         1        32        11                  71

            AGE        = 50 to 69
            CENTER$    = Tokyo

            MinBengn  MaxBengn  MinMalig  MaxMalig     Total      N
           +----------------------------------------+
Alive      |  83.64     71.43     68.97     62.07   |   74.17     89
Dead       |  16.36     28.57     31.03     37.93   |   25.83     31
           +----------------------------------------+
Total       100.00    100.00    100.00    100.00      100.00
   N            55         7        29        29                 120

            AGE        = 50 to 69
            CENTER$    = Boston

            MinBengn  MaxBengn  MinMalig  MaxMalig     Total      N
           +----------------------------------------+
Alive      |  74.36     60.00     69.23     76.92   |   72.95     89
Dead       |  25.64     40.00     30.77     23.08   |   27.05     33
           +----------------------------------------+
Total       100.00    100.00    100.00    100.00      100.00
   N            78         5        26        13                 122
```

```
AGE            = 50 to 69
CENTER$        = Glamorgn

        MinBengn  MaxBengn  MinMalig  MaxMalig    Total      N
       +--------------------------------------+
Alive  |  76.47    100.00     65.85     76.92  |   73.39     80
Dead   |  23.53      .00      34.15     23.08  |   26.61     29
       +--------------------------------------+
Total    100.00    100.00    100.00    100.00     100.00
   N        51         4         41        13                109

AGE            = 70 & Over
CENTER$        = Tokyo

        MinBengn  MaxBengn  MinMalig  MaxMalig    Total      N
       +--------------------------------------+
Alive  |  66.67    100.00     33.33     83.33  |   68.42     13
Dead   |  33.33      .00      66.67     16.67  |   31.58      6
       +--------------------------------------+
Total    100.00    100.00    100.00    100.00     100.00
   N         9         1          3         6                 19

AGE            = 70 & Over
CENTER$        = Boston

        MinBengn  MaxBengn  MinMalig  MaxMalig    Total      N
       +--------------------------------------+
Alive  |  59.09    100.00     62.50     25.00  |   58.90     43
Dead   |  40.91      .00      37.50     75.00  |   41.10     30
       +--------------------------------------+
Total    100.00    100.00    100.00    100.00     100.00
   N        44         1         24         4                 73

AGE            = 70 & Over
CENTER$        = Glamorgn

        MinBengn  MaxBengn  MinMalig  MaxMalig    Total      N
       +--------------------------------------+
Alive  |  61.11    100.00     80.00     57.14  |   68.29     28
Dead   |  38.89      .00      20.00     42.86  |   31.71     13
       +--------------------------------------+
Total    100.00    100.00    100.00    100.00     100.00
   N        18         1         15         7                 41
```

The percentage of women surviving for each age-by-center combination is reported in the first row of each panel. From the marginal *Total* down the right column, we see that the younger women treated in Tokyo have the best survival rate (84.77%). This is the row total (128) divided by the total for the stratum (151).

Summary

Computation

All computations are in double precision.

References

Afifi, A.A., and Clark, V. 1984. *Computer-aided multivariate analysis.* Belmont, Calif.: Lifetime Learning.

Morrison, A.S., Black, M.M., Lowe, C.R., MacMahon, B., and Yuasa, S.Y. 1973. Some international differences in histology and survival in breast cancer. *International Journal of Cancer*, 11: 261–267.

3

Tests and Measures for Two-Way Tables

Leland Wilkinson and Laszlo Engelman

For two-way tables, Crosstabs (XTAB command) provides 20 tests of significance or measures of association. Each is appropriate for a particular table structure (rows by columns). In addition, for some measures, the categories are assumed to be ordered (for example, low, medium, and high). Here are the statistics available for each table structure:

2 x 2 Tables

Pearson chi-square
Likelihood ratio chi-square
Yates' corrected chi-square
Fisher's exact test
Odds ratio
Yule's *Q* and *Y*

2 x k Tables

Ordered categories
Cochran's test of linear trend

R x R Tables

McNemar's chi-square
Cohen's kappa

R x C Tables

Unordered categories
Pearson chi-square
Likelihood ratio chi-square
Phi
Cramer's *V*
Contingency
Uncertainty
Goodman-Kruskal's lambda

Ordered categories
Kendall's tau *b*
Stuart's tau *c*
Goodman-Kruskal's gamma
Spearman's rho
Somers' *d*

For one-way tables with binomially or multinomially distributed data, confidence intervals on the cell proportions are available. Crosstabs also has the Mantel-Haenszel statistic for testing the association between two binary variables controlling for a stratification variable.

Many other nonparametric statistics are computed elsewhere in SYSTAT. For example, Correlations calculates matrices of coefficients like Spearman's rho, Kendall's tau *b*, Guttman's mu2, and Goodman-Kruskal's gamma, and the tetrachoric correlation.

Note: See Chapter 2 for a description of table layouts and how to request tables of counts and percentages and label categories.

Overview

Tests and measures
Organizing your data
Getting started

Examples

Tests and Measures for Two-way Tables

Overview

Crosstabs on the **Stats** menu provides these dialog boxes for frequency tables:

One-way   Chi-square test, frequency counts, percentages, and other options for individual table factors

Two-way   Tests and measures, frequency counts, percentages, and other options for two-way tables

Multiway   Frequency counts and percentages for multiway tables plus the Mantel-Haenszel test for k 2×2 tables

Tests and measures

On the first page of this chapter, the tests and measures for two-way tables are listed. The most familiar test for two-way tables is the **Pearson chi-square** test for independence of table rows and columns. The **Likelihood ratio chi-square** is an alternative to the Pearson chi-square and is used as a test statistic for loglinear models. Other tests and measures are appropriate for specific table structures, and some depend on the fact that the categories of the factor are ordered. The Pearson and Likelihood ratio chi-square statistics apply to $R \times C$ tables—categories need not be ordered.

2 x 2 tables

When the table has only two rows or two columns, the chi-square test is also a test for equality of proportions. The chi-square statistic is only an approximation and does not work well for small samples. In such situations, consider **Fisher's exact test**. It counts all possible outcomes exactly. **Yates' corrected chi-square test** is an attempt to adjust the Pearson chi-square statistic for small samples. It has come into disfavor for being unnecessarily conservative in many instances. The **odds (cross-product) ratio** is used frequently to measure the association between two dichotomous variables. It is the ratio of the product of the major diagonal cell frequencies to the product of the minor diagonal counts and is 1.0 when there is no association. **Yule's Q** and **Yule's Y** measure dominance in a 2×2 table. If either off diagonal cell is 0, both statistics are equal; otherwise, they are less than 1. These statistics are 0 if, and only if, the chi-square statistic is 0; therefore, the null hypothesis that the measure is 0 can be tested by the chi-square test. When counts in a 2×2 table arise from bivariate normal distribution, the **tetrachoric correlation** should be considered (see Chapter 9).

**2 x k
tables
with ordered
categories**

When one table factor is dichotomous and the other has ordered categories, **Cochran's test of linear trend** is designed to reveal whether proportions increase (or decrease) linearly across the ordered categories— that is, is the slope of a regression line significant?

**R x R
square
tables**

McNemar's chi-square test of symmetry is used for $R \times R$ square tables (the number of rows equals the number of columns). This structure arises when the same subjects are measured twice, as in a paired comparisons t test (for example, before and after an event) or when subjects are paired or matched (cases and controls). This test ignores the counts along the diagonal of the table and tests if the counts in cells above the diagonal differ from those below the diagonal (the counts along the diagonal are for subjects who did not change). A significant result indicates a greater change in one direction than another.

The table structure for **Cohen's kappa** looks like that of McNemar's in that the row and column categories are the same. But here the focus shifts to the diagonal: Are the counts along the diagonal significantly greater than those expected by chance alone? Because each subject is classified or rated twice, kappa is a measure of interrater agreement.

Another difference between McNemar and Cohen's kappa is that the former is a "test" with a chi-square statistic, degrees of freedom, and an associated p value, while kappa is a measure. Its "size" is judged by using an asymptotic standard error to construct a t statistic (that is, measure divided by standard error) to test whether kappa differs from 0. Values of Kappa greater than 0.75 indicate strong agreement beyond chance; between 0.40 and 0.79 means fair to good; and below 0.40, poor agreement.

**General
R x C
tables**

Phi, Cramer's V, and **Contingency coefficient** are measures suitable for testing independence of table factors as you would with Pearson's chi-square. They are designed for comparing results of $R \times C$ tables with different sample sizes. (Note that the expected value of the Pearson chi-square is proportional to the total table size.) The three measures are scaled differently, but all test the same null hypothesis. Use the probability printed with the Pearson chi-square to test that these measures are 0. For tables with two rows and two columns (a 2×2 table), Phi and Cramer's V are the same.

R x C
tables
with ordered
categories

Five of the measures for two-way tables are appropriate when both categorical variables have ordered categories (always, sometimes, never or none, minimal moderated, severe). These are **Goodman-Kruskal's gamma**, **Kendall's tau-b**, **Stuart's tau-c**, **Spearman's rho**, and **Somers' d**. The first three measures differ only in how ties are treated; the fourth is like the usual Pearson correlation except that the rank order of each value is used in the computations instead of the value itself. Somers' d is an asymmetric measure; in SYSTAT, the column variable is considered to be the dependent variable.

k x 2 x 2
tables

If you have a series of k 2×2 tables ($k \times 2 \times 2$), the **Mantel-Haenszel test** tests whether a combined estimate of the odds ratio across the tables differs from 1.0.

Organizing your data

There are two ways to organize data for tables:

– The usual cases-by-variables data file
– Cell counts with cell identifiers

For example, if you want to analyze this table about applicants to business schools:

		Status	
		admit	deny
Sex	male	420	90
	female	150	25

you could enter one case for each of the 685 applicants, or you could enter four cases:

SEX$	STATUS$	COUNT
Male	Admit	420
Male	Deny	90
Female	Admit	150
Female	Deny	25

For this method, the cell counts in the third column are identified by specifying:

```
FREQUENCY = count
```

Getting started   For frequency counts, percentages, and confidence intervals of single variables, use **Stats**➠**Crosstabs**➠**One-way**. (See Chapter 2 for more information.)

For frequency counts, percentages, and tests and measures of association for the crosstabulation of two factors, use **Stats**➠**Crosstabs**➠**Two-way**. (See Chapter 2 for more information.)

For statistics and significance tests for two-way tables, use **Stats**➠**Crosstabs**➠**Two-way**➠**Statistics**.

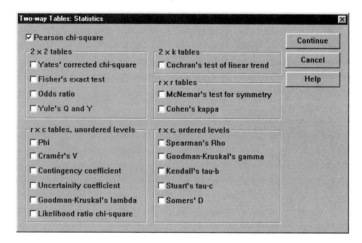

For frequency counts and percentages for series of two-way tables stratified by all combinations of values of additional table factors, use **Stats**➠**Crosstabs**➠**Multiway**. (See Chapter 2 for more information.)

In each dialog box, identify your table factors. Optionally, request **List layout** to display output in list format, **Include missing values** to add an additional category to each table factor for missing category codes and/or percentages, and **Save last table as data file** to save cell frequencies in a SYSTAT data file. For two-way tables, SYSTAT also saves expected values, deviates, and standardized deviates.

Using commands

To form one-way tables in XTAB, specify:

```
XTAB
USE filename
PRINT / options
TABULATE rowvar * colvar / options
```

For two-way tables, specify:

```
XTAB
USE filename
PRINT / options
TABULATE rowvar * colvar / options
```

When using table input (each case is a cell count with category identifiers), specify:

```
XTAB
USE filename
FREQ countvar
PRINT / options
TABULATE...
```

Examples

This section defines statistics and describes Crosstabs features and options in nine examples. If you start reading a later example, you may need to scan earlier examples for more information. You may also want to review Chapter 2, where you learn how to:

- Request a table in standard or list format
- Input cell frequencies
- Request percentages of row, column, or sample totals
- Define, label, and order categories
- Include or exclude a table category for codes that are missing

For the first seven examples in this section, use **Stats▪▶Crosstabs▪▶Two-way**; for the eighth example, use **Stats▪▶Crosstabs▪▶One-way**; and for the ninth, use **Stats▪▶Crosstabs▪▶Multiway**.

3.1 An R x C table

For the *SURVEY2* data introduced in Chapter 2, you study the relation between marital status and age. This is a general $R \times C$ table—while the categories for *AGE* are ordered, those for *MARITAL* are not. The usual Pearson chi-square statistic is used to test the association between the two factors. This statistic is the default for Crosstabs.

The data file is the usual cases-by-variables rectangular file with one record for each person. You use **Data▪▶Label** to split the continuous variable *AGE* into four categories and add names like '30 to 45' for the output. In the last chapter, you found too few *separated* people to tally, so here you use **Label** to eliminate them and also to reorder the categories of *MARITAL* that remain. Under **Stats▪▶Crosstabs▪▶Two-way**, select *AGE* as the row variable and *MARITAL* as the column variable. To supplement the results, request **Row percents**.

```
XTAB
  USE survey2
  LABEL age /    .. 29='18 to 29',
              30 .. 45='30 to 45',
              46 .. 60='46 to 60',
              60 ..   ='Over 60'
  LABEL marital / 2='Married', 3='Divorced',
              1='Never'
  PRINT / ROWPCT
  TABULATE age * marital
```

> *Note:*   *When using the **Label** dialog box, you can omit quotes around category names. With commands, you can omit them if the name has no embedded blanks or symbols (the name, however, is displayed in capital letters).*

```
Frequencies
 AGE (rows) by MARITAL (columns)

           Married  Divorced    Never     Total
         +----------------------------+
18 to 29 |   17        5          53    |    75
         |                             |
30 to 45 |   48       21           9    |    78
         |                             |
46 to 60 |   39       12           8    |    59
         |                             |
Over 60  |   23        5           3    |    31
         +----------------------------+
Total        127       43          73       243


Row percents
 AGE (rows) by MARITAL (columns)

           Married  Divorced    Never     Total      N
         +----------------------------+
18 to 29 |  22.67    6.67       70.67   |  100.00     75
         |                             |
30 to 45 |  61.54   26.92       11.54   |  100.00     78
         |                             |
46 to 60 |  66.10   20.34       13.56   |  100.00     59
         |                             |
Over 60  |  74.19   16.13        9.68   |  100.00     31
         +----------------------------+
Total       52.26   17.70       30.04      100.00
   N         127       43          73                243

Test statistic                      Value      DF        Prob
   Pearson Chi-square                87.761    6.000      0.000
```

Even though the χ^2 statistic is highly significant ($\chi^2 = 87.761$, *p* value < 0.0005), from the table of *Row Percents*, you see that 70.67% of the youngest age group fall in the "Never married" category. Many of these people may be too young to consider marriage.

Eliminating a stratum

If you eliminate the subjects in the youngest group, is there an association between marital status and age? Here, **Data**➠**Select Cases** omits the youngest group; alternatively, you could respecify **Label** and omit the youngest group.

```
SELECT age > 29
PRINT / CHISQ  PHI  CRAMER  CONT
TAB age * marital
SELECT
```

```
Frequencies
AGE (rows) by MARITAL (columns)

              Married  Divorced    Never     Total
           +---------------------------------+
 30 to 45  |    48        21         9     |      78
           |                               |
 46 to 60  |    39        12         8     |      59
           |                               |
 Over 60   |    23         5         3     |      31
           +---------------------------------+
 Total         110        38        20         168

Test statistic                    Value        DF         Prob
   Pearson Chi-square             2.173      4.000        0.704

Coefficient                       Value    Asymptotic Std Error
  Phi                             0.114
  Cramer V                        0.080
  Contingency                     0.113
```

The proportion of married people is larger within the 'Over 60' group than for the '30 to 45' group—74.19% of the former are married while 61.54% of the latter are married. The youngest stratum has the most divorced people. However, you cannot say these proportions differ significantly (χ^2 = 2.173, p value = 0.704).

Extended results

Crosstabs provides three modes or categories of output (**Short, Medium,** and **Long**)—each has statistics or features associated with it. Use **Edit**➠**Options** to specify the mode (see *SYSTAT: Data* for more information). With commands, SHORT, MEDIUM, and LONG are arguments of the PRINT command.

The **Short** mode is assumed unless you already specified a different mode in the current run. With **Short**, for two-way tables, Crosstabs prints the frequency tables and the chi-square statistic associated with each. The output in Example 3.1 illustrates **Short** plus a request for row percentages.

```
PRINT / ROWPCT
```

By specifying **Medium**, you get the frequencies and statistic provided by **Short**, plus the statistics applicable to your table structure:

2 x 2 tables
Likelihood ratio chi-square
Yates' corrected chi-square
Fisher's exact test
Odds ratio (cross-product ratio) and Ln(odds) with its standard error
Yule's Q and Y

2 x k tables
Cochran's test of linear trend on proportions

R x R tables
McNemar's test for symmetry
Cohen's kappa measure of agreement

R x C tables, unordered levels
Phi, a function of chi-square that does not increase with n
Cramer's V
Contingency coefficient C
Uncertainty coefficient
Goodman and Kruskal's lambda

R x C tables, ordered levels
Spearman's rho or rank correlation
Goodman-Kruskal's gamma
Kendall's tau-b
Stuart's tau-c
Somers' d

k x 2 x 2 tables
Mantel-Haenszel for a combined estimate of the odds ratio

For tetrachoric correlations, see Chapter 9.

With **Long**, you get the statistics listed for **Short** and **Medium** plus:

Expected values for each two-way table cell
Deviates (observed − expected values) for each two-way table cell
Standardized deviates (observed − expected) / SQR (expected)

As options, you can include statistics from a larger category. For example,

```
PRINT NONE   / CHISQ     Only the chi-square statistic
PRINT SHORT  / PHI       A table and a χ²  statistic plus φ
PRINT MEDIUM / EXPECT    Applicable statistics listed under Medium plus
                             expected values
```

Notice that NONE is available in command mode; thus, as options, you can request specific statistics from any category.

| Confidence intervals for one-way table proportions | For one-way tables with binomially or multinomially distributed data, you can request **Confidence intervals** on the cell proportions (see Example 3.8). Specify the level n ($0 \le n \le 1$). With commands: |

```
TABULATE varlist / CONFI=n
```

| Requesting percentages | It is often helpful to view tabulated data as proportions of a total rather than as raw frequencies. Crosstabs provides three options for percentages: |

Table percents	Replace each cell frequency with its percentage of the total table count
Row percents	Replace each cell frequency with its percentage of the row total
Column percents	Replace each cell frequency with its percentage of the column total

With commands:

```
PRINT SHORT / ROWPCT  PERCENT  CHI  GAMMA
```

For examples of percentages, see Example 2.5 in Chapter 2.

| List layout | **List layout** is available for one-way, two-way, and multiway tables. For each variable (or unique cross-classification of two or more variables), this feature provides counts, cumulative counts, percentages of the total sample, and cumulative percentages. See examples in Chapter 2. With commands: |

```
PRINT argument / LIST
TABULATE var1 * var2
```

3.2 An R x C table with Long results

This example illustrates LONG results and table input. It uses the *AGE* by *CENTER$* table from the cancer study described in Example 2.3 in Chapter 2.

```
XTAB
   USE cancer
   FREQ = number
   PRINT LONG
   LABEL age / 50='Under 50', 60='50 to 69',
              70='70 & Over'

   TABULATE  center$ * age
```

```
Frequencies
  CENTER$ (rows) by AGE (columns)

             Under 50  50 to 69  70 & Over      Total
           +-----------------------------------+
  Boston   |   58       122        73       |    253
           |                                |
  Glamorgn |   71       109        41       |    221
           |                                |
  Tokyo    |  151       120        19       |    290
           +-----------------------------------+
  Total       280       351       133          764


Expected values
  CENTER$ (rows) by AGE (columns)

             Under 50  50 to 69  70 & Over
           +-----------------------------------+
  Boston   |  92.72     116.23     44.04    |
           |                                |
  Glamorgn |  80.99     101.53     38.47    |
           |                                |
  Tokyo    | 106.28     133.23     50.48    |
           +-----------------------------------+


Deviates: (Observed-Expected)
  CENTER$ (rows) by AGE (columns)

             Under 50  50 to 69  70 & Over
           +-----------------------------------+
  Boston   | -34.72      5.77      28.96    |
           |                                |
  Glamorgn |  -9.99      7.47       2.53    |
           |                                |
  Tokyo    |  44.72    -13.23     -31.48    |
           +-----------------------------------+


Standardized deviates: (Observed-Expected)/SQR(Expected)
  CENTER$ (rows) by AGE (columns)

             Under 50  50 to 69  70 & Over
           +-----------------------------------+
  Boston   |  -3.61       .53       4.36    |
           |                                |
  Glamorgn |  -1.11       .74        .41    |
           |                                |
  Tokyo    |   4.34     -1.15      -4.43    |
           +-----------------------------------+

Test statistic                        Value        DF        Pro
  Pearson Chi-square                  74.039     4.000      0.000
  Likelihood ratio Chi-square         76.963     4.000      0.000
  McNemar Symmetry Chi-square         79.401     3.000      0.000

Coefficient                           Value     Asymptotic StdError
  Phi                                  0.311
  Cramer V                             0.220
  Contingency                          0.297
  Goodman-Kruskal Gamma               -0.417        0.043
  Kendall Tau-B                       -0.275        0.030
  Stuart Tau-C                        -0.265        0.029
  Cohen Kappa                         -0.113        0.022
  Spearman Rho                        -0.305        0.033
  Somers D    (column dependent)      -0.267        0.030
  Lambda      (column dependent)       0.075        0.038
  Uncertainty (column dependent)       0.049        0.011
```

The null hypothesis for the Pearson chi-square test is that the table factors are independent. You reject the hypothesis ($\chi^2 = 74.039$, p value < 0.0005). You worry about the analysis of the full table with four factors in the cancer study because you see an imbalance between *AGE* and study *CENTER*. The researchers in Tokyo entered a much larger proportion of younger women than did the researchers in the other cities.

Notice that with LONG, SYSTAT reports all statistics for an $R \times C$ table including those that are appropriate when both factors have ordered categories (gamma, tau-b, tau-c, rho, and Spearman's rho). In the examples that follow, you request specific statistics appropriate for each table structure.

3.3 The odds (or cross-product) ratio

For a 2×2 table with cell counts a, b, c, and d:

Exposure

		yes	no
Disease	**yes**	a	b
	no	c	d

where, if you call the Disease "yes" people *sick* and the Disease "no" people *well*, the **odds ratio** (or **cross-product ratio**) is:

$$\frac{\text{odds that a sick person is exposed}}{\text{odds that a well person is exposed}} = \frac{a/b}{c/d} = \frac{ad}{bc}$$

If the odds for the sick and disease-free people are the same, the value of the odds ratio is 1.0.

As an example, continue using the *SURVEY2* file and study the association between gender and depressive illness using **Stats⟫Crosstabs⟫Two-way** to select *SEX$* and *CASECONT*. Use **Statistics** to select **Odds ratio**. Be careful to order your table factors so that your odds ratio is constructed correctly. Here you use **Data⟫Label** to do this and to add category names to the output.

```
XTAB
   USE survey2
   LABEL casecont / 1='Depressed', 0='Normal'
   PRINT / FREQ  ODDS
   TABULATE sex$ * casecont
```

```
Frequencies
 SEX$ (rows) by CASECOUNT (columns)

            Depressed    Normal      Total
           +--------------------+
 Female    |    36         116  |     152
           |                    |
 Male      |     8          96  |     104
           +--------------------+
 Total          44         212        256

 Test statistic                    Value      DF       Prob
   Pearson Chi-square              11.095    1.000     0.001

 Coefficient                        Value    Asymptotic Std Error
   Odds Ratio                       3.724
   Ln(Odds)                         1.315             0.415
```

The odds a female is depressed are 36 to 116; the odds for a male, 8 to 96; and the odds ratio is 3.724. Thus, in this sample, females are almost four times more likely to be depressed than males. But, does our sample estimate differ significantly from 1.0? Because the distribution of the odds ratio is very skewed, significance is determined by examining *Ln(Odds)*, the natural logarithm of the ratio, and the standard error of the transformed ratio. Note the symmetry when ratios are transformed:

$$
\begin{array}{cc}
3 & \text{Ln } 3 \\
2 & \text{Ln } 2 \\
1 & \text{Ln } 0 \\
1/2 & -\text{Ln } 2 \\
1/3 & -\text{Ln } 3 \\
\end{array}
$$

The value of *Ln(Odds)* here is 1.315 with a standard error of 0.415. Constructing an approximate 95% confidence interval using the statistic plus or minus two times its standard error:

$$1.315 \pm 2*0.415 = 1.315 \pm 0.830$$

results in: .485 < Ln(Odds) ratio < 2.145

Because 0 is not included in the interval, the *Ln(Odds)* ratio differs significantly from 0, and the odds ratio differs from 1.0.

Using the calculator to take antilogs of the limits. You can use SYSTAT's calculator to take antilogs of the limits EXP(.485) and EXP(2.145) and obtain a confidence interval for the odds ratio:

$$
\begin{array}{ccccc}
e^{.485} & < & \text{odds ratio} & < & e^{2.145} \\
1.624 & < & \text{odds ratio} & < & 8.542 \\
\end{array}
$$

That is, for the lower limit, type CALC EXP(.485).

Notice that the proportion of females who are depressed is 0.2368 (from a table of row percentages not displayed here) and the proportion of males is 0.0769, so you also reject the hypothesis of equality of proportions ($\chi^2 = 11.095$ with p value = 0.001).

3.4 Fisher's exact test

Here is another 2×2 table. Let's say that you are interested in how salaries of female executives compare with those of male executives at a particular firm. The accountant there will not give you salaries in dollar figures, but does tell you whether the executives salaries are *low* or *high*:

	Low	High
Male	2	7
Female	5	1

The sample size is very small. When a table has only two rows and two columns and PRINT=MEDIUM is set as the length (**Edit➧Options➧ Length: Medium**), SYSTAT reports results of five additional tests and measures: Fisher's exact test, the odds ratio (and Ln(Odds)), Yates' corrected chi-square, and Yules' Q and Y.) By setting PRINT=SHORT, you request three of these: Fisher's exact test, the chi-square test, and Yates' corrected chi-square.

```
XTAB
   USE salary
   FREQ = count
   LABEL sex      / 1='male', 2='female'
   LABEL earnings / 1='low',  2='high'
   PRINT / FISHER  CHISQ  YATES
   TABULATE sex * earnings
```

```
Frequencies
 SEX (rows) by EARNINGS (columns)

               low      high    Total
            +------------------+
   male     |    2        7    |    9
   female   |    5        1    |    6
            +------------------+
   Total         7        8        15


WARNING: More than one-fifth of fitted cells are sparse (frequency < 5).
The following significance tests are suspect.

Test statistic                      Value       DF       Prob
   Pearson Chi-square                5.402    1.000      0.020
   Yates corrected Chi-square        3.225    1.000      0.073
   Fisher exact test (two-tail)                          0.041
```

Notice that SYSTAT warns you that results are suspect because the counts in the table are too low (sparse). Technically, the message says that more than one-fifth of the cells have expected values (*Fitted* values) less than 5.

The *p* value for the *Pearson Chi-Square* (0.020) leads you to believe that sex and earnings are *not* independent. But you just read a warning about suspect results. This warning applies to the Pearson chi-square test but not to Fisher's exact test. Fisher's test counts all possible outcomes exactly, including the ones that produce an interaction greater than what you observe. The Fisher exact test *p* value is also significant. On this basis, you reject the null hypothesis of independence (no interaction between sex and earnings).

Results for small samples, however, can be fairly sensitive. One case can matter. What if the accountant forgets one well-paid male executive?

```
Frequencies
 SEX (rows) by EARNINGS (columns)

               low      high    Total
         +-------------------+
  male   |    2        6     |    8
  female |    5        1     |    6
         +-------------------+
  Total       7        7         14


WARNING: More than one-fifth of fitted cells are sparse (frequency < 5).
The following significance tests are suspect.

Test statistic                    Value        DF       Prob
  Pearson Chi-square              4.667      1.000      0.031
  Yates corrected Chi-square      2.625      1.000      0.105
  Fisher exact test (two-tail)                          0.103
```

The results of the Fisher exact test indicates that you cannot reject the null hypothesis of independence. It is too bad that you do not have the actual salaries. Much information is lost when a quantitative variable like salary is dichotomized into "low" and "high."

What is a small expected value?

In larger contingency tables, you do not want to see any expected values less than 1.0 or more than 20% of the values less than 5. For large tables with too many small expected values, there is no remedy but to combine categories or possibly omit a category that has very few observations.

3.5 Cochran's test of linear trend

When one table factor is dichotomous and the other has three or more ordered categories (for example, low, median, high), Cochran's test of linear trend is used to test the null hypothesis that β, the slope of a regression line across the proportions, is 0. For example, in studying the relation of depression and education, you form this table for the *SURVEY2* data and plot the proportion depressed:

	dropout	HS grad	college	degree +
Depressed	14	18	11	1
Normal	36	80	75	21
P_i	.28	.18	.13	.05

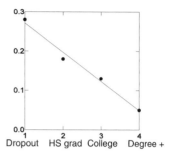

If you regress the proportions on scores 1, 2, 3, and 4 assigned by SYSTAT to the ordered categories, you can test whether the slope is significant.

This is what you do in this example. You also explore the relation of depression to health. Use **Data➠Label** to define and label categories and then use **Stats➠Crosstabs➠Two-way**, selecting *CASECOUNT* as the row variable, *EDUCATN* and *HEALTHY* as column variables, and **Frequencies** and **Column percents**. Using **Statistics**, choose **Cochran's test of linear trend**. With commands:

```
XTAB
   USE survey2
   LABEL casecount   /   1='Depressed',   0='Normal'
   LABEL educatn / 1,2='Dropout'      3='HS grad',
                   4,5='College'      6,7='Degree +'
   LABEL healthy /   1='Excellent',   2='Good',
                     3,4='Fair/Poor'

   PRINT / FREQ  COLPCT  COCHRAN

   TABULATE casecount * educatn
   TAB       casecount * healthy
```

❶
```
Frequencies
  CASECOUNT (rows) by EDUCATN (columns)

             Dropout   HS grad   College  Degree +      Total
           +---------------------------------------+
Depresse   |    14        18         11        1    |       44
           |                                        |
Normal     |    36        80         75       21    |      212
           +---------------------------------------+
Total            50        98         86       22          256
```

```
Column percents
  CASECOUNT (rows) by EDUCATN (columns)

             Dropout   HS grad   College  Degree +      Total        N
           +---------------------------------------+
Depresse   |   28.00     18.37     12.79     4.55   |     17.19       44
           |                                        |
Normal     |   72.00     81.63     87.21    95.45   |     82.81      212
           +---------------------------------------+
Total         100.00    100.00    100.00   100.00        100.00
    N            50        98         86       22                     256

Test statistic                     Value          DF          Prob
  Pearson Chi-square               7.841        3.000         0.049
  Cochran's Linear Trend           7.681        1.000         0.006
```

❷
```
Frequencies
  CASECOUNT (rows) by HEALTHY (columns)

           Excellent   Good  Fair/Poor      Total
           +-------------------------------+
Depresse   |    16        15        13     |       44
           |                               |
Normal     |   105        78        29     |      212
           +-------------------------------+
Total          121        93        42            256
```

```
Column percents
  CASECOUNT (rows) by HEALTHY (columns)

           Excellent   Good  Fair/Poor      Total        N
           +-------------------------------+
Depresse   |   13.22     16.13     30.95   |     17.19       44
           |                               |
Normal     |   86.78     83.87     69.05   |     82.81      212
           +-------------------------------+
Total         100.00    100.00    100.00        100.00
    N           121        93        42                      256

Test statistic                     Value          DF          Prob
  Pearson Chi-square               7.000        2.000         0.030
  Cochran's Linear Trend           5.671        1.000         0.017
```

The highlighted numbers below correspond to those in the output.

❶ As the level of education increases, the proportion of depressed subjects decreases (Cochran $\chi^2 = 7.681$, $df = 1$, and p value = 0.006). 28% of those not graduating from high school (*Dropout*) are depressed, … , and 4.55% of those with advanced degrees are depressed. Notice that the Pearson chi-square is marginally significant (p value = 0.049). It simply tests the hypothesis that the four proportions are equal, rather than decreasing linearly.

❷ The proportion of depressed subjects tends to increase linearly from 0.13 to 0.31 as health deteriorates (p value = 0.017).

3.6
Tests when
categories
are ordered

You now focus on statistics for studies where both table factors have a few ordered categories. For example, a teacher evaluating the activity level of schoolchildren may feel that she can't score them from 1 to 20, but that she could categorize the activity of each child as sedentary, normal, or hyperactive. Here you study the relation of health status with age. Use **Data**➠**Label** to define and label the categories. Notice that variables can be string values—for example, "low", "medium", and "high". If your category codes are character valued, use **Data**➠**Order** to order them.

Use **Stats**➠**Crosstabs**➠**Two-way**➠**Statistics** to obtain the Spearman rank correlation, **Spearman's rho**, and **Goodman-Kruskal's gamma**. For Spearman's rho, instead of using actual data values, the indices of the categories are used to compute the usual correlation. Gamma measures the probability of getting like (as opposed to unlike) orders of values. Its numerator is identical to that of Kendall's tau-*b* and Stuart's tau-*c*.

```
XTAB
   USE survey2
   LABEL healthy /   1='Excellent', 2='Good',
                     3,4='Fair/Poor'
   LABEL age      /     .. 29='18 to 29',
                    30 .. 45='30 to 45',
                    46 .. 60='46 to 60',
                    60 ..    ='Over 60'

PRINT / FREQ  ROWP  GAMMA  RHO

TABULATE  healthy * age
```

```
Frequencies
 HEALTHY (rows) by AGE (columns)

          18 to 29  30 to 45  46 to 60   Over 60     Total
         +-----------------------------------------------+
 Excellen|     43        48        25         5 |    121
         |
 Good    |     30        23        24        16 |     93
         |
 Fair/Poo|      6         9        15        12 |     42
         +-----------------------------------------------+
 Total         79        80        64        33      256

 Row percents
 HEALTHY (rows) by AGE (columns)

          18 to 29  30 to 45  46 to 60   Over 60     Total      N
         +-----------------------------------------------+
 Excellen|   35.54     39.67     20.66      4.13 |  100.00    121
         |
 Good    |   32.26     24.73     25.81     17.20 |  100.00     93
         |
 Fair/Poo|   14.29     21.43     35.71     28.57 |  100.00     42
         +-----------------------------------------------+
 Total       30.86     31.25     25.00     12.89    100.00
 N              79        80        64        33                256

 Test statistic                    Value         DF        Prob
   Pearson Chi-square             29.380      6.000       0.000

 Coefficient                      Value    Asymptotic Std Error
   Goodman-Kruskal Gamma          0.346                   0.072
   Spearman Rho                   0.274                   0.058
```

Not surprisingly, as age increases, health status tends to deteriorate. In the table of row percentages, notice that among those with "Excellent" health, 4.13% are in the oldest age group; in the "Good" category, 17.2% are in the oldest group; and in the "Fair/Poor" category, 28.57% are in the oldest group. The value of gamma is 0.346; rho is 0.274. Here are **confidence intervals** (value ± 2 * *Asymptotic Std Error*) for each statistic:

$$0.202 \leq 0.346 \leq 0.490$$
$$0.158 \leq 0.274 \leq 0.390$$

Because 0 is in neither interval, you conclude that there is an association between health and age.

$$-0.528 \leq -0.294 \leq -0.060$$
$$-0.309 \leq -0.171 \leq -0.033$$

3.7 McNemar's test of symmetry

In November of 1993, the U.S. Congress approved the North American Free Trade Agreement (NAFTA). Let's say that two months before the approval and *before* the televised debate between Vice President Al Gore and businessman Ross Perot, political pollsters queried a sample of 350 people, asking "Are you *For*, *Unsure*, or *Against* NAFTA?" Immediately *after* the debate, the pollsters contacted the same people and asked the question a second time. Here are the responses:

		After the debate		
		for	unsure	against
Before the debate	for	51	22	28
	unsure	46	18	27
	against	52	49	57

The pollsters wonder, "Is there a shift in opinion about NAFTA?" The study design for the answer is similar to a paired *t* test—each subject has two responses. The row and column categories of our table are the same variable measured at different points in time.

Because the data are already tabulated, you enter one record for each of the nine cells with the frequency count and category identifiers:

BEFORE$	AFTER$	COUNT
for	for	51
for	unsure	22
for	against	28
unsure	for	46
unsure	unsure	18
unsure	against	27
against	for	52
against	unsure	49
against	against	57

Use **Data**➠**Frequency** to identify *COUNT* as a **Frequency** variable and use **Data**➠**Order** to ensure that the row and column categories are ordered the same. Using **Stats**➠**Crosstabs**➠**Two-way**, request **Frequencies** and **Table percents** (percentages of the total count). Under **Statistics**, request the **McNemar's test for symmetry** and the usual **Pearson chi-square**.

```
XTAB
   USE nafta
   FREQ = count
   ORDER before$ after$ / SORT='for','unsure','against'

   PRINT / FREQ  MCNEMAR  CHI  PERCENT

   TABULATE before$ * after$
```

```
Frequencies
 BEFORE$ (rows) by AFTER$ (columns)

               for    unsure   against     Total
         +----------------------------+
  for    |    51       22        28    |     101
         |                            |
  unsure |    46       18        27    |      91
         |                            |
  against|    52       49        57    |     158
         +----------------------------+
  Total       149       89       112        350


Percents of total count
 BEFORE$ (rows) by AFTER$ (columns)

               for    unsure   against     Total       N
         +----------------------------+
  for    |   14.57     6.29      8.00  |    28.86      101
         |                            |
  unsure |   13.14     5.14      7.71  |    26.00       91
         |                            |
  against|   14.86    14.00     16.29  |    45.14      158
         +----------------------------+
  Total      42.57    25.43     32.00     100.00
    N        149       89       112                   350

 Test statistic                       Value       DF       Prob
   Pearson Chi-square                 11.473     4.000     0.022
   McNemar Symmetry Chi-square        22.039     3.000     0.000
```

The McNemar test of symmetry focuses on the counts in the off-diagonal cells (those along the diagonal are not used in the computations). You are investigating the direction of change in opinion. First, how many respondents became *more negative* about NAFTA?

- Among those who initially responded *for*, 22 (6.29%) are now *unsure* and 28 (8%) are now *against*.
- Among those who were *unsure* before the debate, 27 (7.71%) answered *against* afterwards.

The three cells in the upper-right contain counts for those who became more unfavorable and comprise 22% (6.29 + 8.00 + 7.71) of the sample. The three cells on the lower left contain counts for people who became more positive about NAFTA (46, 52, and 49) or 42% of the sample.

The null hypothesis for the McNemar test is that these changes are equal. The chi-square statistic for this test is 22.039 with 3 *df* and $p \leq 0.0005$. You reject the null hypothesis. The pro-NAFTA shift in opinion is significantly greater than the anti-NAFTA shift.

You also clearly reject the null hypothesis that the row (*BEFORE$*) and column (*AFTER$*) factors are independent ($\chi^2 = 11.473$, *df* = 4, and $p = 0.022$). However, a test of independence does not answer your original question about change of opinion and its direction.

3.8 Confidence intervals for one-way table percentages

If your data are binomially or multinomially distributed, you may want confidence intervals on the cell proportions. The **Confidence intervals** option under **One-way** produces large sample confidence intervals on the cell proportions with the 1–α level you specify. These confidence intervals are based on an approximation by Bailey (1980). SYSTAT uses that reference's approximation number 6 with a continuity correction, which fits closely the real intervals for the binomial on even small samples and performs well when population proportions are near 0 or 1. The confidence intervals are scaled on a percentage scale for compatibility with the other Crosstabs output.

Here is an example using data from Davis (1977) on the number of buses failing after driving a given distance (one of 10 distances). Print the percentages of the 161 buses failing in each distance category to see the cover of the intervals.

First identify *COUNT* as the count variable under **Data**➠**Frequency**, then use **Stats**➠**Crosstabs**➠**One-way** to choose *DISTANCE*. Select **Frequencies** and **Percents**. With commands:

```
XTAB
  USE buses
  FREQ = count
  PRINT NONE / FREQ  PERCENT
  TABULATE distance / CONFI=.95
```

```
Frequencies
 Values for DISTANCE
                 1.00      2.00      3.00      4.00      5.00      6.00
            +-----------------------------------------------------------+
            |    6        11        16        25        34        46    |
            +-----------------------------------------------------------+

                 7.00      8.00      9.00     10.00     Total
            +-----------------------------------------------+
            |   33        16         2         2    |        191
            +-----------------------------------------------+


Percents of total count
 Values for DISTANCE
                 1.00      2.00      3.00      4.00      5.00      6.00
            +-----------------------------------------------------------+
            |  3.14      5.76      8.38     13.09     17.80     24.08   |
            +-----------------------------------------------------------+

                 7.00      8.00      9.00     10.00     Total       N
            +-----------------------------------------------+
            | 17.28      8.38      1.05      1.05   |      100.00    191
            +-----------------------------------------------+


 95 percent approximate confidence intervals scaled as cell percents
 Values for DISTANCE
                 1.00      2.00      3.00      4.00      5.00
            +---------------------------------------------------+
            |  8.23     11.87     15.26     21.00     26.45     |
            |   .55      1.90      3.55      6.91     10.56     |
            +---------------------------------------------------+

                 6.00      7.00      8.00      9.00     10.00
            +---------------------------------------------------+
            | 33.42     25.85     15.26      4.91      4.91     |
            | 15.74     10.14      3.55       .00       .00     |
            +---------------------------------------------------+
```

There are six buses in the first distance category; this is 3.14% of the 191
buses. The confidence interval for this percentage ranges from 0.55 to
8.23%.

3.9
Mantel-
Haenszel test

For any $k \times 2 \times 2$ table, if the output mode is **Medium** or if you select the **Mantel-Haenszel test**, SYSTAT produces the Mantel-Haenszel statistic without continuity correction. This tests the association between two binary variables controlling for a stratification variable. The Mantel-Haenszel test is often used to test the effectiveness of a treatment on an outcome, to test the degree of association between the presence or absence of a risk factor and the occurrence of a disease, or to compare two survival distributions.

A study by Ansfield, et al. (1977) examined the responses of two different groups of patients (colon or rectum cancer and breast cancer) to two different treatments:

CANCER$	TREAT$	RESPONSE$	NUMBER
Colon-Rectum	a	Positive	16.000
Colon-Rectum	b	Positive	7.000
Colon-Rectum	a	Negative	32.000
Colon-Rectum	b	Negative	45.000
Breast	a	Positive	14.000
Breast	b	Positive	9.000
Breast	a	Negative	28.000
Breast	b	Negative	29.000

Here are the data rearranged:

	Breast Cancer		Colon Rectum	
	Positive	Negative	Positive	Negative
Treatment A	14	28	16	32
Treatment B	9	29	7	45

The odds ratio (cross-product ratio) for the first 2×2 table is:

odds (biopsy positive, given treatment A) = 14/28 divided by
odds (biopsy positive, given treatment B) = 9/29

or 14/28 divided by 9/29=1.6

Similarly, for the second table, the odds ratio is:

16/32 divided by 7/45=3.2

If the odds for treatments A and B are identical, the ratios would both be 1.0. For these data, the breast cancer patients on treatment A are 1.6 both times more likely to have a positive biopsy than patients on treatment B; while, for the colon-rectum, those on "A" are 3.2 times more likely to have a positive biopsy than those on "B". (To ask SYSTAT to compute these odds ratios, see Example 3.3.) But can you say these estimates differ significantly from 1.0? After adjusting for the total frequency in each table, the Mantel-Haenszel statistic combines odd ratios across tables.

Use **Stats➠Crosstabs➠Multiway**, specify *TREAT$* as the **Row variable**, *RESPONSE$* as the **Column variable**, and *CANCER$* as the **Strata variable**. Also select **Mantel-Haenszel test for 2 x 2 sub-tables**. With commands, the stratification variable *CANCER$* must be the first variable listed.

```
XTAB
    USE ansfield
    FREQ = number
    ORDER response$ / SORT='Positive','Negative'

    PRINT / MANTEL

    TABULATE cancer$ * treat$ * response$
```

```
Frequencies
  TREAT$ (rows) by RESPONSE$ (columns)
            CANCER$      = Breast

            Positive  Negative      Total
          +--------------------+
  a       |     14        28    |      42
  b       |      9        29    |      38
          +--------------------+
  Total         23        57           80

            CANCER$      = Colon-Rectum

            Positive  Negative      Total
          +--------------------+
  a       |     16        32    |      48
  b       |      7        45    |      52
          +--------------------+
  Total         23        77          100

    Mantel-Haenszel statistic  =      2.277
    Mantel-Haenszel Chi-square =      4.739  Probability =    0.029
```

SYSTAT prints a chi-square test for testing whether this combined estimate equals 1.0 (that odds for A and B are the same). The probability associated with this chi-square is 0.029, so you reject the hypothesis that the odds ratio is 1.0 and conclude that treatment A is less effective—more patients on treatment A have positive biopsies after treatment than patients on treatment B.

One assumption required for the Mantel-Haenszel chi-square test is that the odds ratios are homogenous across tables. For your example, the second odds ratio is twice as large as the first. You can use loglinear models to test if a cancer by treatment interaction is needed to fit the cells of the three-way table defined by cancer, treatment, and response. The difference between this model and one without the interaction was not significant (a chi-square of 0.36 with 1 *df*).

References

Ansfield, F., et al. 1977. A phase III study comparing the clinical utility of four regimens of 5-fluorouracil. *Cancer*, 39: 34-40.

Bailey, B.J.R. 1980. Large sample simultaneous confidence intervals for the multinomial probabilities based on transformations of the cell frequencies. *Technometrics*, 22: 583-589.

Davis, D.J. 1977. An analysis of some failure data. *Journal of the American Statistical Association*, 72: 113–150.

Fleiss, J.L. 1981. *Statistical methods for rates and proportions*. 2nd ed. New York: John Wiley & Sons, Inc.

Descriptive Statistics

Leland Wilkinson and Laszlo Engelman

The Crosstabs and Descriptive Statistics procedures provide a broad variety of descriptive statistics:

- Crosstabs offers frequency counts, percentages, and cumulative percentages.

- Descriptive Statistics offers the usual mean, standard deviation, and standard error appropriate for data that follow a normal distribution. It also provides the median, minimum, maximum, and range. A confidence interval for the mean and standard errors for skewness and kurtosis can be requested. A stem-and-leaf plot is available for assessing distributional shape and identifying outliers.

Both Crosstabs and Descriptive Statistics provide stratified analyses—that is, you can request results separately for each level of a grouping variable (such as *SEX$*) or for each combination of levels of two or more grouping variables.

In Descriptive Statistics, you can save a file of aggregate statistics. For example, if your input file has exam scores for 300 students from 10 schools, create a new file containing 10 records (one per school). On each record, include the average math score, average verbal score, maximum math score, and verbal standard deviation for the students from one school.

Overview

Frequencies, Percentages, and Cumulative Percentages

Stem-and-Leaf Plots

Descriptive Statistics

Overview

For the statistics in this chapter, use these submenus under **Stats:**

Crosstabs	**One-way** for frequency counts and percentages of individual variables
	Two-way for cross-tabulated variables
Descriptive Statistics	**Stem-and-Leaf** for stem-and-leaf diagrams
	Basic Statistics for basic descriptive statistics
	Cronbach's Alpha for Cronbach's alpha

Note: In this chapter, the **List layout** option on **Crosstabs** is used.

Selecting a statistic

There are many ways to describe data, although not all descriptors are appropriate for a given sample. Means and standard deviations are useful for data that follow a normal distribution, but are poor descriptors when the distribution is highly skewed or has outliers, subgroups, or other anomalies. Some statistics, such as the mean and median, describe the center of a distribution. These estimates are called **measures of location**. Others, such as the standard deviation, describe the **spread** of the distribution.

Before deciding *what* you want to describe (location, spread, and so on), you should consider what *type* of variables are present. Are the values of a variable *unordered categories, ordered categories, counts,* or *measurements*?

For many statistical purposes, counts are treated as measured variables. Such variables are called **quantitative** if it makes sense to do arithmetic on their values. Means and standard deviations are appropriate for quantitative variables that follow a normal distribution. Often, however, real data do not meet this assumption of normality. A descriptive statistic is called **robust** if the calculations are insensitive to violations of the assumption of normality. Robust measures include the median, quartiles, frequency counts, and percentages.

Before requesting descriptive statistics, first scan graphical displays to see if the shape of the distribution is symmetric, if there are outliers, and if the sample has subpopulations. If the latter is true, then the sample is not *homogeneous*, and the statistics should be calculated for each subgroup separately.

In this chapter, we:

— Introduce frequencies and percentages as descriptors for numeric and string variables with unordered categories (Crosstabs).

— Add cumulative percentages for variables with ordered categories (Crosstabs).

— Continue with robust statistics, such as the median, for quantitative variables that may not be normally distributed (Descriptive Statistics).

— Move to descriptors, such as the mean and standard deviation, that assume normality (Descriptive Statistics).

Getting started

For frequency counts and percentages of single variables, use **Stats⭢Crosstabs⭢One-way**; and for frequency counts and percentages of cross-tabulated variables, use **Stats⭢Crosstabs⭢Two-way**. These dialog boxes are displayed in Chapter 4.

For stem-and-leaf plots, use **Stats⭢Descriptive Statistics⭢Stem-and-Leaf**:

For robust and normal theory statistics, use **Stats**➡**Descriptive Statistics**➡**Basic Statistics:**

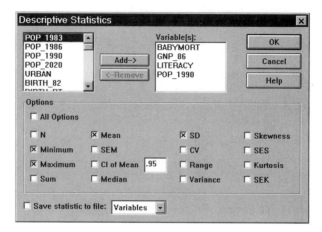

For Cronbach's alpha, use **Stats**➡**Descriptive Statistics**➡**Cronbach's Alpha:**

Using commands

To generate the statistics, choose your data by typing USE *filename,* and continue as follows:

Single variables
```
XTAB
    TAB varlist / LIST
```

Cross-tabulated variables
```
XTAB
    TAB varlist * var / LIST
```

Stem-and-leaf
```
STATISTICS
    STEM varlist
```

Univariate statistics
```
STATISTICS
    STATISTICS varlist / options
```
options identify the statistics to compute

Cronbach's alpha
```
STATISTICS
    CRONBACH varlist
```

Frequencies, Percentages, and Cumulative Percentages

The **List layout** option on the **Crosstabs** dialog boxes reports the number of times (count) each distinct value occurs, the percentage this count is of the total sample size, and its cumulative percentage. Variables can have numeric or character values, and their categories can be ordered or unordered.

4.1 Character variables with unordered categories

This example uses the *OURWORLD* file, which contains data for 57 countries (cases). **List layout** is used to request frequency counts and percentages for the values of *GOV$* (government type), *GROUP$* (European, Islamic, or New World), and *COUNTRY$* (country name).

Use **Stats ▸ Crosstabs ▸ One-way** to identify your variables and select **List layout**. With commands:

```
XTAB
    USE ourworld
    TAB gov$ group$ country$ / LIST
```

Count	Cum Count	Pct	Cum Pct	GOV$
32	32	56.1	56.1	Democracy
13	45	22.8	78.9	Military
12	57	21.1	100.0	OneParty

Count	Cum Count	Pct	Cum Pct	GROUP$
20	20	35.1	35.1	Europe
16	36	28.1	63.2	Islamic
21	57	36.8	100.0	NewWorld

Count	Cum Count	Pct	Cum Pct	COUNTRY$
1	1	1.8	1.8	Afghanistan
1	2	1.8	3.5	Algeria
1	3	1.8	5.3	Argentina
1	4	1.8	7.0	Austria
1	5	1.8	8.8	Bangladesh
1	6	1.8	10.5	Barbados
1	7	1.8	12.3	Belgium
1	8	1.8	14.0	Bolivia
1	9	1.8	15.8	Brazil
1	10	1.8	17.5	Canada
1	11	1.8	19.3	Chile

*** *we omit Colombia through Sweden* ***

Count	Cum Count	Pct	Cum Pct	COUNTRY$
1	50	1.8	87.7	Switzerland
1	51	1.8	89.5	Trinidad
1	52	1.8	91.2	Turkey
1	53	1.8	93.0	UK
1	54	1.8	94.7	Uruguay
1	55	1.8	96.5	Venezuela
1	56	1.8	98.2	WGermany
1	57	1.8	100.0	Yemen

The results for *GOV$* are displayed in the first panel. Under *Count*, we see that 32 of the 57 countries in our sample (or looking at *Pct*, this is 56.1% of the countries) report *Democracy* as their type of government, 22.8% report *Military*, and 21.1%, *One Party*. From the second panel, we see that 35.1% of the nations in our sample are from *Europe*, 28.1% are *Islamic*, and 36.8% are *New World*.

The results for *COUNTRY$* are displayed in the last panel. Each name occurs once, as we hoped would be true, and the names are listed alphabetically. If you want to list the names in the order in which they appear in your file, specify **Data➠Order➠Select sort** as **None**.

Cross-
classifications

In the example above, we report results for each distinct value of each variable. You can also obtain results for each combination of levels of two or more grouping variables. Usually these results are displayed as two-way or multiway tables. However, when some cells are empty, **List layout** provides a compact display of results.

Use **Stats➠Crosstabs➠Two-way** to select the variables *GROUP$* and *GOV$*, and select the **List layout** option. With commands:

```
TAB gov$ * group$ / LIST
```

Count	Cum Count	Pct	Cum Pct	GOV$	GROUP$
16	16	28.1	28.1	Democracy	Europe
4	20	7.0	35.1	OneParty	Europe
4	24	7.0	42.1	Democracy	Islamic
7	31	12.3	54.4	Military	Islamic
5	36	8.8	63.2	OneParty	Islamic
12	48	21.1	84.2	Democracy	NewWorld
6	54	10.5	94.7	Military	NewWorld
3	57	5.3	100.0	OneParty	NewWorld

In *Europe*, there are four times as many nations with a *Democracy* as *One Party* governments (28.1% versus 7%); and there is no entry for *Military* government. Among the *Islamic* countries, there are more *Military* governments than either of the other types. More than half of the *New World* countries (21.1% versus 10.5% + 5.3%) report *Democracy*.

4.2
Numeric
variables

Here we show results of the **List layout** option for two quantitative variables: *BABYMORT* (infant mortality rate for 1990) and *GNP_86* (GNP per capita in 1986). Use **Stats**➠**Crosstabs**➠**One-way** to choose the variables *BABYMORT* and *GNP_86*, and select **List layout**. With commands:

```
XTAB
    USE ourworld
    TAB babymort gnp_86  / LIST
```

❶
```
             Cum           Cum
  Count     Count   Pct    Pct  BABYMORT
     1         1    1.8    1.8    5
    10        11   17.5   19.3    6
     5        16    8.8   28.1    7
     2        18    3.5   31.6   10
     1        19    1.8   33.3   11
     1        20    1.8   35.1   12
     1        21    1.8   36.8   13
     1        22    1.8   38.6   14
     1        23    1.8   40.4   15
     3        26    5.3   45.6   16
     1        27    1.8   47.4   18
     2        29    3.5   50.9   22
     1        30    1.8   52.6   27
     1        31    1.8   54.4   30
     1        32    1.8   56.1   32
     1        33    1.8   57.9   38
     1        34    1.8   59.6   49
     2        36    3.5   63.2   61
     2        38    3.5   66.7   62
     1        39    1.8   68.4   64
     2        41    3.5   71.9   67
     1        42    1.8   73.7   69
     1        43    1.8   75.4   74
     2        45    3.5   78.9   87
     2        47    3.5   82.5  107
     1        48    1.8   84.2  110
     2        50    3.5   87.7  116
     2        52    3.5   91.2  125
     1        53    1.8   93.0  129
     1        54    1.8   94.7  136
     1        55    1.8   96.5  140
     1        56    1.8   98.2  147
     1        57    1.8  100.0  154
```

❷
```
             Cum           Cum
  Count     Count   Pct    Pct  GNP_86
     1         1    2.0    2.0  120
     1         2    2.0    4.0  160
     1         3    2.0    6.0  180
     1         4    2.0    8.0  230
     1         5    2.0   10.0  280
```
*** *we omit GNP values between 280 and 1320* ***
```
     1        21    2.0   42.0  1320
     1        22    2.0   44.0  1480
     1        23    2.0   46.0  1810
     1        24    2.0   48.0  1830
     1        25    2.0   50.0  1900
     1        26    2.0   52.0  2020
```
*** *we omit GNP values between 2020 and 12080* ***
```
     1        44    2.0   88.0  12080
     1        45    2.0   90.0  12160
     1        46    2.0   92.0  12600
     1        47    2.0   94.0  13160
     1        48    2.0   96.0  14120
     1        49    2.0   98.0  15400
     1        50    2.0  100.0  17680
```

The highlighted numbers below correspond to those in the output:

❶ Each infant mortality rate in our sample is listed on the right side of the *BABYMORT* panel. One country (*Count*=1) has a rate of 5, 10 countries have a rate of 6, and so on. The country with the lowest infant mortality rate had 5 babies (from each 1000 live births) die during their first year of life. The country with the worst rate (bottom of the panel) had 154 out of every 1000 babies die. By using **Data➠Select cases** and specifying BABYMORT=5 and listing *COUNTRY$*, we learn that the country with the lowest infant mortality rate is Switzerland. Changing the **Select cases** condition to BABYMORT>150, we find Afghanistan.

The *Cum Count* (cumulative count) is the sum of all *Counts* up to and including the current count. For the infant mortality rate of 6, the *Cum Count* is 11 (the 10 countries with a rate of 6, plus the one country with 5). According to the cumulative percentage column (*Cum Pct*), we see that the median infant mortality rate is 22 (the *Cum Pct* of 50% falls at 22 deaths). Roughly 25% of the countries have a rate greater than 74 deaths per 1000 live births (*Cum Pct* is 75.4%). One-third of the 57 countries (33.3%) have 11 or fewer infant deaths per 1000 live births. These last two descriptive statements are appropriate for any distribution with ordered values.

❷ On the far right, we see that the smallest GNP per capita in 1986 is $120 per person and the largest is $17,680. Note that the total count for *BABYMORT* is 57, while it is 50 for *GNP_86*. Seven countries did not report a GNP. In the next run, we select **Include missing values** on the **One-way** dialog box to include a category for the missing observations and then reexamine the percentages.

Including a category for missing

In output ❷ above, SYSTAT omits a category for the seven countries that did not report a GNP. Here we add a category for *missing* and study how results change.

Select **Include missing values** and **List layout** on the **One-way** dialog box. With commands:

```
TAB gnp_86 / MISS  / LIST
```

```
              Cum              Cum
     Count   Count    Pct      Pct  GNP_86
       7        7    12.3     12.3  .
       1        8     1.8     14.0  120
       1        9     1.8     15.8  160
       1       10     1.8     17.5  180
       1       11     1.8     19.3  230
       1       12     1.8     21.1  280
      ***  we omit GNP values between 280 and 1320  ***
       1       28     1.8     49.1  1320
       1       29     1.8     50.9  1480
       1       30     1.8     52.6  1810
       1       31     1.8     54.4  1830
       1       32     1.8     56.1  1900
       1       33     1.8     57.9  2020
     ***we omit GNP values between 2020 and 12080  ***
       1       51     1.8     89.5  12080
       1       52     1.8     91.2  12160
       1       53     1.8     93.0  12600
       1       54     1.8     94.7  13160
       1       55     1.8     96.5  14120
       1       56     1.8     98.2  15400
       1       57     1.8    100.0  17680
```

The category for the missing GNP values appears at the top of the table—
12.3% of the countries in this sample did not report a GNP. In the
previous panel, a GNP of $280 is the 10th percentile; here, $280 is the
21st percentile. In the previous panel, the median is $1,900; here, it is
$1,480. What should you say in a report? From the available
information, you can state that among the 50 nations that report GNP
per capita, the median is $1,900.

4.3
Results
by groups

You can use the **By Groups** feature to calculate and display results
separately for each value of a grouping variable (or each unique
combination of two or more grouping variables). Grouping variables can
be numeric or string (that is, to stratify the analysis by sex, the values of
the grouping variable could be 1 and 2 or *Male* and *Female*). You can use
this feature with all statistics in this chapter. We examine infant mortality
rates, *BABYMORT*, grouped by the type of nation: *European, Islamic,* or *New
World.* These category names are stored in the variable *GROUP$.* First go to
the **Data**➨**By Groups** and select *GROUP$* as the variable. Then proceed to
Stats➨**Crosstabs**➨**One-way.**

```
XTAB
    USE ourworld
    BY group$
    TAB babymort / LIST
    BY
```

Remember to disengage **By Groups**. It remains in effect until you turn it off.

```
The following results are for:

   GROUP$      - Europe

                Cum              Cum
    Count      Count    Pct      Pct  BABYMORT
      1          1      5.0      5.0    5
     10         11     50.0     55.0    6
      4         15     20.0     75.0    7
      1         16      5.0     80.0   10
      1         17      5.0     85.0   11
      1         18      5.0     90.0   13
      1         19      5.0     95.0   14
      1         20      5.0    100.0   15

The following results are for:

   GROUP$      = Islamic

                Cum              Cum
    Count      Count    Pct      Pct  BABYMORT
      1          1      6.3      6.3   30
      1          2      6.3     12.5   64
      1          3      6.3     18.8   67
      1          4      6.3     25.0   74
      2          6     12.5     37.5   87
      1          7      6.3     43.8  107
      1          8      6.3     50.0  110
      2         10     12.5     62.5  116
      1         11      6.3     68.8  125
      1         12      6.3     75.0  129
      1         13      6.3     81.3  136
      1         14      6.3     87.5  140
      1         15      6.3     93.8  147
      1         16      6.3    100.0  154

The following results are for:

   GROUP$      - NewWorld

                Cum              Cum
    Count      Count    Pct      Pct  BABYMORT
      1          1      4.8      4.8    7
      1          2      4.8      9.5   10
      1          3      4.8     14.3   12
      3          6     14.3     28.6   16
      1          7      4.8     33.3   18
      2          9      9.5     42.9   22
      1         10      4.8     47.6   27
      1         11      4.8     52.4   32
      1         12      4.8     57.1   38
      1         13      4.8     61.9   49
      2         15      9.5     71.4   61
      2         17      9.5     81.0   62
      1         18      4.8     85.7   67
      1         19      4.8     90.5   69
      1         20      4.8     95.2  107
      1         21      4.8    100.0  125
```

The 11 countries with the lowest infant mortality rates are tallied in the *European* panel (their rates are 5 and 6 deaths), and the five countries with the highest rates are tallied in the *Islamic* panel (their rates are more than 125 deaths). Using the *Cum Pct* column, we estimate the median infant mortality rates for these groups as 6 deaths for European nations, 110 deaths for the Islamic nations, and 32 deaths for countries in the *New World*.

Stem-and-Leaf Plots

In this section, we describe more statistics for quantitative variables that do not require normality. We use the **Stem-and-Leaf** procedure on the **Descriptive Statistics** menu to request the median, the first and third quartiles (**hinges**, or 25th and 75th percentiles), and the minimum and maximum values. Note that the median, minimum, and maximum are also available with the descriptive panel of statistics described in the next section.

The stem-and-leaf plot is useful for assessing distributional shape and identifying outliers. Values that are markedly different from the others in the sample are labeled as **outside values**—that is, the value is more than 1.5 **hspreads** outside its hinge (the **hspread** is the distance between the lower and upper hinges, or quartiles). Under normality, this translates into roughly 2.7 standard deviations from the mean.

4.4
The median
and hinges

We request robust statistics for infant mortality, *BABYMORT*, used in the previous examples and add *POP_1990* (1990 population in millions), and *LITERACY* (percentage of the population who can read). Use **Stats**➟ **Descriptive Statistics**➟**Stem-and-Leaf** to select variables. With commands:

```
STATISTICS
    USE ourworld
    STEM babymort pop_1990 literacy
```

❶
```
        Stem and Leaf Plot of variable:      BABYMORT, N = 57

Minimum:         5.000
Lower hinge:         7.000
Median:         22.000
Upper hinge:        74.000
Maximum:       154.000

            0 H 5666666666677777
            1   00123456668
            2 M 227
            3   028
            4   9
            5
            6   11224779
            7 H 4
            8   77
            9
           10   77
           11   066
           12   559
           13   6
           14   07
           15   4
```

❷
```
        Stem and Leaf Plot of variable:      POP_1990, N = 57

Minimum:         0.263
Lower hinge:         6.142
Median:         10.354
Upper hinge:        25.567
Maximum:       152.505

            0   00122333444
            0 H 5556667777788899
            1 M 0000034
            1   556789
            2   14
            2 H 56
            3   23
            3   79
            4
            4
            5   1
         ***Outside Values***
            5   6677
            6   2
           11   48
           15   2
```

❸
```
        Stem and Leaf Plot of variable:      LITERACY, N = 57

Minimum:        11.600
Lower hinge:        55.000
Median:         88.000
Upper hinge:        99.000
Maximum:       100.000

            1   1258
            2   035689
            3   1
            4
            5 H 002556
            6   355
            7   0446
            8 M 03558
            9 H 03344457888889999999999999
           10   00
```

The highlighted numbers below correspond to those in the output:

❶ In a stem-and-leaf plot, the digits of each number are separated into a stem and a leaf. The stems are listed as a column on the left, and the leaves for each stem are in a row on the right. For infant mortality (*BABYMORT*), the *Maximum* number of babies who die in their first year of life is 154 (out of 1,000 live births). Look for this value at the bottom of the *BABYMORT* display. The stem for 154 is 15, and the leaf is 4. The *Minimum* value for this variable is 5—its leaf is 5 with a stem of 0.

Compare the results for *BABYMORT* with those from Crosstabs, where we estimated the median as 22 deaths during the first year of life for every 1,000 live births. The same value is printed here as the *Median* in the top panel and marked by an *M* in the plot. The hinges, marked by *H*'s in the plot, are 7 and 74 deaths, meaning that 25% of the countries in our sample have a death rate of 7 or less, and another 25% have a rate of 74 or higher.

The sample does not appear homogeneous—there is one gap between 49 and 61 deaths and another between 87 and 107. These gaps are more noticeable in this display than from those in Example 4.2.

❷ For these 57 countries, the median population size is 10.354, or more than 10 million people. One-quarter of the countries have a population of 6.142 million or less. The largest country (Brazil) has more than 152 million people. The largest stem for *POP_1990* is 15, like that for *BABYMORT*. This 15 comes from 152.505, so the 2 is the leaf and the 0.505 is lost.

The plot for *POP_1990* is very right-skewed. Notice that a real number line extends from the minimum stem of 0 (0.623) to the stem of 5 for 51 million. The values below *Outside Values* (stems of 5, 6, 11, and 25 with 8 leaves) do not fall along a number line, so the right tail of this distribution extends further than one would think at first glance. In the next example, we investigate how the shape of this distribution changes when the population values are transformed to log units.

❸ The median indicates that half of the countries in our sample have a *LITERACY* rate of 88% or better. The *Upper hinge* is 99%, so more than one-quarter of the countries have a rate of 99% or better. In the country with the lowest rate (Somalia), only 11.6% of the people can read. The stem for 11.6 is 1 (the 10's digit), and the leaf is 1 (the units digit). The 0.6 is not part of the display. For stem 10, there are two leaves that are 0—so two countries have 100% literacy rates (Finland and Norway). Notice the 11 countries (at the top of the plot) with very low rates. Is there a separate subgroup here? After exploring the effect of a transformation on the population variable, we stratify *LITERACY* by country type in order to check for subpopulations.

4.5 Transformations

Because the distribution of *POP_1990* is very skewed, it may not be suited for analyses based on normality. To find out, we transform the population values to log base 10 units using the L10 function, available on **Data⟶Transform⟶Let**. With commands:

```
STATISTICS
    USE ourworld
    LET logpop90=L10(pop_1990)
    STEM logpop90
```

```
        Stem and Leaf Plot of variable:    LOGPOP90, N = 57
Minimum:       -0.581
Lower hinge:        0.788
Median:        1.015
Upper hinge:        1.408
Maximum:        2.183
            -0   5
         ***Outside Values***
            0   01
            0   33
            0   445
            0 H 6667777
            0   888888899999
            1 M 00000111
            1   2222233
            1 H 445555
            1   777777
            1
            2   001
            2
```

For the untransformed values of the population in ❷ above, the stem-and-leaf plot identifies eight outliers. Here, there is only one outlier. More important, however, is the fact that the shape of the distribution for these transformed values is much more symmetric.

4.6 Subpopulations

In Example 4.3, **Data⟶By Groups** is used to request separate tabulations for each level of a grouping variable. Here, we stratify the values of *LITERACY* for countries grouped as *European*, *Islamic*, and *New World*.

Use **Data⟶By Groups** to select *GROUP$* as the grouping variable. Then use **Stats⟶Descriptive Statistics⟶Stem-and-Leaf** to select *LITERACY*. With commands:

```
STATISTICS
    USE ourworld
    BY group$
    STEM literacy
    BY
```

```
The following results are for:
    GROUP$       = Europe

         Stem and Leaf Plot of variable:      LITERACY, N = 20

Minimum:       83.000
Lower hinge:        98.000
Median:        99.000
Upper hinge:        99.000
Maximum:      100.000

              83   0
              93   0
              95   0
         ***Outside Values***
              97   0
              98 H 000
              99 H 00000000000
             100   00

    GROUP$       = Islamic

         Stem and Leaf Plot of variable:      LITERACY, N = 16

Minimum:       11.600
Lower hinge:        19.000
Median:        28.550
Upper hinge:        53.500
Maximum:       70.000

               1 H 1258
               2 M 05689
               3   1
               4
               5 H 0255
               6   5
               7   0

    GROUP$       = NewWorld

         Stem and Leaf Plot of variable:      LITERACY, N = 21

Minimum:       23.000
Lower hinge:        74.000
Median:        85.600
Upper hinge:        94.000
Maximum:       99.000

               2   3
         ***Outside Values***
               5   0
               5   6
               6   3
               6   5
               7 H 44
               7   6
               8   0
               8 M 558
               9 H 03444
               9   8899
```

The *LITERACY* rates for *Europe* and the *Islamic* nations do not even overlap. The rates range from 83% to 100% for the Europeans and 11.6% to 70% for the Islamics. Earlier, 11 countries were identified that have rates of 31% or less. From these stratified results, we learn that 10 of the countries are *Islamic* and 1 (Haiti) is from the *New World*. The Haitian rate (23%) is identified as outlier with respect to the values of the other New World countries.

Descriptive Statistics

Most of the statistics in this section (for example, the mean, standard deviation, variance, standard error of the mean, skewness, kurtosis, and coefficient of variation) require that the variables follow a normal distribution. Exceptions include the median, the minimum and maximum values, and the range.

Use **Stats** ➡ **Descriptive Statistics** ➡ **Basic Statistics** to request these statistics. You can select the descriptors you want or use SYSTAT's default set (number of cases, minimum and maximum values, mean, and standard deviation). Select **All Options** to request all of the statistics. If you do not select any variables, SYSTAT computes statistics for every numeric variable in your file.

For descriptors within subgroups, use **Data** ➡ **By Groups**. Any statistics calculated can be saved in a SYSTAT file. For example, you could save one record with the mean and standard deviation for each cell in an analysis.

**4.7
The default
statistics**

This example uses the *OURWORLD* data file, containing one record for each of 57 countries, and requests the default set of statistics for *BABYMORT* (infant mortality), *GNP_86* (GNP per capita in 1986), *LITERACY* (percentage of the population who can read), and *POP_1990* (population, in millions, in 1990).

The Statistics procedure knows only that these are numeric variables—it does not know if the mean and standard deviation are appropriate descriptors for their distributions. In the previous examples, we learned that the distribution of infant mortality is right-skewed and has distinct subpopulations, the GNP is missing for 12.3% of the countries, and the distribution of *LITERACY* is left-skewed and has distinct subgroups. In Example 4.5, a log transformation markedly improves the symmetry of the population values. This example ignores those findings.

After identifying your data, use **Stats** ➡ **Descriptive Statistics** ➡ **Basic Statistics** to select *BABYMORT*, *GNP_86*, *LITERACY*, and *POP_1990*. With commands:

```
STATISTICS
    USE ourworld
    STATISTICS babymort gnp_86 literacy pop_1990
```

```
Total Observations: 57

                       BABYMORT       GNP_86      LITERACY      POP_1990

    N of cases               57           50            57            57
    Minimum               5.000      120.000        11.600         0.263
    Maximum             154.000    17680.000       100.000       152.505
    Mean                 48.140     4310.800        73.563        22.800
    Standard Dev         47.236     4905.877        29.765        30.366
```

For each variable, SYSTAT prints the number of cases (*N of cases*) with
data present. Note that the sample size for *GNP_86* is 50, or 7 less than the
Total Observations reported at the top of the panel. For each variable,
Minimum is the smallest value and **Maximum**, the largest. Thus, the
lowest infant mortality rate is 5 deaths (per 1,000 live births), and the
highest is 154 deaths. In a symmetric distribution, the mean and median
are approximately the same. In Example 4.4, the median for *POP_1990* is
10.354 million people. Here, the mean is 22.8 million—more than
double the median. This estimate of the mean is quite sensitive to the
extreme values in the right tail.

Standard Dev, or standard deviation, measures the spread of the values in
each distribution. When the data follow a normal distribution, we expect
roughly 95% of the values to fall within two standard deviations of the mean.

The ALL option

Select **All Options** to display all the statistics. With commands:

```
STATISTICS babymort gnp_86 literacy pop_1990 / ALL
```

```
Total Observations: 57

                       BABYMORT       GNP_86      LITERACY      POP_1990

    N of cases               57           50            57            57
    Minimum               5.000      120.000        11.600         0.263
    Maximum             154.000    17680.000       100.000       152.505
    Range               149.000    17560.000        88.400       152.242
    Sum                2744.000   215540.000      4193.100      1299.615
    Median               22.000     1960.000        88.000        10.354
    Mean                 48.140     4310.800        73.563        22.800
    95% CI Upper         60.674     5705.035        81.461        30.857
    95% CI Lower         35.607     2916.565        65.666        14.743
    Std. Error            6.256      693.796         3.942         4.022
    Standard Dev         47.236     4905.877        29.765        30.366
    Variance           2231.194 2.40676E+07       885.931       922.066
    C.V.                  0.981        1.138         0.405         1.332
    Skewness(G1)          0.819        1.159        -0.864         2.525
    SE Skewness           0.324        0.346         0.324         0.324
    Kurtosis(G2)         -0.745        0.024        -0.726         6.610
    SE Kurtosis           0.649        0.693         0.649         0.649
```

The **range** is the difference between the minimum and maximum values. The **variance** is the square of the standard deviation (SD). **Standard error** (*Std. Error*), produced by the **SEM** option, is the standard error of the mean $SD/\sqrt{n}$.

95% CI Upper and *95% CI Lower* are, respectively, the upper and lower endpoints of the 95% confidence interval for the mean:

Mean + $t_{0.975}(df)$ * Std. Error

If you want to select a different level of confidence, type the value in the box. The command option is CONFI = n.

Skewness or **G1** measures the symmetry of the sample distribution; **kurtosis** or **G2**, its peakedness. These measures are centered at 0. A positive value for skewness indicates a long right tail; a negative value, a long left tail. A positive value for kurtosis indicates that the tails of the distribution are longer than those of a normal distribution; a negative value, shorter tails (becoming like those of a box-shaped uniform distribution). What is an extreme *negative* or *positive* value, extreme enough for us to reject normality? **SE Skewness**, is the standard error of G1, and **SE Kurtosis**, the standard error of G2. If the interval of G1 or G2 plus or minus two times its standard error does not include 0, the measure is considered extreme. Thus, *BABYMORT*, *GNP_86*, and *POP_1990* have an extreme positive value (are right-skewed), and *LITERACY* is left-skewed. *POP_1990* appears to be the most skewed (2.525 ± 2*0.324). Since skewness and kurtosis are sensitive to anomalies in the distribution, you should study them in conjunction with a boxplot or a stem-and-leaf plot. **Sum** is the total of the observations in the sample. *C.V.* is the **coefficient of variation** (SD/Mean). In a sample with an odd number of cases, the **median** is the middle observation when the data are ordered. When the sample size is even, the median is the average of the pair of observations occupying the two central positions. More simply, just remember that half the values in the sample are larger, half are smaller.

4.8 Requesting specific statistics and trans- formations

Here, we request the median, mean (plus its standard error and 95% confidence interval), and skewness and kurtosis with their standard errors. We also look more at distributional shape and study the effect of a symmetrizing transformation for *POP_1990*.

After selecting your variables, select the statistics you want. With commands:

```
STATISTICS
USE ourworld
LET logpop90 = L10(pop_1990)
STATISTICS babymort gnp_86 literacy pop_1990 logpop90,
                        / MEDIAN  MEAN   CIM,
                          SEM  SKEWNESS  SES,
                          KURTOSIS  SEK
```

```
Total Observations: 57


                    BABYMORT     GNP_86    LITERACY    POP_1990    LOGPOP90

N of cases                57         50          57          57          57
Median                22.000   1960.000      88.000      10.354       1.015
Mean                  48.140   4310.800      73.563      22.800       1.067
95% CI Upper          60.674   5705.035      81.461      30.857       1.207
95% CI Lower          35.607   2916.565      65.666      14.743       0.926
Std. Error             6.256    693.796       3.942       4.022       0.070
Skewness(G1)           0.819      1.159      -0.864       2.525      -0.287
SE Skewness            0.324      0.346       0.324       0.324       0.324
Kurtosis(G2)          -0.745      0.024      -0.726       6.610       0.633
SE Kurtosis            0.649      0.693       0.649       0.649       0.649
```

The distribution of *LOGPOP90* can be considered symmetric (−0.287 ± 2 * 0.324), while that of the untransformed data is very right-skewed.

Using SYSTAT's calculator to transform results. An approximate 95% confidence interval for the mean of *POP_1990* is:

22.8 ± 2.003 * 4.022   *or*   14.743 to 30.857 million people

The 95% confidence interval for the *LOGPOP90* mean of 1.067 extends from 0.926 to 1.207 (in base 10 log units). We can use SYSTAT's calculator to transform the mean and end points of the interval to get a mean of 11.668, with a confidence interval ranging from 8.433 to 16.106 million people. For example, type

```
CALC 10^.926
```

to get the value 8.433 for the lower end of the interval and

```
CALC 10^1.207
```

to get 16.106 for the upper end. Notice that the interval resulting from the transformation (8.4, 16.1) is much smaller than that found using the untransformed values (14.7, 30.9).

4.9 Saving By Group results

For each level of one or more grouping variables, SYSTAT can compute statistics and write the statistics to a file. Here we first save one statistic for the levels of a single grouping variable. Then we save several statistics for the cross-classifications of two or more grouping variables.

Note: *If you only want to view the within-group statistics (and don't need a SYSTAT data file of them), omit the* **SAVE** *step.*

One statistic and one grouping variable

For European, Islamic, and New World countries, we save the median infant mortality rate, gross national product, literacy rate, and 1990 population. Use **Data**➡**By Groups** to select *GROUP$* as the variable. In **Stats**➡**Descriptive Statistics**➡**Basic Statistics**, select your statistic and variables as usual. When you select **Save statistics to file**, a dialog box appears in which you type the name of the file for the results.

```
STATISTICS
  USE ourworld
  BY group$
  SAVE mystats
  STATISTICS babymort gnp_86 literacy pop_1990 / MEDIAN
  BY
```

The text results that appear on the screen are shown below (they can also be sent to a text file).

```
The following results are for:
   GROUP$      = Europe

                  BABYMORT      GNP_86    LITERACY    POP_1990

   N of cases          20          18          20          20
   Median           6.000    9610.000      99.000      10.462

   GROUP$      = Islamic

                  BABYMORT      GNP_86    LITERACY    POP_1990

   N of cases          16          12          16          16
   Median         113.000     335.000      28.550      16.686

   GROUP$      = NewWorld

                  BABYMORT      GNP_86    LITERACY    POP_1990

   N of cases          21          20          21          21
   Median          32.000    1275.000      85.600       7.241
```

The *MYSTATS* data file (created in the SAVE step) is shown below:

Case	GROUP$	STATISTIC$	BABYMORT	GNP_86	LITERACY	POP_1990
1	Europe	N of cases	20	18	20	20
2	Europe	Median	6	9610	99	10.462
3	Islamic	N of cases	16	12	16	16
4	Islamic	Median	113	335	28.550	16.686
5	NewWorld	N of cases	21	20	21	21
6	NewWorld	Median	32	1275	85.6	7.241

Use a statement such as this to eliminate the sample size records:

```
SELECT statistic$ <> 'N of cases'
```

Multiple statistics and grouping variables

If you want to save two or more statistics for each unique cross-classification of the values of the grouping variables, SYSTAT can write the results in two ways:

1. A separate record for each statistic. The values of a new variable named *STATISTICS$* identify the statistics.

or

2. One record containing all the requested statistics. SYSTAT generates these variable names to label the results.

N of cases	NU*cccccccc*	Std. Error	SE*cccccccc*
Minimum	MI*cccccccc*	Standard Dev	SD*cccccccc*
Maximum	MA*cccccccc*	Variance	VA*cccccccc*
Range	RA*cccccccc*	C.V.	CV*cccccccc*
Sum	SU*cccccccc*	Skewness (G1)	SK*cccccccc*
Median	MD*cccccccc*	SE Skewness	ES*cccccccc*
Mean	ME*cccccccc*	Kurtosis (G2)	KU*cccccccc*
95% CI Upper	CU*cccccccc*	SE Kurtosis	EK*cccccccc*
95% CI Lower	CL*cccccccc*		

The first two letters of the name identify the statistic; *n*, the order in which you selected each variable, and *cccccccc*, the first eight letters of the variable name (see the example below). If you specify a different level for the confidence interval, your specification replaces "95."

The first layout is the default; the second is obtained by selecting **Aggregate** on the **Save statistic to file** drop-down list. With commands:

```
SAVE filename / AGG
```

As examples, we add to the previous example by including the mean and standard error of the mean and *GOV$* as a second grouping variable. That is, we request descriptive statistics for the cross-classification of type of country with government. The nine cells for which we compute statistics are shown here (the number of countries is displayed in each cell):

| | | | GOV$ | |
		Democracy	Military	One Party
	Europe	16	0	4
GROUP$	Islamic	4	7	5
	New World	12	6	3

Note the empty cell in the first row. We illustrate both file layouts—a separate record for each statistic and one record for all results.

Note: *The screen output associated with each layout for saving statistics is the same and looks like the output at the beginning of this example.*

One record per statistic. The following commands are used to compute and save statistics for the combinations of *GROUP* and *GOV$* shown in the table above:

```
BY group$ gov$
SAVE mystats2
STATISTICS babymort gnp_86 literacy pop_1990,
                      / MEDIAN  MEAN  SEM
BY
```

The *MYSTATS2* file with 32 cases and seven variables is shown below:

Case	GROUP$	GOV$	STATISTC$	BABYMORT	GNP_86	LITERACY	POP_1990
1	Europe	Democracy	N of Cases	16.000	16.000	16.000	16.000
2	Europe	Democracy	Mean	6.875	9770.000	97.250	22.427
3	Europe	Democracy	Std. Error	0.547	1057.226	1.055	5.751
4	Europe	Democracy	Median	6.000	10005.000	99.000	9.969
5	Europe	OneParty	N of Cases	4.000	2.000	4.000	4.000
6	Europe	OneParty	Mean	11.500	2045.000	98.750	20.084
7	Europe	OneParty	Std. Error	1.708	25.000	0.250	6.036
8	Europe	OneParty	Median	12.000	2045.000	99.000	15.995
9	Islamic	Democracy	N of Cases	4.000	4.000	4.000	4.000
10	Islamic	Democracy	Mean	91.000	700.000	37.300	12.761
11	Islamic	Democracy	Std. Error	23.083	378.660	9.312	5.315
12	Islamic	Democracy	Median	97.000	370.000	29.550	12.612
13	Islamic	OneParty	N of Cases	5.000	3.000	5.000	5.000
14	Islamic	OneParty	Mean	109.800	1016.667	29.720	15.355
15	Islamic	OneParty	Std. Error	15.124	787.196	9.786	3.289
16	Islamic	OneParty	Median	116.000	280.000	18.000	15.862
17	Islamic	Military	N of Cases	7.000	5.000	7.000	7.000
18	Islamic	Military	Mean	110.857	458.000	37.886	51.444
19	Islamic	Military	Std. Error	11.801	180.039	7.779	18.678
20	Islamic	Military	Median	116.000	350.000	29.000	51.667
21	NewWorld	Democracy	N of Cases	12.000	12.000	12.000	12.000
22	NewWorld	Democracy	Mean	44.667	2894.167	85.800	26.490
23	NewWorld	Democracy	Std. Error	9.764	1085.810	3.143	11.926
24	NewWorld	Democracy	Median	35.000	1645.000	86.800	15.102
25	NewWorld	OneParty	N of Cases	3.000	2.000	3.000	3.000
26	NewWorld	OneParty	Mean	14.667	2995.000	90.500	4.441
27	NewWorld	OneParty	Std. Error	1.333	2155.000	8.251	3.153
28	NewWorld	OneParty	Median	16.000	2995.000	98.500	2.441
29	NewWorld	Military	N of Cases	6.000	6.000	6.000	6.000
30	NewWorld	Military	Mean	53.167	1045.000	63.000	6.886
31	NewWorld	Military	Std. Error	13.245	287.573	10.820	1.515
32	NewWorld	Military	Median	55.000	780.000	60.500	5.726

The average infant mortality rate for European democratic nations is 6.875 (case 2), while the median is 6.0 (case 4).

One record for all statistics. Instead of four records (cases) for each combination of *GROUP$* and *GOV$*, we specify **Aggregate** on the **Save statistic to file** drop-down list to prompt SYSTAT to write one record for each cell:

```
BY group$ gov$
SAVE mystats3 / AG
STATISTICS babymort gnp_86 literacy pop_1990,
                  / MEDIAN  MEAN  SEM
BY
```

The *MYSTATS3* file, with 8 cases and 18 variables, is shown below. (We separated them into two panels and shortened the variable names):

Case	GROUP$	GOV$	NU1BABYM	ME1BABYM	SE1BABYM	MD1BABYM	NU2GNP_8	ME2GNP_8	SE2GNP_8	MD2GNP_8
1	Europe	Democracy	16	6.875	0.547	6.0	16	9770.000	1057.226	10005
2	Europe	OneParty	4	11.500	1.708	12.0	2	2045.000	25.000	2045
3	Islamic	Democracy	4	91.000	23.083	97.0	4	700.000	378.660	370
4	Islamic	OneParty	5	109.800	15.124	116.0	3	1016.667	787.196	280
5	Islamic	Military	7	110.857	11.801	116.0	5	458.000	180.039	350
6	NewWorld	Democracy	12	44.667	9.764	35.0	12	2894.167	1085.810	1645
7	NewWorld	OneParty	3	14.667	1.333	16.0	2	2995.000	2155.000	2995
8	NewWorld	Military	6	53.167	13.245	55.0	6	1045.000	287.573	780

NU3LITER	ME3LITER	SE3LITER	MD3LITER	NU4POP_1	ME4POP_1	SE4POP_1	MD4POP_1
16	97.250	1.055	99.0	16	22.427	5.751	9.969
4	98.750	0.250	99.0	4	20.084	6.036	15.995
4	37.300	9.312	29.5	4	12.761	5.315	12.612
5	29.720	9.786	18.0	5	15.355	3.289	15.862
7	37.886	7.779	29.0	7	51.444	18.678	51.667
12	85.800	3.143	86.8	12	26.490	11.926	15.102
3	90.500	8.251	98.5	3	4.441	3.153	2.441
6	63.000	10.820	60.5	6	6.886	1.515	5.726

Note that there are no European countries with *Military* governments, so no record is written. The full variable names are as follows:

NU1BABYMORT	MD1BABYMORT	ME1BABYMORT	SE1BABYMORT	NU2GNP_86	MD2GNP_86
ME2GNP_86	SE2GNP_86	NU3LITERACY	MD3LITERACY	ME3LITERACY	SE3LITERACY
NU4POP_1990	MD4POP_1990	ME4POP_1990	SE4POP_1990		

T Tests

Laszlo Engelman

T-test provides three types of tests:

- The **two-sample *t* test** (*independent t* test), to compare the means of one variable for two groups of cases

- The **paired comparison *t* test** (*dependent t* test), to compare the means of two variables for a single group

- The **one-sample *t* test**, to compare the mean of one variable with a known or hypothesized value

T Tests

Overview

Overview

The following menus are available from **t-test** on the **Stats** menu:

Two Groups   Two-sample (*independent*) *t* test
Paired   Paired comparison (*dependent*) *t* test
One Sample   One-sample *t* test

Diagrams of the data structure for these tests make their use more clear. In the following diagrams, imagine that the rows are cases and the columns are variables.

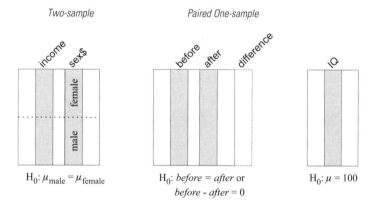

For the two-sample *t* test, the values of the variable of interest (*INCOME*) are stored in a single column, and SYSTAT uses codes of a grouping variable (*SEX$*) to separate the cases into two groups (the codes can be numbers or characters). For each case in a paired *t* test, SYSTAT computes the differences between values of two variables (columns) and tests if the average differs from 0. For the one-sample *t* test, values of a single variable are compared against a constant you specify.

Getting started   For a two-sample *t* test, use Stats⇒ t-test⇒Two Groups:

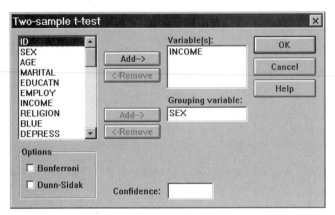

For a paired comparison *t* test, use Stats⇒ t-test⇒Paired:

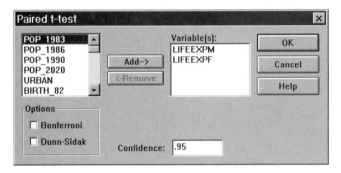

For a one-sample *t* test, use Stats⇒ t-test⇒One Sample:

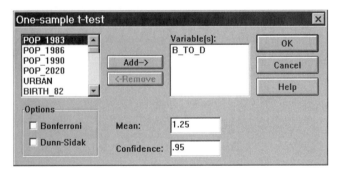

From each dialog box, choose **Bonferroni** or **Dunn-Sidak** probabilities as protection for multiple tests. Use **Confidence** to specify the level of confidence for the difference between means or, for the one-sample *t* test, the difference between the mean and the hypothesized value.

Using commands

To request a *t* test, first identify your data:

    USE *filename*

Then specify TTEST as the procedure name and continue:

Two-sample   TEST *varlist* * *grpvar* / *options*

Paired comparison   TEST *varlist* / *options*

One-sample   TEST *varlist* = *constant* / *options*

Two-Sample T Test

One of the most common situations encountered in statistical practice is that of comparing means for two groups of cases. For example, does the average response for a treatment group differ from that for the control group? The two-sample *t* test (or *independent t* test) addresses this problem. Ideally, for this test, the subjects would be randomly assigned to the two groups, so that any differences in response are due to the treatment (or lack of treatment) and not to other factors. This is not the case in Example 5.1, where average income for males and females is compared—a person is not randomly assigned to be a male or a female. In such situations, the researcher should explore the data carefully to ensure that differences in other factors are not masking or enhancing a significant difference in means. For example, differences in income may be influenced by education and not by sex alone.

For the tests in this section, we use **Stats**➠**t-test**➠**Two Groups**.

5.1 Income differences for males and females

Do males tend to earn more than females? We use the *SURVEY2* data to test whether the average income for males differs from that for females:

$$H_0: \ \mu_{female} = \mu_{male}$$

The *SURVEY2* data file has one case for each subject, with the annual income (*INCOME*) and a numeric or character code to identify the sex (the values *Female* and *Male* are stored in the grouping variable *SEX$*). Note that the cases do not need to be ordered by the values of the grouping variable.

Before displaying the *Quick Graph*, which SYSTAT automatically provides with each test, we show alternative ways of viewing these data— a box-and-whiskers plot, a dual histogram, and a kernel density estimator for each group:

```
TTEST
    USE survey2
    DENSITY income * sex$ / BOX  TRANS
```

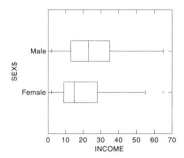

Following are two more ways to view these data:

```
DENSITY income / DUAL=sex$  FILL=0,1
DENSITY income / GROUP=sex$  OVERLAY KERNEL
DASH=1,6
```

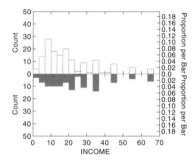 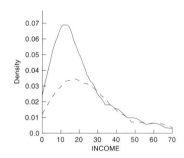

Following is the *t* test. Under **Stats**⟹**t-test**⟹**Two Groups**, select *INCOME* as the **Variable** and *SEX$* as the **Grouping variable**. With commands:

```
TEST income * sex$
```

```
Categorical values encountered during processing are:
SEX$ (2 levels)
   Male Female

Two-sample t test on INCOME grouped by SEX$

   Group          N          Mean          SD
     Male         104        24.971        16.418
     Female       152        20.257        14.828

     Separate Variance t =      2.346 DF =  206.2   Prob =    0.020
     Difference in Means =      4.715  95.00% CI =    0.753 to  8.676


     Pooled Variance t =        2.391 DF =  254     Prob =    0.018
     Difference in Means =      4.715  95.00% CI     0.832 to  8.597
```

❶ (marker next to Group/Male/Female block)

❷ (marker next to Separate Variance block)

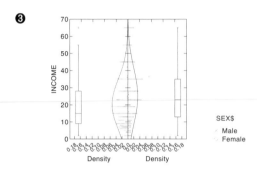

❸

The highlighted numbers below correspond to those in the output:

❶ The average yearly income for males in this sample is almost $5,000 more than that for females ($24,971 versus $20,257). The standard deviation (*SD*) for males (16.4) is also larger than that for females (14.8).

❷ Two tests are computed for comparing group means. The **pooled variance *t* test** is usually the first two-sample *t* test introduced in elementary textbooks. It assumes that the population variances for the two groups are equal—that is, the shapes of the distributions are the same. The **separate variance *t* test** does not require equal variances. Following are the formulas for the test statistics:

Separate variance   *Pooled variance*

$$t = \frac{\bar{x}_1 - \bar{x}_2}{\sqrt{\left(\dfrac{s_1^2}{n_1} + \dfrac{s_2^2}{n_2}\right)}} \qquad t = \frac{\bar{x}_1 - \bar{x}_2}{\sqrt{s_p^2\left(\dfrac{1}{n_1} + \dfrac{1}{n_2}\right)}}$$

where:

$$s_p^2 = \frac{(n_1-1)s_1^2 + (n_2-1)s_2^2}{n_1 + n_2 - 2}$$

$\bar{x}_i$ = mean of group *i*

n_i = number of observations in group *i*

s_i^2 = sample variance in group *i*

The degrees of freedom for the pooled test are $(n_1 + n_2 - 2)$. The degrees of freedom for the separate variance test are computed—the formula involves s_1, s_2, n_1, and n_2.

The *p* values (*Prob*) for both tests indicate a significant difference in the average incomes of males and females. That is, for the separate variance test, $t = 2.346$ with 206.2 degrees of freedom and an associated probability of 0.02. The values for the pooled test are $t = 2.391$, $df = 254$, and *p* value = 0.018. Which result should you use? Use the pooled test when you are comfortable that the population variances in the two groups are equal. Scan graphical displays for similar shapes and note that the more the sample variances differ, the more the degrees of freedom for the separate variance test drop. You pay a penalty for unequal variances—diminished degrees of freedom mean that your effective sample size decreases. Here, we would use the separate variance *t* test.

The **difference in means** is $4,715. The separate variances estimate of the 95% confidence interval for this mean difference extends from $753 to $8,676. Note that the interval using the pooled variance estimate is shorter.

❸ For each group, three graphical displays are combined in this *Quick Graph*: a boxplot displaying the sample median, quartiles, and outliers (if any), a normal curve calculated using the sample mean and standard deviation, and a dit plot displaying each observation. The median incomes differ more than the mean incomes displayed in ❶ above. The distribution of female incomes is more right-skewed than the distribution of male incomes. The boxplot and normal curve indicate that the distribution of male incomes is fairly symmetric.

To omit this display, specify GRAPH=NONE or deselect **Statistical Quick Graphs** in the **Edit➠Options** dialog box.

5.2 Tests for several variables

In Example 5.1, we examined the results for a single two-sample *t* test. SYSTAT allows you to request tests for several variables with one specification. The *p* value associated with the *t* test assumes that you are making one and only one test. The probability of finding a significant difference by chance alone increases rapidly with the number of tests. So, you should avoid requesting tests for many variables and reporting only those that appear to be significant.

Bonferroni and Dunn-Sidak adjustments

What do you do when you want to study test results for several variables? As protection for multiple testing, use the Bonferroni or Dunn-Sidak adjustment to the probabilities.

In the **Stats**➠**t-test**➠**Two Groups** dialog box, specify:

Bonferroni To allow for multiple tests, this adjustment multiplies the usual probability by the number of tests.

Dunn-Sidak The adjusted probability for n independent tests is computed as $1 - (1 - p)n$.

Note that if you expand the formula stated for Dunn-Sidak:

$$1 - \left(1 - np + \binom{n}{2}p^2 - \binom{n}{3}p^3 + \dots + p^n \right)$$

the first 1's cancel, leaving the Bonferroni adjustment of np. The remaining terms for the Dunn-Sidak approach 0 for a very small p.

How do developed and emerging nations differ? We use the *OURWORLD* file with data for 57 countries. Variables recorded for each case (country) include *URBAN* (percentage of the population living in urban areas), *LIFEEXPF* (years of life expectancy for females), *LIFEEXPM* (years of life expectancy for males), and *GDP$* (grouping variable with codes *Developed* and *Emerging*).

Select **Stats**➠**t-test**➠**Two Groups** and select *URBAN*, *LIFEEXPF*, and *LIFEEXPM* as **Variable(s)** and *GDP$* as the **Grouping variable**. Also select **Bonferroni** and/or **Dunn-Sidak**. Because we expect the probabilities to be small, we also set **Decimal places** to 8 in the **Edit**➠**Options** dialog box to display more digits following the decimal point. With commands:

```
TTEST
    USE ourworld
    FORMAT=8
    TEST urban lifeexpf lifeexpm * gdp$ / BONF DUNN
    FORMAT
```

Following are the results (we used an editor to delete the difference in means and confidence intervals):

```
❶  Two-sample t test on URBAN grouped by GDP$


      Group              N        Mean          SD
      Developed         29   66.10344828   16.84243095
      Emerging          27   38.55555556   19.69446134

      Separate Variance t =   5.60601759 DF =   51.4    Prob =   0.00000083

                                    Dunn-Sidak Adjusted Prob =   0.00000248
                                    Bonferroni Adjusted Prob =   0.00000248

      Pooled Variance t =   5.63775382 DF =   54    Prob =   0.00000065
                                    Dunn-Sidak Adjusted Prob =   0.00000194
                                    Bonferroni Adjusted Prob =   0.00000194

❷  Two-sample t test on LIFEEXPF grouped by GDP$


      Group              N        Mean          SD
      Developed         30   77.43333333    4.47740164
      Emerging          27   62.00000000   11.03490964

      Separate Variance t =   6.78218993 DF =   33.6    Prob =   0.00000009
                                    Dunn-Sidak Adjusted Prob =   0.00000027
                                    Bonferroni Adjusted Prob =   0.00000027

      Pooled Variance t =   7.04827872 DF =   55    Prob =   0.00000000
                                    Dunn-Sidak Adjusted Prob =   0.00000001
                                    Bonferroni Adjusted Prob =   0.00000001

❸  Two-sample t test on LIFEEXPM grouped by GDP$


      Group              N        Mean          SD
      Developed         30   70.83333333    3.83345822
      Emerging          27   58.70370370    9.96846883

      Separate Variance t =   5.93974079 DF =   32.9    Prob =   0.00000117
                                    Dunn-Sidak Adjusted Prob =   0.00000351
                                    Bonferroni Adjusted Prob =   0.00000351

      Pooled Variance t =   6.18109495 DF =   55    Prob =   0.00000008
                                    Dunn-Sidak Adjusted Prob =   0.00000025
                                    Bonferroni Adjusted Prob =   0.00000025
```

The highlighted numbers below correspond to those in the output:

❶ On the average, 66.1% of the inhabitants of developed nations live in urban areas, while 38.6% of those in emerging nations live in urban areas. Note that the sample size, *N,* is 29 + 27 = 56, but there are 57 cases in the *OURWORLD* file (the value of *URBAN* for Belgium is missing). Compare the *DF* for the two tests—51.4 versus 54. Thus, considering graphical displays (not shown), the standard deviations, and the small difference between the *DF*'s for the two tests, we are not uncomfortable reporting results for the pooled variance test. Significantly more people in developed nations live in urban areas than do people in emerging nations (t = 5.638, *df* = 54, *p* value < 0.0005).

Simply view this output as an illustration of the mechanics of the adjustment features. A difference between a probability of 0.00000083 and 0.00000248 is negligible, considering possible problems in sampling, errors in the data, or a failure to meet necessary assumptions. However, if you scan the results for 100 variables, a probability of 0.0006 for a separate variance t test is not significant when multiple testing is considered, since the Bonferroni adjusted probability would be 0.06.

❷ The standard deviation (*SD*) for the emerging nations is more than two times larger than that for the developed nations, and the *DF* for the separate variance test drops to 33.6. Using the separate variance test, we conclude that an average life expectancy of 77.4 years differs significantly from 62 years ($t = 6.782$, $df = 33.6$, p value < 0.0005).

❸ Conclusions regarding male life expectancy are similar to those for females, except that for males, life expectancy is, on the average, shorter than that for females—70.8 years in developed nations and 58.7 in emerging nations. You could use a paired t test to check if the sex difference is significant (see Example 5.4).

**5.3
Meeting
assumptions**

Should you transform your data before analysis? Most analyses have assumptions. If your data do not meet the necessary assumptions, the probabilities with the statistics may be suspect. Before a t test, we look for:

— **Violations of the equal variance assumption.** When the shapes of the distributions differ markedly, it is legitimate to use the separate variance t test. *However, you pay a penalty in that the degrees of freedom are reduced.* This means that, effectively, you have a smaller sample, making it harder to detect a significant difference when one truly exists.

— **Symmetry.** The mean of each group should fall approximately in the middle of the spread.

— **Gross outliers.** Values that stand apart from the others can shift the sample mean away from the population mean and inflate the standard deviation used in the denominator of the test statistic.

Frequently, unequal variance can be solved by log transforming or taking the square root of each observation and using the transformed values in the analysis. If the transformation succeeds in equalizing the variances, you can then use the results of the pooled variance test with its full degrees of freedom. Note that symmetry often improves when the variances become equal. Transformations are most effective when the size of each standard deviation is related to its group mean—for example, the more variable group has the larger mean.

In this example, we examine the dollar amounts that Islamic and New World countries spend per person on health. We request tests of health dollars as measured, in square root units, and for log-transformed values. We use **Data ➡ Transform ➡ Let** to transform the values of *HEALTH* (that is, *SQHEALTH = SQR(HEALTH)*). Since SYSTAT requires that the grouping variable has two values, we use **Data ➡ Select Cases** to remove the European countries from the sample (that is, *GROUP$ <>* 'Europe'). With commands:

```
TTEST
    USE ourworld
    SELECT group$ <>'Europe'

    TEST health * group$

    LET sqhealth=SQR(health)
    TEST sqhealth * group$

    LET lghealth=L10(health)
    TEST lghealth * group$
    SELECT
```

Following are the results (again, we omit the differences in means and confidence intervals):

```
Categorical values encountered during processing are:
GROUP$ (2 levels)
   Islamic NewWorld

Two-sample t test on HEALTH grouped by GROUP$

    Group            N        Mean            SD
    Islamic         15       20.336        41.736
    NewWorld        21       85.955       200.531

       Separate Variance t =    -1.456 DF =   22.4    Prob =    0.159
       Pooled Variance t =      -1.243 DF =   34      Prob =    0.222


Two-sample t test on SQHEALTH grouped by GROUP$

    Group            N        Mean            SD
    Islamic         15        3.194         3.295
    NewWorld        21        6.890         6.357

       Separate Variance t =    -2.271 DF =   31.5    Prob =    0.030
       Pooled Variance t =      -2.057 DF =   34      Prob =    0.047


Two-sample t test on LGHEALTH grouped by GROUP$

    Group            N        Mean            SD
    Islamic         15        0.664         0.777
    NewWorld        21        1.442         0.622

       Separate Variance t =    -3.214 DF =   25.9    Prob =    0.003
       Pooled Variance t =      -3.338 DF =   34      Prob =    0.002
```

❷

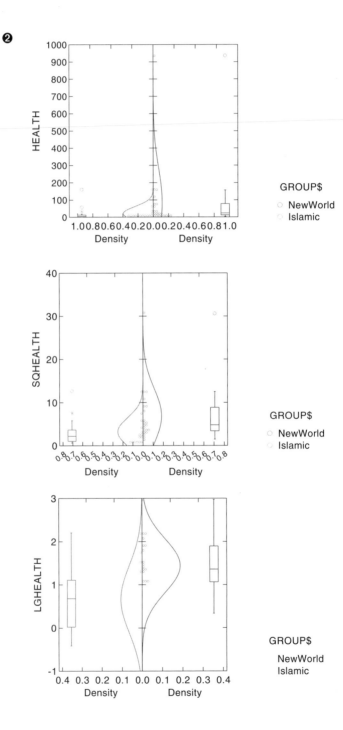

GROUP$

○ NewWorld
○ Islamic

GROUP$

○ NewWorld
○ Islamic

GROUP$

NewWorld
Islamic

❶ The output includes the results for dollars spent per person for health as recorded (*HEALTH*), in square root units (*SQHEALTH*), and in log units (*LGHEALTH*). In the top panel, it appears that New World countries spend considerably more than Islamic nations ($85.96 versus $20.34, on the average). For these untransformed samples, however, this difference is not significant ($t = -1.456$, $df = 22.4$, p value = 0.159). Now let's vet the effect of transforming the data.

For the untransformed data, the standard deviation for the New World countries (200.531) is almost *five* times larger than that for the Islamic nations (41.736). For *SQHEALTH*, the former is approximately two times larger than the latter. For *LGHEALTH*, the difference has reversed. The Islamic group exhibits more spread. Some analysts might want to try a transform between a square root and a log. For example,

```
LET cuberoot = HEALTH^.333
```

But remember, we are selecting a transform using samples of 15 and 21 per group—and the results will have to be explained to others. The graphical displays and test results for the logged data appear to be okay. We conclude that, on the average, New World countries spend significantly more for health than do Islamic nations ($t = -3.338$, $df = 34$, p value = 0.002 for data analyzed in log units).

❷ Each *Quick Graph* combines three graphical displays: a boxplot displays the sample median, quartiles, and outliers (if any); a normal curve calculated using the sample mean and standard deviation; and a dit plot that displays each observation. In the boxplots and normal curves, notice that the shapes of the Islamic and New World distributions are most similar for the data in log units. Canada and Libya are *far outside values* in the boxplots for the raw data and the data in square root units. The log transformation tames these outliers.

Paired Comparison T Test

In each two-sample *t* test example above, we compared the average of one variable for two groups of cases. For the paired (or *dependent*) *t* test, we compare the means of two variables (columns). Often, the study design for this test involves measuring each subject twice: *before* and *after* some kind of treatment or intervention. We are interested in whether the means of the two measures differ—or, equivalently, whether the average of the differences (of the two values for each case) differs from 0.

For the tests in this section, use **Stats**➠**t-test**➠**Paired**.

**5.4
Life
expectancy**

Do females live longer than males? For each of the 57 countries in the *OURWORLD* data file, life expectancy is recorded for females and males. Each case (country) has two measures in the same units (years of life expectancy), so we use the paired comparison *t* test to test if the means are equal.

Following are box-and-whiskers plots of the variables and the difference between male and female life expectancy for each country:

```
TTEST
    USE ourworld
    DENSITY lifeexpf / BOX   TRANS

    DENSITY lifeexpm / BOX   TRANS

    LET dif = lifeexpf - lifeexpm
    DENSITY dif / BOX   TRANS   XLAB='Difference'
```

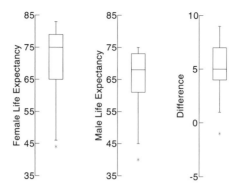

The graphs confirm that females tend to live longer, and that only two countries have negative differences (males live longer than females).

To test whether the average difference departs from 0, use **Stats**➟ **t-test**➟**Paired** and select *LIFEEXPF* and *LIFEEXPM* as **Variable(s)**. We omit SYSTAT's automatic *Quick Graph* by deselecting **Statistical Quick Graphs** in the **Edit**➟**Options** dialog box. With commands:

```
GRAPH NONE
TEST lifeexpf lifeexpm
```

```
Paired samples t test on LIFEEXPF vs LIFEEXPM with 57 cases

    Mean LIFEEXPF    =      70.123
    Mean LIFEEXPM    =      65.088
     Mean Difference =       5.035    95%CI =     4.409 to      5.661
       SD Difference =       2.337                        t =     16.264
                                      DF =   56   Prob =     0.000
```

In the sample, females, on the average, tend to live 70.123 years and males tend to live 65.088 years. The *Mean Difference* between female and male life expectancy is 5.035 years. A 95% confidence interval (*95%CI*) for this difference in means extends from 4.409 years to 5.661 years. The interval is computed as follows:

Mean Difference $\pm\ t_{0.975}$ (*DF*) * (SD Difference)

A difference of 5.035 years departs significantly from 0 ($t = 16.264$, $df = 56$, p value < 0.005). Females do tend to live longer. To calculate the t statistic manually, first, for each country, compute the difference between female and male life expectancy. Then, compute the average and the standard deviation (SD) of the differences. Finally, calculate t where n is the number of countries (or pairs):

$$t = \frac{\text{average of the differences}}{\text{SD}/\sqrt{n}}$$

Matched pairs t test

Mathematically, the matched pairs *t* test is the same as the paired *t* test. Both *t* statistics are used to test whether the average of a set of differences is 0. The difference between the tests is one of study design. Instead of analyzing the differences between the two measures for each subject, we analyze the difference in values for two subjects who have been matched on a variable that is related to the measure studied. For example, cholesterol levels are known to increase with age; so if you want to compare cholesterol levels for a treatment group against those for a control group, you might match a 24-year-old in the treatment group with a 24-year-old in the control group, a 53-year-old treatment subject with a 53-year-old control subject, and so on. The goal is to remove variability due to age from the analysis.

The data for each matched pair must be entered as one record (for example, enter the values for a treatment subject and follow them with the data for his or her matched control subject). Be sure to give the variables unique names such as *CHOL_T* and *CHOL_C* to distinguish the treatment and control values. Continue by specifying your analysis as described for the paired *t* test.

Note: For more information, see SYSTAT: Data.

Multiple testing

Just as with the two-sample *t* test, the probability for the paired test is appropriate for one and only one test. If you want to make statements regarding significance for several pairs of variables, use the **Bonferroni** or **Dunn-Sidak** options described in Example 5.2.

One-Sample T Test

The goal in a **one-sample t test** is to test if the mean of a single sample differs from a hypothesized population value. For example, you read that in the United States, the average IQ is 100, and for students in a statistics class, the average IQ is 123.5. Are the statistics students smarter than the average person? To answer this question in SYSTAT, request a one-sample t test to compare the average sample IQ with the constant 100.

For the tests in this section, use **Stats**➟**t-test**➟**One Sample**.

**5.5
Population
growth**

Will Europe's population remain stable? You read that for the population to remain stable, the ratio of the birth rate to the death rate should not exceed 1.25—that is, five births for every four deaths. Should you reject the null hypothesis that the average European birth-to-death ratio is 1.25?

$$H_0: \mu = 1.25$$

First, use **Data**➟**Select Cases** to select Europe as the value of *GROUP$*. Next, use **Stats**➟**t-test**➟**One Sample** and select *B_TO_D* as the **Variable** and type 1.25 in the **Mean** text box. With commands:

```
TTEST
    USE ourworld
    SELECT group$ = 'Europe'
    TEST b_to_d = 1.25
```

```
One-sample t test of b_to_d with 20 cases;   Ho: Mean =      1.250

     Mean =      1.257
       SD =      0.213
                                           DF =   19   t =      0.147
                                                   Prob =      0.884
```

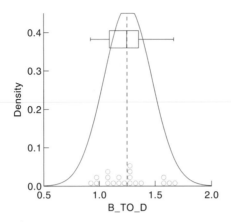

The average birth-to-death ratio for the European countries in the sample is 1.257. We are unable to reject the null hypothesis that the population value is 1.25 ($t = 0.147$, $df = 19$, p value = 0.884). We have no evidence that Europe's population will increase in size.

Do we reach the same conclusion for Islamic nations? Repeat the previous steps, except under **Data➧Select Cases**, specify Islamic as *GROUP$*.

```
SELECT group$ = 'Islamic'
TEST b_to_d = 1.25
SELECT
```

```
One-sample t test of B_TO_D with 16 cases;   Ho: Mean =        1.250

    Mean =        3.478
      SD =        1.179
                                      DF =    15   Prob =    t =    7.557
                                                            0.000
```

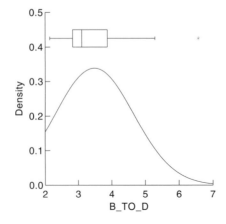

The average birth-to-death ratio for the Islamic countries is 3.478 (more than 2 1/2 times greater than that of the Europeans). The Islamic birth-to-death ratio differs significantly from 1.25 ($t = 7.557$, $df = 15$, p value < 0.0005). We anticipate a population explosion among these nations.

Multiple testing

The Bonferroni and Dunn-Sidak adjustments to probability levels (described in Example 5.2 and Example 5.5) are available for protection for multiple testing.

Analysis of Variance

Leland Wilkinson and Mark Coward

SYSTAT handles a wide variety of balanced and unbalanced analysis of variance designs. The Analysis of Variance (ANOVA) procedure includes all interactions in the model and tests them automatically; it also provides pairwise mean comparisons, analysis of covariance, and repeated measures designs.

The General Linear Model (GLM) procedure is used for randomized block designs, incomplete block designs, fractional factorials, Latin square designs, and analysis of covariance with one or more covariates. GLM also includes repeated measures, split plot, and crossover designs. It includes both univariate and multivariate approaches to repeated measures designs.

For models with fixed and random effects, you can define error terms for specific hypotheses. You can also do stepwise ANOVA (that is, Type I sums of squares). Categorical variables are entered or deleted in blocks, and you can examine interactively or automatically all combinations of interactions and main effects.

GLM also features the means model for missing cells designs. Widely favored for this purpose by statisticians (Searle, 1987; Hocking, 1985; Milliken and Johnson, 1984), the means model allows tests of hypotheses in missing cells designs (using what are often called Type IV sums of squares). Furthermore, the means model allows direct tests of simple hypotheses (for example, within levels of other factors). Finally, the means model allows easier use of population weights to reflect differences in subclass sizes.

After you have estimated your ANOVA model, it is easy to test post hoc pairwise differences in means or to test any contrast across cell means, including simple effects.

For both ANOVA and GLM, group sizes can be unequal for combinations of grouping factors; but for repeated measures designs, each subject must have complete data. You can use numeric or character values to code grouping variables.

You can store results of the analysis (predicted values and residuals) for further study and graphical display. In ANCOVA, you can save adjusted cell means.

Overview

Overview

The **Stats** menu has two items for doing analysis of variance. The first, **Analysis of Variance (ANOVA)**, is for factorial ANOVA and ANCOVA and for simple repeated measures designs. The second, **General Linear Model (GLM)**, is for more general analysis of variance models.

Because the ANOVA procedure has fewer options, it is easier to use than GLM when you are doing simple analysis of variance. ANOVA includes all interactions in the model and tests them automatically. You can specify covariates and save residuals. You can specify any model with GLM, including those you specify with ANOVA and Regression. With GLM, you must specify the interactions you want to test. You identify categorical independent variables, and SYSTAT generates a set of design variables for them.

Stepwise model building is available with GLM. You can do this in one of three ways: use the default values; specify your own selection criteria; or, at each step, interactively select a variable to add or remove from the model.

Getting started   To request an analysis of variance in ANOVA, use **Stats⮕Analysis of Variance⮕Estimate Model**:

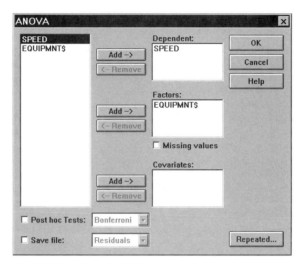

For repeated measures designs, use **Stats⮕Analysis of Variance⮕ Estimate Model** and select **Repeated**.

To request an analysis of variance in GLM, use **Stats⮕General Linear Model⮕Estimate Model**:

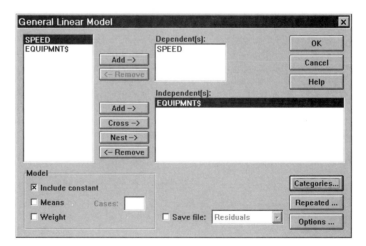

For repeated measures designs, use **Stats**➠**General Linear Model**➠**Estimate Model** and select **Repeated**.

After using ANOVA or GLM to estimate your model, select either **Stats**➠**General Linear Model**➠**Hypothesis Test** or **Stats**➠**Analysis of Variance**➠**Hypothesis Test** to test hypotheses about cell means or model effects.

Using commands   With commands:

```
ANOVA
   USE filename
   CATEGORY
   DEPEND
   SAVE filename
   ESTIMATE
```

or

```
GLM
   USE filename)
   CATEGORY
   MODEL
   SAVE filename
   ESTIMATE
```

To use ANOVA for analysis of covariance, insert the COVARIANCE command before ESTIMATE.

After using ANOVA or GLM to estimate a model, use a HYPOTHESIS paragraph to test its parameters. Begin each test with HYPOTHESIS and end with TEST.

```
HYPOTHESIS
   EFFECT or WITHIN
   ERROR
   POST or CONTRAST or SPECIFY
   AMATRIX
   CMATRIX
   TEST
```

Factorial Designs

A two-sample t test is used to test the difference in means of two groups. When there are more than two groups, **AN**alysis **O**f **VA**riance (ANOVA) is used. For example, is there a difference in average response among groups A, B, C, and D? Or do we reject the null hypothesis:

$$H_0 : \mu_a = \mu_b = \mu_c = \mu_d$$

For two groups, the t test and analysis of variance are the same (the F statistic from ANOVA results is the square of the two-sample pooled variance t statistic). Both test statistics compare the variability among group means (numerator) to the variability within each group (denominator).

The examples in this chapter use **Analysis of Variance** (ANOVA) and **General Linear Model** (GLM) from the **Stats** menu.

6.1 One-way ANOVA

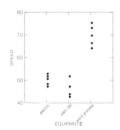

How does equipment influence typing performance? The first example uses a one-way design to compare average typing speed for three groups of typists. Fourteen beginning typists were randomly assigned to three types of machines and given speed tests. Here are their typing speeds in words per minute, plus a dit plot of the data values:

electric	plain old	word processor
52	52	67
47	43	73
51	47	70
49	44	75
53		64

For each typist, there is one record (case) with two entries: typing speed (*SPEED*) and a character (or numeric) code for the machine used (*EQUIPMNT$*). The data are stored in the SYSTAT data file named *TYPING*. The average speeds for the typists in the three groups are 50.4, 46.5, and 69.8 words per minute, respectively. To test the hypothesis that the three samples have the same population average speed, begin by using **File➡Open** to open the *TYPING* file. Then use **Stats➡Analysis of Variance➡Estimate Model** and identify *SPEED* as the dependent variable and *EQUIPMNT$* as a factor. With commands:

```
ANOVA
   USE typing
   CATEGORY equipmnt$
   DEPEND speed
   ESTIMATE
```

❶
```
Categorical values encountered during processing are:
EQUIPMNT$ (3 levels)
   electric, plain old, word process
```

❷
```
Dep Var: SPEED N: 14 Multiple R:  0.952 Squared multiple R:  0.907
```

❸
```
                        Analysis of Variance

  Source           Sum-of-Squares   DF  Mean-Square    F-Ratio      P

  EQUIPMNT$            1469.357      2     734.679      53.520
  0.000

  Error                151.000      11     13.727
```

The highlighted numbers below correspond to those in the output:

❶ SYSTAT lists the character codes it finds for the grouping variable *EQUIPMNT$*.

❷ For the dependent variable *SPEED*, SYSTAT reads 14 cases. The multiple correlation (*Multiple R*) for *SPEED* with the two design variables for *EQUIPMNT$* is 0.952. The square of this correlation (*Squared multiple R*) is 0.907. The grouping structure explains 90.7% of the variability of *SPEED*.

❸ The layout of this ANOVA table is standard in elementary texts; you will find formulas and definitions there. *F-Ratio* is the *Mean-Square* for *EQUIPMNT$* divided by the *Mean-Square* for *Error*. The distribution of the *F-Ratio* is sensitive to the assumption of equal population group variances. The *p* value is the probability of exceeding the *F-Ratio* when the group means are equal. The *p* value printed here is 0.000, so it is less than 0.0005. If the population means are equal, it would be very unusual to find sample means that differ as much as these—you could expect such a large *F-Ratio* fewer than five times out of 10,000.

❹ A *Quick Graph* (not shown here) appears after the ANOVA table. The residuals from each estimated cell mean are plotted on the vertical axis against the estimated cell mean on the horizontal axis.

Pairwise mean comparisons

The results in the ANOVA table above clearly indicate a significant difference among the means, but they do not indicate which mean differs from another.

To report which pairs of means differ significantly, you might think of computing a two-sample *t* test for each pair; however, do *not* do this. The probability associated with the two-sample *t* test assumes that *only one test is performed.* When several means are tested pairwise, the probability of finding one significant difference by chance alone increases rapidly with the number of pairs. If you use a 0.05 significance level to test that means *A* and *B* are equal and to test that means *C* and *D* are equal, the overall *acceptance region* is now 0.95 x 0.95, or 0.9025. Thus, the acceptance region for two independent comparisons carried out simultaneously is about 90%, and the *critical region* is 10% (instead of the desired 5%). For six pairs of means tested at the 0.05 significance level, the probability of a difference falling in the critical region is not 0.05 but

$$1-(0.95)^6 = 0.265$$

For 10 pairs, this probability increases to 0.40. The result of following such a strategy is to declare differences as significant when they are not.

SYSTAT provides two ways to request procedures that provide protection for multiple tests:

- **Stats⟩⟩Analysis of Variance⟩⟩Estimate Model** offers Bonferroni, Tukey, and Scheffé from the **Post hoc Tests** drop-down list. It also provides Fisher's LSD, which offers no protection.

  With commands:
  ```
  DEPEND varlist / BONF or TUKEY    or
                   SCHEFFE or LSD
  ```

- **Stats⟩⟩General Linear Model⟩⟩Pairwise Comparisons** offers the same procedures plus Dunnett's test. You can only access the **Pairwise Comparisons** dialog box after you run ANOVA.

There is an abundance of literature covering multiple comparisons (see Miller, 1985); however, a few points are worth noting here:

- If you have a small number of groups, the Bonferroni pairwise procedure will often be more powerful (sensitive). For more groups, consider the Tukey method. Try all the methods in ANOVA (except Fisher's LSD) and pick the best one.

- All possible pairwise comparisons are a waste of power. Think about a meaningful subset of comparisons and test this subset with Bonferroni levels. To do this, divide your critical level, say 0.05, by the number of comparisons you are making. You will almost always have more power than with any other pairwise multiple comparison procedures.

- Some popular multiple comparison procedures are not found in SYSTAT. Duncan's test, for example, does not maintain its claimed protection level. Other stepwise multiple range tests, such as Newman-Keuls, have not been conclusively demonstrated to maintain overall protection levels for all possible distributions of means.

To request the Bonferroni method for the typing speed data, use **Stats➠Analysis of Variance➠Estimate Model**, select **Post hoc Tests**, and choose **Bonferroni** from the drop-down list. Use **Data➠Order** for sorting the categories of the design. With commands, specify (before ESTIMATE in the previous example):

```
ORDER equipmnt$ / SORT='plain old' 'electric',
                              'word process'
DEPEND speed / BONF
```

❶
```
COL/
ROW EQUIPMNT$
   1  plain old
   2  electric
   3  word process
Using least squares means.
Post Hoc test of SPEED
---------------------------------------------------------------
```

❷
```
Using model MSE of 13.727 with 11 DF.
Matrix of pairwise mean differences:

                        1           2          3
              1       0.0
              2       3.900       0.0
              3      23.300      19.400      0.0
```

❸
```
Bonferroni Adjustment.
Matrix of pairwise comparison probabilities:

                        1           2          3
              1       1.000
              2       0.435       1.000
              3       0.000       0.000      1.000
```

The highlighted numbers below correspond to those in the output.

❶ SYSTAT assigns a number to each of the three groups and uses those numbers in the output panels that follow.

❷ In the first column, you can read differences in average typing speed for the group using *plain old* typewriters. In the second row, you see that they average 3.9 words per minute fewer than those using *electric* typewriters; but in the third row, you see that they average 23.3 minutes fewer than the group using *word processors*. To see whether these differences are significant, look at the probabilities in the corresponding locations in the table at the bottom.

❸ The probability associated with 3.9 is 0.435, so you are unable to detect a difference in performance between the *electric* and *plain old* groups. The probabilities in the third row are both 0.000, indicating that the *word processor* groups average significantly more words per minute than the *electric* and *plain old* groups.

Saving residuals and other results

To save residuals and other results, use **Stats➠Analysis of Variance➠ Estimate Model**, select **Save file**, and choose from the drop-down list:

Residuals	Saves predicted values, residuals, Studentized residuals, leverage for each observation, Cook's distance measure, and the standard error of predicted values. (Only the predicted values and residuals are appropriate for ANOVA.) This is the default.
Residuals/Data	Saves residuals and the data from the original file.
Adjusted	Saves least squares estimates of cell means adjusted for covariates.
Adjusted/Data	Saves least squares estimates of cell means adjusted for covariates and the data from the original file.
Model	Saves design variables.

The usual SAVE options (SINGLE and DOUBLE) also apply. With commands:

```
SAVE filename / RESID, DATA, ADJUST, MODEL
```

6.2 Assumptions and contrasts

An important assumption in analysis of variance is that the population variances are equal—that is, that the groups have approximately the same spread. When variances differ markedly, a transformation may remedy the problem. For example, sometimes it helps to take the square root of each value of the outcome variable (or log transform each value) and use the transformed value in the analysis. In this example, you:

– Analyze the square root of the dependent variable *INCOME*
– Request results for males only

Does average income vary by education? Use a subset of the cases from the *SURVEY2* data file to compare average income for five groups of subjects. Look at those who:

- Did not graduate from high school (*HS dropout*)
- Graduated from high school (*HS grad*)
- Attended some college (*Some college*)
- Graduated from college (*College grad*)
- Have a masters or Ph.D degree (*Degree +*)

The null hypothesis is:

$$H_0 : \mu_d = \mu_g = \mu_s = \mu_c = \mu_+$$

where μ_i is the mean of group i.

In Chapter 5, you compared average incomes for males and females and found that males in the surveyed community earn significantly more than females (almost $25,000 per year versus $20,257). In order to form homogeneous groups, you focus on males by using **Data⟶Select cases** and specifying *SEX$* = 'Male'.

For each subject (case) in the *SURVEY2* data file, use the variables *INCOME* and *EDUC$*. The means, standard deviations, and sample sizes for the five groups are shown below:

	HS dropout	HS grad	Some college	College grad	Degree +
mean	$13,389	$21,231	$29,294	$30,937	38,214
sd	10,639	13,176	16,465	16,894	18,230
n	18	39	17	16	14

Visually, as you move across the groups, you see that average income increases. But considering the variability within each group, you might wonder if the differences are significant. Also there is a relationship between the means and standard deviations—as the means increase, so do the standard deviations. They should be independent. If you take the square root of each income value using a **LET** statement (see below), there is less variability among the standard deviations, and the relation between the means and standard deviations is weaker:

	HS dropout	HS grad	Some college	College grad	Degree +
mean	3.371	4.423	5.190	5.305	6.007
sd	1.465	1.310	1.583	1.725	1.516

After the ANOVA results, you can say more about the assumptions that are necessary for a valid analysis.

For this example, use **Data⟶Label** to form five categories from the seven codes stored in the variable *EDUCATN*. The resulting categories appear in the output in the same order that they are specified in **Label**. To compute the square root of each income value, use **Data⟶Transform⟶Let**.

Then, for a one-way ANOVA, use **Stats⟶Analysis of Variance⟶Estimate Model**, identify *EDUCATN* as a factor, and identify the square root of income as the dependent measure to analyze. With commands:

```
ANOVA
    USE survey2
    SELECT sex$ = 'Male'
    LET sqrt_inc = SQR(income)

    LABEL educatn / 1,2='HS dropout' 3='HS grad',
                    4='Some college' 5='College grad',
                    6,7='Degree +'
    CATEGORY educatn

    DEPEND sqrt_inc
    ESTIMATE
```

❶
```
Categorical values encountered during processing are:
EDUCATN (5 levels)
    HS dropout, HS grad, Some college, College grad, Degree +
```

❷
```
Dep Var: SQRT_INC N: 104 Multiple R:  0.491 Squared multiple R:  0.241
```

❸
```
                          Analysis of Variance

Source               Sum-of-Squares   DF  Mean-Square     F-Ratio       P

EDUCATN                      68.624    4       17.156       7.854
0.000

Error                       216.256   99        2.184
```

The highlighted numbers below correspond to those in the output:

❶ SYSTAT identifies five levels in the grouping variable *EDUCATN*.

❷ The sample size is 104 for this analysis of the dependent variable *SQRT_INC*. The multiple correlation between *SQRT_INC* and the four design variables for *EDUCATN* is 0.491. (The square of this value is 0.241).

❸ In the ANOVA table, you can identify a significant difference among the four means ($F=7.854$, p value < 0.0005).

Data screening and assumptions

Most analyses have assumptions. If your data do not meet the necessary assumptions, then the resulting probabilities for the statistics may be suspect. Before an ANOVA, look for:

– Violations of the equal variance assumption. Your groups should have the same dispersion or spread (their shapes do not differ markedly).
– Symmetry. The mean of each group should fall roughly in the middle of the spread (the within-group distributions are not extremely skewed).
– Independence of the group means and standard deviations (the size of the group means is not related to the size of their standard deviations).
– Gross outliers (no values stand apart from the others in the batch).

Graphical displays are useful for checking assumptions. For analysis of variance, try dit plots, box-and-whisker displays, or bar charts with standard error bars. Here is a bar chart for the data as recorded and a bar chart for after the YPOW option is used to take square roots. The example uses LABEL and CATEGORY.

```
USE survey2
SELECT sex$ = 'Male'
LABEL educatn / 1,2='HS dropout', 3='HS grad',
                4='Some college', 5='College grad',
                6,7='Degree +'
CATEGORY educatn
BAR income * educatn / SERROR  FILL=.5
BAR income * educatn / SERROR  FILL=.35    YPOW=.5
```

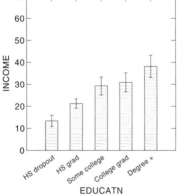 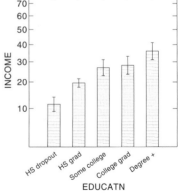

On the left, you can see a relation between the height of the bars (means) and the length of the error bars (standard errors)—that is, the smaller means have shorter error bars than the larger means. After transformation, there is less difference in length among the error bars.

Tukey pairwise mean comparisons

Example 6.1 uses the Bonferroni method to identify significant differences in pairs of means. This example uses the Tukey method. Which method is better? Hopefully, you reach the same conclusion using either method. When the number of comparisons is very large, the Tukey procedure may be more sensitive in detecting difference; when the number of comparisons is small, Bonferroni may be more sensitive.

What group mean differs from another? Specify your ANOVA by using **Stats ▸ Analysis of Variance ▸ Estimate Model** and specifying *SQRT_INC* as the dependent variable. This time, select **Tukey** from the **Post hoc Tests** drop-down list. With commands:

```
DEPEND sqrt_inc / TUKEY
ESTIMATE
```

```
COL/
ROW EDUCATN
  1  HS dropout
  2  HS grad
  3  Some college
  4  College grad
  5  Degree +
Using least squares means.
Post Hoc test of SQRT_INC
-------------------------------------------------------------

Using model MSE of 2.184 with 99 DF.
Matrix of pairwise mean differences:

                1         2         3         4         5
        1     0.0
        2     1.052     0.0
        3     1.819     0.767     0.0
        4     1.935     0.883     0.116     0.0
        5     2.636     1.584     0.817     0.701     0.0

Tukey HSD Multiple Comparisons.
Matrix of pairwise comparison probabilities:

                1         2         3         4         5
        1     1.000
        2     0.100     1.000
        3     0.004     0.387     1.000
        4     0.002     0.268     0.999     1.000
        5     0.000     0.008     0.545     0.694     1.000
```

The layout of the output panels for the Tukey method is the same as that described for the Bonferroni method in Example 6.1. Look first at the probabilities in the bottom table. Four of the probabilities indicate significant differences (they are < 0.05). In the first column, row 3, the average income for high school dropouts differs from those with some college ($p=0.004$), from college graduates ($p=0.002$), and also from those with advanced degrees ($p < 0.0005$). The fifth row shows that the differences between those with advanced degrees and the high school graduates are significant ($p=0.008$).

Linear and quadratic contrasts

Contrasts are used to test relationships among means. A contrast is a linear combination of means μ_i with coefficients α_i:

$$\alpha_1\mu_1 + \alpha_2\mu_2 + \ldots + \alpha_k\mu_k = 0$$

where $\alpha_1 + \alpha_2 + \ldots + \alpha_k = 0$. In SYSTAT, hypotheses can be specified about contrasts and tests performed. Typically, the hypothesis has the form:

$$H_0: \alpha_1\mu_1 + \alpha_2\mu_2 + \ldots + \alpha_k\mu_k = 0$$

The test statistic for a contrast is similar to that for a two-sample t test; the result of the contrast (a relation among means, such as mean A minus mean B) is in the numerator of the test statistic, and an estimate of within-group variability (the pooled variance estimate or the error term from the ANOVA) is part of the denominator.

You can select contrast coefficients to test:

- Pairwise comparisons (test for a difference between two particular means)
- A linear combination of means that are meaningful to the study at hand (compare two treatments versus a control mean)
- Linear, quadratic, or the like increases (decreases) across a set of ordered means (that is, you might test a linear increase in sales by comparing people with *no* training, those with *moderate* training, and those with *extensive* training)

Many experimental design texts place coefficients for linear and quadratic contrasts for three groups, four groups, and so on, in a table. SYSTAT allows you to type your contrasts or select a polynomial option. A polynomial contrast of order 1 is linear; of order 2, quadratic; of order 3, cubic; and so on.

In this example, five groups are ordered by their level of education, so you use these coefficients to test linear and quadratic contrasts:

Linear	−2	−1	0	1	2
Quadratic	2	−1	−2	−1	2

Then you ask, "Is there a linear increase in average income across the five ordered levels of education?" "A quadratic change?" Use **Stats**➠**Analysis of Variance**➠**Hypothesis Test** and specify *EDUCATN* as the effect. Next, select **Contrast**. You can either type **–2 –1 0 1 2** in the text box or select

Polynomial and set **Order** to 1 for a linear contrast. For the quadratic contrast, either type **2 –1 –2 –1 2** in the text box or select **Polynomial** and set **Order** to 2.

With commands:

```
HYPOTHESIS
NOTE 'Test of linear contrast',
     'across ordered group means'
EFFECT = educatn
CONTRAST [-2 -1 0 1 2]
TEST

HYPOTHESIS
NOTE 'Test of quadratic contrast',
     'across ordered group means'
EFFECT = educatn
CONTRAST [2 -1 -2 -1 2]
TEST
SELECT
```

```
                        Test of linear contrast
                       across ordered group means

Test for effect called:      EDUCATN

A Matrix

                        1          2          3          4          5
                        0.0     -4.000     -3.000     -2.000     -1.000

Test of Hypothesis

     Source        SS        DF        MS          F           P

  Hypothesis     63.542      1      63.542      29.089      0.000
     Error      216.256     99       2.184
```

```
                        Test of quadratic contrast
                       across ordered group means

Test for effect called:      EDUCATN

A Matrix

                        1          2          3          4          5
                        0.0        0.0     -3.000     -4.000     -3.000

Test of Hypothesis

     Source        SS        DF        MS          F           P

  Hypothesis      2.202      1       2.202       1.008      0.318
     Error      216.256     99       2.184
```

The F statistic for testing the linear contrast is 29.089 (p value < 0.0005); for testing the quadratic contrast, it is 1.008 (p value $= 0.318$). Thus, you can report that there is a highly significant linear increase in average income across the five levels of education and that you have not found a quadratic component in this increase.

6.3
One-way
ANOVA in GLM

To introduce the General Linear Model procedure, start with a one-way analysis of variance. The following data, *KENTON*, are from Neter, Wasserman, and Kutner (1985). The data comprise unit sales of a cereal product under different types of package designs. Ten stores were selected as experimental units. Each store was randomly assigned to sell one of the package designs (each design was sold at two or three stores).

PACKAGE	SALES
1	12
1	18
2	14
2	12
2	13
3	19
3	17
3	21
4	24
4	30

Numbers are used to code the four types of package designs; alternatively, you could have used words. Neter, Wasserman, and Kutner report that cartoons are part of designs 1 and 3 but not designs 2 and 4; designs 1 and 2 have three colors; and designs 3 and 4 have five colors. Thus, string codes for *PACKAGE$* might have been 'Cart 3,' 'NoCart 3,' 'Cart 5,' and 'NoCart 5.' Notice that the data does not need to be ordered by *PACKAGE* as shown here. Use **Stats**➠**General Linear Model**➠**Estimate Model**. Select *SALES* as the dependent variable and *PACKAGE* as the independent variable. Select the **Categories** button and move *PACKAGE* into the **Categorical Variable(s)** list. With commands:

```
GLM
    USE kenton
    CATEGORY package
    MODEL sales=CONSTANT + package
    GRAPH NONE
    ESTIMATE
```

In ANOVA, the following commands are used instead of the MODEL statement in GLM:

```
ANOVA
    DEPEND sales
    CATEGORY package
    ESTIMATE
```

```
Categorical values encountered during processing are:
PACKAGE (4 levels)
         1        2        3        4

Dep Var: SALES N: 10 Multiple R:  0.921 Squared multiple R:  0.849

                         Analysis of Variance

Source            Sum-of-Squares  DF  Mean-Square    F-Ratio      P

PACKAGE                  258.000   3       86.000     11.217   0.007

Error                     46.000   6        7.667
```

This is the standard analysis of variance table. The F ratio (11.217) appears significant, so you could conclude that the package designs differ significantly in their effects on sales, provided the assumptions are valid.

Pairwise multiple comparisons

Example 6.1 introduced pairwise mean comparison procedures and illustrated how to request them using **Stats**➠**Analysis of Variance**➠ **Estimate Model**. This example illustrates some of the options available under **Stats**➠**General Linear Model**➠**Pairwise Comparisons**: Bonferroni, Tukey-Kramer HSD, Scheffé, Fischer's LSD, and Dunnett's test.

The Dunnett test is available only with one-way designs. Dunnett requires the value of a control group against which comparisons are made. By default, two-sided tests are computed. One-sided Dunnett tests are also available. Incidentally, for Dunnett's tests on *experimental* data, you should use the one-sided option unless you cannot predict from theory whether your experimental groups will have higher or lower means than the control.

Comparisons for the pairwise methods are made across all pairs of least squares group means for the design term which is specified. For a multiway design, marginal cell means are computed for the effects specified before the comparisons are made.

To determine significant differences, simply look for pairs with probabilities below your critical value (for example, 0.05 or 0.01). All multiple comparison methods handle unbalanced designs correctly. Results are also appropriate for analysis of covariance and any general linear model.

After you estimate your ANOVA model, it is easy to do post hoc tests. To do a Tukey HSD test, first estimate the model, then specify these commands:

```
HYPOTHESIS
POST package / TUKEY
TEST
```

```
COL/
ROW PACKAGE
  1   1
  2   2
  3   3
  4   4
Using least squares means.
Post Hoc test of SALES

Using model MSE of 7.667 with 6 DF.
Matrix of pairwise mean differences:

                    1          2          3          4
          1       0.0
          2      -2.000      0.0
          3       4.000      6.000      0.0
          4      12.000     14.000      8.000      0.0


Tukey HSD Multiple Comparisons.
Matrix of pairwise comparison probabilities:

                    1          2          3          4
          1       1.000
          2       0.856      1.000
          3       0.452      0.131      1.000
          4       0.019      0.006      0.071      1.000
```

Results show that sales for the fourth package design (five colors and no cartoons) are significantly larger than those for packages 1 and 2. The difference between designs 4 and 3 is almost significant (p value = 0.071). None of the other pairs differ significantly.

This example uses contrasts to compare the first and third packages. The coefficients are (1, 0, –1, 0). With commands:

```
HYPOTHESIS
EFFECT = package
CONTRAST [1 0 -1 0]
TEST
```

You specify one contrast, so your test has one degree of freedom; therefore, the contrast matrix has one row of numbers. These numbers are the same ones you see in ANOVA textbooks, although SYSTAT offers one advantage—you do not have to standardize them so that their sum of squares is 1.

```
Test for effect called:      PACKAGE

A Matrix

                   1           2           3           4
                 0.0         1.000        0.0        -1.000

Test of Hypothesis

       Source        SS        DF        MS           F            P

   Hypothesis      19.200       1      19.200       2.504        0.165
       Error       46.000       6       7.667
```

The F statistic (2.504) is not significant, so you cannot conclude that the impact of the first and third package designs on sales is significantly different. Incidentally, the **A** matrix contains the contrast. The first column (0) corresponds to the constant in the model, and the remaining three columns (1 0 −1) correspond to the dummy variables for *PACKAGE*.

Now, let's compare the average performance of the first three packages with the last:

```
HYPOTHESIS
EFFECT = package
CONTRAST [1 1 1 −3]
TEST
```

```
Test for effect called:     PACKAGE

A Matrix
                        1           2           3           4
                        0.0         4.000       4.000       4.000

Test of Hypothesis

        Source      SS        DF       MS          F           P

    Hypothesis   204.000      1      204.000     26.609       0.002
        Error     46.000      6        7.667
```

The last package design is significantly different from the other three taken as a group. Notice that the **A** matrix looks much different this time. Because the effects sum to 0, the last effect is minus the sum of the other three; that is, because $\alpha_1 + \alpha_2 + \alpha_3 + \alpha_4 = 0$, where α_i is the effect for level i of *PACKAGE*, then

$$\alpha_4 = -(\alpha_1 + \alpha_2 + \alpha_3)$$

and the contrast is

$$\alpha_1 + \alpha_2 + \alpha_3 - 3\alpha_4$$

which is:

$$\alpha_1 + \alpha_2 + \alpha_3 - 3(-\alpha_1 - \alpha_2 - \alpha_3)$$

which simplifies to:

$$4\alpha_1 + 4\alpha_2 + 4\alpha_3$$

Remember, SYSTAT does all this work automatically.

Orthogonal polynomials

To construct orthogonal polynomials for your between-groups factors, use **Stats⫸General Linear Model⫸Hypothesis Test**, type **package** in the **Effects** text box, and select **Contrast**. In the **Contrast** dialog box, select **Polynomial** and type **2** in the **Order** text box. Constructing orthogonal polynomials for between-group factors is useful when the levels of a factor are ordered. (The package designs do not have this order.) With commands:

```
HYPOTHESIS
EFFECT = package
CONTRAST / POLYNOMIAL ORDER=2
TEST
```

```
Test for effect called:     PACKAGE

A Matrix
                      1          2          3          4
                    0.0      0.000     -1.000     -1.000
Test of Hypothesis

       Source       SS        DF        MS          F          P

   Hypothesis    60.000       1      60.000      7.826      0.031
        Error    46.000       6       7.667
```

Make sure that the levels of the factor—after they are sorted by the procedure numerically or alphabetically—are ordered meaningfully on a latent dimension. If you need a specific order, use **Data⫸Label** or **Data⫸Order**; otherwise, the results will not make sense. In the example, the significant quadratic effect is the result of the fourth package having a much larger sales volume than the other three.

Effects and dummy variables

You can use **MODEL** in GLM instead of **DEPEND** in ANOVA to get the same results. If you want to see the estimates of the effects when you use ANOVA, set **PRINT=LONG** before you do the analysis. The effects in a least squares analysis of variance are associated with a set of dummy variables that SYSTAT generates automatically. Ordinarily, you do not have to concern yourself with these dummy variables; however, if you want to see them, you can save them in a SYSTAT file by using either **Stats⫸Analysis of Variance⫸Estimate Model** or **Stats⫸General Linear Model⫸ Estimate Model** and selecting **Model** from the **Save file** drop-down list.

To view the file, use **Data⟶List Cases:**

SALES	X(1)	X(2)	X(3)
12	1	0	0
18	1	0	0
14	0	1	0
12	0	1	0
13	0	1	0
19	0	0	1
17	0	0	1
21	0	0	1
24	−1	−1	−1
30	−1	−1	−1

The variables $X(1)$, $X(2)$, and $X(3)$ are the *effects coding* dummy variables generated by the procedure. All cases in the first cell are associated with dummy values 1 0 0; those in the second cell with 0 1 0; the third, 0 0 1; and the fourth, −1 −1 −1. Other least squares programs use different methods to code dummy variables. The coding used by SYSTAT is most widely used and guarantees that the effects sum to 0.

If you had used *dummy coding*, these dummy variables would be saved:

SALES	X(1)	X(2)	X(3)
12	1	0	0
18	1	0	0
14	0	1	0
12	0	1	0
13	0	1	0
19	0	0	0
19	0	0	1
17	0	0	1
21	0	0	1
24	0	0	0
30	0	0	0

This coding yields parameter estimates which are the differences between the mean for each group and the mean of the last group.

Printing effects (beta coefficients)

When **Print** is set to **Long**, SYSTAT displays the estimates of ANOVA effects (beta coefficients) in your model. To set Print to Long, use **Edit⟶Options** and select **Long** from the **Length** drop-down list. With commands, PRINT=LONG.

6.4
Two-way
analysis of
variance

Consider the following two-way analysis of variance design from Afifi and Azen (1972), cited in Kutner (1974), and reprinted in BMDP manuals. The dependent variable, *SYSINCR*, is the change in systolic blood pressure after administering one of four different drugs to patients with one of three different diseases. Patients were assigned randomly to one of the possible drugs.

	DISEASE 1	DISEASE 2	DISEASE 3
DRUG 1	42	33	31
	44	26	-3
	36	33	25
	13	21	25
	19		24
	22		
DRUG2	28	34	3
	23	33	26
	34	31	28
	42	36	32
	13		4
			16
DRUG3	1	11	21
	29	9	1
	19	7	9
		1	3
		-6	
DRUG4	24	27	22
	9	12	7
	22	12	25
	-2	-5	5
	15	16	12
		15	

The data are stored in the SYSTAT file *AFIFI*:

DRUG	DISEASE	SYSINCR
1	1	42
1	1	44
1	1	36
*** we omit cases 4-56 ***		
4	3	5
4	3	12

To request a least squares two-way analysis of variance, use **Stats**➡ **Analysis of Variance**➡**Estimate Model** and select *SYSINCR* as the dependent variable and *DRUG* and *DISEASE* as the factors. From the **Save file** drop-down list, choose **Residuals/Data**. With commands:

```
ANOVA
    USE afifi
    CATEGORY drug disease
    DEPEND sysincr
    SAVE myresids / RESID  DATA
    ESTIMATE
```

Because this is a factorial design, ANOVA automatically generates an interaction term (*DRUG*DISEASE*). You can do the same analysis with GLM:

```
GLM
    USE afifi
    CATEGORY drug disease
    MODEL sysincr = CONSTANT + drug + disease +,
                    drug*disease
    SAVE myresids / RESID  DATA
    ESTIMATE
```

```
Dep Var: SYSINCR N: 58 Multiple R:  0.675 Squared multiple R:  0.456

                      Analysis of Variance

Source            Sum-of-Squares   DF   Mean-Square    F-Ratio      P

DRUG                   2997.472     3      999.157       9.046     0.000
DISEASE                 415.873     2      207.937       1.883     0.164
DRUG*DISEASE            707.266     6      117.878       1.067     0.396

Error                  5080.817    46      110.453

Durbin-Watson D Statistic      2.414
First Order Autocorrelation   -0.223
Residuals have been saved.
```

If you have an orthogonal design (equal number of cases in every cell), you will find that the ANOVA table is the same one you get with any standard ANOVA program. SYSTAT can handle nonorthogonal designs, however, as in the present example. To understand the sources for sums of squares, you must know something about least squares ANOVA.

As with one-way ANOVA, your specifying factor levels causes SYSTAT to create dummy variables out of the classifying input variable. SYSTAT creates one fewer dummy variables than categories specified.

Coding of the dummy variables is the classic analysis of variance parameterization, in which the sum of effects estimated for a classifying variable is 0 (Scheffé, 1959). In our example, *DRUG* has four categories; therefore, SYSTAT creates three dummy variables with the following scores for subjects at each level:

1	0	0	for *DRUG*=1 subject
0	1	0	for *DRUG*=2 subjects
0	0	1	for *DRUG*=3 subjects
−1	−1	−1	for *DRUG*=4 subjects

Because *DISEASE* has three categories, SYSTAT creates two dummy variables to be coded as follows:

1	0	for *DISEASE*=1 subject
0	1	for *DISEASE*=2 subjects
-1	-1	for *DISEASE*=3 subjects

Now, because there are no continuous predictors in the model (unlike the analysis of covariance), you have a complete design matrix of dummy variables as follows (*DRUG* is labeled with an *A*, *DISEASE* with a *B*, and the grand mean with an *m*):

Design Matrix

Treatment		*mean*	*drug effects*			*disease effects*		*interaction effects*					
A	B	m	a1	a2	a3	b1	b2	a1b1	a1b2	a2b1	a2b2	a3b1	a3b2
1	1	1	1	0	0	1	0	1	0	0	0	0	0
1	2	1	1	0	0	0	1	0	1	0	0	0	0
1	3	1	1	0	0	-1	-1	-1	-1	0	0	0	0
2	1	1	0	1	0	1	0	0	0	1	0	0	0
2	2	1	0	1	0	0	1	0	0	0	1	0	0
2	3	1	0	1	0	-1	-1	0	0	-1	-1	0	0
3	1	1	0	0	1	1	0	0	0	0	0	1	0
3	2	1	0	0	1	0	1	0	0	0	0	0	1
3	3	1	0	0	1	-1	-1	0	0	0	0	-1	-1
4	1	1	-1	-1	-1	1	0	-1	0	-1	0	-1	0
4	2	1	-1	-1	-1	0	1	0	-1	0	-1	0	-1
4	3	1	-1	-1	-1	-1	-1	1	1	1	1	1	1

If you use **General Linear Model** instead of **Analysis of Variance**, you must select the variables in the order shown above if you want the columns to correspond to this example.

This example is used to explain how SYSTAT gets an error term for the ANOVA table. Because it is a least squares program, the error term is taken from the residual sum of squares in the regression onto the above dummy variables. For nonorthogonal designs, this choice is identical to that produced by BMDP2V and SPSS GLM with Type III sum of squares. These, in general, will be the hypotheses you want to test on unbalanced experimental data. You can construct other types of sums of squares by using **Stats➠General Linear Model➠Hypothesis Test➠A matrix** or by running your ANOVA model using the **Stepwise** options in **Stats➠General Linear Model➠Estimate Model➠Options**. Consult the references if you do not already know what these sums of squares mean. An example is given below in the section on unbalanced designs.

Post hoc
tests

It is evident that only the main effect for *DRUG* is significant; therefore, you might want to test some contrasts on the *DRUG* effects. A simple way would be to use **Stats**➠**General Linear Model**➠**Pairwise Comparisons**, type **Drug** in the **Groups** text box, and select **Bonferroni** to test all pairwise comparisons of marginal drug means. With commands:

```
HYPOTHESIS
POST drug / BONFERRONI
TEST
```

The layout of the output resulting from these instructions or commands is similar to that for the Tukey results in Example 6.2.

To test specific contrasts on marginal and cell means, use **Stats**➠**General Linear Model**➠**Hypothesis Test**, type **Drug** in the **Effects** text box, and select **Contrast**. In the **Contrast** dialog box, type **1 0 –1 0** to specify a contrast between the first and third drug. With commands:

```
HYPOTHESIS
EFFECT = drug
CONTRAST [1 0 –1 0]
TEST
```

You need four numbers (1 0 –1 0) because *DRUG* has four levels. Notice the A matrix in the output below. SYSTAT automatically takes into account the degree of freedom 1ost in the design coding. Also notice that you do not need to normalize contrasts or rows of the A matrix to unit vector length, as in some ANOVA programs. If you use (2 0 –2 0) or (0.707 0 –0.707 0) instead of (1 0 –1 0), you get the same sum of squares. Here is the result of the above hypothesis test:

```
Test for effect called:      DRUG

A Matrix

                        1           2          3          4          5
                        0.0         1.000      0.0        -1.000     0.0

                        6           7          8          9          10
                        0.0         0.0        0.0        0.0        0.0

                        11          12
                        0.0         0.0

Test of Hypothesis

     Source        SS         DF        MS          F            P

   Hypothesis    1697.545      1      1697.545     15.369       0.000
       Error     5080.817     46       110.453
```

You cannot use **Contrast** to specify coefficients for interaction terms. It creates an A matrix only for main effects.

Here is one more example that tests the first against the fourth drug:

```
HYPOTHESIS
EFFECT = drug
CONTRAST [1  0  0 −1]
TEST
```

```
Test for effect called:      DRUG

A Matrix

                         1           2           3           4           5
                         0.0         2.000       1.000       1.000       0.0

                         6           7           8           9           10
                         0.0         0.0         0.0         0.0         0.0

                         11          12
                         0.0         0.0

Test of Hypothesis

       Source        SS          DF         MS            F              P

    Hypothesis    1178.892      1       1178.892      10.673         0.002
       Error      5080.817      46       110.453
```

Notice that in the **A** matrix created by this contrast, you get (2 1 1) in place of the three design variables corresponding to the appropriate columns of the **A** matrix.

Because you selected the reduced form for coding of design variables in which sums of effects are 0, you have the following restriction for the *DRUG* effects:

$$\alpha_1 + \alpha_2 + \alpha_3 + \alpha_4 = 0$$

where α_i is the effect for that level of *DRUG*. This means that

$$\alpha_4 = -(\alpha_1 + \alpha_2 + \alpha_3)$$

and the contrast *DRUG(1)–DRUG(4)* is equivalent to

$$\alpha_1 - [- (\alpha_1 + \alpha_2 + \alpha_3)] = 0$$

which is

$$2\alpha_1 + \alpha_2 + \alpha_3$$

Tests of simple effects

Now you can do simple contrasts between drugs within levels of disease, although the lack of a significant *DRUG* *DISEASE* interaction does not justify it. To show how it is done, consider a contrast between the first and third levels of *DRUG* for the first *DISEASE* only. You must specify the contrast in terms of the cell means. Use the terminology:

MEAN (DRUG *index,* DISEASE *index*) = μ_{ij}

You want to contrast cell means μ_{12} and μ_{31}. These are composed of:

$$\mu_{11} = \mu + \alpha_1 + \beta_1 + \alpha\beta_{11} \quad \mu_{31} = \mu + \alpha_3 + \beta_1 + \alpha\beta_{31}$$

Therefore, the difference between these two means is:

$$\mu_{11} - \mu_{31} = \alpha_1 - \alpha_3 + \alpha\beta_{11} - \alpha\beta_{31}$$

Now, if you look back at the illustration of the design matrix above, you can find these terms and construct an **A** matrix that picks up each one at the appropriate column. Here are the column labels of the design matrix (a means *DRUG* and b means *DISEASE*) to serve as a column ruler over the **A** matrix specified in this hypothesis paragraph. (You can use a single space between columns—an extra space appears here to accommodate the labels in the column ruler.)

Design matrix

m	a1	a2	a3	b1	b2	a1b1	a1b2	a2b1	a2b2	a3b1	a3b2
0	1	0	−1	0	0	1	0	0	0	−1	0

```
HYPOTHESIS
AMATRIX [0  1  0 -1  0  0  1  0  0  0 -1  0]
TEST
```

After you understand how specifying factor levels (or, with the command interface, *CATEGORY*) codes design variables and how the model sentence orders them, you can take any standard ANOVA text like Winer (1971) or Scheffé (1959) and construct an **A** matrix for any linear contrast.

Contrasting marginal and cell means

Now look at how to contrast cell means directly without being concerned about how they are coded. Use **Stats⇒General Linear Model⇒Hypothesis Test⇒Specify** and type **[drug[1]=drug[3]]** to test the first level of *DRUG* against the third (contrasting the marginal means). With commands:

```
HYPOTHESIS
SPECIFY drug[1] = drug[3]
TEST
```

To contrast the first against the fourth with commands:

```
HYPOTHESIS
    SPECIFY drug[1] = drug[4]
    TEST
```

Finally, here is the simple contrast of the first and third levels of *DRUG* for the first *DISEASE* only.

```
HYPOTHESIS
    SPECIFY drug[1] disease[1] = drug[3] disease[1]
    TEST
```

Screening results   Let's examine these data in more detail. To save the residuals in a file, use either **Stats**➠**General Linear Model**➠**Estimate Model** or **Stats**➠ **Analysis of Variance**➠**Estimate Model** and choose **Residuals/Data** from the **Save file** drop-down list. Specify *MYRESIDS* as the filename. To analyze the residuals to examine the ANOVA assumptions, open the file *MYRESIDS* and use **Graph**➠**Plot**. First, plot residuals against estimated values (cell means) to check for homogeneity of variance. Use the Studentized residuals to reference them against a *t* distribution. Notice that the value at the bottom of the following plot badly skews the data in its cell (which happens to be *DRUG1, DISEASE3*). With commands:

```
PLOT student * estimate / SYM=1  FILL=1
```

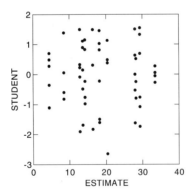

The following example is a stem-and-leaf plot of Studentized residuals:

```
STATS
    USE myresids
    STEM student
```

```
          Stem and Leaf Plot of Variable:  STUDENT    , N =   58

Minimum is:       -2.647
Lower Hinge is:       -0.761
Median is:        0.101
Upper Hinge is:       0.698
Maximum is:        1.552

              -2   6
              -2
              -1   987666
              -1   410
              -0 H 9877765
              -0   432222000
               0 M 0001222333444
               0 H 55666888
               1   011133444
               1   55
```

Notice that the smallest value seems to be out of line. A t statistic value of -2.647 corresponds to $p < 0.01$, and you would not expect one this small to show up in a sample of only 58 independent values. This is the same point that appeared at the bottom of the previous plot.

Now, look at the boxplot of the dependent variable against the four drug groups. The outlier stands out clearly in the first group.

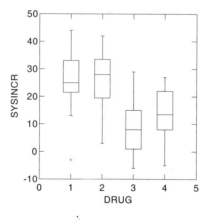

To see the effect of this outlier, delete the observation with the outlying Studentized residual. Then, run the analysis again. Here is the ANOVA output for the revised data:

```
Dep Var: SYSINCR     N:   57   Multiple R:  .710    Squared Multiple R:  .503

                           Analysis of Variance

Source        Sum-of-Squares   DF  Mean-Square    F-Ratio       P

DRUG             3344.064      3    1114.688       11.410      0.000
DISEASE           232.826      2     116.413        1.192      0.313
DRUG*DISEASE      676.865      6     112.811        1.155      0.347

Error            4396.367     45      97.697
```

The differences are not substantial. Nevertheless, notice that the disease effect is substantially attenuated when only one case out of 58 is deleted. Daniel (1960) gives an example in which one outlying case alters the fundamental conclusions of a designed experiment. The *F* test is robust to certain violations of assumptions, but factorial ANOVA is not robust against outliers. You should routinely do these plots for ANOVA.

6.5 Single degree-of-freedom designs

The following data (*REACT*) involve yields of a chemical reaction under various combinations of four binary factors (*A*, *B*, *C*, and *D*). Two reactions were observed under each combination of experimental factors, so the number of cases per cell is two.

A	B	C	D	YIELD
1	1	1	1	15
1	1	1	1	779
1	1	1	2	999
1	1	1	2	990
1	1	2	1	499
1	1	2	1	212
1	1	2	2	286
1	1	2	2	611
1	2	1	1	438
1	2	1	1	239
1	2	1	2	926
1	2	1	2	787
1	2	2	1	871
1	2	2	1	303
1	2	2	2	891
1	2	2	2	663
2	1	1	1	177
2	1	1	1	831
2	1	1	2	222
2	1	1	2	182
2	1	2	1	342
2	1	2	1	426
2	1	2	2	416
2	1	2	2	910
2	2	1	1	474
2	2	1	1	328
2	2	1	2	70
2	2	1	2	121
2	2	2	1	569
2	2	2	1	111
2	2	2	2	771
2	2	2	2	119

To analyze these data in a four-way ANOVA, use **Stats**➠**Analysis of Variance**➠**Estimate Model**. Move *YIELD* to the **Dependent** list and move *A*, *B*, *C*, and *D* to the **Factors** list. With commands:

```
ANOVA
   USE react
   CATEGORY a, b, c, d
   DEPEND yield
   ESTIMATE
```

You can see the advantage of ANOVA over GLM when you have several factors; you have to select only the main effects. With GLM, you have to specify the interactions and identify which variables are categorical (that is, *a*, *b*, *c*, and *d*). The following example is the full model using GLM:

```
MODEL yield = CONSTANT + a + b + c + d +,
              a*b + a*c + a*d + b*c + b*d + c*d +,
              a*b*c + a*b*d + a*c*d + b*c*d +,
              a*b*c*d
```

```
Dep Var: YIELD N: 32 Multiple R:  0.755 Squared multiple R:  0.570

                        Analysis of Variance
Source           Sum-of-Squares   DF   Mean-Square    F-Ratio     P
A                    369800.000    1    369800.000      4.651   0.047
B                      1458.000    1      1458.000      0.018   0.894
C                      5565.125    1      5565.125      0.070   0.795
D                    172578.125    1    172578.125      2.170   0.160
A*B                   87153.125    1     87153.125      1.096   0.311
A*C                  137288.000    1    137288.000      1.727   0.207
A*D                  328860.500    1    328860.500      4.136   0.059
B*C                   61952.000    1     61952.000      0.779   0.390
B*D                    3200.000    1      3200.000      0.040   0.844
C*D                    3160.125    1      3160.125      0.040   0.844
A*B*C                 81810.125    1     81810.125      1.029   0.326
A*B*D                  4753.125    1      4753.125      0.060   0.810
A*C*D                415872.000    1    415872.000      5.230   0.036
B*C*D                     4.500    1         4.500      0.000   0.994
A*B*C*D               15051.125    1     15051.125      0.189   0.669

Error               1272247.000   16     79515.437
```

The output shows a significant main effect for the first factor (*A*) plus one significant interaction (*A*C*D*). Let's look at the study more closely. Because this is a single degree-of-freedom study (a $2n$ factorial), each effect estimate is normally distributed if the usual assumptions for the experiment are valid. All the effects estimates, except the constant, have zero mean and common variance (because dummy variables were used in their computation). Thus, you can compare them to a normal distribution. SYSTAT remembers your last selections. To save the effects into a SYSTAT file, while in **Stats**➟**General Linear Model**➟**Estimate Model**, select **Coefficients** from the **Save file** drop-down list, and specify a filename. With commands:

```
SAVE effects / COEF
ESTIMATE
```

This reestimates the model and saves the regression coefficients (effects). The file has one case with 16 variables (CONSTANT plus 15 effects). The effects are labeled *X(1)*, *X(2)*, and so on because they are related to the dummy variables, not the original variables *A*, *B*, *C*, and *D*. Let's transpose this file into a new file containing only the 15 effects.

```
USE effects
DROP constant
TRANSPOSE
SELECT case > 1
```

Now, do a probability plot of the effects:

```
PPLOT col(1) / FILL=1 SYMBOL=1  XLABEL='Estimates of
         Effects'
```

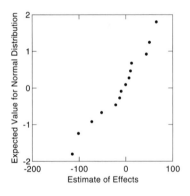

These effects are indistinguishable from a random normal variable. They plot almost on a straight line. What does it mean for the study and for the significant *F* tests?

It's time to reveal that the data were produced by a random number generator.

- If you are doing a factorial analysis of variance, the *p* values you see on the output are not adjusted for the number of factors. If you do a three-way design, look at seven tests (excluding the constant). For a four-way design, examine 15 tests. Out of 15 *F* tests on random data, expect to find at least one test approaching significance. You have two significant and one almost significant, which is not far out of line. The probabilities for each separate *F* test need to be corrected for the experiment-wise error rate. Some authors devote entire chapters to fine distinctions between multiple comparison procedures and then illustrate them within a multi-factorial design not corrected for the experiment-wise error rate just demonstrated. Remember this: a factorial design *is* a multiple comparison. If you have a single degree-of-freedom study, use the procedure you used to draw a probability plot of the effects. Any effect that is really significant will become obvious.

– If you have a factorial study with more degrees of freedom on some factors, use the Bonferroni critical value for deciding which effects are significant. It guarantees that the Type I error rate for the study will be no greater than the level you choose. In the above example, this value is 0.05/15 (that is, 0.003).

– Multiple *F* tests based on a common denominator (mean square error in this example) are correlated. This complicates the problem further. In general, the greater the discrepancy between numerator and denominator degrees of freedom and the smaller the denominator degrees of freedom, the greater the dependence of the tests. The Bonferroni tests are best in this situation, although Feingold and Korsog (1986) offer some useful alternatives.

6.6 Unbalanced designs

An unbalanced factorial design occurs when the numbers of cases in cells are unequal and not proportional across rows or columns. The following is an example of a 2×2 design:

	B1	B2
A1	1 2	5 3 4
A2	6 7 9 8 4	2 1 5 3

Unbalanced designs require a least squares procedure like General Linear Model because the usual maximum likelihood method of adding up sums of squared deviations from cell means and the grand mean does not yield maximum likelihood estimates of effects. General Linear Model adjusts for unbalanced designs when you get an ANOVA table to test hypotheses.

However, the estimates of effects in the unbalanced design are no longer orthogonal (and thus statistically independent) across factors and their interactions. This means that the sum of squares associated with one factor depends on the sum of squares for another or its interaction.

Analysts accustomed to using multiple regression have no problem with this situation because they assume that their independent variables in a model are correlated. Experimentalists, however, often have difficulty speaking of a main effect *conditioned* on another. Consequently, there is extensive literature on hypothesis testing methodology for unbalanced designs (for example, Speed and Hocking, 1976, and Speed, Hocking, and Hackney, 1978), and there is no consensus on how to test hypotheses with nonorthogonal designs.

Some statisticians advise you to do a series of hierarchical tests beginning with interactions. If the highest-order interactions are insignificant, drop them from the model and recompute the analysis. Then, examine the lower-order interactions. If they are insignificant, recompute the model with main effects only. Some computer programs automate this process and print sums of squares and *F* tests according to the hierarchy (ordering of effects) you specify in the model. SPSS GLM, for example, calls these Type I sums of squares.

This procedure is analogous to stepwise regression in which hierarchical subsets of models are tested. This example assumes you have specified the following model:

```
Y = CONSTANT + a + b + c + a*b + a*c + b*c + a*b*c
```

The hierarchical approach tests the following models:

```
Y = CONSTANT + a + b + c + a*b + a*c + b*c + a*b*c
Y = CONSTANT + a + b + c + a*b + a*c + b*c
Y = CONSTANT + a + b + c + a*b + a*c
Y = CONSTANT + a + b + c + a*b
Y = CONSTANT + a + b + c
Y = CONSTANT + a + b
Y = CONSTANT + a
```

The problem with this approach, however, is that plausible subsets of effects are ignored if you examine only one hierarchy. The following model, which may be the best fit to the data, is never considered:

```
Y = CONSTANT + a + b + a*b
```

Furthermore, if you decide to examine all the other plausible subsets, you are really doing all possible subsets regression, and you should use Bonferroni confidence levels before rejecting a null hypothesis. The example above has 127 possible subset models (excluding ones without a CONSTANT). Interactive stepwise regression allows you to explore subset models under your control.

If you have done an experiment and have decided that higher-order effects (interactions) are of enough theoretical importance to include in your model, you should condition every test on all other effects in the model you selected.

This is the classical approach of Fisher and Yates. It amounts to using the default F values on the ANOVA output, which are the same as the SPSS Type III sums of squares.

Probably the most important reason to stay with one model is that if you eliminate a series of effects that are not quite significant (say, $p = 0.06$), you could end up with an incorrect subset model because of the dependencies among the sums of squares. In summary, if you want other sums of squares, compute them. You can supply the mean square error to customize sums of squares by using **Stats**➟**General Linear Model**➟ **Hypothesis Test**, selecting MSE, and specifying the mean square error and degrees of freedom.

6.7 Randomized block designs

A randomized block design is like a factorial design without an interaction term. The following example is from Neter, Wasserman, and Kutner (1985). Five blocks of judges were given the task of analyzing three treatments. Judges are stratified within blocks, so the interaction of blocks and treatments cannot be analyzed. These data are in the file BLOCK. Use **Stats**➟**General Linear Model**➟**Estimate Model**. Move JUDGMENT to the **Dependent(s)** list and move BLOCK and TREAT into the **Independent(s)** list. Select **Categories** and move BLOCK and TREAT into the **Categorial Variable(s)** list.

BLOCK	TREAT	JUDGMENT
1	1	1
1	2	5
1	3	8
2	1	2
2	2	8

BLOCK	TREAT	JUDGMENT
2	3	14
3	1	7
3	2	9
3	3	16
4	1	6
4	2	13
4	3	18
5	1	12
5	2	14
5	3	17

```
GLM
   USE block
   CATEGORY block, treat
   MODEL judgment = CONSTANT + block + treat
   ESTIMATE
```

You must use GLM instead of ANOVA because you do not want the
*BLOCK*TREAT* interaction in the model.

```
Dep Var: JUDGMENT N: 15 Multiple R:  0.970 Squared multiple R:  0.940

                          Analysis of Variance

   Source           Sum-of-Squares  DF  Mean-Square   F-Ratio      P

   BLOCK                   171.333   4      42.833     14.358    0.001
   TREAT                   202.800   2     101.400     33.989    0.000
   Error                    23.867   8       2.983
```

6.8 Incomplete block designs

Randomized blocks can be used in factorial designs as well. Here is an example from John (1971). The data (in the file *JOHN*) involve an experiment with three treatment factors (*A, B,* and *C*) plus a blocking variable with eight levels. Notice that data were collected on 32 of the possible 64 experimental situations.

BLOCK	A	B	C	Y
1	1	1	1	101
1	2	1	2	373
1	1	2	2	398
1	2	2	1	291
2	1	1	2	312
2	2	1	1	106
2	1	2	1	265
2	2	2	2	450
3	1	1	1	106
3	2	2	1	306
3	1	1	2	324
3	2	2	2	449
4	1	2	1	272
4	2	1	1	89
4	1	2	2	407

BLOCK	A	B	C	Y
4	2	1	2	338
5	1	1	1	87
5	2	1	2	324
5	1	2	1	279
5	2	2	2	471
6	1	1	2	323
6	2	1	1	128
6	1	2	2	423
6	2	2	1	334
7	1	1	1	131
7	2	1	1	103
7	1	2	2	445
7	2	2	2	437
8	1	1	2	324
8	2	1	2	361
8	1	2	1	302
8	2	2	1	272

Use **Stats**➠**General Linear Model**➠**Estimate Model** and select *Y* as the dependent variable. Select *BLOCK* and use **Add** to move it into the **Independent(s)** list. Move *A*, *B*, and *C* into the **Independent(s)** list in the same manner. To create the *A*B* term, add *A* to the **Independent(s)** list, then select *B* and use **Cross** to move it to the **Independent(s)** list. Create *A*C* and *B*C* in the same way. To create the term *A*B*C*, add *A* to the **Independent(s)** list, select *B* and use **Cross** to move it to the **Independent(s)** list, and select *C* and use **Cross** to move it to the **Independent(s)** list. Finally, select the **Categories** button and move *BLOCK*, *A*, *B*, and *C* into the **Categorical Variable(s)** list. Again, you must use **General Linear Model** instead of **Analysis of Variance** because you do not want interactions with *BLOCK* in the model. With commands:

```
GLM
    USE john
    CATEGORY block, a, b, c
    MODEL y = CONSTANT + block + a + b + c +,
             a*b + a*c + b*c + a*b*c
    ESTIMATE
```

```
Dep Var: Y N: 32 Multiple R:  0.994 Squared multiple R:  0.988

                         Analysis of Variance

Source           Sum-of-Squares   DF   Mean-Square   F-Ratio      P

BLOCK               2638.469      7     376.924       1.182     0.364
A                   3465.281      1    3465.281      10.862     0.004
B                 161170.031      1  161170.031     505.209     0.000
C                 278817.781      1  278817.781     873.992     0.000
A*B                   28.167      1      28.167       0.088     0.770
A*C                 1802.667      1    1802.667       5.651     0.029
B*C                11528.167      1   11528.167      36.137     0.000
A*B*C                 45.375      1      45.375       0.142     0.711

Error               5423.281     17     319.017
```

6.9 Fractional factorial designs

Sometimes a factorial design involves so many combinations of treatments that certain cells must be left empty to save experimental resources. At other times, a complete randomized factorial study is designed, but loss of subjects leaves one or more cells completely missing. These models are similar to incomplete block designs because not all effects in the full model can be estimated. Usually, certain interactions must be left out of the model.

The following example uses some experimental data that contain values in only 8 out of 16 possible cells. Each cell contains two cases. The pattern of nonmissing cells makes it possible to estimate only the main effects plus 3 two-way interactions. The data are in the file *FRACTION*.

A	B	C	D	Y
1	1	1	1	7
1	1	1	1	3
2	2	1	1	1
2	2	1	1	2
2	1	2	1	12
2	1	2	1	13
1	2	2	1	14
1	2	2	1	15
2	1	1	2	8
2	1	1	2	6
1	2	1	2	12
1	2	1	2	10
1	1	2	2	6
1	1	2	2	4
2	2	2	2	6
2	2	2	2	7

```
GLM
    USE fraction
    CATEGORY a, b, c, d
    MODEL y = CONSTANT + a + b + c + d + a*b + a*c + b*c
    ESTIMATE
```

Again, you must use GLM instead of ANOVA to omit the higher way interactions that ANOVA automatically generates.

```
Dep Var: Y N: 16 Multiple R:  0.972 Squared multiple R:  0.944

                        Analysis of Variance
    Source         Sum-of-Squares   DF  Mean-Square    F-Ratio      P

    A                    16.000      1      16.000       8.000    0.022
    B                     4.000      1       4.000       2.000    0.195
    C                    49.000      1      49.000      24.500    0.001
    D                     4.000      1       4.000       2.000    0.195
    A*B                 182.250      1     182.250      91.125    0.000
    A*C                  12.250      1      12.250       6.125    0.038
    B*C                   2.250      1       2.250       1.125    0.320

    Error                16.000      8       2.000
```

When missing cells turn up by chance rather than by design, you may not know which interactions to eliminate. When you attempt to fit the full model, SYSTAT informs you that the design is singular. In that case, you may need to try several models before finding an estimable one. It is usually best to begin by leaving out the highest order interaction (A∗B∗C∗D in this example). Continue with subset models until you get an ANOVA table.

Looking for an estimable model is not the same as analyzing the data with stepwise regression because you are not looking at p values. After you find an estimable model, stop and settle with the statistics printed in the ANOVA table.

6.10 Mixed models

Mixed models involve combinations of fixed and random factors in an ANOVA. Fixed factors are assumed to be comprised of an exhaustive set of categories (for example, males and females), while random factors have category levels that are assumed to have been randomly sampled from a larger population of categories (for example, classrooms or word stems). Because of the mixing of fixed and random components, expected mean squares for certain effects are different from those for fully fixed or fully random designs. **General Linear Model** can handle mixed models because **Stats⟹General Linear Model⟹Hypothesis Test** lets you specify error terms for specific hypotheses.

For example, let's reanalyze the *AFIFI* data with a mixed model instead of a fully fixed factorial. This time, you are interested in the four drugs as wide-spectrum disease killers. Because each drug is now thought to be effective against diseases in general, you have sampled three random diseases to assess the drugs. This implies that *DISEASE* is a random factor and *DRUG* remains a fixed factor. In this case, the error term for *DRUG* is the *DRUG∗DISEASE* interaction. To test the effect, run the same analysis you already performed to get the ANOVA table. Use **Stats⟹Analysis of Variance⟹Estimate Model**, select *SYSINCR* as the dependent variable, and select *DRUG* and *DISEASE* as factors. With commands:

```
ANOVA
   USE afifi
   CATEGORY drug, disease
   DEPEND sysincr
   ESTIMATE
```

The output for these commands is shown in Example 6.4. Now use Stats⟶General Linear Model⟶Hypothesis Test and type **Drug** in the Effects text box. In the **Error Term** group, select **Between Subject(s) Effect(s)** and type **Drug*Disease** as the error term. With commands:

```
HYPOTHESIS
EFFECT = drug
ERROR = drug*disease
TEST
```

```
Test for effect called:    DRUG

Test of Hypothesis

        Source       SS       DF      MS          F          P

    Hypothesis    2997.472    3    999.157      8.476      0.014
         Error     707.266    6    117.878
```

6.11 Nested designs

Nested designs resemble factorial designs with certain cells missing (incomplete factorials). This is because one factor is *nested* under another, so that not all combinations of the two factors are observed. For example, in an educational study, classrooms are usually nested under schools because it is impossible to have the same classroom existing at two different schools (except as antimatter). The following example (in which teachers are nested within schools) is from Neter, Wasserman, and Kutner (1985). The data (learning scores) look like this:

	TEACHER1	TEACHER2
SCHOOL1	25	14
	29	11
SCHOOL2	11	22
	6	18
SCHOOL3	17	5
	20	2

In the study, there are actually six teachers, not just two; thus, the design really looks like this:

	TEACHER1	TEACHER2	TEACHER3	TEACHER4	TEACHER5	TEACHER6
SCHOOL1	25	14				
	29	11				
SCHOOL2			11	22		
			6	18		
SCHOOL3					17	5
					20	2

The data are set up in the file *SCHOOLS*.

TEACHER	SCHOOL	LEARNING
1	1	25
1	1	29
2	1	14
2	1	11
3	2	11
3	2	6
4	2	22
4	2	18
5	3	17
5	3	20
6	3	5
6	3	2

Use **Stats⇒General Linear Model⇒Estimate Model**, and select
LEARNING as the dependent variable. Add *SCHOOL* to the **Independent(s)**
list, then add *SCHOOL* to the **Independent(s)** list again. Next, select
TEACHER and use **Nest** to nest the teachers within the schools
(*TEACHER* (*SCHOOL*)). Select the **Categories** button and move *TEACHER* and
SCHOOL into the **Categorical Variable(s)** list. With commands:

```
GLM
    USE schools
    CATEGORY teacher, school
    MODEL learning = CONSTANT + school + teacher(school)
    ESTIMATE
```

```
Dep Var: LEARNING N: 12 Multiple R:  0.972 Squared multiple R:  0.945

                        Analysis of Variance

Source             Sum-of-Squares  DF  Mean-Square    F-Ratio      P

SCHOOL                    156.500   2       78.250     11.179   0.009
TEACHER(SCHOOL)           567.500   3      189.167     27.024   0.001

Error                      42.000   6        7.000
```

Your data can use any codes for *TEACHER*, including a separate code for
every teacher in the study, as long as each different teacher within a given
school has a different code. GLM will use the nesting specified in the
MODEL statement to determine the pattern of nesting. You can, for
example, allow teachers in different schools to share codes.

This example is a balanced nested design. Unbalanced designs (unequal
number of cases per cell) are handled automatically in SYSTAT because
the estimation method is least squares.

6.12
Split plot
designs

The split plot design is closely related to the nested design. In the split plot, however, plots are often considered a random factor; therefore, you have to construct different error terms to test different effects. The following example involves two treatments: A (between plots) and B (within plots). The numbers in the cells are the *YIELD* of the crop within plots.

	A1		A2	
	PLOT1	PLOT2	PLOT3	PLOT4
B1	0	3	4	5
B2	0	1	2	4
B3	5	5	7	6
B4	3	4	8	6

Here are the data from the *PLOTS* data file in the form needed by ANOVA:

PLOT	A	B	YIELD
1	1	1	0
1	1	2	0
1	1	3	5
1	1	4	3
2	1	1	3
2	1	2	1
2	1	3	5
2	1	4	4
3	2	1	4
3	2	2	2
3	2	3	7
3	2	4	8
4	2	1	5
4	2	2	4
4	2	3	6
4	2	4	6

To analyze this design, you need two different error terms. For the Between Plots effects (*A*), you need "PLOTS within *A*." For the Within Plots effects (*B* and *A*B*), you need "B by PLOTS within *A*."

Fit the
saturated
model

First, fit the saturated model with all the effects and then use the items on the **General Linear Model** dialog box to specify different error terms. Use **Stats⟹General Linear Model⟹Estimate Model**, select *YIELD* as the dependent variable, and add *A* and *B* to the **Independent(s)** list. To obtain the term *A*B*, add *A* to the **Independent(s)** list, select *B*, and use **Cross** to move it to the **Independent(s)** list. To obtain the term *PLOT(A)*, add *A* to the **Independent(s)** list, select *PLOT*, and use **Nest** to move it to the **Independent(s)** list. To obtain *B*PLOT(A)*, add *A* to the **Independent(s)** list, select *PLOT*, and use **Nest** to move it to the **Independent(s)** list. Select

B and use **Cross** to move it to the **Independent(s)** list. Finally, select the **Categories** button and move *PLOT*, *A*, and *B* into the **Categorical Variable(s)** list. With commands:

```
GLM
    USE plots
    CATEGORY plot, a, b
    MODEL yield = CONSTANT + a + b + a*b + plot(a) +,
                  b*plot(a)
    ESTIMATE
```

```
Dep Var: YIELD N: 16 Multiple R:  1.000 Squared multiple R:  1.000

                         Analysis of Variance

Source            Sum-of-Squares  DF  Mean-Square    F-Ratio      P
A                        27.563    1      27.563         .         .
B                        42.687    3      14.229         .         .
A*B                       2.188    3       0.729         .         .
PLOT(A)                   3.125    2       1.562         .         .
B*PLOT(A)                 7.375    6       1.229         .         .

Error                     0.000    0          .
```

Between-plots effects

You do not get a full ANOVA table because the model is perfectly fit. The coefficient of determination (*Squared multiple R*) is 1. Now you have to use some of the effects as error terms. First, test for between-plots effects, namely *A*. Use **Stats▸General Linear Model▸Hypothesis Test**. Type **A** in the **Effects** text box and type **plot(a)** in the **Between Subject(s) Effect(s)** text box. With commands:

```
HYPOTHESIS
    EFFECT = a
    ERROR = plot(a)
    TEST
```

```
Test for effect called:     A

Test of Hypothesis

       Source        SS        DF       MS          F          P
   Hypothesis     27.563        1     27.563      17.640      0.052
        Error      3.125        2      1.562
```

Within-plots effects

To do the within-plots effects (*B*), use **Stats▸General Linear Model▸Hypothesis Test**. Type **B** in the **Effects** text box and type **B*plot(a)** in the **Between Subject(s) Effect(s)** text box. With commands:

```
HYPOTHESIS
    EFFECT = b
```

```
ERROR = b*plot(a)
TEST
```

```
Test for effect called:     B

Test of Hypothesis

      Source        SS      DF      MS         F         P

   Hypothesis    42.687     3    14.229    11.576     0.007
      Error       7.375     6     1.229
```

Finally, do *A*B* with the same error term. Use **Stats**➠**General Linear Model**➠**Hypothesis Test**. Type **A*B** in the **Effects** text box and type **B*plot(a)** in the **Between Subject(s) Effect(s)** text box. With commands:

```
HYPOTHESIS
EFFECT = a*b
ERROR = b*plot(a)
TEST
```

```
Test for effect called:     A*B

Test of Hypothesis

      Source        SS      DF      MS         F         P

   Hypothesis     2.188     3     0.729    0.593     0.642
      Error       7.375     6     1.229
```

This analysis is the same as that for a repeated measures design with subjects as *PLOT*, groups as *A*, and trials as *B*. Because this method becomes unwieldy for a large number of plots (subjects), SYSTAT offers a more compact method for repeated measures analysis, which is discussed later in this chapter.

6.13
Latin square designs

A Latin square design imposes a pattern on treatments in a factorial design to save experimental effort or reduce within cell error. As in the nested design, not all combinations of the square and other treatments are measured, so the model lacks certain interaction terms between squares and treatments. GLM can analyze these designs easily if an extra variable denoting the square is included in the file. The following fixed effects example is from Neter, Wasserman, and Kutner (1985). The *SQUARE* variable is represented in the cells of the design. For simplicity, the dependent variable, *RESPONSE*, has been left out.

	day1	day2	day3	day4	day5
week1	D	C	A	B	E
week2	C	B	E	A	D
week3	A	D	B	E	C
week4	E	A	C	D	B
week5	B	E	D	C	A

You would set up the data as shown below (the *LATIN* file).

DAY	WEEK	SQUARE	RESPONSE
1	1	D	18
1	2	C	17
1	3	A	14
1	4	E	21
1	5	B	17
2	1	C	13
2	2	B	34
2	3	D	21
2	4	A	16
2	5	E	15
3	1	A	7
3	2	E	29
3	3	B	32
3	4	C	27
3	5	D	13
4	1	B	17
4	2	A	13
4	3	E	24
4	4	D	31
4	5	C	25
5	1	E	21
5	2	D	26
5	3	C	26
5	4	B	31
5	5	A	7

To do the analysis, use **Stats**➧**General Linear Model**➧**Estimate Model**. Move *RESPONSE* to the **Dependent(s)** list and move *DAY*, *WEEK*, and *SQUARE* to the **Independent(s)** list. With commands:

```
GLM
    USE latin
    CATEGORY day, week, square
    MODEL response = CONSTANT + day + week + square
    ESTIMATE
```

```
Dep Var: RESPONSE N: 25 Multiple R:  0.931 Squared multiple R:  0.867

                        Analysis of Variance

Source          Sum-of-Squares  DF  Mean-Square   F-Ratio      P

DAY                     82.000   4       20.500     1.306   0.323
WEEK                   477.200   4      119.300     7.599   0.003
SQUARE                 664.400   4      166.100    10.580   0.001

Error                  188.400  12       15.700
```

6.14
Crossover and changeover designs

In crossover designs, an experiment is divided into periods, and the treatment of a subject changes from one period to the next. Changeover studies often use designs similar to a Latin square. A problem with these designs is that there may be a residual or carry-over effect of a treatment into the following period. This can be minimized by extending the interval between experimental periods; however, this is not always feasible. Fortunately, there are methods to assess the magnitude of any carry-over effects that may be present.

Two-period crossover designs can be analyzed as repeated-measures designs (see below). More complicated crossover designs can also be analyzed by SYSTAT, and carry-over effects can be assessed. Cochran and Cox (1957) present a study of milk production by cows under three different feed schedules: *A* (roughage), *B* (limited grain), and *C* (full grain). The design of the study has the form of two 3×3 Latin squares:

	COW					
	Latin square 1			Latin square 2		
Period	I	II	III	IV	V	VI
1	A	B	C	A	B	C
2	B	C	A	C	A	B
3	C	A	B	B	C	A

The data are set up in the *WILLIAMS* data file as follows:

COW	SQUARE	PERIOD	FEED	CARRY	RESIDUAL	MILK
1	1	1	1	1	0	38
1	1	2	2	1	1	25
1	1	3	3	2	2	15
2	1	1	2	1	0	109
2	1	2	3	2	2	86
2	1	3	1	2	3	39
3	1	1	3	1	0	124
3	1	2	1	2	3	72
3	1	3	2	1	1	27
4	2	1	1	1	0	86
4	2	2	3	1	1	76
4	2	3	2	2	3	46
5	2	1	2	1	0	75
5	2	2	1	2	2	35
5	2	3	3	1	1	34
6	2	1	3	1	0	101
6	2	2	2	2	3	63
6	2	3	1	2	2	1

PERIOD is nested within each Latin square (the periods for cows in one square are unrelated to the periods in the other). The variable *RESIDUAL* indicates the treatment of the preceding period. For the first period for each cow, there is no preceding period.

```
GLM
    USE williams
    CATEGORY cow, period, square, residual, carry, feed
    MODEL milk = CONSTANT + cow + feed +,
                 period(square) + residual(carry)
    ESTIMATE
```

```
Dep Var: MILK N: 18 Multiple R:  0.995 Squared multiple R:  0.990

                            Analysis of Variance

Source            Sum-of-Squares  DF  Mean-Square  F-Ratio     P
COW                   3835.950     5      767.190   15.402   0.010
FEED                  2854.550     2     1427.275   28.653   0.004
PERIOD(SQUARE)        3873.950     4      968.488   19.443   0.007
RESIDUAL(CARRY)        616.194     2      308.097    6.185   0.060

Error                  199.250     4       49.813
```

There is a significant effect of feed on milk production and an insignificant residual or carry-over effect in this instance. To replicate the Cochran and Cox Type I sums of squares analysis, you must fit a new model to get their sums of squares. The following commands test the *COW* effect. Notice that the *Error* specification uses the mean square error (MSE) from the previous analysis. It also contains the error degrees of freedom (4) from the previous model.

```
GLM
    USE williams
    CATEGORY cow
    MODEL milk = CONSTANT + cow
    ESTIMATE

    HYPOTHESIS
    EFFECT = cow
    ERROR = 49.813(4)
    TEST
```

```
Dep Var: MILK N: 18 Multiple R:  0.533 Squared multiple R:  0.284

                            Analysis of Variance

Source            Sum-of-Squares  DF  Mean-Square  F-Ratio     P
COW                   5781.111     5     1156.222    0.952   0.484
Error                14581.333    12     1215.111
```

```
Test for effect called:     COW

Test of Hypothesis

        Source      SS      DF      MS          F         P

    Hypothesis   5781.111    5    1156.222    23.211    0.005
         Error    199.252    4      49.813
```

The remaining term, *PERIOD*, requires a different model. *PERIOD* is nested with *SQUARE*.

```
GLM
    USE williams
    CATEGORY period square
    MODEL milk = CONSTANT + period(square)
    ESTIMATE

    HYPOTHESIS
    EFFECT = period(square)
    ERROR = 49.813(4)
    TEST
```

```
Dep Var: MILK N: 18 Multiple R:  0.751 Squared multiple R:  0.564

                          Analysis of Variance

Source              Sum-of-Squares   DF   Mean-Square   F-Ratio      P

PERIOD(SQUARE)          11489.111     4     2872.278     4.208     0.021
Error                    8873.333    13      682.564
```

```
Test for effect called:     PERIOD(SQUARE)

Test of Hypothesis

        Source       SS      DF      MS          F         P

    Hypothesis   11489.111    4    2872.278    57.661    0.001
         Error     199.252    4      49.813
```

6.15 Missing cells designs: the means model

When cells are completely missing in a factorial design, parameterizing a model can be difficult. The full model cannot be estimated. GLM offers a means model parameterization so that missing cell parameters can be dropped automatically from the model, and hypotheses for main effects and interactions can be tested by specifying cells directly. Examine Searle (1987); Hocking, (1985); or Milliken and Johnson (1984) for more information in this area.

Widely favored for this purpose by statisticians (Searle, 1987; Hocking, 1985; Milliken and Johnson, 1984), the means model allows:

- Tests of hypotheses in missing cells designs (using Type IV sums of squares)

- Tests of simple hypotheses (for example, within levels of other factors)

- The use of population weights to reflect differences in subclass sizes

Coding for the means model

Effects coding is the default for GLM. Alternatively, means models code predictors as cell means rather than effects which differ from a grand mean. To code the model as a string of cell means instead of ANOVA effects, use **Stats**➠**General Linear Model**➠**Estimate Model** and select **Means**. With commands, use the MODEL command with the MEANS option. The constant is omitted, and the predictors are 1 for a case belonging to a given cell and 0 for all others. When cells are missing, GLM automatically excludes null columns and estimates the submodel.

The categorical variables are specified in the MODEL statement differently for a means model than for an effects model. Here are some examples:

```
MODEL y = a*b / MEANS
MODEL y = group*age*school$ / MEANS
```

The first two models generate fully factorial designs (*A* by *B* and *GROUP* by *AGE* by *SCHOOL$*). Notice that they omit the constant and main effects parameters because the means model does not include effects or a grand mean. Nevertheless, the number of parameters is the same in the two models. For a 2×3 design (two levels of *A* and three levels of *B*), here are the effects model and the means model, respectively:

```
MODEL y = CONSTANT + A + B + A*B
```

A	B	m	a1	b1	b2	a1b1	a1b2
1	1	1	1	1	0	1	0
1	2	1	1	0	1	0	1
1	3	1	1	-1	-1	-1	-1
2	1	1	-1	1	0	-1	0
2	2	1	-1	0	1	0	-1
2	3	1	-1	-1	-1	1	-1

```
MODEL y = A*B / MEANS
```

A	B	a1b1	a1b2	a1b3	a2b1	a2b2	a2b3
1	1	1	0	0	0	0	0
1	2	0	1	0	0	0	0
1	3	0	0	1	0	0	0
2	1	0	0	0	1	0	0
2	2	0	0	0	0	1	0
2	3	0	0	0	0	0	1

Means and effects models can be blended for incomplete factorials and others designs. All crossed terms (for example, *A*∗*B*) will be coded with means design variables (provided the MEANS option is present), and the remaining terms will be coded as effects. The constant must be omitted, even in these cases, because it is collinear with the means design variables. All covariates and effects coded factors must precede the crossed factors in the MODEL statement.

Here is an example, assuming *A* has four levels, *B* has two, and *C* has three. In this design, there are 24 possible cells, but only 12 are nonmissing. The treatment combinations are partially balanced across the levels of *B* and *C*.

```
MODEL y = A + B*C / MEANS
```

A	B	C	a1	a2	a3	b1c1	b1c2	b1c3	b2c1	b2c2	b2c3
1	1	1	1	0	0	1	0	0	0	0	0
3	1	1	0	0	1	1	0	0	0	0	0
2	1	2	0	1	0	0	1	0	0	0	0
4	1	2	-1	-1	-1	0	1	0	0	0	0
1	1	3	1	0	0	0	0	1	0	0	0
4	1	3	-1	-1	-1	0	0	1	0	0	0
2	2	1	0	1	0	0	0	0	1	0	0
3	2	1	0	0	1	0	0	0	0	1	0
2	2	2	0	1	0	0	0	0	0	1	0
4	2	2	-1	-1	-1	0	0	0	0	1	0
1	2	3	1	0	0	0	0	0	0	0	1
3	2	3	0	0	1	0	0	0	0	0	1

Nutritional knowledge survey

The following example, which uses the data file *MJ202*, is from Milliken and Johnson (1984). The data are from a home economics survey experiment. *DIFF* is the change in test scores between pre-test and post-test on a nutritional knowledge questionnaire. *GROUP* classifies whether or not a subject received food stamps. *AGE* designates four age groups, and *RACE$* was their term for designating *Whites*, *Blacks*, and *Hispanics*.

	Group 0				Group 1			
	1	2	3	4	1	2	3	4
W	1	3	6		9	10	13	15
H			5				12	
B		2	4	7	8		11	14

Shading denotes cells where no data were collected. Numbers within cells refer to cell designations in the Fisher LSD pairwise mean comparisons at the end of this example.

GROUP	AGE	RACE$	DIFF	GROUP	AGE	RACE$	DIFF
0	1	W	5	1	2	W	3
0	1	W	−2	1	2	W	3
0	1	W	−10	1	2	W	7
0	2	B	−4	1	2	W	7
0	2	B	0	1	2	W	4
0	2	B	5	1	3	B	1
0	2	B	−6	1	3	B	5
0	2	B	2	1	3	B	15
0	2	W	7	1	3	B	9
0	2	W	2	1	3	H	0
0	2	W	−13	1	3	W	4
0	2	W	2	1	3	W	5
0	2	W	3	1	3	W	0
0	2	W	3	1	3	W	5
0	2	W	−4	1	3	W	2
0	2	W	−5	1	3	W	8
0	3	B	3	1	3	W	1
0	3	B	−14	1	3	W	−2
0	3	B	−14	1	3	W	6
0	3	B	−1	1	3	W	6
0	3	B	3	1	3	W	4
0	3	B	1	1	3	W	−5
0	3	H	−1	1	3	W	6
0	3	H	6	1	3	W	3
0	3	W	−20	1	3	W	4
0	3	W	6	1	3	W	5
0	3	W	9	1	3	W	12
0	3	W	−5	1	3	W	3
0	3	W	3	1	3	W	8
0	3	W	−1	1	3	W	3
0	3	W	3	1	3	W	8
0	3	W	0	1	3	W	13
0	3	W	4	1	3	W	4
0	3	W	−3	1	3	W	7
0	3	W	2	1	3	W	9
0	3	W	3	1	3	W	3
0	3	W	−5	1	3	W	12
0	3	W	2	1	3	W	11
0	3	W	−1	1	3	W	4
0	3	W	−1	1	3	W	12
0	3	W	6	1	4	B	−3
0	3	W	−8	1	4	W	−6
0	3	W	0	1	4	W	−5
0	3	W	2	1	4	W	5
0	4	B	0	1	4	W	8
1	1	B	4	1	4	W	5
1	1	B	4	1	4	W	6
1	1	W	−8	1	4	W	7
1	1	W	9	1	4	W	6
1	2	W	5	1	4	W	2
1	2	W	0	1	4	W	7
1	2	W	10	1	4	W	5

First, fit the model. Use **Stats**➡**General Linear Model**➡**Estimate Model**, select **Means**, and deselect **Include constant**. Move *DIFF* to the **Dependent(s)** list. Move *GROUP* to the **Independent(s)** list, and then use **Cross** to move *AGE* and *RACE$* to the **Independent(s)** list. Select **Categories** and move *GROUP*, *AGE*, and *RACE$* to the **Categorical Variable(s)** list. With commands:

```
GLM
    USE mj202
    CATEGORY group age race$
    MODEL diff = group*age*race$ / MEANS
    ESTIMATE
```

```
Means Model

Dep Var: DIFF N: 107 Multiple R:  0.538 Squared multiple R:  0.289

                        Unweighted Means Model

                        Analysis of Variance

    Source      Sum-of-Squares   DF  Mean-Square     F-Ratio       P
    Model           1068.546     14    76.325          2.672     0.003
    Error           2627.472     92    28.559
```

Now you need to test the *GROUP* main effect. The following notation is equivalent to Milliken and Johnson's. Because of the missing cells, the *GROUP* effect must be computed over means which are balanced across the other factors.

In the drawing at the beginning of this example, notice that this specification contrasts all the numbered cells in group 0 (except 2) with all the numbered cells in group 1 (except 8 and 15).

```
    HYPOTHESIS
    NOTE 'GROUP MAIN EFFECT
    SPECIFY ,
    group[0] age[1] race$[W] + group[0] age[2] race$[W] +,
    group[0] age[3] race$[B] + group[0] age[3] race$[H] +,
    group[0] age[3] race$[W] + group[0] age[4] race$[B] =,
    group[1] age[1] race$[W] + group[1] age[2] race$[W] +,
    group[1] age[3] race$[B] + group[1] age[3] race$[H] +,
    group[1] age[3] race$[W] + group[1] age[4] race$[B]
    TEST
```

```
                        GROUP MAIN EFFECT

Contrasting using unweighted means.

Hypothesis.

A Matrix

                    1           2           3           4           5
                 -1.000        0.0       -1.000      -1.000      -1.000
```

	6	7	8	9	10
	-1.000	-1.000	0.0	1.000	1.000
	11	12	13	14	15
	1.000	1.000	1.000	1.000	0.0

Null hypothesis value for D
              0.0

Test of Hypothesis

Source	SS	DF	MS	F	P
Hypothesis	75.738	1	75.738	2.652	0.107
Error	2627.472	92	28.559		

The computations for the *AGE* main effect are similar:

```
HYPOTHESIS
NOTE 'AGE MAIN EFFECT'
SPECIFY ,
GROUP[1] AGE[1] RACE$[B] + GROUP[1] AGE[1] RACE$[W] =,
GROUP[1] AGE[4] RACE$[B] + GROUP[1] AGE[4] RACE$[W];

GROUP[0] AGE[2] RACE$[B] + GROUP[1] AGE[2] RACE$[W] =,
GROUP[0] AGE[4] RACE$[B] + GROUP[1] AGE[4] RACE$[W];

GROUP[0] AGE[3] RACE$[B] + GROUP[1] AGE[3] RACE$[B] +,
GROUP[1] AGE[3] RACE$[W] =,
GROUP[0] AGE[4] RACE$[B] + GROUP[1] AGE[4] RACE$[B] +,
GROUP[1] AGE[4] RACE$[W]
TEST
```

AGE MAIN EFFECT

Hypothesis.

A Matrix

		1	2	3	4	5
	1	0.0	0.0	0.0	0.0	0.0
	2	0.0	-1.000	0.0	0.0	0.0
	3	0.0	0.0	0.0	-1.000	0.0

		6	7	8	9	10
	1	0.0	0.0	-1.000	-1.000	0.0
	2	0.0	1.000	0.0	0.0	-1.000
	3	0.0	1.000	0.0	0.0	0.0

		11	12	13	14	15
	1	0.0	0.0	0.0	1.000	1.000
	2	0.0	0.0	0.0	0.0	1.000
	3	-1.000	0.0	-1.000	1.000	1.000

D Matrix

1	0.0
2	0.0
3	0.0

Test of Hypothesis

Source	SS	DF	MS	F	P
Hypothesis	41.526	3	13.842	0.485	0.694
Error	2627.472	92	28.559		

The *GROUP* by *AGE* interaction requires more complex balancing. It is derived from a subset of the means in the following specified combination. Again, check Milliken and Johnson to see the correspondence.

```
HYPOTHESIS
NOTE 'GROUP BY AGE INTERACTION'
SPECIFY ,
group[0] age[1] race$[W] - group[0] age[3] race$[W] -,
group[1] age[1] race$[W] + group[1] age[3] race$[W] +,
group[0] age[3] race$[B] - group[0] age[4] race$[B] -,
group[1] age[3] race$[B] + group[1] age[4] race$[B]=0.0;


group[0] age[2] race$[W] - group[0] age[3] race$[W] -,
group[1] age[2] race$[W] + group[1] age[3] race$[W] +,
group[0] age[3] race$[B] - group[0] age[4] race$[B] -,
group[1] age[3] RACE$[B] + group[1] age[4] race$[B]=0.0;


group[0] age[3] race$[B] - group[0] age[4] race$[B] -,
group[1] age[3] race$[B] + group[1] age[4] race$[B]=0.0
   TEST
```

```
                    GROUP BY AGE INTERACTION

Hypothesis.
                  *** We omit the A and D matrices ***

Test of Hypothesis

     Source        SS        DF       MS         F          P

  Hypothesis    91.576        3     30.525     1.069      0.366
     Error    2627.472       92     28.559
```

The following commands are needed to produce the rest of Milliken and Johnson's results. The remaining output is not listed.

```
HYPOTHESIS
   NOTE 'RACE$ MAIN EFFECT'
   SPECIFY ,
group[0] age[2] race$[B] + group[0] age[3] race$[B] +,
group[1] age[1] race$[B] + group[1] age[3] race$[B] +,
group[1] age[4] race$[B] =,
group[0] age[2] race$[W] + group[0] age[3] race$[W] +,
group[1] age[1] race$[W] + group[1] age[3] race$[W] +,
group[1] age[4] race$[W];

group[0] age[3] race$[H] + group[1] age[3] race$[H] =,
group[0] age[3] race$[W] + group[1] age[3] race$[W]
   TEST
```

```
HYPOTHESIS
NOTE 'GROUP*RACE$
SPECIFY ,
group[0] age[3] race$[B] - group[0] age[3] race$[W] -,
group[1] age[3] race$[B] + group[1] age[3] race$[W]=0.0;

group[0] age[3] race$[H] - group[0] age[3] race$[W] -,
group[1] age[3] race$[H] + group[1] age[3] race$[W]=0.0
  TEST
    HYPOTHESIS
    NOTE 'AGE*RACE$'
    SPECIFY ,
group[1] age[1] race$[B] - group[1] age[1] race$[W] -,
group[1] age[4] race$[B] + group[1] age[4] race$[W]=0.0;

group[0] age[2] race$[B] - group[0] age[2] race$[W] -,
group[0] age[3] race$[B] + group[0] age[3] race$[W]=0.0;

group[1] age[3] race$[B] - group[1] age[3] race$[W] -,
group[1] age[4] race$[B] + group[1] age[4] race$[W]=0.0
  TEST
```

Finally, Milliken and Johnson do pairwise comparisons:

```
HYPOTHESIS
POST group*age*race$ / LSD
TEST
```

Here is the matrix of comparisons printed by ANOVA. The matrix of
mean differences has been omitted.

```
COL/
ROW   GROUP           AGE       RACE$
  1         0.000       1.000 W
  2         0.000       2.000 B
  3         0.000       2.000 W
  4         0.000       3.000 B
  5         0.000       3.000 H
  6         0.000       3.000 W
  7         0.000       4.000 B
  8         1.000       1.000 B
  9         1.000       1.000 W
 10         1.000       2.000 W
 11         1.000       3.000 B
 12         1.000       3.000 H
 13         1.000       3.000 W
 14         1.000       4.000 B
 15         1.000       4.000 W

USING UNWEIGHTED MEANS.

POST HOC TEST OF      DIFF


USING MODEL MSE OF        28.559 WITH      92. DF.
FISHER'S LEAST-SIGNIFICANT-DIFFERENCE TEST.
MATRIX OF PAIRWISE COMPARISON PROBABILITIES:
                      1            2            3            4            5
```

1	1.000				
2	0.662	1.000			
3	0.638	0.974	1.000		
4	0.725	0.323	0.295	1.000	
5	0.324	0.455	0.461	0.161	1.000
6	0.521	0.827	0.850	0.167	0.497
7	0.706	0.901	0.912	0.527	0.703
8	0.197	0.274	0.277	0.082	0.780
9	0.563	0.778	0.791	0.342	0.709
10	0.049	0.046	0.042	0.004	0.575
11	0.018	0.016	0.015	0.002	0.283
12	0.706	0.901	0.912	0.527	0.703
13	0.018	0.007	0.005	0.000	0.456
14	0.914	0.690	0.676	0.908	0.403
15	0.090	0.096	0.090	0.008	0.783
	6	7	8	9	10
6	1.000				
7	0.971	1.000			
8	0.292	0.543	1.000		
9	0.860	0.939	0.514	1.000	
10	0.026	0.392	0.836	0.303	1.000
11	0.010	0.213	0.451	0.134	0.425
12	0.971	1.000	0.543	0.939	0.392
13	0.000	0.321	0.717	0.210	0.798
14	0.610	0.692	0.288	0.594	0.168
15	0.059	0.516	0.930	0.447	0.619
	11	12	13	14	15
11	1.000				
12	0.213	1.000			
13	0.466	0.321	1.000		
14	0.082	0.692	0.124	1.000	
15	0.219	0.516	0.344	0.238	1.000

Within group 0 (cells 1-7), there are no significant pairwise differences in average test score changes. The same is true within group 1 (cells 8-15). Average changes for group 1 *Blacks* and *Whites* in age group 3 (cells 11 and 13) differ significantly from average changes for group 0 subjects of the same race and age (cells 6 and 4).

6.16 Separate variance hypothesis tests

Analysis of variance assumes that the data within cells are independent and normally distributed with equal variances. This is the ANOVA equivalent of the regression assumptions for residuals. When the homogeneous variance part of the assumptions is false, it is sometimes possible to adjust the degrees of freedom to produce approximately distributed F statistics.

Levene (1960) proposed a test for unequal variances. You can use this test to determine whether you need an unequal variance F test. Simply fit your model in ANOVA and save residuals. Then transform the residuals into their absolute values. Merge these with your original grouping variable(s). Then redo your ANOVA on the absolute residuals. If it is significant, then you should consider using the separate variances test.

Before doing all this work, you should do a boxplot by groups to see whether the distributions differ. If you see few differences in the spread of the boxes, Levene's test is unlikely to be significant.

The following data (from the *MJ20* data file) are from Milliken and Johnson (1984). They are the results of a paired-associate learning task. *GROUP* describes the type of drug administered; *LEARNING* is the amount of material learned during testing.

GROUP	LEARNING	GROUP	LEARNING
1	1	3	11
1	8	3	7
1	9	3	8
1	9	3	10
1	4	3	12
1	0	3	5
1	1	4	13
2	12	4	14
2	10	4	14
2	13	4	17
2	13	4	11
2	12	4	14
2	10	4	13
3	12	4	14
3	4		

First, do Levene's test:

```
ANOVA
    USE mj20
    SAVE mjresids / RESID DATA
    DEPEND learning
    CATEGORY group
    ESTIMATE

    USE mjresids
    LET residual = ABS(residual)
    CATEGORY group
    DEPEND residual
    ESTIMATE
```

Here is the ANOVA table of the absolute residuals:

```
Dep Var: RESIDUAL N: 29 Multiple R:  0.675 Squared multiple R:  0.455

                        Analysis of Variance
 Source            Sum-of-Squares   DF   Mean-Square   F-Ratio      P
 GROUP                    30.603    3        10.201     6.966    0.001
 Error                    36.608   25         1.464
```

Notice that the F is significant, indicating that the separate variances test is advisable. Let's do several single degree-of-freedom tests, following Milliken and Johnson. The first is for comparing all drugs against the control:

```
ANOVA
    USE mj20
    CATEGORY group
    DEPEND learning
    ESTIMATE

    HYPOTHESIS
    SPECIFY 3*group[1] = group[2] +group[3] + group[4],
            / SEPARATE
    TEST
```

Here is the output. The ANOVA table has been omitted because it is not valid when variances are unequal.

```
Using separate variances estimate for error term.

Hypothesis.

A Matrix

                          1            2            3            4
                          0.0         -4.000        0.0          0.0

Null hypothesis value for D
                          0.0

Test of Hypothesis

Source          SS            DF            MS             F             P

Hypoth       242.720         1          242.720        18.115        0.004
Error         95.085      7.096         13.399
```

Next, test the hypothesis that groups 2 and 3 together are not significantly different from group 4:

```
    HYPOTHESIS
    SPECIFY 2*group[4] = group[2] + group[3],
            / SEPARATE
    TEST
```

```
Using separate variances estimate for error term.

Hypothesis.

A Matrix

                          1            2            3            4
                          0.0         2.000        3.000        3.000

Null hypothesis value for D
                          0.0

Test of Hypothesis

Source          SS            DF            MS             F             P

Hypoth        65.634         1          65.634         17.819        0.001
Error         61.852      16.792        3.683
```

6.17
Analysis of
covariance

In some situations, a covariate (or in the language of regression, an independent variable) can add variability to the measure under study (the dependent variable). An analysis of covariance adjusts or removes the variability in the dependent variable due to the covariate. For example, assume that you want to compare the average cholesterol level for a group of subjects taking a new drug (T) with the average for a control group (C). The ages of the subjects vary from 30 to 80 years. Because cholesterol increases with age, the variability of the cholesterol values within each group is considerably greater than it would be if each sample comprised only 50 year olds.

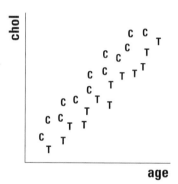

Fit a line to these data that has the same slope that you would get if you fit each group separately. (We assume the lines are parallel.) Now, derive a new data value for each subject—the difference between his or her cholesterol level and the value on the line at his or her age. Notice that most of the values for the control group are positive, while those for the treatment group are negative. These new values are independent of age. If you used a two-sample t test to compare the average differences (or residuals) for the two groups, you would probably find a highly significant difference in the group means. If you repeat the t test using the original cholesterol values, you may be unable to detect a significant difference.

Analysis of covariance improves the sensitivity of detecting differences among group means by removing unwanted variability due to one or more covariates. In addition to the usual assumptions required for an ANOVA, your data must satisfy the following:

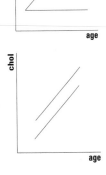

- **The slopes of the regression lines for each group must be equal.** That is, the lines must be *parallel*. Examine the drawings on the left. From the top figure, you can see that there is no difference in cholesterol for the young people, while the difference is quite extreme for the older people. If a figure for your data is similar to this, you should *not* do an analysis of covariance. Ideally, the slopes of the lines should look like those in the lower figure.

- **Within each group, the dependent variable is related linearly to the covariate.** if not, a transformation might remedy this problem.

- **The within-group slope of the dependent variable on the covariate differs from 0.** If the slope is 0, the covariate does not remove unwanted variability; at the same time, it takes away a degree of freedom from the error term.

- **The value of the covariates should be similar for each group.** Examine the results carefully if you find the ages of the Treatment group are centered around 35 years, those of the Control group are centered around 65 years, and there is little overlap.

Winer (1971) uses the *COVAR* data file for an analysis of covariance in which X is the covariate and *TREAT* is the treatment. The data are organized as shown below:

TREAT	X	Y
1	3	6
1	1	4
⋮	⋮	⋮
1	4	6
2	4	8
⋮	⋮	⋮
2	2	7
3	3	6
⋮	⋮	⋮
3	4	7

Cases do not need to be ordered by the grouping variable *TREAT*.

Before analyzing the data with an analysis of covariance model, be sure there is no significant interaction between the covariate and the treatment. The assumption of no interaction is often called the *homogeneity of slopes* assumption because it is tantamount to saying that the slope of the regression line of the dependent variable onto the covariate should be the same in all cells of the design. To do this, see "Homogeneity of slopes (parallelism)" on p. 182.

Now, fit the usual analysis of covariance model by using **Stats ➠Analysis of Variance ➠Estimate Model** and by specifying *Y* as the dependent outcome variable, *TREAT* as the factor or grouping variable, and *X* as the covariate. With commands:

```
ANOVA
   USE covar
   CATEGORY treat
   DEPEND y
   COVARIATE x
   ESTIMATE
```

```
Categorical values encountered during processing are:
TREAT (3 levels)
        1       2       3

Dep Var: Y N: 21 Multiple R:  0.916 Squared multiple R:  0.839

                      Analysis of Variance

Source            Sum-of-Squares  DF  Mean-Square   F-Ratio     P

TREAT                  16.932      2      8.466      13.970    0.000
X                      16.555      1     16.555      27.319    0.000

Error                  10.302     17      0.606
```

The treatment adjusted for the covariate is significant. There is a significant difference among the three treatment groups. Also notice that the coefficient for the covariate is significant ($F = 27.319$, $p < 0.0005$). If it were not, the analysis of covariance could be taking away a degree of freedom without reducing mean square error enough to help you.

For incomplete factorials and similar designs, you still must specify a model to do analysis of covariance.

Saving adjusted cell means

To save adjusted cell means, use **Stats➠Analysis of Variance➠Estimate Model** and specify the ANOVA design as above. Select **Save file**, and then choose **Adjusted** or **Adjusted/Data** from the drop-down list to indicate the results to save. With commands (insert before **ESTIMATE**):

```
   SAVE filename / ADJUST    DATA
```

ESTIMATE, a variable in the saved file, is computed for each case, so there are duplicates for cases in the same cell. For multivariate designs, this variable has subscripts for different dependent variables (for example, *ESTIMATE(1)*, *ESTIMATE(2)*, and so on). Use **Data➠List Cases** to print these values. To merge the estimates with the original data, use **Data➠Merge** or use **Stats➧Analysis of Variance➧Estimate Model**, select **Save file**, and choose an option that includes **Data** from the drop-down list.

SYSTAT computes the adjusted cell means the same way it computes estimates when saving residuals. Model terms (main effects and interactions) that do not contain categorical variables (covariates) are incorporated into the equation by adding the product of the coefficient and the mean of the term for computing estimates. The grand mean (CONSTANT) is included in computing the estimates.

Homogeneity of slopes (parallelism)

Parallelism is easy to test with a preliminary model. Use General Linear Model to estimate this model with the interaction between treatment (*TREAT*) and covariate (*X*) in the model. With commands:

```
GLM
    USE covar
    CATEGORY treat
    MODEL y = CONSTANT + treat + x + treat*x
    ESTIMATE
```

```
Dep Var: Y N: 21 Multiple R:  0.921 Squared multiple R:  0.849

                        Analysis of Variance

   Source          Sum-of-Squares   DF   Mean-Square    F-Ratio       P

   TREAT                   6.693    2        3.346       5.210      0.019
   X                      15.672    1       15.672      24.399      0.000
   TREAT*X                 0.667    2        0.334       0.519      0.605

   Error                   9.635   15        0.642
```

The probability value for the treatment by covariate interaction is 0.605, so the assumption of homogeneity of slopes is plausible.

Repeated Measures and Multivariate ANOVA

In factorial ANOVA designs, each subject is measured once. For example, the assumption of independence would be violated if a subject is measured first as a control group member and later as a treatment group member.

In a repeated measures design, the same variable is measured several times for each subject (case). A paired-comparison *t* test is the most simple form of a repeated measures design (for example, each subject has a *before* and *after* measure). In the first repeated measures example (Example 6.18), each rat is weighed once a week for five weeks. In Example 6.20, each subject is measured under four experimental conditions.

Usually it is not necessary for you to understand how SYSTAT carries out calculations; however, repeated measures is an exception. It is helpful to understand the quantities SYSTAT derives from your data. First, remember how to calculate a paired-comparison *t* test by hand:

- For each subject, compute the difference between the two measures.
- Calculate the average of the differences.
- Calculate the standard deviation of the differences.
- Calculate the test statistic using this mean and standard deviation.

SYSTAT derives similar values from your repeated measures and uses them in analysis-of-variance computations to test changes across the repeated measures (within-subjects) as well as differences between groups of subjects (between-subjects.) Tests of the within-subjects values are called polynomial tests of order 1, 2,..., up to *k*, where *k* is one less than the number of repeated measures. The first polynomial is used to test linear changes (for example, do the repeated responses increase (or decrease) around a line with a significant slope?). The second polynomial tests if the responses fall along a *quadratic* curve, and so on.

For each case, SYSTAT uses **orthogonal contrast coefficients** to derive one number for each polynomial. For the coefficients of the linear polynomial, SYSTAT uses (−1, 0, 1) when there are three measures; (−3, −1, 1, 3) when there are four measures; and so on. When there are three repeated measures, SYSTAT multiplies the first by –1, the second by 0, and the third by 1, and sums these products (this sum is then multiplied by a constant to make the sum of squares of the coefficients equal to 1). Notice that when the responses are the same, the result of the polynomial contrast is 0; when the responses fall closely along a line with a steep slope, the polynomial differs markedly from 0.

For the coefficients of the quadratic polynomial, SYSTAT uses (1, –2, 1) when there are three measures; (1, –1, –1, 1) when there are four measures; and so on. The cubic and higher-order polynomials are computed in a similar way.

Let's continue the discussion for a design with three repeated measures. Assume that you record body weight once a month for three months for rats grouped by diet. (Diet A includes a heavy concentration of alcohol and Diet B consists of normal lab chow.) For each rat, SYSTAT computes a linear component and a quadratic component. SYSTAT also sums the weights to derive a *total* response. These derived values are used to compute two analysis of variance tables:

- The *total* response is used to test **between-group** differences; that is, the total is used as the dependent variable in the usual factorial ANOVA computations. In the example, this test compares total weight for Diet A against that for Diet B. This is analogous to a two-sample *t* test using total weight as the dependent variable.

- The linear and quadratic components are used to test changes across the repeated measures (**within-subjects**) and also to test the interaction of the within-factor with the grouping factor. If the test for the linear component is significant, you can report a significant linear increase in weight over the three months. If the test for the quadratic component is also significant (but much less so than the linear component), you might report that growth is predominantly linear, but there is a significant curve in the upward trend.

- A significant interaction between Diet (the between-group factor) and the linear component across time might indicate that the slopes for Diet A and Diet B differ. This test may be the most important one for the experiment.

For a discussion of assumptions needed for a valid repeated measures ANOVA, see the next example.

6.18
One-way
repeated
measures

In this example, six rats were weighed at the end of each of five weeks. The weights are set up in the *RATS* file like this:

WEIGHT(1)	WEIGHT(2)	WEIGHT(3)	WEIGHT(4)	WEIGHT(5)
1	4	5	10	10
2	9	10	7	7
3	6	7	8	8
4	7	9	8	9
3	6	7	8	9
2	3	5	7	7

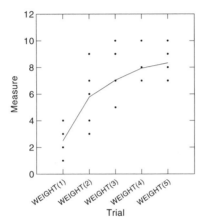

ANOVA is the simplest way to analyze this one-way model. Because we have no categorical variable(s), SYSTAT generates only the constant (grand mean) in the model. To see the results of the individual single degree-of-freedom orthogonal polynomials, use **Edit➠Options** and select **Medium** from the **Length** drop-down list. Next, use **Stats➠ Analysis of Variance➠Estimate Model** and select *WEIGHT(1)*, *WEIGHT(2)*, *WEIGHT(3)*, *WEIGHT(4)*, and *WEIGHT(5)* as the dependent variables. Select the **Repeated** button and select **Perform repeated measures analysis**. In the **Name** text box labeled **First**, type **Time**; in the **Levels** text box, type **5**. The **Metric** text box is left empty. With commands:

```
ANOVA
   USE rats
   PLOT weight(1 .. 5) / REPEAT  SMOOTH=LOWESS
   DEPEND weight(1 .. 5) / REPEAT NAME='Time'
   PRINT MEDIUM
   ESTIMATE
```

The dependent variables in the model are treated as a set of repeated measures. SYSTAT also generates equally spaced polynomials and partitions the hypotheses according to the proper effects. Univariate sums of squares are derived from the orthogonal components used in the multivariate calculations.

```
Number of cases processed: 6
Dependent variable means

                 WEIGHT(1)   WEIGHT(2)   WEIGHT(3)   WEIGHT(4)   WEIGHT(5)

                   2.500       5.833       7.167       8.000       8.333


-----------------------------------------------------------------------------
Univariate and Multivariate Repeated Measures Analysis


Within Subjects
---------------

Source            SS          DF          MS          F       P      G-G     H-F

Time            134.467        4        33.617     16.033   0.000   0.004   0.002
Error            41.933       20         2.097

Greenhouse-Geisser Epsilon:        0.3420
Huynh-Feldt Epsilon       :        0.4273
-----------------------------------------------------------------------------


Single Degree of Freedom Polynomial Contrasts
---------------------------------------------

Polynomial Test of Order 1 (Linear)

Source            SS          DF          MS             F              P

Time            114.817        1        114.817        38.572         0.002
Error            14.883        5          2.977


Polynomial Test of Order 2 (Quadratic)

Source            SS          DF          MS             F              P

Time             18.107        1         18.107         7.061         0.045
Error            12.821        5          2.564

-----------------------------------------------------------------------------
               *** We omit Polynomial Tests of Orders 3 and 4 ***

Multivariate Repeated Measures Analysis

Test of: Time               Hypoth. DF   Error DF      F            P
  Wilks' Lambda=     0.011        4          2        43.007       0.023
  Pillai Trace =     0.989        4          2        43.007       0.023
  H-L Trace    =    86.014        4          2        43.007       0.023
```

The output contains both univariate and multivariate statistics. Like all standard ANOVA procedures, the univariate repeated measures approach requires that the distributions within cells be normal. The univariate repeated measures approach also requires that the covariances between all possible pairs of repeated measures be equal. (Actually, the requirement is slightly less restrictive, but this difference is of little practical importance.) Of course, the usual ANOVA requirement that all variances within cells are equal still applies; thus, the covariance matrix of the measures should have a constant diagonal and equal elements off the diagonal. This assumption is called **compound symmetry**.

The multivariate analysis at the bottom of the output does not require compound symmetry. It requires that the covariance matrices within groups (there is only one group in this example) be equivalent and that they be based on multivariate normal distributions. If the classical assumptions hold, then you should generally ignore the multivariate tests at the bottom of the output and stay with the classical univariate ANOVA table because the multivariate tests will be generally less powerful.

There is a middle approach. The Greenhouse-Geiser and Huynh-Feldt statistics are used to adjust the probability for the classical univariate tests when compound symmetry fails. (Huynh-Feldt is a more recent adjustment to the conservative Greenhouse-Geiser statistic.) If the Huynh-Feldt p values are substantially different from those under the column directly to the right of the F statistic, then you should be aware that compound symmetry has failed. In this case, compare the adjusted p values under Huynh-Feldt to those for the multivariate tests.

If all else fails, the single degree-of-freedom polynomial tests can always be trusted. If there are several to examine, however, remember that you may want to use Bonferroni adjustments to the probabilities. That is, divide the normal value (for example, 0.05) by the number of polynomial tests you want to examine. You need to make a Bonferroni adjustment only if you are unable to use the summary univariate or multivariate tests to protect the overall level; otherwise, you can examine the polynomials without penalty if the overall test is significant.

The polynomial tests are not simply a fall-back, however. Here, they indicate that most of the trials effect can be accounted for by a linear trend across time. In fact, the sum of squares for *TIME* is 134.467, and the sum of squares for the linear trend is almost as large (114.817). Thus, the linear polynomial accounts for roughly 85% of the change across the repeated measures.

Unevenly spaced polynomials

Sometimes the underlying metric of the profiles is not evenly spaced. Let's assume that the fifth weight was measured after the tenth week instead of the fifth. In that case, the default polynomials have to be adjusted for the uneven spacing. These adjustments do not affect the overall repeated measures tests of each effect (univariate or multivariate), but they partition the sums of squares differently for the single degree-of-freedom tests. Use **Stats⟩Analysis of Variance⟩Estimate Model⟩ Repeated**, type **Time** in the **Name** text box, **5** in the **Levels** text box, and **1 2 3 4 10** in the **Metric** text box. With commands:

```
DEPEND weight(1 .. 5) / REPEAT=5(1 2 3 4 10),
                                NAME='Time'
ESTIMATE
```

After estimating the model as described above, specify:

```
HYPOTHESIS
WITHIN='Time'
CONTRAST / POLYNOMIAL  METRIC=1,2,3,4,10
TEST
```

The last point has been spread out further to the right. Notice how the significance tests below for the linear and quadratic trends differ from the previous ones. Before, the linear trend was strongest; now, the quadratic polynomial has the most significant results (F=107.9, $p < 0.0005$).

```
Univariate and Multivariate Repeated Measures Analysis

Within Subjects
---------------

Source           SS        DF        MS        F       P      G-G    H-F

Time          134.467       4      33.617   16.033   0.000   0.004  0.002
Error          41.933      20       2.097

Greenhouse-Geisser Epsilon:        0.3420
Huynh-Feldt Epsilon      :         0.4273
-----------------------------------------------------------------------------

Single Degree of Freedom Polynomial Contrasts
---------------------------------------------

Polynomial Test of Order 1 (Linear)

Source           SS        DF        MS            F              P

Time           67.213       1      67.213       23.959         0.004
Error          14.027       5       2.805


Polynomial Test of Order 2 (Quadratic)

Source           SS        DF        MS            F              P

Time           62.283       1      62.283      107.867         0.000
Error           2.887       5       0.577

           *** We omit Polynomial Tests of Orders 3 and 4 ***
-----------------------------------------------------------------------------

Multivariate Repeated Measures Analysis

Test of: Time              Hypoth. DF   Error DF      F          P
  Wilks' Lambda=    0.011       4           2       43.007      0.023
  Pillai Trace =    0.989       4           2       43.007      0.023
  H-L Trace    =   86.014       4           2       43.007      0.023
```

The univariate F tests for the polynomials are different, but the multivariate test is unchanged because it measures variation across all components.

Difference contrasts

If you do not want to use polynomials, you can specify a C matrix that contrasts adjacent weeks. Use **Stats⮕General Linear Model⮕ Hypothesis Test** and type **Time** in the **Within** text box. Next, select the **Contrast** button and select **Difference**. After estimating the model:

```
HYPOTHESIS
WITHIN='Time'
CONTRAST / DIFFERENCE
TEST
```

Notice the C matrix that this command generates:

```
Hypothesis.

C Matrix

                    1           2           3           4           5
            1    1.000      -1.000        0.0         0.0         0.0
            2    0.0         1.000       -1.000       0.0         0.0
            3    0.0         0.0          1.000      -1.000       0.0
            4    0.0         0.0          0.0         1.000      -1.000


Univariate F Tests

Effect      SS         DF      MS          F           P

1         66.667       1     66.667      17.241       0.009
Error     19.333       5      3.867
2         10.667       1     10.667      40.000       0.001
Error      1.333       5      0.267
3          4.167       1      4.167       0.566       0.486
Error     36.833       5      7.367
4          0.667       1      0.667       2.500       0.175
Error      1.333       5      0.267

Multivariate Test Statistics

            Wilks' Lambda =     0.011
             F-Statistic =     43.007     DF =   4,   2      Prob =     0.023

             Pillai Trace =     0.989
             F-Statistic =     43.007     DF =   4,   2      Prob =     0.023

     Hotelling-Lawley Trace =   86.014
             F-Statistic =     43.007     DF =   4,   2      Prob =     0.023
```

In this case, each of the univariate F tests covers the significance of the difference between the adjacent weeks indexed by the C matrix. For example, $F=17.241$ shows that the first and second weeks differ significantly. Unlike polynomials, these contrasts are not orthogonal.

Summing effects

To sum across weeks, use **Stats➡General Linear Model➡Estimate Model**, select **Contrast**, and then select **Sum**. With commands:

```
HYPOTHESIS
WITHIN='Time'
CONTRAST / SUM
TEST
```

In this example, you are testing whether the overall weight (across weeks) significantly differs from 0. Naturally, the F value is significant. Notice the C matrix that is generated. It is simply a set of 1's that, in the equation BC'=0, sum all the coefficients in B. In a group-by-trials design, this C matrix is useful for pooling trials and analyzing group effects.

```
Hypothesis.
C Matrix

                    1         2         3         4         5
                 1.000     1.000     1.000     1.000     1.000

Test of Hypothesis

Source       SS      DF       MS          F          P

Hypothesis 6080.167   1   6080.167     295.632     0.000
Error       102.833   5     20.567
```

Special contrasts

To test any arbitrary contrast effects between dependent variables, you can use C matrix, which has the same form (without a column for the **CONSTANT**) as A matrix. The following commands test a linear trend across the five trials:

```
HYPOTHESIS
CMATRIX [-2 -1 0 1 2]
TEST
```

```
Hypothesis.
C Matrix

                    1         2         3         4         5
                -2.000    -1.000     0.0       1.000     2.000

Test of Hypothesis

Source       SS      DF       MS          F          P

Hypothesis 1148.167   1   1148.167     38.572     0.002
Error       148.833   5     29.767
```

6.19
One grouping and one within factor with ordered levels

The following example uses estimates of population for 1983, 1986, and 1990 and projections for 2020 for 57 countries from the *OURWORLD* data file. The data are log transformed before analysis. Here you compare trends in population growth for European and Islamic countries. The variable *GROUP$* contains codes for these groups plus a third code for New World countries (use **Data**➡**Select cases** to exclude these countries from this analysis). With commands:

```
SELECT group$ <> 'NewWorld'
```

Here is a bar chart of the data after using YLOG to log tranform them:

```
BAR pop_1983 .. pop_2020 / REPEAT  OVERLAY YLOG,
                           GROUP=group$ SERROR,
                           FILL=.35, .8
```

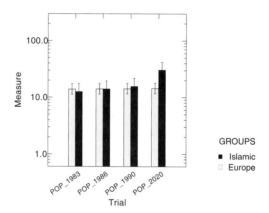

After using **Data**➡**Select Cases** to exclude the New World countries, use **Data**➡**Transform**➡**Let** to log transform the population variables. Then use **Stats**➡**Analysis of Variance**➡**Estimate Model**, select the population measures as dependent variables, and select *GROUP$* as the factor. Next, select the **Repeated** button and check **Perform repeated measures analysis**. In the **Name** text box, type **Time**; in the **Levels** text box, type **4** to specify that our model has four repeated measures. With commands:

```
ANOVA
   USE ourworld
   SELECT group$ <> 'NewWorld'
   CATEGORY group$
   LET(pop_1983, pop_1986, pop_1990, pop_2020) = L10(@)
   DEPEND pop_1983 pop_1986 pop_1990 pop_2020 /,
                           REPEAT=4 NAME='Time'
   ESTIMATE
```

```
Single Degree of Freedom Polynomial Contrasts
---------------------------------------------

Polynomial Test of Order 1 (Linear)

Source                SS        DF      MS           F            P

Time                0.675       1     0.675       370.761       0.000
Time*GROUP$         0.583       1     0.583       320.488       0.000
Error               0.062      34     0.002


Polynomial Test of Order 2 (Quadratic)

Source                SS        DF      MS           F            P

Time                0.132       1     0.132        92.246       0.000
Time*GROUP$         0.128       1     0.128        89.095       0.000
Error               0.049      34     0.001


Polynomial Test of Order 3 (Cubic)

Source                SS        DF      MS           F            P

Time                0.028       1     0.028        96.008       0.000
Time*GROUP$         0.027       1     0.027        94.828       0.000
Error               0.010      34     0.000
--------------------------------------------------------------------


Multivariate Repeated Measures Analysis

Test of: Time              Hypoth. DF   Error DF     F           P
   Wilks' Lambda=    0.063       3         32      157.665     0.000
   Pillai Trace =    0.937       3         32      157.665     0.000
   H-L Trace    =   14.781       3         32      157.665     0.000

Test of: Time*GROUP$       Hypoth. DF   Error DF     F           P
   Wilks' Lambda=    0.076       3         32      130.336     0.000
   Pillai Trace =    0.924       3         32      130.336     0.000
   H-L Trace    =   12.219       3         32      130.336     0.000
```

The within-subjects results indicate highly significant linear, quadratic, and cubic changes across time. The pattern of change across time for the two groups also differs significantly (that is, the *TIME* * *GROUP$* interactions are highly significant for all three tests). There is a larger gap in time between 1990 and 2020 than between the other values. Let's incorporate "real time" in the analysis.

```
DEPEND pop_1983 pop_1986 pop_1990 pop_2020 /,
                    REPEAT=4(83,86,90,120) NAME='TIME'
ESTIMATE
```

The results for the orthogonal polynomials are shown below (the rest of the output is the same as that shown above).

```
Single Degree of Freedom Polynomial Contrasts

Polynomial Test of Order 1 (Linear)

Source              SS        DF      MS          F           P

Time                0.831     1       0.831       317.273     0.000
Time*GROUP$         0.737     1       0.737       281.304     0.000
Error               0.089     34      0.003

Polynomial Test of Order 2 (Quadratic)

Source              SS        DF      MS          F           P

Time                0.003     1       0.003       4.402       0.043
Time*GROUP$         0.001     1       0.001       1.562       0.220
Error               0.025     34      0.001

Polynomial Test of Order 3 (Cubic)

Source              SS        DF      MS          F           P

Time                0.000     1       0.000       1.653       0.207
Time*GROUP$         0.000     1       0.000       1.733       0.197
Error               0.006     34      0.000
```

When the values for *POP_2020* are positioned on a real time line, the tests for quadratic and cubic polynomials are no longer significant. The test for the linear *TIME * GROUP$* interaction, however, remains highly significant, indicating that the slope across time for the Islamic group is significantly steeper than that for the European countries.

6.20
Two grouping and one within factor

Repeated measures enables you to handle grouping factors automatically. The following example is from Winer (1971). There are two grouping factors (*ANXIETY* and *TENSION*) and one trials factor. The data are entered in the file *REPEAT1* as follows:

ANXIETY	TENSION	TRIAL(1)	TRIAL(2)	TRIAL(3)	TRIAL(4)
1	1	18	14	12	6
1	1	19	12	8	4
1	1	14	10	6	2
1	2	16	12	10	4
1	2	12	8	6	2
1	2	18	10	5	1
2	1	16	10	8	4
2	1	18	8	4	1
2	1	16	12	6	2
2	2	19	16	10	8
2	2	16	14	10	9
2	2	16	12	8	8

Here is a dot display of the average responses across trials for each of the four combinations of *ANXIETY* and *TENSION*.

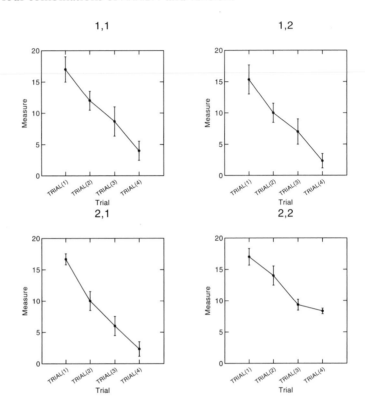

First, adjust the output length by using **Edit➡Options** and setting the **Length** to **Medium**. Next, use **Stats➡Analysis of Variance➡Estimate Model** and select *ANXIETY* and *TENSION* as the factors and the *TRIAL* variables as dependent. Then, select **Repeated** and check **Perform repeated measures analysis**. In the **Name** text box, type **Trial**. With commands:

```
ANOVA
    USE repeat1
    DOT trial(1..4) / Group=anxiety,tension,
        line,repeat,serror
    CATEGORY anxiety  tension
    DEPEND trial(1 .. 4) / REPEAT NAME='Trial'
    PRINT MEDIUM
    ESTIMATE
```

The model also includes an interaction between the grouping factors (*ANXIETY*∗*TENSION*).

```
Univariate and Multivariate Repeated Measures Analysis

Between Subjects
----------------

Source          SS        DF      MS          F           P

ANXIETY         10.083    1       10.083      0.978       0.352
TENSION          8.333    1        8.333      0.808       0.395
ANXIETY
*TENSION        80.083    1       80.083      7.766       0.024
Error           82.500    8       10.312


Within Subjects
---------------

Source          SS        DF       MS         F       P       G-G     H-F

Trial          991.500    3        330.500    152.051 0.000   0.000   0.000
Trial
*ANXIETY         8.417    3          2.806    1.291   0.300   0.300   0.301
Trial
*TENSION        12.167    3          4.056    1.866   0.162   0.197   0.169
Trial
*ANXIETY
*TENSION        12.750    3          4.250    1.955   0.148   0.185   0.155
Error           52.167    24         2.174

Greenhouse-Geisser Epsilon:         0.5361
Huynh-Feldt Epsilon     :           0.9023
-----------------------------------------------------------------------------


Single Degree of Freedom Polynomial Contrasts
---------------------------------------------

Polynomial Test of Order 1 (Linear)

Source          SS        DF      MS           F           P

Trial          984.150    1       984.150      247.845     0.000
Trial
*ANXIETY         1.667    1         1.667      0.420       0.535
Trial
*TENSION        10.417    1        10.417      2.623       0.144
Trial
*ANXIETY
*TENSION         9.600    1         9.600      2.418       0.159
Error           31.767    8         3.971


Polynomial Test of Order 2 (Quadratic)

Source          SS        DF      MS           F           P

Trial            6.750    1         6.750      3.411       0.102
Trial
*ANXIETY         3.000    1         3.000      1.516       0.253
Trial
*TENSION         0.083    1         0.083      0.042       0.843
Trial
*ANXIETY
*TENSION         0.333    1         0.333      0.168       0.692
Error           15.833    8         1.979


Polynomial Test of Order 3 (Cubic)

Source          SS        DF      MS           F           P

Trial            0.600    1         0.600      1.051       0.335
Trial
*ANXIETY         3.750    1         3.750      6.569       0.033
Trial
*TENSION         1.667    1         1.667      2.920       0.126
Trial
*ANXIETY
*TENSION         2.817    1         2.817      4.934       0.057
Error            4.567    8         0.571
-----------------------------------------------------------------------------


Multivariate Repeated Measures Analysis

Test of: Trial              Hypoth. DF  Error DF    F           P
```

```
Wilks' Lambda=      0.015      3           6       127.686     0.000
Pillai Trace =      0.985      3           6       127.686     0.000
H-L Trace    =     63.843      3           6       127.686     0.000

Test of: Trial                 Hypoth. DF  Error DF      F          P
          *ANXIETY
Wilks' Lambda=      0.244      3           6         6.183      0.029
Pillai Trace =      0.756      3           6         6.183      0.029
H-L Trace    =      3.091      3           6         6.183      0.029

Test of: Trial                 Hypoth. DF  Error DF      F          P
          *TENSION
Wilks' Lambda=      0.361      3           6         3.546      0.088
Pillai Trace =      0.639      3           6         3.546      0.088
H-L Trace    =      1.773      3           6         3.546      0.088

Test of: Trial                 Hypoth. DF  Error DF      F          P
          *ANXIETY
          *TENSION
Wilks' Lambda=      0.328      3           6         4.099      0.067
Pillai Trace =      0.672      3           6         4.099      0.067
H-L Trace    =      2.050      3           6         4.099      0.067
```

In the within-subjects table, you see that the trial effect is highly significant ($F=152.1$, $p< 0.0005$) and that the linear trend across trials (Polynomial Order 1) is highly significant ($F=247.8$, $p< 0.0005$). The hypothesis sums of squares for the linear, quadratic, and cubic polynomials sum to the total hypothesis sum of squares for trials (that is, $984.15 + 6.75 + 0.60=991.5$). Notice that the total sum of squares is 991.5, while that for the linear trend is 984.15. This means that the linear trend accounts for more than 99% of the variability across the four trials. The assumption of compound symmetry is *not* required for the test of linear trend—so you can report, "There is a highly significant linear decrease across the four trials ($F=247.8$, $p< 0.0005$)."

6.21 Two trial factors

Repeated measures enables you to handle several trials factors, so we include an example with two trial factors. It is an experiment from Winer (1971) which has one grouping factor (*NOISE*) and two trials factors (*PERIODS* and *DIALS*). The trials factors must be sorted into a set of dependent variables (one for each pairing of the two factors groups). It is useful to label the levels with a convenient mnemonic.

The file is set up with variables *P1D1* through *P3D3*. Variable *P1D2* means a score in the *PERIODS* = 1, *DIALS* = 2 cell. The data are in the file *REPEAT2*.

NOISE	P1D1	P1D2	P1D3	P2D1	P2D2	P2D3	P3D1	P3D2	P3D3
1	45	53	60	40	52	57	28	37	46
1	35	41	50	30	37	47	25	32	41
1	60	65	75	58	54	70	40	47	50
2	50	48	61	25	34	51	16	23	35
2	42	45	55	30	37	43	22	27	37
2	56	60	77	40	39	57	31	29	46

With commands:

```
ANOVA
    USE repeat2
    CATEGORY noise
    DEPEND p1d1 .. p3d3 / REPEAT=3,3,
                            NAMES='period','dial'
    PRINT MEDIUM
    ESTIMATE
```

This example is an alternative specification using GLM:

```
GLM
    USE repeat2
    CATEGORY noise
    MODEL p1d1 .. p3d3 = CONSTANT + noise /,
                            REPEAT=3,3 NAMES='period','dial'
    PRINT MEDIUM
    ESTIMATE
```

Notice that **REPEAT** specifies that the two trials factors have three levels each. ANOVA assumes the subscript of the first factor will vary slowest in the ordering of the dependent variables. If you have two repeated factors (*DAY* with four levels and *AMPM* with two levels), you should select eight dependent variables and type **Repeat=4,2**. The repeated measures are selected in the following order:

```
DAY1_AM DAY1_PM DAY2_AM DAY2_PM DAY3_AM DAY3_PM DAY4_AM
DAY4_PM
```

From this indexing, it generates the proper main effects and interactions. When more than one trial factor is present, ANOVA lists each dependent variable and the associated level on each factor.

```
Dependent variable means
                        P1D1        P1D2        P1D3        P2D1        P2D2
                        48.000      52.000      63.000      37.167      42.167

                        P2D3        P3D1        P3D2        P3D3
                        54.167      27.000      32.500      42.500

-----------------------------------------------------------------------------

Univariate and Multivariate Repeated Measures Analysis

Between Subjects
----------------
Source          SS        DF      MS              F           P
NOISE           468.167   1       468.167         0.752       0.435
Error           2491.111  4       622.778
```

```
Within Subjects
----------------

Source            SS         DF       MS        F        P      G-G     H-F

period          3722.333     2     1861.167   63.389   0.000   0.000   0.000
period*NOISE     333.000     2      166.500    5.671   0.029   0.057   0.029
Error            234.889     8       29.361

Greenhouse-Geisser Epsilon:      0.6476
Huynh-Feldt Epsilon     :        1.0000
dial            2370.333     2     1185.167   89.823   0.000   0.000   0.000
dial*NOISE        50.333     2       25.167    1.907   0.210   0.215   0.210
Error            105.556     8       13.194

Greenhouse-Geisser Epsilon:      0.9171
Huynh-Feldt Epsilon     :        1.0000
period*dial       10.667     4        2.667    0.336   0.850   0.729   0.850
period*dial

*NOISE            11.333     4        2.833    0.357   0.836   0.716   0.836
Error            127.111    16        7.944

Greenhouse-Geisser Epsilon:      0.5134
Huynh-Feldt Epsilon     :        1.0000
--------------------------------------------------------------------------


Single Degree of Freedom Polynomial Contrasts
---------------------------------------------

Polynomial Test of Order 1 (Linear)

Source            SS         DF       MS            F               P

period          3721.000     1     3721.000      73.441          0.001
period*NOISE     225.000     1      225.000       4.441          0.103
Error            202.667     4       50.667

dial            2256.250     1     2256.250     241.741          0.000
dial*NOISE         6.250     1        6.250       0.670          0.459
Error             37.333     4        9.333

period*dial        0.375     1        0.375       0.045          0.842
period*dial

*NOISE             1.042     1        1.042       0.125          0.742
Error             33.333     4        8.333

Polynomial Test of Order 2 (Quadratic)

Source            SS         DF       MS            F               P

period             1.333     1        1.333       0.166          0.705
period*NOISE     108.000     1      108.000      13.407          0.022
Error             32.222     4        8.056

dial             114.083     1      114.083       6.689          0.061
dial*NOISE        44.083     1       44.083       2.585          0.183
Error             68.222     4       17.056

period*dial        3.125     1        3.125       0.815          0.418
period*dial

*NOISE             0.125     1        0.125       0.033          0.865
Error             15.333     4        3.833
```

*** *We omit Polynomial Tests of Order 3 and 4* ***

```
Multivariate Repeated Measures Analysis

Test of: period            Hypoth. DF   Error DF     F           P
  Wilks' Lambda=    0.051        2          3      28.145      0.011
  Pillai Trace =    0.949        2          3      28.145      0.011
  H-L Trace    =   18.764        2          3      28.145      0.011

Test of: period*NOISE       Hypoth. DF   Error DF     F           P
  Wilks' Lambda=    0.156        2          3       8.111      0.062
  Pillai Trace =    0.844        2          3       8.111      0.062
  H-L Trace    =    5.407        2          3       8.111      0.062

Test of: dial              Hypoth. DF   Error DF     F           P
  Wilks' Lambda=    0.016        2          3      91.456      0.002
  Pillai Trace =    0.984        2          3      91.456      0.002
```

```
      H-L Trace    =     60.971      2           3         91.456      0.002

Test of: dial*NOISE              Hypoth. DF  Error DF       F          P
  Wilks' Lambda=         0.565      2           3         1.155      0.425
  Pillai Trace =         0.435      2           3         1.155      0.425
  H-L Trace    =         0.770      2           3         1.155      0.425

Test of: period*dial             Hypoth. DF  Error DF       F          P
  Wilks' Lambda=         0.001      4           1       331.445      0.041
  Pillai Trace =         0.999      4           1       331.445      0.041
  H-L Trace    =      1325.780      4           1       331.445      0.041

Test of: period*dial             Hypoth. DF  Error DF       F          P
         *NOISE
  Wilks' Lambda=         0.000      4           1       581.875      0.031
  Pillai Trace =         1.000      4           1       581.875      0.031
  H-L Trace    =      2327.500      4           1       581.875      0.031
```

6.22 Repeated measures analysis of covariance

Repeated measures analysis of covariance works similarly if the covariate does not vary within subjects (that is, across trials). To do repeated measures ANCOVA, where the covariate varies within subjects, you would have to set up your model like a split plot with a different record for each measurement.

This example is from Winer (1971). This design has two trials (*DAY1* and *DAY2*), one covariate (*AGE*), and one grouping factor (*SEX*). The data are in the file *WINER*.

SEX	AGE	DAY(1)	DAY(2)
1	3	10	8
1	5	15	12
1	8	20	14
1	2	12	6
2	1	15	10
2	8	25	20
2	10	20	15
2	2	15	10

```
ANOVA
   USE winer
   CATEGORY sex
   DEPEND day(1 .. 2) / REPEAT  NAME='day'
   COVARIATE age
   ESTIMATE
```

To use GLM:

```
GLM
   USE winer
   CATEGORY sex
   MODEL day(1 .. 2) = CONSTANT + sex + age /,
                       REPEAT  NAME='day'
   ESTIMATE
```

The *F* statistics for the covariate and its interactions, namely *AGE* (13.587) and *DAY*AGE* (0.102), are not ordinarily published; however, they help you understand the adjustment made by the covariate.

```
Dependent variable means

                     DAY(1)      DAY(2)

                     16.500      11.875


--------------------------------------------------------------------

Univariate Repeated Measures Analysis
Between Subjects
----------------

Source          SS          DF      MS              F               P

SEX             44.492      1       44.492          3.629           0.115
AGE             166.577     1       166.577         13.587          0.014
Error           61.298      5       12.260

Within Subjects
---------------

Source          SS          DF      MS          F       P       G-G     H-F

day             22.366      1       22.366      17.899  0.008   .       .
day*SEX         0.494       1       0.494       0.395   0.557   .       .
day*AGE         0.127       1       0.127       0.102   0.763   .       .
Error           6.248       5       1.250

Greenhouse-Geisser Epsilon:         .
Huynh-Feldt Epsilon       :         .
```

This analysis did not test the homogeneity of slopes assumption. If you want to test the homogeneity of slopes assumption, run the following model first:

```
MODEL day(1 .. 2) = CONSTANT + sex + age + sex*age /,
                    REPEAT
```

Then check to see if the *SEX*AGE* interaction is significant.

6.23 Covariance alternatives to repeated measures

Analysis of covariance offers an alternative to repeated measures in a pre-post design. You can use the pre-test as a covariate in predicting the post-test. This example shows how to do a two-group, pre-post design:

```
GLM
    USE filename
    CATEGORY group
    MODEL post = CONSTANT + group + pre
    ESTIMATE
```

When using this design, be sure to check the homogeneity of slopes assumption. Use the following commands to check that the interaction term, *GROUP*PRE*, is not significant.

```
GLM
    USE filename
    CATEGORY group
    MODEL post = CONSTANT + group + pre + group*pre
    ESTIMATE
```

6.24 Weighting means

Sometimes you want to weight the cell means when you test hypotheses in ANOVA. Suppose you have an experiment in which a few rats died before its completion. You do not want the hypotheses tested to depend upon the differences in cell sizes (which are presumably random). Here is an example from Morrison (1976). The data (*MOTHERS*) are hypothetical profiles on three scales of mothers in each of four socioeconomic classes.

CLASS	SCALE(1)	SCALE(2)	SCALE(3)
1	19	20	18
1	20	21	19
1	19	22	22
1	18	19	21
1	16	18	20
1	17	22	19
1	20	19	20
1	15	19	19
2	12	14	12
2	15	15	17
2	15	17	15
2	13	14	14
2	14	16	13
3	15	14	17
3	13	14	15
3	12	15	15
3	12	13	13
4	8	9	10
4	10	10	12
4	11	10	10
4	11	7	12

Morrison analyzes these data with the multivariate profile model for repeated measures. Because the hypothesis of parallel profiles across classes is not rejected, you can test whether the profiles are level. That is, do the scales differ when we pool the classes together?

Pooling unequal classes can be done by weighting each according to sample size or averaging the means of the subclasses. First, let's look at the model. Notice in the output below that the dependent variable means differ from the CONSTANT. The CONSTANT in this case is a mean of the cell means rather than the mean of all the cases. Use **Stats⟶General Linear Model⟶Estimate Model**. Select *SCALE(1)*, *SCALE(2)*, and *SCALE(3)* as dependent variables and select *CLASS* as an independent variable. Select **Categories** and move *CLASS* into the **Categorical Variable(s)** list. With commands:

```
GLM
    USE mothers
    CATEGORY class
    MODEL scale(1 .. 3) = CONSTANT + class
    ESTIMATE
```

```
Dependent variable means

                        SCALE(1)    SCALE(2)    SCALE(3)
                         14.524      15.619      15.857


                         -1
Estimates of effects  B = (X'X)  X'Y
                          SCALE(1)    SCALE(2)    SCALE(3)

    CONSTANT               13.700      14.550      14.988

    CLASS      1            4.300       5.450       4.763

    CLASS      2            0.100       0.650      -0.787

    CLASS      3           -0.700      -0.550       0.012


Squared multiple correlations
                        SCALE(1)    SCALE(2)    SCALE(3)
                         0.816       0.917       0.858
      *** We omit the default tests of effects for CONSTANT and CLASS ***
```

Now, test the hypothesis of equality of scale parameters without weighting the cell means:

```
HYPOTHESIS
EFFECT = CONSTANT
CMATRIX [1 -1  0;
         0  1 -1]
TEST
```

```
Test for effect called:      CONSTANT
C Matrix

                           1              2           3
                1       1.000         -1.000        0.0
                2       0.0            1.000       -1.000


Univariate F Tests

    Effect         SS          DF        MS            F            P

        1       14.012         1       14.012        4.652        0.046
    Error       51.200        17        3.012
        2        3.712         1        3.712        1.026        0.325
    Error       61.500        17        3.618

Multivariate Test Statistics

            Wilks' Lambda =        0.564
               F-Statistic =        6.191    DF =   2,  16    Prob =       0.010

             Pillai Trace =        0.436
               F-Statistic =        6.191    DF =   2,  16    Prob =       0.010

  Hotelling-Lawley Trace =        0.774
               F-Statistic =        6.191    DF =   2,  16    Prob =       0.010
```

If you believe (as Morrison does) that the differences in cell sizes reflect population subclass proportions, then you need to weight the cell means to get a grand mean, namely:

$$8\mu_1 + 5\mu_2 + 4\mu_3 + 4\mu_4$$

Expressed in terms of our analysis of variance parameterization, this is:

$$8(\mu + \alpha_1) + 5(\mu + \alpha_2) + 4(\mu + \alpha_3) + 4(\mu + \alpha_4)$$

Because the sum of effects is 0 for a classification and because you do not have an independent estimate of *CLASS4*, this expression is equivalent to:

$$8(\mu + \alpha_1) + 5(\mu + \alpha_2) + 4(\mu + \alpha_3) + 4(\mu - \alpha_1 - \alpha_2 - \alpha_3)$$

which works out to one of the following two expressions:

$$21\mu + 4\alpha_1 + \alpha_2$$
$$21\mu + 4\alpha_1 + \alpha_2 + 0\alpha_3$$

Use **AMATRIX** to test this hypothesis.

```
HYPOTHESIS
AMATRIX [21  4  1  0]
CMATRIX [1 -1  0;
         0  1 -1]
TEST
```

```
Hypothesis.

A Matrix
                           1            2           3           4
                        21.000       4.000       1.000        0.0

C Matrix
                           1            2           3
                 1      1.000       -1.000        0.0
                 2       0.0         1.000      -1.000

Univariate F Tests

     Effect        SS         DF        MS            F              P

        1        25.190        1       25.190        8.364         0.010
     Error       51.200       17        3.012
        2         1.190        1        1.190        0.329         0.574
     Error       61.500       17        3.618

Multivariate Test Statistics

          Wilks' Lambda =          0.501
             F-Statistic =          7.959     DF =   2,  16     Prob =      0.004

          Pillai Trace =           0.499
             F-Statistic =          7.959     DF =   2,  16     Prob =      0.004

   Hotelling-Lawley Trace =        0.995
             F-Statistic =          7.959     DF =   2,  16     Prob =      0.004
```

This is the multivariate F statistic that Morrison gets. For these data, we prefer the weighted means analysis (the second one) because these differences in cell frequencies probably reflect population base rates. They are not random like the dead rats experiment. You can accomplish this same result more easily using the mean model (see Example 6.15).

```
GLM
    USE mothers
    CATEGORY class
    MODEL scale(1 .. 3) = class / MEANS
    ESTIMATE

    HYPOTHESIS
    SPECIFY 8*class[1] + 5*class[2] + 4*class[3] +,
            4*class[4] = 0
    CMATRIX [1 -1  0;
             0  1 -1]
    TEST
```

```
Dependent variable means

                     SCALE(1)    SCALE(2)    SCALE(3)

                      14.524      15.619      15.857


Unweighted Means Model
```

```
A Matrix

                        1          2          3          4
                     -8.000     -5.000     -4.000     -4.000

C Matrix

                        1          2          3
                1     1.000     -1.000      0.0
                2     0.0        1.000     -1.000

D Matrix

                        1          2
                     0.0        0.0

Univariate F Tests

    Effect          SS         DF        MS           F            P

        1         25.190        1       25.190       8.364        0.010
    Error         51.200       17        3.012
        2          1.190        1        1.190       0.329        0.574
    Error         61.500       17        3.618

Multivariate Test Statistics

            Wilks' Lambda =      0.501
               F-Statistic =     7.959     DF =   2,  16     Prob =      0.004

              Pillai Trace =     0.499
               F-Statistic =     7.959     DF =   2,  16     Prob =      0.004

   Hotelling-Lawley Trace =      0.995
               F-Statistic =     7.959     DF =   2,  16     Prob =      0.004
```

6.25
Issues in repeated measures analysis

As you have seen, repeated measures designs can be generated in SYSTAT with a single procedure. You need not worry about weighting cases in unbalanced designs or selecting error terms. The program does this automatically; however, you should keep the following in mind:

– The sums of squares for the univariate F tests are pooled across subjects within groups and their interactions with trials. This means that the traditional analysis method has highly restrictive assumptions. You must assume that the variances within cells are homogeneous and that the covariances across all pairs of cells are equivalent (compound symmetry). There are some mathematical exceptions to this requirement, but they rarely occur in practice. Furthermore, the compound symmetry assumption rarely holds for real data.

– Compound symmetry is *not* required for the validity of the single degree-of-freedom polynomial contrasts. These polynomials partition sums of squares into orthogonal components. You should routinely examine the magnitude of these sums of squares relative to the hypothesis sum of squares for the corresponding univariate repeated measures F test when your trials are ordered on a scale.

– Think of the repeated measures output as an expanded traditional ANOVA table. The effects are printed in the same order as they appear in Winer (1971) and other texts, but they include the single degree-of-freedom and multivariate tests to protect you from false conclusions. If you are satisfied that both are in agreement, you can delete the additional lines in the output file.

– You can test any hypothesis after you have estimated a repeated measures design and examined the output. For example, you can use **Stats**➧**General Linear Model**➧**Hypothesis Test**, select **Contrast**, and use **Polynomial** with **Metric** to test single degree-of-freedom components in an unevenly spaced design. You can also use **Difference** to do post hoc tests on adjacent trials.

This example tests adjacent trials within the first level of *ANXIETY*:

```
GLM
    USE repeat1
    CATEGORY anxiety, tension
    MODEL trial(1 .. 4) = CONSTANT + anxiety + tension +,
                          anxiety*tension  / REPEAT,
                          NAME='trial'
    ESTIMATE

    HYPOTHESIS
    WITHIN = 'trial'
    CONTRAST / DIFFERENCE
    AMATRIX [0 1 0 0]
    TEST
```

If you want other contrasts on the trials factor, use **Stats**➧**General Linear Model**➧**Hypothesis Test** and the **C matrix** option.

```
    HYPOTHESIS
    WITHIN = 'trial'
    CMATRIX [-3 -1  1  3]
    TEST
```

This hypothesis is equivalent to a linear contrast on the *TRIAL*∗*ANXIETY* interaction. You get the same *F* statistic as the program prints in the first single degree-of-freedom polynomial contrast for the within subjects test of *TRIAL*∗*ANXIETY*.

6.26
Hotelling's T²

You can use **General Linear Model** to calculate Hotelling's T^2 statistic.

One-sample test

For example, to get a one-sample test for the variables X and Y, select both X and Y as dependent variables.

```
GLM
    USE filename
    MODEL x, y = CONSTANT
    ESTIMATE
```

The F test for **CONSTANT** is the statistic you want. It is the same as the Hotelling's T^2 for the hypothesis that the population means for X and Y are 0.

You can also test against the hypothesis that the means of X and Y have particular nonzero values, for example 10 and 15, by using **Stats**➠ **General Linear Model**➠**Hypothesis Test** and the **D matrix** option.

```
HYPOTHESIS
DMATRIX [10 15]
TEST
```

Two-sample test

For a two-sample test, you must provide a categorical independent variable that represents the two groups.

```
GLM
    CATEGORY group
    MODEL x,y = CONSTANT + group
    ESTIMATE
```

Hotelling's T^2, the simplest form of multivariate analysis of variance, is discussed fully in the next section.

6.27
Multivariate analysis of variance

The following data (in the file *MANOVA*) comprise a hypothetical experiment on rats assigned randomly to one of three drugs. Weight loss in grams was observed for the first and second weeks of the experiment. The data were analyzed in Morrison (1976) with a two-way multivariate analysis of variance (a two-way MANOVA.)

SEX	DRUG	WEEK(1)	WEEK(2)
1	1	5	6
1	1	5	4
1	1	9	9
1	1	7	6
1	2	7	6
1	2	7	7
1	2	9	12
1	2	6	8
1	3	21	15
1	3	14	11
1	3	17	12
1	3	12	10
2	1	7	10
2	1	6	6
2	1	9	7
2	1	8	10
2	2	10	13
2	2	8	7
2	2	7	6
2	2	6	9
2	3	16	12
2	3	14	9
2	3	14	8
2	3	10	5

You can use ANOVA to set up the MANOVA model for complete factorials.

```
ANOVA
    USE manova
    CATEGORY sex, drug
    DEPEND week(1 .. 2)
    ESTIMATE
```

You can also use GLM to set up the MANOVA model. With this approach, the design does not have to be a complete factorial. With commands:

```
GLM
    USE manova
    CATEGORY sex, drug
    MODEL week(1 .. 2) = CONSTANT + sex + drug +,
                         sex*drug
    ESTIMATE
```

Notice that the only difference between an ANOVA and MANOVA model is that a MANOVA model has more than one dependent variable.

```
Dependent variable means
                          WEEK(1)     WEEK(2)
                           9.750       8.667

                              -1
Estimates of effects   B = (X'X)  X'Y
                              WEEK(1)     WEEK(2)

   CONSTANT                    9.750       8.667

   SEX        1                0.167       0.167

   DRUG       1               -2.750      -1.417

   DRUG       2               -2.250      -0.167

   SEX        1
   DRUG       1               -0.667      -1.167

   SEX        1
   DRUG       2               -0.417      -0.417

Squared multiple correlations
                          WEEK(1)     WEEK(2)
                           0.770       0.378
```

Notice that each column of the **B** matrix is now assigned to a separate dependent variable. It is as if we had done two runs of an ANOVA. The numbers in the matrix are the analysis of variance effects estimates.

Testing hypotheses

With more than one dependent variable, you do not get a single ANOVA table; instead, each hypothesis is tested separately. **Effects** on the **Hypothesis Test** dialog box operates the way you have seen before; it tests independent variables. Here are three hypotheses. Extended output for the second hypothesis is used to illustrate the detailed output.

```
HYPOTHESIS
EFFECT = sex
TEST

PRINT = LONG

HYPOTHESIS
EFFECT = drug
TEST

PRINT = SHORT

HYPOTHESIS
EFFECT = sex*drug
TEST
```

Here are the collected results:

SEX

```
Test for effect called:     SEX

Univariate F Tests

    Effect          SS        DF       MS              F            P

WEEK(1)            0.667       1       0.667          0.127        0.726
       Error      94.500      18       5.250
WEEK(2)            0.667       1       0.667          0.105        0.749
       Error     114.000      18       6.333

Multivariate Test Statistics

            Wilks' Lambda =        0.993
             F-Statistic =        0.064    DF =   2,  17     Prob =      0.938

             Pillai Trace =        0.007
             F-Statistic =        0.064    DF =   2,  17     Prob =      0.938

   Hotelling-Lawley Trace =        0.008
             F-Statistic =        0.064    DF =   2,  17     Prob =      0.938
```

DRUG

```
Test for effect called:     DRUG

Null hypothesis contrast AB

                      WEEK(1)      WEEK(2)

             1        -2.750       -1.417
             2        -2.250       -0.167


                       -1
Inverse contrast A(X'X)  A'

                       1           2
             1        0.083
             2       -0.042       0.083


                                                    -1   -1
Hypothesis sum of product matrix   H = B'A'(A(X'X)  A')   AB

                      WEEK(1)      WEEK(2)

   WEEK(1)            301.000
   WEEK(2)             97.500       36.333


Error sum of product matrix G = E'E

                      WEEK(1)      WEEK(2)

   WEEK(1)             94.500
   WEEK(2)             76.500      114.000


Univariate F Tests

    Effect          SS        DF       MS              F            P

WEEK(1)           301.000      2      150.500         28.667       0.000
       Error      94.500      18       5.250
WEEK(2)            36.333      2       18.167          2.868       0.083
       Error     114.000      18       6.333

Multivariate Test Statistics

            Wilks' Lambda =        0.169
             F-Statistic =       12.199    DF =   4,  34     Prob =      0.000
```

```
              Pillai Trace =        0.880
              F-Statistic =         7.077   DF =   4,  36    Prob =       0.000

     Hotelling-Lawley Trace =       4.640
              F-Statistic =        18.558   DF =   4,  32    Prob =       0.000

                    THETA = 0.821 S =  2, M =-0.5, N =  7.5 Prob =       0.000

Test of Residual Roots

   Roots 1 through 2
      Chi-Square Statistic =        36.491       DF = 4

   Roots 2 through 2
      Chi-Square Statistic =         1.262       DF = 1

Canonical Correlations

                         1            2
                     0.906        0.244

Dependent variable canonical coefficients standardized
by conditional (within groups) standard deviations

                         1            2
      WEEK(1)        1.437       -0.352
      WEEK(2)       -0.821        1.231

Canonical loadings (correlations between conditional
dependent variables and dependent canonical factors)

                         1            2
      WEEK(1)        0.832        0.555
      WEEK(2)        0.238        0.971
```

SEX by DRUG

```
Test for effect called:      SEX*DRUG

Univariate F Tests

     Effect          SS        DF       MS          F           P

WEEK(1)           14.333        2      7.167      1.365        0.281
     Error        94.500       18      5.250
WEEK(2)           32.333        2     16.167      2.553        0.106
     Error       114.000       18      6.333

Multivariate Test Statistics

              Wilks' Lambda =       0.774
              F-Statistic =         1.159   DF =   4,  34    Prob =       0.346

              Pillai Trace =        0.227
              F-Statistic =         1.152   DF =   4,  36    Prob =       0.348

     Hotelling-Lawley Trace =       0.290
              F-Statistic =         1.159   DF =   4,  32    Prob =       0.347

                    THETA = 0.221 S =  2, M =-0.5, N =  7.5 Prob =       0.295
```

Default output

Matrix formulas (that are something long) make explicit the hypothesis being tested. For MANOVA, hypotheses are tested with sums of squares and cross products matrices. Before printing the multivariate tests, however, ANOVA prints the univariate tests. Each of these F statistics is constructed in the same way as the ANOVA model. The sums of squares for hypothesis and error are taken from the diagonals of the respective sum of product matrices. The univariate F test for the *WEEK(1) DRUG* effect, for example, is computed from 301.0/2 over 94.5/18, or hypothesis mean square divided by error mean square. The next statistics printed are for the multivariate hypothesis. Wilks' Lambda (likelihood ratio criterion) varies between 0 and 1. Schatzoff (1966) has tables for its percentage points. The following F statistic is Rao's approximate (sometimes exact) F statistic corresponding to the likelihood ratio criterion (see Rao, 1973). Pillai's trace and its F approximation are taken from Pillai (1960). The Hotelling-Lawley trace and its F approximation are documented in Morrison (1976). The last statistic is the largest root criterion for Roy's union-intersection test (see Morrison, 1976). Charts of the percentage points of this statistic, found in Morrison and other multivariate texts, are taken from Heck (1960).

The probability value printed for Theta is not an approximation. It is what you find in the charts. In the first hypothesis, all the multivariate statistics have the same value for the F approximation because the approximation is exact when there are only two groups (see Hotelling's T^2 in Morrison, 1976). In these cases, Theta is not printed because it has the same probability value as the F statistic.

Because you requested extended output for the second hypothesis, you get additional material.

Bartlett's residual root (eigenvalue) test. The chi-square statistics follow Bartlett (1947). The probability value for the first chi-square statistic should correspond to that for the approximate multivariate F statistic in large samples. In small samples, they might be discrepant, in which case you should generally trust the F statistic more. The subsequent chi-square statistics are recomputed, leaving out the first and later roots until the last root is tested. These are sequential tests and should be treated with caution, but they can be used to decide how many dimensions (roots and canonical correlations) are significant. The number of significant roots corresponds to the number of significant p values in this ordered list.

Canonical coefficients. Information on the canonical variates is printed next. Dimensions with insignificant chi-square statistics in the prior tests should be ignored in general. Corresponding to each canonical correlation is a canonical variate, whose coefficients have been standardized by the within-groups standard deviations. If you want to standardize these variates by the total (sample) standard deviations, use **Stats⇒General Linear Model⇒Hypothesis Test** and select **Sample**. With commands (insert this command prior to TEST):

```
STANDARDIZE = TOTAL
```

Continue with the other test specifications described above.

The default option for **Standardize** is **Within groups. Sample** (or TOTAL) is generally used for canonical correlation analysis or multivariate regression when groups are not present to introduce covariation among variates.

Finally, the canonical loadings are printed. These are correlations and, thus, provide information different from the canonical coefficients. In particular, you can identify suppressor variables in the multivariate system by looking for differences in sign between the coefficients and the loadings (which is the case with these data). See Bock (1975) and Wilkinson (1975, 1977) for an interpretation of these variates.

6.28 Multivariate analysis of covariance

Multivariate analysis of covariance is a extension of the univariate model discussed in a previous section. If you have a one-way or complete factorial design, you can use ANOVA to select covariate terms. You can use GLM the same way; just select the dependent variable and select one or more covariate variables. To select independent variables that are categorical design factors, use **Stats**➧**General Linear Model**➧**Estimate Model**, and select your independent variables. Select the **Categories** button and move the independent variables that are categorical design factors into the **Categorical Variable(s)** list.

More About Analysis of Variance

Often, you will want to examine the influence of categorical variables (such as gender, species, country, and experimental group) on continuous variables. The model equations for this case, called *analysis of variance,* are the same as the ones discussed in Chapter 8. However, you have to figure out a numerical coding for categories so that you can use the codes in an equation as the independent variable(s).

Effects coding

This example continues from the accounting firm example in Chapter 8. The following data file, *EARNBILL,* shows the breakdown of accountants sampled by sex. Because *SEX* is a categorical variable (numerical values assigned to *MALE* or *FEMALE* are arbitrary), a code variable with the values 1 or –1 is used. It doesn't matter which group is assigned –1, as long as the other is assigned 1.

EARNINGS	SEX	CODE
86	female	–1
67	female	–1
95	female	–1
105	female	–1
86	female	–1
82	male	1
140	male	1
145	male	1
144	male	1
184	male	1

There is nothing wrong with plotting earnings against the code variable, as long as you realize that the slope of the line is arbitrary because it depends on how you assign your codes. By changing the values of the code variable, you can change the slope. Here is a plot with the least squares regression line superimposed.

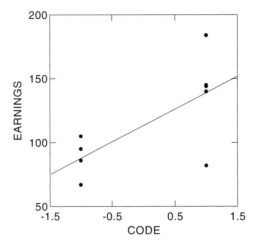

Let's do a regression on the data using these codes. Here are the coefficients as computed by ANOVA:

```
Variable    Coefficients
Constant        113.400
Code             25.600
```

Notice that *Constant* (113.4) is the mean of all the data. It is also the regression intercept because the codes are symmetrical about 0. The coefficient for *Code* (25.6) is the slope of the line. It is also one half the difference between the means of the groups. This is because the codes are exactly two units apart. This slope is often called an *effect* in the analysis of variance because it represents the amount that the categorical variable *SEX* affects *BILLINGS*. In other words, the effect of *SEX* can be represented by the amount that the mean for males differs from the overall mean.

Means coding

The effects coding model is useful because the parameters (constant and slope) can be interpreted as an overall level and as the effect(s) of treatment, respectively. Another model, however, which yields the means of the groups directly is called the means model. Here are the codes for this model.

EARNINGS	SEX	CODE1	CODE2
86	female	1	0
67	female	1	0
95	female	1	0
105	female	1	0
86	female	1	0
82	male	0	1
140	male	0	1
145	male	0	1
144	male	0	1
184	male	0	1

Notice that *CODE1* is non-zero for all females, and *CODE2* is non-zero for all males. To estimate a regression model with these codes, you must leave out the constant. With only two groups, there are not more than two distinct pieces of information needed to distinguish them. Here are the coefficients for these codes in a model without a constant:

```
Variable    Coefficient

Code1            87.800
Code2           139.000
```

Notice that the coefficients are now the means of the groups.

Models

Let's look at the algebraic models for each of these codings. Recall that the regression model looks like this:

$$y = \beta_0 + \beta_1 x_1 + \varepsilon$$

For the effects model, it is convenient to modify this notation as follows:

$$y_j = \mu + \alpha_j + \varepsilon$$

When x (the code variable) is -1, α_j is equivalent to α_1; when x is 1, α_j is equivalent to α_2. This shorthand will help you later when dealing with models with many categories. For this model, the μ parameter stands for the grand (overall) mean, and the α parameter stands for the effect. In this model, our best prediction of the score of a group member is derived from the grand mean plus or minus the deviation of that group from this grand mean.

The means model looks like this:

$$y_j = \mu_j + \varepsilon$$

In this model, our best prediction of the score of a group member is the mean of that group.

Hypotheses

As with regression, we are usually interested in testing hypotheses concerning the parameters of the model. Here are the hypotheses for the two models:

$$H_0: \alpha_1 = \alpha_2 = 0 \qquad \text{(effects model)}$$
$$H_0: \mu_1 = \mu_2 \qquad \text{(means model)}$$

The tests of this hypothesis compare variation between the means to variation within each group, which is mathematically equivalent to testing the significance of coefficients in the regression model. For your example, the F ratio in the analysis of variance table tells you that the coefficient for *SEX* is significant at $p = 0.019$, which is less than the conventional 0.05 value. Thus, on the basis of this sample and the validity of our usual regression assumptions, you can conclude that women earn significantly less than men in this firm.

```
Dep Var:earnings     N:   10    Multiple R:  .719    Squared Multiple R:  .517
                              Analysis Of Variance

   Source    Sum-of-squares   Df  Mean-square     F-ratio        P
    Sex           6553.600     1     6553.600       8.563      0.019
   Error          6122.800     8      765.350
```

The nice thing about realizing that ANOVA is specially-coded regression is that the usual assumptions and diagnostics are appropriate in this context. You can plot residuals against estimated values, for example, to check for homogeneity of variance.

Multi-group ANOVA

When there are more groups, the coding of categories becomes more complex. For the effects model, there are one fewer coding variables than number of categories. For two categories, you need only one coding variable; for three categories, you need two coding variables:

Category	Code	
1	1	0
2	0	1
3	−1	−1

For the means model, the extension is straightforward:

Category	Code		
1	1	0	0
2	0	1	0
3	0	0	1

For multi-group ANOVA, the models have the same form as for the two-group ANOVA above. The corresponding hypotheses for testing whether there are differences between means are:

H_0: $\alpha_1 = \alpha_2 = \alpha_3 = 0$ (effects model)

H_0: $\mu_1 = \mu_2 = \mu_3$ (means model)

You do not need to know how to produce coding variables to do ANOVA. SYSTAT does this for you automatically. All you need is a single variable that contains different values for each group. SYSTAT translates these values into different codes. It is important to remember, however, that regression and analysis of variance are not fundamentally different models. They are both instances of the general linear model.

Factorial ANOVA

It is possible to have more than one categorical variable in ANOVA. When this happens, you code each categorical variable exactly the same way as you do with multi-group ANOVA. The coded design variables are then added as a full set of predictors in the model.

ANOVA factors can interact. For example, a treatment may enhance bar pressing by male rats, yet suppress bar pressing by female rats. To test for this possibility, you can add (to your model) variables which are the product of the *main effect* variables already coded. This is similar to what you do when you construct polynomial models. For example, this is a model without an interaction:

```
MODEL y = CONSTANT + treat + sex
```

This is a model which contains interaction:

```
MODEL y = CONSTANT + treat + sex + treat*sex
```

If the hypothesis test of the coefficients for the *TREAT*SEX* term is significant, then you must qualify your conclusions by referring to the interaction. You might say, "It works one way for males and another for females."

Types of sums of squares

SPSS and some other programs print several types of sums of squares for testing hypotheses. The standard type printed in SPSS is Type III.

Type I. Type I sums of squares are computed from the difference between the residual sums of squares of two different models. The particular models needed for the computation depend on the order of the variables in the MODEL statement. For example, if the model is

```
MODEL y = CONSTANT + a + b + a*b
```

then the sum of squares for $A*B$ is produced from the difference between SSE (sum of squared error) in the two following models:

```
MODEL y = CONSTANT + a + b
MODEL y = CONSTANT + a + b + a*b
```

Similarly, the Type I sums of squares for B in this model are computed from the difference in SSE between the following models:

```
MODEL y = CONSTANT + a
MODEL y = CONSTANT + a + b
```

Finally, the Type I sums of squares for A is computed from the difference in residual sums of squares for the following:

```
MODEL y = CONSTANT
MODEL y = CONSTANT + a
```

In summary, to compute sums of squares, move from right to left and construct models which differ by the right-most term only.

Type II. Type II sums of squares are computed similarly to Type I except that main effects and interactions determine the ordering of differences instead of the MODEL statement order. For the above model, Type II sums of squares for the interaction are computed from the difference in residual sums of squares for the following models:

```
MODEL y = CONSTANT + a + b
MODEL y = CONSTANT + a + b + a*b
```

For the B effect, difference the following models:

```
MODEL y = CONSTANT + a + b
MODEL y = CONSTANT + a
```

For the A effect, difference the following (this is not the same as for Type I):

```
MODEL y = CONSTANT + a + b
MODEL y = CONSTANT + b
```

In summary, include interactions of the same order as well as all lower order interactions and main effects when differencing to get an interaction. When getting sums of squares for a main effect, difference against all other main effects only.

Type III. Type III sums of squares are the default for ANOVA and are much simpler to understand. Simply difference from the full model, leaving out only the term in question. For example, the Type III sum of squares for *A* is taken from the following two models:

```
MODEL y = CONSTANT + b + a*b
MODEL y = CONSTANT + a + b + a*b
```

Type IV. Type IV sums of squares are designed for missing cells designs and are not easily presented in the above terminology. They are produced by balancing over the means of nonmissing cells not included in the current hypothesis.

SYSTAT's sums of squares

Printing more than one sum of squares in a table is potentially confusing to users. There is a strong temptation to choose the most significant sum of squares without understanding the hypothesis being tested.

A Type I test is produced by first estimating the full models and noting the error term. Then, each effect is entered sequentially and tested with the error term from the full model. Later, effects are conditioned on earlier effects, but earlier effects are not conditioned on later effects. A Type II test is produced most easily with interactive stepping (STEP). Type III is printed in the regression and ANOVA table. Finally, Type IV is produced by the careful use of SPECIFY in testing means models. The advantage of this approach is that the user is always aware that sums of squares depend on explicit mathematical models rather than additions and subtractions of dimensionless quantities.

Summary

Computation

Centered sums of squares and cross products are accumulated using provisional algorithms. Linear systems, including those involved in hypothesis testing, are solved by using forward and reverse sweeping (Dempster, 1969). Eigensystems are solved with Householder tridiagonalization and implicit QL iterations. For further information, see Wilkinson and Reinsch (1971) or Chambers (1977).

References

Affifi, A.A. and Clark, V. 1984. *Computer-aided multivariate analysis.* Belmont, Calif.: Lifetime Learning Publications.

Afifi, A.A., and Azen, S.P. 1972. *Statistical analysis: a computer-oriented approach.* New York: Academic Press.

Bartlett, M.S. 1947. Multivariate analysis. *Journal of the Royal Statistical Society*, Series B, 9: 176-197.

Bock, R.D. 1975. *Multivariate statistical methods in behavioral research.* New York: McGraw-Hill.

Cochran and Cox 1957. *Experimental designs.* 2nd ed. New York: John Wiley & Sons, Inc.

Daniel, C. 1960. Locating outliers in factorial experiments. *Technometrics*, 2: 149-156.

Feingold, M., and Korsog, P.E. 1986. The correlation and dependence between two f statistics with the same denominator. *The American Statistician*, 40: 218-220.

Heck, D.L. 1960. Charts of some upper percentage points of the distribution of the largest characteristic root. *Annals of Mathematical Statistics*, 31: 625-642.

Hocking, R.R. 1985. *The analysis of linear models.* Monterey, Calif.: Brooks/Cole.

John, P.W.M. 1971. *Statistical design and analysis of experiments.* New York: MacMillan, Inc.

Kutner, M.H. 1974. Hypothesis testing in linear models (Eisenhart Model I). *The American Statistician*, 28: 98-100.

Levene, H. 1960. Robust tests for equality of variance. I. Olkin, ed., *Contributions to Probability and Statistics*. Palo Alto, Calif.: Stanford University Press, 278-292.

Miller, R. 1985. Multiple comparisons. Kotz, S., and Johnson, N.L., eds., *Encyclopedia of Statistical Sciences*, vol. 5. New York: John Wiley & Sons, Inc., 679-689.

Milliken, G.A., and Johnson, D.E. 1984. Analysis of messy data, Vol. 1: *Designed Experiments*. New York: Van Nostrand Reinhold Company.

Morrison, D.F. 1976. *Multivariate statistical methods*. New York: McGraw-Hill.

Neter, J., and Wasserman, W., and Kutner, M. 1985. *Applied linear statistical models*, 2nd ed. Homewood, Ill.: Richard E. Irwin, Inc.

Pillai, K.C.S. 1960. *Statistical table for tests of multivariate hypotheses*. Manila: The Statistical Center, University of Phillipines.

Rao, C.R. 1973. *Linear statistical inference and its applications*, 2nd ed. New York: John Wiley & Sons, Inc.

Schatzoff, M. 1966. *Exact distributions of Wilk's likelihood ratio criterion*. *Biometrika*, 53: 347-358.

Scheffé, H. 1959. *The analysis of variance*. New York: John Wiley & Sons, Inc.

Searle, S.R. 1971. *Linear models*. New York: John Wiley & Sons, Inc.

Searle, S.R. 1987. *Linear models for unbalanced data*. New York: John Wiley & Sons, Inc.

Speed, F.M., and Hocking, R.R. 1976. The use of the r( )- notation with unbalanced data. *The American Statistician*, 30: 30-33.

Speed, F.M., Hocking, R.R., and Hackney, O.P. 1978. Methods of analysis of linear models with unbalanced data. *Journal of the American Statistical Association*, 73: 105-112.

Wilkinson, L. 1975. Response variable hypotheses in the multivariate analysis of variance. *Psychological Bulletin*, 82: 408-412.

Wilkinson, L. 1977. Confirmatory rotation of MANOVA canonical variates. *Multivariate Behavioral Research*, 12: 487-494.

Winer, B.J. 1971. *Statistical principles in experimental design*, 2nd ed. New York: McGraw-Hill.

Nonparametric Statistics

Leland Wilkinson

Stats➠**Nonparametric Tests** computes nonparametric statistics for:

- Testing differences for a single variable across two or more independent groups of cases: the Mann-Whitney rank sum test, the Kruskal-Wallis one-way analysis of variance, and the Kolmogorov-Smirnov two-sample test.

- Testing differences among two or more dependent variables: the Sign test, the Wilcoxon signed rank test, and the Friedman two-way ANOVA (or repeated measures) test.

- Studying the distribution of a single variable: the Kolmogorov-Smirnov one-sample test and the Wald-Wolfowitz runs test.

Overview

Getting started

Independent Samples

Related Variables

One-Sample Tests

Summary

Computation

Nonparametric Statistics

Overview

The statistics in **Stats→Nonparametric Tests** are appropriate for testing independent groups, related variables, or a single sample. The **Stats→Nonparametric Tests** menu offers the following submenus:

Kruskal-Wallis	Mann-Whitney and Kruskal-Wallis tests
Two sample KS	Kolmogorov-Smirnov two-sample test
Sign	Sign test
Wilcoxon	Wilcoxon signed-rank test
Friedman	Friedman test
One sample KS	Kolmogorov-Smirnov test
Wald-Wolfowitz Runs	Wald-Wolfowitz runs test

For measuring differences of a single variable across two or more independent groups of cases, **Stats→Nonparametric Tests** provides **Kruskal-Wallis** and **Two sample KS**. For differences among related or several dependent variables, it provides **Sign**, **Wilcoxon**, and **Friedman**. For studying the distribution of a single variable, it provides **One sample KS** and **Wald-Wolfowitz Runs**.

Many nonparametric statistics are computed elsewhere in SYSTAT. **Stats→Correlations** calculates matrices of coefficients, such as Spearman's rho, Kendall's tau-*b*, Guttman's *mu2*, and Goodman-Kruskal gamma. **Stats→Descriptive Statistics→Basic Statistics** offers stem-and-leaf plots, and **Graph→Box Plot** offers boxplots with medians and quartiles. **Stats→Time Series** can perform nonmetric smoothing. **Stats→Crosstabs** can be used for chi-square tests of independence. **Stats→Multidimensional Scaling** (MDS) and **Stats→Cluster Analysis** work with nonmetric data matrices. Finally, you can use **Data→Rank** to compute a variety of rank order statistics.

A word of advice. Beware of using nonparametric procedures to rescue bad data. These procedures were, in most cases, designed to apply to data that were categorical or ranked in the first place, such as rank judgments and binary data. If you have data that violate distributional assumptions for linear models, you should consider transformations or robust models before retreating to nonparametrics.

We caution you that *nonparametric* doesn't mean that all assumptions are dropped. For example, the Mann-Whitney test assumes that the shapes of the distributions are the same.

Getting started

To request a nonparametric test, use **Stats**➠**Nonparametric Tests**. Because there are several nonparametric tests dialog boxes, the boxes will be displayed as they are discussed.

With commands

First specify your data:

USE *filename*

Then continue as follows:

Differences across groups

```
KRUSKAL varlist * grpvar
KS varlist * grpvar
```

Differences among variables

```
SIGN varlist
WILCOXON varlist
FRIEDMAN varlist
```

Single variable

```
KS varlist / options
```

where options are UNIVORM, NORMAL, T, F, CHISQ, GAMMA, BETA, EXP, LOGISTIC, RANGE, WEIBULL, BINOMIAL POISSON, LILLIEFORS distributions

```
RUNS varlist / CUT=n
```

Independent Samples

In this section, we use **Stats⇒Nonparametric Tests⇒Kruskal-Wallis** for the Kruskal-Wallis and Mann-Whitney tests, and **Stats⇒Nonparametric Tests⇒Two sample KS** for the Kolmogorov-Smirnov two-sample test to measure differences across independent groups of cases for a single variable.

For the Kruskal-Wallis test, the values of a variable are transformed to ranks (ignoring group membership) to test that there is no shift in the center of the groups (that is, the centers do not differ). This is the nonparametric analog of a one-way analysis of variance. When there are only two groups, this procedure reduces to the Mann-Whitney test, the nonparametric analog of the two-sample t test.

The Kolmogorov-Smirnov two-sample test measures the discrepancy between two-sample cumulative distribution functions.

For the Kruskal-Wallis test, use **Stats⇒Nonparametric Tests⇒Kruskal-Wallis**:

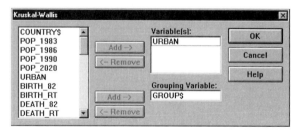

For the two-sample Kolmogorov-Smirnov test, use **Stats⇒ Nonparametric Tests⇒Two sample KS**:

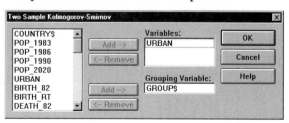

7.1
Kruskal-Wallis

For two or more independent groups, the Kruskal-Wallis test statistic tests whether the *k* samples come from identically distributed populations. (For two groups, this is the Mann-Whitney test. See Example 7.2.)

In this example, we compare the percentage of people who live in cities (*URBAN*) for three groups of countries: European, Islamic, and New World. We use the *OURWORLD* data file that has one record for each of 57 countries with the variables *URBAN* and *GROUP$*. Here is a boxplot of *URBAN* grouped by *GROUP$*. Use the **Graph** menu to create boxplots.

```
NPAR
    USE ourworld
    DENSITY urban * group$ / BOX  TRANS
```

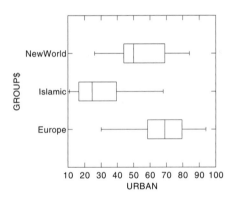

The median of each distribution is marked by the vertical bar inside the box: the median for *European* countries is 69%; for *Islamic* countries, 24.5%; and for *NewWorld* countries, 50%. We ask, "Is there a difference in typical values of *URBAN* among these groups of countries?"

Use **Stats**⟹**Nonparametric Tests**⟹**Kruskal-Wallis** and specify *URBAN* for **Variable(s)** and *GROUP$* for **Grouping Variable**. With commands:

```
NPAR
    USE ourworld
    KRUSKAL urban * group$
```

```
Kruskal-Wallis One-Way Analysis of Variance for 56 cases
Dependent variable is URBAN
 Grouping variable is GROUP$

    Group      Count    Rank Sum

    Europe       19      765.00
    Islamic      16      198.00
    NewWorld     21      633.00

Kruskal-Wallis Test Statistic =       25.759
 Probability is          0.000 assuming Chi-square distribution with 2 DF
```

We conclude that urbanization differs markedly across the three groups of countries (p value < 0.0005).

7.2 Mann-Whitney

When there are only two groups, **Kruskal-Wallis** provides the Mann-Whitney test. Note that your grouping variable must contain exactly two values. Here we modify the one-way ANOVA example above by deleting the Islamic group. We ask, "Do European nations tend to be more urban than New World countries?" We use **Data**➠**Select cases** and specify GROUP$<>Islamic to eliminate the Islamic countries. Then use **Stats**➠ **Nonparametric Tests**➠**Kruskal-Wallis** and repeat the same steps from Example 7.1. With commands:

```
NPAR
    USE ourworld
    SELECT group$ <> 'Islamic'
    KRUSKAL urban * group$
```

```
Kruskal-Wallis One-Way Analysis of Variance for 40 cases
Dependent variable is URBAN
 Grouping variable is GROUP$

    Group      Count    Rank Sum

    Europe       19      475.00
    NewWorld     21      345.00

Mann-Whitney U test statistic =      285.000
 Probability is         0.020
Chi-square approximation =          5.370 with 1 DF
```

The percentage of population living in urban areas is significantly greater for *European* countries than for *New World* countries (p value = 0.02).

**7.3
Kolmogorov-
Smirnov
two-sample
test**

The Kolmogorov-Smirnov test compares two-sample cumulative distribution functions. You assume that both samples come from exactly the same distribution. The distributions can be organized as two variables (two columns) or as a single variable (column) with a second variable that identifies group membership. The latter layout is necessary when sample sizes differ.

Separate samples. When each distribution is stored as a single column (single variables), use **Variables** under **Stats**➧**Nonparametric Tests**➧ **Two sample KS** to select both variables.

One variable plus grouping. When the distribution is stored as a single variable and there is a grouping variable to identify the samples, use **Stats**➧**Nonparametric Tests**➧**Two sample KS**. Identify the variables of interest with **Variable** and the grouping variable with **Grouping Variable**.

In this example, we test if the distributions of *URBAN*, the proportion of people living in cities, for European and New World countries have the same mean, standard deviation, and shape. Again, we eliminate the Islamic countries. Under **Stats**➧**Nonparametric Tests**➧**Two sample KS**, select *URBAN* as **Variable** and *GROUP$* as **Grouping Variable**.

```
NPAR
    USE ourworld
    SELECT group$ <> 'Islamic'
    KS urban * group$
```

```
Kolmogorov-Smirnov Two Sample Test results
  Maximum differences for pairs of groups
                      Europe      NewWorld
      Europe          0.0
    NewWorld          0.519        0.0

  Two-sided probabilities
                      Europe      NewWorld
      Europe          1.000
    NewWorld          0.009        1.000
```

The two distributions differ significantly (p value=0.009).

Related Variables

Use the tests in this section to identify differences among related variables. **Stats⊯➡Nonparametric Tests⊯➡Sign**, **Stats⊯➡Nonparametric Tests⊯➡Wilcoxon**, and **Stats⊯➡Nonparametric Tests⊯➡Friedman** work in similar ways (there are no special features or options associated with these tests):

- For each case, **Stats⊯➡Nonparametric Tests⊯➡Sign** computes the sign of the difference between two variables.

- **Stats⊯➡Nonparametric Tests⊯➡Wilcoxon** uses the rank order of the differences between two variables and is the nonparametric analog of the paired *t* test.

- Within each case, **Stats⊯➡Nonparametric Tests⊯➡Friedman** ranks the values of two or more variables from smallest to largest. This is the nonparametric analog of a repeated measures analysis of variance.

For a sign test, use **Stats⊯➡Nonparametric Tests⊯➡Sign**:

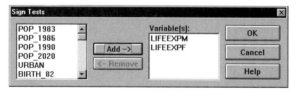

For a Wilcoxon signed-rank test, use **Stats⊯➡Nonparametric Tests⊯➡Wilcoxon**:

For a Friedman test, use **Stats⊯➡Nonparametric Tests⊯➡Friedman**:

7.4
The Sign and
Wilcoxon
tests

A need for comparing variables arises frequently in *before and after* studies where each subject is measured before a treatment and again afterwards. Here your goal is to determine if any difference in response can be attributed to chance alone. As a test, researchers often use the Sign test or the Wilcoxon signed-rank test. For these tests, the measurements need not be collected at different points in time; they simply can be two measures on the same scale for which you want to test differences.

Here, for a sample of countries (not subjects), we ask, "Does life expectancy differ for males and females?" Using the *OURWORLD* data, we compare *LIFEEXPF* and *LIFEEXPM*.

Here are stem-and-leaf plots for each distribution. Use the **Graph** menu to create stem-and-leaf plots.

```
STATISTICS
    USE ourworld
    STEM lifeexpf lifeexpm / LINES=10
```

```
Stem and Leaf Plot of variable:  LIFEEXPF, N = 57
        Minimum:        44.000
        Lower hinge:        65.000
        Median:         75.000
        Upper hinge:        79.000
        Maximum:        83.000

            4    4
            4    679
            5    0234
            5    55667
            6    4
            6  H 567788889
            7    01344
            7  H 5666777778889999
            8    0000111111223
```

```
Stem and Leaf Plot of variable:    LIFEEXPM, N = 57
        Minimum:        40.000
        Lower hinge:        61.000
        Median:         68.000
        Upper hinge:        73.000
        Maximum:        75.000

            4    0
        * * * Outside Values * * *
            4    56789
            5    122334
            5    6
            6  H 01222444
            6  M 5556778899
            7  H 001111223333333334444
            7    55555
```

Median life expectancy for females is 75 years; for males, 68 years.

Sign test

The sign test counts the number of times male life expectancy is greater than that for females and vice versa. This test is attractive because of its simplicity and the fact that the variance of the first measure in each pair may differ from that of the second. However, you may be losing information since the magnitude of each difference is ignored.

To request the sign test, use **Stats➠Nonparametric Tests➠Sign** and select *LIFEEXPF* and *LIFEEXPM*. With commands:

```
NPAR
    USE ourworld
    SIGN lifeexpf lifeexpm
```

```
Sign test results

  Counts of differences (row variable greater than column)

                    LIFEEXPM      LIFEEXPF

  LIFEEXPM                 0            2
  LIFEEXPF                55            0

  Two-sided probabilities for each pair of variables

                    LIFEEXPM      LIFEEXPF

  LIFEEXPM              1.000
  LIFEEXPF              0.000         1.000
```

For each case, SYSTAT first reports the number of differences that were positive and the number that were negative. In two countries (Afghanistan and Bangladesh), the males live longer than the females; the reverse is true for the other 55 countries. Note that the layout of this output allows reports for many pairs of variables (see below).

In the *Two-sided probabilities* panel, the smaller count of differences (positive or negative) is compared to the total number of non-zero differences. Nonparametric Tests computes a sign test on all possible pairs of specified variables. For each pair, the difference between values on each case is calculated, and the number of positive and negative differences is printed. The lesser of the two types of difference (positive or negative) is then compared to the total number of non-zero differences. From this comparison, the probability is computed according to the binomial (for a total less than or equal to 25) or a normal approximation to the binomial (for a total greater than 25). A correction for continuity (0.5) is added to the normal approximation's numerator, and the denominator is computed from the null value of 0.5. The large sample test is thus equivalent to a chi-square test for an underlying proportion of 0.5. The probability for our test is 0.000 (or < 0.0005). We conclude that there is a significant difference in life expectancy; females tend to live longer.

Wilcoxon signed-rank test	The Wilcoxon signed-rank test also uses the differences but incorporates information about the magnitude of each difference.

Select **Stats**➠**Nonparametric Tests**➠**Wilcoxon** and specify *LIFEEXPF* and *LIFEEXPM*. With commands:

```
NPAR
    USE ourworld
    WILCOXON lifeexpf lifeexpm
```

```
Wilcoxon Signed Ranks Test Results

  Counts of differences (row variable greater than column)

                   LIFEEXPM     LIFEEXPF

  LIFEEXPM               0            2
  LIFEEXPF              55            0


  Z = (Sum of signed ranks)/square root(sum of squared ranks)

                   LIFEEXPM     LIFEEXPF

  LIFEEXPM            0.000
  LIFEEXPF            6.535        0.000


  Two-sided probabilities using normal approximation

                   LIFEEXPM     LIFEEXPF

  LIFEEXPM            1.000
  LIFEEXPF            0.000        1.000
```

The *Counts of differences* reported with **Sign** are also reported with **Wilcoxon**. In the Wilcoxon test, the absolute values of all non-zero differences are ranked. For ties, the average rank is assigned. The sum of the ranks associated with positive differences and the sum of ranks associated with negative differences are then computed. The test statistic is the lesser of these two sums. Two-tail probabilities are computed from an approximate normal variate (Z in the output) constructed from this statistic (for example, Marascuilo & McSweeney, 1977, p. 338). The Z for our test is 6.535 with a probability less than 0.0005. As with the sign test, we conclude that females tend to live longer.

Multiple variables	SYSTAT can compute a sign or Wilcoxon test on all pairs of specified variables (or all numeric variables in your file). To illustrate the layout of the output, we add two more variables to our last request for a sign test: the birth-to-death ratios in 1982 and 1990.

Use **Stats**➠**Nonparametric Tests**➠**Sign**➠**Variable(s)** to select *B_TO_D82*, *B_TO_D*, *LIFEEXPM*, and *LIFEEXPF*. With commands:

```
NPAR
   USE ourworld
   SIGN b_to_d82 b_to_d lifeexpm lifeexpf
```

```
Sign test results

   Counts of differences (row variable greater than column)

                    B_TO_D82     LIFEEXPM     LIFEEXPF     B_TO_D

   B_TO_D82               0            0            0          17
   LIFEEXPM              57            0            2          57
   LIFEEXPF              57           55            0          57
   B_TO_D                36            0            0           0

   Two-sided probabilities for each pair of variables

                    B_TO_D82     LIFEEXPM     LIFEEXPF     B_TO_D

   B_TO_D82           1.000
   LIFEEXPM           0.000        1.000
   LIFEEXPF           0.000        0.000        1.000
   B_TO_D             0.013        0.000        0.000        1.000
```

The results contain some meaningless data. SYSTAT has ordered the variables as they appear in the data file. When you specify more than two variables, there may be just a few numbers of interest. In the first column, the birth-to-death ratio in 1982 is compared with the birth-to-death ratio in 1990—and with "male and female life expectancy!" Only the last entry is relevant—36 countries have larger ratios in 1990 than they did in 1982. In the last column, you see that 17 countries have smaller ratios in 1990. The life expectancy comparisons you saw in the last example are in the middle of this table. In the *Two-sided probabilities* panel, the probability for the birth-to-death ratio comparison (0.013) is at the bottom of the first column. We conclude that the ratio is significantly larger in 1990 than it was in 1982. Does this mean that the number of births is increasing or that the number of deaths is decreasing?

7.5 Friedman Test

This example is a nonparametric extension of the paired *t* test where, instead of two measures, each subject has *n* measures (*n* > 2). Or, in other terms, it is a nonparametric analog of a repeated measures analyses of variance with one group. We use the Friedman test. It is often used for analyzing rankings of three or more objects by multiple judges. That is, there is one case for each judge and the variables are the judges ratings of several types of wine, consumer products, or even how a set of mothers relate to their children. The Friedman statistic is used to test the hypothesis that there is no systematic response or pattern across the variables (ratings).

Instead of ratings, we study dollars that each country spends per person for education, health, and the military. We ask, "Do the typical values for the three expenditures differ significantly?" We stratify our analysis and look within each type of country separately. Here are the median expenditures:

	EDUCATN	HEALTH	MILITARY
Europe	$496.28	502.01	271.15
Islamic	13.67	4.28	22.80
NewWorld	57.39	22.73	29.02

To group the analysis by type of country, use **Data**➠**By Groups** and select *GROUP$*. To request the Friedman test, use **Stats**➠**Nonparametric Tests**➠**Friedman** and select *EDUC*, *HEALTH*, and *MIL* under **Variable(s)**. With commands:

```
NPAR
   USE ourworld
   BY group$
   FRIEDMAN educ health mil
```

❶
```
The following results are for:

   GROUP$      = Europe


Friedman Two-Way Analysis of Variance Results for 20 cases.


   Variable         Rank Sum

   EDUC                43.000
   HEALTH              52.000
   MIL                 25.000


Friedman Test Statistic =       18.900
Kendall Coefficient of Concordance =        0.472
Probability is        0.000 assuming Chi-square distribution with 2 DF
The following results are for:

   GROUP$      = Islamic
```

❷
```
Friedman Two-Way Analysis of Variance Results for 15 cases.


   Variable         Rank Sum

   EDUC                37.500
   HEALTH              17.000
   MIL                 35.500


Friedman Test Statistic =       17.033
Kendall Coefficient of Concordance =        0.568
Probability is        0.000 assuming Chi-square distribution with 2 DF
The following results are for:

   GROUP$      = NewWorld
```

❸ Friedman Two-Way Analysis of Variance Results for 21 cases.

Variable	Rank Sum
EDUC	56.000
HEALTH	31.500
MIL	38.500

Friedman Test Statistic =   15.167
Kendall Coefficient of Concordance =   0.361
Probability is   0.001 assuming Chi-square distribution with 2 DF

The highlighted numbers below correspond to those in the output:

❶ Results for the 20 European countries. The **Friedman test** transforms the data for each country to ranks ("1" for the smallest value, "2" for the next, and "3" for the largest) and then sums the ranks for each variable. Thus, if each country spent the least on the military, the *Rank Sum* for *MIL* would be 20. The largest the *Rank Sum* could be is 60 (20×3). Here, no expenditure is always the smallest or largest. But still we reject that the expenditures are equal (Friedman statistic = 18.90, p value < 0.0005). The **Kendall coefficient of concordance** is an estimate of the average correlation among the expenditures.

❷ For the 15 Islamic countries, we reject the hypothesis that the three expenditures are equal (17.03, p value < 0.0005).

❸ For the 21 New World countries, we find a significant difference in the pattern of expenditures (15.17, p value = 0.001).

One-Sample Tests

For studying the distribution of a single variable, **Stats**➠**Nonparametric Tests** offers the Kolmogorov-Smirnov one-sample test and the Wald-Wolfowitz runs procedure. For the former, the sample cumulative distribution is compared to that of a specific distribution. Use the runs test to detect serial patterns in a run of numbers.

For the one-sample Kolmogorov-Smirnov test, use **Stats**➠ **Nonparametric Tests**➠**One sample KS:**

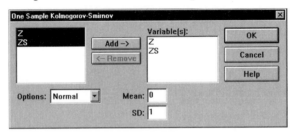

For the Wald-Wolfowitz runs test, use **Stats**➠**Nonparametric Tests**➠**Wald-Wolfowitz Runs:**

7.6 Kolmogorov-Smirnov one-sample test

The Kolmogorov-Smirnov one-sample test is used to compare the shape and location of a sample distribution.

| Uniform | Exp | Normal | Logistic | t | Range | F |
| Weibull | ChiSq | Binomial | Gamma | Poisson | Beta | |

You can specify parameters for these distributions.

The Kolmogorov-Smirnov test and its generalizations are among the handiest of distribution free tests. The test statistic is based on the maximum difference between two cumulative distribution functions. In the one-sample test, one of the CDF's is continuous and the other is discrete. Thus, it is a companion test to a probability plot. SYSTAT also provides **Lilliefors**. This test automatically standardizes the variables you select and tests whether the standardized versions are normally distributed.

As an example, we use SYSTAT's random number generator to make a normally distributed random number and then test it for normality. We use the variable Z as our normal random number and the variable ZS as a standardized copy of Z. This may seem strange because normal random numbers are expected to have a mean of 0 and a standard deviation of 1. This is not exactly true in a sample, however, so we standardize the observed values to make a variable that has exactly a mean of 0 and a standard deviation of 1.

With commands:

```
BASIC
   NEW
   REPEAT 50
   LET z=zrn
   LET zs=z
   RUN
   SAVE NORM
   STAND ZS/SD
```

Next, we use **Stats▸Descriptive Statistics▸Basic Statistics** to see the mean and standard deviation of our two variables. Remember, if you correlated these two variables with **Stats▸Correlations**, the Pearson correlation would be 1. Only their mean and standard deviations differ. Here are the results:

```
Total Observations:    50

                           Z           ZS

   N of cases             50           50
   Minimum            -2.194       -2.271
   Maximum             1.832        1.932
   Mean               -0.018        0.000
   Standard Dev        0.958        1.000
```

Finally, we test Z for normality with **Nonparametric Tests**. We use the *NORM* data file. Use **Stats▸Nonparametric Tests▸One sample KS**. Select Z and ZS as variables, select **Normal** under **Options**, and specify 0 as the mean and 1 as the standard deviation.

With commands:

```
NPAR
    USE norm
    KS z zs / NORMAL
```

```
Kolmogorov-Smirnov One Sample Test using Normal(0.00,1.00) distribution
    Variable      N-of-Cases      MaxDif  Probability (2-tail)
       Z              50            .069         .969
       ZS             50            .065         .983
```

Why are the probabilities different? The Kolmogorov-Smirnov one-sample test pays attention to the shape, location, and scale of the sample distribution. *Z* and *ZS* have the same shape in the population (they are both normal). Because *ZS* has been standardized, however, it has a different location.

Thus, you should never use the Kolmogorov-Smirnov test with the normal distribution on a variable you have standardized. The probability printed for *ZS* (0.983) is misleading. If you select **ChiSq**, **Normal**, or **Uniform**, you are assuming that the variable you are testing has been randomly sampled from a standard normal, uniform (0 to 1), or chi-square (with stated degrees of freedom) population.

Lilliefors test

Here we perform a Lilliefors test. Note that **Lilliefors** automatically standardizes the variables you list and tests whether the standardized versions are normally distributed. Select **Lilliefors** under **Options**. With commands:

```
    KS z zs / LILLIEFORS
```

```
Kolmogorov-Smirnov One Sample Test using Normal(0.00,1.00) distribution
    Variable      N-of-Cases      MaxDif  Lilliefors Probability (2-tail)
       Z              50            .065         .895
       ZS             50            .065         .895
```

Notice the probabilities are smaller this time even though *Maxdif* is the same as before. The probability values for *Z* and *ZS* (0.895) are the same because this test pays attention only to the shape of the distribution and not to the location or scale. Neither significantly differs from normal.

This example was constructed to contrast **Normal** and **Lilliefors**. Many statistical package users do a Kolmogorov-Smirnov test for normality on their standardized data without realizing that they should instead do a Lilliefors test.

One last point: The Lilliefors test can be used for residual analysis in regression. Just standardize your residuals and use **Nonparametric Tests** to test them for normality. If you do this, you should always look at the corresponding normal probability plot.

7.7
Wald-
Wolfowitz
runs test

The Wald-Wolfowitz runs test detects serial patterns in a run of numbers. For example, you toss a coin 20 times and find four runs of heads or tails:

HTHHHHHHHHHHTTTTTTTTTT

The runs test measures such behavior for dichotomous (or binary) variables. For continuous variables, use **Stats**➡**Nonparametric Tests**➡**Wald-Wolfowitz Runs** and **Cut** to define a cutpoint to see whether values fluctuate in patterns above and below this cutpoint. This feature is useful for studying trends in residuals from a regression analysis.

We use the *OURWORLD* file. We cut *MIL* (dollars per person each country spends on the military) at its median (you can use the **Stats**➡**Descriptive Statistics**➡**Basic Statistics** procedure to find the median) and see whether countries with higher military expenditures are grouped together in the file. Select **Stats**➡**Nonparametric Tests**➡**Wald-Wolfowitz Runs** and select MIL. Enter 53.889 as the **Cut**. With commands:

```
NPAR
    USE ourworld
    RUNS mil / CUT=53.889
```

Wald-Wolfowitz runs test using cutpoint =		53.889			
Variable	Cases LE Cut	Cases GT Cut	Runs	Z	Probability (2-tail)
MIL	28	28	17	-3.237	0.001

The test is significant (p value = 0.001). The military expenditures are not ordered randomly in the file.

Here is a scatterplot of the military expenditures against the case number (order of each country in the file). Use **Graph**➡**Scatterplot** to create a scatterplot. We add a dotted line at the cutpoint of 53.889. The European countries are first in the file, followed by Islamic and New World. Iraq, Libya, and Canada stand apart from the other countries in their group.

With commands:

```
IF (country$='Iraq' or country$='Libya' or,
    country$='Canada') THEN LET country2$=country$
PLOT mil / LINE DASH=11 YLIM=53.9 LABEL=country2$
```

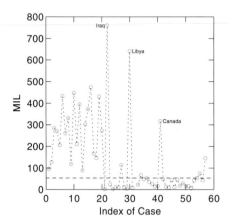

Be careful when you use a cutpoint on a continuous variable, however. Your conclusions can change depending on the cutpoint you use. Remember some of the warnings cited above about using nonparametrics on continuous data. They are no panacea.

Summary

Computation

Probabilities for the Kolmogorov-Smirnov statistic for $n < 25$ are computed with an asymptotic negative exponential approximation.

Lilliefors probabilities are computed by a nonlinear approximation to Lilliefors' table. Dallal and Wilkinson (1986) recomputed Lilliefors' study using up to a million replications for estimating critical values. They found a number of Lilliefors' value to be incorrect. Consequently, the SYSTAT approximation uses the corrected values. The approximation discussed in Dallal and Wilkinson and used in SYSTAT differs from the tabled values by less than 0.01 and by less than 0.001 for $p < 0.05$.

References

Conover, W.J. 1980. *Practical nonparametric statistics*. 2nd ed. New York: John Wiley & Sons, Inc.

Hollander, M., and Wolfe, D.A. 1973. *Nonparametric statistical methods*. New York: John Wiley & Sons, Inc.

Lehmann, E.L. 1975. *Nonparametrics*. San Francisco: Holden-Day, Inc.

Marascuilo, L.A., and McSweeney, M. 1977. *Nonparametric and distribution-free methods for the social sciences*. Belmont, Calif.: Wadsworth Publishing.

Mosteller, F., and Rourke, R.E.K. 1973. *Sturdy statistics*. Reading, Mass.: Addison-Wesley.

Siegel, S. 1956. *Nonparametric statistics for the behavioral sciences*. New York: McGraw-Hill.

8

Linear Regression

Leland Wilkinson and Mark Coward

Linear Regression and General Linear Model (GLM) estimate and test simple and multiple linear regression models. The model for *simple* linear regression is

$$y = \beta_0 + \beta_1 x_1 + \varepsilon$$

where y is the *dependent* variable, x is the *independent* variable, β_0 is the intercept, and β_1 is the slope of the line of best fit. The model for *multiple* linear regression is

$$y = \beta_0 + \beta_1 x_1 + \beta_2 x_2 + ... + \beta_p x_p + \varepsilon$$

Variations of this model include mixture models (constraining the independent variables to sum to a constant), polynomial regression, and stepwise regression (choosing a subset of predictors from among many candidates). For the latter, you can direct SYSTAT *interactively*, specifying which variable to enter or remove at each step, or let SYSTAT automatically select variables. For mixture models and polynomial regression, use **General Linear Model**. Stepwise procedures are available in both Linear Regression and General Linear Model.

Once the parameters of a model (β_i) have been estimated, you can use **General Linear Model** to test that a coefficient (or a set of coefficients) is 0 or to test that a coefficient equals a hypothesized value.

For each model you fit, SYSTAT reports R^2, adjusted R^2, the standard error of the estimate, and an ANOVA table for assessing the fit of the model. For each variable in the model, the output includes the estimate of the regression coefficient, the standard error of the coefficient and standardized coefficient, tolerance, and an F statistic for measuring the usefulness of the variable in the model.

You can store results of the analysis (predicted values, residuals, and diagnostics that identify unusual cases) for further use in examining assumptions. Input can be the usual cases-by-variables, covariance, correlation, or sum of squares and cross-products matrix.

Linear Regression

Overview

The **Stats** menu contains two procedures for regression. The first, **Linear Regression**, is for simple regression, multiple regression, and stepwise regression models. The second, **General Linear Model**, is for more general regression models with interactions and/or dummy variables.

Linear Regression is easier to use than General Linear Model when you are doing simple regression, multiple regression, or stepwise regression because it has fewer options. To include interaction terms in your model or for mixture models, use General Linear Model. With Linear Regression, all independent variables must be continuous; in General Linear Model, you can identify categorical independent variables and SYSTAT will generate a set of design variables for each. Both General Linear Model and Linear Regression allow you to save residuals.

The ability to do stepwise regression is available with both Linear Regression and General Linear Model. You can do this in one of three ways: use the default values, specify your own selection criteria, or at each step, interactively select a variable to add or remove from the model.

In this documentation and command interface, the Linear Regression and General Linear Model features (and also those for ANOVA) are part of a larger procedure called MGLH (multivariate general linear hypothesis) in previous SYSTAT releases.

Getting started   To request a regression analysis, use **Stats**➡**Linear Regression**.

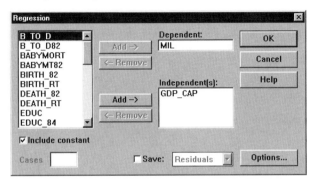

If you want to save residuals and other results from fitting your model, select **Save** in the **Linear Regression** dialog box.

For stepwise model building, click **Options**, select **Stepwise** in the **Options** dialog box, and select the stepwise criteria you want to use. For *automatic stepping*, continue by selecting **Automatic**. For *interactive stepping*, select **Interactive**.

Simple Linear Regression

You should read this section sequentially because the models are presented in order of increasing complexity. Information on interpreting a given part of the output is presented with the first example that generates it.

**8.1
Simple linear
regression**

As our first example, we explore the relation between gross domestic product per capita (*GDP_CAP*) and spending on the military (*MIL*) for 57 countries that report this information to the United Nations—we want to see if a measure of the financial well being of a country is useful for predicting its military expenditures. Our model is:

$$\text{military spending} = \beta_0 + \beta_1 \, \text{gdp\_cap} + \varepsilon$$

We use **Scatterplot** on the **Graph** menu to look at the data:

```
USE ourworld
    PLOT mil * gdp_cap / SMOOTH=LOWESS LABLE=name$,
                         YLAB="Military Spending"
```

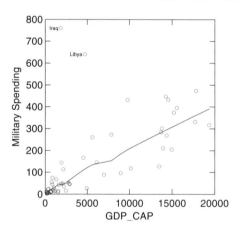

To obtain this scatterplot, we created a new variable, *NAME$*, that had missing values for all countries except Libya and Iraq. We then used the new variable to label plot points. For more information about scatterplots, see *SYSTAT: Graphics.*

Iraq and Libya stand apart from the other countries—they spend considerably more for the military than countries with similar *GDP_CAP* values. The smoother indicates that the relationship between the two variables is fairly linear. Distressing, however, is the fact that many points clump in the lower left corner. Many data analysts would want to study the data after log transforming both variables. We do this in Example 8.2, but now we estimate the coefficients for the data as recorded.

After reading the *OURWORLD* data file, use **Stats**➠**Linear Regression** and then select *MIL* as the **Dependent** variable and *GDP_CAP* as the **Independent** variable. With commands:

```
REGRESS
    USE ourworld
    MODEL mil = CONSTANT + gdp_cap
    ESTIMATE
```

❶
```
1 case(s) deleted due to missing data.

Dep Var: MIL   N: 56   Multiple R: 0.646   Squared multiple R: 0.417

Adjusted squared multiple R: 0.407   Standard error of estimate: 136.154

Effect        Coefficient    Std Error    Std Coef Tolerance    t    P(2 Tail)
```
❷
```
CONSTANT         41.857       24.838        0.0        .       1.685   0.098
GDP_CAP           0.019        0.003        0.646    1.000     6.220   0.000


                       Analysis of Variance

Source          Sum-of-Squares   DF  Mean-Square    F-Ratio       P
```
❸
```
Regression        717100.891     1   717100.891     38.683      0.000

Residual         1001045.288    54    18537.876
- - - - - - - - - - - - - - - - - - - - - - - - - - - - - - - - - - - - - - - -

***WARNING***
Case      22 is an outlier        (Studentized Residual =        6.956)
Case      30 is an outlier        (Studentized Residual =        4.348)
```

The highlighted numbers below correspond to those in the output:

❶ SYSTAT reports that data are missing for one case. In the next line, it reports that 56 cases are used ($N = 56$). In the regression calculations, SYSTAT uses only the cases that have complete data for the variables in the model. However, when only the dependent variable is missing, SYSTAT computes a predicted value, its standard error, and a leverage diagnostic for the case. In this sample, Afghanistan did not report military spending.

When there is only one independent variable, *Multiple R* (0.646) is the simple correlation between *MIL* and *GDP_CAP*. *Squared multiple R*

(0.417) is the square of this value, and it is the proportion of the total variation in the military expenditures accounted for by *GDP_CAP* (*GDP_CAP* explains 41.7% of the variability of *MIL*). Use the *Sum-of-Squares* in the *Analysis of Variance* table to compute it:

$$\frac{717100.891}{717100.891 + 1001045.288}$$

Adjusted squared multiple R is of interest for models with more than one independent variable, so we explain it in Example 8.4. The *Standard error of estimate* (136.154) is the square root of the residual mean square (18537.876) in the ANOVA table.

❷ The estimates of the regression coefficients are 41.857 and 0.019, so the equation is:

mil = 41.857 + 0.019 * gdp_cap

The **Standard Errors** (*Std Error*) of the estimated coefficients are in the next column and the **Standardized Coefficients** (*Std Coef*) follow. The latter are called **beta weights** by some social scientists. *Tolerance* is not relevant when there is only one predictor, so we define it in the multiple linear regression example below.

Next are *t* statistics (*t*)—the first (1.685) tests the significance of the difference of the constant from 0 and the second (6.220) tests the significance of the slope, which is equivalent to testing the significance of the correlation between military spending and *GDP_CAP*.

❸ The *F-Ratio* in the *Analysis of Variance* table is used to test the hypothesis that the slope (β_1) is 0 (or, for multiple regression, that $\beta_1, \ldots \beta_p = 0$). The *F* is large when the independent variable(s) helps to explain the variation in the dependent variable. Here, there is a significant linear relation between military spending and *GDP_CAP*. Thus, we reject the hypothesis that the slope of the regression line is zero (*F-Ratio* = 38.683, *p* value (*P*) < 0.0005).

How good is the fit? It appears from the results above that *GDP_CAP* is useful for predicting spending on the military—that is, countries that are financially sound tend to spend more on the military than poorer nations. These numbers, however, do not provide the complete picture. Notice that SYSTAT warns us that two countries (Iraq and Libya) with unusual values could be distorting the results. We recommend that you use **Save**

to save the residuals and other diagnostic statistics (see Example 8.3). But first, we want to explore the effect of log transforming the variables.

Regression without the constant

You can delete the constant from your regression (that is, regression through the origin) by deselecting **Include constant** in the **Linear Regression** dialog box. You almost never want to remove the constant and you should be familiar with no-constant regression terminology before considering it.

Cross-validation

If you identify a weight variable (which has 0 or 1 for each case) by using **Data➠Weight** before computing a model, SYSTAT computes predicted values for cases with zero weight, even though they are not included in the cases used to compute the regression equation.

8.2 Transforming the data

The data in the scatterplot in Example 8.1 are not well suited for linear regression, as the heavy concentration of points in the lower left corner of the graph shows. Here are the same data plotted in log units:

```
REGRESS
    USE ourworld
    PLOT mil * gdp_cap / SMOOTH=LOWESS,
           LABEL=country$,
           XLAB='GDP per capita',
           YLAB='Military Spending',
           XLOG  YLOG
```

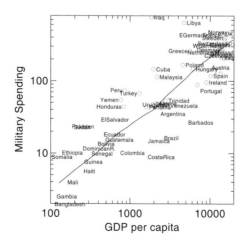

Except possibly for Iraq and Libya, the configuration of these points is better for linear modeling than that in Example 8.1.

We now transform both the y and x variables and refit the model. The revised model is:

$$\text{log\_mil} = \beta_0 + \beta_1 \, \text{log\_gdp} + \varepsilon$$

Specify the transformations under **Data➠Transform** and then specify the model as in Example 8.1. With commands:

```
REGRESS
    USE ourworld
    LET log_mil = L10(mil)
    LET log_gdp = L10(gdp_cap)
    MODEL log_mil =  CONSTANT + log_gdp
    ESTIMATE
```

```
 1 case(s) deleted due to missing data.

 Dep Var: LOG_MIL    N: 56    Multiple R: 0.857    Squared multiple R: 0.734

 Adjusted squared multiple R: 0.729    Standard error of estimate: 0.346

 Effect           Coefficient    Std Error    Std Coef Tolerance    t    P(2 Tail)

 CONSTANT           -1.308          0.257         0.0         .     -5.091    0.000
 LOG_GDP             0.909          0.075         0.857     1.000   12.201    0.000

                           Analysis of Variance

 Source          Sum-of-Squares   DF  Mean-Square    F-Ratio       P

 Regression           17.868       1     17.868      148.876     0.000
 Residual              6.481      54      0.120

 ***WARNING***
 Case        22 is an outlier        (Studentized Residual =        4.004)
 Durbin-Watson D Statistic     1.810
 First Order Autocorrelation   0.070
```

The *Squared multiple R* for the variables in log units is 0.734 (versus 0.417 for the untransformed values). That is, we have gone from explaining 41.7% of the variability of military spending to 73.4% by using the log transformations. The *F* ratio is now 148.876—it was 38.683. Notice that we now have only one outlier (Iraq).

The calculator

But what *is* the estimated model now?

$$\text{log\_mil} = -1.308 + 0.909 * \text{log\_gdp}$$

However, many people don't think in "log units." Let's transform this equation (exponentiate each side of the equation):

$$10^{\text{log\_mil}} = 10^{(-1.308 + 0.909 * \text{log\_gdp})}$$

$$mil = 10^{\beta_0 + \beta_1 \log x}$$

$$mil = 10^{\beta_0} \times x^{\beta_1}$$

military spending = 0.049 gdp$^{0.909}$

We used the calculator to compute 0.049. Type:

CALC 10^-1.308

and SYSTAT returns 0.049.

Comparing models graphically

Let's overlay the fits for the transformed data (dashed line) and the untransformed values (solid line) on a scatterplot of the data.

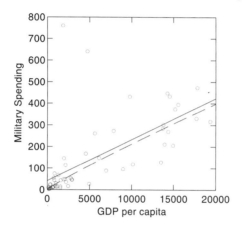

The dashed line is the line of best fit for the untransformed values, and the solid line is the fit for the log-transformed variables.

8.3 Saving residuals and diagnostics

SYSTAT can save the following results from the regression analysis:

Residuals	Predicted values, residuals, Studentized residuals, leverage for each observation, Cook's distance measure, and the standard error of predicted values. Definitions follow.
Partial	Partial residuals. Definitions follow.
Model	The variables in the model are added to the statistics listed under **Residuals**.
Coefficients	Estimates of the regression coefficients.

Residuals

When you select **Residuals**, the saved file contains three variables with the following labels:

ESTIMATE   Estimated (predicted) values
RESIDUAL   Residuals
LEVERAGE   Leverage for each observation

If the model has only one dependent variable, three additional variables are saved:

STUDENT   Studentized residuals
COOK   Cook's D values
SEPRED   Standard error of predicted values

In this example, we continue with Example 8.2 and save the residuals and diagnostics along with the data. After selecting the dependent and independent variables, select **Save** and select **Residual/Data** from the drop-down list. When you click **OK** to run the procedure, SYSTAT will prompt you to enter a filename. Type the filename *MYRESULT*. With commands, type:

```
SAVE myresult / DATA  RESID
```

before **ESTIMATE**. The results are stored in the file *MYRESULT*.

In the definitions that follow, we say more about the diagnostics and the Durbin-Watson D statistic.

Studentized residuals. The Studentized residuals are the true "external" kind discussed in Velleman and Welsch (1981). Use these statistics to identify outliers in the dependent variable space. Under normal regression assumptions, they have a t distribution with $(N - p - 1)$ degrees of freedom, where N is the total sample size and p is the number of predictors (including the constant). Here are stem-and-leaf plots of the residuals and Studentized residuals:

```
STATS
   USE myresult
   STEM residual student
```

```
Stem and Leaf Plot of variable:              Stem and Leaf Plot of
RESIDUAL, N = 56                             variable:     STUDENT, N = 56
         Minimum:        -0.644                       Minimum:        -1.923
         Lower hinge:    -0.246                        Lower hinge:     -0.719
         Median:         -0.031                        Median:         -0.091
         Upper hinge:     0.203                         Upper hinge:     0.591
         Maximum:         1.216                         Maximum:         4.004

         -6   42                                        -1   986
         -5   6                                         -1   32000
         -4   42                                        -0 H 88877766555
         -3   554000                                    -0 M 443322111000
         -2 H 65531                                       0   000022344
         -1   9876433                                     0 H 555889999
         -0 M 98433200                                    1   0223
          0   222379                                      1   5
          1   1558                                        2   3
          2 H 009                              * * * Outside Values * * *
          3   0113369                                     4   0
          4   27
          5   1                                 1 cases with missing values
          6                                     excluded from plot.
          7   7
    * * * Outside Values * * *
         12   1

 1 cases with missing values
 excluded from plot.
```

Iraq's residual is 1.216 and is identified as an *Outside Value*. The value of its Studentized residual is 4.004, which is very extreme for the *t* distribution.

Other diagnostics. Leverage is discussed in Belsley, Kuh, and Welsch (1980) and Velleman and Welsch (1981). Leverage helps to identify outliers in the independent variable space. Leverage has an average value of p/N, where p is the number of estimated parameters (including the constant) and N is the number of cases. What is a high value of leverage? In practice, it is useful to examine the values in a stem-and-leaf plot and identify those that stand apart from the rest of the sample. However, various rules of thumb have been suggested. For example, values of leverage less than 0.2 appear to be safe; between 0.2 and 0.5, risky; and above 0.5, to be avoided. Another says that if $p > 6$ and $(N - p) > 12$, use $3p/N$ as a cutoff. SYSTAT uses an F approximation to determine this value for warnings (Belsley, Kuh, and Welsch, 1980).

Cook (1977) discusses the Cook statistic. Cook represents the influence of an observation on the estimates of the regression coefficients. Its formula combines leverage and Studentized residuals. As a rule of thumb, under the normal regression assumptions, Cook can be compared to an F distribution with p and $N - p$ degrees of freedom.

A graphical look at diagnostics

Let's plot the Studentized residuals (to identify outliers in the y-space) against leverage (to identify outliers in the x-space) and use Cook's distance measure to scale the size of each plot symbol. In a second plot, we display the corresponding country names. Use the data file *MYRESULT*, created earlier in this example.

```
USE myresult
PLOT student * leverage / SIZE=cook
PLOT student * leverage / LABEL=country
```

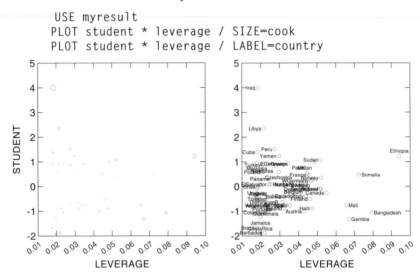

The case with the most influence on the estimates of the regression coefficients stands out at the top left (that is, it has the largest plot symbol). From the plot on the right, we identify this country as Iraq. Its value of Cook's distance measure is large because its Studentized residual is extreme. On the other hand, Ethiopia (furthest to the right), the case with the next most influence, has a large value of Cook's distance because its value of leverage is large. Gambia has the third largest Cook value, and Libya, the fourth.

Partial residuals

Partial residuals allows you to save partial residuals:

```
MODEL Y = CONSTANT + X1 + X2 + X3
```

The saved file contains the following:

YPARTIAL(1): residual of *Y*	=	*CONSTANT + X2 + X3*
XPARTIAL(1): residual of *X1*	=	*CONSTANT + X2 + X3*
YPARTIAL(2): residual of *Y*	=	*CONSTANT + X1 + X3*
XPARTIAL(2): residual of *X2*	=	*CONSTANT + X1 + X3*
YPARTIAL(3): residual of *Y*	=	*CONSTANT + X1 + X2*
XPARTIAL(3): residual of *X3*	=	*CONSTANT + X1 + X2*

The three correlations between the respective *YPARTIAL(i)* and *XPARTIAL(i)* variables are in fact partial correlations, and correspond to the *F* statistic for the variables included in the model.

Durbin-Watson statistic

When you select **Save**, the first-order autocorrelation and Durbin-Watson statistic are added to the output. To compute additional autocorrelations or partial autocorrelations, select **Stats⟹Time Series⟹ACF** or **Stats⟹Time Series⟹PACF**.

Deleting an outlier

In the plots above, we identified Iraq as the case with the greatest influence on the estimates of the regression coefficients. Let's remove it from the regression analysis and check SYSTAT's warnings.

continuing from Example 8.2

```
SELECT mil < 700
MODEL log_mil = CONSTANT + log_gdp
SAVE junk / RESID
ESTIMATE
SELECT
```

```
Dep Var:     LOG_MIL N: 55 Multiple R: 0.886 Squared multiple R: 0.785

Adjusted squared multiple R:  0.781    Standard error of estimate:     0.306

Effect        Coefficient    Std Error    Std Coef Tolerance    t    P(2 Tail)

CONSTANT        -1.353         0.227        0.0        .      -5.949   0.000
LOG_GDP          0.916         0.066        0.886     1.000   13.896   0.000

                        Analysis of Variance

Source         Sum-of-Squares    DF    Mean-Square    F-Ratio      P

Regression          18.129        1       18.129      193.107    0.000
Residual             4.976       53        0.094


Durbin-Watson D Statistic     1.763
First Order Autocorrelation   0.086

Residuals have been saved.
```

Now there are no warnings about outliers.

Printing residuals and diagnostics

Let's use **List Cases** on the **Data** menu to look at some of the values in the *MYRESULT* file created in Example 8.3. We use the country name as the **ID Variable** for the listing.

```
USE myresult
IDVAR = country$
FORMAT 10 3
LIST cook  leverage  student  mil  gdp_cap
```

* Case ID *	COOK	LEVERAGE	STUDENT	MIL	GDP_CAP
Ireland	0.013	0.032	-0.891	95.833	8970.885
Austria	0.023	0.043	-1.011	127.237	13500.299
Belgium	0.000	0.044	-0.001	283.939	13724.502
Denmark	0.000	0.045	-0.119	269.608	14363.064
...					
Gambia	0.062	0.067	-1.328	2.500	229.913
Iraq	0.118	0.019	4.004	760.000	1863.509
...					
Libya	0.056	0.022	2.348	640.513	4738.055
Somalia	0.009	0.072	0.473	8.846	201.798
Afghanistan	.	0.075	.	.	189.128

The value of *MIL* for Afghanistan is missing, so Cook's distance measure and Studentized residuals are not available (periods are inserted for these values in the listing).

Multiple Linear Regression

8.4
Six independent variables

In this example, we build a multiple regression model to predict total employment using values of six independent variables. The data were originally used by Longley (1967) to test the robustness of least-squares packages to multicollinearity and other sources of ill-conditioning. SYSTAT can print the estimates of the regression coefficients with more "correct" digits than the solution provided by Longley himself if you select **Edit**➠**Options** and change the value for **Decimal places**. By default, the first three digits after the decimal are displayed. These data are also used in Example 8.5 to illustrate how to build a regression model in a stepwise manner.

DEFLATOR	GNP	UNEMPLOY	ARMFORCE	POPULATN	TIME	TOTAL
83.0	234289	2356	1590	107608	1947	60323
88.5	259426	2325	1456	108632	1948	61122
88.2	258054	3682	1616	109773	1949	60171
89.5	284599	3351	1650	110929	1950	61187
96.2	328975	2099	3099	112075	1951	63221
98.1	346999	1932	3594	113270	1952	63639
99.0	365385	1870	3547	115094	1953	64989
100.0	363112	3578	3350	116219	1954	63761
101.2	397469	2904	3048	117388	1955	66019
104.6	419180	2822	2857	118734	1956	67857
108.4	442769	2936	2798	120445	1957	68169
110.8	444546	4681	2637	121950	1958	66513
112.6	482704	3813	2552	123366	1959	68655
114.2	502601	3931	2514	125368	1960	69564
115.7	518173	4806	2572	127852	1961	69331
116.9	554894	4007	2827	130081	1962	70551

The model is:

$$\text{total} = \beta_0 + \beta_1 \text{ deflator} + \beta_2 \text{ gnp} + \beta_3 \text{ unemploy} +, \\ \beta_4 \text{ armforce} + \beta_5 \text{ population} + \beta_6 \text{ time}$$

Use **Stats**➠**Linear Regression** as described in Example 8.1 to specify the model (only now select six independent variables instead of one). With commands:

```
REGRESS
   USE longley
   MODEL total = CONSTANT + deflator + gnp + unemploy +,
             armforce + populatn + time
   ESTIMATE
```

```
Dep Var:        TOTAL N: 16 Multiple R: 0.998 Squared multiple R: 0.995

Adjusted squared multiple R:  0.992     Standard error of estimate:     304.854

Effect          Coefficient    Std Error    Std Coef  Tolerance     t   P(2 Tail)

CONSTANT      -3482258.635   890420.384        0.0        .       -3.911    0.004
DEFLATOR           15.062       84.915        0.046      0.007     0.177    0.863
GNP                -0.036        0.033       -1.014      0.001    -1.070    0.313
UNEMPLOY           -2.020        0.488       -0.538      0.030    -4.136    0.003
ARMFORCE           -1.033        0.214       -0.205      0.279    -4.822    0.001
POPULATN           -0.051        0.226       -0.101      0.003    -0.226    0.826
TIME             1829.151      455.478        2.480      0.001     4.016    0.003

                    Analysis of Variance

Source         Sum-of-Squares   DF  Mean-Square    F-Ratio       P

Regression        1.84172E+08    6  3.06954E+07    330.285     0.000
Residual           836424.056    9    92936.006
```

The *Adjusted squared multiple R* is 0.992. The formula for this statistic is:

$$\text{adjusted squared multiple R} = R^2 - \frac{(p-1)}{(n-p)} \times (1 - R^2)$$

where n is the number of cases and p is the number of predictors, including the constant.

Notice the extremely small tolerances in the output. **Tolerance** is 1 minus the multiple correlation between a predictor and the remaining predictors in the model. These tolerances signal that the predictor variables are highly intercorrelated—a worrisome situation. This *multicollinearity* can inflate the standard errors of the coefficients, thereby attenuating the associated F statistics, and can threaten computational accuracy.

After the output is displayed, you can use General Linear Model to test hypotheses involving linear combinations of regression coefficients.

Extended output

Extended regression output is available when you select **Edit**➠**Options** and set **Length** to **Long**. With commands, insert PRINT=LONG before ESTIMATE. This option inserts the following output between the regression coefficients and the analysis of variance table printed above:

```
Eigenvalues of unit scaled X'X
                        1          2          3          4          5
                      6.861      0.082      0.046      0.011      0.000

                        6          7
                      0.000      0.000

Condition indices

                        1          2          3          4          5
                      1.000      9.142     12.256     25.337    230.424

                        6          7
                   1048.080  43275.042

                        1          2          3          4          5
         CONSTANT     0.000      0.000      0.000      0.000      0.000
         DEFLATOR     0.000      0.000      0.000      0.000      0.457
         GNP          0.000      0.000      0.000      0.001      0.016
         UNEMPLOY     0.000      0.014      0.001      0.065      0.006
         ARMFORCE     0.000      0.092      0.064      0.427      0.115
         POPULATN     0.000      0.000      0.000      0.000      0.010
         TIME         0.000      0.000      0.000      0.000      0.000

                        6          7
         CONSTANT     0.000      1.000
         DEFLATOR     0.505      0.038
         GNP          0.328      0.655
         UNEMPLOY     0.225      0.689
         ARMFORCE     0.000      0.302
         POPULATN     0.831      0.160
         TIME         0.000      1.000

Correlation matrix of regression coefficients

                   CONSTANT   DEFLATOR    GNP       UNEMPLOY   ARMFORCE
         CONSTANT     1.000
         DEFLATOR    -0.205      1.000
         GNP          0.816     -0.649      1.000
         UNEMPLOY     0.836     -0.555      0.946      1.000
         ARMFORCE     0.550     -0.349      0.469      0.619      1.000
         POPULATN    -0.411      0.659     -0.833     -0.758     -0.189
         TIME        -1.000      0.186     -0.802     -0.824     -0.549

                   POPULATN    TIME
         POPULATN     1.000
         TIME         0.388      1.000
```

SYSTAT computes these statistics by scaling the columns of the X matrix so that the diagonal elements of $X'X$ are 1's and then factoring the $X'X$ matrix. In the Longley example, most of the eigenvalues of $X'X$ are nearly 0, showing that the predictor variables comprise a relatively redundant set. The *Condition indices* are the square roots of the ratios of the largest eigenvalue to each successive eigenvalue. A condition index greater than 15 indicates a possible problem, and an index greater than 30 suggests a serious problem with collinearity (Belsley, Kuh, and Welsh, 1980). The condition indices in the Longley example show a tremendous collinearity problem.

The *Variance Proportions* are the proportions of the variance of the estimates accounted for by each principal component associated with each of the above eigenvalues. You should begin to worry about collinearity when a component associated with a high condition index contributes substantially to the variance of two or more variables. This is certainly the case with the last component of the Longley data. *TIME*, *GNP*, and *UNEMPLOY* load highly on this component. See Belsley, Kuh, and Welsch (1980) for more information about these diagnostics.

Finally, SYSTAT gives the *Correlation matrix of regression coefficients*. In the Longley data, these estimates are highly correlated, further indicating that there are too many correlated predictors in the equation to provide stable estimates.

Saving residuals

As in Example 8.2, you should save the residuals and diagnostics. Plot the residuals against the independent variables and estimated values. In this example, the saved file contains the Longley variables, *ESTIMATE*, *RESIDUAL*, *LEVERAGE*, *STUDENT*, *COOK*, and *SEPRED*. However, before starting the regression analysis, you should have examined a scatterplot matrix of the Longley variables.

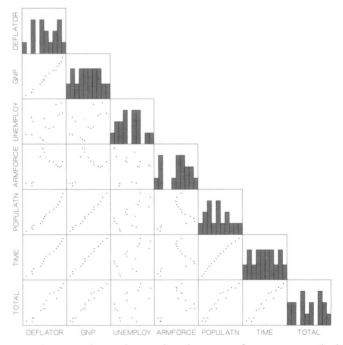

Notice the severely nonlinear distributions of *ARMFORCE* with the other variables, as well as the near perfect correlations among several of the predictors. There is also a sharp discontinuity between post-war and 1950's behavior on *ARMFORCE*.

8.5 Stepwise regression

In SYSTAT, multiple linear regression models can be fit in a stepwise manner (that is, variables can be entered into, or removed from, the model one at a time). Stepwise regression can be done in two ways:

- **By user intervention.** At each step, you select a variable to enter or remove.
- **Automatically.** At each step, SYSTAT selects a variable to enter or remove (see selection criteria below).

In this example, we illustrate both approaches. You can use Linear Regression or General Linear Model to request stepwise regression. Select **Stats➝Linear Regression➝Options** and select **Stepwise** in the **Linear Regression Options** dialog box. For stepwise regression, the following options are available:

Backward
: The default method. Begin with all candidate variables in the model. At each step, SYSTAT removes the variable with the largest Remove value.

Forward
: Begin with no variables in the model, and at each step, SYSTAT adds the variable with the smallest Enter value.

Automatic
: At each step, SYSTAT automatically removes (the default) or adds a variable to your model. Because backward stepwise regression is the default, you must include Forward with Automatic to perform automatic forward stepwise regression.

Interactive
: You interactively select the variable to move.

Probability
: Probability of F-to-enter limit and probability of F-to-remove limit. Default = 0.15.

F-statistic
: F-to-enter limit (default = 4.0) and F-to-remove limit (default = 3.9).

Force=n
: Force the first n variables into the model. Default = 0.

SYSTAT allows you to control the entry and deletion of variables at each step. This way, you can explore possibilities that the automatic stepwise procedure may miss. Using interactive stepwise regression will help convince you that there may be several candidate models in typical data whose performance is relatively indistinguishable from the automatically selected model. For the mechanics of how to enter or delete a variable, see "Interactive stepping" on p. 271.

Use **Forward** and **Backward** to select forward and backward stepping. Forward stepping begins with no variables in the equation, enters the most "significant" predictor at the first step, and continues adding and deleting variables until none can "significantly" improve the fit. Backward stepping begins with all candidate variables, removes the least "significant" predictor at the first step, and continues until no "insignificant" variables remain. The quotation marks are used deliberately, because tests of significance in stepwise regression cannot be derived from the usual F statistic printed in the output.

You can specify your own alpha-to-enter and alpha-to-remove values with **Enter** and **Remove**. Do not make alpha-to-remove less than alpha-to-enter, or you can cycle variables in and out of the equation (stepping automatically stops if this happens). The default values for these options are **Enter** = 0.15 and **Remove** = 0.15. These values are appropriate for predictor variables that are relatively independent. If your predictor variables are highly correlated, you should consider lowering the **Enter** and **Remove** values well below 0.05. You can also force the first n variables in your equation by specifying **Force** = n. For example, a value of 3 for **Force** will force the first three variables into the equation.

Tolerance prevents entry into the equation whose tolerance is below the specified value. When there are high correlations among the independent variables, the estimates of the regression coefficients can become unstable. Tolerance is a measure of this condition. It is $(1 - R^2)$, one minus the squared multiple correlation between a predictor and the other predictors included in the model. (Note that the dependent variable is not used.) By setting a minimum tolerance value, variables highly correlated with others already in the model are not allowed to enter.

See Example 8.5 for more information about these options.

Automatic
stepping

Here is an example of forward automatic stepping using the *LONGLEY* data. After selecting your variables, click **Options**, and select **Stepwise**, **Forward**, **Automatic**. With commands:

```
REGRESS
    USE longley
    MODEL total = CONSTANT + deflator + gnp + unemploy +,
                  armforce + populatn + time
    START / FORWARD
    STEP / AUTO
    STOP
```

❶ Step # 0 R = 0.000 R-Square = 0.000

Effect	Coefficient	Std Error	Std Coef	Tol.	DF	F	'p'
In							
‾1 Constant							
Out	Part. Corr.						
‾2 DEFLATOR	0.971	.	.	1.00000	1	230.089	0.000
3 GNP	0.984	.	.	1.00000	1	415.103	0.000
4 UNEMPLOY	0.502	.	.	1.00000	1	4.729	0.047
5 ARMFORCE	0.457	.	.	1.00000	1	3.702	0.075
6 POPULATN	0.960	.	.	1.00000	1	166.296	0.000
7 TIME	0.971	.	.	1.00000	1	233.704	0.000

❷ Step # 1 R = 0.984 R-Square = 0.967

Term entered: GNP

Effect	Coefficient	Std Error	Std Coef	Tol.	DF	F	'p'
In							
‾1 Constant							
3 GNP	0.035	0.002	0.984	1.00000	1	415.103	0.000
Out	Part. Corr.						
‾2 DEFLATOR	-0.187	.	.	0.01675	1	0.473	0.504
4 UNEMPLOY	-0.638	.	.	0.63487	1	8.925	0.010
5 ARMFORCE	0.113	.	.	0.80069	1	0.167	0.689
6 POPULATN	-0.598	.	.	0.01774	1	7.254	0.018
7 TIME	-0.432	.	.	0.00943	1	2.979	0.108

Step # 2 R = 0.990 R-Square = 0.981

Term entered: UNEMPLOY

Effect	Coefficient	Std Error	Std Coef	Tol.	DF	F	'p'
In							
‾1 Constant							
3 GNP	0.038	0.002	1.071	0.63487	1	489.314	0.000
4 UNEMPLOY	-0.544	0.182	-0.145	0.63487	1	8.925	0.010
Out	Part. Corr.						
‾2 DEFLATOR	-0.073	.	.	0.01603	1	0.064	0.805
❸ 5 ARMFORCE	-0.479	.	.	0.48571	1	3.580	0.083
6 POPULATN	-0.164	.	.	0.00563	1	0.334	0.574
7 TIME	0.308	.	.	0.00239	1	1.259	0.284

Step # 3 R = 0.993 R-Square = 0.985

Term entered: ARMFORCE

Effect	Coefficient	Std Error	Std Coef	Tol.	DF	F	'p'
In							
‾1 Constant							
3 GNP	0.041	0.002	1.154	0.31838	1	341.684	0.000
4 UNEMPLOY	-0.797	0.213	-0.212	0.38512	1	13.942	0.003
5 ARMFORCE	-0.483	0.255	-0.096	0.48571	1	3.580	0.083
Out	Part. Corr.						
2 DEFLATOR	0.163	.	.	0.01318	1	0.299	0.596
6 POPULATN	-0.376	.	.	0.00509	1	1.813	0.205
7 TIME	0.830	.	.	0.00157	1	24.314	0.000

❹ Step # 4 R = 0.998 R-Square = 0.995

Term entered: TIME

Effect	Coefficient	Std Error	Std Coef	Tol.	DF	F	'p'

```
 In
 ---
  1 Constant
  3 GNP            -0.040     0.016   -1.137 0.00194  1   5.953  0.033
  4 UNEMPLOY       -2.088     0.290   -0.556 0.07088  1  51.870  0.000
  5 ARMFORCE       -1.015     0.184   -0.201 0.31831  1  30.496  0.000
  7 TIME         1887.410   382.766    2.559 0.00157  1  24.314  0.000

 Out            Part. Corr.
 ---
  2 DEFLATOR        0.143      .        .    0.01305  1   0.208  0.658
  6 POPULATN       -0.150      .        .    0.00443  1   0.230  0.642
```

- Type **STOP**.

❺
```
Dep Var: TOTAL   N: 16   Multiple R: 0.998   Squared multiple R: 0.995

Adjusted squared multiple R: 0.994   Standard error of estimate: 279.396

Effect        Coefficient    Std Error    Std Coef Tolerance    t    P(2 Tail)

CONSTANT    -3598729.374   740632.644       0.0        .     -4.859   0.001
GNP               -0.040        0.016      -1.137    0.002    -2.440   0.033
UNEMPLOY          -2.088        0.290      -0.556    0.071    -7.202   0.000
ARMFORCE          -1.015        0.184      -0.201    0.318    -5.522   0.000
TIME            1887.410      382.766       2.559    0.002     4.931   0.000

                    Analysis of Variance

Source        Sum-of-Squares   DF   Mean-Square    F-Ratio      P

Regression      1.84150E+08     4   4.60375E+07    589.757    0.000
Residual         858680.406    11     78061.855
```

In four steps, SYSTAT entered four predictors. None was removed, resulting in a final equation with a constant and four predictors. Here's what we see along the way. The highlighted numbers below correspond to those in the output:

❶ Step 0. No variables are in the model. *GNP* has the largest simple correlation and *F*, so SYSTAT enters it at step 1. Note at this step that the **partial correlation**, *Part Corr*, is the simple correlation of each predictor with total.

❷ With *GNP* in the equation, *UNEMPLOY* is now the best candidate.

❸ The *F* for *ARMFORCE* is 3.58, when *GNP* and *UNEMPLOY* are included in the model.

❹ SYSTAT finishes by entering *TIME*.

❺ To get more information about this last model, type **STOP**. For this final model, SYSTAT uses all cases with complete data for *GNP*, *UNEMPLOY*, *ARMFORCE*, and *TIME*. Thus, when some values in the sample are missing, the sample size may be larger here than for the last step in the stepwise process (there, cases are omitted if any value is missing among the six candidate variables). If you don't want to stop here, you could move more variables in (or out) as described below.

Customized
stepping

You can adjust values for the automated procedure using **Enter**, **Remove**, **Force**, and **Tolerance**.

Discussion

If you are thinking of testing hypotheses after automatically fitting a subset model, don't bother. Stepwise regression programs are the most notorious source of pseudo "p values" in the field of automated data analysis. Statisticians seem to be the only ones who know these are not "real" p values. The automatic stepwise option is provided to select a subset model for prediction purposes. It should never be used without cross-validation.

If you still want some sort of confidence estimate on your subset model, you might look at tables in Wilkinson (1979), Rencher and Pun (1980), and Wilkinson and Dallal (1982). These tables provide null hypothesis R^2 values for selected subsets given the number of candidate predictors and final subset size. If you don't know this literature already, you will be surprised at how large multiple correlations from stepwise regressions on random data can be. For a general summary of these and other problems, see Hocking (1983). For more specific discussions of variable selection problems, see the previous references and Flack and Chang (1987), Freedman (1983), and Lovell (1983). Stepwise regression is probably the most abused computerized statistical technique ever devised. If you think you need automated stepwise regression to solve a particular problem, it is almost certain that you do not. Professional statisticians rarely use automated stepwise regression because it does not necessarily find the "best" fitting model, the "real" model, or alternative "plausible" models. Furthermore, the order in which variables enter or leave a stepwise program is usually of no theoretical significance. You are always better off thinking about why a model could generate your data and then testing that model.

Interactive
stepping

Interactive stepping helps you to explore model building in more detail. With data that are as highly intercorrelated as the *LONGLEY* data, interactive stepping reveals the dangers of thinking that the automated result is the only acceptable subset model. In this example, we use interactive stepping to explore the *LONGLEY* data further. That is, after specifying a model that includes all of the candidate variables available as above, we request backward stepping by selecting **Stepwise**, **Backward**, and **Interactive** in the **Linear Regression Options** dialog box. After reviewing the results at each step, we use **Step** to move a variable in (or out) of the model. When finished, we select **Stop** for final model. With commands:

```
START / BACK
```

We summarize the commands later. Here is the output with our actions:

```
Step # 0 R =  0.998 R-Square =  0.995

  Effect            Coefficient   Std Error  Std Coef   Tol.   DF      F      'P'

  In

  ‾1 Constant
   2 DEFLATOR          15.062        84.915    0.046 0.00738   1    0.031   0.863
   3 GNP               -0.036         0.033   -1.014 0.00056   1    1.144   0.313
   4 UNEMPLOY          -2.020         0.488   -0.538 0.02975   1   17.110   0.003
   5 ARMFORCE          -1.033         0.214   -0.205 0.27863   1   23.252   0.001
   6 POPULATN          -0.051         0.226   -0.101 0.00251   1    0.051   0.826
   7 TIME            1829.151       455.478    2.480 0.00132   1   16.127   0.003

  Out              Part. Corr.

  ‾  none
```

We begin with all variables in the model. See Example 8.4 for a complete table of this model. We remove *DEFLATOR* because it has an unusually low tolerance and F value.

- Following the prompt (>), type **STEP DEFLATOR** and press Enter.

```
Dependent Variable TOTAL
Minimum tolerance for entry into model = 0.000100
Backward stepwise with Alpha-to-Enter=0.150 and Alpha-to-Remove=0.150

Step # 1 R =  0.998 R-Square =  0.995
Term removed: DEFLATOR

  Effect            Coefficient   Std Error  Std Coef   Tol.   DF      F      'P'

  In

  ‾1 Constant
   3 GNP               -0.032         0.024   -0.905 0.00097   1    1.744   0.216
   4 UNEMPLOY          -1.972         0.386   -0.525 0.04299   1   26.090   0.000
   5 ARMFORCE          -1.020         0.191   -0.202 0.31723   1   28.564   0.000
   6 POPULATN          -0.078         0.162   -0.154 0.00423   1    0.230   0.642
   7 TIME            1814.101       425.283    2.459 0.00136   1   18.196   0.002

  Out              Part. Corr.

  ‾2 DEFLATOR          0.059            .         .   0.00738   1    0.031   0.863
```

POPULATN has the lowest F statistic and, again, a low tolerance.

- Type **STEP POPULATN**.

```
Step # 2 R = 0.998 R-Square = 0.995
Term removed: POPULATN

Effect              Coefficient   Std Error   Std Coef    Tol.   DF      F      'P'

In

 1 Constant
 3 GNP                  -0.040       0.016      -1.137   0.00194  1   5.953   0.033
 4 UNEMPLOY             -2.088       0.290      -0.556   0.07088  1  51.870   0.000
 5 ARMFORCE             -1.015       0.184      -0.201   0.31831  1  30.496   0.000
 7 TIME               1887.410     382.766       2.559   0.00157  1  24.314   0.000

Out                 Part. Corr.

 2 DEFLATOR              0.143         .           .     0.01305  1   0.208   0.658
 6 POPULATN             -0.150         .           .     0.00443  1   0.230   0.642
```

GNP and *TIME* both have low tolerance values. They could be highly correlated with one another, so we will take each out and examine the behavior of the other when we do.

- Type **STEP TIME** to remove *TIME*.

```
Step # 3 R = 0.993 R-Square = 0.985
Term removed: TIME

Effect              Coefficient   Std Error   Std Coef    Tol.   DF      F      'P'

In

 1 Constant
 3 GNP                   0.041       0.002       1.154   0.31838  1 341.684  0.000
 4 UNEMPLOY             -0.797       0.213      -0.212   0.38512  1  13.942   0.003
 5 ARMFORCE             -0.483       0.255      -0.096   0.48571  1   3.580   0.083

Out                 Part. Corr.

 2 DEFLATOR              0.163         .           .     0.01318  1   0.299   0.596
 6 POPULATN             -0.376         .           .     0.00509  1   1.813   0.205
 7 TIME                  0.830         .           .     0.00157  1  24.314   0.000
```

- Type **STEP TIME** to reenter *TIME*.

```
Step # 4 R = 0.998 R-Square = 0.995
Term entered: TIME
Effect              Coefficient   Std Error   Std Coef    Tol.   DF      F      'P'

In

 1 Constant
 3 GNP                  -0.040       0.016      -1.137   0.00194  1   5.953   0.033
 4 UNEMPLOY             -2.088       0.290      -0.556   0.07088  1  51.870   0.000
 5 ARMFORCE             -1.015       0.184      -0.201   0.31831  1  30.496   0.000
 7 TIME               1887.410     382.766       2.559   0.00157  1  24.314   0.000

Out                 Part. Corr.

 2 DEFLATOR              0.143         .           .     0.01305  1   0.208   0.658
 6 POPULATN             -0.150         .           .     0.00443  1   0.230   0.642
```

- Type **STEP GNP** to remove GNP.

```
Step # 5 R = 0.996 R-Square = 0.993
 Term removed: GNP
 Effect          Coefficient   Std Error   Std Coef   Tol.     DF        F      'P'

 In
 ‾‾
  1 Constant
  4 UNEMPLOY        -1.470        0.167      -0.391   0.30139   1   77.320   0.000
  5 ARMFORCE        -0.772        0.184      -0.153   0.44978   1   17.671   0.001
  7 TIME           956.380       35.525       1.297   0.25701   1  724.765   0.000
 Out             Part. Corr.

  ‾‾
  2 DEFLATOR       -0.031          .           .      0.01385   1    0.011   0.920
  3 GNP            -0.593          .           .      0.00194   1    5.953   0.033
  6 POPULATN       -0.505          .           .      0.00889   1    3.768   0.078
```

We are comfortable with the tolerance values in both models with three variables. With *TIME* in the model, the smallest F is 17.671 and with *GNP* in the model, the smallest F is 3.580. Furthermore, with *TIME*, the squared multiple correlation is 0.993 and with *GNP*, it is 0.985. Let's stop the stepping and view more information about the last model.

- Type **STOP**.

```
Dep Var: TOTAL   N: 16   Multiple R: 0.996   Squared multiple R: 0.993

Adjusted squared multiple R: 0.991   Standard error of estimate: 332.084

Effect        Coefficient    Std Error    Std Coef  Tolerance      t    P(2 Tail)

CONSTANT      -1797221.112   68641.553       0.0        .       -26.183   0.000
UNEMPLOY           -1.470        0.167      -0.391     0.301      -8.793   0.000
ARMFORCE           -0.772        0.184      -0.153     0.450      -4.204   0.001
TIME              956.380       35.525       1.297     0.257      26.921   0.000

                          Analysis of Variance

Source          Sum-of-Squares   DF   Mean-Square    F-Ratio       P

Regression       1.83685E+08      3   6.12285E+07    555.209     0.000
Residual         1323360.743     12    110280.062
```

Our final model includes only *UNEMPLOY*, *ARMFORCE*, and *TIME*. Notice that its multiple correlation (0.996) is not significantly smaller than that for the automated stepping (0.998). Here are the commands we used:

```
REGRESS
   USE longley
   MODEL total=constant + deflator + gnp + unemploy +,
            armforce + populatn + time
   START / BACK
   STEP deflator
   STEP populatn
   STEP time
   STEP time
   STEP gnp
   STOP
```

More about Regression

Linear models are models based on *lines*. More generally, they are based on linear surfaces, such as lines, planes, and hyperplanes. Linear models are widely applied because lines and planes often appear to successfully describe the relations among variables measured in the real world. We begin by examining the equation for a straight line, and then move to more complex linear models.

Simple linear models

A linear model looks like this:

$$y = a + bx$$

This is the equation for a straight line that you learned in school. The quantities in this equation are:

y Dependent variable.

x Independent variable.

a Value of y when x is 0. This is sometimes called a y-intercept (where a line intersects the y-axis in a graph when x is 0).

b Slope of the line, or the number of units y changes when x changes by one unit.

Let's look at an example. Accounting firms typically fine tune their partners' earnings according to many factors. Here are actual billings and earnings for one small firm:

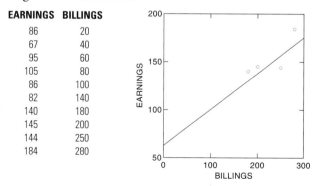

EARNINGS	BILLINGS
86	20
67	40
95	60
105	80
86	100
82	140
140	180
145	200
144	250
184	280

Regression can help fit a line for predicting earnings from billings. To fit this line, specify *EARNINGS* as the dependent variable and *BILLINGS* as the independent variable in a model statement. The *y*-intercept is 62.8 thousand dollars and the slope is 0.375. These values do not predict any single accountant's earnings exactly. They describe the whole firm well in the sense that, on average, the line predicts a given earnings value fairly closely from a given billings value.

Estimation and inference

We often want to do more with such data than draw a line on a picture. In order to generalize, formulate a policy, or test a hypothesis, we need to make an inference. To make an inference about compensation, we need to include a term for random error. The error parameter is usually called ε:

$$y = a + bx + \varepsilon$$

We use Greek letters for unobservable quantities and Roman letters for observable quantities. Notice that ε is a random variable. It varies like any other variable (for example, *x*), but it varies randomly, like the tossing of a coin. Since ε is random, the model forces *y* to be random as well. We are saying with our model that earnings are only partly predictable from billings. They vary slightly according to many other factors, which we assume are random.

Standard errors

There are several statistics relevant to the estimation of α and β. Usually, researchers want to test the null hypothesis that $\beta = 0$. The estimate of the slope β for our data is 0.375. We need a measure of how variable we could expect our estimates to be if we continued to sample data from our population and use least squares. A statistic calculated by Regression shows what we could expect this variation to be. It is called, appropriately, the standard error of estimate, or *Std Error* in the output. The standard error of the *y*-intercept, or regression constant, is in the first row of the coefficients: 10.440. The standard error of the billing coefficient, or slope, is 0.065. Look for these numbers in the following output:

```
Dep Var:EARNINGS      N:   10    Multiple R:  .897    Squared Multiple R:  .804
Adjusted squared multiple R:  .779      Standard error of estimate:      17.626

   Variable    Coefficient    Std Error    Std Coef Tolerance    T    P(2 tail)

CONSTANT          62.838        10.440      0.000  .             6.019   0.000
 BILLINGS          0.375         0.065      0.897 1.0000000      5.728   0.000


                         Analysis of Variance

   Source    Sum-of-Squares   DF   Mean-Square    F-Ratio     P

Regression      10191.109      1    10191.109      32.805    0.000
  Residual       2485.291      8      310.661
```

Hypothesis
testing

The t statistic, 5.728, is the ratio of the *BILLINGS* slope coefficient to its standard error (0.375 to 0.065). If the value of t is well above 2.0 or below 2.0, we are willing to reject the null hypothesis that the slope is 0.

At the bottom of the output, we get an analysis of variance table that tests the goodness of fit of the entire model. The null hypothesis corresponding to the F ratio (32.805) and its associated p value is that the billing variable coefficient is equal to 0. This test overwhelmingly rejects the null hypothesis ($p < 0.001$).

The multiple
correlation

In the output is the *Squared multiple R statistic*. This is the proportion of the total variation in the dependent variable (earnings) accounted for by the linear prediction using billings. The value here (0.804) tells us that approximately 80% of the variation in earnings can be accounted for by a linear prediction from billings. The rest of the variation, as far as this model is concerned, is random error. The square root of this statistic is called, not surprisingly, the multiple correlation. The *Adjusted squared multiple correlation* (0.779) is what we would expect the squared multiple correlation to be if we used the model we just estimated on a new sample of 10 accountants in the firm. It is smaller than the squared multiple correlation because the coefficients were optimized for this sample rather than for the new one.

Regression
diagnostics

We do not need to understand the mathematics of how a line is fitted to use regression. You can fit a line to any x–y data by the method of least squares. The computer doesn't care where the numbers come from. To have a model and estimates that mean something, however, you should be sure that the assumptions are reasonable and that the sample data appear to be sampled from a population that meets the assumptions.

The sample analogs of the errors in the population model are the **residuals**—the differences between the observed and predicted values of the dependent variable. There are many diagnostics you can perform on the residuals. Here are the most important ones:

• The errors are normally distributed. Draw a normal probability plot (**Probability Plot**) of the residuals:

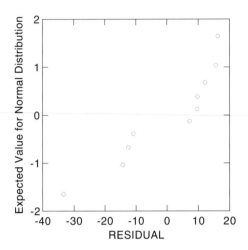

The residuals should fall approximately on a diagonal straight line in this plot. When the sample size is small, as in the accounting example, the line may be quite jagged. It is difficult to tell by any method whether a small sample is from a normal population. You can also plot a histogram or stem-and-leaf plot of the residuals to see if they are lumpy in the middle with thin, symmetric tails.

- The errors have constant variance. Plot the residuals against the estimated values. The following plot shows Studentized residuals (*STUDENT*) against estimated values (*ESTIMATE*). Studentized residuals follow approximately a *t* distribution, which means we can spot large values (greater than 2 or 3 in absolute magnitude) as possible problems.

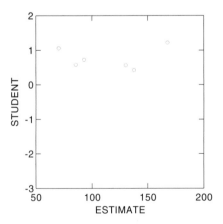

The residuals should be arranged in a horizontal band within 2 or 3 units around 0 in this plot. Again, since there are so few observations, it is difficult to tell whether they violate this assumption in this case. There is only one particularly large residual, and it is toward the middle of the values. This accountant billed $140,000 and is earning only $80,000. He or she might have a gripe about supporting a higher share of the firm's overhead.

- The errors are independent. Several plots can be done. Look at the plot of residuals against estimated values above. Make sure that the residuals are randomly scattered above and below the 0 horizontal and that they do not track in a snaky way across the plot. If they look as if they were shot at the plot by a horizontally moving machine gun, then they are probably not independent of each other. You may also want to plot residuals against other variables, such as time, orientation, or other ways that might influence the variability of your dependent measure.

  Stats➠**Time Series**➠**ACF** measures whether the residuals are serially correlated. Here is an autocorrelation plot:

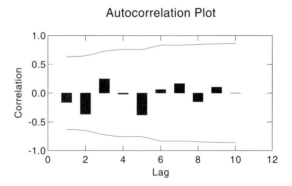

Autocorrelation Plot

All of the bars should be within the parentheses if each residual is not predictable from the one preceding it, and the one preceding that, and the one preceding that, and so on.

- All of the members of the population are described by the same linear model. Plot Cook's distance (*COOK*) against the estimated values.

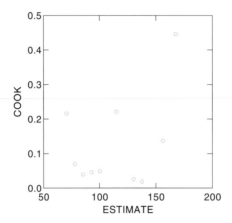

Cook's distance measures the influence of each sample observation on the coefficient estimates. Observations that are far from the average of all of the independent variable values or that have large residuals tend to have a large Cook's distance value (say, greater than 2). Cook's D actually follows closely an F distribution, so aberrant values depend on the sample size. We don't want to find a large Cook's D value for an observation because it would mean that the coefficient estimates would change substantially if we deleted that observation. While none of the Cook values are extremely large in our example, could it be that the largest one in the upper right corner is the founding partner in the firm? Despite large billings, this partner is earning more than the model predicts.

In conclusion, keep in mind that all our diagnostic tests are themselves a form of inference. We can assess theoretical errors only through the dark mirror of our observed residuals. Despite this caveat, testing assumptions graphically is critically important. You should never publish regression results until you have examined these plots.

Multiple regression

A multiple linear model has more than one independent variable:

$$y = a + bx + cz$$

This is the equation for a plane in three-dimensional space. The parameter a is still an intercept term. It is the value of y when x and z are 0. The parameters b and c are still slopes. One gives the slope of the plane along the x dimension and the other along the z dimension. The statistical model has the same form:

$$y = \alpha + \beta x + \gamma z + \varepsilon$$

Before we run out of letters for independent variables, let's switch to a more frequently used notation:

$$y = \beta_0 + \beta_1 x_1 + \beta_2 x_2 + \varepsilon$$

Notice that we are still using Greek letters for unobservables and Roman letters for observables.

Now, let's look at our accounting data again. We have learned that there is another variable that appears to determine earnings—the number of hours billed per year by each accountant. Here is an expanded listing of the data:

EARNINGS	BILLINGS	HOURS
86	20	1771
67	40	1556
95	60	1749
105	80	1754
86	100	1594
82	140	1400
140	180	1780
145	200	1737
144	250	1645
184	280	1863

For our model, β_1 is the coefficient for *BILLINGS*, and β_2 is the coefficient for *HOURS*. Fitting this model involves no more work than fitting the simple regression model.

```
USE earnbill
MODEL earnings = CONSTANT + billings + hours
ESTIMATE
```

We specify one dependent and two independent variables and estimate the model as before. Here is the result:

```
Dep Var:    EARNINGS N: 10 Multiple R: 0.998 Squared multiple R: 0.996

Adjusted squared multiple R:  0.995     Standard error of estimate:      2.678

Effect          Coefficient    Std Error     Std Coef Tolerance    t     P(2

CONSTANT         -139.925        11.116        0.0        .      -12.588
BILLINGS            0.333         0.010        0.797    0.951     32.690
HOURS               0.124         0.007        0.449    0.951     18.429

                          Analysis of Variance

Source          Sum-of-Squares   DF  Mean-Square    F-Ratio      P

Regression         12626.210      2    6313.105     880.493    0.000
Residual              50.190      7       7.170
```

This time, we have one more row in our regression table for *HOURS*. Notice that its coefficient (0.124) is smaller than that for *BILLINGS* (0.333). This is partly due to the different scales of the variables. *HOURS* are measured in larger numbers than *BILLINGS*. If we want to compare the influence of each independent of scales, we should look at the standardized coefficients. Here, we still see that *BILLINGS* (0.797) plays a greater role in predicting *EARNINGS* than *HOURS* (0.449). Notice also that both coefficients are highly significant and that the overall model is highly significant, as shown in the analysis of variance table.

Variable selection

In applications, you may not know which subset of predictor variables in a larger set constitute a "good" model. There are many strategies for identifying a good subset—forward selection, backward elimination, stepwise (either a forward or backward type), and all subsets. Forward selection begins with the "best" predictor, adds the next "best," and continues entering variables to improve the fit. Backward selection begins with all candidate predictors in an equation and removes the least useful one at a time as long as the fit is not substantially "worsened." **Stepwise** begins as either forward or backward, but allows "poor" predictors to be removed from the candidate model or "good" predictors to reenter the model at any step. Finally, all subsets methods compute all possible subsets of predictors for each model of a given size (number of predictors) and choose the "best" one.

Bias and variance tradeoff. Submodel selection is a tradeoff between bias and variance. By decreasing the number of parameters in the model, its predictive capability is enhanced because the variance of the parameter estimates decreases. On the other side, bias may increase because the "true model" may have a higher dimension. So, we'd like to balance smaller variance against increased bias. There are two aspects to variable selection: selecting the dimensionality of the submodel (how many variables to include) and evaluating the model selected. After you determine the dimension, there may be several alternative subsets that perform equally well. Then, knowledge of the subject matter, how accurately individual variables are measured, and what a variable "communicates" can guide selection of the model to report.

A strategy. If you are in an exploratory phase of research, you might try the following version of backward stepping. First, fit a model using all candidate predictors. Then identify the least "useful" variable, remove it from the model list, and fit a smaller model. Evaluate your results and select another variable to remove. Continue removing variables. For a given size model, you may want to remove alternative variables (that is, first remove variable *a*, evaluate results, replace *a* and remove *b*, etc.).

Removal criteria. Decisions about which variable to remove should be based on statistics and diagnostics in the output, especially graphical displays of these values, and your knowledge of the problem at hand. As a guideline, consider models that include only variables that have absolute "*t*" values well above 2.0 and "tolerance" values greater than 0.1. We use quotation marks here because *t* and other statistics do not have their usual distributions when you are selecting subset models.

Evaluation criteria. There is no one test to identify the dimensionality of the best submodel. Recent research by Leo Breiman emphasizes the usefulness of cross-validation techniques involving 80% random subsamples. Sample 80% of your file, fit a model, use the resulting coefficients on the remaining 20% to obtain predicted values, and then compute for this smaller sample. In over-fitting situations, the discrepancy R^2 between the R^2 for the 80% sample and the 20% sample can be dramatic.

A warning. If you do not have extensive knowledge of your variables and expect this strategy to help you to find a "true" model, you can get into a lot of trouble. Automatic stepwise regression programs cannot do your work for you. You must be able to examine graphics and make intelligent choices based on theory and prior knowledge. Otherwise, you will be arriving at nonsense. See Example 8.5 for more information.

Testing Hypotheses

After your initial Linear Regression analysis, you can use the advanced hypothesis testing features available with General Linear Model. In this section, we describe features available with **General Linear Model**➠ **Hypothesis Test** to test whether:

- A single regression coefficient is 0 (**Specify** or **Effects**).
- The coefficients for two variables simultaneously are 0 (**Specify** or **Effects**).
- Two coefficients are equal (**Specify** or **Effects**).
- A coefficient is, say, three times larger than another (**Specify** or **A matrix**).
- One coefficient is equal to 30 and another equal to 50 (**Specify** or **Effects** and **D matrix**).
- The difference between the coefficients is 30 (**Specify** or **A matrix** and **D matrix**).

Within, Contrast, and **Error Term** are more appropriate for analysis of variance. The following items, which are described in Chapter 12, are used for discriminant analysis and canonical correlation.

- **Priors.** Specify prior probabilities for discriminant analysis.
- **Standardize (Within groups, Sample).** Standardize canonical coefficients using total sample or within-groups covariance matrix.
- **Save scores and results.** Save MANOVA or canonical variable (discriminant) scores and predicted group membership into a file.

For factor analysis, see Chapter 12, and use:

- **Factor (Hypothesis, Error).** Compute principal components on the hypothesis (between-subjects) or error (within-subjects) correlation, covariance, or SSCP matrix.
- **Covariance, SSCP, Correlations.** Specify type of matrix to factor.
- **Rotate.** Rotate canonical factors.

Effects

Effects is where you specify the variable(s) whose coefficient you want to test. For example, for testing:

$$H_0: \beta_i = 0$$

type the name of the variable in the **Effects** text box. For testing:

$$H_0: \beta_i = \beta_2 = 0$$

type the names of the two variables connected by an ampersand (&). The resulting p values are the same as the ones for the tests of significance of the coefficients in the regression output. (See Example 8.6.)

Specify

To define your test, select **Specify** and type your expression in the **Equation** text box. For example, if *GNP* and *ARMFORCE* are variable names from the last regression model estimated, type:

GNP=0	To test whether the coefficient is 0.
GNP=ARMFORCE	To test whether the two coefficients are equal.
3*GNP=ARMFORCE	To test whether 3 times the *GNP* coefficient equals the *ARMFORCE* coefficient.
GNP= -.05 ARMFORCE=10	To simultaneously test that the GNP and *ARMFORCE* coefficients equal specific values.
GNP-ARMFORCE=1.5	To test whether the difference between the coefficients is 1.5.

Multiple expressions must be separated by a semicolon, as in:

gnp=-.05; armforce=16

With commands:

```
HYPOTHESIS
SPECIFY gnp=-.05; armforce=16
TEST
```

Options for Specify. **Pooled**, the default, uses the usual residual error (within cell) as the error term. **Separate** is used in ANOVA when cell variances are unequal.

A matrix and D matrix

Using **A matrix**, **C matrix**, and **D matrix**, you can test *any* general linear hypothesis. (Note that **Specify** described above is much easier to use in most circumstances.) The **C matrix** is used to test hypotheses for repeated measures analysis of variance designs and models with multiple dependent variables. **A matrix** and **D matrix** are used to test hypotheses in regression. Linear hypotheses in regression have the form $A\beta = D$, where **A** is a matrix of linear weights on coefficients across the independent variables (the rows of β), β is the matrix of regression coefficients, and **D** is a null hypothesis matrix (usually a null matrix). The **A** and **D** matrices may be specified in several alternative ways, and if they are not specified, they have default values.

The **A** matrix has as many columns as there are regression coefficients (including the constant) in your model. The number of rows in **A** determine how many degrees of freedom your hypothesis involves. The **D** matrix, if you use it, must have the same number of rows as **A**. For univariate multiple regression, **D** has only one column. For multivariate models (multiple dependent variables), the **D** matrix has one column for each dependent variable.

As an example, look at the *LONGLEY* data below that have six independent variables. The columns of the **A** matrix represent:

```
CONSTANT DEFLATOR GNP UNEMPLOY ARMFORCE POPULATN TIME
```

To test that the coefficients for *GNP* and *ARMFORCE* are simultaneously 0, select **A matrix** and type these values in the text box:

```
0 0 1 0 0 0 0;
0 0 0 0 1 0 0
```

adding a semicolon and pressing Enter at the end of each row.

To test whether the coefficient for *ARMFORCE* equals 10.0, type these values in the **A matrix** text box:

```
0 0 0 0 1 0 0
```

Then select **D matrix** and type the number 10 in the text box.

See Example 8.8 for more **A** and **D** matrix applications in regression.

8.6
One
regression
coefficient
$H_0 : B_i = 0$

Using **Hypothesis**, you can test single regression coefficients, several coefficients, linear combinations of coefficients, and nonzero null hypotheses.

Most regression programs print tests of significance for each coefficient in an equation. General Linear Model has a powerful additional feature—post hoc tests of regression coefficients. To demonstrate these tests, we continue with the *LONGLEY* data and examine whether the *DEFLATOR* coefficient differs significantly from 0. First, we estimate the coefficients for a model with six predictors:

```
REGRESS
    USE longley
    MODEL total = CONSTANT + deflator + gnp + unemploy +,
                  armforce + populatn + time
    ESTIMATE / TOL=.00001
```

```
Dep Var: TOTAL    N: 16    Multiple R: 0.998    Squared multiple R: 0.995

Adjusted squared multiple R: 0.992    Standard error of estimate: 304.854

Effect          Coefficient      Std Error     Std Coef Tolerance      t    P(2 Tail)

CONSTANT      -3482258.635     890420.384        0.0        .        -3.911    0.004
DEFLATOR            15.062         84.915        0.046      0.007      0.177    0.863
GNP                 -0.036          0.033       -1.014      0.001     -1.070    0.313
UNEMPLOY            -2.020          0.488       -0.538      0.030     -4.136    0.003
ARMFORCE            -1.033          0.214       -0.205      0.279     -4.822    0.001
POPULATN            -0.051          0.226       -0.101      0.003     -0.226    0.826
TIME              1829.151        455.478        2.480      0.001      4.016    0.003

                        Analysis of Variance

Source          Sum-of-Squares    DF   Mean-Square      F-Ratio      P

Regression        1.84172E+08      6   3.06954E+07      330.285    0.000
Residual           836424.056      9     92936.006
```

After reviewing the results, select **Stats➠General Linear Model➠ Hypothesis Test** and select *DEFLATOR* as the **Effect**. With commands:

```
HYPOTHESIS
EFFECT = deflator
TEST
```

```
Test for Effect called:     DEFLATOR

Test of Hypothesis

      Source        SS       DF      MS          F         P

  Hypothesis    2923.976      1    2923.976    0.031     0.863
       Error  836424.056      9   92936.006
```

Notice that the *Error Sum of Squares* (836424.056) is the same as the output *Residual Sum of Squares* at the bottom of the ANOVA table. The probability level (0.863) is the same also.

You can test all of the coefficients in the equation this way, individually, or choose **All** to generate separate hypothesis tests for each predictor or type:

```
HYPOTHESIS
ALL
TEST
```

8.7 Two regression coefficients
$H_0 : \beta_1 = \beta_2 = 0$

You may wonder why you need to bother with testing when the regression output gives you the same numbers. After specifying your model, try this one:

```
HYPOTHESIS
EFFECT = deflator & gnp
TEST
```

```
Test for effect called:      DEFLATOR
                         and
                             GNP

A Matrix

                          1          2          3          4          5
                  1      0.0      1.000      0.0        0.0        0.0
                  2      0.0      0.0        1.000      0.0        0.0

                          6          7
                  1      0.0        0.0
                  2      0.0        0.0
Test of Hypothesis

      Source       SS        DF       MS            F          P

  Hypothesis   149295.592     2    74647.796       0.803      0.478
      Error    836424.056     9    92936.006
```

This time, the *Error* sum of squares is the same as before, but the *Hypothesis* sum of squares is different. We just tested the hypothesis that the *DEFLATOR* and *GNP* coefficients simultaneously are 0.

The **A** matrix printed above the test specifies the hypothesis that we tested. It has two degrees of freedom (see the *F* statistic) because the **A** matrix has two rows—one for each coefficient. If you know some matrix algebra, you can see that the matrix product **AB** using this **A** matrix and **B** as a column matrix of regression coefficients picks up only two coefficients: *DEFLATOR* and *GNP*. Notice that our hypothesis had the following matrix equation: **AB** = **0**, where **0** is a null matrix.

If you don't know matrix algebra, don't worry; the ampersand method is equivalent. You can ignore the **A** matrix in the output.

Two coefficients with an A matrix
$H_0: \beta_1 = \beta_2 = 0$

If you are experienced with matrix algebra, however, you can specify your own matrix by using **A matrix**. When typing the matrix, be sure to separate cells with spaces and press Enter between rows. The following simultaneously tests that *DEFLATOR* = 0 and *GNP* = 0:

```
HYPOTHESIS
AMATRIX [0 1 0 0 0 0;
         0 0 1 0 0 0]
TEST
```

You get the same output as above.

Why bother with **A matrix** when the you can use **Effect**? Because in the **A matrix** you can use any numbers, not just 0's and 1's. Here is a bizarre matrix:

1.0 3.0 0.5 64.3 3.0 2.0 0.0

You may not want to test this kind of hypothesis on the *LONGLEY* data, but there are important applications in the analysis of variance where you might. We will see some of these later in the chapter.

8.8 A nonzero null hypothesis with a D matrix
$H_0: \beta_1 = 30$

You can test nonzero null hypotheses with a **D** matrix, often in combination using **Contrast** or **A matrix**. Here, we test whether the *DEFLATOR* coefficient significantly differs from 30:

```
HYPOTHESIS
AMATRIX [0 1 0 0 0 0]
DMATRIX [30]
TEST
```

Specify as an alternative to A and D matrices
$H_0: \beta_1 = 30$

The commands that test whether *DEFLATOR* differs from 30 can be performed more efficiently using **Specify**.

```
HYPOTHESIS
SPECIFY [deflator=30]
TEST
```

More Examples

8.9 Regression with ecological or grouped data

If you have aggregated data, weight the regression by a count variable. This variable, n_i, should represent the counts of observations (n) contributing to the ith case. If n is not an integer, SYSTAT truncates it to an integer before using it as a weight. The regression results are identical to those produced if you had typed in each case n_i times.

We use, for this example, an ecological or grouped data file, *PLANTS*:

CO2	SPECIES	COUNT
12	1	10
14	2	9
13	3	15
11	5	22
11	6	20

The total, N, for this regression is 76. The commands are:

```
REGRESS
    USE plants
    FREQ=count
    MODEL co2 = CONSTANT + species
    ESTIMATE
```

```
Dep Var: CO2   N: 76   Multiple R: 0.757   Squared multiple R: 0.573

Adjusted squared multiple R: 0.567   Standard error of estimate: 0.729

Effect         Coefficient   Std Error   Std Coef Tolerance     t    P(2 Tail)

CONSTANT          13.738        0.204       0.0        .      67.273   0.000
SPECIES           -0.466        0.047      -0.757    1.000    -9.961   0.000

                          Analysis of Variance

Source         Sum-of-Squares   DF   Mean-Square   F-Ratio     P

Regression          52.660       1      52.660      99.223    0.000
Residual            39.274      74       0.531
```

8.10 Regression without the constant

To regress without the constant (intercept) term, or through the origin, remove the constant from the list of independent variables. **Regress** adjusts accordingly. The commands are:

```
REGRESS
    MODEL dependent = var1 + var2
    ESTIMATE
```

Some users are puzzled when they see a model without a constant having a higher multiple correlation than a model that includes a constant. How can a regression with fewer parameters predict "better" than another? It doesn't. The total sum of squares must be redefined for a regression model with zero intercept. It is no longer centered about the mean of the dependent variable. Other definitions of sums of squares can lead to strange results, such as negative multiple correlations. If your constant is actually near 0, then including or excluding the constant makes little difference in the output. Kvålseth (1985) discusses the issues involved in summary statistics for zero-intercept regression models. The definition of R^2 used in SYSTAT is Kvålseth's formula 7. This was chosen because it retains its PRE (percentage reduction of error) interpretation and is guaranteed to be in the (0,1) interval.

How, then, do you test the significance of a constant in a regression model? Include a constant in the model as usual and look at its test of significance. In Example 8.6 with the *LONGLEY* data, the F statistic for the constant is 15.294.

If you have a zero-intercept model where it is appropriate to compute a coefficient of determination and other summary statistics about the centered data, use **Stats**➠**General Linear Model**➠**Options** and select **Mixture model**. This option analyzes mixture models and is discussed in Example 8.11. It provides Kvålseth's formula 1 for R^2 and uses centered total sum of squares for other summary statistics.

8.11 Mixture models

Mixture models decompose the effects of mixtures of variables on a dependent variable. They differ from ordinary regression models because the independent variables sum to a constant value. The regression model, therefore, does not include a constant, and the regression and error sums of squares have one less degree of freedom. Marquardt and Snee (1974) and Diamond (1981) discuss these models and their estimation.

Here is an example using the *PUNCH* data file from Cornell (1985). The study involved effects of various mixtures of watermelon, pineapple, and orange juice on taste ratings by judges of a fruit punch.

WATRMELN	PINEAPPL	ORANGE	TASTE
1.0	0.0	0.0	4.3
1.0	0.0	0.0	4.7
1.0	0.0	0.0	4.8
0.0	1.0	0.0	6.2
0.0	1.0	0.0	6.5
0.0	1.0	0.0	6.3
0.5	0.5	0.0	6.3
0.5	0.5	0.0	6.1
0.5	0.5	0.0	5.8
0.0	0.0	1.0	7.0
0.0	0.0	1.0	6.9
0.0	0.0	1.0	7.4
0.5	0.0	0.5	6.1
0.5	0.0	0.5	6.5
0.5	0.0	0.5	5.9
0.0	0.5	0.5	6.2
0.0	0.5	0.5	6.1
0.0	0.5	0.5	6.2

Use **Stats**➟**General Linear Model**. Select *TASTE* for the **Dependent** variable. Select *WATRMELN*, *PINEAPPL*, and *ORANGE* as **Independent** variables. Select *WATRMELN* again, click **Add** to add it to the Independent list. Then select *PINEAPPL* and click **Cross**. *WATRMELN*PINEAPPL* should appear in the Independent list. Using the same method, add *WATRMELN*ORANGE* and *PINEAPPL*ORANGE* to the Independent list.

Click **Options** in the **General Linear Model** dialog box and select **Mixture model**. Return to the main dialog box (click **Continue**) and deselect (uncheck) **Include Constant**.

```
GLM
    USE punch
    MODEL taste = watrmeln + pineappl + orange,
                + watrmeln*pineappl,
                + watrmeln*orange,
                + pineappl*orange
    ESTIMATE / MIX
```

```
Model contains no constant
Assuming Mixture Model

Dep Var: TASTE   N: 18   Multiple R: 0.969   Squared multiple R: 0.939

Adjusted squared multiple R: 0.913   Standard error of estimate: 0.232

Effect        Coefficient   Std Error   Std Coef Tolerance     t    P(2 Tail)

WATRMELN          4.600       0.134        3.001    0.667   34.322    0.000
PINEAPPL          6.333       0.134        4.131    0.667   47.255    0.000
ORANGE            7.100       0.134        4.631    0.667   52.975    0.000
WATRMELN
*PINEAPPL          2.400       0.657        0.320    0.667    3.655    0.003
WATRMELN
*ORANGE            1.267       0.657        0.169    0.667    1.929    0.078
PINEAPPL
*ORANGE           -2.200       0.657       -0.293    0.667   -3.351    0.006
```

```
                          Analysis of Variance
 Source           Sum-of-Squares   DF  Mean-Square   F-Ratio     P

 Regression           9.929         5     1.986      36.852    0.000
 Residual             0.647        12     0.054
```

Not using **Mix** produces a much larger R^2 (0.999) and an F value of 2083.371, both of which are inappropriate for these data. Notice that the Regression sum of squares has five degrees of freedom instead of six as in the usual zero-intercept regression model. We have lost one degree of freedom because the predictors sum to 1.

8.12 Partial correlations

Partial correlations are easy to compute with General Linear Model. The partial correlation of two variables (*a* and *b*) controlling for the effects of a third (*c*) is the correlation between the residuals of each (*a* and *b*) after each has been regressed on the third (*c*). You can therefore use **General Linear Model** to compute an entire matrix of partial correlations.

First, you need to select **Edit**➠**Options** and select **Long** for **Length**. Then use **Stats**➠**General Linear Model**, select the variables for which you want partial correlations as the **Dependent** variables, and select the control variable as the **Independent** variable. For example, to compute the matrix of partial correlations for *Y1*, *Y2*, *Y3*, *Y4*, and *Y5*, controlling for the effects of *X*, select *Y1* through *Y5* as dependent variables and *X* as the independent variable. With commands:

```
GLM
    MODEL y(1 .. 5) = CONSTANT + x
    PRINT=LONG
    ESTIMATE
```

Look for the *Residual Correlation Matrix* in the output; it is the matrix of partial correlations among the *y*'s given *x*. If you want to compute partial correlations for several *x*'s, just select them (also) as independent variables.

More Features

Multivariate regression

We can extend the multiple regression equation to several dependent variables:

$$y_1 = \beta_{01} + \beta_{11}x_{11} + \beta_{21}x_{21} + \varepsilon_1$$
$$y_2 = \beta_{02} + \beta_{12}x_{12} + \beta_{22}x_{22} + \varepsilon_2$$
$$y_3 = \beta_{03} + \beta_{13}x_{13} + \beta_{23}x_{23} + \varepsilon_3$$

Each equation is for predicting a different dependent variable. For example, we might want to predict earnings, office size, and expense accounts from billings and hours in our accounting firm. We can't show you a picture of the resulting predictions because they would have too many dimensions to represent on paper. Nevertheless, you should know that multivariate regression is a simple extension of multiple regression.

Matrix notation

The multivariate equations get messy when we have a lot of x and y variables. There is a simpler *matrix* notation that mathematicians use for representing arrays of variables. You don't need to understand matrix algebra to benefit from looking at the matrix representation of multiple regression. Here it is:

$$\mathbf{Y} = \mathbf{XB} + \mathbf{E}$$

Notice the parallels to the multivariate equations. We have collected all of the y variables into the columns of matrix Y, all of the x variables into the columns of X, and so on.

The multivariate general linear hypothesis

Let's now see how we test hypotheses using the *multivariate general linear model*. Since the matrix notation works for single variables as well as for many, we can use a simple matrix equation to describe every model from simple through multivariate regression. Every hypothesis can be specified as another type of simple matrix equation:

$$\mathbf{ABC'} = \mathbf{D}$$

In addition to the **B** matrix, which contains the regression coefficients that appeared in the matrix model above, there are three new matrices in this equation:

A   Matrix that specifies weights we want to use on the independent variable coefficients.

C   Matrix that operates similarly on the dependent variable coefficients.

D   Matrix of null hypothesis values.

The apostrophe or prime mark (') after the C matrix denotes a transpose. It means that we flip over the C matrix so that its number of rows matches the number of columns in **B**.

General Linear Model allows you to input actual values for the A, C, and D matrices. You may never need to use them because in almost every application, the values in them are either 1 or 0 and **General Linear Model** has automatic settings for these instances. Their advantage, however, is that verbal descriptions can be ambiguous, so a statistician cannot be sure what hypothesis is being tested. When unusual hypotheses are tested, sometimes this is the only way to be sure that the test is specified correctly.

Using an SSCP, covariance, or correlation matrix as input

Normally for a regression analysis, you use a cases-by-variables data file. You can, however, use a covariance or correlation matrix saved (from **Correlations**) as input. If you use a matrix as input, specify the sample size that generated the matrix where the number you type is an integer greater than 2.

You can enter an SSCP, covariance, or correlation matrix by typing it into the Data Editor Worksheet, by using BASIC, or by saving it in a SYSTAT file. Be sure to include the dependent as well as independent variables.

SYSTAT needs the sample size to calculate degrees of freedom, so you need to enter the original sample size in the **Cases** text box. Linear Regression determines the type of matrix (SSCP, covariance, etc.) and adjusts appropriately. With a correlation matrix, the raw and standardized coefficients are the same. Therefore, the **Include constant** option is disabled when using SSCP, covariance, or correlation matrices. Because these matrices are centered, the constant term has already been removed.

The following two analyses of the same data file produce identical results (except that you don't get residuals with the second). In the first, we use the usual cases-by-variables data file. In the second, we use the CORR command to save a covariance matrix and then analyze that matrix file with the REGRESS command.

Here are the usual instructions for a regression analysis:

```
REGRESS
    USE filename
    MODEL Y = X(1) + X(2) + X(3)
    ESTIMATE
```

Here, we compute a covariance matrix and use it in the regression analysis:

```
CORR
    USE filename1
    SAVE filename2
    COVARIANCE X(1) X(2) X(3) Y

REGRESS
    USE filename2
    MODEL Y = X(1) + X(2) + X(3) / N=40
    ESTIMATE
```

The triangular matrix input facility is useful for "meta-analysis" of published data and missing-value computations. There are a few warnings, however. First, if you input correlation matrices from textbooks or articles, you may not get the same regression coefficients as those printed in the source. Because of round-off error, printed and raw data can lead to different results. Second, if you use pairwise deletion with **Corr**, the degrees of freedom for hypotheses will not be appropriate. You may not even be able to estimate the regression coefficients because of singularities.

In general, when an incomplete data procedure is used to estimate the correlation matrix, the estimate of regression coefficients and hypothesis tests produced from it are optimistic. You can correct for this by specifying a sample size smaller than the number of actual observations (preferably, set it equal to the smallest number of cases used for any pair of variables), but this is a crude guess that you could refine only by doing Monte Carlo simulations. There is no simple solution. Beware, especially, of multivariate regressions (or MANOVA, etc.) with missing data on the dependent variables. You can usually compute coefficients, but results from hypothesis tests are particularly suspect.

Coding for dummy variables

For each categorical variable that you select in General Linear Model, SYSTAT generates a set of design variables. In the computations, SYSTAT regresses the dependent variables onto the design variables. For a given categorical variable, there will be one fewer design variable than the number of levels.

By default, SYSTAT produces parameter estimates that are differences from group means. Clicking **Categories** in the **General Linear Model** dialog box and selecting **Dummy** for selected categorical variables produces estimates that are differences from the last group. For more information, see Chapter 6.

Extended output

With **Edit▸Options**, if you set **Length** to **Long** (with commands, PRINT=LONG), Linear Regression and General Linear Model produce extended output. For Linear Regression, the Long setting adds the following output: eigenvalues of the unit-scaled matrix $X'X$, condition indices, variance proportions, and a correlation matrix of regression coefficients. For hypothesis testing, **Long** adds A and D matrices, the matrix of contrasts, and the inverse of the cross-product of contrasts. For multivariate regression, you also get hypothesis and error sum of product matrices, tests of residual roots, canonical correlations, coefficients, and loadings.

The inverse of the contrasts basis matrix is $A(X'X)-1A'$. The latter contrast can be used for constructing simultaneous confidence intervals on regression coefficients or contrasts of coefficients (Morrison, 1976). SYSTAT does not compute the inverse of $X'X$ to solve for regression coefficients because this introduces inaccuracies. You can display it, however, by letting the **A matrix** default to the identity matrix.

References

Belsley, D.A., Kuh, E., and Welsch, R.E. 1980. *Regression diagnostics: Identifying influential data and sources of collinearity.* New York: John Wiley & Sons, Inc.

Flack. V.F., and Chang P.C. 1987. Frequency of selecting noise variables in subset regression analysis: A simulation study. *The American Statistician,* 41: 84-86.

Freedman, D.A. 1983. A note on screening regression equations. *The American Statistician,* 37: 152-155.

Hocking, R.R. 1983. Developments in linear regression methodology: 1959-82. *Technometrics,* 25: 219-230.

Lovell, M.C. 1983. Data Mining. *The Review of Economics and Statistics,* 65: 1-12.

Rencher, A.C., and Pun, F.C. 1980. Inflation of R-squared in best subset regression. *Technometrics,* 22: 49-54.

Velleman, P.F., and Welsch, R.E. 1981. Efficient computing of regression diagnostics. *The American Statistician,* 35: 234-242.

Wilkinson, L. 1979. Tests of significance in stepwise regression. *Psychological Bulletin,* 86: 168-174.

Wilkinson, L., and Dallal, G.E. 1982. Tests of significance in forward selection regression with an F-to-enter stopping rule. *Technometrics,* 24: 25-28.

Weisberg, S. 1985. *Applied linear regression.* New York: John Wiley & Sons, Inc.

Correlations, Similarities, and Distance Measures

Leland Wilkinson, Laszlo Engelman, and Rick Marcantonio

Correlations computes correlations and measures of similarity and distance. It prints the resulting matrix and, if requested, saves it in a SYSTAT file for further analysis, such as multidimensional scaling, cluster, or factor analysis. As a *Quick Graph*, Correlations includes a SPLOM (matrix of scatterplots) where the data in each plot correspond to a value in the matrix.

For continuous data, Correlations provides the Pearson correlation, covariances, and sums of squares of deviations from the mean and sums of cross-products of deviations (SSCP). In addition to the usual probabilities, the Bonferroni and Dunn-Sidak adjustments are available with Pearson correlations. If distances are desired, Euclidean or city-block distances are available. Similarity measures for continuous data include the Bray-Curtis coefficient and the QSK quantitative symmetric coefficient (or Kulczynski measure).

For rank-order data, Correlations provides Goodman-Kruskal's gamma, Guttman's mu2, Spearman's rho, and Kendall's tau.

For binary data, Correlations provides S2, the positive matching dichotomy coefficient; S3, Jaccard's dichotomy coefficient; S4, the simple matching dichotomy coefficient; S5, Anderberg's dichotomy coefficient; and S6, Tanimoto's dichotomy coefficient. When underlying distributions are assumed to be normal, the tetrachoric correlation is available.

When data are missing, listwise and pairwise deletion methods are available for all measures. An EM algorithm is an option for maximum likelihood estimates of correlation, covariance, and cross-products of deviations matrices. For robust ML estimates where outliers are downweighted, the user can specify the degrees of freedom for the t distribution or contamination for a normal distribution. Correlations includes a graphical display of the pattern of missing values. Little's MCAR test is printed with the display. The EM algorithm also identifies cases with extreme Mahalanobis distances.

Hadi's robust outlier detection and estimation procedure is an option for correlations, covariances, and SSCP; cases identified as outliers by the procedure are not used to compute estimates.

Overview

Correlations, Similarities, and Distance Measures

Overview

Correlations on the **Stats** menu provides the following types of correlation and similarity measures:

Pearson	Pearson correlations
Covariance	Covariances
SSCP	Sums of squares of deviations from the mean and cross-products of deviations
Euclidean	Normalized Euclidean distances
City	City-block distances
Bray-Curtis	Bray-Curtis similarity coefficients
QSK	Quantitative symmetric similarity coefficients (also called Kulczynski measures)
Spearman	Spearman rank-order correlations
Gamma	Goodman-Kruskal gamma coefficients
Tau	Kendall's tau-*b* coefficient
Mu2	Guttman's mu2 monotonicity coefficients
Tetra	Tetrachoric correlations
S2, S3, S4, S5, S6	Dichotomy coefficients

Getting started For a full matrix or a portion of a matrix, and distance or similarity measures, use **Stats ⟹ Correlations**:

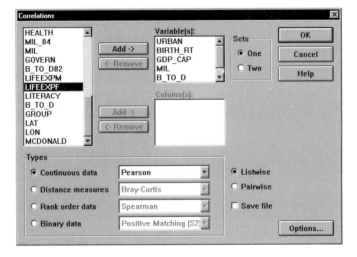

For probabilities associated with each correlation coefficient, Expectation Maximization estimation, and Hadi outlier identification and estimation, use **Stats ➡ Correlations ➡ Options**:

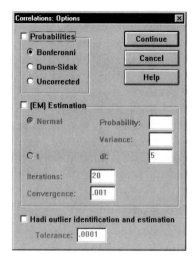

Using commands

First, choose what data to use:

    USE *filename*

Then, choose your measure and type:

Full matrix   *MEASURE varlist / options*

Portion of matrix   *MEASURE rowlist * collist / options*

Correlations, Covariances, and SSCP

Correlations computes many different measures of the strength of association between variables. The most popular measure, and the one after which Correlations is named, is the Pearson correlation. The **Pearson correlation** coefficient varies between −1 and +1. A Pearson correlation of 0 indicates that neither of two variables can be predicted from the other by using a linear equation. A Pearson correlation of 1 indicates that one variable can be predicted perfectly by a positive linear function of the other, and vice versa. And a value of −1 indicates the same, except that the function has a negative sign for the slope of the line.

The **Pearson**, **Covariance**, and **SSCP** measures are related. The entries in an SSCP matrix are sums of squares of deviations (from the mean) and sums of cross-products of deviations. If you divide each entry by $(n-1)$, variances result from the sums of squares, and covariances result from the sums of cross-products. When you divide each covariance by the product of the standard deviations (of the two variables), the result is a correlation.

Correlations provides the same options for these three measures, except those that produce probabilities (**Bonferroni**, **Dunn-Sidak**, and **Uncorrected**) are available only with **Pearson**.

Even if your goal is another similarity or distance measure and not Pearson correlations, you should skim this section because the following common features are illustrated:

- Formatting the matrix of results
- Transforming variables
- Estimating correlations (or other measures) when some values are missing
- Producing separate results for subgroups
- Saving correlations or a matrix of measures

The scatterplot matrix *Quick Graph* feature is also introduced.

9.1
Pearson
correlations

This example uses data from the *OURWORLD* file that contains records (cases) for 57 countries. We are interested in correlations among variables recording the percentage of the population living in cities, birth rate, gross domestic product per capita, dollars expended per person for the military, ratio of birth rates to death rates, life expectancy (in years) for males and females, percentage of the population who can read, and gross national product per capita in 1986.

Use **Correlations**➠ **Continuous data**➠ **Pearson** and select *URBAN*, *BIRTH_RT*, *GDP_CAP*, *MIL*, *B_TO_D*, *LIFEEXPM*, *LIFEEXPF*, *LITERACY*, and *GNP_86* as variables. With commands:

```
CORR
    USE ourworld
    PEARSON urban birth_rt gdp_cap mil b_to_d lifeexpm,
        lifeexpf literacy gnp_86
```

❶
```
Pearson correlation matrix

              URBAN BIRTH_RT  GDP_CAP      MIL   B_TO_D LIFEEXPM LIFEEXPF
URBAN         1.000
BIRTH_RT     -0.800    1.000
GDP_CAP       0.625   -0.762    1.000
MIL           0.597   -0.672    0.899    1.000
B_TO_D       -0.307    0.511   -0.659   -0.607    1.000
LIFEEXPM      0.776   -0.922    0.664    0.582   -0.211    1.000
LIFEEXPF      0.801   -0.949    0.704    0.619   -0.265    0.989    1.000
LITERACY      0.800   -0.930    0.637    0.562   -0.274    0.911    0.935
GNP_86        0.592   -0.689    0.964    0.873   -0.560    0.633    0.665

           LITERACY   GNP_86
LITERACY      1.000
GNP_86        0.611    1.000

Number of observations: 49
```

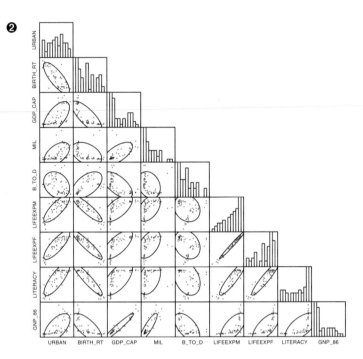

The highlighted numbers below correspond to those in the output:

❶ The correlations for all pairs of the nine variables are shown here. The bottom of the output panel shows that the sample size is 49, but the data file has 57 countries. If a country has one or more missing values, SYSTAT, by default, omits all of the data for the case. This is called **listwise deletion**. In Example 9.3, for each pair of variables, we use all available data. This is called **pairwise deletion**. In Example 9.4, we select **EM**, or the maximum likelihood method, for estimating correlations when data are missing

❷ This *Quick Graph* is a SPLOM—that is, a matrix of scatterplots with one plot for each entry in the correlation matrix. To turn this feature off, deselect **Statistical Quickgraphs** in the **Edit ➡ Options** dialog box (with commands: GRAPH=NONE).

The display shows histograms of each variable on the diagonal and scatterplots of each variable against the other. For example, the plot of *BIRTH_RT* against *URBAN* is at the top left under the histogram for *URBAN*. To identify the *x* and *y* variables in a particular plot, look at the bottom of its column for the name of the *x* variable and in its row for the *y* variable. To characterize the relation within each plot, SYSTAT adds a 75% ellipse that assumes a Gaussian (normal) bivariate distribution. The center of each ellipse is the sample mean of the *x* and *y* variables in the plot, its axes are determined by the standard deviations of *x* and *y*, and its orientation is determined by the sample covariance between *x* and *y*. In Example 9.2, we'll discuss further the configuration of points in these plots and the need for a transformation.

Requesting means

When you select **Output Results ▶ Long** in the **Edit ▶ Options** dialog box (with commands: PRINT=LONG), SYSTAT prints the mean of each variable for the 49 cases (that is, the cases that have no values missing for the nine-variable subset). This option is also available with **Covariance** and **SSCP**.

```
Means
              URBAN BIRTH_RT  GDP_CAP      MIL   B_TO_D LIFEEXPM LIFEEXPF
             52.878   25.959 5484.213  116.136    2.885   65.429   70.571

            LITERACY   GNP_86
             74.727 4210.408
```

Altering the format

The correlation matrix above wraps (the results for nine variables do not fit in one panel). You can use the **Data/Output Format** options in the **Edit ▶ Options** dialog box to squeeze in more results by specifying **Field width** and **Decimal places**. For example, the same correlations printed in fields 7 characters wide (the default is 12) and also 6 characters wide are shown below. For the latter, we request only 2 digits to the right of the decimal instead of 3.

continuing from the previous correlation matrix
```
FORM 7 3
PEARSON urban birth_rt gdp_cap mil b_to_d,
        lifeexpm lifeexpf literacy gnp_86

FORM 6 2
PEARSON urban birth_rt gdp_cap mil b_to_d,
        lifeexpm lifeexpf literacy gnp_86
```

With commands, press F9 to retrieve the previous PEARSON statement instead of retyping it.

```
Pearson correlation matrix

          URBAN BIRTH_  GDP_CA    MIL B_TO_D LIFEEX LIFEEX LITERA GNP_86
URBAN     1.000
BIRTH_RT  -0.800  1.000
GDP_CAP    0.625 -0.762  1.000
MIL        0.597 -0.672  0.899  1.000
B_TO_D    -0.307  0.511 -0.659 -0.607  1.000
LIFEEXPM   0.776 -0.922  0.664  0.582 -0.211  1.000
LIFEEXPF   0.801 -0.949  0.704  0.619 -0.265  0.989  1.000
LITERACY   0.800 -0.930  0.637  0.562 -0.274  0.911  0.935  1.000
GNP_86     0.592 -0.689  0.964  0.873 -0.560  0.633  0.665  0.611  1.000

Number of observations: 49

Pearson correlation matrix

          URBAN BIRTH GDP_C    MIL B_TO_ LIFEE LIFEE LITER GNP_8
URBAN     1.00
BIRTH_RT  -0.80  1.00
GDP_CAP    0.62 -0.76  1.00
MIL        0.60 -0.67  0.90  1.00
B_TO_D    -0.31  0.51 -0.66 -0.61  1.00
LIFEEXPM   0.78 -0.92  0.66  0.58 -0.21  1.00
LIFEEXPF   0.80 -0.95  0.70  0.62 -0.26  0.99  1.00
LITERACY   0.80 -0.93  0.64  0.56 -0.27  0.91  0.93  1.00
GNP_86     0.59 -0.69  0.96  0.87 -0.56  0.63  0.67  0.61  1.00

Number of observations: 49
```

Notice that while the top row of variable names is truncated to fit within the field specification, the row names remain complete.

Requesting a portion of a matrix

You can request that only a portion of the matrix (correlations or any other measure in this chapter) be computed. Select **Two** from the **Sets** options in the **Correlations** dialog box, select *LIFEEXPM*, *LIFEEXPF*, *LITERACY*, and *GNP_86* as variables, and then select *URBAN*, *BIRTH_RT*, *GDP_CAP*, *MIL*, and *B_TO_D* as columns.

```
FORMAT
PEARSON lifeexpm lifeexpf literacy gnp_86 *,
        urban birth_rt gdp_cap mil b_to_d
```

```
Pearson correlation matrix

           URBAN   BIRTH_RT   GDP_CAP      MIL    B_TO_D
LIFEEXPM   0.776    -0.922     0.664     0.582    -0.211
LIFEEXPF   0.801    -0.949     0.704     0.619    -0.265
LITERACY   0.800    -0.930     0.637     0.562    -0.274
GNP_86     0.592    -0.689     0.964     0.873    -0.560

Number of observations: 49
```

These correlations are from the lower left corner of the first matrix.

9.2
Transforma-
tions

Correlations, covariances, and SSCP measure linear relations. If linearity does not hold for your variables, your results may be meaningless. A good way to assess linearity, the presence of outliers, and other anomalies is to vet the plot for each pair of variables in the scatterplot matrix above. The relation of *GDP_CAP* to *BIRTH_RT*, *B_TO_D*, *LIFEEXPM*, and *LIFEEXPF* does not appear to be linear. Also, the points in the *MIL* versus *GDP_CAP* and *GNP_86* versus *MIL* displays clump in the lower left corner.

It is not wise to use correlations for describing these relations. Therefore, you can log transform *GDP_CAP*, *MIL*, and *GNP_86*.

Correlations for transformed values

We now transform *GDP_CAP*, *MIL*, and *GNP_86* and request correlations for the variables from the previous example (use **Data ➧ Transform**):

```
LET gdp_cap = L10(gdp_cap)
LET     mil = L10(mil)
LET  gnp_86 = L10(gnp_86)
```

or use SYSTAT's shortcut notation:

```
LET (gdp_cap,mil,gnp_86)=L10(@)
```

After transforming the variables, use **Correlations ➧ Continuous data ➧ Pearson** and select *URBAN*, *BIRTH_RT*, *GDP_CAP*, *MIL*, *B_TO_D*, *LIFEEXPM*, *LIFEEXPF*, *LITERACY*, and *GNP_86* as variables. With commands:

```
continuing from Example 9.1
LET (gdp_cap,mil,gnp_86) = L10(@)
PRINT = LONG
PEARSON urban birth_rt gdp_cap mil b_to_d,
        lifeexpm lifeexpf literacy gnp_86
```

❶ Means

	URBAN	BIRTH_RT	GDP_CAP	MIL	B_TO_D	LIFEEXPM	LIFEEXPF
	52.878	25.959	3.370	1.695	2.885	65.429	70.571

	LITERACY	GNP_86
	74.727	3.279

❷ Pearson correlation matrix

	URBAN	BIRTH_RT	GDP_CAP	MIL	B_TO_D	LIFEEXPM	LIFEEXPF
URBAN	1.000						
BIRTH_RT	-0.800	1.000					
GDP_CAP	0.764	-0.919	1.000				
MIL	0.680	-0.801	0.895	1.000			
B_TO_D	-0.307	0.511	-0.529	-0.537	1.000		
LIFEEXPM	0.776	-0.922	0.860	0.727	-0.211	1.000	
LIFEEXPF	0.801	-0.949	0.895	0.763	-0.265	0.989	1.000
LITERACY	0.800	-0.930	0.834	0.714	-0.274	0.911	0.935
GNP_86	0.775	-0.879	0.974	0.877	-0.441	0.861	0.886

	LITERACY	GNP_86
LITERACY	1.000	
GNP_86	0.840	1.000

Number of observations: 49

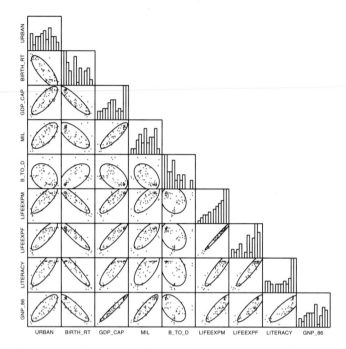

In the scatterplot matrix, linearity has improved in the plots involving *GDP_CAP*, *MIL*, and *GNP_86*.

❶ These means are computed using the 49 cases that have all values present for the nine variables selected.

❷ Look at the difference between the correlations before and after transformation.

	Transformation			Transformation			Transformation	
	no	yes		no	yes		no	yes
gdp_cap vs.			mil vs.			gnp_86 vs.		
urban	.625	.764	urban	.597	.680	urban	.592	.775
birth_rt	-.762	-.919	birth_rt	-.672	-.801	birth_rt	-.689	-.879
lifeexpm	.664	.860	lifeexpm	.582	.727	lifeexpm	.633	.861
lifeexpf	.704	.895	lifeexpf	.619	.763	lifeexpf	.665	.886
literacy	.637	.834	literacy	.562	.714	literacy	.611	.840

After log transforming the variables, linearity has improved in the plots, and many of the correlations are stronger.

9.3
Missing data:
Complete pairs

Because eight cases have one or two values missing, none of their data are used in the first two examples. This is called **listwise deletion**, or *using complete cases only*. SYSTAT provides two other approaches for estimating correlations when data are missing. Select:

Listwise	If any variable you specify has a missing value, the case is omitted from the computation. This is the default.
Pairwise	Correlations are computed separately for each pair of variables, using only cases that have both values.
EM	A maximum likelihood Expectation Maximization method is used to estimate correlations. **EM** is available from **Stats➧Correlations➧Options**. See Example 9.4.

Listwise and **Pairwise** are available for all **Correlations** correlations, similarity measures, and distances. **EM** is available for **Pearson**, **Covariance**, and **SSCP**.

With pairwise deletion, you get the same correlation (covariance or sum of cross-products) for two variables containing missing data if you select them alone or with other variables containing missing data. With listwise deletion, correlations under these circumstances may differ, depending on the pattern of how values of the other variables are missing. If you use pairwise deletion to compute an SSCP matrix, the sums of squares and cross-products are weighted by N/n, where N is the number of cases in the whole file and n is the number of cases with nonmissing values in a given pair.

Pairwise deletion is one of the worst ways to handle missing values. If as few as 20% of the values in a data matrix are missing, it is not difficult to find two correlations that were computed using substantially different subsets of the cases. In such cases, it is common to encounter error messages that the matrix is singular in regression programs and to get eigenvalues less than 0.

But, more important, *classical statistical analyses require complete cases*. For exploration, this restriction can be circumvented by identifying one or more variables that are not needed, deleting them, and requesting the desired analysis—there should be more complete cases for this smaller set of variables.

If you have missing values, you may want to compare results from pairwise deletion with those from the EM method in Example 9.4. Or, you may want to take the time to replace the missing values in the raw data by examining similar cases or variables with nonmissing values. One way to do this is to compute a regression equation to predict each variable from nonmissing data on other variables and then use that equation to predict missing values. For more information about missing values, see Little and Rubin (1987). This example uses the same variables used in Example 9.1, with the transformations from Example 9.2 still in effect. Select **Correlations ⇒ Pairwise** to estimate correlations. With commands:

```
continuing with the transformations from Example 9.2
GRAPH = NONE
PRINT = LONG
CORR
PEARSON urban birth_rt gdp_cap mil b_to_d,
        lifeexpm lifeexpf literacy gnp_86 / PAIR
```

```
Means
                    URBAN      BIRTH_RT       GDP_CAP           MIL        B_TO_D
                   52.821        26.351         3.372         1.775         2.873
                 LIFEEXPM      LIFEEXPF       LITERACY        GNP_86
                   65.088        70.123        73.563         3.293

Pearson correlation matrix

                    URBAN      BIRTH_RT       GDP_CAP           MIL        B_TO_D
URBAN               1.000
BIRTH_RT           -0.781         1.000
GDP_CAP             0.778        -0.895         1.000
MIL                 0.683        -0.687         0.857         1.000
B_TO_D             -0.248         0.535        -0.472        -0.377         1.000
LIFEEXPM            0.796        -0.892         0.854         0.696        -0.172
LIFEEXPF            0.816        -0.924         0.891         0.721        -0.230
LITERACY            0.807        -0.930         0.832         0.646        -0.291
GNP_86              0.775        -0.881         0.974         0.881        -0.455
                 LIFEEXPM      LIFEEXPF       LITERACY        GNP_86
LIFEEXPM            1.000
LIFEEXPF            0.989         1.000
LITERACY            0.911         0.937         1.000
GNP_86              0.863         0.888         0.842         1.000

Pairwise frequency table

                    URBAN      BIRTH_RT       GDP_CAP           MIL        B_TO_D
URBAN                  56
BIRTH_RT               56            57
GDP_CAP                56            57            57
MIL                    55            56            56            56
B_TO_D                 56            57            57            56            57
LIFEEXPM               56            57            57            56            57
LIFEEXPF               56            57            57            56            57
LITERACY               56            57            57            56            57
GNP_86                 49            50            50            50            50
                 LIFEEXPM      LIFEEXPF       LITERACY        GNP_86
LIFEEXPM               57
LIFEEXPF               57            57
LITERACY               57            57            57
GNP_86                 50            50            50            50
```

The sample size for each variable is reported as the diagonal of the *Pairwise frequency table*; sample sizes for complete pairs of cases are reported off the diagonal. There are 57 countries in this sample—56 reported the percentage living in cities (*URBAN*), and 50 reported the gross national product per capita in 1986 (*GNP_86*). There are 49 countries that have values for *both* variables.

The means are printed because we specified PRINT=LONG. Since **Pairwise** is requested, all available values are used to compute each mean—that is, these means are the same as those computed in the **Stats** procedure.

9.4 Missing data: EM estimation

Instead of pairwise deletion, many data analysts prefer to use an EM algorithm when estimating correlations, covariances, or an SSCP matrix. For these measures, **EM** is available from **Stats**➧**Correlations**➧ **Options**. EM uses the maximum likelihood method to compute the estimates. This procedure defines a model for the partially missing data and bases inferences on the likelihood under that model. Each iteration consists of an E step and an M step. The E step finds the conditional expectation of the "missing" data given the observed values and current estimates of the parameters. These expectations are then substituted for the "missing" data. For the M step, maximum likelihood estimation is performed as though the missing data had been filled in. "Missing" data is enclosed in quotation marks because the missing values are not being directly filled but, rather, functions of them are used in the loglikelihood.

You should take care in assessing the pattern of how the values are missing. Given variables *X* and *Y* (age and income, for example), is the probability of a response:

1. Independent of the values of *X* and *Y*? That is, is the probability that income is recorded the same for all people regardless of their ages or incomes? The recorded or observed values of income form a random subsample of the true incomes for all of the people in the sample. Little and Rubin call this pattern **MCAR**, for *Missing Completely At Random*.

2. Dependent on *X* but not on *Y*? In this case, the probability that income is recorded depends on the subject's age, so the probability varies by age but not by income *within that age group*. This pattern is called **MAR**, for *Missing At Random*.

3. Dependent on *Y* and possibly *X* also? In this case, the probability that income is present varies by the value of income within each age group. This is not an unusual pattern for real-world applications.

To use the EM algorithm, your data should be MCAR or at least MAR.

Request long output by selecting **Output Results**➡**Long** in the **Edit**➡**Options** dialog box. *COUNTRY$* is defined as an ID variable by selecting it in the **Data**➡**ID Variable** dialog box. This example uses the same variables used in Example 9.1, with the transformations from Example 9.2 still in effect. Choose the EM algorithm by selecting **Stats**➡**Correlations**➡**Options**. In addition to EM estimates of the means, this provides the pattern of where values are missing and Little's MCAR test.

continuing with the transformations from Example 9.2
```
IDVAR = country$
GRAPH = NONE
PRINT = LONG
PEARSON urban birth_rt gdp_cap mil b_to_d lifeexpm,
        lifeexpf literacy gnp_86 / EM
```

❶
EM Algorithm	Iteration	Maximum Error	-2*log(likelihood)
	1	1.092328	24135.483249
	2	1.023878	7625.491302
	3	0.643113	6932.605472
	4	0.666125	6691.458724
	5	0.857590	6573.199525
	6	2.718236	6538.852550
	7	0.728468	6531.689766
	8	0.196577	6530.369252
	9	0.077590	6530.167056
	10	0.034510	6530.159651
	11	0.016278	6530.176410
	12	0.007986	6530.190050
	13	0.004050	6530.198695
	14	0.002120	6530.203895
	15	0.001145	6530.207008
	16	0.000637	6530.208887

❷
```
No.of  Missing value patterns

Cases  (X=nonmissing; .=missing)
 49    XXXXXXXX
  1    .XXXXXXX
  6    XXXXXXXX.

  1    XXX.XXXX.
```

❸
```
Little MCAR test statistic:   782751.151  df =   23  prob = 0.000
```

❹
```
EM estimate of means
                  URBAN     BIRTH_RT    GDP_CAP        MIL       B_TO_D
                 53.152       26.351      3.372      1.754        2.873
               LIFEEXPM     LIFEEXPF    LITERACY     GNP_86
                 65.088       70.123     73.563      3.284
```

❺
```
EM estimated correlation matrix
```

	URBAN	BIRTH_RT	GDP_CAP	MIL	B_TO_D
URBAN	1.000				
BIRTH_RT	-0.782	1.000			
GDP_CAP	0.779	-0.895	1.000		
MIL	0.700	-0.697	0.863	1.000	
B_TO_D	-0.259	0.535	-0.472	-0.357	1.000
LIFEEXPM	0.796	-0.892	0.854	0.713	-0.172
LIFEEXPF	0.816	-0.924	0.891	0.738	-0.230
LITERACY	0.808	-0.930	0.832	0.668	-0.291
GNP_86	0.796	-0.831	0.968	0.874	-0.342
	LIFEEXPM	LIFEEXPF	LITERACY	GNP_86	
LIFEEXPM	1.000				
LIFEEXPF	0.989	1.000			
LITERACY	0.911	0.937	1.000		
GNP_86	0.863	0.885	0.828	1.000	

If PRINT=LONG is omitted, the first four output panels are not printed. The highlighted numbers below correspond to those in the output:

❶ SYSTAT reports information about the iterations needed to reach a solution.

❷ Pattern of values missing. Forty-nine cases in the sample are complete (an *X* is printed for each of the nine variables). Periods are inserted where data are missing. The value of the first variable, *URBAN*, is missing for one case, while the value of the last variable, *GNP_86*, is missing for six cases. The last row of the pattern indicates that the values of the fourth variable, *MIL*, and the last variable, *GNP_86*, are both missing for one case.

❸ Little's MCAR test has a probability less than 0.0005, indicating that we reject the hypothesis that the nine missing values are randomly missing. This test has limited power when the sample of incomplete cases is small and it also offers no direct evidence on the validity of the MAR assumption.

❹ *EM estimate of means.* Compare these means with the means from the other methods.

❺ *EM estimated correlation matrix.*

Options
for EM

EM provides options for controlling the computation (**Iterations** and **Convergence**) and downweighting the influence of outliers on the estimates (**t** and **Normal**):

Normal=*n1, n2*   ML estimates for contaminated multivariate normal samples, where *n1* is the probability of contamination and *n2* is the variance ($\sigma^2/n1$) of the contamination. See "Robust estimates" below.

t=*df*   ML estimates for a *t* distribution sample, where *df* is the degrees of freedom. The default is 5. See "Robust estimates" below.

Iterations=*n*   Maximum number of iterations for computing the estimates. The default is 20.

Convergence=*n*   Convergence criterion. If the relative change of covariance entries are all less than this value, convergence is assumed. The default is 0.001.

With commands:

```
PEARSON or COVA or SSCP / EM ITER=n, CONV=n, TOL=n,
                              T=df, NORMAL=n1,n2
```

Robust estimates

Both the multivariate t and contaminated normal models downweight the influence of outliers (observations with large squared distances). Downweighting for the latter tends to be concentrated in a few outlying cases, while that for the former is more spread out. For these methods, the pattern of how values are missing is assumed to be MCAR or MAR.

For the t distribution, use **t** to specify the known degrees of freedom, v, for the t distribution. The degree of downweighting is inversely related to v. For example, try values like 4 or 6 and choose the one that produces the largest maximized loglikelihood. For the contaminated normal, SYSTAT assumes that the distribution is a mixture of $N(\mu,\sigma^2)$ and $N(\mu, \sigma^2/\lambda)$ with π probability of contamination. Use **Normal** to specify π and λ. For example, let $\pi = 0.10$ (for 10% contamination) and $\lambda = 0.008$.

Outliers

When PRINT=LONG, **EM** also identifies outliers. There were none in the current run. The outlier report from another run is shown here:

```
Case Iraq is an outlier. Mahalanobis D^2=26.284893  z=3.086498
```

The case label *Iraq* is printed because we specified *COUNTRY$* as an ID variable.

9.5 Bonferroni and Dunn-Sidak adjusted probabilities

Pearson provides three options for displaying the probability associated with each correlation coefficient. These options are available from Stats➠Correlations➠Options.

Bonferroni	An adjustment is made to the probability that allows for multiple testing—that is, use these probabilities when scanning a matrix for significant correlations.
Dunn-Sidak	An adjustment similar to that of the Bonferroni. See Chapter 5 for comments about the formula.
Uncorrected	The usual probability associated with a single correlation coefficient. Appropriate only if, a priori, you select a specific correlation to report.

With commands:

```
PEARSON varlist / BONF  DUNN  PROB
```

We now request the usual probabilities for the Example 9.3 correlation matrix computed with pairwise deletion and Bonferroni adjustments for the same matrix and for that obtained via EM estimation in Example 9.4. To request the probabilities, choose **Probabilities** and **Uncorrected** from **Stats ⇒ Correlations ⇒ Options**.

continuing from Example 9.4
```
PEARSON urban birth_rt gdp_cap mil b_to_d,
        lifeexpm lifeexpf literacy gnp_86 / PAIR PROB
```

Probabilities for a single correlation

The *p* values that are appropriate for making statements regarding one specific correlation are shown here. They are associated with the Pearson correlations in Example 9.3.

```
Bartlett Chi-square statistic:    815.067 DF=36 Prob= 0.000

Matrix of Probabilities

                 URBAN      BIRTH_RT      GDP_CAP         MIL      B_TO_D
URBAN            0.0
BIRTH_RT         0.000       0.000
GDP_CAP          0.000       0.000        0.0
MIL              0.000       0.000        0.000        0.0
B_TO_D           0.065       0.000        0.000        0.004       0.0
LIFEEXPM         0.000       0.000        0.000        0.000       0.202
LIFEEXPF         0.000       0.000        0.000        0.000       0.085
LITERACY         0.000       0.000        0.000        0.000       0.028
GNP_86           0.000       0.000        0.000        0.000       0.001
                 LIFEEXPM    LIFEEXPF     LITERACY      GNP_86
LIFEEXPM         0.0
LIFEEXPF         0.000       0.0
LITERACY         0.000       0.000        0.0
GNP_86           0.000       0.000        0.000        0.0
```

This results in *p* values for each correlation in the matrix. By themselves, these values are not very informative. These *p* values are pseudo-probabilities because *they do not reflect the number of correlations being tested*. If pairwise deletion is used, the problem is even worse, although many statistics packages print probabilities as if they meant something in this case, too.

SYSTAT computes the Bartlett chi-square test whenever you request probabilities for more than one correlation. This tests a global hypothesis concerning the significance of all of the correlations in the matrix

$$\chi^2 = \left\{ N - 1 - \frac{(2p+1)}{6} \right\} ln|\mathbf{R}|$$

where N is the total sample size (or the smallest sample size for any pair in the matrix if pairwise deletion is used), p is the number of variables, and $|R|$ is the determinant of the correlation matrix. This test is sensitive to non-normality, and the test statistic is only asymptotically distributed (for large samples) as chi-square. Nevertheless, it can serve as a guideline.

If the Bartlett test is not significant, don't even look at the significance of individual correlations. In this example, the test is significant, which indicates that there may be some real correlations among the variables. The Bartlett test is sensitive to non-normality and can be used only as a guide. Even if the Bartlett test is significant, you cannot accept the nominal p values as the true family probabilities associated with each correlation.

Bonferroni probabilities with pairwise deletion

Let's now examine the probabilities adjusted by the Bonferroni method that provides protection for multiple tests. (Again, they are associated with the Pearson correlations in Example 9.3.) Remember that the log-transformed values from the previous request are still in effect. To request the probabilities, choose **Probabilities** and **Bonferroni** from **Stats**➠**Correlations**➠**Options**.

```
PEARSON urban birth_rt gdp_cap mil b_to_d lifeexpm,
        lifeexpf literacy gnp_86 / PAIR BONF
```

```
Bartlett Chi-square statistic:    815.067 DF=36 Prob= 0.000

Matrix of Bonferroni Probabilities

             URBAN BIRTH_RT  GDP_CAP     MIL   B_TO_D LIFEEXPM LIFEEXPF
URBAN        0.0
BIRTH_RT     0.000   0.0
GDP_CAP      0.000   0.000    0.000
MIL          0.000   0.000    0.000    0.0
B_TO_D       1.000   0.001    0.008    0.151   0.0
LIFEEXPM     0.000   0.000    0.000    0.000   1.000    0.0
LIFEEXPF     0.000   0.000    0.000    0.000   1.000    0.000    0.0
LITERACY     0.000   0.000    0.000    0.000   1.000    0.000    0.000
GNP_86       0.000   0.000    0.000    0.000   0.032    0.000    0.000

            LITERACY  GNP_86
LITERACY     0.0
GNP_86       0.000    0.0
```

*** *We omit the pairwise frequency table. See Example 9.3.* ***

Compare these results with those for the 36 tests in the previous panel. Notice that some correlations, such as those for *B_TO_D* with *MIL*, *LITERACY*, and *GNP_86*, are no longer significant.

Bonferroni
probabilities
for EM
estimates

The Bonferroni adjusted probabilities for the EM estimated matrix in Example 9.4 are shown here. (Remember that the log transformations are still in effect.)

```
PEARSON urban birth_rt gdp_cap mil b_to_d lifeexpm,
            lifeexpf literacy gnp_86 / EM  BONF
```

```
Bartlett Chi-square statistic:    821.288 DF=36 Prob= 0.000

Matrix of Bonferroni Probabilities

              URBAN BIRTH_RT  GDP_CAP     MIL   B_TO_D LIFEEXPM LIFEEXPF
  URBAN       0.0
  BIRTH_RT    0.000    0.0
  GDP_CAP     0.000    0.000    0.0
  MIL         0.000    0.000    0.000    0.0
  B_TO_D      1.000    0.001    0.008    0.248    0.0
  LIFEEXPM    0.000    0.000    0.000    0.000    1.000    0.000
  LIFEEXPF    0.000    0.000    0.000    0.000    1.000    0.000    0.0
  LITERACY    0.000    0.000    0.000    0.000    1.000    0.000    0.000
  GNP_86      0.000    0.000    0.000    0.000    0.537    0.000    0.000

              LITERACY  GNP_86
  LITERACY    0.0
  GNP_86      0.000     0.000
```

*** We omit the pairwise frequency table. See Example 9.3. ***

9.6
Hadi
robust outlier
detection

The **Hadi** outlier identification and estimation option is available with **Pearson**, **Covariance**, and **SSCP** and works for complete cases only (that is, listwise deletion). To request the probabilities, choose **Probabilities** and **Uncorrected** from the **Stats**➠**Correlations**➠**Options** dialog box. It identifies specific cases as outliers (if there are any) and then uses the acceptable cases to compute the requested measure in the usual way. Following are the steps for this procedure:

– Compute a "robust" covariance matrix by finding the median (instead of the mean) for each variable and using $\Sigma(x_i - median)^2$ in the calculation of each covariance. If the resulting matrix is singular, reconstruct another after inflating the smallest eigenvalues by a small amount.

– Use this robust estimate of the covariance matrix to compute Mahalanobis distances and then use the distance to rank the cases.

– Use the half of the sample with the lowest ranks to compute the usual covariance matrix (that is, deviations from the mean).

– Use this covariance matrix to compute new distances for the complete sample and rerank the cases.

– After ranking, select the same number of cases with small ranks as before but add the case with the next largest rank and repeat the

process, each time updating the covariance matrix, computing and sorting new distances, and increasing the subsample size by one.
- Continue adding cases until the entering one exceeds an internal limit based on a chi-square statistic (see Hadi, 1994). The cases remaining (not entered) are identified as outliers.
- Use the cases that are not identified as outliers to compute the measure requested in the usual way.

With commands:

```
PEARSON or COVA or SSCP varlist/ HADI
```

If only one or two variables have outliers among many well behaved variables, the outliers may be masked. Let's look for outliers among four variables. Use **Stats**➦**Correlations**➦ **Continuous data**➦**Pearson** and select *GDP_CAP*, *MIL*, *B_TO_D*, and *LITERACY* as variables. The transformations from Example 9.2 are still in effect for *GDP_CAP* and *MIL. COUNTRY$* is defined as an ID variable by selecting it in the **Data**➦ **ID Variable** dialog box. To request Hadi outlier identification, use **Stats**➦**Correlations**➦ **Options**➦**Pearson**➦**Hadi outlier identification and estimation**.
With commands:

```
CORR
    USE ourworld
    LET (gdp_cap, mil) = L10(@)
    GRAPH = NONE
    PRINT = LONG
    IDVAR = country$
    PEARSON gdp_cap mil b_to_d literacy / HADI
```

❶
```
These 15 outliers are identified:
       Case       Distance
   -----------   -----------
Venezuela         4.48653
CostaRica         4.55336
Senegal           4.66615
Sudan             4.74882
Ethiopia          4.82013
Pakistan          5.05827
Libya             5.10295
Haiti             5.44901
Bangladesh        5.47974
Yemen             5.84027
Gambia            5.84202
Iraq              5.84507
Guinea            6.12308
Somalia           6.18465
Mali              6.30091
```

❷
```
Means of variables of non-outlying cases
               GDP_CAP     MIL   B_TO_D LITERACY
                 3.634   1.967    2.533   88.183
```

❸
```
HADI estimated correlation matrix

               GDP_CAP     MIL   B_TO_D LITERACY
GDP_CAP          1.000
MIL              0.860   1.000
B_TO_D          -0.839  -0.753    1.000
LITERACY         0.729   0.642   -0.698    1.000

Number of observations: 56
```

The highlighted numbers below correspond to those in the output:

❶ Fifteen countries are identified as outliers. We suspect that the sample may not be homogeneous and we will request a plot after viewing this output. The panel is set to PRINT=LONG; the country names appear because we specified *COUNTRY$* as an ID variable.

❷ The means are printed because we specified PRINT=LONG.

❸ These correlations are computed using the 30 or so cases that are not identified as outliers.

Let's look at this sample graphically and identify countries as European (E), Islamic (I), or New World (N).

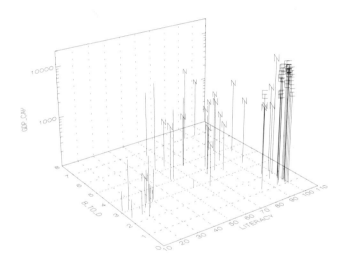

Stratifying the analysis

We'll use **Hadi** for each of the three groups separately.

continuing from the previous run
```
BY group$
PEARSON gdp_cap mil b_to_d literacy / HADI
BY
```

The request for extended output is still in effect. For clarity, we edited the following output by moving the panels of means to the end:

```
The following results are for:

   GROUP$      = Europe

These 1 outliers are identified:
    Case      Distance
------------  ------------
Portugal       5.72050

HADI estimated correlation matrix

                GDP_CAP        MIL       B_TO_D    LITERACY
GDP_CAP          1.000
MIL              0.474      1.000
B_TO_D          -0.092     -0.173      1.000
LITERACY         0.259      0.263      0.136      1.000

Number of observations: 20

The following results are for:

   GROUP$      = Islamic

HADI estimated correlation matrix

                GDP_CAP        MIL       B_TO_D    LITERACY
GDP_CAP          1.000
MIL              0.877      1.000
B_TO_D           0.781      0.882      1.000
LITERACY         0.600      0.605      0.649      1.000

Number of observations: 15

The following results are for:

   GROUP$      = NewWorld

HADI estimated correlation matrix

                GDP_CAP        MIL       B_TO_D    LITERACY
GDP_CAP          1.000
MIL              0.674      1.000
B_TO_D          -0.246     -0.287      1.000
LITERACY         0.689      0.561     -0.045      1.000

Number of observations: 21
```

*** *Here are the means for European countries* ***
```
Means of variables of non-outlying cases
                GDP_CAP      MIL    B_TO_D  LITERACY
                  4.059    2.404     1.260    98.316
```

*** *For Islamic countries* ***
```
Means of variables of non-outlying cases
                GDP_CAP      MIL    B_TO_D  LITERACY
                  2.764    1.400     3.547    36.733
```

*** *For New World countries* ***
```
Means of variables of non-outlying cases
                GDP_CAP      MIL    B_TO_D  LITERACY
                  3.214    1.466     3.951    79.957
```

When computations are done separately for each group, Portugal is the only outlier, and the within-groups correlations differ markedly from group to group and from those for the complete sample. By scanning the means, we also see that the centroids for the three groups are quite different.

Tolerance

Variables are not used in this procedure if their R^2 (with the other variables) is greater than 1—the value set for **Tolerance**. Use the **Tolerance** option to change this. The default is 0.0001.

Saving correlations or other measures

To save a correlation matrix or other measure computed in **Correlations**, select **Save file** in the **Correlations** dialog box. With commands:

```
SAVE filename
```

The results are stored in a SYSTAT file. SYSTAT automatically defines the type of file:

CORR	Pearson, Spearman, gamma, mu2, tau, tetra
DISS	City and Euclidean
COVA	Covariance
SSCP	SSCP
SIMI	BC, QSK, S2, S3, S4, S5, S6
RECT	Rectangular (see note below)

Note: *If you request a rectangular section of a matrix (rowlist * collist), SYSTAT saves the union of the row and column variables (a triangle), not just the rectangle of measures that are printed.*

You can change the file type with the following commands:

```
TYPE = CORR or DISS or COVA or SSCP or SIMI or RECT
```

Dissimilarity and Distance Measures for Continuous Data

Correlations offers two dissimilarity measures and two distance measures:

Bray-Curtis	Bray-Curtis (BC) dissimilarity measure for continuous data.
QSK	Quantitative symmetric dissimilarity coefficient, also called the Kulczynski measure.
Euclidean	Root mean squared Euclidean distance. (The normalized Euclidean distances are root mean squared distances, which keeps them from getting out of hand when the sample size is large.)
City	City-block distance (sum of absolute discrepancies).

Euclidean and city-block distance measures have been widely available in software packages for many years; Bray-Curtis and QSK are less common. For each pair of variables,

$$\text{Bray-Curtis} = \frac{\sum_k |x_{ik} - x_{jk}|}{\sum_k x_{ik} + \sum_k x_{jk}}$$

$$\text{QSK} = 1 - \frac{1}{2}\left[\sum_k \min(x_{ik}, x_{jk}) \cdot \left(\frac{1}{\sum_k x_{ik}} + \frac{1}{\sum_k x_{jk}} \right) \right]$$

where i and j are variables and k is cases. After an extensive computer simulation study, Faith, Minchin, and Belbin (1987) concluded that BC and QSK were "effective as robust measures," in terms of both rank and linear correlation. The use of these measures is similar to that for correlations (**Pearson, Covariance,** and **SSCP**), except the **EM, Prob, Bonferroni, Dunn-Sidak,** and **Hadi** options are not available.

Missing data

Listwise and **Pairwise** are available. See Example 9.3.

Measures for Rank-Order Data

Correlations provides the following measures for rank-order data:

Spearman   Spearman rank-order correlation coefficients

Gamma   Goodman-Kruskal's gamma coefficients (Goodman and Kruskal, 1954)

Mu2   Guttman's mu2 monotonicity coefficients (Shye, 1978)

Tau   Kendall's tau-*b* coefficients

If your data are simply ranks of attributes, or if you want to see how well variables are associated when you pay attention to rank ordering, you should consider these measures. The one closest to **Pearson** is **Spearman**. Spearman's rho is simply a Pearson correlation computed on the same data after converting them to ranks.

9.7
Spearman
correlations

As an example, we request **Spearman** correlations for the same data used in Example 9.1 and Example 9.2 (after transforming variables). It is often useful to compute both a **Spearman** and a **Pearson** matrix using the same data. The absolute difference between the two can reveal unusual features such as outliers and highly skewed distributions.

```
CORR
    USE ourworld
    GRAPH = NONE
    SPEARMAN urban birth_rt gdp_cap mil b_to_d,
             lifeexpm lifeexpf literacy gnp_86 / PAIR
```

```
Spearman correlation matrix

            URBAN BIRTH_RT  GDP_CAP     MIL   B_TO_D LIFEEXPM LIFEEXPF
   URBAN    1.000
BIRTH_RT   -0.749    1.000
 GDP_CAP    0.777   -0.874    1.000
     MIL    0.678   -0.670    0.848    1.000
  B_TO_D   -0.381    0.689   -0.597   -0.498    1.000
LIFEEXPM    0.731   -0.856    0.834    0.633   -0.410    1.000
LIFEEXPF    0.771   -0.902    0.910    0.709   -0.501    0.965    1.000
 LITERACY   0.760   -0.868    0.882    0.696   -0.576    0.813    0.866
  GNP_86    0.767   -0.847    0.973    0.867   -0.543    0.834    0.901

          LITERACY   GNP_86
 LITERACY   1.000
  GNP_86    0.909    1.000

    *** We have omitted the pairwise frequency table. See Example 9.3. ***
```

Note that many of these correlations are closer to the Pearson correlations for the log-transformed data in Example 9.2 than they are to the correlations for the raw data in Example 9.1.

Missing data

Listwise and Pairwise are available. See Example 9.3.

Measures for Binary Data

Correlations offers the following association measures for binary data:

S2	Positive matching dichotomy coefficients
S3	Jaccard's dichotomy coefficients
S4	Simple matching dichotomy coefficients
S5	Anderberg's dichotomy coefficients
S6	Tanimoto's dichotomy coefficients
Tetra	Tetrachoric correlation

S2 to S6 similarity coefficients. These coefficients relate variables whose values may represent the presence or absence of an attribute or simply two values. The similarity coefficients S2–S6 work only for dichotomous data scored as 0 or 1 (or any two numbers). They are documented in Gower (1985). These coefficients were chosen for SYSTAT because they are *metric* and produce symmetric positive semidefinite (Gramian) matrices, provided that you do not use the pairwise deletion option. This makes them suitable for multidimensional scaling and factoring as well as clustering. The following table shows how the similarity coefficients are computed:

$$S2 = \frac{a}{a + b + c + d}$$
Proportion of pairs with both values present

$$S3 = \frac{a}{a + b + c}$$
Proportion of pairs with both values present *given* that at least one occurs

$$S4 = \frac{a + d}{a + b + c + d}$$
Proportion of pairs where the values of both variables agree

$$S5 = \frac{a}{a + 2(b + c)}$$ S3 standardized by all possible patterns of agreement and disagreement

$$S6 = \frac{a + d}{a + 2(b + c) + d}$$ S4 standardized by all possible patterns of agreement and disagreement

When the absence of an attribute in both variables is deemed to convey no information, d should not be included in the coefficient (see S3 and S5).

Tetrachoric correlation. While the data for this measure are binary, they are assumed to be a random sample from a bivariate normal distribution. For example, let's draw a horizontal line and a vertical line on this bivariate normal distribution and count the number of observations in each quadrant.

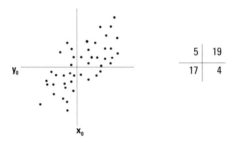

A large proportion of the observations fall in the upper right and lower left quadrants because the relationship is positive (the Pearson correlation is approximately 0.80). Correspondingly, if there were a strong negative relationship, the points would concentrate in the upper left and lower right quadrants. If the original observations are no longer available, but you do have the frequency counts for the four quadrants, try a tetrachoric correlation.

The computations for the tetrachoric correlation begin by finding estimates of the inverse cumulative marginal distributions:

$$z \text{ value for } x_0 = \Phi^{-1}\left(\frac{17 + 5}{45}\right) \text{ and } z \text{ value for } y_0 = \Phi^{-1}\left(\frac{17 + 4}{45}\right)$$

and using these values as limits when integrating the bivariate normal density expressed in terms of ρ, the correlation, and then solving for ρ.

If you have the original data, don't bother dichotomizing them because the tetrachoric correlation has an efficiency of 0.40 compared with the efficient Pearson correlation estimate.

9.8
S2 and S3
coefficients

The choice among the binary S measures depends on what you want to state about your variables. In this example, we request **S2** and **S3** to study responses made by 256 subjects to a depression inventory (Afifi and Clark, 1984). These data are stored in the *SURVEY2* data file that has one record for each respondent with answers to 20 questions about depression. Each subject was asked, for example, "Last week, did you cry less than 1 day (code 0), 1 to 2 days (code 1), 3 to 4 days (code 2), or 5 to 7 days (code 3)?" The distributions of the answers appear to be Poisson, so they are not satisfactory for Pearson correlations. Here we dichotomize the behaviors or feelings as "Did it occur or did it not?" by using transformations of the form:

```
LET blue = blue <> 0
```

The result is true (1) when the behavior or feeling is present or false (0) when it is absent. We use SYSTAT's shortcut notation to do this for seven of the 20 questions. From the dialog boxes, use **Data ➠ Transform** to transform variables. For each pair of feelings or behaviors, **S2** indicates the proportion of subjects with both, and **S3** indicates the proportion of times both occurred given that one occurs. To perform this example, use **Stats ➠ Correlations ➠ Binary Data ➠ Positive Matching** (**S2**) and select the transformed variables *BLUE, DEPRESS, CRY, SAD, NO_EAT, GETGOING*, and *TALKLESS*. Then, run the example again, using **Stats ➠ Correlations ➠ Binary Data ➠ Jaccard** (**S3**) and the same variables.

```
CORR
 USE survey2
 LET (blue,depress,cry,sad,no_eat,getgoing,talkless),
    = @ <> 0
 GRAPH = NONE
 S2 blue depress cry sad no_eat getgoing talkless
 S3 blue depress cry sad no_eat getgoing talkless
```

```
S2 binary similarity coefficients

              BLUE DEPRESS    CRY     SAD   NO_EAT GETGOING TALKLESS
     BLUE    1.000
  DEPRESS    0.207   1.000
      CRY    0.090   0.113   1.000
      SAD    0.188   0.313   0.117   1.000
   NO_EAT    0.117   0.129   0.051   0.137   1.000
 GETGOING    0.180   0.309   0.086   0.258   0.152   1.000
 TALKLESS    0.117   0.156   0.059   0.145   0.098   0.172   1.000

Number of observations: 256

S3 binary similarity coefficients

              BLUE DEPRESS    CRY     SAD   NO_EAT GETGOING TALKLESS
     BLUE    1.000
  DEPRESS    0.442   1.000
      CRY    0.303   0.257   1.000
      SAD    0.410   0.625   0.288   1.000
   NO_EAT    0.306   0.239   0.155   0.273   1.000
 GETGOING    0.303   0.488   0.152   0.395   0.248   1.000
 TALKLESS    0.306   0.305   0.183   0.294   0.248   0.289   1.000

Number of observations: 256
```

The frequencies for *DEPRESS* and *SAD* are:

		Sad	
		1	0
Depress	1	80	20
	0	28	128

For S2, the result is 80/256 = 0.313; for S3, 80/128 = 0.625.

9.9 Tetrachoric correlation

As an example, we use the bivariate normal data described in the introduction to this section. We begin by entering the data as a table and saving them in a SYSTAT data file named *TETRA*.

x	y	count
0	0	17
1	0	4
0	1	5
1	1	19

```
USE tetra
FREQ = count
TETRA x y
```

```
Tetrachoric correlations

                  X       Y
     X         1.000
     Y         0.810   1.000

Number of observations: 45
```

For our single pair of variables, the tetrachoric correlation is 0.81.

Missing data	Listwise and **Pairwise** are available. See Example 9.3.

Summary

Computation

The computational algorithms use provisional means, sums of squares, and cross-products (Spicer, 1972).

For the rank-order coefficients (**Gamma**, **Mu2**, **Spearman**, and **Tau**), keep in mind that these are time consuming. **Spearman** requires sorting and ranking the data before doing the same work done by **Pearson**. The **Gamma** and **Mu2** items require computations between all possible pairs of observations. Thus, their computing time is combinatoric.

References

Afifi, A.A., and Clark, V. 1984. *Computer-aided multivariate analysis.* Belmont, Calif.: Lifetime Learning Publications.

Faith, D.P., Minchin, P., and Belbin, L. 1987. Compositional dissimilarity as a robust measure of ecological distance. *Vegetatio*, 69: 57–68.

Goodman, L.A., and Kruskal, W.H. 1954. Measures of association for cross-classification. *Journal of the American Statistical Association*, 49: 732–764.

Gower, J.C. 1985. Measures of similarity, dissimilarity, and distance. In Kotz, S., and Johnson, N.L. *Encyclopedia of Statistical Sciences*, vol. 5. New York: John Wiley & Sons, Inc.

Hadi, A.S. 1994. A modification of a method for the detection of outliers in multivariate samples. In *Journal of the Royal Statistical Society,* Series (B), 56: No. 2.

Little, R.J.A., and Rubin, D.B. 1987. *Statistical analyses with missing data.* New York: John Wiley & Sons, Inc.

Shye, S., ed. 1978. *Theory construction and data analysis in the behavioral sciences.* San Francisco: Jossey-Bass, Inc.

10

Cluster Analysis

Leland Wilkinson, Laszlo Engelman, James Corter, and Mark Coward

Stats➡Cluster Analysis provides three classes of clustering: **Join**, **Kmeans**, and **Additive Trees**. **Join** comprises hierarchical linkage methods. **Kmeans** performs the k means splitting method, which is not necessarily hierarchical. **Additive Trees** forms trees whose path (branch) lengths represent similarities among objects.

Stats➡Cluster Analysis➡Join clusters cases, variables, or both variables and cases simultaneously, while Stats➡Cluster Analysis➡Kmeans clusters cases only. Stats➡Cluster Analysis➡Additive Trees clusters a similarity or dissimilarity matrix. Eight distance metrics are available with the **Join** and **Kmeans** methods, including metrics for quantitative variables and frequency count data. **Join** provides six measures for amalgamating (or linking) objects and displays the results as a tree (dendrogram) or as a polar dendrogram. When the **Matrix** option is used to cluster cases and variables simultaneously, SYSTAT uses a gray-scale or color spectrum to represent the data values.

For each cluster, **Kmeans** prints descriptive statistics for each variable and the distance from each case to its center. Within each cluster for each variable, **Kmeans** also features a profile display that shows how the average for the cluster departs from the mean of the complete sample.

Join operates on a rectangular SYSTAT file or a file containing a symmetric matrix, such as those produced by **Correlations**. **Additive Trees** requires a file containing a symmetric matrix. You can use the **Correlations** procedure to produce a symmetric matrix if your data are rectangular. **Kmeans** works on the usual cases-by-variables data file only. You can save cluster identifiers in a SYSTAT file.

Cluster Analysis

Overview

Stats⇒**Cluster Analysis** provides **Join** for hierarchical clustering methods, **Kmeans** for the k means splitting method, and **Additive Trees** for additive trees.

Cluster analysis is a multivariate procedure for detecting natural groupings in data. The objects in these groups may be:

— **Cases** (observations or rows of a data file). For example, if health indicators (numbers of doctors, nurses, hospital beds, life expectancy, and so on) are recorded for countries (cases), then developed nations may form a subgroup or cluster separate from emerging countries. Use **Kmeans** or **Join**.

— **Variables** (characteristics or columns of the data). For example, if causes of death (cancer, cardiovascular, lung disease, accidents, and so on) are variables recorded for each U.S. state (case), the results may show that accidents and illnesses are relatively independent. Use **Join**.

— **Cases and variables** (individual entries in the data matrix). For example, certain wines (variables) may be associated with good years (cases) of production. Other wines have other years that are better. Use **Join** with the **Matrix** option.

A cluster analysis of cases resembles discriminant analysis in one respect—the researcher seeks to classify a set of objects into subgroups, but neither the number nor members of the subgroups are known.

The cluster literature is diverse and contains many descriptive synonyms: hierarchical clustering (McQuitty, 1960; Johnson, 1967); single linkage clustering (Sokal and Sneath, 1963), and joining (Hartigan, 1975). Output from hierarchical methods can be represented as a tree (Hartigan, 1975) or dendrogram (Sokal and Sneath, 1963). The linkage of each object or group of objects is shown as a joining of branches in a tree. The "root" of the tree is the linkage of all clusters into one set, and the ends of the branches lead to each separate object.

In the first four examples, the data are economic indicators, demographic variables, and other measures recorded for 30 countries. The analyses use:

- **Kmeans** and **Join** to cluster countries (cases) (Example 10.1 and Example 10.2)
- **Join** to cluster variables (Example 10.3)
- **Join** with the **Matrix** option to cluster cases and variables simultaneously (Example 10.4)

The data in the file *SUBWORLD* are a subset of cases and variables from the *OURWORLD* file:

URBAN	Percentage of the population living in cities
BIRTH_RT	Births per 1000 people
DEATH_RT	Deaths per 1000 people
B_TO_D	Ratio of births to deaths
BABYMORT	Infant deaths during the first year per 1000 live births
GDP_CAP	Gross domestic product per capita (in U.S. dollars)
LIFEEXPM	Years of life expectancy for males
LIFEEXPF	Years of life expectancy for females
EDUC	U.S. dollars spent per person on education
HEALTH	U.S. dollars spent per person on health
MIL	U.S. dollars spent per person on the military
LITERACY	Percentage of the population who can read

The distributions of the economic variables (*GDP_CAP*, *EDUC*, *HEALTH*, and *MIL*) are skewed with long right tails, so these variables are analyzed in log units.

Missing data

In Stats⟶Cluster Analysis, all distances are computed with pairwise deletion of missing values. See Chapter 9 for a description of this method.

Since missing data are excluded from distance calculations by pairwise deletion, they do not directly influence clustering when you use the **Matrix** option for **Join**. To use the **Matrix** display to analyze patterns of missing data, create a new file in which missing values are recoded to 1 and all other values to 0. Then use **Join** with **Matrix** to see whether missing values cluster together in a systematic pattern.

Getting started

Both Stats⟶Cluster Analysis⟶Kmeans and Stats⟶Cluster Analysis⟶Join read rectangular SYSTAT data files. **Join** can read a file that contains an SSCP, a covariance, a correlation, or a dissimilarity matrix. Stats⟶Cluster Analysis⟶Additive Trees requires a file containing a symmetric matrix. When reading a data file, **Cluster Analysis** recognizes its type. **Cluster Analysis** ignores missing values in its calculations.

For a hierarchical cluster analysis, use Stats⟶Cluster Analysis⟶Join:

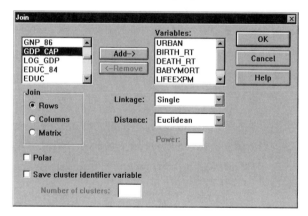

For a *k* means cluster analysis, use **Stats**⮞**Cluster Analysis**⮞**Kmeans**:

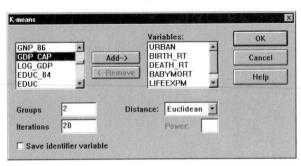

For additive trees, use **Stats**⮞**Cluster Analysis**⮞**Additive Trees**:

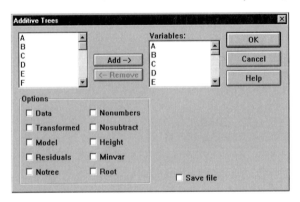

K Means Clustering

Stats➠**Cluster Analysis**➠**Kmeans** produces *k* means clustering. This method splits a set of objects into a selected number of groups by maximizing between-cluster variation relative to within-cluster variation. It is similar to doing a one-way analysis of variance where the groups are unknown and the largest *F* value is sought by reassigning members to each group.

Kmeans starts with one cluster and splits it into two clusters by picking the case farthest from the center as a *seed* for a second cluster and assigning each case to the nearest center. It continues splitting one of the clusters into two (and reassigning cases) until *n* (specified with **Groups**) clusters are formed. **Kmeans** reassigns cases until the within-groups sum of squares can no longer be reduced.

Kmeans uses a rectangular data matrix only. To keep the influence of all variables comparable, use **Data**➠**Standardize** to transform the values of each variable to *z*-scores (the **SD** option) or to a 0,1 scale (**Range**).

The first example uses few features specific to **Cluster Analysis**. After describing the output, however, it defines options, including distance metrics.

10.1 Clustering cases

The first example clusters countries (cases). The variables are the demographic variables, economic indicators, and other measures described in the introduction. Because the economic variables have skewed distributions, use **Data**➠**Transform** to transform them. Also select **Data**➠**Standardize**➠**SD** and **Data**➠**ID Variable** to identify *COUNTRY$* as a variable with values to label the output. Use **Stats**➠**Cluster Analysis**➠**Kmeans** to select the 12 variables.

Use the default Euclidean distance metric for the data standardized with the **SD** option. Use **Groups** to arbitrarily request four clusters. With commands:

```
CLUSTER
    USE subworld
    IDVAR = country$
    LET (gdp_cap, educ, mil, health) = L10(@)
    STANDARDIZE / SD
    KMEANS urban birth_rt death_rt babymort lifeexpm,
           lifeexpf gdp_cap b_to_d literacy educ,
           mil health / NUMBER=4
```

Note that **KMEANS** must be specified last.

❶ Distance metric is Euclidean distance

K-means splitting cases into 4 groups

❷ Summary statistics for 1 clusters

Variable	Minimum	Mean	Maximum	St.Dev.
URBAN	-2.01	-0.00	1.59	1.00
BIRTH_RT	-1.14	0.00	1.69	1.00
DEATH_RT	-1.28	0.00	3.08	1.00
BABYMORT	-0.85	0.00	2.41	1.00
GDP_CAP	-2.00	0.00	1.28	1.00
EDUC	-2.41	-0.00	1.28	1.00
HEALTH	-2.22	-0.00	1.31	1.00
MIL	-1.76	-0.00	1.46	1.00
LIFEEXPM	-2.78	-0.00	0.99	1.00
LIFEEXPF	-2.47	-0.00	1.07	1.00
LITERACY	-2.27	-0.00	0.75	1.00
B_TO_D	-1.09	-0.00	2.42	1.00

❸ Summary statistics for all cases

Variable	Between SS	DF	Within SS	DF	F-Ratio
URBAN	18.606	3	9.394	25	16.506
BIRTH_RT	26.204	3	2.796	26	81.226
DEATH_RT	23.663	3	5.337	26	38.422
BABYMORT	26.028	3	2.972	26	75.887
GDP_CAP	26.959	3	2.041	26	114.446
EDUC	25.371	3	3.629	26	60.593
HEALTH	24.923	3	3.077	25	67.488
MIL	24.787	3	3.213	25	64.289
LIFEEXPM	24.750	3	4.250	26	50.473
LIFEEXPF	25.927	3	3.073	26	73.121
LITERACY	24.854	3	4.146	26	51.947
B_TO_D	22.292	3	6.708	26	28.800
** TOTAL **	294.362	36	50.638	309	

❹ Cluster 1 of 4 contains 12 cases

Members			Statistics			
Case	Distance	Variable	Minimum	Mean	Maximum	St.Dev.
Austria	0.28	URBAN	-0.17	0.60	1.59	0.54
Belgium	0.09	BIRTH_RT	-1.14	-0.93	-0.83	0.10
Denmark	0.19	DEATH_RT	-0.77	0.00	0.26	0.35
France	0.14	BABYMORT	-0.85	-0.81	-0.68	0.05
Switzerland	0.26	GDP_CAP	0.33	1.01	1.28	0.26
UK	0.14	EDUC	0.47	0.95	1.28	0.28
Italy	0.16	HEALTH	0.52	0.99	1.31	0.23
Sweden	0.23	MIL	0.28	0.81	1.11	0.25
WGermany	1.31	LIFEEXPM	0.23	0.75	0.99	0.23
Poland	1.39	LIFEEXPF	0.43	0.79	1.07	0.18
Czechoslov	0.26	LITERACY	0.54	0.72	0.75	0.06
Canada	1.30	B_TO_D	-1.09	-0.91	-0.46	0.18

⑤   Cluster 2 of 4 contains 5 cases

```
        Members                         Statistics
     Case      Distance | Variable   Minimum    Mean   Maximum   St.Dev.
  Ethiopia       0.40   | URBAN        -2.01    -1.69    -1.29     0.30
  Guinea         0.52   | BIRTH_RT      1.46     1.58     1.69     0.10
  Somalia        0.38   | DEATH_RT      1.28     1.85     3.08     0.76
  Afghanistan    0.38   | BABYMORT      1.38     1.88     2.41     0.44
  Haiti          0.30   | GDP_CAP      -2.00    -1.61    -1.27     0.30
                        | EDUC         -2.41    -1.58    -1.10     0.51
                        | HEALTH       -2.22    -1.64    -1.29     0.44
                        | MIL          -1.76    -1.51    -1.37     0.17
                        | LIFEEXPM     -2.78    -1.90    -1.38     0.56
                        | LIFEEXPF     -2.47    -1.91    -1.48     0.45
                        | LITERACY     -2.27    -1.83    -0.76     0.62
                        | B_TO_D       -0.38    -0.02     0.25     0.26
```

----

⑥   Cluster 3 of 4 contains 11 cases

```
        Members                         Statistics
     Case      Distance | Variable   Minimum    Mean   Maximum   St.Dev.
  Argentina      0.45   | URBAN        -0.88     0.16     1.14     0.76
  Brazil         0.32   | BIRTH_RT     -0.60     0.07     0.92     0.49
  Chile          0.40   | DEATH_RT     -1.28    -0.70     0.00     0.42
  Colombia       0.42   | BABYMORT     -0.70    -0.06     0.55     0.47
  Uruguay        0.61   | GDP_CAP      -0.75    -0.38     0.04     0.28
  Ecuador        0.36   | EDUC         -0.89    -0.39     0.14     0.36
  ElSalvador     0.52   | HEALTH       -0.91    -0.47     0.28     0.38
  Guatemala      0.65   | MIL          -1.25    -0.59     0.37     0.49
  Peru           0.37   | LIFEEXPM     -0.63     0.06     0.77     0.49
  Panama         0.51   | LIFEEXPF     -0.57     0.04     0.61     0.44
  Cuba           0.58   | LITERACY     -0.94     0.20     0.73     0.51
                        | B_TO_D       -0.65     0.63     1.68     0.76
```

----

⑦   Cluster 4 of 4 contains 2 cases

```
        Members                         Statistics
     Case      Distance | Variable   Minimum    Mean   Maximum   St.Dev.
  Iraq           0.29   | URBAN        -0.30     0.06     0.42     0.51
  Libya          0.29   | BIRTH_RT      0.92     1.27     1.61     0.49
                        | DEATH_RT     -0.77    -0.77    -0.77     0.0
                        | BABYMORT      0.44     0.47     0.51     0.05
                        | GDP_CAP      -0.25     0.05     0.36     0.43
                        | EDUC         -0.04     0.44     0.93     0.68
                        | HEALTH       -0.51    -0.04     0.42     0.66
                        | MIL           1.34     1.40     1.46     0.08
                        | LIFEEXPM     -0.09    -0.04     0.02     0.08
                        | LIFEEXPF     -0.30    -0.21    -0.11     0.13
                        | LITERACY     -0.94    -0.86    -0.77     0.12
                        | B_TO_D        1.61     2.01     2.42     0.57
```

Cluster Profile Plots

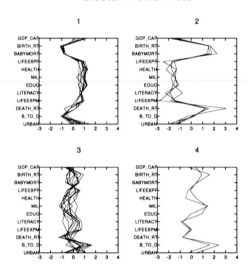

Cluster Profile Plots

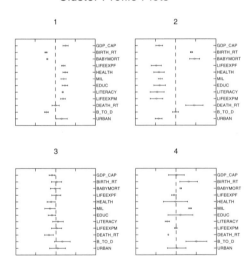

The highlighted numbers below correspond to those in the output:

❶ SYSTAT reports the distance metric used for this analysis and that four clusters are formed.

❷ Descriptive statistics for each variable are given for the complete sample. The standardized data are used.

❸ For each variable, **Cluster Analysis** compares the between-cluster mean square (*Between SS/DF*) to the within-cluster mean square (*Within SS/DF*) and reports the *F-Ratio*. Do not use these F ratios to test significance, because the clusters are formed to characterize differences. The log of gross domestic product (GDP_CAP) and BIRTH_RT are better discriminators between countries than URBAN or DEATH_RT. For a good graphical view of the separation of the clusters, you might rotate the data using the three variables with the highest F ratios.

❹ For each of the 12 countries (cases) in cluster 1, **Cluster Analysis** prints its *Distance* from the center of cluster 1. Descriptive statistics for these countries appear on the right. The standard scores for LITERACY range from 0.54 to 0.75 with an average of 0.72. B_TO_D ranges from −1.09 to −0.46. Thus, for these predominantly European countries, literacy is well above the average for the sample and the birth-to-death ratio is below average.

❺ Descriptive statistics for the five countries in cluster 2 are printed next. Here, LITERACY ranges from −2.27 to −0.76 in these countries, and B_TO_D ranges from −0.38 to 0.25. Thus, the countries in cluster 2 have a lower literacy rate and a greater potential for population growth than those in cluster 1.

❻ Descriptive statistics for the 11 countries in cluster 3 appear next.

❼ Iraq and Libya form the fourth cluster. The average birth-to-death ratio is 2.01, the highest among the four clusters.

❽ Parallel coordinate plot. The variables in this *Quick Graph* are ordered by their F ratio in ❸. In the top left plot, there is one line for each country in cluster 1 that connects its z-scores for each of the variables. Zero marks the average for the complete sample. The lines for these 12 countries all follow a similar pattern: above average values for GDP_CAP, below for BIRTH_RT, and so on. The lines in cluster 3 do not follow such a tight pattern. To omit this display, specify GRAPH=NONE or deselect **Edit➭Options➭Statistical Quickgraphs**.

❾ The variables in this **cluster profile** are ordered by the *F* ratios printed in panel ❸. The vertical lines under each cluster number indicate the grand mean across all data. The mean within each cluster is marked by an open circle (∘). The horizontal lines indicate one standard deviation above or below the mean. The countries in cluster 1 have above average means of gross domestic product, life expectancy, literacy, and urbanization, and spend considerable money on health care and the military, while the means of their birth rates, infant mortality rates, and birth-to-death ratios are low. The opposite is true for cluster 2.

Case labels

Cases are denoted in tree and matrix displays with case numbers. If you have a character variable in your data file, use **Data**➞**ID Variable** to label cases with their values shown.

Number of groups

You can change the number of groups formed with the **Groups** option by specifying any integer value up to the number of cases in the file. Because a *k* means clustering for one number of groups may not correspond to that for a different number, try runs with different numbers. It is best to have a general idea of how many groups to expect in your data. Requesting more and more clusters eventually can reveal more noise than information about your data.

Results for 2, 3, ..., *k* clusters. If you request long output by selecting **Edit**➞**Options**➞**Output Results**➞**Long** and specify *k* for **Groups**, **Cluster Analysis** reports results for two clusters, three clusters, up to and including *k* clusters.

Number of iterations

You can use **Iterations** to specify the number of iterations used to reallocate cases. With commands:

```
KMEANS varlist / ITER=n
```

The default value is 50. You should rarely need more.

Saving cluster membership

Type or select **Save** to save a file of identifiers. If you type

    SAVE *filename* / DATA

the cluster indices are saved as a new variable with the data currently in use.

Distance metrics

Cluster Analysis can use the raw data or standardized data to compute distances and cluster centers. Euclidean, the default distance measure, is sensitive to the units in which variables are measured. For example, *LITERACY* values of 11% to 99% dominate *EDUC* values of 0 to 3. Standardization is a remedy for this problem.

Standardizing the data. If your data are not on common scales, you should consider standardizing them using **Data**➡**Standardize** or the STANDARDIZE command.

Metrics. **Cluster Analysis** provides these metrics under **Stats**➡**Cluster Analysis**➡**Kmeans**➡**Distance** for computing distances for the raw or standardized data:

Euclidean	Normalized Euclidean distance (root mean-squared distance). Use for continuous or ratio scales. This is the default.
Gamma	1-(Goodman-Kruskal gamma coefficient). Use with rank order or ordinal scales.
Pearson	1-(Pearson product-moment correlation coefficient). Use with continuous data.
Rsquared	1-(square of Pearson product-moment correlation). Use with continuous data.
Minkowski	pth root of the mean pth powered coordinated distances. (Use $p=1$ for city-block distance, and $p=2$ for Euclidean.) Use with continuous data.
Chisquare	Chi-square measure for each $2 \times n$ frequency table. Use with frequency count data.
Phisquare	Phi-square (chi-square/total) measure for each $2 \times n$ frequency table. Use with frequency count data.
MW	Minimum within sum of squares deviations. Use with continuous data.

When using commands, add one of the following to your option list:

GAMMA	PEARSON	RSQUARED	EUCLIDEAN
MINKOWSKI	CHISQUARE	PHISQUARE	MW

Hierarchical Clusters: Join

Stats➠**Cluster Analysis**➠**Join** produces hierarchical clusters that are displayed in a tree. Select:

Rows   Cluster rows (cases). This is the default. See Example 10.2.

Columns   Cluster columns (variables). See Example 10.3.

Matrix   Cluster rows and columns at the same time. Both rows and columns are permuted to bring similar rows and columns next to one another. The permuted matrix is displayed using the Tukey gapping method. See Example 10.4.

You can also cluster a similarity or dissimilarity matrix directly.

Join provides eight **Distance** metrics and six **Linkage** (amalgamation) methods. These metrics and methods are defined following the Example 10.2 output.

10.2 Clustering cases

This example uses the *SUBWORLD* data and **Stats**➠**Cluster Analysis**➠**Join** to cluster cases. Use **Data**➠**ID Variable** to specify *COUNTRY$* as the ID variable, and use **Data**➠**Standardize** to standardize the data (as in Example 10.1).

```
CLUSTER
    USE subworld
    IDVAR = country$
    LET (gdp_cap, educ, mil, health) = L10(@)
    STANDARDIZE / SD
    JOIN urban birth_rt death_rt babymort lifeexpm,
         lifeexpf gdp_cap b_to_d literacy educ,
         mil health
```

❶
```
Distance metric is Euclidean distance
Single linkage method (nearest neighbor)
```

❷
```
Cluster       and   Cluster        Were joined   No. of members
containing          containing     at distance   in new cluster
WGermany            Belgium           0.087           2
WGermany            Denmark           0.111           3
WGermany            UK                0.113           4
Sweden              WGermany          0.128           5
Austria             Sweden            0.161           6
Austria             France            0.194           7
Austria             Italy             0.194           8
Austria             Canada            0.211           9
Uruguay             Argentina         0.215           2
Switzerland         Austria           0.236          10
Czechoslov          Poland            0.241           2
Switzerland         Czechoslov        0.260          12
Guatemala           ElSalvador        0.315           2
Guatemala           Ecuador           0.316           3
Uruguay             Chile             0.370           3
Cuba                Uruguay           0.374           4
Haiti               Somalia           0.397           2
Switzerland         Cuba              0.403          16
Guatemala           Brazil            0.417           4
Peru                Guatemala         0.421           5
Colombia            Peru              0.443           6
Ethiopia            Haiti             0.474           3
Panama              Colombia          0.516           7
Switzerland         Panama            0.556          23
Libya               Iraq              0.570           2
Afghanistan         Guinea            0.583           2
Ethiopia            Afghanistan       0.597           5
Switzerland         Libya             0.860          25
Switzerland         Ethiopia          0.908          30
Switzerland         Ethiopia          0.908          30
```

❸

Cluster Tree

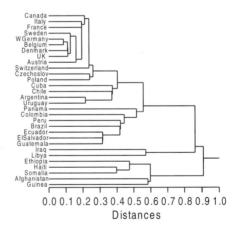

The highlighted numbers below correspond to those in the output:

❶ SYSTAT reports the distance metric and the linkage method.

❷ The joining history. The countries at the top of the panel are joined first at a distance of 0.087. The last entry represents the joining of the largest two clusters to form one cluster of all 30 countries. Switzerland is in one of the clusters, Ethiopia in the other.

❸ The **tree diagram** is printed with a unique ordering in which every branch is lined up so that most similar objects are closest to each other. If a perfect *seriation* (one-dimensional ordering) exists in the data, the tree reproduces it. The algorithm for ordering the dendrogram is given in Gruvaeus and Wainer (1972). This ordering may differ from that of trees printed by other clustering programs if they do not use a seriation algorithm to order branches. The advantage of using seriation is most apparent for single linkage clusters. Because the example joins rows (cases) and uses *COUNTRY* as an **ID Variable**, the branches of the tree are labeled with countries. If you join columns (variables), then variable names are used. The scale for the joining distances is printed at the bottom.

If you have have selected long output results using **Edit➧Options** or PRINT=LONG, an ASCII tree is produced instead of the *Quick Graph*. This option is useful if you are joining more than 100 objects.

In ❷ and ❸, notice that Iraq and Libya, which form their own cluster as they did in the k means analysis, are the second to last cluster to link with others. They join with all the countries listed above them at a distance of 0.583. Finally, at a distance of 0.908, the five countries at the bottom of the display are added to form one big cluster.

A polar dendrogram

Here the **Polar** option is used for the same cluster analysis:

Cluster Tree

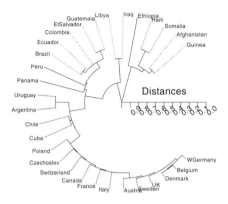

Distance metrics

Initially, **Join** considers each object (case or variable) as a separate cluster. It begins by joining the two "closest" objects as a cluster and continues (in a stepwise manner) joining an object with another object, an object with a cluster, or a cluster with another cluster until all objects are combined into one cluster.

By default, **Join** computes normalized **Euclidean** distances. Normalized distances are root mean-squared distances. Normalizing by the sample size allows comparison of clusters across different size samples with or without missing data. Without missing data, normalized and regular **Euclidean** distances cluster identically.

If a case has one or more values missing, the remaining values are used in the computations; that is, distances are computed between each pair of cases (or variables) by using the values that are complete for both numbers of the pair.

In addition to **Euclidean**, **Join** provides seven metrics for **Distance**:

Gamma	**Pearson**	**Rsquared**	**Minkowski**
Chisquare	**Phisquare**	**Percent**	

With commands:

```
JOIN varlist / DISTANCE=method
```

where *method* is one of the eight metrics described on p. 345.

Percent (the only distance metric not defined previously) is the percentage of disagreement (or mismatches) among values. It is used with categorical or nominal scales.

Before you compute a distance measure, you may want to use **Data➠Standardize** to standardize the variables.

All of these distance indices are computed across columns if you join rows, and across rows if you join columns. Missing values are excluded from all computations. Profiles that are missing all their values are as far apart as possible.

Matrices computed with **Stats➠Correlations** can be passed to **Cluster Analysis** for joining. A variety of similarity and dissimilarity coefficients can be computed, including several that are popular for binary data. **Cluster Analysis** automatically recognizes whether the matrix is a similarity or dissimilarity matrix. Just remember, if you want to cluster cases instead of variables, you must transpose the raw data matrix before computing a similarity or dissimilarity matrix in **Correlations**.

Linkage (amalgamation) methods

Various methods are available for computing the distance of one object (or cluster) from another and to determine whether the two should be merged in a given step.

Single. Use the distance between the two closest members of two clusters, often called **single linkage clustering** (Hartigan, 1975); tends to produce long, stringy clusters. If you use a SYSTAT file that contains a similarity or dissimilarity matrix, you get what Johnson (1967) calls hierarchical clustering via the **min method**. If you use a rectangular matrix, this option produces a single linkage clustering (the default).

Complete. Uses the most distant pair of objects in two clusters to compute between-cluster distances; tends to produce compact, globular clusters. If you use a similarity or dissimilarity matrix from a SYSTAT file, you get **Johnson's max method**.

Centroid. Uses the average value of all objects in a cluster (the cluster centroid) as the reference point for distances to other objects or clusters (Sokal and Michener, 1958).

Average. Averages all distances between pairs of objects in different clusters to decide how far apart they are (Sokal and Michener, 1958).

Median. Similar to **Average** linkage, except medians are used (Gower, 1967).

Ward. Ward's method (Ward, 1963). Resembles **Centroid** linkage, but adjusts for covariances.

For some data, the last four methods cannot produce a hierarchical tree with strictly increasing amalgamation distances. In these cases, you may see stray branches that do not connect to others. If this happens, you should consider **Single** or **Complete** linkage. For more information on these problems, see Fisher and Van Ness (1971). These reviewers concluded that these and other problems made **Centroid**, **Average**, **Median**, and **Ward** (as well as *k* means) "inadmissible" clustering procedures. In practice and in Monte Carlo simulations, however, they sometimes perform better than **Single** and **Complete** linkage, which Fisher and Van Ness considered "admissible." Milligan (1980) tested all of the hierarchical joining methods in a large Monte Carlo simulation of clustering algorithms. Consult his paper for further details. With commands:

```
JOIN varlist / LINKAGE=method
```

where *method* is one of the linkage methods listed above.

Case labels

Cases are denoted in tree and matrix displays with case numbers. If you have a character variable in your data file, you can label cases with its values. Select **Data➧ID Variable** or the IDVAR command.

Saving cluster membership

To save cluster membership identifiers in a file, use **Save cluster identification variable**. Use **Number of clusters** to type the number of identifiers to save. You must be joining rows, not columns.

For example, if you have 50 cases and 7 variables and you specify six clusters, SYSTAT joins the 50 cases 44 times to reduce the set of objects to six clusters and saves the integer identifiers for these six clusters in a SYSTAT file. If you don't know how many clusters are in your data, you should examine your tree display after a trial run to find relatively clear breaks between branches. Draw a vertical line at several positions along the tree and look for a cut that produces fairly distinct clumps of branches. Then choose the number of branches crossing your cut line for the desired number of clusters.

Cluster identifiers can be added to the original data. To save the cluster indices as a new variable with the data, specify:

```
SAVE filename / DATA NUMBER=n
```

**10.3
Clustering
variables**

This example joins columns (*variables*) instead of rows (*cases*) to see which
variables cluster together. This example also uses **Stats⏵Cluster
Analysis⏵Join⏵Columns** to join columns rather than rows.

```
USE subworld
IDVAR = country$
LET (gdp_cap, educ, mil, health) = L10(@)
STANDARDIZE / SD
JOIN urban birth_rt death_rt babymort lifeexpm,
     lifeexpf gdp_cap b_to_d literacy educ,
     mil health / COLS
```

```
Distance metric is 1-Pearson correlation coefficient
Single linkage method (nearest neighbor)

Cluster        and  Cluster        Were joined   No. of members
containing          containing     at distance   in new cluster
------------        ------------   ------------   ---------------
LIFEEXPF            LIFEEXPM            0.144            2
HEALTH              GDP_CAP             0.239            2
EDUC                HEALTH              0.286            3
LIFEEXPF            LITERACY            0.379            3
BABYMORT            BIRTH_RT            0.386            2
EDUC                LIFEEXPF            0.444            6
MIL                 EDUC                0.474            7
MIL                 URBAN               0.541            8
B_TO_D              BABYMORT            0.832            3
B_TO_D              DEATH_RT            0.840            4
MIL                 B_TO_D              1.538           12
```

Cluster Tree

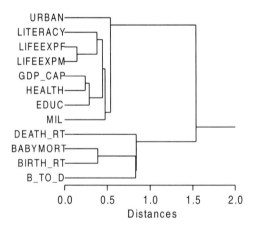

The scale at the bottom of the tree for the distance (1–*r*)ranges from 0.0
to 1.5. The smallest distance is 0.011—thus, the correlation of *LIFEEXPM*
with *LIFEEXPF* is 0.989.

10.4 Clustering variables and cases simultaneously

To produce a shaded display of the original data matrix in which rows and columns are permuted according to an algorithm in Gruvaeus and Wainer (1972), use the **Stats**➧**Cluster Analysis**➧**Join**➧**Matrix** option. Different shadings or colors represent the magnitude of each number in the matrix (Ling, 1973).

If you use the **Matrix** option with Euclidean distance, be sure that the variables are on comparable scales, because both rows and columns of the matrix are clustered. Joining a matrix containing inches of annual rainfall and annual growth of trees in feet, for example, would split columns more by scales than by covariation. In cases like this, to standardize your data before joining, use **Data**➧**Standardize** with the **Range** option.

```
USE subworld
IDVAR = country$
LET (gdp_cap, educ, mil, health) = L10(@)
STANDARDIZE / SD
JOIN urban birth_rt death_rt babymort lifeexpm,
      lifeexpf gdp_cap b_to_d literacy educ,
      mil health / MATRIX
```

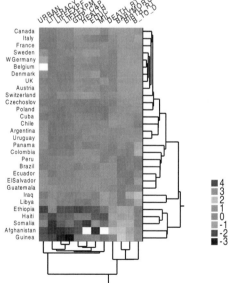

Permuted Data Matrix

This clustering reveals three groups of countries and two groups of variables. The countries with more urban dwellers and literate citizens, longest life-expectancies, highest gross domestic product, and most expenditures on health care, education, and the military are on the top left of the data matrix; countries with the highest rates of death, infant mortality, birth, and population growth (see *B_TO_D*) are on the lower right. You can also see that, consistent with the previous **Kmeans** and **Join** examples, Iraq and Libya spend much more on military, education, and health than their immediate neighbors.

The Guttman simplex is not a necessary consequence of the two-way clustering and permutation algorithm. Data frequently have an irregular or stepwise structure. The multitrait-multimethod matrix of Campbell and Fiske (1959) is a good example. If you permute a symmetric matrix of correlations from **Stats**➠**Correlations**, you may encounter this structure.

Matrix clustering is especially useful for displaying large correlation matrices. You may want to cluster the correlation matrix this way and then use the ordering to produce a scatterplot matrix that is organized by the multivariate structure. See *SYSTAT: Graphics* for more information about scatterplot matrices.

10.5 Distance matrix input

This example clusters a matrix of distances. The data, stored as a dissimilarity matrix in the *CITIES* data file, are airline distances in hundreds of miles between 10 global cities. The data are adapted from Hartigan (1975).

	BERLIN	BOMBAY	CAPETOWN	CHICAGO	LONDON	MONTREAL	NEWYORK	PARIS	SANFRAN	SEATTLE
BERLIN	0									
BOMBAY	39	0								
CAPETOWN	60	51	0							
CHICAGO	44	81	85	0						
LONDON	6	45	60	40	0					
MONTREAL	37	75	79	8	33	0				
NEWYORK	40	78	78	7	35	3	0			
PARIS	5	44	58	41	2	34	36	0		
SANFRAN	57	84	103	19	54	25	26	56	0	
SEATTLE	51	77	102	17	48	23	24	50	7	0

```
CLUSTER
  USE cities
```

```
         JOIN berlin bombay capetown chicago london,
           montreal newyork paris sanfran seattle
```

```
Single linkage method (nearest neighbor)

Cluster     and  Cluster      Were joined  No. of members
containing       containing   at distance  in new cluster
------------     ------------  -----------  --------------
PARIS            LONDON            2.000          2
NEWYORK          MONTREAL          3.000          2
BERLIN           PARIS             5.000          3
CHICAGO          NEWYORK           7.000          3
SEATTLE          SANFRAN           7.000          2
SEATTLE          CHICAGO          17.000          5
BERLIN           SEATTLE          33.000          8
BOMBAY           BERLIN           39.000          9
BOMBAY           CAPETOWN         51.000         10
```

Cluster Tree

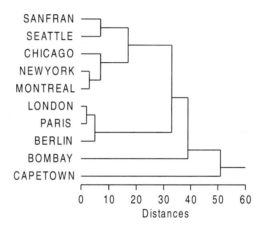

The tree is printed in seriation order. Imagine a trip around the globe to these cities. SYSTAT has identified the shortest path between cities. The itinerary begins at San Francisco, leads to Seattle, Chicago, New York, and so on, and ends in Capetown.

Note that the *CITIES* data file contains the distances between the cities; SYSTAT did not have to compute those distances. When you save the file, be sure to save it as a dissimilarity matrix. For more information about reading and saving files, see *SYSTAT: Data*.

This example is used both to illustrate direct distance input and to give you an idea of the kind of information contained in the order of the SYSTAT cluster tree. For distance data, the seriation reveals shortest paths; for typical sample data, the seriation is more likely to replicate in new samples so that you can recognize cluster structure.

Additive Trees

**10.6
Additive trees
example**

Additive trees were developed by Sattath and Tversky (1977) for modeling similarity/dissimilarity data, which are not fit well by hierarchical joining trees. Hierarchical trees imply that all within-cluster distances are smaller than all between-cluster distances and that within-cluster distances are equal. This so-called "ultrametric" condition seldom applies to real similarity data from direct judgment. Additive trees, on the other hand, represent similarities with a network model in the shape of a tree. Distances between objects are represented by the lengths of the branches connecting them in the tree.

This example uses the *ROTHKOPF* data file, which is also used in Chapter 6.

```
CLUSTER
    USE rothkopf
    ADD a .. z
```

```
Similarities linearly transformed into distances.
77.000 needed to make distances positive.
104.000 added to satisfy triangle inequality.
Checking 14950 quadruples.
Checking 1001 quadruples.
Checking 330 quadruples.
Checking 70 quadruples.
Checking 1 quadruples.

Stress formula 1      =      0.061
Stress formula 2      =      0.399
r(monotonic) squared  =      0.841
r-squared (p.v.a.f.)  =      0.788


Node      Length  Children Variable
   1      23.396            A
   2      15.396            B
   3      14.813            C
   4      13.313            D
   5      24.125            E
   6      34.837            F
   7      15.917            G
   8      27.875            H
   9      25.604            I
  10      19.833            J
  11      13.688            K
  12      28.620            L
  13      21.812            M
  14      22.187            N
  15      19.083            O
  16      14.167            P
  17      18.958            Q
  18      21.437            R
  19      28.000            S
  20      23.875            T
  21      23.000            U
  22      27.125            V
  23      21.562            W
  24      14.604            X
  25      17.187            Y
  26      18.042            Z
```

```
27    16.943    1,    9
28    15.380    2,   24
29    15.716    3,   25
30    19.583    4,   11
31    26.062    5,   20
32    23.843    7,   15
33     6.114    8,   22
34    17.175   10,   16
35    18.807   13,   14
36    13.784   17,   26
37    15.663   18,   23
38     8.886   19,   21
39     4.562   27,   35
40     1.700   29,   36
41     8.799   33,   38
42     4.180   39,   31
43     1.123   12,   28
44     5.049   34,   40
45     2.467   42,   41
46     4.585   30,   43
47     2.616   32,   44
48     2.730    6,   37
49     0.0     45,   48
50     3.864   46,   47
51     0.0     50,   49
```

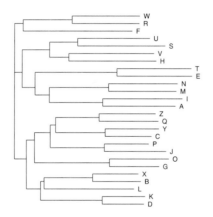

Valid print options for **Additive Trees** are:

Data   Raw data matrix.

Transformed   Data, after transformation into distance-like numbers.

Model   Model (tree) distances.

Residuals   Residuals matrix.

Notree   Omit printing of the tree graph.

Nonumbers   Omit numbering of objects in the tree graph.

Nosubtract   Specify an additive constant. The default assumption is interval-scale data; this implies complete freedom in choosing an additive constant. Therefore, the primary approach is to either add *or* subtract an additive constant to exactly satisfy the triangle inequality: $d(i,j)+d(i,k) <= d(j,k)$ for all *i,j,k, and* $d(i,j) + d(i,k) = d(j,k)$ for some *i,j,k.* However, if **Nosubtract** is specified, strict inequality is allowed; that is, if $d(i,j) + d(i,k) > d(j,k)$ holds for all *i,j,k* in the data, no constant is subtracted.

Height Request printing of the distance of each node from the root.

Minvar Combine the last few remaining clusters into the root node. If **Minvar** is specified, the program will search for the root that minimizes the variance of the distances from the root to the leaves.

Root Specify where the root is to be placed. If this option is requested, this keyword must be followed by two node numbers, for exampke, ROOT 12 13 . Note that the two nodes specified must be contiguous in the tree structure. A previous run will generally be necessary to determine the correct node numbers.

Summary

Computation

Join follows the standard hierarchical amalgamation method described in Hartigan (1975). The algorithm in Gruvaeus and Wainer (1972) is used to order the tree.

Kmeans follows the algorithm described in Hartigan (1975). Modifications from Hartigan and Wong (1979) improve speed. There is an important difference between SYSTAT's **Kmeans** algorithm and that of Hartigan (or implementations of Hartigan's in BMDP, SAS, and SPSS). In SYSTAT, seeds for new clusters are chosen by finding the case farthest from the centroid of its cluster. In Hartigan's algorithm, seeds form new clusters are chosen by splitting on the variable with largest variance.

References

Campbell, D.T., and Fiske, D.W. 1959. Convergent and discriminant validation by the multitrait-multimethod matrix. *Psychological Bulletin,* 56: 81-105.

Fisher, L., and Van Ness, J.W. 1971. Admissible clustering procedures. *Biometrika*, 58: 91-104.

Gower, J.C. 1967. A comparison of some methods of cluster analysis. *Biometrics,* 23: 623-637.

Gruvaeus, G., and Wainer, H. 1972. Two additions to hierarchical cluster analysis. *The British Journal of Mathematical and Statistical Psychology,* 25: 200-206.

Guttman, L. 1944. A basis for scaling qualitative data. *American Sociological Review*, 139-150.

Hartigan, J.A. 1975. *Clustering algorithms*. New York: John Wiley & Sons, Inc.

Johnson, S.C. 1967. Hierarchical clustering schemes. *Psychometrika,* 32: 241-254.

Ling, R.F. 1973. A computer generated aid for cluster analysis. *Communications of the ACM,* 16: 355-361.

MacQueen, J. 1967. Some methods for classification and analysis of multivariate observations. *5th Berkeley symposium on mathematics, statistics, and probability*, Vol. 1: 281–298.

McQuitty, L.L. 1960. Hierarchical syndrome analysis. *Educational and Psychological Measurement*, 20: 293-303.

Milligan, G.W. 1980. An examination of the effects of six types of error perturbation on fifteen clustering algorithms. *Psychometrika*, 45: 325-342.

Sattath, S., and Tversky, A. 1977. Additive similarity trees. *Psychometrika*, 42: 319-345.

Sokal, R.R., and Michener, C.D. 1958. A statistical method for evaluating systematic relationships. *University of Kansas Science Bulletin*, 38: 1409-1438.

Sokal, R.R., and Sneath, P.H.A. 1963. *Principles of numerical taxonomy*. San Francisco: W.H. Freeman and Company.

Wainer, H., and Schacht, S. 1978. Gappint. *Psychometrika*, 43: 203-212.

Ward, J.H. 1963. Hierarchical grouping to optimize an objective function. *Journal of the American Statistical Association*, 58: 236-244.

Wilkinson, L. 1978. Permuting a matrix to a simple structure. *Proceedings of the American Statistical Association*.

11

Discriminant Analysis

Laszlo Engelman

Discriminant Analysis provides linear or quadratic functions of the variables that "best" separate cases into two or more predefined groups. The variables in the linear function can be selected in a forward or backward stepwise manner, either interactively by the user or automatically by SYSTAT. For the latter at each step, SYSTAT enters the variable that contributes most to the separation of the groups (or removes the variable that is least useful). Contrasts that emphasize the difference between specific groups can be used to guide variable selection. Cases can be classified even if they are not used in the computations.

Print options allow the user to select panels of output to display, including group means, variances, covariances, and correlations. Available at each step are discriminant functions, F statistics for entering or removing variables, Wilks' lambda or U statistics (with an approximate F statistic), F statistics for pairwise differences between-group means, and classification and jackknife classification matrices with the percentage for correct classification. For each case, the user can request posterior probabilities for its assignment to each group, Mahalanobis distances to the centroid of each group, and canonical variable scores. Coefficients for canonical variables in the original units or standardized data are available. Users can also request eigenvalues, canonical correlations, and the Lawley-Hotelling and Pillai traces with their associated approximate F statistics. Users can save posterior probabilities, Mahalanobis distances, and canonical variable scores.

Discriminant Analysis

Overview

Overview

Discriminant analysis is related to both multivariate analysis of variance and multiple regression. The cases are grouped in cells like a one-way multivariate analysis of variance and the predictor variables form an equation like that for multiple regression. In Discriminant Analysis, Wilks' lambda, the same test statistic used in multivariate ANOVA, is used to test the equality of group centroids. Discriminant Analysis can be used not only to test multivariate differences among groups, but also to explore:

– Which variables are most useful for discriminating among groups
– If one subset of variables performs equally well as another
– Which groups are most alike and most different

The examples that follow present approaches for selecting variables and evaluating the resulting models.

Getting started

To request your analysis, use Stats⮞Discriminant Analysis:

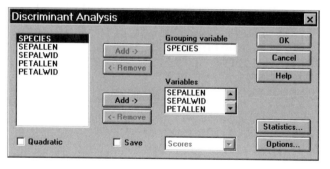

For controls for stepwise model building and tolerance, use **Stats**▸
Discriminant Analysis▸**Options:**

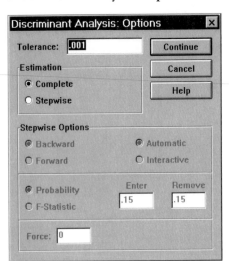

Using commands

Choose your data by typing **USE** *filename* and continue as follows:

```
DISCRIM
```

basic
```
     MODEL grpvar = varlist
     PRINT / options
     SAVE / options
     ESTIMATE
```

stepwise
```
     Instead of ESTIMATE, specify START
     START / options
```
where options are BACKWARD, FORWARD etc...
```
     STEP varlist, + or -, / options
       ⋮
     STEP
     STOP
```

Contrasts and priors

Contrasts and priors are available with commands. For a discussion of contrasts, see Example 11.5. Unless stated otherwise, a case is assumed a priori to have equal probability of being in any group. If prior probabilities are stated, they affect only the constant term of the classification function and the computation of the posterior probabilities. The prior probabilities of the groups used in the analysis should sum to 1.

Extended results

Discriminant Analysis allows you to control what panels appear in the output. You can request preassigned sets of reports by using **Edit**➧ **Options** and choosing the **Length** of output as **Short**, **Medium**, or **Long**.

You can also select or add reports individually by using **Stats**➧ **Discriminant Analysis**➧**Statistics** and selecting the desired output elements. For example, the output in Example 11.1 illustrates the panels printed by default and a request for group means (**Means**).

Short

The **Short** mode is assumed unless you already specified a different argument in this run. For **Short**, panels are:

FMatrix	Between-groups F matrix
FStats	F-to-enter or F-to-remove statistics (linear model only)
Eigen	Eigenvalues and canonical correlations
CMeans	Canonical scores for group centroids
Sum	Summary of the variable moved at each step in stepwise analyses
Class	Classification matrix
JClass	Jackknifed classification matrix

With commands, the respective options are:

FMATRIX   FSTATS   EIGEN   CMEANS   SUM   CLASS
JCLASS

Medium

By specifying **Medium**, you obtain the panels listed for **Short**, and:

Means	Group frequencies and means
Wilks'	Wilks' lambda with approximate F
CFunc	Coefficients for classification functions
Traces	Lawley-Hotelling, Pillai, and Wilks' trace
CDFunc	Coefficients for canonical variables
SCDFunc	Standardized coefficients for canonical variables

With commands, the respective options are:

MEANS   WILKS   CFUNC   TRACES   CDFUNC   SCDFUNC

Long

With **Long**, you get the panels listed for **Short** and **Medium**, and:

WCov	Pooled within-group covariance matrix
WCorr	Pooled within-group correlation matrix

TCov	Total covariance matrix
TCorr	Total correlation matrix
GCov	Groupwise covariance matrices (quadratic model only) and test for equality of covariance matrices
GCorr	Groupwise correlation matrices (quadratic model only)

Mahalanobis distances, posterior probabilities, and canonical scores for each case must be specified individually. These will not be printed by using **Edit▸Options** and selecting **Long** for **Length**.

Mahal	Mahalanobis distances and posterior probabilities
CScore	Canonical scores for each case

With commands, the respective options are:

```
WCOV    WCORR   TCOV    TCORR   GCOV    GCORR
MAHAL   CSCORE
```

You can specify individual panels by specifying the particular option. For example, with commands:

PRINT SHORT / CFUNC   All **Short** panels and classification functions

The Basics

We define statistics and describe Discriminant Analysis options in seven examples. Interpretation of a specific output panel is presented with the first output that generates the panel. If you start reading a later example, you may need to look at an earlier example for explanations.

11.1
The Fisher
iris data

In this example, we examine measurements made on 150 iris flowers: sepal length, sepal width, petal length, and petal width (in centimeters). The data are from Fisher (1936) and are grouped by species: Setosa, Versicolor, and Virginica (coded as 1, 2, and 3, respectively).

The goal of the discriminant analysis is to find a linear combination of the four measures that best classifies or discriminates among the three species (groups of flowers). Here is a SPLOM of the four measures with within-group bivariate confidence ellipses and normal curves.

```
DISCRIM
   USE iris
   SPLOM sepallen..petalwid / HALF GROUP=species ELL,
                              DENSITY=NORM  OVERLAY
```

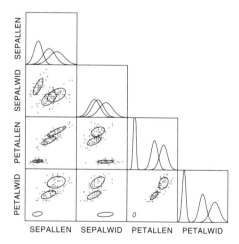

Let's see what a default analysis tells us about the separation of the groups and the usefulness of the variables for the classification. Using **Data**➠ **Label**, assign names to the numeric *SPECIES* codes. Use **Stats**➠ **Discriminant Analysis** to select *SPECIES* as the **Grouping variable** and *SEPALLEN, SEPALWID, PETALLEN,* and *PETALLWID* as the **Variables** in the model. In the **Statistics** subdialog box, select **Means** to request the group means. With commands:

```
USE iris
LABEL species / 1='Setosa', 2='Versicolor',
                 3='Virginica'
MODEL species = sepallen .. petalwid
PRINT / MEANS
ESTIMATE
```

Note the shortcut notation (..) in the MODEL statement for listing consecutive variables in the file (otherwise, simply list each variable name separated by a space).

❶ Group frequencies

```
-----------------
                Setosa Versicol Virginic
Frequencies        50       50       50
```

Group means

```
----------
SEPALLEN         5.006    5.936    6.588
SEPALWID         3.428    2.770    2.974
PETALLEN         1.462    4.260    5.552
PETALWID         0.246    1.326    2.026
```

❷ Between groups F-matrix -- df =   4   144

```
                 Setosa Versicol Virginic
Setosa              0.0
Versicolor      550.189    0.0
Virginica      1098.274  105.313    0.0
```

❸

Variable	F-to-remove	Tolerance		Variable	F-to-enter	Tolerance
2 SEPALLEN	4.72	0.347993				
3 SEPALWID	21.94	0.608859				
4 PETALLEN	35.59	0.365126				
5 PETALWID	24.90	0.649314				

❹ Classification matrix (cases in row categories classified into columns).

```
--------------------
            Setosa Versicol Virginic %correct
Setosa         50       0        0     100
Versicolor      0      48        2      96
Virginica       0       1       49      98

Total          50      49       51      98
```

Jackknifed classification matrix

```
-------------------------------
            Setosa Versicol Virginic %correct
Setosa         50       0        0     100
Versicolor      0      48        2      96
Virginica       0       1       49      98

Total          50      49       51      98
```

❺

	Eigen values	Canonical correlations	Cumulative proportion of total dispersion
	32.192	0.985	0.991
	0.285	0.471	1.000

Canonical scores of group means

Setosa	7.608	.215
Versicolor	-1.825	-.728
Virginica	-5.783	.513

❻

Canonical Scores Plot

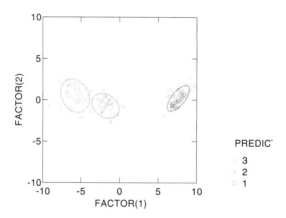

The highlighted numbers below correspond to those in the output:

❶ *Group frequencies.* The count of flowers within each group and the means for each variable. If the group code or one or more measures is missing, the case is not used in the analysis.

❷ *Between groups F matrix.* For each pair of groups, use these *F* statistics to test the equality of group means. These values are proportional to distance measures and are computed from Mahalanobis D^2 statistics. Thus, the centroids for Versicolor and Virginica are closest (105.3); those for Setosa and Virginica (1098.3) are furthest apart. *Note*: if you explore differences among several pairs, don't use the probabilities associated with these *F*'s as a test because of the simultaneous inference problem. Compare the relative size of these values with the distances between-group means in the canonical variable plot below.

❸ *F statistics and Tolerance.* Use *F-to-remove* statistics to determine the relative importance of variables included in the model. The numerator degrees of freedom for each F is the number of groups minus 1, and the denominator df is the (total sample size) – (number of groups) – (number of variables in the model) + 1. For these data, 3–1 and 150–3–4+1 or 2 and 144. Because you may be scanning F's for several variables, do not use the probabilities from the usual F tables for a test. Here we conclude that *SEPALLEN* is least helpful for discriminating among the species (F=4.72). See Example 11.2 for a discussion of *F-to-enter* and Example 11.3 for a discussion of *Tolerance*.

❹ *Classification tables*. In the *Classification matrix*, each case is classified into the group where the value of its **classification function** is largest (these functions are defined in Example 11.3). For Versicolor (row name), 48 flowers are classified correctly and 2 are misclassified (classified as Virginica)—96% of the Versicolor flowers are classified correctly. Overall, 98% of the flowers are classified correctly (see the last row of the table). The results in the first table can be misleading because we evaluated the classification rule using the same cases used to compute it. They may provide an overly optimistic estimate of the rule's success. The *Jackknifed classification matrix* attempts to remedy the problem by using functions computed from all of the data *except* the case being classified. The method of leaving out one case at a time is called the **jackknife** and is one form of cross-validation (see also Example 11.7).

For these data, the results are the same. If the percentage for correct classification is considerably lower in the *Jackknife* panel than in the first matrix, you may have too many predictors in your model.

❺ *Eigenvalues, Canonical correlations, Cumulative proportion of total dispersion, and Canonical scores of group means*. The **first canonical variable** is the linear combination of the variables that best discriminates among the groups; the second canonical variable is orthogonal to the first and is the next best combination of variables, and so on. For our data, the first eigenvalue (32.2) is very large relative to the second, indicating that the first canonical variable captures most of the difference among the groups—at the right of this panel, notice that it accounts for more than 99% of the total dispersion of the groups.

The **canonical correlation** between the first canonical variable and a set of two dummy variables representing the groups is 0.985; the correlation between the second canonical variable and the dummy variables is 0.471. (The number of dummy variables is the number of group minus 1.) Finally, the canonical variables are evaluated at the group means. That is, in the canonical variable plot, the centroid for the Setosa flowers is (7.608, 0.215), Versicolor is (–1.825, –0.728), and so on, where the first canonical variable is the x coordinate and the second, the y coordinate.

❻ *Canonical scores plot.* The axes of this *Quick Graph* are the first two canonical variables, and the points are the canonical variable scores. The confidence ellipses are centered on the centroid of each group. The Setosa flowers are well differentiated from the others. There is some overlap between the other two groups. Look for outliers in these displays because they can affect your analysis.

When the analysis has more than two canonical variables, SYSTAT displays a SPLOM of the first three canonical variables. To omit the *Quick Graph*, use **Edit➧Options** and deselect **Statistical Quickgraphs** (with commands, type GRAPH=NONE).

Classification functions

The classification functions are not printed in Example 11.1. If you replace the PRINT request with:

```
PRINT NONE / CFUNC
```

and rerun the example, the only output is:

```
Classification functions
-----------------------
              Setosa Versicol Virginic
  Constant   -86.308  -72.853 -104.368
  SEPALLEN    23.544   15.698   12.446
  SEPALWID    23.588    7.073    3.685
  PETALLEN   -16.431    5.211   12.767
  PETALWID   -17.398    6.434   21.079
```

These functions are defined in Example 11.3.

Stepwise Modeling

In the previous example, we knew what variables to include in the model because we were replicating a classical problem. For many applications, it is unclear just which variables to use, and a key goal may be to identify a relevant subset of predictors. There is no one exact procedure for identifying the *best* subset, and there is no ideal test to tell you that you have found it. There are many strategies for identifying a "good" model. In Discriminant Analysis, you can build a model in a *stepwise* manner, entering or removing a variable from the model at each step. If you begin by identifying the variable for which the group means are most different, using it in a one-variable discriminant function, and then continue by adding the next "best" variable step by step, the method is called **forward** selection. If you start with a model that contains all possible candidate variables, and remove the least useful variable at each step, the method is called **backward** selection. In Discriminant Analysis, you can ask SYSTAT to select a variable to move at each step or you can interactively select the variable to move after studying results and graphics for the current step. We call the former **automatic** stepping and the later **interactive** stepping. We illustrate these methods in the next three examples.

For either method, the problem is to determine just where to stop adding (or removing) variables. This problem is the same as that for stepwise regression. We suggest that you read "Variable selection" on p. 282 in Chapter 8 for more information, especially the material about the usefulness of cross-validation techniques.

11.2 Automatic forward stepping	Our problem for this example is to derive a rule for classifying countries as European, Islamic, or New World. We know that strong correlations exist among the candidate predictor variables, so we are curious about just which subset will be useful. Here are the candidate predictors:

URBAN	Percentage of the population living in cities
BIRTH_RT	Births per 1000 people in 1990
DEATH_RT	Deaths per 1000 people in 1990
B_TO_D	Ratio of births to deaths in 1990
BABYMORT	Infant deaths during the first year per 1000 live births
GDP_CAP	Gross domestic product per capita (in U.S. dollars)
LIFEEXPM	Years of life expectancy for males
LIFEEXPF	Years of life expectancy for females
EDUC	U.S. dollars spent per person on education in 1986
HEALTH	U.S. dollars spent per person on health in 1986
MIL	U.S. dollars spent per person on the military in 1986
LITERACY	Percentage of the population who can read

Because the distributions of the economic variables are skewed with long right tails, we log transform *GDP_CAP* and take the square root of *EDUC*, *HEALTH*, and *MIL*. Use **Data⟶Transform⟶Let** and type:

```
LET gdp_cap= L10(gdp_cap)
LET educ= SQR(educ)
LET health= SQR(health)
LET mil= SQR(mil)
```

With commands, use SYSTAT's shortcut notation to request the square root transformations:

```
LET (educ, health, mil) = SQR(@)
```

Use **Stats⟶Discriminant Analysis⟶Options** to request **Automatic Forward** stepping. With commands, use **START** (instead of **ESTIMATE**) with the **FORWARD** option and **STEP** with the **AUTO** option. In Example 11.3, we request automatic backward stepping and in Example 11.4, we illustrate how you can interactively select variables to enter or remove at each step.

Note: *When using the dialog box or commands, it is important to point out that after stepping stops, you need to type STOP to ask SYSTAT to produce the summary table, classification matrices, and information about canonical variables.*

```
DISCRIM
   USE ourworld
   LET  gdp_cap = L10 (gdp_cap)
   LET (educ, health, mil) = SQR(@)

   MODEL group$ = urban birth_rt death_rt babymort,
                  gdp_cap educ health mil b_to_d,
                  lifeexpm lifeexpf literacy
   PRINT / MEANS
   START / FORWARD
   STEP / AUTO
   STOP
```

Note that the initial results appear after **START / FORWARD** is specified. **STEP / AUTO** and **STOP** are selected later, as indicated in the output that follows:

❶

```
Group frequencies
----------------
                Europe  Islamic NewWorld
Frequencies       19       15      21

Group means
-----------
   URBAN        68.789   30.067   56.381
   BIRTH_RT     12.579   42.733   26.952
   DEATH_RT     10.105   13.400    7.476
   BABYMORT      7.895  102.333   42.810
   GDP_CAP       4.043    2.764    3.214
   EDUC         21.527    6.416    8.962
   HEALTH       21.954    3.194    6.890
   MIL          15.975    7.543    6.090
   B_TO_D        1.266    3.547    3.951
   LIFEEXPM     72.368   54.400   66.619
   LIFEEXPF     79.526   57.133   71.571
   LITERACY     97.526   36.733   79.957
```

❷

Variable	F-to-remove	Tolerance	Variable	F-to-enter	Tolerance
			6 URBAN	23.20	1.000000
			8 BIRTH_RT	103.50	1.000000
			10 DEATH_RT	14.41	1.000000
			12 BABYMORT	53.62	1.000000
			16 GDP_CAP	59.12	1.000000
			19 EDUC	27.12	1.000000
			21 HEALTH	49.62	1.000000
			23 MIL	19.30	1.000000
			34 B_TO_D	31.54	1.000000
			30 LIFEEXPM	37.08	1.000000
			31 LIFEEXPF	50.30	1.000000
			32 LITERACY	63.64	1.000000

```
STEP arguments: var_name or indices, - (minus) removes, + (plus) enters a
     variable, no argument for SYSTAT to select. To end stepping, type STOP.
```

- With commands, type STEP / AUTO.

```
*************** Step   1  --  Variable BIRTH_RT Entered  ***************
```
❸ Between groups F-matrix -- df =   1   52
```
-------------------------------------------------
            Europe  Islamic NewWorld
Europe      0.0
Islamic     206.588   0.0
NewWorld    55.856    59.063    0.0

  Variable   F-to-remove Tolerance | Variable    F-to-enter Tolerance
-----------------------------------+------------------------------------
  8 BIRTH_RT    103.50  1.000000   |   6 URBAN       1.26   0.724555
                                   |  10 DEATH_RT   19.41   0.686118
                                   |  12 BABYMORT    2.13   0.443802
                                   |  16 GDP_CAP     4.56   0.581395
                                   |  19 EDUC        5.12   0.831381
                                   |  21 HEALTH      9.52   0.868614
                                   |  23 MIL         8.55   0.907501
                                   |  34 B_TO_D     14.94   0.987994
                                   |  30 LIFEEXPM    4.31   0.437850
                                   |  31 LIFEEXPF    3.58   0.371618
                                   |  32 LITERACY   10.32   0.324635

*************** Step   2  --  Variable DEATH_RT Entered  ***************
```
❹ Between groups F-matrix -- df =   2   51
```
-------------------------------------------------
            Europe  Islamic NewWorld
Europe      0.0
Islamic     120.130   0.0
NewWorld    59.759    29.766    0.0

  Variable   F-to-remove Tolerance | Variable    F-to-enter Tolerance
-----------------------------------+------------------------------------
  8 BIRTH_RT    118.41  0.686118   |   6 URBAN       0.07   0.694384
 10 DEATH_RT     19.41  0.686118   |  12 BABYMORT    1.83   0.279580
                                   |  16 GDP_CAP     7.88   0.520784
                                   |  19 EDUC        5.03   0.812622
                                   |  21 HEALTH      6.47   0.864170
                                   |  23 MIL        13.21   0.789555
                                   |  34 B_TO_D      0.82   0.186108
                                   |  30 LIFEEXPM    3.34   0.158185
                                   |  31 LIFEEXPF    5.20   0.120507
                                   |  32 LITERACY    2.22   0.265285

*************** Step   3  --  Variable MIL Entered  ***************

Between groups F-matrix  --  df =    3    50
-------------------------------------------------
            Europe  Islamic NewWorld
Europe      0.0
Islamic     80.760    0.0
NewWorld    55.650    24.674    0.0

  Variable   F-to-remove Tolerance | Variable    F-to-enter Tolerance
-----------------------------------+------------------------------------
  8 BIRTH_RT     77.85  0.683054   |   6 URBAN       3.87   0.509585
 10 DEATH_RT     25.39  0.596945   |  12 BABYMORT    1.02   0.258829
 23 MIL          13.21  0.789555   |  16 GDP_CAP     0.67   0.304330
                                   |  19 EDUC        0.01   0.534243
                                   |  21 HEALTH      1.24   0.652294
                                   |  34 B_TO_D      0.81   0.186064
                                   |  30 LIFEEXPM    0.28   0.135010
                                   |  31 LIFEEXPF    1.34   0.091911
                                   |  32 LITERACY    3.51   0.252509

STEP arguments: var_name or indices, - (minus) removes, + (plus) enters a
       variable, no argument for SYSTAT to select. To end stepping, type STOP.
```

- When using the dialog box or commands, type STOP.

❺

Variable entered or removed	F-to-enter or F-to-remove	Number of variables in model	Wilks' lambda	Approx. F-value	DF1	DF2	p-tail
BIRTH_RT	103.495	1	0.2008	103.4953	2	52	0.00000
DEATH_RT	19.406	2	0.1140	50.0200	4	102	0.00000
MIL	13.212	3	0.0746	44.3576	6	100	0.00000

❻ Classification matrix (cases in row categories classified into columns.

	Europe	Islamic	NewWorld	%correct
Europe	19	0	0	100
Islamic	0	13	2	87
NewWorld	2	2	17	81
Total	21	15	19	89

Jackknifed classification matrix

	Europe	Islamic	NewWorld	%correct
Europe	19	0	0	100
Islamic	0	13	2	87
NewWorld	2	3	16	76
Total	21	16	18	87

❼

Eigen values	Canonical correlations	Cumulative proportion of total dispersion
5.247	0.916	0.821
1.146	0.731	1.000

Canonical scores of group means

Europe	-2.938	.409
Islamic	2.481	1.243
NewWorld	.886	-1.258

❽

Canonical Scores Plot

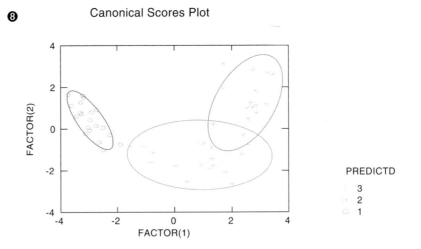

The highlighted numbers below correspond to those in the output:

❶ *Group frequencies.* From the panel of group means, note that, on the average, the percentage of the population living in cities (*URBAN*) is 68.8% in Europe, 30.1% in Islamic nations, and 56.4% in the New

World. The *LITERACY* rates for these same groups are 97.5%, 36.7%, and 80.0%, respectively.

❷ *F statistics*. In Example 11.1, *F*-to-remove statistics are defined. Here are *F*-to-enter statistics for each variable not in the functions. When no variables are in the model, each *F* is the same as that for a one-way analysis of variance. Thus, group differences are the strongest for *BIRTH_RT* ($F=103.5$) and weakest for *DEATH_RT* ($F=14.41$). At later steps, each *F* corresponds to the *F* for a one-way analysis of covariance where the covariates are the variables already included.

❸ At step 1, SYSTAT enters *BIRTH_RT* because its *F*-to-enter is largest in the last panel and now displays the same *F* in the *F*-to-remove panel. *BIRTH_RT* is correlated with several candidate variables, so notice how their *F*-to-enter values drop when *BIRTH_RT* enters (for example, for *GDP_CAP*, from 59.1 to 4.6). *DEATH_RT* now has the highest *F*-to-enter, so SYSTAT will enter it at step 2. From the between-groups *F*-matrix (defined above), note that when *BIRTH_RT* is used alone, Europe and Islamic countries are the groups that differ most (206.6), and Europe and the New World are the groups that differ least (55.9).

❹ After *DEATH_RT* enters, the *F*-to-enter for *MIL* (money spent per person on the military) is largest, so SYSTAT enters it at step 3. SYSTAT's default limit for *F*-to-enter values is 4.0. No variable has an *F*-to-enter above the limit, so the stepping stops. Also, all *F*-to-remove values are greater than 3.9, so no variables are removed.

❺ *Summary table*. There is one line in this table for each variable moved into the model. The *F*-to-enter (*F*-to-remove) is printed for each along with Wilks' lambda and its approximate *F* statistic, numerator and denominator degrees of freedom, and tail probability.

❻ *Classification matrices* (defined in Example 11.1). From the biased estimate in the first matrix, our three-variable rule classifies 89% of the countries correctly. For the jackknifed results, this percentage drops to 87%. All of the European nations are classified correctly (100%), while almost one-fourth of the New World countries are misclassified (two as Europe and three as Islamic). These countries can be identified by selecting **Mahal** in the **Statistics** subdialog box—the posterior probability for each case belonging to each group is printed. You will find, for example, that Canada is misclassified as European and that Haiti and Bolivia are misclassified as Islamic.

❼ The first canonical variable accounts for 82.1% of the dispersion, and from the *Canonical scores of group means*, the groups are ordered from left to right: Europe, New World, and then Islamic. The second canonical variable contrasts Islamic versus New World (1.243 versus −1.258).

❽ In this canonical variable plot, the European nations (on the left) are well separated from the other groups. The plus sign (+) next to the European confidence ellipse is Canada. If you are unsure about which ellipse corresponds to what group, look at the group means in ❼.

Options for stepwise model building

When building models in a stepwise manner, use **Stats**➧**Discriminant Analysis**➧**Options** and select **Stepwise**. Use these options for controlling the computations:

Tolerance=n	Matrix inversion tolerance limit. The default is 0.001.
Backward	Initialize the procedure for backward stepping.
Forward	Initialize the procedure for forward stepping. SYSTAT reports results for step 0. If omitted, all specified variables that surpass **Enter** or **Remove** limits are entered or removed from the model.
Automatic	SYSTAT selects a variable to move at each step.
Interactive	You interactively select the variable to move.
Probability	Probability of F-to-enter limit and probability of F-to-remove limit. The default is 0.15.
F-statistic	F-to-enter limit (the default is 4.0) and F-to-remove limit (the default is 3.9).
Force=n	Force the first n variables into the model. The default is 0.

We use **Forward** and **Backward** in Example 11.2 and Example 11.3. Comments are made regarding **Enter** and **Remove** values in Example 11.1, Example 11.2, and Example 11.3. **Force** is usually used in automatic stepwise model building to ensure that the first n variables remain in the model regardless of their F-to-remove or F-to-enter values.

When using commands for stepwise modeling, use START instead of ESTIMATE. START initiates stepwise model building and is followed by STEP to execute the process.

```
START / FORWARD or BACK, TOL=n, FENTER=n,
            FREMOVE=n, FORCE=n, ENTER=n, REMOVE=n
```

The **Tolerance** option controls the matrix inversion tolerance limit. Tolerance is a guard against computational problems when the variables are highly correlated. The default is 0.001. With commands:

```
ESTIMATE / TOL=n
```

Automatic stepping

When you specify **START**, SYSTAT reports F-to-enter statistics for each variable (for forward stepping), or F-to-remove statistics (for backward stepping). To request that SYSTAT select variables one by one to enter (or remove), select **Automatic**. With commands, here is the minimum you need (as illustrated in Example 11.2 and Example 11.3):

```
          ⋮                           ⋮
   START / FORWARD            START / BACKWARD
   STEP / AUTO                STEP / AUTO
```

When stepping stops, both command users and dialog box users type **STOP**. This signals that model building has ended. SYSTAT then forms classification tables and computes the canonical variable coefficients and scores.

Interactive stepping

Professional data analysts rarely use automatic stepwise procedures, instead preferring to guide the variable selection process themselves using statistics in the output, plots, and, most important, knowledge of the theory in the subject area and the meaning of the variables.

If you want to interactively guide the selection of variables at each step, use **Stats**➠**Discriminant Analysis**➠**Options** and select **Stepwise** and **Interactive**. The rest of the interactive stepping process must be done with commands. Here is the minimum you need:

```
          ⋮                           ⋮
   START / FORWARD            START / BACKWARD
   STEP                       STEP
          ⋮                           ⋮
```

If you want to limit the number of steps, specify **NUMBER=n**. The default is 2 times the number of candidate variables.

Specifying **STEP** alone causes SYSTAT to select the same variable as in automatic stepping (that is, values of **FENTER** and **FREMOVE** are used).

More likely, at each step, you will want to name a variable to move. For example,

$$\vdots$$

```
START / FORWARD
STEP literacy
STEP gdp_cap
STEP lifeexpf lifeexpm
```

$$\vdots$$

```
STOP
```

Note that when stepping is completed, both command users and dialog box users must type STOP. Here are the commands to identify one or more variables to move:

Example	Argument	Definition
STEP +	+ (*a plus*)	Enter the variable with the largest *F*-to-enter value, irrespective of the FENTER limit.
STEP -	- (*a minus*)	Remove the variable with the smallest *F*-to-remove value, irrespective of the FREMOVE limit.
STEP mil	*varlist*	Move one or more variables (*varlist*) in (or out) of the model, irrespective of FENTER and FREMOVE limits.
AUTO	AUTO	Switch to an automatic stepping mode.

We illustrate interactive stepping in Example 11.4.

11.3 Automatic backward stepping

It is possible that classification rules for other subsets of the variables perform better than that found using forward stepping—especially when there are correlations among the variables. We try backward stepping.

Use **Data**➡**ID Variable** and select *COUNTRY$* (the name of the country will label each case in this panel). Continue by using **Stats**➡**Discriminant Analysis**➡**Options** and selecting **Stepwise** and **Backward**. Use **Stats**➡**Discriminant Analysis**➡**Statistics** and request that the classification functions be printed at each step (**CFunc**). For when the stepping is finished, also request Mahalanobis distances and posterior probabilities (**MAHAL**) and the coefficients for the canonical variables (**CDFunc** and **SCDFunc**).

continuing with the data transformations in Example 11.2

```
MODEL group$ = urban birth_rt death_rt babymort,
               gdp_cap educ health mil b_to_d,
               lifeexpm lifeexpf literacy
PRINT SHORT / CFUNC
IDVAR = country$
START / BACKWARD

STEP / AUTO
PRINT / MAHAL TRACES CDFUNC SCDFUNC
STOP
```

Note that we request STEP after an initial report and PRINT and STOP later.

❶ Between groups F-matrix -- df =   12   41

```
            Europe  Islamic NewWorld
Europe      0.0
Islamic     25.306   0.0
NewWorld    18.060   7.375   0.0
```

❷ Classification functions

```
            Europe    Islamic   NewWorld
Constant  -4408.400 -4396.890 -4408.530
   URBAN     -2.417    -2.357    -2.287
BIRTH_RT     41.979    43.168    43.132
DEATH_RT     50.020    48.154    48.195
BABYMORT      9.319     9.381     9.346
 GDP_CAP    243.669   234.516   237.080
    EDUC      2.008     4.045     3.428
  HEALTH    -17.971   -19.853   -19.307
     MIL     -9.842   -10.175   -10.608
   B_TO_D    -59.655   -62.245   -61.820
LIFEEXPM     -9.822    -9.154    -9.495
LIFEEXPF     93.593    93.093    93.411
LITERACY      7.591     7.583     7.718
```

❸

Variable	F-to-remove	Tolerance	Variable	F-to-enter	Tolerance
6 URBAN	2.17	0.436470			
8 BIRTH_RT	2.01	0.059623			
10 DEATH_RT	2.26	0.091463			
12 BABYMORT	0.10	0.083993			
16 GDP_CAP	0.62	0.143526			
19 EDUC	6.12	0.065095			
21 HEALTH	5.36	0.083198			
23 MIL	7.11	0.323519			
34 B_TO_D	0.55	0.136148			
30 LIFEEXPM	0.26	0.036088			
31 LIFEEXPF	0.07	0.012280			
32 LITERACY	1.45	0.177756			

- With commands, type STEP / AUTO.

```
*************** Step  1  --  Variable LIFEEXPF Removed  ***************

Between groups F-matrix  --  df =   11    42
------------------------------------------------
              Europe  Islamic NewWorld
Europe         0.0
Islamic       28.200   0.0
NewWorld      20.169   8.209   0.0

Classification functions
----------------------
              Europe  Islamic NewWorld
Constant    -2135.287-2147.992-2144.271
  URBAN       -0.869   -0.817   -0.742
  BIRTH_RT    20.147   21.452   21.343
  DEATH_RT    29.388   27.631   27.603
  BABYMORT     3.751    3.842    3.789
  GDP_CAP    292.124  282.713  285.441
  EDUC        -3.883   -1.815   -2.452
  HEALTH      -5.835   -7.782   -7.195
  MIL         -6.977   -7.325   -7.748
  B_TO_D     -13.746  -16.581  -16.000
  LIFEEXPM    32.720   33.161   32.963
  LITERACY     5.534    5.537    5.665

  Variable   F-to-remove Tolerance | Variable   F-to-enter  Tolerance
--------------------------------------+----------------------------------
  6 URBAN          2.45   0.466202 | 31 LIFEEXPF     0.07   0.012280
  8 BIRTH_RT       3.04   0.077495 |
 10 DEATH_RT       2.45   0.100658 |
 12 BABYMORT       0.41   0.140589 |
 16 GDP_CAP        0.68   0.144854 |
 19 EDUC           6.71   0.066537 |
 21 HEALTH         6.78   0.092071 |
 23 MIL            7.39   0.328943 |
 34 B_TO_D         0.70   0.148030 |
 30 LIFEEXPM       0.24   0.077817 |
 32 LITERACY       1.48   0.185492 |
```

❹
```
*************** Step  2  --  Variable LIFEEXPM Removed  ***************
```
            *** We omit the output for Steps 2-6. See comment ❹ below. ***

```
*************** Step  7  --  Variable URBAN Removed  ***************
```
❺
```
Between groups F-matrix  --  df =    5    48
------------------------------------------------
              Europe  Islamic NewWorld
Europe         0.0
Islamic       61.590   0.0
NewWorld      40.935   15.600   0.0

Classification functions
----------------------
              Europe  Islamic NewWorld
Constant     -22.483  -38.431  -17.698
BIRTH_RT       0.300    1.337    0.938
DEATH_RT       1.422    0.659    0.259
EDUC          -0.179    1.301    0.851
HEALTH         0.748   -0.882   -0.398
MIL            0.754    0.418    0.179

  Variable   F-to-remove Tolerance | Variable   F-to-enter  Tolerance
--------------------------------------+----------------------------------
  8 BIRTH_RT      27.89   0.622699 |  6 URBAN         3.65   0.504724
 10 DEATH_RT      15.51   0.583392 | 12 BABYMORT      1.12   0.243722
 19 EDUC           5.20   0.083925 | 16 GDP_CAP       1.20   0.171233
 21 HEALTH         6.67   0.102470 | 34 B_TO_D        1.24   0.180347
 23 MIL            7.42   0.501019 | 30 LIFEEXPM      0.02   0.123573
                                   | 31 LIFEEXPF      0.49   0.076049
                                   | 32 LITERACY      3.42   0.250341
```

- Type PRINT / MAHAL TRACE CDFUNC SCDFUNC.
- Type STOP.

❻

```
Variable      F-to-enter  Number of
entered or      or        variables     Wilks'    Approx.
  removed   F-to-remove   in model      lambda    F-value  DF1  DF2  p-tail
-----------  -----------  ---------   ----------  --------  ---  ---  ------
LIFEEXPF         0.068        11        0.0405    15.1458   22   84   0.00000
LIFEEXPM         0.237        10        0.0410    16.9374   20   86   0.00000
BABYMORT         0.219         9        0.0414    19.1350   18   88   0.00000
B_TO_D           0.849         8        0.0430    21.4980   16   90   0.00000
GDP_CAP          1.429         7        0.0457    24.1542   14   92   0.00000
LITERACY         2.388         6        0.0505    27.0277   12   94   0.00000
URBAN            3.655         5        0.0583    30.1443   10   96   0.00000
```

✱✱✱ *The panel of Mahalanobis distances and posterior probabilities appears here.*
   We move it below for discussion. See **❿** .   ✱✱✱

❼
```
Classification matrix (cases in row categories classified into columns.
---------------------
         Europe  Islamic  NewWorld  %correct
Europe      19       0        0       100
Islamic      0      13        2        87
NewWorld     1       2       18        86

  Total     20      15       20        91

Jackknifed classification matrix
---------------------------------
         Europe  Islamic  NewWorld  %correct
Europe      19       0        0       100
Islamic      0      13        2        87
NewWorld     1       2       18        86

  Total     20      15       20        91

            Eigen       Canonical     Cumulative proportion
            values    correlations     of total dispersion
          ---------   ------------    ---------------------
            6.984        0.935               0.859
            1.147        0.731               1.000
```

❽
```
         Wilks' lambda=       0.058
            Approx.F=        30.144  DF= 10,     96  p-tail=  0.0000

        Pillai's trace=       1.409
            Approx.F=        23.360  DF= 10,     98  p-tail=  0.0000

Lawley-Hotelling trace=       8.131
            Approx.F=        38.215  DF= 10,     94  p-tail=  0.0000
```

❾
```
Canonical discriminant functions
--------------------------------
                    1          2
Constant         -1.984     -5.402
   URBAN            .          .
BIRTH_RT          0.160      0.041
DEATH_RT         -0.159      0.277
BABYMORT           .          .
 GDP_CAP           .          .
    EDUC          0.236      0.006
  HEALTH         -0.260     -0.002
     MIL         -0.074      0.150
  B_TO_D           .          .
LIFEEXPM           .          .
LIFEEXPF           .          .
LITERACY           .          .
```

```
Canonical discriminant functions -- standardized by within variances
---------------------------------------------------------------------
                    1         2
    URBAN           .         .
  BIRTH_RT        0.974     0.251
  DEATH_RT       -0.519     0.905
  BABYMORT          .         .
   GDP_CAP          .         .
      EDUC        1.557     0.041
    HEALTH       -1.557    -0.009
       MIL       -0.391     0.795
    B_TO_D          .         .
  LIFEEXPM          .         .
  LIFEEXPF          .         .
   LITERACY         .         .
```

⑩ Canonical scores of group means

```
-------------------------------
Europe       -3.389     .410
Islamic       2.864    1.243
NewWorld      1.020   -1.259
```

Canonical Scores Plot

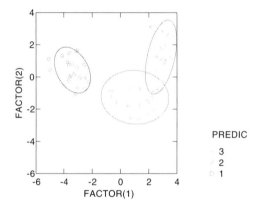

The highlighted numbers below correspond to those in the output:

❶ Before stepping starts, SYSTAT uses all candidate variables to compute classification functions that follow. A variable is omitted only if it fails the *Tolerance* limit. When all 12 variables are included, the *F*'s in the *Between-groups F-matrix* indicate relations similar to those among the groups in Example 11.2, step 3.

❷ *Classification functions.* This panel displays coefficients for functions used to classify cases into groups. That is, for each case, SYSTAT computes three functions. The first is:

-4408.4 − 2.417 urban + 41.979 birth_rt + ... + 7.591 literacy

Each case is assigned to the group with the largest value.

❸ *Tolerance* measures the correlation of a candidate variable with the variables included in the model, and its values range from 0 to 1.0. If a variable is highly correlated with one or more of the others, the value of *Tolerance* is very small and the resulting estimates of the discriminant function coefficients may be very unstable. To avoid a loss of accuracy in the matrix inversion computations, you rarely should set the value of this limit to a lower value (the default is 0.001). *LIFEEXPF*, female life expectancy, has a very low *Tolerance* value, so it may be redundant or highly correlated with another variable or a linear combination of other variables. The *Tolerance* value of *LIFEEXPM*, male life expectancy, is also low—these two measures of life expectancy may be highly correlated with one another. Notice also that the value for *BIRTH_RT* is very low (0.059623) and its *F*-to-remove value is 2.01—its *F*-to-enter at step 0 in the last example was 103.5.

At step 1, SYSTAT removes *LIFEEXPF* from the model, because its *F*-to-remove is the smallest. After female life expectancy is removed, the *Tolerance* value for male life expectancy is still low (0.077817).

❹ *Step 2.* SYSTAT continues removing variables one by one. We omit the output for steps 2 through 6. See the summary table in ❻.

❺ *Step 7.* No variable has an *F*-to-remove value less than 3.9, so the stepping stops. The final model found by backward stepping includes five variables: *BIRTH_RT*, *DEATH_RT*, *EDUC*, *HEALTH*, and *MIL*. We are not happy, however, with the low tolerance values for the last two variables. The model found via automatic forward stepping did not include *EDUC* or *HEALTH* (their *F*-to-enter statistics at step 3 are 0.01 and 1.24, respectively). *URBAN* and *LITERACY* appear more likely candidates, but their *F*'s are still less than 4.0.

❻ *Summary table.* Here, we add *Tolerance* to some of the summary results:

Step	Variable Removed	F	Tolerance
1	LIFEEXPF	0.07	0.012
2	LIFEEXPM	0.24	0.078
3	BABYMORT	0.22	0.204
4	B_TO_D	0.85	0.163
5	GDP_CAP	1.43	0.160
6	LITERACY	2.39	0.247
7	URBAN	3.65	0.505

❼ *Classification matrices.* In both classification matrices, 91% of the countries are classified correctly using the five-variable discriminant functions. This is a slight improvement over the three-variable model from the last example, where the percentages were 89% for the first matrix and 87% for the *Jackknifed* results. The improvement from 87% to 91% is because two New World countries are now classified correctly. We add two variables and gain two correct classifications.

❽ *Wilks' lambda, Pillai's trace*, and *Lawley-Hotelling trace*. Wilks' lambda (or *U* statistic), a multivariate analysis of variance statistic that varies between 0 and 1, tests the equality of group means for the variables in the discriminant functions. Wilks' lambda is transformed to an *Approximate F* statistic for comparison with the *F* distribution. Here the associated probability is less than 0.00005, indicating a highly significant difference among the groups. The Lawley-Hotelling trace and its *F* approximation are documented in Morrison (1976). When there are only two groups, it and Wilks' lambda are equivalent. Pillai's trace and its *F* approximation are taken from Pillai (1960).

❾ *Canonical discriminant functions* (or canonical variables). Here are coefficients of the canonical variables computed first for the data as input and then for the standardized values. For the unstandardized data, the first canonical variable is:

  -1.984 + .160 birth_rt − .159 death_rt + .236 educ − .260 health − .074 mil

The coefficients are adjusted so that the overall mean of the corresponding scores is 0 and the pooled within-group variances are 1. After standardizing, the first canonical variable is:

  0.974 birth_rt − .519 death_rt + 1.557 educ − 1.557 health − .391 mil

Usually, one uses the latter set of coefficients to interpret what variables "drive" each canonical variable. Here, *EDUC* and *HEALTH*, the variables with low tolerance values, have the largest coefficients, and they appear to cancel one another. Also, in the final model, the size of their *F*-to-remove values indicates they are the least useful variables in the model. This indicates that we do not have an optimum set of variables. These two variables contribute little alone, while together they enhance the separation of the groups. This suggests that the difference between *EDUC* and *HEALTH* could be a useful variable (for example, LET diff = educ - health). We did this and here is the first canonical variable for standardized values (we omit the constant):

  1.024 birth_rt − 0.539 death_rt − .480 mil + .553 diff

⑩ From the *Canonical* scores of the group means for the first canonical variable, the groups line up with Europe first, then New World in the middle, and Islamic on the right. In the second dimension, *DEATH_RT* and *MIL* (military expenditures) appear to separate Islamic and New World countries.

Compare the plot of canonical variable scores on p. 384 with that in Example 11.2. The configuration of the groups is similar. Canada, a lone "+" among the "o"s falls within the European confidence ellipse.

Mahalanobis distances and posterior probabilities

For Mahalanobis distances, use **Stats**➨**Discriminant Analysis**➨ **Statistics** and select **Mahal**. Note that you must do this even if you have selected **Long** as the output **Length** in the **Edit**➨**Options** dialog box. With commands, even if you have already specified PRINT=LONG, you must type PRINT / MAHAL to obtain Mahalanobis distances.

```
                        Mahalanobis distance-square from group means and
                          Posterior probabilities for group membership
                Priors =      .333          .333            .333
                              Europe       Islamic       NewWorld

          Europe
          ------------
          Ireland           3.0 1.00     33.7  .00     13.6  .00
          Austria           4.0 1.00     37.7  .00     19.8  .00
          Belgium      *     .3 1.00     42.7  .00     26.0  .00
          Denmark           9.1 1.00     37.6  .00     24.9  .00
          Finland           2.1 1.00     40.5  .00     22.3  .00
          France            2.3 1.00     45.5  .00     29.1  .00
          Greece            5.7 1.00     48.6  .00     28.3  .00
          Switzerland      11.9 1.00     71.7  .00     48.3  .00
          Spain             3.6 1.00     42.8  .00     18.9  .00
          UK                2.1 1.00     42.8  .00     29.9  .00
          Italy              .6 1.00     44.7  .00     23.0  .00
          Sweden            4.3 1.00     51.7  .00     35.9  .00
          Portugal          3.6 1.00     40.4  .00     18.8  .00
          Netherlands       2.1 1.00     43.9  .00     24.2  .00
          WGermany          6.0 1.00     65.8  .00     45.5  .00
          Norway            5.3 1.00     38.5  .00     28.4  .00
          Poland            2.7  .99     29.5  .00     12.5  .01
          Hungary           4.4 1.00     39.8  .00     24.3  .00
          EGermany          8.0 1.00     42.4  .00     31.9  .00
          Czechoslov        1.8 1.00     40.9  .00     25.1  .00

          Islamic
          ------------
          Gambia           43.2  .00      2.9 1.00     15.3  .00
          Iraq             71.3  .00     23.5 1.00     41.7  .00
          Pakistan         38.7  .00       .5  .98      8.6  .02
          Bangladesh       37.2  .00      2.0  .91      6.8  .09
          Ethiopia         40.5  .00      1.1  .99     10.0  .01
          Guinea           41.2  .00      8.0 1.00     24.1  .00
          Malaysia   -->   36.6  .00      7.7  .17      4.5  .83
          Senegal          42.8  .00       .9  .98      9.1  .02
          Mali             49.3  .00      5.5 1.00     23.5  .00
          Libya            60.3  .00     15.6 1.00     30.1  .00
          Somalia          50.0  .00      1.1 1.00     13.1  .00
          Afghanistan *      .        .        .        .
          Sudan            43.8  .00       .3  .99     10.1  .01
          Turkey     -->   25.0  .00      7.2  .05      1.5  .95
          Algeria          43.1  .00      4.1  .79      6.7  .21
          Yemen            57.4  .00      3.1 1.00     23.2  .00
```

```
NewWorld
------------
Argentina              11.5   .03    19.8   .00     4.4   .97
Barbados               16.4   .00    20.9   .00     4.7  1.00
Bolivia        -->     27.7   .00     3.4   .56     3.8   .44
Brazil                 27.4   .00    11.5   .00      .6  1.00
Canada         -->      6.7  1.00    35.9   .00    19.3   .00
Chile                  21.1   .00    15.7   .00     1.5  1.00
Colombia               35.2   .00    13.9   .00     1.9  1.00
CostaRica              34.8   .00    21.1   .00     5.5  1.00
Venezuela              41.2   .00    13.4   .01     4.6   .99
DominicanR.            26.0   .00    13.2   .00     1.3  1.00
Uruguay                13.6   .07    22.9   .00     8.6   .93
Ecuador                32.8   .00     8.6   .02     1.0   .98
ElSalvador             35.3   .00     7.5   .07     2.5   .93
Jamaica                25.6   .00    19.1   .00     1.9  1.00
Guatemala              37.6   .00     4.5   .33     3.1   .67
Haiti          -->     37.9   .00     2.0   .99    10.6   .01
Honduras               39.8   .00     6.4   .27     4.5   .73
Trinidad               34.1   .00    11.4   .03     4.1   .97
Peru                   20.2   .00    10.5   .02     2.4   .98
Panama                 23.8   .00    16.5   .00     2.4  1.00
Cuba                   12.0   .03    18.5   .00     5.1   .97

        -->    case misclassified
         *     case has missing values
```

For each case (up to 250 cases), the *Mahalanobis distance squared* (D^2) is computed to each group mean. The closer a case is to a particular mean, the more likely it belongs to that group. The *posterior probability* for the distance of a case to a mean is the ratio of EXP(-D^2/2) for the group divided by the sum of EXP(-D^2/2) for all groups (prior probabilities, if specified, affect these computations).

An arrow (-->) marks incorrectly classified cases and an asterisk (*) flags cases with missing values. New World countries Bolivia and Haiti are classified as Islamic, and Canada is classified as Europe. Note that even though an asterisk marks Belgium, results are printed—the value of the unused candidate variable *URBAN* is missing. No results are printed for Afghanistan, because *MIL*, a variable in the final model, is missing.

You can identify cases with all large distances as outliers. A case can have a 1.0 probability of belonging to a particular group but still have a large distance. Look at Iraq. It is correctly classified as Islamic, but its distance is 23.5. The distances in this panel are distributed approximately as a chi-square with degrees of freedom equal to the number of variables in the function.

Saving distances, probabilities, and canonical variable scores

For each case, you can save the group membership predicted by the model (named *PREDICTD*) and a misclassification indicator named *CORRECT* (0=misclassification, 1=correct prediction). Use **Stats ➠ Discriminant Analysis**, select **Save**, and choose from the drop-down list:

Scores   Canonical variable scores, the default. Also includes the grouping variable and the **ID Variable**, if specified.

Scores/Data	The canonical variable scores and the data (with transformations created in the current run).
Distances	Mahalanobis distances from each case to each group centroid and the posterior probability of the case's membership in each group. Also includes the grouping variable and the **ID Variable**, if specified.
Distances/Data	Mahalanobis distances and the data (with transformations created in the current run).

If no option is selected, **Scores** is assumed. The saved variables containing canonical variable scores are named *SCORE(1)*, *SCORE(2)*, and so on; the Mahalanobis distances, *DISTANCE(1)*, *DISTANCE(2)*, and so on; and the posterior probabilities, *PROB(1)*, *PROB(2)*, and so on. You cannot save **Scores** and **Distances** together, but you can save both with **Data**. With commands, type

```
SAVE mycanvar / SCORE DATA
```

before **START** to save the canonical variable scores with the data. Scatterplots of the saved data are shown below:

```
PLOT score(2) * score(1) / LABEL=country$,
                XLABEL='First Canonical Variable',
                YLABEL='Second Canonical Variable'
```

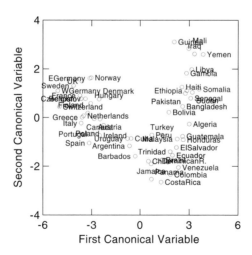

When the groups are plotted individually, it is easy to see that Turkey and Malaysia are misclassified as New World, Canada as Europe, and Haiti and Bolivia as Islamic:

```
PLOT score(2) * score(1) / LABEL=country$,
                                GROUP=group$  ROW=1
```

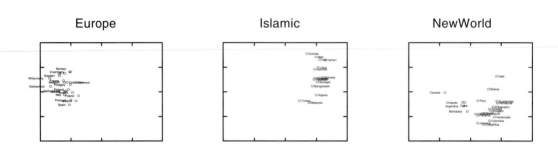

11.4 Interactive stepping

Automatic forward and backward stepping can produce different sets of predictor variables, and still other subsets of the variables may perform equally as well or possibly better. Here we use interactive stepping to explore alternative sets of variables.

Let's say you decide not to include birth and death rates in the model because the rates are changing rapidly for several nations (that is, we omit these variables from the model). We also add the difference between *EDUC* and *HEALTH* as a candidate variable.

SYSTAT provides several ways to specify which variables to move in (or out) from the model.

continuing with the data transformations in Example 11.2
```
LET diffrnce = educ - health

MODEL group$ = urban birth_rt death_rt babymort,
               gdp_cap educ health mil b_to_d,
               lifeexpm lifeexpf literacy  diffrnce
PRINT SHORT / SCDFUNC
GRAPH=NONE
START / BACK
```

After interpreting these commands and printing ❶ in the output below, SYSTAT waits for us to enter **STEP** instructions. Here is a summary of the **STEP** arguments (variable numbers are visible in the output):

a. STEP birth_rt   Remove two variables
death_rt

b. STEP lifeexpf   Remove one variable

c. STEP -   Remove lifeexpm

d. STEP -   Remove babymort

e. STEP -   Remove urban

f. STEP -   Remove gdp_cap

g. STEP educ   Remove educ and health;
health diffrnce   add diffrnce

h. STEP +   Enter gdp_cap

STOP

- Note that the seventh **STEP** specification (**g**) removes *EDUC* and *HEALTH* and enters *DIFFRNCE*. Remember, after the last step, type **STOP** for the canonical variable results and other summaries.

```
         *** We omit the between-groups F-matrix (see Example 11.3) ***

   Variable    F-to-remove  Tolerance |  Variable     F-to-enter  Tolerance
--------------------------------------+-----------------------------------
   6 URBAN          2.17    0.436470   | 40 DIFFRNCE        0.00   0.000000
   8 BIRTH_RT       2.01    0.059623   |
  10 DEATH_RT       2.26    0.091463   |
  12 BABYMORT       0.10    0.083993   |
  16 GDP_CAP        0.62    0.143526   |
  19 EDUC           6.12    0.065095   |
  21 HEALTH         5.36    0.083198   |
  23 MIL            7.11    0.323519   |
  34 B_TO_D         0.55    0.136148   |
  30 LIFEEXPM       0.26    0.036088   |
  31 LIFEEXPF       0.07    0.012280   |
  32 LITERACY       1.45    0.177756   |

STEP arguments: var_name or indices. -(minus) removes,+(plus) enters variable,
     no argument for SYSTAT to select. To end stepping, type STOP.
```

- Type **STEP** birth_rt death_rt

```
**************** Step   1  --  Variable BIRTH_RT Removed  ****************

Between groups F-matrix  -- df =   11     42
-----------------------------------------------
              Europe  Islamic NewWorld
Europe         0.0
Islamic       26.367   0.0
NewWorld      18.039   8.240    0.0

   Variable    F-to-remove  Tolerance |  Variable     F-to-enter  Tolerance
--------------------------------------+-----------------------------------
   6 URBAN          2.64    0.437926   |  8 BIRTH_RT       2.01   0.059623
  10 DEATH_RT       2.00    0.092765   | 40 DIFFRNCE       0.00   0.000000
  12 BABYMORT       0.14    0.091364   |
  16 GDP_CAP        1.40    0.150944   |
  19 EDUC           5.99    0.065824   |
  21 HEALTH         4.24    0.090886   |
  23 MIL            5.92    0.384992   |
  34 B_TO_D         0.35    0.329976   |
  30 LIFEEXPM       0.42    0.036548   |
  31 LIFEEXPF       0.96    0.015962   |
  32 LITERACY       1.79    0.292005   |

**************** Step   2  --  Variable DEATH_RT Removed  ****************

Between groups F-matrix  -- df =   10     43
-----------------------------------------------
              Europe  Islamic NewWorld
```

```
Europe        0.0
Islamic      27.816    0.0
NewWorld     18.173    9.279     0.0

  Variable    F-to-remove  Tolerance  |  Variable    F-to-enter  Tolerance
-----------------------------------------------------------------------------
  6 URBAN        2.20      0.452548   |   8 BIRTH_RT     1.75     0.060472
 12 BABYMORT     0.23      0.108992   |  10 DEATH_RT     2.00     0.092765
 16 GDP_CAP      1.14      0.153540   |  40 DIFFRNCE     0.00     0.000000
 19 EDUC         6.52      0.065850   |
 21 HEALTH       6.28      0.093470   |
 23 MIL          6.69      0.385443   |
 34 B_TO_D       6.48      0.651944   |
 30 LIFEEXPM     0.51      0.036592   |
 31 LIFEEXPF     0.28      0.019231   |
 32 LITERACY     1.89      0.312350   |
```

- Type **STEP** lifeexpf

```
**************** Step   3  --  Variable LIFEEXPF Removed  ****************

Between groups F-matrix  --  df =   9    44
---------------------------------------------
             Europe  Islamic NewWorld
Europe        0.0
Islamic      31.164    0.0
NewWorld     20.461   10.475     0.0

  Variable    F-to-remove  Tolerance  |  Variable    F-to-enter  Tolerance
-----------------------------------------------------------------------------
  6 URBAN        2.27      0.472161   |   8 BIRTH_RT     1.88     0.086049
 12 BABYMORT     0.79      0.147553   |  10 DEATH_RT     1.31     0.111768
 16 GDP_CAP      1.80      0.171189   |  31 LIFEEXPF     0.28     0.019231
 19 EDUC         7.51      0.066995   |  40 DIFFRNCE    10.26     0.000500
 21 HEALTH       7.37      0.095626   |
 23 MIL          6.88      0.389511   |
 34 B_TO_D       6.49      0.683545   |
 30 LIFEEXPM     0.28      0.151179   |
 32 LITERACY     2.44      0.338715   |
```

- Type **STEP–** (minus) to remove the variable with the lowest *F*-to-remove value.

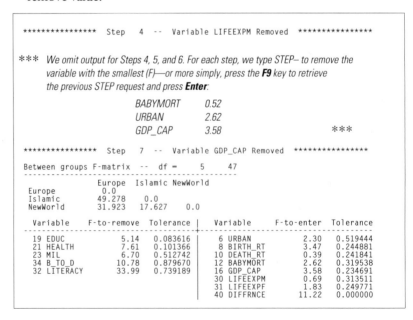

```
**************** Step   4  --  Variable LIFEEXPM Removed  ****************

***   We omit output for Steps 4, 5, and 6. For each step, we type STEP– to remove the
      variable with the smallest (F)—or more simply, press the F9 key to retrieve
      the previous STEP request and press Enter:

              BABYMORT    0.52
              URBAN       2.62
              GDP_CAP     3.58                          ***

**************** Step   7  --  Variable GDP_CAP Removed  ****************

Between groups F-matrix  --  df =   5    47
---------------------------------------------
             Europe  Islamic NewWorld
Europe        0.0
Islamic      49.278    0.0
NewWorld     31.923   17.627     0.0

  Variable    F-to-remove  Tolerance  |  Variable    F-to-enter  Tolerance
-----------------------------------------------------------------------------
 19 EDUC         5.14      0.083616   |   6 URBAN        2.30     0.519444
 21 HEALTH       7.61      0.101366   |   8 BIRTH_RT     3.47     0.244881
 23 MIL          6.70      0.512742   |  10 DEATH_RT     0.39     0.241841
 34 B_TO_D      10.78      0.879670   |  12 BABYMORT     2.62     0.319538
 32 LITERACY    33.99      0.739189   |  16 GDP_CAP      3.58     0.234691
                                      |  30 LIFEEXPM     0.69     0.313511
                                      |  31 LIFEEXPF     1.83     0.249771
                                      |  40 DIFFRNCE    11.22     0.000000
```

- Type STEP edu health diffrnce.

```
**************** Step   8  --  Variable EDUC Removed  ****************

    *** We omit Steps 8 and 9 where EDUC (19) and HEALTH (21) are removed. ***

**************** Step  10  --  Variable DIFFRNCE Entered  ****************

Between groups F-matrix  --  df =    4    49
----------------------------------------
          Europe  Islamic NewWorld
Europe     0.0
Islamic   60.897    0.0
NewWorld  38.792   22.475    0.0

  Variable  F-to-remove  Tolerance |  Variable   F-to-enter  Tolerance
--------------------------------------+-----------------------------------
  23 MIL         16.65   0.683968   |   6 URBAN        2.50   0.522963
  34 B_TO_D      13.97   0.900149   |   8 BIRTH_RT     3.89   0.246110
  32 LITERACY    47.38   0.792219   |  10 DEATH_RT     0.41   0.241913
  40 DIFFRNCE     6.98   0.772114   |  12 BABYMORT     3.26   0.333341
                                    |  16 GDP_CAP      4.30   0.372308
                                    |  19 EDUC         0.94   0.514966
                                    |  21 HEALTH       0.94   0.628279
                                    |  30 LIFEEXPM     0.98   0.326826
                                    |  31 LIFEEXPF     2.40   0.269658
```

- Type STEP+ (plus) to enter *GDP_CAP* with its *F* of 4.30.

```
**************** Step  11  --  Variable GDP_CAP Entered  ****************

Between groups F-matrix  --  df =    5    48
----------------------------------------
          Europe  Islamic NewWorld
Europe     0.0
Islamic   57.542    0.0
NewWorld  35.743   18.688    0.0

  Variable  F-to-remove  Tolerance |  Variable   F-to-enter  Tolerance
--------------------------------------+-----------------------------------
  16 GDP_CAP      4.30   0.372308   |   6 URBAN        2.72   0.513543
  23 MIL          5.88   0.478530   |   8 BIRTH_RT     1.04   0.189556
  34 B_TO_D       9.46   0.887953   |  10 DEATH_RT     1.00   0.215879
  32 LITERACY    12.31   0.609614   |  12 BABYMORT     0.71   0.256567
  40 DIFFRNCE     8.37   0.735173   |  19 EDUC         0.36   0.324618
                                    |  21 HEALTH       0.36   0.396047
                                    |  30 LIFEEXPM     0.04   0.259888
                                    |  31 LIFEEXPF     0.24   0.180725
```

- Type STOP.

```
Variable    F-to-enter  Number of
entered or     or       variables     Wilks'     Approx.
 removed    F-to-remove  in model      lambda     F-value  DF1  DF2   p-tail
----------  ----------  ---------   ----------  ---------  ---  ---  -------
BIRTH_RT       2.011       11         0.0444      14.3085   22   84  0.00000
DEATH_RT       2.002       10         0.0486      15.2053   20   86  0.00000
LIFEEXPF       0.275        9         0.0492      17.1471   18   88  0.00000
LIFEEXPM       0.277        8         0.0498      19.5708   16   90  0.00000
BABYMORT       0.524        7         0.0510      22.5267   14   92  0.00000
URBAN          2.615        6         0.0568      25.0342   12   94  0.00000
GDP_CAP        3.583        5         0.0655      27.9210   10   96  0.00000
EDUC           5.143        4         0.0795      31.1990    8   98  0.00000
HEALTH         2.438        3         0.0874      39.7089    6  100  0.00000
DIFFRNCE       6.986        4         0.0680      34.7213    8   98  0.00000
GDP_CAP        4.298        5         0.0577      30.3710   10   96  0.00000

Classification matrix (cases in row categories classified into columns.
----------------------
          Europe  Islamic NewWorld  %correct
Europe      19       0        0       100
Islamic      0      14        1        93
NewWorld     1       1       19        90

  Total     20      15       20        95
```

```
Jackknifed classification matrix
------------------------------
            Europe  Islamic NewWorld %correct
  Europe      19       0       0       100
  Islamic      0      12       3        80
  NewWorld     1       3      17        81

    Total     20      15      20        87

            Eigen      Canonical    Cumulative proportion
            values    correlations    of total dispersion
          ---------   ------------   ---------------------
            6.319        0.929             0.822
            1.369        0.760             1.000

Canonical discriminant functions -- standardized by within variances
--------------------------------------------------------------------
                  1        2
  URBAN           .        .
  BIRTH_RT        .        .
  DEATH_RT        .        .
  BABYMORT        .        .
  GDP_CAP       0.687    0.038
  EDUC            .        .
  HEALTH          .        .
  MIL           0.068    0.840
  B_TO_D       -0.446   -0.504
  LIFEEXPM        .        .
  LIFEEXPF        .        .
  LITERACY      0.390   -0.857
  DIFFRNCE     -0.638   -0.029


Canonical scores of group means
-------------------------------
  Europe      3.162    .535
  Islamic    -2.890   1.281
  NewWorld    -.796  -1.399
```

Here is a summary of results for the models estimated in Example 11.2, Example 11.3, and Example 11.4:

Model	% Correct	
Automatic	**Class**	**Jackknife**
Forward		
1. BIRTH_RT DEATH_RT MIL	89	87
Backward		
2. BIRTH_RT DEATH_RT MIL EDUC HEALTH	91	91
Interactive (ignoring BIRTH_RT and DEATH_RT)		
3. MIL B_TO_D LITERACY	84	84
4. MIL B_TO_D LITERACY EDUC HEALTH	91	89
5. MIL B_TO_D LITERACY DIFFRNCE	91	89
6. MIL B_TO_D LITERACY DIFFRNCE GDP_CAP	95	87

Notice that the largest difference between the two classification methods (95% versus 87%) occurs for the last model, which includes the most variables. A difference like this one (8%) can indicate overfitting of correlated candidate variables. Since the jackknifed results can still be overly optimistic, we show how to do cross-validation in Example 11.7.

More Features

11.5 Contrasts

Contrasts are available with commands only. When you have specific hypotheses about differences among particular groups, you can specify one or more contrasts to direct the entry (or removal) of variables into the model.

According to the jackknifed classification results in Example 11.2 through Example 11.4, the European countries are always classified correctly (100% correct). All of the misclassifications are New World countries classified as Islamic or vice versa. In order to maximize the difference between the second (Islamic) and third groups (New World), we specify contrast coefficients with commands:

```
CONTRAST [0 -1 1]
```

If we want to specify linear and quadratic contrasts across four groups, we could specify:

```
CONTRAST [-3 -1 1 3; -1 1 1 -1]
```

or

```
CONTRAST [-3 -1  1  3
          -1  1  1 -1]
```

Here we use the first contrast and request interactive forward stepping. Compare these results with those in Example 11.2, where the three variables *BIRTH_RT*, *DEATH_RT*, and *MIL* are included in the final model.

```
continuing with the data transformations in Example 11.2
MODEL group$ = urban birth_rt death_rt babymort,
               gdp_cap educ health mil b_to_d,
               lifeexpm lifeexpf literacy
CONTRAST [0 -1 1]
PRINT / SHORT
START / FORWARD

STEP literacy
STEP mil
STEP urban
STOP
```

After viewing the results, remember to cancel the contrast if you plan to do other discriminant analyses:

CONTRAST / CLEAR

❶
Variable	F-to-remove	Tolerance	Variable	F-to-enter	Tolerance
			6 URBAN	21.87	1.000000
			8 BIRTH_RT	59.06	1.000000
			10 DEATH_RT	28.79	1.000000
			12 BABYMORT	44.12	1.000000
			16 GDP_CAP	14.32	1.000000
			19 EDUC	1.30	1.000000
			20 HEALTH	3.34	1.000000
			23 MIL	0.65	1.000000
			34 B_TO_D	1.12	1.000000
			30 LIFEEXPM	35.00	1.000000
			31 LIFEEXPF	43.16	1.000000
			32 LITERACY	64.84	1.000000

```
STEP arguments: var_name or indices, - (minus) removes, + (plus) enters a
     variable, no argument for SYSTAT to select. To end stepping, type STOP.

**************** Step   1  --  Variable LITERACY Entered  ****************
```

*** We omit results for Step 1, Step 2, and Step 3. ***

❷
Variable entered or removed	F-to-enter or F-to-remove	Number of variables in model	Wilks' lambda	Approx. F-value	DF1	DF2	p-tail
LITERACY	64.844	1	0.4450	64.8444	1	52	0.00000
MIL	9.963	2	0.3723	42.9917	2	51	
URBAN	2.953	3	0.3515	30.7433	3	50	0.00000

❸ Classification matrix (cases in row categories classified into columns)

	Europe	Islamic	NewWorld	%correct
Europe	18	0	1	95
Islamic	0	14	1	93
NewWorld	2	3	16	76
Total	20	17	18	87

Jackknifed classification matrix

	Europe	Islamic	NewWorld	%correct
Europe	18	0	1	95
Islamic	0	14	1	93
NewWorld	2	3	16	76
Total	20	17	18	87

❹
Eigen values	Canonical correlations	Cumulative proportion of total dispersion
1.845	0.805	1.000

Canonical scores of group means

Europe	.882
Islamic	-2.397
NewWorld	.914

The highlighted numbers below correspond to those in the output:

❶ Compare these *F-to-enter* values with those in ❷, Example 11.2. The statistics here indicate that for the economic variables (*GDP_CAP*, *EDUC*, *HEALTH*, and *MIL*), differences between the second and third groups are much smaller than those when European countries are included.

❷ *Summary table.* *LITERACY* has the largest *F-to-enter* in ❶, so we enter it first. Next we enter *MIL*. We enter *URBAN*, even though its *F* statistic is rather small.

❸ The *Jackknifed classification matrix* indicates that using *LITERACY*, *MIL*, and *URBAN*, 87% of the countries are classified correctly. This is the same percentage correct as in ❻, Example 11.2 for the model with *BIRTH_RT*, *DEATH_RT*, and *MIL*. Here, however, one fewer Islamic country is misclassified, and one European country is now classified incorrectly.

❹ Since a single contrast has one degree of freedom, only one dimension is defined—that is, there is only one eigenvalue and one canonical variable.

11.6
A quadratic model

One of the assumptions necessary for linear discriminant analysis is equality of covariance matrices. Within group scatterplot matrices (SPLOM's) provide a picture of how measures co-vary. Here we add 85% ellipses of concentration to enhance our view of the bivariate relations. Since our sample sizes do not differ markedly (15 to 21 countries per group), the ellipses for each pair of variables should have approximately the same shape and tilt across groups if the equality of covariance assumption holds.

```
DISCRIM
   USE ourworld
   LET(educ, health, mil) = SQR(@)
   STAND
   SPLOM birth_rt death_rt educ health mil / HALF ROW=1,
                              GROUP=group$  ELL=.85
DENSITY=NORMAL
```

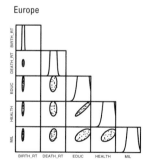

Europe

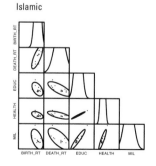

Islamic

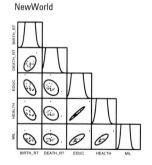

NewWorld

Because for most pairs of variables the length, width, and tilt of the ellipses vary markedly across groups, the assumption of equal covariance matrices has not been met.

Fortunately, the quadratic model does not require equality of covariances. However, it has a different problem: it requires a larger minimum sample size than that needed for the linear model. For five variables, for example, the linear and quadratic models, respectively, for each group are:

$$f = a + bx_1 + cx_2 + dx_3 + ex_4 + fx_5$$

$$f = a + bx_1 + cx_2 + dx_3 + ex_4 + fx_5 + gx_1x_2 + \ldots + px_4x_5 + qx_1^2 + \ldots + ux_5^2$$

So the linear model has six parameters to estimate for each group and the quadratic has 21. These parameters aren't all independent, so we don't require as many as 3×21 cases for a quadratic fit.

Here we select **Quadratic** on the **Discriminant Analysis** dialog box to fit a quadratic model using the subset of variables identified with backward stepping in Example 11.3. Following this, we examine results for the subset identified in Example 11.4 before *EDUC* and *HEALTH* are removed.

```
USE ourworld
LET (educ, health, mil) = SQR(@)
MODEL group$ = birth_rt death_rt,
               educ health mil / QUAD
PRINT SHORT / GCOV WCOV GCOR  CFUNC  MAHAL
IDVAR = country$
ESTIMATE


MODEL group$ = educ health mil b_to_d,
               literary / QUAD
ESTIMATE
```

Results for the first model ❶

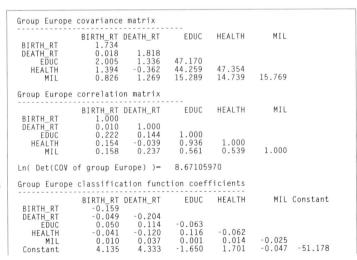

```
Group Europe covariance matrix
------------------------------------------
          BIRTH_RT DEATH_RT   EDUC   HEALTH     MIL
BIRTH_RT    1.734
DEATH_RT    0.018    1.818
    EDUC    2.005    1.336   47.170
  HEALTH    1.394   -0.362   44.259   47.354
     MIL    0.826    1.269   15.289   14.739   15.769

Group Europe correlation matrix
------------------------------------------
          BIRTH_RT DEATH_RT   EDUC   HEALTH     MIL
BIRTH_RT    1.000
DEATH_RT    0.010    1.000
    EDUC    0.222    0.144    1.000
  HEALTH    0.154   -0.039    0.936    1.000
     MIL    0.158    0.237    0.561    0.539    1.000

Ln( Det(COV of group Europe) )=    8.67105970
```

❷
```
Group Europe classification function coefficients
------------------------------------------
          BIRTH_RT DEATH_RT   EDUC   HEALTH      MIL  Constant
BIRTH_RT   -0.159
DEATH_RT   -0.049   -0.204
    EDUC    0.050    0.114   -0.063
  HEALTH   -0.041   -0.120    0.116   -0.062
     MIL    0.010    0.037    0.001    0.014   -0.025
Constant    4.135    4.333   -1.650    1.701   -0.047  -51.178
```

❸ Group Islamic covariance matrix

```
              BIRTH_RT DEATH_RT    EDUC    HEALTH     MIL
BIRTH_RT       48.638
DEATH_RT       27.543   25.543
    EDUC      -19.873  -20.369   33.751
  HEALTH      -10.926  -10.619   18.831   10.860
     MIL      -15.590  -28.499   36.679   19.323   66.018
```

Group Islamic correlation matrix

```
              BIRTH_RT DEATH_RT    EDUC    HEALTH     MIL
BIRTH_RT        1.000
DEATH_RT        0.781    1.000
    EDUC       -0.490   -0.694    1.000
  HEALTH       -0.475   -0.638    0.984    1.000
     MIL       -0.275   -0.694    0.777    0.722    1.000
```

Ln(Det(COV of group Islamic))= 10.34980794

Group Islamic classification function coefficients

```
              BIRTH_RT DEATH_RT    EDUC    HEALTH      MIL Constant
BIRTH_RT       -0.024
DEATH_RT        0.070   -0.075
    EDUC        0.010   -0.073   -0.358
  HEALTH       -0.042    0.133    1.093   -0.895
     MIL        0.026   -0.047    0.049   -0.036   -0.019
Constant        0.949   -0.596    1.282   -0.999   -0.396  -20.449
```

❹ Group NewWorld covariance matrix

```
              BIRTH_RT DEATH_RT    EDUC    HEALTH     MIL
BIRTH_RT       60.248
DEATH_RT        9.574    8.162
    EDUC      -30.857   -6.223   45.045
  HEALTH      -27.930   -5.296   41.630   40.410
     MIL      -15.414   -1.740   18.309   17.291   12.237
```

Group NewWorld correlation matrix

```
              BIRTH_RT DEATH_RT    EDUC    HEALTH     MIL
BIRTH_RT        1.000
DEATH_RT        0.432    1.000
    EDUC       -0.592   -0.325    1.000
  HEALTH       -0.566   -0.292    0.976    1.000
     MIL       -0.568   -0.174    0.780    0.778    1.000
```

Ln(Det(COV of group NewWorld))= 11.46371023

Group NewWorld classification function coefficients

```
              BIRTH_RT DEATH_RT    EDUC    HEALTH      MIL Constant
BIRTH_RT       -0.008
DEATH_RT        0.012   -0.040
    EDUC       -0.008   -0.021   -0.126
  HEALTH        0.004    0.011    0.242   -0.133
     MIL       -0.011    0.020    0.023    0.021   -0.058
Constant        0.435    0.264    0.826   -0.654    0.523  -13.312
```

❺ Test for equality of covariance matrices
```
    Chisquare=  139.5799      df=     30    prob=  0.0000
```

Between groups F-matrix -- df =   5   49

```
              Europe  Islamic NewWorld
Europe         0.0
Islamic       64.453    0.0
NewWorld      43.144   15.920    0.0
```

❻
```
                    Mahalanobis distance-square from group means and
                    Posterior probabilities for group membership
         Priors =        .333       .333       .333
                      Europe     Islamic   NewWorld
```

✱✱✱ *We omit the distances and probabilities for the Europe and Islamic groups*

NewWorld

```
Argentina          48.1  .00   45.2  .00    3.8 1.00
Barbados           31.8  .00   65.0  .00    6.5 1.00
Bolivia      -->  369.3  .00    4.1  .65    4.2  .35
Brazil            133.3  .00    9.4  .03    1.1  .97
```

```
Canada      -->   14.5  .88  533.6  .00   15.7  .12
Chile             66.6  .00   16.6  .00    1.8 1.00
Colombia         161.1  .00    9.2  .04    1.8  .96
CostaRica        181.6  .00   93.2  .00    7.8 1.00
Venezuela        180.9  .00   16.6  .01    6.0  .99
DominicanR.      175.3  .00   21.5  .00    2.3 1.00
Uruguay           23.1  .00   38.4  .00    5.8 1.00
Ecuador          212.2  .00    5.8  .13     .8  .87
ElSalvador       312.9  .00   10.0  .03    2.0  .97
Jamaica           73.8  .00   20.2  .00    2.5 1.00
Guatemala        404.9  .00    6.0  .17    1.7  .83
Haiti       -->  792.1  .00    3.9  .99   11.2  .01
Honduras         395.9  .00   16.1  .00    4.1 1.00
Trinidad         164.1  .00   38.0  .00    5.6 1.00
Peru             167.6  .00   18.9  .00    4.9 1.00
Panama           133.9  .00   97.7  .00    3.4 1.00
Cuba              33.6  .00   39.7  .00    6.8 1.00
        -->   case misclassified
         *    case has missing values
```

❼ Classification matrix (cases in row categories classified into columns.

	Europe	Islamic	NewWorld	%correct
Europe	20	0	0	100
Islamic	0	14	1	93
NewWorld	1	2	18	86
Total	21	16	19	93

Jackknifed classification matrix

	Europe	Islamic	NewWorld	%correct
Europe	20	0	0	100
Islamic	0	13	2	87
NewWorld	1	2	18	86
Total	21	15	20	91

Eigen values	Canonical correlations	Cumulative proportion of total dispersion
7.226	0.937	0.862
1.152	0.732	1.000

❽   *** *We omit the Eiginvalues, canonical discriminant functions, etc.* ***

❶ The within group correlation and covariance matrices for the 20 European countries.

❷ *Discriminant function coefficients for the European group.* Look at the quadratic function displayed at the beginning of this example. For our data,

a=-51.178, b=4.135, c=4.333, d=-1.650, e=1.701, f=-0.047,
    g=-0.049, …, p=0.014, q=-0.159, …, and u=-0.025
or

f=-51.178 + 4.135 birth_rt + … -0.049 birth_rt*death_rt + …
    -0.159 birth_rt^2 + … -0.025 mil^2

❸ Covariance and correlation matrices for the 15 Islamic countries, followed by their discriminant functions.

❹ Similar results for the 21 New World countries.

❺ Chi-square test for equality of covariance matrices. The results are highly significant ($p < 0.00005$). Thus, we reject the hypothesis of equal covariance matrices.

❻ Mahalanobis distances and posterior probabilities for the current model. Only four cases are misclassified: Turkey as a New World country, Canada as European, and Haiti and Bolivia as Islamic.

❼ The classification matrix indicates that 93% of the countries are correctly classified; using the jackknifed results, the percentage drops to 91%. The latter percentage agrees with that for the linear model using the same variables.

❽ The canonical discriminant functions and other results we delete are just like those at the end of Example 11.3, except here our sample has one more country. A case was deleted in the earlier example because one of the candidate variables (not entered) has a missing value.

Results for the second model

```
***  We omit panels like those labeled ❶, ❷, ❸, ❹, and ❺ in the
     output above. The results for this model are similar.         ***

Between groups F-matrix  --  df =    5    49
------------------------------------------------
              Europe  Islamic NewWorld
Europe        0.0
Islamic       51.515   0.0
NewWorld      33.603  17.991   0.0

                 Mahalanobis distance-square from group means and
                   Posterior probabilities for group membership
         Priors =     .333          .333          .333
                    Europe        Islamic      NewWorld

   ***  We omit the distance and probabilities for the Europe and Islamic groups.
            (Turkey is no longer misclassified.)  ***

NewWorld
------------
Argentina         30.9  .00   48.3  .00    4.3 1.00
Barbados          35.5  .00   68.7  .00    7.4 1.00
Bolivia          186.2  .00   10.1  .08    2.2  .92
Brazil           230.8  .00    8.1  .13    1.2  .87
Canada     -->    19.4  .74  524.3  .00   16.3  .26
Chile            144.3  .00   17.2  .00    1.6 1.00
Colombia         475.1  .00   29.8  .00    1.9 1.00
CostaRica        834.5  .00  190.5  .00   10.3 1.00
Venezuela        932.5  .00   83.6  .00    8.8 1.00
DominicanR.      267.4  .00   18.6  .00    2.0 1.00
Uruguay           15.2  .04   60.5  .00    3.9  .96
Ecuador          276.0  .00   11.5  .02    1.0  .98
ElSalvador       498.0  .00   17.6  .00    1.7 1.00
Jamaica          312.0  .00   15.5  .00     .7 1.00
Guatemala        501.3  .00    7.9  .24    2.5  .76
Haiti      -->   648.4  .00    4.6  .99   10.2  .01
Honduras         688.1  .00   31.8  .00    4.0 1.00
Trinidad         315.4  .00   43.1  .00    4.6 1.00
Peru             179.9  .00   16.3  .02    5.1  .98
Panama           411.0  .00  109.7  .00    3.6 1.00
Cuba              54.7  .00   54.5  .00    6.8 1.00

      -->   case misclassified
        *   case has missing values

Classification matrix (cases in row categories classified into columns)
-------------------
           Europe  Islamic NewWorld %correct
Europe       20       0       0      100
```

```
Islamic              0      15      0     100
NewWorld             1       1     19      90

Total               21      16     19      96

Jackknifed classification matrix
- - - - - - - - - - - - - - - - - - - - - - - -
                Europe  Islamic NewWorld %correct
Europe            19       0       1       95
Islamic            0      14       1       93
NewWorld           1       1      19       90

Total             20      15      21       93

            Eigen     Canonical    Cumulative proportion
            values   correlations   of total dispersion
          - - - - -  - - - - - - -  - - - - - - - - - - - -
            5.585       0.921             0.801
            1.391       0.763             1.000

Canonical scores of group means
- - - - - - - - - - - - - - - - - - - - - -
Europe      -2.916    .501
Islamic      2.725   1.322
NewWorld      .831  -1.422
```

This model does slightly better than the first one—the classification matrices here show that 96% and 93%, respectively, are classified correctly. This is because Turkey and Bolivia are classified correctly here and misclassified with the first model.

11.7 Cross-validation

At the end of Example 11.4, we reported the percentage of correct classification for six models. The same sample was used to compute the estimates and evaluate the success of the rules. We also reported results for the jackknifed classification procedure that removes and replaces one case at a time. This approach, however, may still give an overly optimistic picture. Ideally, we should try the rules on a new sample and compare results with those for the original data. Since this usually isn't practical, researchers often use a **cross-validation** procedure—that is, they randomly split the data into two samples, use the first sample to estimate the classification functions, and then use the resulting functions to classify the second sample. The first sample is often called the **learning sample** and the second, the **test sample**. The proportion of correct classification for the test sample is an empirical measure for the success of the discrimination.

Cross-validation is easy to implement in Discriminant Analysis. Cases assigned a weight of zero are not used to estimate the discriminant functions, but are classified into groups. In this example, we generate a uniform random number (values range from 0 to 1.0) for each case, and when it is less than 0.65, the value 1.0 is stored in a new weight variable named *CASE_USE*. If the random number is equal to or greater than 0.65, a zero is placed in the weight variable. So, approximately 65% of the cases have a weight of 1.0 and 35%, a weight of zero.

We now request a cross-validation for each of the six models listed at the end of Example 11.4.

1. BIRTH_RT DEATH_RT MIL
2. BIRTH_RT DEATH_RT MIL EDUC HEALTH
3. MIL B_TO_D LITERACY
4. MIL B_TO_D LITERACY EDUC HEALTH
5. MIL B_TO_D LITERACY DIFFRNCE
6. MIL B_TO_D LITERACY DIFFRNCE GDP_CAP

Use interactive forward stepping to "toggle" variables in and out of the model subsets. Use **Data ➡ Weight** to identify the *CASE_USE* variable.

continuing with the data transformations in Example 11.2
```
LET diffrnce = educ - health
LET case_use = URN < .65
WEIGHT = case_use

MODEL group$ = urban birth_rt death_rt babymort,
               gdp_gap educ health mil b_to_d,
               lifeexpm lifeexpf literacy diffrnce
PRINT  NONE / FSTATS  CLASS  JCLASS
GRAPH  NONE
START / FORWARD
```

In the output that follows, we construct sets of variables for each model like this:
```
STEP  birth_rt death_rt mil,
STEP  educ health
```
and so on...

Here are the results from the first **STEP** specification after variable 23, *MIL*, enters:

```
    Variable   F-to-remove  Tolerance |   Variable    F-to-enter  Tolerance
----------------------------------------+---------------------------------------
    8 BIRTH_RT    57.86    0.640126  |   6 URBAN        7.41    0.415097
   10 DEATH_RT    24.56    0.513344  |  12 BABYMORT     0.20    0.234804
   23 MIL         13.43    0.760697  |  16 GDP_CAP      3.22    0.394128
                                     |  19 EDUC         2.00    0.673136
                                     |  21 HEALTH       4.68    0.828565
                                     |  34 B_TO_D       0.16    0.209796
                                     |  30 LIFEEXPM     0.42    0.136526
                                     |  31 LIFEEXPF     0.83    0.104360
                                     |  32 LITERACY     1.54    0.244547
                                     |  40 DIFFRNCE     5.23    0.784797
```

❶
```
Classification matrix (cases in row categories classified into columns)
---------------------
              Europe  Islamic NewWorld %correct
    Europe      13       0       0       100
    Islamic      0       8       1        89
    NewWorld     0       1      15        94

    Total       13       9      16        95
```

❷
```
Classification of cases with zero weight or frequency
----------------------------------------------------
              Europe  Islamic NewWorld %correct
    Europe       6       0       0       100
    Islamic      0       4       2        67
    NewWorld     2       0       3        60

    Total        8       4       5        76
```

❸
```
Jackknifed classification matrix
--------------------------------
              Europe  Islamic NewWorld %correct
    Europe      13       0       0       100
    Islamic      0       8       1        89
    NewWorld     1       1      14        88

    Total       14       9      15        92
```

The highlighted numbers below correspond to those in the output:

❶ This classification table presents results for the learning sample or the cases with *CASE_USE* values of 1.0. Overall, 95% of these countries are classified correctly. The sample size is 13+9+16=38—or 67.9% of the original sample of 56 countries.

❷ Test sample results. The percentage of correct classification for the 17 countries that are not used to compute the estimates drops to 76%.

❸ Jackknifed results for the learning sample. Notice that the percentages of correct classification are closer to those for the learning sample in ❶ than for the test sample in ❷.

Now we add the variables *EDUC* and *HEALTH* by specifying:

```
STEP educ health
```

Here are the results after *HEALTH* enters:

```
 Variable   F-to-remove  Tolerance  |   Variable   F-to-enter  Tolerance
---------------------------------------+------------------------------------------
  8 BIRTH_RT    21.13    0.588377   |    6 URBAN        6.50    0.414511
 10 DEATH_RT    16.52    0.508827   |   12 BABYMORT     0.07    0.221475
 19 EDUC         2.24    0.103930   |   16 GDP_CAP      3.06    0.242491
 21 HEALTH       4.88    0.127927   |   34 B_TO_D       0.32    0.198963
 23 MIL          5.68    0.567128   |   30 LIFEEXPM     0.05    0.117494
                                    |   31 LIFEEXPF     0.04    0.080161
                                    |   32 LITERACY     1.75    0.238831
                                    |   40 DIFFRNCE     0.00    0.000000
```

❹ Classification matrix (cases in row categories classified into columns)

```
-------------
            Europe  Islamic NewWorld %correct
Europe        13       0       0       100
Islamic        0       8       1        89
NewWorld       0       1      15        94

  Total       13       9      16        95
```

❺ Classification of cases with zero weight or frequency

```
-------------
            Europe  Islamic NewWorld %correct
Europe         6       0       0       100
Islamic        0       5       1        83
NewWorld       1       0       4        80

  Total        7       5       5        88
```

Jackknifed classification matrix

```
-------------
            Europe  Islamic NewWorld %correct
Europe        13       0       0       100
Islamic        0       8       1        89
NewWorld       0       1      15        94

  Total       13       9      16        95
```

❹ After adding *EDUC* and *HEALTH*, the results here for the learning sample do not differ from those in ❶ above.

❺ For the test sample, the addition of *EDUC* and *HEALTH* increases the percentage correct from 76% to 88%.

We continue by issuing the **STEP** specifications listed above, each time noting the total percentage correct as well as the percentages for the Islamic and New World groups. After scanning the classification results from both the test sample and the learning sample jackknifed panel, we conclude that model 2 (*BIRTH_RT*, *DEATH_RT*, *MIL*, *EDUC*, and *HEALTH*) is best and that model 1 performs the worst.

Classifying new cases

Group membership is known in the current example. Use **Data**➠ **Weight** to assign a case frequency of zero to some countries so their values are not used in the computations, but at the same time they are classified. What if you have cases where the group membership is unknown? For example, you might want to apply the rules developed for one sample to a new sample.

When the value of the grouping variable is missing, SYSTAT still classifies the case. For example, we set the group code for New World countries to missing:

```
IF group$ = 'NewWorld' THEN LET group$ = ' '
```

and request automatic forward stepping for the model stated above:

```
    ⋮
PRINT / MAHAL
START / FORWARD
STEP / AUTO
STOP
```

Here are the Mahalanobis distances and posterior probabilities for the countries with missing group codes and also the classification matrix. The weight variable is not used here.

```
                  Mahalanobis distance-square from group means and
                  Posterior probabilities for group membership
        Priors =        .500             .500
                      Europe          Islamic

  Not Grouped
  ------------
  Argentina    *     28.6 1.00       59.6  .00
  Barbados     *     25.9 1.00       71.9  .00
  Bolivia      *    120.7  .00        2.7 1.00
  Brazil       *    115.7  .00       10.0 1.00
  Canada       *      2.1 1.00      124.1  .00
  Chile        *     63.2  .00       35.5 1.00
  Colombia     *    204.0  .00       22.4 1.00
  CostaRica    *    306.5  .00       60.8 1.00
  Venezuela    *    297.0  .00       49.2 1.00
  DominicanR.  *    129.9  .00       10.8 1.00
  Uruguay      *     12.5 1.00       91.4  .00
  Ecuador      *    149.3  .00        8.4 1.00
  ElSalvador   *    183.7  .00       10.1 1.00
  Jamaica      *    100.2  .00       32.7 1.00
  Guatemala    *    155.3  .00        5.5 1.00
  Haiti        *    136.8  .00        1.4 1.00
  Honduras     *    216.6  .00       13.2 1.00
  Trinidad     *    132.6  .00       14.0 1.00
  Peru         *     99.4  .00        7.4 1.00
  Panama       *    160.5  .00       18.9 1.00
  Cuba         *     19.4 1.00       70.7  .00

        -->   case misclassified
         *    case not used in computation

  Classification matrix (cases in row categories classified into columns)
  ------------------------
               Europe  Islamic %correct
  Europe         19       0      100
  Islamic         0      15      100

    Total        19      15      100

  Not Grouped     5      16
```

Argentina, Barbados, Canada, Uruguay, and Cuba are classified as European; the other 15 countries are classified as Islamic.

References

Fisher, R.A. 1936. The use of multiple measurements in taxonomic problems. *Annals of Eugenics*, 7: 179-188.

Hill, M.A., and Engelman, L. 1992. Graphical aids for nonlinear regression and discriminant analysis. *Computational Statistics, Vol. 2*, Y. Dodge and J. Whittaker, eds. Proceedings of the 10th Symposium on Computational Statistics Physica-Verlag, 111-126.

Morrison, D.F. 1976. *Multivariate statistical methods*. New York: McGraw-Hill.

Pillai, K.C.S. 1960. *Statistical table for tests of multivariate hypotheses*. Manila: The Statistical Center, University of Phillipines.

12

General Linear Models

Leland Wilkinson and Mark Coward

General Linear Model (GLM) can estimate and test any univariate or multivariate general linear model, including those for multiple regression, analysis of variance or covariance, and other procedures such as discriminant analysis and principal components. We focus on the latter in this chapter. The model is:

$$Y = XB + e$$

where Y is a vector or matrix of dependent variables, X is a vector or matrix of independent variables, B is a vector or matrix of regression coefficients, and e is a vector or matrix of random errors. See Searle (1971), Winer (1971), Neter, Wasserman, and Kutner (1985), or Cohen and Cohen (1983) for details.

In multivariate models, Y is a matrix of continuous measures. The X matrix can be either continuous or categorical dummy variables according to the type of model. For *discriminant analysis*, X is a matrix of dummy variables, as in analysis of variance. For *principal components analysis*, X is a constant (a single column of 1's). For *canonical correlation*, X is usually a matrix of continuous right-hand variables (and Y is the matrix of left-hand variables).

You can estimate the model using either **Stats▬►Analysis of Variance** or **Stats▬►General Linear Model**. After the parameters of a model have been estimated, they can be tested by any general linear hypothesis of the following form:

$$ABC' = D$$

where A is a matrix of linear weights on coefficients across the independent variables (the rows of B), C is a matrix of linear weights on the coefficients across dependent variables (the columns of **B**), **B** is the matrix of regression coefficients or effects, and **D** is a null hypothesis matrix (usually a null matrix).

For the multivariate models described in this chapter, the **C** matrix is an identity matrix, and the **D** matrix is null. The **A** matrix can have several different forms, but these are all submatrices of an identity matrix and are easily formed using **Stats**⟹**General Linear Model**⟹**Hypothesis Test**.

☞ For discriminant analysis, you may prefer to use *Stats*⟹*Discriminant*. See Chapter 11 for more information.

☞ For examples of simple and multiple linear regression, see Chapter 8.

☞ For examples of analysis of variance and analysis of covariance, see Chapter 6.

Overview

Examples

Summary

General Linear Models

Overview

You can specify any multivariate linear model with General Linear Model. For some multivariate models, it may be easier to use ANOVA, which can handle models with multiple dependent variables and zero, one, or more categorical independent variables (that is, only the constant is present in the former). ANOVA automatically generates interaction terms for the design factor.

 To fully appreciate the depth and breadth of general linear models, you may want to read the examples in Chapter 8 and Chapter 6.

Estimating the model

You must estimate your model using either ANOVA or General Linear Model before you can perform hypothesis testing. To use General Linear Model, select **Stats➧General Linear Model➧Estimate Model**.

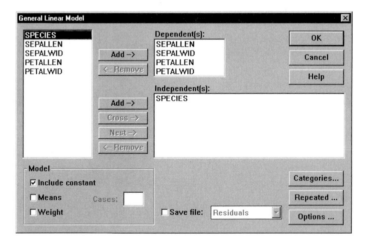

Select variables from the source list at the left to specify dependent and independent variables. After you select independent variables, you can select **Categories** to identify variables that generate design variables. You can also perform repeated measures analysis, change the tolerance, and request stepwise estimation.

SYSTAT generates a set of dummy variables (using Effects coding) for each variable identified by using **Category**. There are one fewer dummy variables than the number of levels for a given categorical variable.

You can specify interactions between independent variables with **Cross** or use **Nest** to nest variables. For example, to specify an interaction between two variables, select both variables in the source list on the left side of the dialog box and click **Cross**. With commands, use asterisks to link interactions (*CARDIO*CANCER*) and parentheses for nesting (*CARDIO(CANCER)*).

Hypothesis testing

After estimating the model, use **Stats**➡**General Linear Model**➡ **Hypothesis Testing** to test your hypothesis.

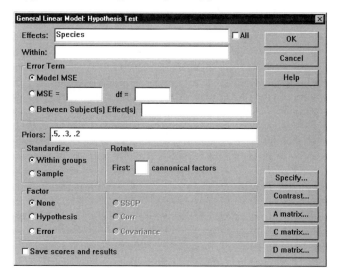

The options you select depend on the type of analysis. For specific types of analyses, see the following sections on discriminant analysis, canonical correlation, and principle components.

Effects. For discriminant analysis, type the name of your grouping variable. For principle components, you don't need to use this text box unless you have a grouping variable for within-groups components. For canonical correlation, use **All** to test all the effects in the model.

Priors. Prior probabilities for discriminant analysis. Type one for each group; separate them by spaces or commas. These probabilities should add up to 1. For example, if you have three groups, priors might be 0.5, 0.3, and 0.2.

Standardize. You can standardize canonical coefficients using total sample or within-groups covariance matrix. In discriminant analysis, **Within groups** is generally used to make comparisons easier when the measures are on different scales. For canonical correlation, **Sample** is used.

Rotate. Specify the number of components to rotate.

Factor. In a factor analysis with grouping variables, you can factor the **Hypothesis** matrix (between groups) or **Error** matrix (within groups). This allows you to compute principal components on the hypothesis or error matrix separately, offering a direct way to compute principal components on residuals of any linear model you wish to fit. You can specify the matrix type as **Correlations**, **SSCP**, or **Covariance**.

Save scores and results. Save a SYSTAT data file containing results. Exactly what is saved depends on the analysis, as described in the following sections for discriminant analysis, canonical correlation, and principle components. (For other models, residuals are saved. For multivariate analyses, these residuals are rarely examined because they are only marginal residuals for each separate dependent variable.) When you save scores and results, extended output is automatically produced. This enables you to see more detailed output when computing these statistics.

Discriminant analysis

Type the name of the grouping variable for **Effects.** Enter the prior probabilities, making sure that they add up to 1. Under **Standardize**, you generally want to select **Within groups** for discriminant analysis; this makes comparisons easier when the measures are on different scales. Specify the number of components to rotate, and select **Specify** for tests of contrasts across levels of the grouping factor.

If you select **Save scores and results**, SYSTAT saves canonical variable scores (*FACTOR*), Mahalanobis distances to each group centroid (*DISTANCE*), posterior probabilities (*PROB*), original group membership (*GROUP*), and membership predicted by the model (*PREDICT*).

Canonical correlation

For canonical correlation, select **All** to test all the effects in the model. This automatically generates separate tests for each effect in the model. Under **Standardize**, select **Sample**. Specify the number of components to rotate.

Principal components

For principal components, you don't need to specify anything for **Effects** unless you have a grouping variable for within-groups components. In a factor analysis with grouping variables, you can factor the **Hypothesis** matrix (between groups) or **Error** matrix (within groups). You can also specify the matrix type as **Correlations**, **SSCP**, or **Covariance**.

If you select **Save scores and results**, scores are saved (*FACTOR*).

Specify and contrast

In the **Hypothesis Test** dialog box, you can use **Specify** and **Contrast** to define contrasts across the levels of a grouping variable.

Specify. Uses GLM's cell means "language" to specify tests of contrasts. You can use this same language to define contrasts across the levels of a grouping variable in a multivariate model. For example, using the *IRIS* data, after you estimate the model as described in Example 12.1, you can test the contrasts (–2, 1, 1) and (0, 1, –1) across the levels of *SPECIES*:

```
SPECIFY  2*SPECIES[1] = SPECIES[2] + SPECIES[3]; ,
              SPECIES[2] = SPECIES[3]
```

Notice that if you enter *both* statements in the **Specify** statement, the results are multivariate test statistics.

Contrast. Specify contrast coefficients. For example, using the *IRIS* data:

```
CONTRAST  [-2  1  1;
               0  1  -1]
```

The output from this test contains the results of the multivariate test for all four dependent measures and the univariate tests for each.

A matrix, C matrix, and D matrix

Contrast, A matrix, C matrix, and **D matrix** are available for hypothesis testing in multivariate models. You can test parameters of the multivariate model estimated or factor the quadratic form of your model into orthogonal components. Linear hypotheses have the form:

$$ABC' = D$$

where **A** is a matrix of linear weights contrasting the coefficient estimates (the rows of **B**). **C** has as many columns as there are dependent variables.

For most multivariate models, **C** is an identity matrix. Finally, **D** is a null hypothesis matrix (usually a null matrix). These matrices (**A**, **C**, and **D**) may be specified in several alternative ways; if they are not specified, they have default values. For more information about these matrices, see Chapter 6 and Chapter 8.

Extended output

General Linear Model produces extended output if you set the output length to **Long** (using either **Edit➡Options** or the PRINT=LONG command) or if you select **Save scores and results** in the **Hypothesis Test** dialog box.

For estimation, extended output adds the following: total sum of product matrix, residual (or pooled within groups) sum of product matrix, residual (or pooled within groups) covariance matrix, and the residual (or pooled within groups) correlation matrix.

For hypothesis testing, extended output adds **A**, **C**, and **D** matrices, the matrix of contrasts, and the inverse of the cross products of contrasts, hypothesis and error sum of product matrices, tests of residual roots, canonical correlations, coefficients, and loadings.

Using an SSCP, covariance, or correlation matrix as input

Normally, you analyze raw cases-by-variables data with General Linear Model. You can, however, use a symmetric matrix data file (for example, a covariance matrix saved in a file from **Correlations**) as input. If you use a matrix as input, you *must* specify a value for **Cases** when estimating the model (under **Group** in the **General Linear Model** dialog box) to specify the sample size of the data file that generated the matrix. The number you specify must be an integer greater than 2.

Be sure to include the dependent as well as independent variables in your matrix. SYSTAT picks out the dependent variable you name in your model.

SYSTAT uses the sample size to calculate degrees of freedom in hypothesis tests. SYSTAT also determines the type of matrix (SSCP, covariance, and so on) and adjusts appropriately. With a correlation matrix, the raw and standardized coefficients are the same; therefore, you cannot include a constant when using SSCP, covariance, or correlation matrices. Because these matrices are centered, the constant term has already been removed.

The triangular matrix input facility is useful for "meta-analysis" of published data and missing value computations; however, you should heed the following warnings. First, if you input correlation matrices from textbooks or articles, you may not get the same regression coefficients as those printed in the source. Because of round-off error, printed and raw data can lead to different results. Second, if you use pairwise deletion with **Correlations**, the degrees of freedom for hypotheses will not be appropriate. You may not even be able to estimate the regression coefficients because of singularities.

In general, correlation matrices containing missing data produce coefficient estimates and hypothesis tests that are optimistic. You can correct for this by specifying a sample size smaller than the number of actual observations (preferably set it equal to the smallest number of cases used for any pair of variables), but this is a guess that you can refine only by doing Monte Carlo simulations. There is no simple solution. Beware, especially, of multivariate regressions (MANOVA and others) with missing data on the dependent variables. You can usually compute coefficients, but hypothesis testing produces results that are suspect.

Examples

The examples in this section illustrate discriminant analysis, within-groups principal components analysis, and canonical correlation analysis. For examples of regression and analysis of variance in General Linear Model, see the examples in Chapter 8 and Chapter 6.

12.1 Discriminant analysis

This example uses the *IRIS* data file. Fisher used these data to illustrate his discriminant function. To define the model, use **Stats**➠**General Linear Model**➠**Estimate Model.**

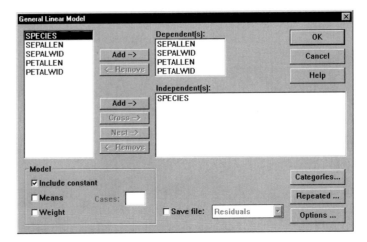

Select *SEPALLEN*, *SEPALWID*, *PETALLEN*, and *PETALWID* as dependent variables and select *SPECIES* as the independent variable. Select **Categories** to specify species as a categorical variable, and be sure that **Include constant** is selected.

With commands:

```
GLM
    USE iris
    CATEGORY species
    MODEL sepallen  sepalwid  petallen  petalwid =,
        CONSTANT + species
    ESTIMATE
```

```
Dependent variable means
                   SEPALLEN    SEPALWID    PETALLEN    PETALWID
                      5.843       3.057       3.758       1.199
                                   -1
Estimates of effects   B = (X'X)   X'Y

                           SEPALLEN    SEPALWID    PETALLEN    PETALWID

   CONSTANT                   5.843       3.057       3.758       1.199

   SPECIES      1            -0.837       0.371      -2.296      -0.953

   SPECIES      2             0.093      -0.287       0.502       0.127


Squared multiple correlations
                   SEPALLEN    SEPALWID    PETALLEN    PETALWID
                      0.619       0.401       0.941       0.929
- - - - - - - - - - - - - - - - - - - - - - - - - - - - - - - - - - - - - - - - - - - - -
```

To compute and save the discriminant function, scores, and classification probabilities, you must test the null hypothesis that the groups are equivalent. To do so, select **Stats**➧**General Linear Model**➧**Hypothesis Test.**

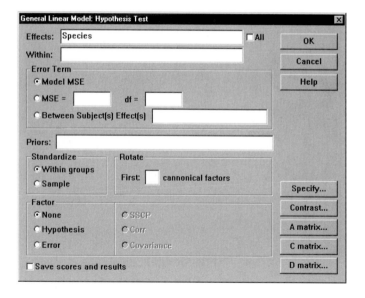

For **Effects**, type Species as shown. In the bottom of the dialog box, make sure that **Save scores and results** is selected. With commands:

```
HYPOTHESIS
EFFECT = species
SAVE canon
TEST
```

SYSTAT saves the canonical scores associated with the hypothesis. The scores are stored in subscripted variables named *FACTOR*. Because the effects involve a categorical variable, the Mahalanobis distances (named *DISTANCE*) and posterior probabilities (named *PROB*) are saved in the same file. These distances are computed in the discriminant space itself. The closer a case is to a particular group's location in that space, the more likely it is that it belongs to that group. The probability of group membership is computed from these distances. A variable named *PREDICT* that contains the predicted group membership is also added to the file.

```
Test for effect called:     SPECIES

Null hypothesis contrast AB

                    SEPALLEN      SEPALWID      PETALLEN      PETALWID
            1        -0.837         0.371        -2.296        -0.953
            2         0.093        -0.287         0.502         0.127


                   -1
Inverse contrast A(X'X)  A'

                     1            2
            1      0.013
            2     -0.007        0.013

                                                  -1   -1
Hypothesis sum of product matrix   H = B'A'(A(X'X)  A')  AB

                    SEPALLEN      SEPALWID      PETALLEN      PETALWID
   SEPALLEN          63.212
   SEPALWID         -19.953        11.345
   PETALLEN         165.248       -57.240       437.103
   PETALWID          71.279       -22.933       186.774        80.413


Error sum of product matrix G = E'E

                    SEPALLEN      SEPALWID      PETALLEN      PETALWID
   SEPALLEN          38.956
   SEPALWID          13.630        16.962
   PETALLEN          24.625         8.121        27.223
   PETALWID           5.645         4.808         6.272         6.157


Univariate F Tests

   Effect          SS         DF        MS            F             P
SEPALLEN         63.212        2      31.606       119.265        0.000
   Error         38.956      147       0.265
SEPALWID         11.345        2       5.672        49.160        0.000
   Error         16.962      147       0.115
PETALLEN        437.103        2     218.551      1180.161        0.000
   Error         27.223      147       0.185
PETALWID         80.413        2      40.207       960.007        0.000
   Error          6.157      147       0.042


Multivariate Test Statistics

          Wilks' Lambda =        0.023
             F-Statistic =      199.145    DF =   8, 288    Prob =    0.000


          Pillai Trace =         1.192
             F-Statistic =       53.466    DF =   8, 290    Prob =    0.000


    Hotelling-Lawley Trace =    32.477
             F-Statistic =      580.532    DF =   8, 286    Prob =    0.000


          THETA = 0.970 S = 2, M = 0.5, N = 71.0 Prob =    0.0

Test of Residual Roots
```

```
     Roots 1 through 2
       Chi-Square Statistic =      546.115      DF = 8

     Roots 2 through 2
       Chi-Square Statistic =       36.530      DF = 3

Canonical Correlations
                              1            2
                           0.985        0.471
Dependent variable canonical coefficients standardized
by conditional (within groups) standard deviations
                              1            2
        SEPALLEN           0.427        0.012
        SEPALWID           0.521        0.735
        PETALLEN          -0.947       -0.401
        PETALWID          -0.575        0.581

Canonical loadings (correlations between conditional
dependent variables and dependent canonical factors)
                              1            2
        SEPALLEN          -0.223        0.311
        SEPALWID           0.119        0.864
        PETALLEN          -0.706        0.168
        PETALWID          -0.633        0.737

Group classification function coefficients
                              1            2            3
        SEPALLEN          23.544       15.698       12.446
        SEPALWID          23.588        7.073        3.685
        PETALLEN         -16.431        5.211       12.767
        PETALWID         -17.398        6.434       21.079

Group classification constants
                              1            2            3
                         -86.308      -72.853     -104.368
Canonical scores have been saved.
--------------------------------------------------------------------
```

The multivariate tests are all highly significant. The *dependent variable canonical coefficients* are used to produce discriminant scores. These coefficients are standardized by the within-groups standard deviations so you can compare their magnitude across variables with different scales. Because they are not raw coefficients, there is no need for a constant. The scores produced by these coefficients have an overall zero mean and a unit standard deviation within groups.

The group classification coefficients and constants comprise the Fisher discriminant functions for classifying the raw data. You can apply these coefficients to new data and assign each case to the group with the largest function value for that case.

Studying saved results

The *CANON* file that was just saved contains the canonical variable scores (*FACTOR(1)* and *FACTOR(2)*), the Mahalanobis distances to each group centroid (*DISTANCE(1)*, *DISTANCE(2)*, and *DISTANCE(3)*), the posterior probability for each case being assigned to each group (*PROB(1)*, *PROB(2)*, and *PROB(3)*), the predicted group membership (*PREDICT*), and the original group assignment (*GROUP*).

To produce a classification table, you can use **Crosstabs** to crosstabulate *GROUP* against *PREDICT*. For a plot of the second canonical variable against the first, you could use **Graph**➠**Scatterplot** to display *FACTOR(2)* by *FACTOR(1)*. However, it is much easier to use discriminant analysis. See Chapter 11 for more information.

Prior probabilities

In this example, there were equal numbers of flowers in each group. Sometimes the probability of finding a case in each group is not the same across groups. To adjust the prior probabilities for this example, specify 0.5, 0.3, and 0.2 after **Priors** in the **Hypothesis Test** dialog box.

General Linear Model uses the probabilities you specify to compute the posterior probabilities that are saved in the file under the variable *PROB*. Be sure to specify a probability for each level of the grouping variable. The probabilities should add up to 1.

12.2 Within-groups principal components analysis

General Linear Model allows you to partial out effects based on grouping variables and to factor residual correlations. If between-group variation is significant, the within-group structure can differ substantially from the total structure (ignoring the grouping variable).

Specify the number of components you want to rotate in the **Hypothesis Test** dialog box. Varimax rotation is used.

> **Note:** If you are just computing principal components on a single sample (no grouping variable), you can obtain more detailed output using Factor Analysis. See Chapter 16 for more information.

The following data (*USSTATES*) comprise death rates by cause from nine census divisions of the country for that year. The divisions are in the column labeled *DIV*, and the U.S. Post Office two-letter state abbreviations follow *DIV*. Other variables include *ACCIDENT*, *CARDIO*, *CANCER*, *PULMONAR*, *PNEU_FLU*, *DIABETES*, *LIVER*, *STATE$*, *FSTROKE*, *MSTROKE*.

The variation in death rates between divisions in these data is substantial. Here is a grouped boxplot of the second variable, *CARDIO*, by division. The other variables show similar regional differences.

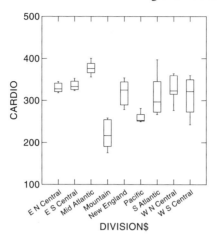

If you analyze these data ignoring *DIVISION$*, the correlations among death rates would be due substantially to between-division differences. You might want to examine the pooled within-region correlations to see if the structure is different when divisional differences are statistically controlled. Accordingly, you will factor the residual correlation matrix after regressing medical variables onto an index variable denoting the census regions:

```
GLM
    USE usstates
    CATEGORY division
    MODEL accident cardio cancer pulmonar pneu_flu,
        diabetes liver fstroke mstroke = CONSTANT,
        + division
    ESTIMATE
```

Next is the hypothesis stage. The following commands compute the principal components on the error (residual) correlation matrix and rotate the first two components to a varimax criterion.

```
HYPOTHESIS
EFFECT = division
FACTOR = ERROR
TYPE   = CORR
ROTATE = 2
TEST
```

The **Factor** options can be used with any hypothesis. Ordinarily, when you test a hypothesis, the matrix product $G^{-1} H$ is factored and the latent roots of this matrix are used to construct the multivariate test statistic (see the references on MANOVA if this is unclear). However, you can use the **Factor** options of **Hypothesis** or **Error** to indicate which matrix—the hypothesis (H) matrix or the error (G) matrix—is to be factored. By computing principal components on the hypothesis or error matrix separately, Factor offers a direct way to compute principal components on residuals of any linear model you wish to fit. You can use any A, C, and/or D matrices in the hypothesis you are factoring, or you can use any of the other commands that create these matrices.

Specify the number of components you want to rotate (by the varimax method) with the **Rotate** option. For other rotations, use **Factor Analysis**.

In the output below, notice the sorted, rotated loadings. The first component rotates to a dimension defined by *CANCER*, *CARDIO*, *PULMONAR*, and *DIABETES*, and the second by a dimension defined by *MSTROKE* and *FSTROKE* (male and female stroke rates). *ACCIDENT* also loads on the second factor but is not independent of the first. *LIVER* does not load highly on either factor.

```
Factoring Error Matrix
                      1          2          3          4          5
          1        1.000
          2        0.280      1.000
          3        0.188      0.844      1.000
          4        0.307      0.676      0.711      1.000
          5        0.113      0.448      0.297      0.396      1.000
          6        0.297      0.419      0.526      0.296     -0.123
          7       -0.005      0.251      0.389      0.252     -0.138
          8        0.402     -0.202     -0.379     -0.190     -0.110
          9        0.495     -0.119     -0.246     -0.127     -0.071


                      6          7          8          9
          6        1.000
          7       -0.025      1.000
          8       -0.151     -0.225      1.000
          9       -0.076     -0.203      0.947      1.000

Latent roots
                      1          2          3          4          5
                   3.341      2.245      1.204      0.999      0.475

                      6          7          8          9
                   0.364      0.222      0.119      0.033
Loadings
                      1          2          3          4          5
          1        0.191      0.798      0.128     -0.018     -0.536
          2        0.870      0.259     -0.097      0.019      0.219
          3        0.934      0.097      0.112      0.028      0.183
          4        0.802      0.247     -0.135      0.120     -0.071
          5        0.417      0.146     -0.842     -0.010     -0.042
          6        0.512      0.218      0.528     -0.580      0.068
          7        0.391     -0.175      0.400      0.777     -0.044
          8       -0.518      0.795      0.003      0.155      0.226
          9       -0.418      0.860      0.025      0.138      0.204


                      6          7          8          9
          1        0.106     -0.100     -0.019     -0.015
          2        0.145     -0.254      0.177      0.028
          3        0.039     -0.066     -0.251     -0.058
          4       -0.499      0.085      0.044      0.015
          5        0.216      0.220     -0.005     -0.002
          6        0.093      0.241      0.063      0.010
          7        0.154      0.159      0.046      0.009
          8       -0.041      0.056      0.081     -0.119
          9        0.005      0.035     -0.101      0.117

Rotated loadings on first 2 principal components
                      1          2
          1        0.457      0.682
          2        0.906     -0.060
          3        0.909     -0.234
          4        0.838     -0.047
          5        0.441     -0.008
          6        0.556      0.027
          7        0.305     -0.300
          8       -0.209      0.925
          9       -0.093      0.951

Sorted rotated loadings on first 2 principal components
(loadings less than .25 made 0.)
                      1          2
          1        0.909      0.0
          2        0.906      0.0
          3        0.838      0.0
          4        0.556      0.0
          5        0.0        0.951
          6        0.0        0.925
          7        0.457      0.682
          8        0.305     -0.300
          9        0.441      0.0
```

12.3
Canonical
correlation
analysis

Suppose you have 10 dependent variables, *MMPI(1)* to *MMPI(10)*, and 3 independent variables, *RATER(1)* to *RATER(3)*. Enter the following commands to obtain the canonical correlations and dependent canonical coefficients.

```
GLM
    USE datafile
    MODEL mmpi(1 .. 10) = CONSTANT + rater(1) +,
                          rater(2) + rater(3)

    ESTIMATE

    PRINT=LONG

    HYPOTHESIS
    STANDARDIZE
    EFFECT=rater(1) & rater(2) & rater(3)
    TEST
```

The canonical correlations are displayed; if you want, you can rotate the dependent canonical coefficients by using the **Rotate** option.

To obtain the coefficients for the independent variables, run **GLM** again with the model reversed:

```
MODEL rater(1 .. 3) = CONSTANT + mmpi(1) + mmpi(2),
                      + mmpi(3) + mmpi(4) + mmpi(5),
                      + mmpi(6) + mmpi(7) + mmpi(8),
                      + mmpi(9) + mmpi(10)
ESTIMATE
HYPOTHESIS
STANDARDIZE = TOTAL
EFFECT = mmpi(1) & mmpi(2) & mmpi(3) & mmpi(4) &,
         mmpi(5) & mmpi(6) & mmpi(7) & mmpi(8) &,
         mmpi(9) & mmpi(10)
TEST
```

Summary

Computation

Centered sums of squares and cross products are accumulated using provisional algorithms. Linear systems, including those involved in hypothesis testing, are solved by using forward and reverse sweeping (Dempster, 1969). Eigensystems are solved with Householder tridiagonalization and implicit QL iterations. For further information, see Wilkinson and Reinsch (1971) or Chambers (1977).

References

Cohen, J., and P. Cohen. 1983. *Applied multiple regression/correlation analysis for the behavioral sciences*. 2nd ed. Hillsdale, N.J.: Lawrence Erlbaum.

Linn, R. L., Centra, J. A., and Tucker, L. 1975. Between, within, and total group factor analyses of student ratings of instruction. *Multivariate Behavioral Research*, 10: 277-288.

Neter, J., Wasserman,W., and Kutner, M. 1985. *Applied linear statistical models*. 2nd ed. Homewood, Illinois: Richard E. Irwin, Inc.

Searle, S. R. 1971. *Linear models*. New York: John Wiley & Sons, Inc.

Winer, B. J. 1971. *Statistical principles in experimental design*. 2nd ed. New York: McGraw-Hill.

13

Designs for Quality Improvement

Herb Stenson

Design of Experiments generates design matrices for a variety of ANOVA and mixture models. You can use **Design of Experiments** as an online library of experimental designs, which can be saved to a SYSTAT file. You can run the associated experiment, add the values of a dependent variable to the same file, and analyze the experimental data by using **General Linear Model** (or another SYSTAT statistical procedure).

Design of Experiments provides *complete* and *incomplete* factorial designs. Complete factorial designs are simplest and have two or three levels of each factor. Two-level designs can have two to seven factors, and three-level designs can have two to five factors.

Incomplete designs offered by **Design of Experiments** include: Latin square designs with 3 to 12 levels per factor; selected two-level designs described by Box, Hunter, and Hunter (1978) with 3 to 11 factors and from 4 to 128 runs; 13 of the most popular Taguchi (1987) designs; all of the Plackett and Burman (1946) two-level designs with 4 to 100 runs; the six 3-, 5-, and 7-level designs described by Plackett and Burman; and the set of 10 three-level designs described by Box and Behnken (1960) in both their blocked and unblocked versions.

Four types of mixture models described by Cornell (1990) are available: Lattice, Centroid, Axial, and Screen designs. The number of factors (components of a mixture) can be as large as your computer's memory allows.

Any design can be replicated as many times as you want, and the runs can be randomized.

Overview

Designs

Designs for Quality Improvement

430

Overview

Modern quality control (or quality improvement, as it is often called) places an emphasis on designing quality into products from the start, as well as monitoring quality during production. In an industrial setting, researchers need information regarding factors that influence the quality of a product. To get this information, they design experiments that vary parameters of the products systematically in order to identify critical factors and important values of those factors. Such research can be costly and time-consuming, so experimental designs that provide the maximum amount of information using the fewest number of runs (trials) are desirable. Such experiments often have only two or three levels for each factor; there cannot be replications; and the design may be an incomplete design, meaning that not all possible combinations of factor levels are used in an experiment. A number of carefully constructed designs are available for such experiments.

Standard two-level and three-level factorial designs can be generated by the **Design of Experiments** procedure. In these designs, each factor has the same number of levels (two or three), and all possible combinations of the factors are present (that is, the design is completely crossed). To decrease the number of runs required, omit some combinations of factors from the experiment. **Design of Experiments** can generate a wide variety of such incomplete factorial designs.

The general approach used in constructing incomplete designs is to be sure that at least the main effects of each factor can be tested. Parsimony is achieved by omitting cells of the design in such a pattern that the main effects can be tested, but some or all of the interactions among factors cannot. The number of testable interactions depends on the particular design, ranging from *none* (for a Latin square design), to *all* (for a complete factorial design). If some, but not all, interactions are included, the highest-order interactions are usually omitted. Main effects of some factors are completely confounded (aliased) with these high-order interactions. Thus, if the effect for a confounded variable is significant, one cannot be sure whether the result is due to the variable itself or to the interaction with which it is confounded. This is the price of parsimony. In addition, in an incomplete design, the omission of cells is such that the remaining cells still form an orthogonal (mutually independent) set, so that the tests of the factors and interactions (if available) are statistically independent.

Various statisticians such as Plackett and Burman (1946), Box and Behnken (1960), Box, Hunter, and Hunter (1978), and Taguchi (1987) have contributed to this effort. It is their experimental designs that are presented here.

In industries such as the petroleum, chemical, or food industries, a special kind of experiment is required that involves testing various mixtures of components to determine the properties of the mixtures. A class of standard experimental designs called mixture models has been developed to meet this need. In mixture models, each row of the design matrix contains a list of the proportions in which each component (column of the model) is present in the mixture represented by that row. Thus, the sum of all the elements in a row must add up to 1. This creates a special degrees-of-freedom problem which is handled properly by the **General Linear Model** procedures when the **Mixture model** option is selected. Four broad classes of mixture models have been identified by Cornell (1990). Each is available in **Design of Experiments**.

Getting started   To perform complete factorial and fractional factorial designs, use Stats➠**Design of Experiments**:

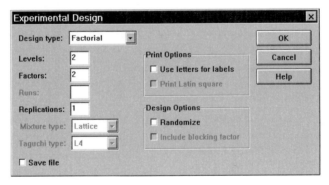

Design type	Choose a design from the drop-down list.
Levels	For factorial, Latin, and mixture designs, this is the number of levels.
Factors	For factorial, BoxHunter, BoxBehnken, and lattice mixture designs, this is the number of factors.
Runs	For Plackett and BoxHunter, this is the number of runs.
Replications	For all designs except BoxBehnken and mixture, this is the number of replications (default=1).
Mixture type	If mixture is the design type, you can specify a mixture type from the drop-down list.
Taguchi type	If Taguchi is the design type, you can specify a Taguchi type from the drop-down list.
Save file	Saves the results of the analysis.
Use letters for labels	Labels the design factors with letters instead of numbers.
Print Latin square	For Latin square designs, you can print the Latin square.
Randomize	Randomizes the runs (cases).
Include blocking factor	For BoxBehnken designs, you can include a blocking factor.

Note: *It is not necessary to have a data file open to use **Design of Experiments**.*

Using commands

To generate a design matrix using commands, type one of the design types with a list of options following the slash.

```
FACTORIAL      BOXHUNTER      LATIN        TAGUCHI
PLACKET        BOXBEHNKEN     MIXTURE
```

For example:

```
DESIGN
    FACTORIAL / LEVELS=2  LETTERS
```

To save the results of the analysis, enter a SAVE command prior to entering the DESIGN command.

Designs

Here is the layout of a complete ANOVA design with three 2-level factors. Each of the factors (A, B, and C) has levels coded as "+" and "–" for *high* and *low* or *on* and *off* settings. There are eight possible experiments:

	C = –			C = +	
	B			B	
	–	+		–	+
A –	1	3	–	5	7
A +	2	4	+	6	8

For example, experiment (or *run*) 2 is carried out with A = "+", B = "–", and C = "–"; experiment 8 is carried out with A = "+", B = "+", and C = "+"; and so on. The following shows how **Design of Experiments** organizes these codes (the same layout is used for the analysis—just add a column with the result of each experiment):

RUN	A	B	C
1	-	-	-
2	+	-	-
3	-	+	-
4	+	+	-
5	-	-	+
6	+	-	+
7	-	+	+
8	+	+	+

These are the design variables that FACTORIAL generates for a complete factorial design. Consider what can be done when the researchers feel that a complete design cannot be carried out because of time or expense constraints. This may not be the case for a simple eight-cell design, but the number of cells (runs) for five factors is 32; for six factors, it is 64. For the latter situations, an incomplete design may be appropriate, given the assumption that certain higher-order interactions are not present. One or more of the main effects is then intentionally confounded with these presumably insignificant interactions.

To illustrate an incomplete design, let's use the simple three-factor situation described above. The C factor is intentionally confounded with the A*B interaction; in other words, C is *aliased* with A*B. In this case, only four experiments are done:

The data file of codes that BOXHUNTER produces looks like this:

RUN	A	B	C
1	-	-	+
2	+	-	-
3	-	+	-
4	+	+	+

Notice that each element of the code for variable C is the product of the corresponding codes for A and B; this is as it should be because C has been aliased with the A*B interaction.

It is easy in **Design of Experiments** to generate design variables for designs like this and for designs that are much more complex. See the examples that follow.

Complete factorial designs

In complete factorial designs, each factor has the same number of levels and all possible combinations of factors are present.

13.1 A 2^3 design

To generate the factorial design at the beginning of this section and save the variables to a file, use **Stats▸Design of Experiments**, and select **Factorial** from the **Design type** drop-down list. Enter 3 in the **Factors** text box and 2 in the **Levels** text box. Select **Save file**. With commands:

```
DESIGN
    SAVE factor
    FACTORIAL / FACTORS=3  LEVELS=2
```

```
Full 2-Level Factorial Design:   8 Runs,  3 Factors

               Factor
        Run    1  2  3

         1     -  -  -
         2     +  -  -
         3     -  +  -
         4     +  +  -
         5     -  -  +
         6     +  -  +
         7     -  +  +
         8     +  +  +
```

13.2
A 2³
design with
replicates

In addition to the example above, if you type 2 in the **Replications** text box, two runs are generated for each combination of factors. With commands:

```
DESIGN
    SAVE factor2
    FACTORIAL / FACTORS=3  LEVELS=2  REPS=2  LETTERS
```

```
Full 2-Level Factorial Design:   16 Runs,  3 Factors

               Factor
        Run    A  B  C

         1     -  -  -
         2     +  -  -
         3     -  +  -
         4     +  +  -
         5     -  -  +
         6     +  -  +
         7     -  +  +
         8     +  +  +
         9     -  -  -
        10     +  -  -
        11     -  +  -
        12     +  +  -
        13     -  -  +
        14     +  -  +
        15     -  +  +
        16     +  +  +
```

Box and Hunter
fractional
factorials

BoxHunter generates design variables for 27 fractional factorial designs for factors with two levels. You can specify 3 to 11 factors. The number of runs can be an even number between 4 and 128 and must exceed the number of factors by at least one. Notice that some combinations of runs and factors can result in complete (and perhaps replicated) factorial designs as opposed to the incomplete designs.

13.3
A 2^3 fractional factorial

To generate the fractional factorial design in the introduction and save the design variables to a file, use **Stats ➤ Design of Experiments**, select **BoxHunter** from the **Design type** drop-down list, enter 3 in the **Factors** text box, and select **Save file**. With commands:

```
DESIGN
     SAVE boxhun1
     BOXHUNTER / FACTORS=3
```

```
Box-Hunter Fractional 2-Level Design:   4 Runs,  3 Factors,  Resolution = 3

                Factor
         Run    1  2  3

          1     -  -  +
          2     +  -  -
          3     -  +  -
          4     +  +  +
```

13.4
Aliases

For seven two-level factors, the number of cells (runs) for a complete factorial is $2^7 = 128$. The following example shows the smallest fractional factorial for estimating main effects. The design codes for the first three factors generate the last four. SYSTAT will report how these codes are generated (or aliased) if you use **Edit ➤ Options** and set **Length** to **Long**. Next, use **Stats ➤ Design of Experiments** and select **BoxHunter** from the **Design type** drop-down list. Enter 7 in the **Factors** text box and 8 in the **Runs** text box. Select **Save file**. With commands:

```
DESIGN
     SAVE boxhun2
     PRINT=LONG
     BOXHUNTER / FACTORS=7   RUNS=8
```

```
Box-Hunter Fractional 2-Level Design:   8 Runs,  7 Factors,  Resolution = 3

                Factor
         Run    1  2  3  4  5  6  7

          1     -  -  -  +  +  +  -
          2     +  -  -  -  -  +  +
          3     -  +  -  -  +  -  +
          4     +  +  -  +  -  -  -
          5     -  -  +  +  -  -  +
          6     +  -  +  -  +  -  -
          7     -  +  +  -  -  +  -
          8     +  +  +  +  +  +  +

         Generators for the Requested Design

             Factor 4 = 1x2.
             Factor 5 = 1x3.
             Factor 6 = 2x3.
             Factor 7 = 1x2x3.
```

The main effect for factor 4 is confounded with the interaction between factors 1 and 2; the main effects for factor 5 is confounded with the interaction between factors 1 and 3; and so on.

Latin squares

Latin square designs have three factors, all with the same number of levels. Because it is assumed that there are no interactions, the structure of a Latin square design is often laid out as a two-way design with the level of the third design factor displayed in each cell. Here is a 6 x 6 Latin square given by Cochran and Cox (1957):

		1	**2**	**3**	**4**	**5**	**6**
	1	6	2	3	4	5	1
	2	2	6	5	3	1	4
Factor A	**3**	1	4	6	2	3	5
	4	4	1	2	5	6	3
	5	3	5	4	1	2	6
	6	5	3	1	6	4	2

(Factor B across the top columns 1–6)

With three six-level factors, there are 216 possible combinations or experiments. By using this Latin square design, only 36 are needed. For example, the "2" in the lower right corner of the diagram indicates an experiment using level 6 of factor A, level 6 of factor B, and level 2 of factor C. The default output shows runs (cells) by design codes for the factors. To obtain the Latin structure as displayed here, use the **Print Latin square** option. **Randomize** randomly permutes the rows and columns of the Latin square. In addition, for four-level designs, a random selection of one of four possible standard squares is made prior to permutations. (For three-level designs, only one standard square exists.)

With commands:

```
LATIN / LEVELS=n  SQUARE  REPS=n  LETTERS  RAND
```

13.5 A 4x4x4 design

To generate a Latin square when each factor has four leveles, use **Stats➡ Design of Experiments** and select **Latin** from the **Design type** drop-down list. Enter 4 in the **Levels** text box and select **Use letters for labels**, **Print Latin square**, and **Save file**. With commands:

```
DESIGN
    LATIN / LEVELS=4  SQUARE  LETTERS
```

```
Latin-Square Design:  4 Factors, Each With  4 Levels

              Factor 2
   Factor 1   1  2  3  4

       1      A  B  C  D
       2      B  C  D  A
       3      C  D  A  B
       4      D  A  B  C
```

If you don't select **Print Latin square**, the results are as follows:

```
SAVE latin
LATIN / LEVELS=4  LETTERS
```

```
Latin-Square by Run:  16 Runs;  3 Factors, Each With  4 Levels

              Factor
       Run    A  B  C

        1     1  1  1
        2     1  2  2
        3     1  3  3
        4     1  4  4
        5     2  1  2
        6     2  2  3
        7     2  3  4
        8     2  4  1
        9     3  1  3
       10     3  2  4
       11     3  3  1
       12     3  4  2
       13     4  1  4
       14     4  2  1
       15     4  3  2
       16     4  4  3
```

13.6
A
permutation

To randomly assign the factors to the cells, select **Randomize** on the
Design of Experiments dialog box. With commands:

```
DESIGN
    SAVE latin2
    LATIN / LEVELS=4  SQUARE  LETTERS  RAND
```

```
Latin-Square Design:  4 Factors, Each With  4 Levels

              Factor 2
   Factor 1   1  2  3  4

       1      D  C  A  B
       2      C  A  B  D
       3      B  D  C  A
       4      A  B  D  C
```

Taguchi designs

In recent years, Taguchi designs have become increasingly popular. These designs allow for a maximum number of main effects to be estimated from a minimum number of runs in the experiment. Use **Stats**➠**Design of Experiments**, select **Taguchi** from the **Design type** drop-down list, and then select the appropriate type from the **Taguchi type** drop-down list.

Type	Runs	Factors	Levels
L4	4	3	2 each
L8	8	7	2 each
L9	9	4	3 each
L12	12	11	2 each
L16	16	15	2 each
LP16	16	5	4 each
L18	18	1 two-level, 7 three-level	
L25	25	6	5 each
L27	27	23	3 each
L32	32	31	2 each
LP32	32	1 two-level, 9 four-level	
L36	36	11 two-level, 12 three-level	
L54	54	1 two-level, 25 three-level	

With commands:

```
TAGUCHI / TYPE=type   REPS=n   RAND   LETTERS
```

13.7 Design L12 with eleven 2-level factors

To obtain a Taguchi L12 design with 11 factors, use **Stats**➠**Design of Experiments**, select **Taguchi** from the **Design type** drop-down list, and then select **L12** from the **Taguchi type** drop-down list. Select **Save file**. With commands:

```
DESIGN
    SAVE taguchi
    TAGUCHI / TYPE=L12
```

```
Taguchi Design L12:  12 Runs; 11 Factors, Each With 2 Levels

        Factor
  Run   1  2  3  4  5  6  7  8  9 10 11

    1   1  1  1  1  1  1  1  1  1  1  1
    2   1  1  1  1  1  2  2  2  2  2  2
    3   1  1  2  2  2  1  1  1  2  2  2
    4   1  2  1  2  2  1  2  2  1  1  2
    5   1  2  2  1  2  2  1  2  1  2  1
    6   1  2  2  2  1  2  2  1  2  1  1
    7   2  1  2  2  1  1  2  2  1  2  1
    8   2  1  2  1  2  2  2  1  1  1  2
    9   2  1  1  2  2  2  1  2  2  1  1
   10   2  2  2  1  1  1  1  2  2  1  2
   11   2  2  1  2  1  2  1  1  1  2  2
   12   2  2  1  1  2  1  2  1  2  2  1
```

13.8
Design L16 with fifteen 2-level factors plus aliases

To obtain a Taguchi L16 design with 15 factors, use **Stats➠Design of Experiments**, select **Taguchi** from the **Design type** drop-down list, and then select **L16** from the **Taguchi type** drop-down list. Select **Save file**. To request a table defining the interaction, use **Edit➠Options** (before using the **Design of Experiments** dialog box) and set **Length** to **Long**. With commands:

```
DESIGN
    SAVE taguch2
    PRINT=LONG
    TAGUCHI / TYPE=L16
```

```
Taguchi Design L16:  16 Runs; 15 Factors, Each With 2 Levels

               Factor
        Run    1  2  3  4  5  6  7  8  9 10 11 12 13 14 15

          1    1  1  1  1  1  1  1  1  1  1  1  1  1  1  1
          2    1  1  1  1  1  1  1  2  2  2  2  2  2  2  2
          3    1  1  1  2  2  2  2  1  1  1  1  2  2  2  2
          4    1  1  1  2  2  2  2  2  2  2  2  1  1  1  1
          5    1  2  2  1  1  2  2  1  1  2  2  1  1  2  2
          6    1  2  2  1  1  2  2  2  2  1  1  2  2  1  1
          7    1  2  2  2  2  1  1  1  1  2  2  2  2  1  1
          8    1  2  2  2  2  1  1  2  2  1  1  1  1  2  2
          9    2  1  2  1  2  1  2  1  2  1  2  1  2  1  2
         10    2  1  2  1  2  1  2  2  1  2  1  2  1  2  1
         11    2  1  2  2  1  2  1  1  2  2  1  2  1  2  1
         12    2  1  2  2  1  2  1  2  1  1  2  1  2  1  2
         13    2  2  1  1  2  2  1  1  2  2  1  1  2  2  1
         14    2  2  1  1  2  2  1  2  1  1  2  2  1  1  2
         15    2  2  1  2  1  1  2  1  2  1  2  2  1  1  2
         16    2  2  1  2  1  1  2  2  1  2  1  1  2  2  1

        Interaction Term(s) for Each Pair of Columns

               Column
Column
               1   2   3   4   5   6   7   8   9  10

        1
        2      3
        3      2   1
        4      5   6   7
        5      4   7   6   1
        6      7   4   5   2   3
        7      6   5   4   3   2   1
        8      9  10  11  12  13  14  15
        9      8  11  10  13  12  15  14   1
       10     11   8   9  14  15  12  13   2   3
       11     10   9   8  15  14  13  12   3   2   1
       12     13  14  15   8   9  10  11   4   5   6   7
       13     12  15  14   9   8  11  10   5   4   7   6   1
       14     15  12  13  10  11   8   9   6   7   4   5   2   3
       15     14  13  12  11  10   9   8   7   6   5   4   3   2   1
```

Plackett-Burman designs

Plackett-Burman designs are a special type of two-level designs that maximize the number of unbiased main effect estimates obtained from as few runs as possible. Designs are also available for factors with three, five, and seven levels. To define the design, use **Stats▸Design of Experiments**, select **Plackett** from the **Design type** drop-down list, and use the **Runs** text box. For two-level designs with one fewer factors than runs, specify the number of runs to be between 4 and 100; otherwise, specify the number of runs as follows for the respective number of factors and levels:

n	Factors	Levels
9	4	3
27	13	3
81	40	3
25	6	5
125	31	5
49	8	7

With commands:

```
PLACKETT / RUNS=n  REPS=n  RAND  LETTERS
```

13.9 Eleven 2-level factors

This design has 11 two-level factors. Compare these design variables with those in Example 13.7. Use **Stats▸Design of Experiments**, select **Plackett i** from the **Design type** drop-down list, and type 12 in the **Runs** text box. With commands:

```
DESIGN
    SAVE plackett
    PLACKETT / RUNS=12
```

```
Plackett-Burman Design:  12 Runs; 11 Factors, Each With 2 Levels

        Factor
  Run   1  2  3  4  5  6  7  8  9 10 11
   1     +  +  -  +  +  +  -  -  -  +  -
   2     +  -  +  +  +  -  -  -  +  -  +
   3     -  +  +  +  -  -  -  +  -  +  +
   4     +  +  +  -  -  -  +  -  +  +  -
   5     +  +  -  -  -  +  -  +  +  -  +
   6     +  -  -  -  +  -  +  +  -  +  +
   7     -  -  -  +  -  +  +  -  +  +  +
   8     -  -  +  -  +  +  -  +  +  +  -
   9     -  +  -  +  +  -  +  +  +  -  -
  10     +  -  +  +  -  +  +  +  -  -  -
  11     -  +  +  -  +  +  +  -  -  -  +
  12     -  -  -  -  -  -  -  -  -  -  -
```

Box and Behnken designs

BoxBehnken generates Box and Behnken designs. Use **Factor** to specify the number of factors. If you also select **Block**, a blocking factor is included:

Factors	With Block
3	No blocking possible
4	3 blocks of 9 cases
5	2 blocks of 23 cases
6	2 blocks of 27 cases
7	2 blocks of 31 cases
9	5 blocks of 26 cases
10	2 blocks of 85 cases
11	No blocking possible
12	2 blocks of 102 cases
16	6 blocks of 66 cases

With commands:

```
BOXBEHNKEN / FACTORS=n  BLOCK  RAND  LETTERS
```

13.10 Three 3-level factors

Each factor in this design has three levels. Use **Stats➠Design of Experiments**, and select **BoxBehnken** from the **Design type** drop-down list. Type 3 in the **Factors** text box. With commands:

```
DESIGN
    SAVE boxbehn
    BOXBEHNKEN / FACTORS=3
```

```
Box-Behnken Design:  15 Runs;  3 Factors, Each With 3 Levels

            Factor
       Run  1  2  3
         1  -  -  0
         2  +  -  0
         3  -  +  0
         4  +  +  0
         5  -  0  -
         6  +  0  -
         7  -  0  +
         8  +  0  +
         9  0  -  -
        10  0  +  -
        11  0  -  +
        12  0  +  +
        13  0  0  0
        14  0  0  0
        15  0  0  0
```

Mixture designs

Mixture generates four types of mixture models: Lattice, Centroid, Axial, and Screen. With Lattice models, you can specify the number of levels or the number of values that each component (factor) assumes, including 0 and 1. For the other mixture models, the number of factors determines the number of levels.

With commands:

```
MIXTURE / TYPE=type FACTORS=n LEVELS=n RAND LETTERS
```

13.11 A lattice design

Each of the three factors in this design has five levels; that is, each component of the mixture is 0%, 25%, 50%, 75%, or 100% of the mixture for a given run, subject to the restriction that the sum of the percentages is 100. Use **Stats** ➡ **Design of Experiments** and select **Mixture** from the **Design type** drop-down list. Type 3 in the **Factors** text box and 5 in the **Levels** text box. With commands:

```
DESIGN
    MIXTURE / TYPE=LATTICE  FACTORS=3  LEVELS=5
```

```
Lattice Mixture Design:  15 Runs;  3 Factors, Each With  5 Levels

              Factor
     Run       1     2     3
      1     1.000  .000  .000
      2      .000 1.000  .000
      3      .000  .000 1.000
      4      .750  .250  .000
      5      .750  .000  .250
      6      .000  .750  .250
      7      .500  .500  .000
      8      .500  .000  .500
      9      .000  .500  .500
     10      .250  .750  .000
     11      .250  .000  .750
     12      .000  .250  .750
     13      .500  .250  .250
     14      .250  .500  .250
     15      .250  .250  .500
```

 After you collect your data, you may want to display it in a triangular scatterplot. See *SYSTAT: Graphics*.

As you can see, the sum of each row in this lattice design is 1.00. See Cornell (1990) for more information on **Lattice** designs. Notice that we selected the number of levels of each component to be 5 in this example. The selection of levels has no effect for the other three types of designs available because the number of factors determines the number of levels for each of them. As Cornell points out, the vast majority of mixture research employs lattice models; however, the other three types included here are useful in specific situations.

Centroid designs

Centroid designs consist of every (non-empty) subset of the components, but only with mixtures in which the components appear in equal proportions. Thus, if we asked for a centroid design with four factors (components), the mixtures in the model would consist of all permutations of the set (1,0,0,0), all permutations of the set (1/2,1/2,0,0), all permutations of the set (1/3,1/3,1/3,0) and the set (1/4,1/4,1/4,1/4). Thus, the number of distinct points is 1 less than 2 raised to the q power, where q is the number of components. See Cornell (1990) for more information on centroid designs.

Axial designs

Axial designs are useful when you want to have mainly complete mixtures in the model. A complete mixture is one in which all components are present to at least some degree (no component has a 0 entry). Such designs allow an in-depth analysis of the response surface for the design. See Cornell (1990) for more information on axial designs.

Screening designs

Screening designs enable you to single out unimportant components from an array of many potential components. Here you do not want to have complete mixtures; instead you want to maximize the number of mixtures containing a few levels of each component. That is, if you want to have a manageable number of runs (mixtures) and there is a large number of components, then you sacrifice the completeness of mixtures in order to screen many components. See Cornell (1990) for more information on screening designs.

References

Box, G.E.P., and Behnken, D.W. 1960. Some new three level designs for the study of quantitative variables. *Technometrics*, vol. 2, 4: 455-475.

Box, G.E.P., Hunter, W.G., and Hunter, J.S. 1978. *Statistics for experimenters.* New York: John Wiley & Sons, Inc.

Cochran, W.G., and Cox, G.M. 1957. *Experimental designs*, 2nd ed. New York: John Wiley & Sons, Inc.

Cornell, J.A. 1990. *Experiments with mixtures.* New York: John Wiley & Sons, Inc.

Plackett, R.L., and Burman, J.P. 1946. The design of optimum multifactor experiments. *Biometrika*, vol. 33: 305-325.

Taguchi, G. 1987. *System of experimental design* (2 volumes). New York: UNIPUB/Kraus International Publications.

Nonlinear Regression

Laszlo Engelman and Leland Wilkinson

Nonlinear Model estimates parameters for a variety of nonlinear models using a Gauss-Newton (SYSTAT computes exact derivatives), Quasi-Newton, or Simplex algorithm. In addition, you can specify a loss function other than least squares, so maximum likelihood estimates can be computed. You can set lower and upper limits on individual parameters. When the parameters are highly intercorrelated, and there is concern about overfitting, you can fix the value of one or more parameters, and Nonlinear Model will test the result against the full model. If the estimates have trouble converging, or they converge to a local minimum, Marquardting is available.

For assessing the certainty of the parameter estimates, Nonlinear Model offers Wald confidence regions and Cook-Weisberg graphical confidence curves. The latter are useful when it is unreasonable to assume that the estimates follow a normal distribution. You can also save values of the loss function for plotting contours in a bivariate display of the parameter space. This allows you to study the combinations of parameter estimates with approximately the same loss function values.

When your response contains outliers, you may want to downweight their residuals using one of Nonlinear Model's robust ψ functions: median, Huber, Hampel, bisquare, t, trim, or the pth power of the absolute value of the residuals.

Nonlinear Regression

The Basics

The Basics

Nonlinear Model estimates parameters for a variety of nonlinear models. Nonlinear Model is available only with SYSTAT commands. You can use these NONLIN commands:

MODEL Specify a general algebraic equation model.

LOSS Specify loss functions other than least squares. (Maximum likelihood estimation, for example, can be accomplished by specifying negative log-likelihood with LOSS.)

FUNPAR Specify functions of parameters and SYSTAT provides estimates with standard errors.

SAVE Save predicted values and residuals.

ROBUST Select a robust ψ function for downweighting the influence of extreme residuals.

ESTIMATE Estimate your model.

FIX Fix the values of one or more parameters and let SYSTAT test whether the results differ from those for the full model.

Getting started You can enter NONLIN commands at the command prompt in the Main window, submit them from the Command Editor, or use **Stats**➠ **Nonlinear Model** and enter and submit them in the **Nonlinear Model** window. To estimate the parameters of a nonlinear regression model, the following commands are available:

```
MODEL var = function
LOSS function
FUNPAR name1 = function1...
ROBUST arguments
RESET dependvar = expression
     weightvar = expression
SAVE filename / options
ESTIMATE / options
FIX / p₁ = n₁, p₂ = n₂,...
```

For a list of options available, see *SYSTAT: Command Reference*.

14.1 Default setup

For this first example, we do not specify any options specific to NONLIN; we simply specify the model using the operators and functions available for SYSTAT's transformations. At the end of the example, we describe options for specifying starting values, specifying bounds for the parameters, controlling convergence, setting the number of iterations and step halvings, specifying tolerance, and selecting an alternative algorithm. Here, we use the default Gauss-Newton algorithm that computes exact derivatives.

The *PATTISON* data are from a 1987 JASA article by C. P. Y. Clarke (Clarke took the data from an unpublished thesis by N. B. Pattinson). For 13 grass samples collected in a pasture, Pattinson recorded the number of weeks since grazing began in the pasture (*TIME*) and the weight of grass (*GRASS*) cut from 10 randomly sited quadrants. He then fit the Mitcherlitz equation. Here is the model with the *Quick Graph* from its fit:

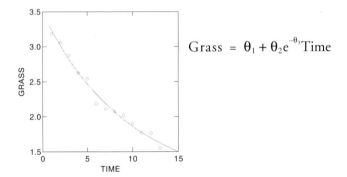

$$Grass \ = \ \theta_1 + \theta_2 e^{-\theta_3} Time$$

Use **Statistics ➡ Nonlinear Model** and type the following commands:

```
NONLIN
    USE pattison
    MODEL grass = p1 + p2*EXP(-p3*time)
    ESTIMATE
```

❶
```
Iteration
No.    Loss        P1           P2           P3
 0 .220818D+02 .101000D+01 .102000D+01 .103000D+01
 1 .120609D+02 .117014D+01 .182736D+00-.152631D+00
 2 .112473D+02 .172163D+01-.530281D-01-.212060D+00
 3 .530076D+01 .272740D+01-.314883D+00 .112491D+00
 4 .281714D+01 .971285D+00 .251024D+01 .186373D+00
 5 .127700D+00 .120930D+01 .223520D+01 .109079D+00
 6 .540618D-01 .966518D+00 .251532D+01 .102374D+00
 7 .534536D-01 .963226D+00 .251890D+01 .103061D+00
 8 .534536D-01 .963120D+00 .251900D+01 .103055D+00
 9 .534536D-01 .963121D+00 .251900D+01 .103055D+00
```

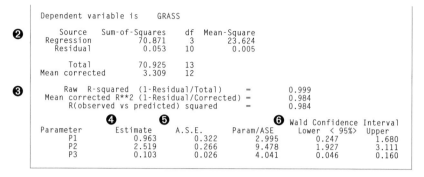

```
Dependent variable is    GRASS

    Source   Sum-of-Squares   df  Mean-Square
  Regression       70.871      3      23.624
  Residual          0.053     10       0.005

     Total          70.925    13
Mean corrected       3.309    12

    Raw  R-squared  (1-Residual/Total)       =      0.999
Mean corrected R**2 (1-Residual/Corrected) =      0.984
        R(observed vs predicted) squared    =      0.984

                                                   Wald Confidence Interval
Parameter     Estimate    A.S.E.    Param/ASE    Lower  < 95%>  Upper
   P1           0.963       0.322       2.995       0.247         1.680
   P2           2.519       0.266       9.478       1.927         3.111
   P3           0.103       0.026       4.041       0.046         0.160
```

The highlighted numbers below correspond to those in the output:

❶ The estimates of parameters converged in nine iterations. At each iteration, Nonlinear Model prints the number of the iteration, the *Loss*, or the residual sum of squares (RSS), and the estimates of the parameters. The residual sum of squares is RSS $= \Sigma(w \cdot (y - \hat{f})^2)$, where y is the observed value, $\hat{f}$ is the estimated value, and w is the value of the case weight (its default is 1.0). At step 0, the estimates of the parameters are the starting values chosen by SYSTAT or specified by the user with the START option of ESTIMATE.

❷ The output includes the following sums of squares (SS):

- *Regression* $\Sigma wy^2 - \Sigma w(y - \hat{f})^2$

- *Residual* $\Sigma w \cdot (y - \hat{f})^2$

- *Total* $\Sigma w \cdot y^2$

- *Mean corrected* $\Sigma w \cdot (y - \bar{y})^2$

❸ The *Raw R-squared* (Regression SS / Total SS) is the proportion of the variation in y that is explained by the sum of squares due to regression. Some researchers object to this measure because the means are not removed. The *Mean corrected R**2* tries to adjust for this. Many researchers prefer the last measure of R^2 (*R(observed vs. predicted) squared*). It is the correlation squared between the observed values and the predicted values ($(r(y,\hat{f})^2)$).

❹ Estimates of the parameters. The estimated model is:

Grass $= 0.963 + 2.519e^{-0.103\text{Time}}$

❺ Asymptotic Standard Error (*A.S.E.*). A period (there is none here) indicates a problem with the estimate (the correlations among the estimated parameters may be very high, or the value of the function may not be affected if the estimate is changed). Read *Param/ASE*, the estimate of each parameter divided by its asymptotic standard error, roughly as a *t* statistic.

❻ The *Wald Confidence Intervals* for the estimates are defined as EST ± *t* × A.S.E for the *t* distribution with residual degrees of freedom (*df* =10 in this example). SYSTAT prints the 95% confidence intervals. Use CONFI=*n* to specify a different confidence level.

Specifying your model

Nonlinear Model uses models resembling those for General Linear Model (GLM). There is one critical difference, however. The Nonlinear Model statement is a literal algebraic expression of variables and parameters. Choose any name you want for these parameters. Any names you specify that are not variable names in your file are assumed to be parameter names. Suppose you specify the following model for the *USSTATES* data:

liver = b0 + b1*wine

Since B0 and B1 are not variables (they are parameters), the following model is the same:

liver = constant + beta*wine

Parameter names can be any names that meet the requirements for SYSTAT numeric variable names (eight characters beginning with a letter). However, unlike variable names, parameter names may not have subscripts.

Any legal SYSTAT expression can be used in a model statement, including trigonometric and other functions, plus the special variables CASE and COMPLETE. The only restriction is that the dependent variable must be a variable in your file. Here is a more complicated example:

cardio=(division<5)*mu1 + (division>=5)*mu2

This model has two parameters (*MU1* and *MU2*). Their values are conditional on the value of *DIVISION*. Notice that the remaining parts of this expression involve relational operations (*DIVISION* >5). SYSTAT evaluates these to 1 (true) or 0 (false).

Piecewise regression. You can fit different curves to different subsets of your data:

$$y = (x<=0)*10 + (x>0 \text{ AND } x<1)*beta*x + (x>=1)*20$$

In this model, y is 10 if x is less than or equal to 0, y is $BETA*x$ if x is greater than 0 and less than 1, and y is 20 if x is greater than or equal to 1. These types of constraints are useful for specifying bounded probability functions such as the cumulative uniform distribution. See Example 14.11.

Missing data. Missing values are handled according to the conventions of SYSTAT BASIC. That is, missing values propagate in algebraic expressions. For example, the result of "$x + .$" is a missing value. The expression "$x = .$" is 1 if x is missing and 0 if it is not. Thus, you can use logical expressions to put conditions on model or loss functions. Consider the following loss function:

$$(x<>.)*(y - \text{estimate})^2 + (x=.)*(z - \text{estimate})^2$$

Illegal expressions (such as division by zero and negative square roots) are set to missing values. Parameter estimates are forced to move away from regions of the parameter space that yield illegal function evaluations.

Using the LOSS command to select subsets. You can use the LOSS command to select subsets of your data. For example,

```
LOSS (case<100)*(y - estimate)^2
```

This function uses the first 99 cases because the loss for the remaining cases is 0 (**CASE** is a built-in variable). If you save residuals, they are computed for all cases using the parameter estimates derived from the subset. Here is how to use all cases where AGE is 25 or 35. The variable AGE does not need to appear in your model statement.

```
LOSS (age=25 OR age=35)*(y - estimate)^2
```

ESTIMATE command	Nonlinear Model provides the **ESTIMATE** command for controlling the computation of your model.

Initial values

Use the **START** option to specify a starting value for each parameter in your model.

START = *n1, n2 ...*   Starting values for the parameters. Default = 0.101, 0.102, 0.103, 0.104, $\cdots$

The values must be in the same order as the parameters. Separate the values with commas or blanks (for example, "1E–5, 123.4, 15" for three parameters). You can specify starting values for some of the parameters and leave blanks for others (for example, "1E–5, , 15"). SYSTAT chooses starting values if you do not. Specify starting values that give the general shape of the function you expect as a result. For example, if you expect that the function is a negative exponential function, then specify initial values that yield a negative exponential function. Also, make sure that the starting values are in a reasonable range. For example, if the function contains **EXP(P*TIME)** and *TIME* ranges from 10,000 to 20,000, then the initial value of *P* should be around 1/10,000. If you specified an initial value such as 0.1, the function would have extremely large values, such as e^{1000}. For example,

```
ESTIMATE / START=1,2,3
```

For examples where starting values are specified, see Example 14.5 (second part), Example 14.7, and Example 14.11.

Parameter bounds

Use the **MINIMUM** and **MAXIMUM** options to specify bounds for your parameters.

MINIMUM = *n1, n2, ...*   Minimum values for the parameters
MAXIMUM = *n1, n2, ...*   Maximum values for the parameters

Specify a value for each parameter, separating them with commas. You can omit a bound for a parameter by typing ", ," (comma space comma). For example, type

```
ESTIMATE / MIN=-1,0,3, MAX=2, ,10
```

to specify minimum values for three parameters and maximum values for the first and third parameters.

Iterations and step halvings

Use the ITER and HALF options to specify the number of iterations or increment halvings.

ITER = n Maximum number of iterations. Default=25.
HALF = n Maximum number of increment halvings. Default=8.

If you do not reach convergence in the number of iterations you specify, you can type ESTIMATE again to continue iterating. For some models with many parameters, you may want to begin with just a few iterations to see if all looks well and then continue.

If the loss increases between two iterations, Nonlinear Model halves the increment size, computes the loss at the midpoint, and compares it to the residual sum of squares at the previous iteration. This process continues until the residual sum of squares is less than that at the previous iteration or until the maximum number of halvings is reached. For example,

```
ESTIMATE / ITER=40  HALF=16
```

Convergence

Use the LCONV and CONV options to specify convergence criteria.

LCONV = n Loss convergence criterion. Default=0.000001.
CONV = n Parameter convergence criterion. Default=0.00001.

When the relative improvement in the loss function for an iteration is less than LCONV, Nonlinear Model declares that a solution has been found. When the largest relative improvement of parameters for an iteration is less than CONV, Nonlinear Model considers that the estimates of the parameters have converged. When both the LCONV and CONV criteria are satisfied, Nonlinear Model declares the problem solved. For example,

```
ESTIMATE / LCONV=.0001  CONV=.001
```

Marquardting

When SYSTAT's default starting values do not lead to a reasonable solution, you can try specifying your own starting values or use the MARQUARDT option of ESTIMATE, which is the Marquardt method of inflating the diagonal of the (Jacobian'Jacobian) matrix by a specified number (n). This speeds convergence when initial values are far from the estimates and when the estimates of the parameters are highly intercorrelated. This method is similar to "ridging," except that the inflation factor n is omitted from final iterations. With commands:

```
ESTIMATE / MARQUARDT=n
```

Tolerance

In order for SYSTAT to invert the matrix of sums of cross-products of the derivatives with respect to the parameters, the matrix cannot be singular. Use TOL to guard against this singularity problem:

TOL = n A check for near singularity when Nonlinear Model inverts the matrix of sums of cross-products of the derivatives. Default=0.0001.

A parameter estimate is not changed at an iteration if more than (1 − TOL) proportion of the sum of squares of partial derivatives with respect to that parameter can be expressed with partial derivatives of other parameters. For example,

```
ESTIMATE / TOL=.001
```

Estimation method

Nonlinear Model provides three algorithms for estimating your model:

GN   Modified Gauss-Newton method that computes exact derivatives. This is the default.

QUASI   Quasi-Newton algorithm that uses numeric estimates of the first and second derivatives.

SIMPLEX   Simplex algorithm that uses a direct search procedure.

The Gauss-Newton method with its exact derivatives produces more accurate estimates of the asymptotic standard errors and covariances and can converge in fewer iterations and more quickly than the other two algorithms.

Both GN and the Quasi-Newton method do not work if the derivatives are undefined in the region in which you are seeking minimum values. Specifically, the first and second derivatives must exist at all points for which the algorithm computes values. However, the algorithms cannot identify situations where the derivatives do not exist. Also, Quasi-Newton cannot detect when derivatives fluctuate rapidly—thus, Gauss-Newton can be more accurate.

The Simplex algorithm does not have this requirement. It calculates a value for your loss function at some point, looks to see if this value is less than values elsewhere, and steps to a new point to try again. When the steps become small, iterations stop.

GN is the fastest method. Simplex is generally slower than the others, particularly for least squares, because Simplex cannot make use of the information in the derivatives to find how far to move its estimates at each step. The above output took 3 iterations using exact derivatives. For the same model, the Quasi-Newton method takes 22 iterations and the Simplex method takes 15 iterations. Also note that one Simplex iteration takes much more time than the others. With commands:

```
ESTIMATE / GN or QUASI or SIMPLEX
```

How Nonlinear Model works. The estimation works as follows: the starting values of the parameters are selected by the program or by you. Then the MODEL statement (if stated) is evaluated for the first case in double precision. The result of this function is called the **estimate**. Then the LOSS statement is evaluated for the first case, using the estimate from the MODEL statement. If you did not include a LOSS statement, then loss is computed by squaring the residual for the first case.

This procedure is repeated for all cases in the file and the loss is summed over cases. The summed loss is then minimized using the Gauss-Newton, Quasi-Newton, or Simplex algorithms. Iterations continue until both convergence criteria are met or the maximum number of iterations is reached.

Loss function

The LOSS feature allows you to compute loss functions other than least squares. We introduce loss functions on p. 470. Type your LOSS statement as you would a MODEL statement. For example:

```
LOSS = ABS(y - estimate)
```

This loss function is least absolute deviations. The word "estimate" in the statement is the fitted value from your model. It is a special Nonlinear Model word, so you should not name a variable "*ESTIMATE*." If you use both MODEL and LOSS, then MODEL defines the parameters (that is, new parameters cannot be introduced in LOSS). Otherwise, the LOSS statement defines the parameters. If you don't specify a MODEL, "estimate" is not defined. If you specify a model, do it *before* specifying the loss function.

Here is what least squares (the default if you do not use LOSS) looks like:

$$(y - estimate)^2$$

The LOSS statement is most useful for computing maximum likelihood estimates.

14.2 Extended output

If you specify the **Long** output results under **Edit➧Options**, casewise predictions and the asymptotic correlation matrix of parameters are printed in addition to the default output. With commands, type

```
PRINT = LONG
```

before **ESTIMATE**.

Predicted values and residuals

For each case, Nonlinear Model prints the observed and predicted value and the residual. Here is the output for the *PATTISON* example above:

```
Case   Observed   Predicted   Residual
  1      3.183       3.235      -0.052
  2      3.059       3.013       0.046
  3      2.871       2.812       0.059
  4      2.622       2.631      -0.009
  5      2.541       2.468       0.073
  6      2.184       2.320      -0.136
  7      2.110       2.188      -0.078
  8      2.075       2.068       0.007
  9      2.018       1.959       0.059
 10      1.903       1.862       0.041
 11      1.770       1.774      -0.004
 12      1.762       1.695       0.067
 13      1.550       1.623      -0.073
```

The asymptotic correlation matrix of parameters

Nonlinear Model computes asymptotic standard errors and correlations by estimating the $(J'J)^{-1}$ matrix after iterations have terminated. The *Asymptotic Correlation Matrix of Parameters* is computed from the asymptotic covariance matrix that inverts $(J'J)^{-1} \times$ RMS, where J is the Jacobian and RMS is the residual mean squared. You should examine your model for redundant parameters. If the $J'J$ matrix is singular (parameters are very highly intercorrelated), SYSTAT prints a period to mark parameters with problems. Here is the *Asymptotic Correlation Matrix of Parameters* for the *PATTISON* example above:

```
Asymptotic Correlation Matrix of Parameters
              P1         P2         P3
  P1       1.000
  P2      -0.972      1.000
  P3       0.984     -0.923      1.000
```

These parameters are highly intercorrelated; the model may be overparameterized. In Example 14.4, we arbitrarily fix the value of one of the parameters, refit the model, and let SYSTAT test this restricted model against the full model.

Problems   You may encounter numerous pitfalls (for example, dependencies, discontinuities, local minima, and so on). Nonlinear Model offers several possibilities to overcome these pitfalls, but in some instances, even your best efforts may be futile.

- Find reasonable starting values by considering approximately what the values should be. Try plotting the data. For example in Example 14.6, you could let DAYS $\rightarrow \infty$ and estimate θ_1 to be approximately 20.
- Try Marquardting.
- Use several different starting values for each method before you feel comfortable with the final estimates. This can help you expose local minima. The Simplex method is most robust against local minima. There is a trade-off, however, because it is considerably slower.
- Try switching back and forth between Gauss-Newton, Quasi-Newton, and Simplex without changing the starting values. That way, one may help you out of a convergence or local minimum problem.
- If you get illegal function values for starting values, try some other estimates. For some functions with many parameters, you may need high quality starting values to get an estimable function at all.
- Never trust the output of an iterative nonlinear estimation procedure until you have plotted estimates against predictors and you have tried several different starting values. SAVE is designed so that you can quickly save estimates, residuals, and model variables and plot them. All of the examples in this chapter were tested this way. Although most began with default starting values for the parameters, they were checked with other starting values.

14.3 Confidence curves and regions

Confidence curves and regions provide information about the certainty of your parameter estimates. The usual Wald confidence intervals (Example 14.1) can be misleading when intercorrelations among the parameters are high.

Confidence curves. Cook and Weisberg construct confidence curves by plotting an assortment of potential estimates of a specific parameter, which we call θ^*, on the y-axis against the absolute value of a t statistic derived from the residual sum of squares (RSS) associated with each θ^*. To obtain the values for the x-axis, SYSTAT:

- Computes the model as usual and saves RSS.
- Fixes the value of the parameter of interest of (for example, the estimate plus half the standard error of the estimate), recomputes the model, and saves RSS*.
- Computes the t statistic:

$$t = \sqrt{\frac{\text{RSS}^* - \text{RSS}}{1} \Big/ \frac{\text{RSS}}{n - p}}$$

- Repeats the above steps for other values of θ^*.

Now SYSTAT plots each θ^* against the absolute value of its associated t^* statistic. Vertical lines at the 90, 95, and 99 percentage points of the t distribution with $(n{-}p)$ degrees of freedom provide a useful frequentist calibration of the plot.

To illustrate the usefulness of confidence curves, we again use the *PATTISON* data. Recall that the estimated model was:

Grass = $0.93 + 2.519e^{-0.103\text{Time}}$

To produce the Cook-Weisberg confidence curves for the model, type

```
SAVE pattci / CI=p1 p2 p3
```

before **ESTIMATE** in the commands. Then, to generate the graphs type:

```
SUBMIT pattci
```

Here are the results:

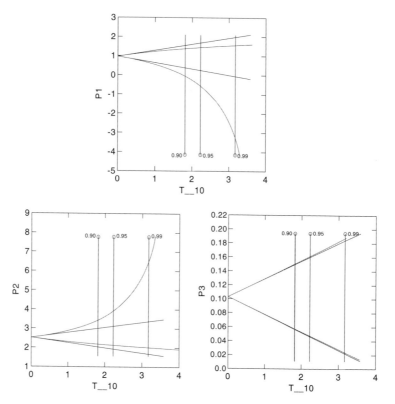

The blue lines are the Wald 95% confidence intervals (see Example 14.1) and the solid curves are the Cook-Weisberg confidence curves. The vertical lines show the 90th, 95th, and 99th percentiles of the t distribution with $n-p = 10$ degrees of freedom.

For P1 and P2, the coverage of the Wald intervals differs makedly from that of the Cook-Weisberg (C-W) curves. The 95% interval for P1 on the C-W curve is approximately from −0.58 to 1.45; the Wald interval extends from 0.247 to 1.68. The steeply descending lower C-W curve indicates greater uncertainty for smaller estimates of P1. For P2, the C-W interval ranges from 2.12 to 3.92; the Wald interval ranges from 1.9 to 3.1. The agreement between the two methods is better for P3. The C-W curves show that the distributions of estimates for P1 and P2 are quite asymetric.

Confidence region. SYSTAT also provides the CR option for confidence regions. When there are more than two parameters in the model, this feature causes Nonlinear Model to search for the best values of the additional parameters for each combination of estimates for the first two parameters. Type:

```
SAVE pattcr / CR=p1 p2
```

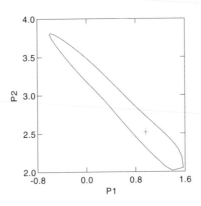

You can specify the level of confidence. For example,

```
SAVE pattcr / CR=p1 p2 CONFI=.90
```

14.4 Evaluating the fit and fixing parameters

In Example 14.1, the R^2 between the observed and predicted values is 0.984, indicating good agreement between the data and fitted values. However, there may be consecutive points across time where the fitted values are consistently overestimated or underestimated. We can look for trends in the residuals by plotting them versus *TIME* and connecting the points with a line. A stem-and-leaf plot will tell us if extreme values are identified as outliers (outside values or far outside values):

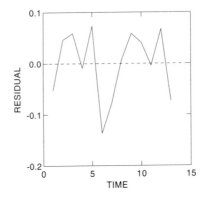

The results of a runs test would not be significant here. The large negative residual in the center of the plot, –0.137, is not identified as an outlier in the stem-and-leaf plot.

We should probably be more concerned about the fact that the parameters are highly intercorrelated: the correlation between P1 and P2 is –0.972, and the correlation between P1 and P3 is 0.984. This might indicate that our model has too many parameters. You can fix one or more parameters and let SYSTAT estimate the remaining parameters. Suppose, for example, that similar studies report a value of P1 close to 1.0. You can fix P1 at 1.0 and then test whether the results differ from the results for the full model.

To do this, first specify the full model as described in Example 14.1. Use FIX to specify the parameter as P1 with a value of 1. Then initiate the estimation process with ESTIMATE:

```
FIX p1=1
ESTIMATE
```

Here are selections from the output:

```
                                                        Wald Confidence Interval
Parameter            Estimate      A.S.E.    Param/ASE    Lower < 95%> Upper
P1                     1.000        0.0          .              .         .
P2                     2.490        0.060      41.662         2.358     2.621
P3                     0.106        0.004      23.728         0.096     0.116

Analysis of the effect of fixing parameter(s)

Source        Sum-of-squares   DF  Mean-square     F-value   p(F-value)

Parameter fix       0.000        1     0.000          0.014       0.908
  Residual          0.053       10     0.005
```

The *Analysis of the effect of fixing parameter(s)* F test tests the hypothesis $H_0 : P_1 = 1.0$. In our output, $F = 0.014$ ($p = 0.908$), indicating that there is no significant difference between the two models. This is not surprising, considering the similarity of the results:

	Three parameters	P1 fixed at 1.0
P1	0.963	1.000
P2	2.519	2.490
P3	0.103	0.106
RSS	0.053	0.054
R**2	0.984	0.984

There are some differences between the two models. The correlation between P2 and P3 is 0.923 for the full model and 0.810 when P1 is fixed. The most striking difference is in the Wald intervals for P2 and P3. When P1 is fixed, the Wald interval for P2 is less than one-fourth of the interval for the full model. The interval for P3 is less than one-fifth the interval for the full model. Let's see what information the C-W curves provide about the uncertainty of the estimates. Here are the curves for the model with P1 fixed:

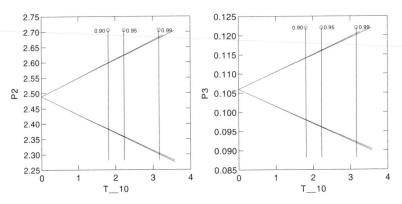

Compare these curves with the curves for the full model. The C-W curve for P2 has straightened out and is very close to the Wald interval. If we were to plot the P2 C-W curve for both models on the same axes, the wedge for the fixed P1 model would be only a small slice of the wedge for the full model.

Saving results and values

In Nonlinear Model, you can save residuals, estimated values, and variables from your model statement, loss function values surrounding the converged minimum, or data for plotting the Cook-Weisberg confidence intervals or two-parameter confidence region. To save, type:

> SAVE *filename* /

Following the slash, type one of the following options:

RESID	Estimated values, residuals, and variables from the model statement.
DATA	Data, estimated values, and residuals.
RS = *pname1*, *pname2*	Save five levels of contours of the loss function surrounding the converged minimum (like a response surface for the loss function in a 2-D parameter space). Specify names of two parameters (*pnamei*). If the names are omitted, SYSTAT assumes the first two parameters in your model. See Example 14.6.

CI = *pname1*, *pname2*...	The data values that Nonlinear Model computes for Cook-Weisberg confidence curves plus commands to plot the values. Specify names of parameters (*pnamei*). You may specify a subset of the parameters. See Example 14.3.
CR = *pname1*, *pname2*	Save a closed curve that defines the 95% confidence region for a pair of parameters surrounding the converged minimum. Specify their names as *pnamei*. Use CONFI to change the size of the region. Differs from RS in that SYSTAT reestimates the whole model when computing each value of the loss function (instead of fixing unspecified parameters at their estimated value). This option is useful when there are more than two parameters. See Example 14.3.
CONFI = *n*	Type *n* to specify the size of the CR confidence region. The default is 0.95.

To enter these options, type:

```
SAVE filename / DATA  or  RESID
              or
SAVE filename / RS=p1,p2  or  CI=p1,p2,...  or
                CR=p1,p2  CONFI=n
```

Requesting RS, CI, and CR in one run. After viewing results for a model, you may repeat SAVE commands to request RS, CI, and CR. Simply type ESTIMATE after each SAVE request. For example, after running Example 14.1, we could type:

```
SAVE curves / CI=p1 p2 p3
ESTIMATE

SAVE region / CR=p1 p2
ESTIMATE

SAVE contour / RS=p1 p2
ESTIMATE
```

and to generate the graphs we would type:

```
SUBMIT curves
SUBMIT region
SUBMIT contour
```

Special Features

In this section, we introduce examples that illustrate how to:

- Estimate functions of parameters and obtain confidence curves for them
- Contour the loss function

14.5 Functions of parameters

Frequently, researchers are not interested in the estimates of the parameters themselves, but instead want to make statements about functions of parameters. For example, in a logistic model, they may want to estimate *LD50* and *LD90* and determine the variability of these estimates. You can specify functions of parameters in Nonlinear Model. SYSTAT evaluates the function at each iteration and prints the standard error and the Wald interval for the estimate after the last iteration. In Example 14.13, we estimate *LD50* for quantile response data.

We look at a quadratic function described by Cook and Weisberg. Here is the *Quick Graph* that results from fitting the model:

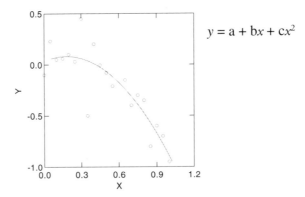

$$y = a + bx + cx^2$$

This function reaches its maximum at $-b/2c$. However, for the data given by Cook and Weisberg, this maximum is close to the smallest x. That is, to the left of the maximum, there is little of the response curve.

In SYSTAT, you can estimate the maximum (and get Wald intervals) directly from the original quadratic by using FUNPAR. With commands:

```
NONLIN
   USE quad
   MODEL y = a + b*x + c*x^2
   FUNPAR max = -b/(2*c)
   ESTIMATE
```

Parameter	Estimate	A.S.E.	Param/ASE	Wald Confidence Interval Lower < 95%>	Upper
A	0.034	0.117	0.292	-0.213	0.282
B	0.524	0.555	0.944	-0.647	1.694
C	-1.452	0.534	-2.718	-2.579	-0.325
MAX	0.180	0.128	1.409	-0.090	0.450

Using the Wald interval, we estimate that the maximum response occurs for an x value between -0.09 and 0.45.

C-W curves

To obtain the C-W confidence curves for *MAX*, we have to re-express the model so that *MAX* is a parameter of the model:

$$b = -2c\text{Max} \quad \text{so,} \quad y = a - (2c\text{Max})x + cx^2$$

The original model is easy to compute because it is linear. The reparameterized model is not as well behaved, so we use estimates from the first run as starting values and request C-W confidence curves:

```
MODEL y=a - (2*c*max)*x + c*x^2
SAVE quadcw / CI=max
ESTIMATE / START=0.034,-1.452, 0.180
SUBMIT quadcw
```

The C-W confidence curves describe our uncertainty about the x value at which the expected response is maximized much better than the Wald interval does.

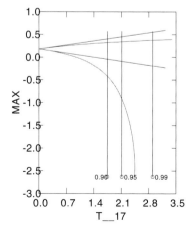

The picture provides clear information about the MAX response in the positive direction. We can be confident that the value is less than 0.4 because the C-W curve is lower than the Wald interval on the 95th percentile line. The lower bound is much less clear; it could certainly be lower than the Wald interval indicates.

14.6
Contouring the
loss function

You can save loss function values along contour curves and then plot the loss function. For this example, we use the *BOD* data (Bates and Watts, 1988). These data were taken from stream samples in 1967 by Marske. Each sample bottle was inoculated with a mixed culture of microorganisms, sealed, incubated, and opened periodically for analysis of dissolved oxygen concentration.

The data are:

DAYS	BOD
1.000	8.300
2.000	10.300
3.000	19.000
4.000	16.000
5.000	15.000
7.000	19.800

$$\text{Bod} = \theta_1(1 - e^{-\theta_2 \text{Days}})$$

where *DAYS* is time in days and *BOD* is the biochemical oxygen demand. The six *BOD* values are averages of two analyses on each bottle. An exponential decay model with a fixed rate constant was estimated to predict biochemical oxygen demand.

Let's look at the contours of the parameter space defined by *THETA_2* with *THETA_1*. We use loss function data values stored in the *BODRS* data file. Here's how we created the file:

```
NONLIN
   USE bod
   MODEL bod = theta_1*(1-EXP(-theta_2*days))
   PRINT=LONG
```

```
SAVE bodrs / RS
ESTIMATE
```

```
Dependent variable is      BOD

      Source   Sum-of-Squares   df   Mean-Square
  Regression      1401.390       2     700.695
   Residual         25.990       4       6.498

      Total       1427.380       6
Mean corrected    107.213        5

      Raw  R-square  (1-Residual/Total)      =      0.982
Mean corrected R**2 (1-Residual/Corrected) =      0.758
      R(observed vs predicted) square       =      0.758

                                                    Wald Confidence Interval
Parameter       Estimate       A.S.E.      Param/ASE    Lower  < 95%>  Upper
THETA_1          19.143         2.496         7.670      12.213        26.072
THETA_2           0.531         0.203         2.615      -0.033         1.095

              BOD           BOD
  Case      Observed      Predicted      Residual
   1          8.300         7.887          0.413
   2         10.300        12.525         -2.225
   3         19.000        15.252          3.748
   4         16.000        16.855         -0.855
   5         15.600        17.797         -2.197
   6         19.800        18.678          1.122

Asymptotic Correlation Matrix of Parameters
                   THETA_1       THETA_2
   THETA_1          1.000
   THETA_2         -0.853         1.000
```

Now we request the plot:

```
SUBMIT bodrs
```

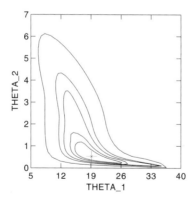

The kidney-shaped area near the center of the plot is the region where the loss function is minimized. Any parameter value combination (that is, any point inside the kidney) produces approximately the same loss function.

Maximum Likelihood Estimation

A maximum likelihood estimate of a parameter is a value of the parameter for a given distribution that has the highest probability of generating the observed sample data. Sometimes maximum likelihood and least squares estimates are the same; at other times they differ. In general, these estimates are found by maximizing the likelihood function L with respect to the parameter vector θ:

$$L = \prod_{i=1}^{n} d(x_i, \theta)$$

where $d(x_i, \theta)$ is the density of the response at each value of x. Equivalently, the negative of the log of the likelihood function can be minimized:

$$-\log L = \sum_{i=1}^{n} \ln(d(x_i, \theta))$$

Here we outline four methods for computing maximum likelihood estimates in NONLIN. To define them, we use a specific model and a specific density. The model is the sum of two exponentials:

$$\hat{y} = p_1 e^{p_2 x} + p_3 e^{p_4 x}$$

and the distribution of y at each x is Poisson:

$$d(x_i, \lambda) = \frac{e^{-\lambda} \lambda^y}{y!}$$

In our definitions, we also use the log of the density:

$$\ln d = -\lambda + y\ln\lambda - \text{LGM}(y + 1)$$

where LGM is the log gamma function for computing $y!$.

Method 1. Set the LOSS function to –ln(density). In NONLIN, you can specify your own loss function. Here we specify the negative of the log of the density function:

$$\text{LOSS} = \lambda - y\ln\lambda + \text{LGM}(y + 1)$$

For the estimate of lambda, we use $\hat{y}$, or **estimate**, as it is known to Nonlinear Model. Using commands, we type:

```
MODEL Y = p1*EXP(p2*x) + p3*EXP(p4*x)
LOSS = estimate - y*LOG(estimate) + LGM(y+1)
ESTIMATE
```

Note that for this method, you need to specify only the loss function. To do this for our example, we would rewrite LOSS, substituting the expression on the right side of the MODEL statement (above) for the word "estimate."

This method can be used for any distribution; however, the estimated standard errors may not be correct. See Example 14.7.

Method 2. Iteratively reweighted least squares. This method is appropriate for distributions belonging to the exponential family (for example, normal, binomial, multinomial, Poisson, and gamma). It provides meaningful standard errors for the parameter estimates and useful residuals. For this method, you define a case weight that is recomputed at each iteration:

$$\text{weight} = \frac{1}{\text{variance}(y_i)}$$

For our Poisson distribution, the mean and variance are equal, so lambda is the variance, and our estimate of the variance is *estimate*. Thus, the weight is:

$$\text{weight} = \frac{1}{\text{estimate}}$$

Here's how to specify this method using NONLIN commands:

```
LET wt=1
WEIGHT = wt
MODEL y = p1*EXP(p2*x) + p2*EXP(p4*x)
RESET wt = 1 / estimate
ESTIMATE / SCALE
```

The standard deviation of the resulting estimates are the usual information theory standard errors. See Example 14.8.

Method 3. Estimate ln(density) and reset the predicted value to y + 1. For this method, the data may follow any distribution and the standard errors are correct, but the method does not yield correct residuals. You define a dummy outcome variable and estimate the log of the density, and then reset the outcome variable to $\hat{y} + 1$ at each iteration. For our example, with commands:

```
LET dummy = 0
MODEL dummy = -p1*EXP(p2*x) - p3*EXP(p4*x),
            + y*LOG(p1*EXP(p2*x) + p3*EXP(p4*x),
            -LGM(y + 1)
RESET dummy = estimate + 1
ESTIMATE / SCALE
```

Method 4. Set the predicted value to zero and define the function as the square root of the negative log density. This method is a variation of method 1, so it is appropriate for data from any distribution and provides estimates of the parameters only. Here we trick NONLIN by setting $y=0$ for all cases:

$$f = \sqrt{-\ln d(x, \theta)} \quad , \text{ so } \Sigma(y - f)^2 \text{ becomes}$$

$$\Sigma(0 - \sqrt{-\ln d(x, q)})^2 = \Sigma -\ln d(x, \theta)$$

For our example, with commands:

```
LET dummy = 0
MODEL dummy = SQR(p1*EXP(p2*x) + p3*EXP(p4*x),
            - y*LOG(p1*EXP(p2*x) + p3*EXP(p4*x),
            + LGM(y + 1)
ESTIMATE
```

14.7 Setting LOSS = –ln(density)

Because NONLIN includes a loss function, you can maximize the likelihood of a function in the model equation. The way to do this is to minimize the negative of the log-likelihood as explained in method 1 on p. 470.

Here is an example using the *IRIS* data. Let's compute the maximum likelihood estimates of the mean and variance of *SEPALWID* assuming a normal distribution for the first species in the *IRIS* data. For a sample of n independent normal random variables, the log-likelihood function is:

$$L(\mu, \sigma^2) = -\frac{n}{2}\ln(2\pi) - \frac{n}{2}\ln(\sigma^2) - \frac{1}{2\sigma^2}\sum(X - \mu)^2$$

However, we can use the ZDF function as a shortcut. In this example, we minimize the negative of the log-likelihood with LOSS and thus maximize the likelihood. SYSTAT's small default starting values for MEAN and SIGMA (0.101 and 0.100) will produce very large z-scores ((x_i - mean) / sigma) and values of the density close to zero, so we arbitrarily select larger starting values. We use the *IRIS* data. Under SELECT, we specify species=1. Then, we type in our LOSS statement (see below). Finally, we use ESTIMATE's START option to specify start values (2,2):

```
NONLIN
   USE iris
   SELECT species=1
   LOSS = -log(zdf(sepalwid,mean,sigma))
   ESTIMATE / START=2,2
```

```
Iteration
 No.   Loss         MEAN        SIGMA
  0 .900717D+02 .200000D+01 .200000D+01
  1 .614505D+02 .331334D+01 .142676D+01
  2 .373247D+02 .346920D+01 .823316D+00
  3 .271437D+02 .345195D+01 .621190D+00
  4 .178069D+02 .343963D+01 .373668D+00
  5 .177826D+02 .343003D+01 .375763D+00
  6 .177819D+02 .342854D+01 .375482D+00
  7 .177818D+02 .342817D+01 .375340D+00
  8 .177818D+02 .342805D+01 .375285D+00
Final value of loss function is      17.782

                                            Wald Confidence Interval
Parameter     Estimate    A.S.E.    Param/ASE    Lower < 95%>  Upper
   MEAN         3.428      0.044      77.896       3.340       3.517
   SIGMA        0.375      0.032      11.890       0.312       0.439
```

Note that the least squares estimate of sigma (0.379) computed in **Statistics** is larger than the biased maximum likelihood estimate here (0.375).

14.8 Iteratively reweighted least squares for a logistic model

In this example, we use method 2, as discussed on p. 471. Cox (1970) reports the following data on tests among objects for failures after certain times. These data are in the *COX* data file—*FAILURE* is the number of failures and *COUNT* is the total number of tests:

TIME	FAILURE	COUNT
7	0	55
14	2	157
27	7	159
51	3	16

Cox uses a logistic model to fit the failures:

$$\text{estimate} = n_i \frac{\text{EXP}(\beta_0 + \beta_1 \text{time})}{1 + \text{EXP}(\beta_0 + \beta_1 \text{time})}$$

where n_i is the count. The log-likelihood function for the logit model is:

$$L(\beta_0, \beta_1) = \sum [p\ln(\text{estimate}) + (1-p)\ln(1\text{-estimate})]$$

where the sum is over all observations. Because the counts differ at each time, the variances of the failures also differ. If *FAILURE* is randomly sampled from a binomial, then

VAR(failure) = estimate*(count − estimate)/count

Therefore, the weight is 1/variance:

wi = count / (estimate*(count-estimate))

We use these variances to weight each case in the estimation. On each iteration, the variances are recalculated from the new estimates and used anew in computing the weighted loss function.

In the following commands, we use RESET to recompute the weight after each iteration. The SCALE option of ESTIMATE rescales the mean square error to 1 at the end of the iterations. The commands are:

```
NONLIN
  USE cox
  PRINT = LONG
  LET w = 1
  WEIGHT = w
  MODEL failure = count*EXP(-b0 - b1*time)/,
                  (1 + EXP(-b0 - b1*time))
  RESET w = count / (estimate*(count-estimate))
  ESTIMATE / SCALE
```

```
Iteration
No.     Loss          B0            B1
  0 .162222D+03 .101000D+00 .102000D+00
  1 .161785D+02 .272314D+01 -.109931D-01
  2 .325354D+01 .419599D+01 -.509510D-01
  3 .754172D+00 .510574D+01 -.736890D-01
  4 .665897D+00 .539079D+01 -.801623D-01
  5 .674806D+00 .541501D+01 -.806924D-01

Dependent variable is  FAILURE

     Source    Sum-of-Squares   DF  Mean-Square
  Regression        13.037       2      6.518
    Residual         0.675       2      0.337

      Total         13.712       4
Mean corrected       5.812       3

      Raw  R-square  (1-Residual/Total)       =        0.951
Mean corrected R**2 (1-Residual/Corrected) =        0.936
       R(observed vs predicted) square       =        0.988
Standard Errors of Parameters are rescaled

                                                   Wald Confidence Interval
Parameter        Estimate      A.S.E.   Param/ASE    Lower < 95%> Upper
       B0           5.415       0.728       7.443       3.989      6.841
       B1          -0.081       0.022      -3.609      -0.125     -0.037

         FAILURE       FAILURE
 Case    Observed     Predicted    Residual   Case Weight
   1        0.0          0.427      -0.427        2.359
   2        2.000        2.132      -0.132        0.475
   3        7.000        6.014       0.986        0.173
   4        3.000        3.427      -0.427        0.371

Asymptotic Correlation Matrix of Parameters
                    B0           B1
        B0        1.000
        B1       -0.910        1.000
```

Jennrich and Moore (1975) show that this method can be used for
maximum likelihood estimation of parameters from a distribution in the
exponential family.

Robust Estimation

When your dependent variable contains outliers, a robust regression procedure can downweight their influence on the parameter estimates. Thus, the resulting estimates reflect the great bulk of the data and are not sensitive to the value of a few unusual cases. Here are the robust estimation procedures with their loss functions. They are available using the ROBUST command.

ABSOLUTE	The sum of absolute values of residuals (1st power).
POWER=n	The sum of nth power of absolute values of residuals. The default is 1.5.
TRIM=n	The n proportion of the residuals (those with the largest absolute values) are trimmed. Then, the sum of squares of the remaining residuals is minimized. The default is 0.05, the proportion trimmed.
HUBER=n	The sum of MAD standardized residuals weighted by Huber (n). The default is 1.7.
HAMPEL=$n1, n2, n3$	The sum of MAD standardized residuals weighted by Hampel $(n1, n2, n3)$. The default is 1.7, 3.4, 8.5.
T=df	The sum of $df/(df+u\verb|^|2)$, where u=residuals/MAD (residuals) and df is the degrees of freedom for the t distribution. The default is 5.0; the df of t.
BISQUARE=n	The sum of MAD standardized residuals weighted by Bisquare (n). The default is 7.0.

The parameters for HUBER, HAMPEL, T, and the BISQUARE are defined in MAD units (median absolute deviations from the median of the residuals).

Each procedure has a ψ function that is used to construct a weight for each residual (that is recomputed at each iteration). Here is the weighting scheme for the Hampel procedure (the heavy line is the Hampel ψ function):

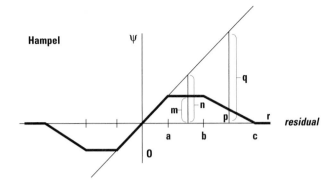

for | residual | < a   the weight (ψ(residual)/residual) is 1.0

a <| residual | < b   the weight is m/n

b <| residual | < c   the weight is p/q

c <| residual | the weight is 0.0

Nonlinear Model's default values for a, b, and c are 1.7, 3.4, and 8.5, respectively. So, if the size of the residual is less than 1.7, the weight is one; if it is over 8.5, the weight is zero. As the residual increases in absolute value, the weight decreases.

With commands:

```
MODEL statement
ROBUST ABSOLUTE or POWER=n or TRIM=n or HUBER=n or
       HAMPEL=n1,n2,n3 or T=n or BISQUARE=n
```

14.9 Measures of location

Robust estimators provide methods other than the mean, median, or mode to estimate the center of a distribution. The sample mean is the least squares estimate of location; that is, it is the point at which the squared deviations of the sample values are at a minimum. (The sample medians minimize absolute deviations instead of squared deviations.) In terms of the ψ weights described above, the usual mean assigns a weight of 1.0 to each observation, while the robust methods assign smaller weights to residuals far from the center.

In this example, we continue using sepal width of the Setosa iris flowers and **SELECT** species=1 (introduced in Example 14.7). We request the usual sample mean and then ask for a 10% trimmed mean, a Hampel estimator, and the median. But first, let's view the distribution graphically. Here are a box-and-whisker display and a dit plot of the data.

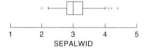 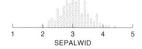

Except for the outlier at the left, the distribution of *SEPALWID* is slightly right-skewed.

Mean

In Example 14.7, we requested maximum likelihood estimates of the mean and standard deviation. Here is the least squares estimate:

```
NONLIN
    USE iris
    SELECT species = 1
    MODEL sepalwid = mean
    ESTIMATE
```

```
Iteration
No.     Loss          MEAN
 0 .560487D+03 .101000D+00
 1 .704080D+01 .342800D+01
 2 .704080D+01 .342800D+01

Dependent variable is SEPALWID

    Source    Sum-of-Squares   DF  Mean-Square
Regression         587.559      1      587.559
  Residual           7.041     49        0.144

     Total          594.600     50
Mean corrected        7.041     49

    Raw  R-square  (1-Residual/Total)       =    0.988
Mean corrected R**2 (1-Residual/Corrected) =    0.0
    R(observed vs predicted) square        =    0.0

                                          Wald Confidence Interval
Parameter      Estimate    A.S.E.   Param/ASE   Lower < 95%> Upper
    MEAN          3.428     0.054      63.946    3.320       3.536
```

Trimmed mean

We enter the following commands after viewing the results for the mean. Note that SYSTAT resets the starting values to their defaults when a new model is specified. If MODEL is not given, SYSTAT uses the final values from the last calculation as starting values for the current task. In Example 14.10, we also request several estimators, but do not respecify the model.

For this trimmed mean estimate, SYSTAT deletes the five cases (0.1 * 50 = 5) with the most extreme residuals.

```
MODEL sepalwid = trimmean
ROBUST TRIM = 0.1
ESTIMATE
```

```
Iteration
No.      Loss        TRIMMEAN
 0 .560487D+03 .101000D+00
 1 .704080D+01 .342800D+01
 2 .344888D+01 .342800D+01
 3 .337200D+01 .338667D+01
 4 .337200D+01 .338667D+01

TRIM robust regression: 45 cases had positive psi-weights.
                  The average psi-weight is 1.00000.

Dependent variable is SEPALWID

Zero weights, Missing data or estimates reduced degrees of freedom
   Source    Sum-of-Squares   DF   Mean-Square
Regression       587.474       1      587.474
   Residual        7.126      44        0.162

     Total        594.600      45
Mean corrected     7.041      44

     Raw  R-square  (1-Residual/Total)       =      0.988
Mean corrected R**2 (1-Residual/Corrected) =      0.0
     R(observed vs predicted) square        =      0.0

                                              Wald Confidence Interval
Parameter        Estimate   A.S.E.   Param/ASE    Lower < 95%> Upper
  TRIMMEAN          3.387    0.060     56.451      3.266      3.508
```

The trimmed estimate deletes the outlier, plus the four flowers on the right side of the distribution with width equal to or greater than 4.0 (if you select the **Long** mode of output, you would see that these flowers have the largest residuals).

Hampel

We now request a Hampel estimator using the default values for its parameters.

```
MODEL sepalwid = hamp_est
ROBUST HAMPEL
ESTIMATE
```

```
Iteration
No.      Loss       HAMP_EST
 0 .560487D+03 .101000D+00
 1 .704080D+01 .342800D+01
 2 .494767D+01 .342800D+01
 3 .493065D+01 .341728D+01
 4 .492759D+01 .341556D+01
 5 .492723D+01 .341535D+01
 6 .492718D+01 .341533D+01
 7 .492718D+01 .341532D+01
 8 .492718D+01 .341532D+01

HAMPEL robust regression:  50 cases had positive psi-weights.
                           The average psi-weight is 0.94311.

Dependent variable is SEPALWID

    Source     Sum-of-Squares   DF   Mean-Square
Regression         587.551       1      587.551
  Residual           7.049      49        0.144

    Total          594.600      50
Mean corrected       7.041      49

    Raw  R-square  (1-Residual/Total)      =      0.988
Mean corrected R**2 (1-Residual/Corrected) =      0.0
       R(observed vs predicted) square     =      0.0

                                              Wald Confidence Interval
Parameter        Estimate     A.S.E.    Param/ASE    Lower < 95%> Upper
HAMP_EST            3.415      0.054      63.673      3.308        3.523
```

The Hampel estimate (3.415) falls in between the trimmed mean and the mean.

Median

We let **NONLIN** minimize the absolute value of the residuals for an estimate of the median.

```
MODEL sepalwid = median
ROBUST ABSOLUTE
ESTIMATE
```

```
Iteration
No.      Loss       MEDIAN
 0 .560487D+03 .101000D+00
 1 .143680D+02 .342800D+01
 2 .142988D+02 .341647D+01
 3 .142499D+02 .340831D+01
 4 .142214D+02 .340357D+01
 5 .142081D+02 .340135D+01
 6 .142028D+02 .340047D+01
 7 .142010D+02 .340016D+01
 8 .142003D+02 .340005D+01
 9 .142001D+02 .340002D+01
10 .142000D+02 .340001D+01
11 .142000D+02 .340000D+01
12 .142000D+02 .340000D+01

ABSOLUTE robust regression:  50 cases had positive psi-weights.
                             The average psi-weight is 2418627.93032.
```

```
Dependent variable is SEPALWID

       Source    Sum-of-Squares    DF   Mean-Square
    Regression        587.520       1      587.520
      Residual          7.080      49        0.144

         Total        594.600      50
  Mean corrected        7.041      49

       Raw  R-square  (1-Residual/Total)      =      0.988
  Mean corrected R**2 (1-Residual/Corrected) =      0.0
        R(observed vs predicted) square      =      0.0

                                                    Wald Confidence Interval
  Parameter          Estimate       A.S.E.   Param/ASE      Lower < 95%> Upper
    MEDIAN              3.400          .          .            .          .
```

If you request the median for these data in the Basic Statistics procedure, the value is 3.4.

14.10 Regression

Usually, you would not use NONLIN for linear regression because GLM is available. If, however, you are concerned about the influence of outliers on the estimates of the coefficients, you should try one of Nonlinear Model's robust procedures. Let's redo Example 8.2 in Chapter 8.

The example uses the *OURWORLD* data file and we model the relation of military expenditures to gross domestic product using information reported by 57 countries to the United Nations. Each country is a case in our file and *MIL* and *GDP_CAP* are our two variables. In Chapter 8, we discovered that both variables require a log transformation, and that Iraq and Libya are outliers.

Here is a scatterplot of the data. The solid line is the least squares line-of-best fit for the complete sample (with its corresponding confidence band); the dotted line (and its confidence band) is the regression line after deleting Iraq and Libya from the sample. How do robust lines fit within original confidence bands?

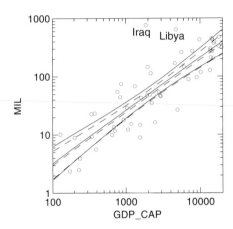

Visually, we see the dotted line-of-best fit falls slightly below the solid line for the complete sample. More striking, however, is the upper curve for the confidence band—the dotted line is considerably lower than the solid one.

Linear

In this section, we display NONLIN results for a least squares regression and then try the ABSOLUTE, HUBER, and TRIM robust estimation procedures.

```
NONLIN
    USE ourworld
    LET log_mil = L10(mil)
    LET log_gdp = L10(gdp_cap)
    MODEL log_mil = intercept + slope*log_gdp
    ESTIMATE
```

```
Dependent variable is LOG_MIL

Zero weights, missing data or estimates reduced degrees of freedom
     Source   Sum-of-Squares   df   Mean-Square
 Regression       194.332       2      97.166
   Residual         6.481      54       0.120

     Total         200.813     56
Mean corrected      24.349     55

        Raw  R-square (1-Residual/Total)        =     0.968
Mean corrected R-square (1-Residual/Corrected) =     0.734
        R(observed vs predicted) square        =     0.734

                                              Wald Confidence Interval
Parameter      Estimate    A.S.E.   Param/ASE    Lower < 95%> Upper
INTERCEPT        -1.308     0.257     -5.091     -1.822      -0.793
SLOPE             0.909     0.075     12.201      0.760       1.058
```

The estimate of the intercept (−1.308) and the slope (0.909) are the same as those produced by GLM. Stem-and-leaf plots of the residuals and studentized residuals are displayed in Chapter 8.

The residual for Iraq (1.216) is identified as an outlier—its Studentized value is 4.004. Libya's residual is 0.77.

1st power

We now estimate the same model using a least absolute values loss function (**first power regression**). We do not respecify the model, so by default, SYSTAT uses our last estimates as starting values. To avoid this, we specify **START** without an argument.

```
ROBUST ABSOLUTE
ESTIMATE / START
```

```
Iteration
 No.     Loss       INTERCEPT    SLOPE
  0 .119361D+03 .101000D+00 .102000D+00
  1 .147084D+02-.130751D+01 .909014D+00
  2 .146579D+02-.135163D+01 .919628D+00
  3 .146302D+02-.138083D+01 .926673D+00
  4 .146142D+02-.140215D+01 .931814D+00
  5 .146139D+02-.140402D+01 .932266D+00
  6 .146135D+02-.140636D+01 .932831D+00
  7 .146130D+02-.140918D+01 .933513D+00
  8 .146125D+02-.141248D+01 .934310D+00
  9 .146118D+02-.141622D+01 .935214D+00
 10 .146111D+02-.142033D+01 .936207D+00
 11 .146104D+02-.142471D+01 .937267D+00
 12 .146096D+02-.142924D+01 .938362D+00
 13 .146089D+02-.143375D+01 .939451D+00
 14 .146082D+02-.143801D+01 .940481D+00
 15 .146075D+02-.141174D+01 .941383D+00
 16 .146070D+02-.144461D+01 .942075D+00
 17 .146068D+02-.144633D+01 .942491D+00
 18 .146066D+02-.144701D+01 .942656D+00
 19 .146066D+02-.144717D+01 .942695D+00
 20 .146066D+02-.144720D+01 .942701D+00
 21 .146066D+02-.144720D+01 .942702D+00

ABSOLUTE robust regression:    56 cases have positive psi-weights
                               The average psi-weight is 40210712082202.71000

Dependent variable is LOG_MIL

Zero weights, missing data or estimates reduced degrees of freedom
   Source    Sum-of-Squares  df  Mean-Square
Regression       194.271      2     97.136
  Residual         6.542     54      0.121

     Total        200.813     56
Mean corrected      24.349    55

     Raw  R-square (1-Residual/Total)       =     0.967
Mean corrected R-square (1-Residual/Corrected) =   0.731
        R(observed vs predicted) square     =     0.734

                                              Wald Confidence Interval
Parameter          Estimate    A.S.E.    Param/ASE    Lower < 95%> Upper
INTERCEPT           -1.447       .           .           .         .
SLOPE                0.943       .           .           .         .
```

Huber

For the Hampel estimator, the weights begin to be less than 1.0 after the value of the first parameter (1.7). For this Huber estimate, we let the weight taper off sooner by setting the parameter at 1.5.

```
ROBUST HUBER = 1.5
ESTIMATE / START
```

```
Iteration
 No.     Loss       INTERCEP     SLOPE
  0 .119361D+03 .101000D+00 .102000D+00
  1 .648115D+01-.130751D+01 .909014D+00
  2 .440129D+01-.130751D+01 .909014D+00
  3 .437575D+01-.133598D+01 .913222D+00
  4 .423449D+01-.134979D+01 .916520D+00
  5 .421525D+01-.136344D+01 .919986D+00
  6 .420907D+01-.136871D+01 .921305D+00
  7 .420581D+01-.137068D+01 .921795D+00
  8 .420451D+01-.137148D+01 .921995D+00
  9 .420399D+01-.137181D+01 .922077D+00
 10 .420378D+01-.137194D+01 .922110D+00
 11 .420369D+01-.137199D+01 .922123D+00
 12 .420366D+01-.137201D+01 .922128D+00
 13 .420364D+01-.137202D+01 .922130D+00
 14 .420364D+01-.137203D+01 .922131D+00
 15 .420363D+01-.137203D+01 .922132D+00
```

```
HUBER robust regression:  56 cases had positive psi-weights.
                          The average psi-weight is 0.92192.

Dependent variable is  LOG_MIL

Zero weights, Missing data or estimates reduced degrees of freedom
   Source    Sum-of-Squares   DF  Mean-Square
   Regression     194.306      2     97.153
   Residual         6.507     54      0.121

      Total        200.813    56
Mean corrected      24.349    55

      Raw  R-square  (1-Residual/Total)       =    0.968
Mean corrected R**2 (1-Residual/Corrected)  =    0.733
      R(observed vs predicted) square         =    0.734

                                                   Wald Confidence Interval
Parameter        Estimate      A.S.E.    Param/ASE    Lower < 95%> Upper
INTERCEPT          -1.372       0.257      -5.331     -1.888    -0.856
   SLOPE            0.922       0.075      12.353      0.772     1.072
```

5% trim

In the linear regression version of this example, we removed Iraq from the sample by specifying:

SELECT mil < 700 *or* SELECT country$ <> 'Iraq'

Here, we ask for 5% trimming (0.05*56=2.8 or 2 cases):

ROBUST TRIM = .05
ESTIMATE / START

```
Iteration
No.     Loss       INTERCEP       SLOPE
 0 .119361D+03 .101000D+00 .102000D+00
 1 .648115D+01-.130751D+01 .909014D+00
 2 .500359D+01-.130751D+01 .909014D+00
 3 .497569D+01-.135311D+01 .915937D+00
 4 .497569D+01-.135311D+01 .915937D+00

TRIM robust regression: 54 cases had positive psi-weights.
                        The average psi-weight is 1.00000.

Dependent variable is  LOG_MIL

Zero weights, Missing data or estimates reduced degrees of freedom
   Source    Sum-of-Squares   DF  Mean-Square
   Regression     194.256      2     97.128
   Residual         6.557     52      0.126

      Total        200.813    54
Mean corrected      24.349    53

      Raw  R-square  (1-Residual/Total)       =    0.967
Mean corrected R**2 (1-Residual/Corrected)  =    0.731
      R(observed vs predicted) square         =    0.734

                                                   Wald Confidence Interval
Parameter        Estimate      A.S.E.    Param/ASE    Lower < 95%> Upper
INTERCEP           -1.332        .          .          .         .
   SLOPE            0.905        .          .          .         .
```

More Examples

The following examples illustrate a few NONLIN applications. Like GLM, it encompasses a variety of models and allows you to solve problems that are often "hard-wired" in other packages.

14.11 Piecewise regression

Sometimes we need to fit two different regression functions to the same data. For example, sales of a certain product might be strongly related to quality when advertising budgets are below a certain level—that is, when sales are generated by "word of mouth." Above this advertising budget level, sales may be less strongly related to quality of goods and more by marketing and advertising factors. In these cases, we can fit different sections of the data with different models. It is easier to combine these into a single model, however.

Here is an example of a quadratic function with a ceiling using data from Gilfoil (1982). This particular study is one of several that show that dialog menu interfaces are preferred by inexperienced computer users and that command based interfaces are preferred by experienced users. The data below are for one subject. The variable *SESSION* is the session number and *TASKS* is the number of user-controlled tasks (as opposed to dialog) chosen by the subject during a session. The data are in the file *LEARN*.

SESSION	TASKS	SESSION	TASKS
1	0	11	5
2	0	12	6
3	0	13	6
4	1	14	6
5	0	15	6
6	1	16	6
7	1	17	6
8	6	18	6
9	6	19	6
10	6	20	6

We fit these data with a quadratic model for earlier sessions and a ceiling for later sessions. We use NONLIN to estimate the point where the learning hits this ceiling (at six tasks). Here is the *Quick Graph* that results from this analysis:

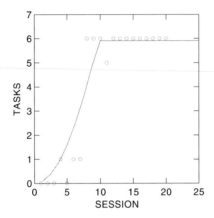

The commands are:

```
NONLIN
    USE learn
    PRINT = LONG
    MODEL tasks = b*session^2*(session<known) +,
                  b*known^2*(session>=known)
    ESTIMATE
```

Note that the expressions (SESSION<KNOWN *and* SESSION>=KNOWN) control which function is to be used—the quadratic or the horizontal line.

```
Dependent variable is TASKS

      Source    Sum-of-Squares   DF   Mean-Square
  Regression        445.582       2      222.791
    Residual         14.418      18        0.801

       Total        460.000      20
Mean corrected      140.000      19

      Raw  R-square  (1-Residual/Total)      =     0.969
Mean corrected R**2 (1-Residual/Corrected) =     0.897
       R(observed vs predicted) square      =     0.912

                                                    Wald Confidence Interval
Parameter      Estimate     A.S.E.    Param/ASE      Lower < 95%> Upper
B                 0.063      0.007       8.762        0.048       0.079
KNOWN             9.660      0.594      16.269        8.412      10.907

             TASKS        TASKS
   Case    Observed     Predicted      Residual
      1       0.0         0.063         -0.063
      2       0.0         0.253         -0.253
      3       0.0         0.570         -0.570
      4       1.000       1.013         -0.013
      5       0.0         1.583         -1.583
      6       1.000       2.280         -1.280
      7       1.000       3.103         -2.103
      8       6.000       4.053          1.947
      9       6.000       5.130          0.870
```

```
        10      6.000       5.909        0.091
        11      5.000       5.909       -0.909
        12      6.000       5.909        0.091
        13      6.000       5.909        0.091
        14      6.000       5.909        0.091
        15      6.000       5.909        0.091
        16      6.000       5.909        0.091
        17      6.000       5.909        0.091
        18      6.000       5.909        0.091
        19      6.000       5.909        0.091
        20      6.000       5.909        0.091

  Asymptotic Correlation Matrix of Parameters
                          B          KNOWN
     B                  1.000
     KNOWN             -0.928        1.000
```

From the *Quick Graph*, we see that the fit at the lower end is not impressive. We might want to fit a truncated logistic model (see below in this chapter) instead of a quadratic because learning is more often represented with this type of function. This model would have a logistic curve at the lower values of *SESSION* and a flat ceiling line at the upper end. We should use a LOSS also to make the fit maximum likelihood.

Piecewise linear regression models with unknown breakpoints can be fitted similarly. These models look like this:

$$y = b0 + b1*x + b2*(x–\text{break})*(x>\text{break})$$

If the break point is known, then you can use GLM to do ordinary regression to fit the separate pieces. See Neter, Wasserman, and Kutner (1985) for an example.

14.12 Kinetic models

You can also use NONLIN to test kinetic models. The following analysis models competitive inhibition for an enzyme inhibitor. The data are adapted from a conference session on statistical computing with microcomputers (Greco, et al., 1982). We will fit three variables: initial enzyme velocity (*V*), concentration of the substrate (*S*), and concentration of the inhibitor (*I*). The parameters of the model are the maximum velocity (*VMAX*), the Michaelis constant (*KM*), and the dissociation constant of the enzyme-inhibitor complex (*KIS*). The model to estimate is:

$$V = VMAX \frac{S}{KM\left(1 + \dfrac{1}{KIS}\right) + S}$$

The data are in the file *ENZYME*.

V	S	I		V	S	I
.021	.25	.5		.545	5.00	.2
.022	.25	.5		.303	.25	.0
.038	.50	.5		.310	.25	.0
.036	.50	.5		.451	.50	.0
.081	1.25	.5		.465	.50	.0
.085	1.25	.5		.752	1.25	.0
.162	2.50	.5		.694	1.25	.0
.150	2.50	.5		.950	2.50	.0
.225	3.75	.5		.929	2.50	.0
.210	3.75	.5		1.020	3.75	.0
.294	5.00	.5		1.013	3.75	.0
.269	5.00	.5		1.072	5.00	.0
.048	.25	.2		1.059	5.00	.0
.048	.25	.2		.323	.25	.0
.088	.50	.2		.310	.25	.0
.089	.50	.2		.479	.50	.0
.188	1.25	.2		.454	.50	.0
.177	1.25	.2		.756	1.25	.0
.318	2.50	.2		.723	1.25	.0
.318	2.50	.2		.964	2.50	.0
.447	3.75	.2		1.054	3.75	.0
.447	3.75	.2		1.040	3.75	.0
.553	5.00	.2		1.094	5.00	.0

```
NONLIN
    USE ENZYME
    PRINT = LONG
    MODEL V = VMAX*S / (KM*(1 + I/KIS) + S)
    ESTIMATE / MIN = 0,0,0
```

```
Dependent variable is V

    Source    Sum-of-Squares   DF   Mean-Square
  Regression       15.404       3      5.135
   Residual         0.014      43      0.000

     Total          15.418     46
Mean corrected       5.763     45

    Raw  R-square  (1-Residual/Total)       =        0.999
Mean corrected R**2 (1-Residual/Corrected) =        0.998
     R(observed vs predicted) square        =        0.998

                                               Wald Confidence Interval
Parameter        Estimate      A.S.E.    Param/ASE    Lower < 95%> Upper
VMAX              1.260         0.012      104.192      1.235       1.284
KM                0.847         0.027       31.876      0.793       0.900
KIS               0.027         0.001       31.033      0.025       0.029

Asymptotic Correlation Matrix of Parameters
                    VMAX          KM          KIS
VMAX               1.000
KM                 0.866        1.000
KIS                0.466        0.673        1.000
```

You could try alternative models for these data such as one for uncompetitive inhibition,

$$V = VMAX \frac{S}{KM + S\left(1 + \dfrac{I}{KII}\right)}$$

or one for noncompetitive inhibition,

$$V = VMAX \frac{S}{KM\left(1 + \dfrac{1}{KIS}\right) + S\left(1 + \dfrac{I}{KII}\right)}$$

where *KII* is the dissociation constant of the enzyme-inhibitor-substrate complex.

14.13 A logistic model for quantal response data

The following data, in the data file *DOSE*, are from a toxicity study for a drug designed to combat tumors. The table shows the proportion of laboratory rats dying (*RESPONSE*) at each dose level (*DOSE*) of the drug. Clinical studies usually scale dose in natural logarithm units, which are listed in the center column (*LOGDOS*). We arbitrarily set the *LOGDOS* to -4 for zero *DOSE* for the purpose of plotting and fitting with a linear model.

Dose	Log Dose	Response
0.00	−4.000	0.026
0.10	−2.303	0.120
0.25	−1.386	0.088
0.50	−0.693	0.169
1.00	0.000	0.281
2.50	0.916	0.443
5.00	1.609	0.632
10.00	2.303	0.718
25.00	3.219	0.820
50.00	3.912	0.852
100.00	4.605	0.879

A model lacking meaning

The plot of *RESPONSE* against *LOGDOSE* is clearly curvilinear. The S-shaped function suggests that we could use a linear model with linear, quadratic, and cubic terms (that is, a polynomial function) to fit a curved line to the data. Here are the results from GLM:

```
Dep Var:RESPONSE      N:   11   Multiple R:  .993   Squared Multiple R:  .986
Adjusted squared multiple R:  .980    Standard Error of Estimate:      0.047

   Variable   Coefficient   Std Error   Std Coef Tolerance    T    P(2 tail)

CONSTANT          0.314       0.021      0.000   .         15.317   0.000
LOGDOSE           0.166       0.013      1.344   .168      12.486   0.000
LOGDOSE*
LOGDOSE           0.009       0.002      0.202   .771       4.027   0.005
LOGDOSE*
LOGDOSE*
LOGDOSE          -0.004       0.001     -0.492   .152      -4.344   0.003
```

Notice that all the coefficients are highly significant and that the overall fit is excellent ($R^2 = 0.986$). Even the tolerances are relatively large, so we need not worry about collinearity. The residual plots for this function are reasonably well behaved. There is no significant autocorrelation in the residuals.

The following figure shows the observed data and the fitted curve:

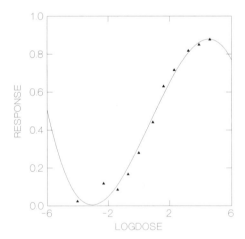

How do the researchers interpret this plot? First of all, the curve is consistent with the printed output; it fits extremely well in the range of the data. Putting the fitted curve into ordinary language, we can say that fewer animals die at lower dosages and more at higher. At the extremes, however, more animals die with extremely low dosages and fewer animals die at extremely high dosages.

This is nonsense. While it is possible to imagine some drugs (arsenic, for example) for which dose-response functions are nonmonotonic, the model we fit makes no sense for a clinical drug of this sort. Second, the cubic function we fit extrapolates beyond the 0–1 response interval. It implies that there is something beyond dying and something less than living. Third, the parameters of the model we fit have no theoretical interpretation.

A logistic model

Clinical researchers usually prefer to fit quantal response data like these with a bounded monotonic response function of the following form:

$$\text{proportion dying} = \alpha + \frac{1 - \alpha}{1 + e^{[\beta - g\,log(\text{dose})]}}$$

α	The background response, or rate of dying
β	A location parameter for the curve
γ	A slope parameter for the curve

Estimating a quantity called *LD50* is the usual purpose of this type of study. *LD50* is the dose at which 50% of the animals are expected to die. *LD50* is:

$$e^{\beta/g}(1 - 2\alpha)^{1/g}$$

Notice how the parameters of this model make theoretical sense. We have a problem, however. We cannot fit an intrinsically nonlinear model like this with a linear regression program. We cannot even transform this equation, using logs or other mathematical operators, to a linear form. The cubic linear model we fit before was nonlinear in the data but linear in the parameters. Linear models involve additive combinations of parameters. The model we want to fit now is nonlinear in the data *and* nonlinear in the parameters.

We need a program that fits this type of model iteratively. NONLIN begins with initial estimates of parameter values and modifies them in small steps until the fit of the curve to the data is as close as possible. Here is the result:

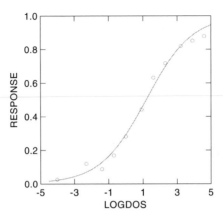

Notice how the curve tapers at the ends so that it is bounded by 0 and 1 on the *RESPONSE* scale. This behavior fits our theoretical ideas about the effect of this drug. The value for *LD50* is 3.262, which is in raw *DOSE* units. The Wald interval in the following output indicates it could vary from 2.48 to 4.04.

Here are the commands we used to estimate the logistic model parameters:

```
USE dose
MODEL response = alpha + (1-alpha)/,
                 (1 + EXP(beta-gamma*logdose))
FUNPAR logld50 = beta/gamma + log(1-2*alpha)/gamma
FUNPAR ld50 = EXP(beta/gamma)*(1-2*alpha)^(1/gamma)
ESTIMATE
```

```
Dependent variable is RESPONSE

    Source    Sum-of-Squares   DF   Mean-Square
  Regression       3.401        3      1.134
  Residual         0.012        8      0.001

    Total          3.412       11
Mean corrected     1.114       10

     Raw  R-square  (1-Residual/Total)      =        0.997
Mean corrected R**2 (1-Residual/Corrected) =        0.989
     R(observed vs predicted) square        =        0.990

                                              Wald Confidence Interval
Parameter      Estimate     A.S.E.   Param/ASE    Lower < 95%> Upper
ALPHA            0.003       0.037      0.089      -0.082      0.089
BETA             0.898       0.190      4.732       0.460      1.335
GAMMA            0.754       0.073     10.394       0.586      0.921
LOGLD50          1.200       0.253      4.742       0.616      1.783
LD50             3.262       0.339      9.620       2.480      4.044
```

Interestingly, this model does not fit significantly better than the cubic polynomial. Both have comparable values of R^2 (for the cubic it is 0.986 and for the logistic it is 0.990). True, the cubic model has four parameters and we have three. Nevertheless, this example should convince you that blind searching for models that produce good fits is not good science. It is even possible that a model with a poorer fit can be the true model generating data and one with a better fit can be bogus.

Summary

Computation

The Quasi-Newton method is described in Fletcher (1972) and is sometimes called modified Fletcher/Powell. Modifications include the LDL'Cholesky factorization in Time Series for ARIMA estimation. The Simplex method is adapted from O'Neill (1971), with several revisions noted in Griffiths and Hill (1985).

The loss function is computed in two steps. First, the MODEL statement is evaluated for a case using current values of the parameters and data. Second, the LOSS statement is evaluated using the estimate (computed as the result of the MODEL statement evaluation) and other parameter and data values. These two steps are repeated for all cases, over which the results of the loss function are summed. The summed loss is then minimized by the Quasi-Newton or Simplex procedure. Step halvings are used in the minimizations when MODEL or LOSS statement evaluations overflow or result in illegal values. If repeated step halvings down to machine epsilon (error limit) fail to remedy this situation, iterations cease with an "Illegal values" message.

Asymptotic standard errors are computed by the central differencing finite approximation of the Hessian matrix. Some nonlinear regression programs compute standard errors by squaring the Jacobian matrix of first derivatives. Others use different methods altogether. For linear models, all valid methods produce identical results. For some nonlinear models, however, the results may differ. The Hessian approach, which works well for nonlinear regression, is also ideally suited for Nonlinear Model's maximum likelihood estimation.

References

Bates, D.M., and Watts, D.G. 1988. *Nonlinear regression and its applications*, New York: John Wiley & Sons, Inc.

Clark, G.P.Y. 1987. Approximate confidence limits for a parameter function in nonlinear regression, *Journal of the American Statistical Association*, 82: 221-230.

Cook, R.D., and Weisberg, S. 1990. Confidence curves in nonlinear regression, *Journal of the American Statistical Association*, 85: 544-551.

Cox, D.R. 1970. *The analysis of binary data*. New York: Halsted Press.

Fletcher, R. 1972. *FORTRAN subroutines for minimization by Quasi-Newton methods*. AERE R. 7125.

Griffiths, P., and Hill, I.D. 1985. *Applied statistics algorithms*. Chichester: Ellis Horwood Limited.

Gilfoil, D.M. 1982. Warming up to computers: A study of cognitive and affective interaction over time, in *Proceedings: Human factors in computer systems*. Washington, D.C.: Association for Computing Machinery.

Greco, W.R., et. al. 1982. ROSFIT: An enzyme kinetics nonlinear regression curve fitting package for a microcomputer. *Computers and Biomedical Research*, 15: 39-45.

Hill, M.A., and Engelman, L. 1992. Graphical aids for nonlinear regression and discriminant analysis. *Computational Statistics,* vol. 2, Y. Dodge and J. Whittaker, eds. Proceedings of the 10th Symposium on Computational Statistics Physica-Verlag, 111–126.

Jennrich, R.I., and Moore, R.H. 1975. Maximum likelihood estimation by means of nonlinear least squares. *Proceedings of the Statistical Computing Section*, American Statistical Association, 57-65.

Neter, J., and Wasserman, W., and Kutner, M. 1985. *Applied linear statistical models*, 2nd ed. Homewood, Ill.: Richard E. Irwin, Inc.

O'Neill, R. 1971. Functions minimization usign a simplex procedure. Algorithms AS 47. *Applied Statistics*, 338.

Rousseeuw, P.J., and Leroy, A.M. 1987. *Robust regression and outlier detection*. New York: John Wiley & Sons, Inc.

Loglinear Models

Laszlo Engelman

Loglinear Model (LOGLIN command) is useful for analyzing relationships among the factors of a multiway frequency table. The loglinear procedure computes maximum likelihood estimates of the parameters of a loglinear model by using the Newton-Ralphson method. For each user-specified model, a test-of-fit of the model is provided, along with observed and expected cell frequencies, estimates of the loglinear parameters (lambdas), standard errors of the estimates, the ratio of each lambda to its standard error, and multiplicative effects (EXP(lambda)).

For each cell, you can request its contribution to the Pearson chi-square or the likelihood ratio chi-square. Deviates, standardized deviates, Freeman-Tukey deviates, and likelihood ratio deviates are available to characterize departures of the observed values from expected values.

When searching for the *best* model, you can request tests after removing each first-order effect or interaction term one at a time individually or hierarchically (when a lower-order effect is removed, so are its respective interaction terms). The models do not need to be hierarchical.

A model can explain the frequencies well in most cells, but poorly in a few. LOGLIN uses Freeman-Tukey deviates to identify the most divergent cell, fit a model without it, and continue in a stepwise manner identifying other outlier cells that depart from your model.

You can specify cells that contain structural zeros (cells that are empty naturally or by design, not by sampling), and fit a model to the subset of cells that remain. A test of fit for such a model is often called a test of quasi-independence.

For each level of a term included in your model, you can save the estimate of lambda, the standard error of lambda, the ratio of lambda to its standard error, the multiplicative effect, and the marginal indices of the effect. Alternatively, for each cell, you can save the observed and expected frequencies and its deviates (listed above), the Pearson and likelihood ratio chi-square contributions to the log-likelihood, and the cell indices.

Overview

Getting started

Examples

Loglinear Models

Overview

The Loglinear Model (LOGLIN command) procedure has the following options:

MODEL   Specify the loglinear model, including both the frequency table and the terms (or effects) in the model to fit.

ZERO   Use CELL to specify the indices of the cells to treat as structural zeros, or use EMPTY to treat all cells with zero frequency or structural zeros.

PRINT   Select specific reports to display.

ESTIMATE   Specify options for controlling the computations.

TABULATE   Specify a frequency table with no analysis.

Researchers fit loglinear models to the cell frequencies of a multiway table in order to describe relationships among the categorical variables that form the table. A loglinear model expresses the logarithm of the expected cell frequency as a linear function of certain parameters in a manner similar to that of analysis of variance. Recall that the **expected value** for a two-way table cell in row i and column j is:

$$\frac{(\text{row } i \text{ total}) \cdot (\text{column } j \text{ total})}{\text{total table count}} \quad \text{or} \quad \frac{R_i \cdot C_j}{\text{total}}$$

Taking natural logarithms:

$$ln\,F_{ij} = ln(1/\text{total}) + ln(R_i) + ln(C_j)$$

So, the computation of the log of the expected value of each cell frequency involves a contribution from the particular row the cell is in and a contribution from its column.

For a two-way table with factors A and B, the complete loglinear model is:

$$ln\,F_{ij} = \theta + \lambda_{A_i} + \lambda_{B_j} + \lambda_{AB_{ij}}$$

where F is the expected value of the cell frequency, i ranges from 1 to the number of rows, j ranges from 1 to the number of columns, θ is the overall mean effect, and the parameters λ sum to 0 over the levels of the row factors and column factors. An important distinction between ANOVA and loglinear modeling is: in the latter, the focus is on the need for interaction terms; in ANOVA, testing for main effects is the primary interest. The usual χ^2 test of independence of two-way table factors tests that the $\lambda_{AB_{ij}}$ interaction terms are 0 for all cells simultaneously.

For a particular cell in a three-way table (a cell in the i row, j column, and k level of the third factor C), the expression is:

$$ln\,F_{ijk} = \theta + \lambda_{A_i} + \lambda_{B_j} + \lambda_{C_k} + \lambda_{AB_{ij}} + \lambda_{AC_{ik}} + \lambda_{BC_{jk}} + \lambda_{ABC_{ijk}}$$

where the λs are the **effects** for variables A, B, and C and sum to 0 when summed over the levels of each index. The **order of the effect** is the number of indices in the subscript.

The loglinear model for a three-way table is **saturated** because it contains all possible terms or effects. Various smaller models can be formed by including only selected combinations of effects (or equivalently testing that certain effects are 0). An important goal in loglinear modeling is "parsimony"—that is, to see how few effects are needed to estimate the cell frequencies. You usually don't want to test that the main effect of a factor is 0 because this is the same as testing that the total frequencies are equal for all levels of the factor. For example, a test that the main effect for *SURVIVE$* (alive, dead) is 0 simply tests whether the total number of survivors equals the number of nonsurvivors. If no interaction terms are included and the test is not significant (that is, the model fits), you can report that the table factors are independent. When there are more than two second-order effects, the test of an interaction is conditional on the other interactions and may not have a simple interpretation.

Getting started   Loglinear analysis is available only by using SYSTAT commands. You can submit LOGLIN commands at the command prompt in the Main window; submit commands from the Command Editor; or use **Stats➠Loglinear Model** and submit commands in the **Loglinear Model** window.

The LOGLIN command offers the following options:

Loglinear model
```
MODEL vars defining table = terms of table
PRINT argument / options
ZERO CELL=n1,n2, ... CELL=... or EMPTY
ESTIMATE / options
```

Multiway table only
```
TABULATE var1 * var2 ...
```

   To display the command prompt in the Main window, use **Edit➠Options** and select **Command Prompt**.

Examples

In this chapter, you use the Morrison breast cancer data stored in the *CANCER* data file (Bishop, et al. (1975)) and treat the data as a four-way frequency table:

CENTER$ Center or city where the data were collected
SURVIVE$ Survival—dead or alive
AGE   Age groups of under 50, 50 to 69, and 70 or over
TUMOR$ Tumor diagnosis (called *INFLAPP* by some researchers)
             with levels
             – Minimal inflammation and benign
             – Greater inflammation and benign
             – Minimal inflammation and malignant
             – Greater inflammation and malignant

The analysis of a multiway table can be separated into three steps:

– First, screen for an appropriate model to test.
– Test the model, and if not significant (meaning it fits), delete one or more effects and compare results. If significant, compare results with those for models with one or more terms.
– For the model you select as best, examine expected values and deviates looking for cells (or layers within the table) with large differences between observed and expected cell counts.

How do you determine which effects or terms to include in your loglinear model? Ideally, by using your knowledge of the subject matter of your study, you have a specific model in mind—that is, you want to make statements regarding the independence of certain table factors. Otherwise, you may want to screen for effects as shown in Example 15.3.

Note: *If you want to form only a multiway table (no analysis is needed), see Example 15.5.*

15.1
A model
for the
CANCER data

This first example uses MODEL to fit a specific model and explains the "short" output panels (obtained by using **Edit▸Options** or the PRINT command to set output length to **Short**). Example 15.2 describes results for the **Medium** mode. Later, Example 15.3 will show how to screen for effects to include when you are uncertain about what model to fit.

For the first model of the *CANCER* data, you include three two-way interactions. Using the first letter of each table factor as a shortcut notation, the model is:

$$ln\,F_{ijkl} \;=\; \theta + C + A + S + T + AC + SC + TC$$

The *CANCER* data include one record for each of the 72 cells formed by the four table factors. Each record includes a variable, *NUMBER*, that has the number of women in the cell plus numeric or character value codes to identify the levels of the four factors that define the cell. (Use **Data▸ Frequency** to tell SYSTAT that *NUMBER* contains cell counts; that is, each record represents more than one case.) For more details about table input, see Example 2.3 in Chapter 2.

The MODEL statement has two parts: table factors and terms (*effects to fit*). Table factors appear to the left of the equal sign and terms are on the right. The layout of the table is determined by the order in which the variables are specified—for example, specify *TUMOR$* last so its levels determine the columns.

The LABEL statement assigns category names to the numeric codes for *AGE*. If the statement is omitted, the data values label the categories. By default, SYSTAT orders string variables alphabetically, so you specify SORT = NONE to list the categories for the other factors as they first appear in the data file.

Use ESTIMATE to select options for controlling the computations. Here you specify DELTA = 0.5 to add 0.5 to each cell frequency. This option is common in multiway table procedures as an aid when some cell sizes are sparse. It is of little use in practice and is used here only to make the results compare with those reported elsewhere.

```
LOGLIN
    USE cancer
    FREQ = number
    LABEL age / 50='Under 50', 60='50 to 69',
             70='70 & Over'
    ORDER center$ survive$ tumor$ / SORT=NONE
    MODEL center$*age*survive$*tumor$ = center$ + age,
                                    + survive$ + tumor$,
                                    + age*center$,
                                    + survive$*center$,
                                    + tumor$*center$
    PRINT SHORT / EXPECT LAMBDAS
    ESTIMATE / DELTA=0.5
```

❶ Number of cells (product of levels):   72
                         Total count: 764

❷ Observed Frequencies

CENTER$	AGE	SURVIVE$	TUMOR$			
			MinMalig	MinBengn	MaxMalig	MaxBengn
Tokyo	Under 50	Dead	9	7	4	3
		Alive	26	68	25	9
	50 to 69	Dead	9	9	11	2
		Alive	20	46	18	5
	70 & Over	Dead	2	3	1	0
		Alive	1	6	5	1
Boston	Under 50	Dead	6	7	6	0
		Alive	11	24	4	0
	50 to 69	Dead	8	20	3	2
		Alive	18	58	10	3
	70 & Over	Dead	9	18	3	0
		Alive	15	26	1	1
Glamorgn	Under 50	Dead	16	7	3	0
		Alive	16	20	8	1
	50 to 69	Dead	14	12	3	0
		Alive	27	39	10	4
	70 & Over	Dead	3	7	3	0
		Alive	12	11	4	1

❸
```
Pearson ChiSquare   57.5272   df  51   Probability  0.24635
      LR ChiSquare   55.8327   df  51   Probability  0.29814
     Raftery's BIC -282.7342
     Dissimilarity    9.9530
```

❹ Expected Values
=============

CENTER$	AGE	SURVIVE$	TUMOR$			
			MinMalig	MinBengn	MaxMalig	MaxBengn
Tokyo	Under 50	Dead	7.852	15.928	7.515	2.580
		Alive	28.076	56.953	26.872	9.225
	50 to 69	Dead	6.281	12.742	6.012	2.064
		Alive	22.460	45.563	21.498	7.380
	70 & Over	Dead	1.165	2.363	1.115	0.383
		Alive	4.166	8.451	3.988	1.369
Boston	Under 50	Dead	5.439	12.120	2.331	0.699
		Alive	10.939	24.378	4.688	1.406
	50 to 69	Dead	11.052	24.631	4.737	1.421
		Alive	22.231	49.542	9.527	2.858
	70 & Over	Dead	6.754	15.052	2.895	0.868
		Alive	13.585	30.276	5.822	1.747
Glamorgn	Under 50	Dead	9.303	10.121	3.476	0.920
		Alive	19.989	21.746	7.468	1.977
	50 to 69	Dead	14.017	15.249	5.237	1.386
		Alive	30.117	32.764	11.252	2.979
	70 & Over	Dead	5.582	6.073	2.086	0.552
		Alive	11.993	13.048	4.481	1.186

❺ Log-Linear Parameters (Lambda)
================================

THETA

1.826

	CENTER$	
Tokyo	Boston	Glamorgn
0.049	0.001	-0.050

	AGE	
Under 50	50 to 69	70 & Over
0.145	0.444	-0.589

SURVIVE$	
Dead	Alive
-0.456	0.456

	TUMOR$		
MinMalig	MinBengn	MaxMalig	MaxBengn
0.480	1.011	-0.145	-1.346

CENTER$	AGE		
	Under 50	50 to 69	70 & Over
Tokyo	0.565	0.043	-0.609
Boston	-0.454	-0.043	0.497
Glamorgn	-0.111	-0.000	0.112

CENTER$	SURVIVE$	
	Dead	Alive
Tokyo	-0.181	0.181
Boston	0.107	-0.107
Glamorgn	0.074	-0.074

```
CENTER$ |                        TUMOR$
        |  MinMalig    MinBengn    MaxMalig    MaxBengn
--------+-------------------------------------------------
Tokyo   |   -0.368      -0.191       0.214       0.345
Boston  |    0.044       0.315      -0.178      -0.181
Glamorgn|    0.323      -0.123      -0.036      -0.164
--------+
```

❻ Lambda / SE(Lambda)
===============================
```
     THETA
------------
    1.826
------------
```

```
              CENTER$
   Tokyo      Boston      Glamorgn
----------------------------------------
   0.596       0.014       -0.586
----------------------------------------
```

```
                 AGE
 Under 50      50 to 69      70 & Over
----------------------------------------
   2.627         8.633        -8.649
----------------------------------------
```

```
       SURVIVE$
  Dead       Alive
---------------------------
  -11.548      11.548
---------------------------
```

```
                   TUMOR$
  MinMalig    MinBengn    MaxMalig    MaxBengn
------------------------------------------------
    6.775       15.730      -1.718      -10.150
------------------------------------------------
```

```
CENTER$ |                  AGE
        |  Under 50      50 to 69      70 & Over
--------+--------------------------------------------
Tokyo   |    7.348         0.576        -5.648
Boston  |   -5.755        -0.618         5.757
Glamorgn|   -1.418        -0.003         1.194
--------+
```

```
CENTER$ |   SURVIVE$
        |  Dead        Alive
--------+-----------------------
Tokyo   |  -3.207       3.207
Boston  |   1.959      -1.959
Glamorgn|   1.304      -1.304
--------+
```

```
CENTER$ |                        TUMOR$
        |  MinMalig    MinBengn    MaxMalig    MaxBengn
--------+-------------------------------------------------
Tokyo   |   -3.862      -2.292       2.012       2.121
Boston  |    0.425       3.385      -1.400      -0.910
Glamorgn|    3.199      -1.287      -0.289      -0.827
--------+
```

❼ Model ln(MLE): -160.563

❽ The 3 most outlandish cells (based on FTD, stepwise):
===

```
                                          CENTER$
                                          | AGE
                                          |  | SURVIVE$
      ln(MLE)  LR_ChiSq  p-value Frequency |  |  | TUMOR$
      --------  --------  -------  --------- -  -  -  -
      -154.685   11.755    0.001       7    1  1  1  2
      -150.685    8.001    0.005       1    2  3  2  3
      -145.024   11.321    0.001      16    3  1  1  1
```

The highlighted numbers below correspond to those in the output.

❶ You entered cases for 72 cells. The total frequency count across these cells is 764—that is, there are 764 women in the sample.

❷ *Observed Frequencies table.* Notice that the order of the factors is the same order you specified using MODEL.

❸ The test-of-fit is not significant for either the Pearson chi-square or the likelihood-ratio test, indicating that your model with its three two-way interactions does not disagree with the observed frequencies. The model statement describes an association between study center and age, survival, and tumor status. However, at each center, the other three factors are independent. Because your overall goal is parsimony, you will explore in Example 15.3 whether any of the interactions can be dropped.

Raftery's BIC (Bayesian Information Criterion) adjusts the chi-square for both the complexity of the model (measured by degrees of freedom) and the size of the sample. It is the likelihood ratio chi-square minus the degrees of freedom for the current model times the natural log of the sample size. If BIC is negative, you can conclude that the model is preferable to the saturated model. When comparing alternative models, select the model with the lowest BIC value.

The *Index of dissimilarity* can be interpreted as the percentage of cases that need to be relocated in order to make the observed and expected counts equal. For these data, you would have to move about 9.95% of the cases to make the expected frequencies fit.

❹ *Expected Values.* These are the F's in the model above and are obtained by fitting the loglinear model to the observed frequencies. Compare these values with those in ❷. To see how they are computed, see ❺.

❺ *Log-Linear Parameters (Lambda).* Here are the parameter estimates for the model you requested. Usually it is of more interest to examine these estimates divided by their standard errors (see ❻). Here, however, you display them in order to relate them to the expected values. For example, the observed frequency for the cell in the upper-left corner (Tokyo, Under 50, Dead, MinMalig) is 9. To find the expected frequency under your model, you add the estimates (from each panel, select the term that corresponds to your cell):

```
theta  1.826      CENTER$   0.049      C*A    0.565
                  AGE       0.145      C*S   -0.181
                  SURVIVE$ -0.456      C*T   -0.368
                  TUMOR$    0.480
```

and then use SYSTAT's calculator to sum the estimates:

$$ln\,F_{1111} = 1.826 + 0.049 + 0.145 - 0.456 + 0.480 + 0.565 - 0.181 - 0.368$$
$$= 2.06$$

that is, type

```
CALC 1.826 + 0.049 +...-0.368
```

and SYSTAT responds 2.06. Take the antilog of this value

```
CALC EXP(2.06)
```

and SYSTAT responds 7.846. In the panel of *Expected Values*, this number is printed as 7.852 (in its calculations, SYSTAT uses more digits following the decimal point). Thus, for this cell, the sample includes nine women (observed frequency) and the model predicts 7.85 women (expected frequency).

❻ *Lambda/SE(Lambda)*. The ratio of the parameter estimates to their asymptotic standard errors. This panel is part of the default output. Examine these values to better understand the relationships among the table factors. Because, for large samples, this ratio can be interpreted as a standard normal deviate (*z*-score), you can use it to indicate significant parameters—for example, for an interaction term, significant positive (or negative) associations. In the *CENTER$* by *AGE* panel, the ratio for young women from Tokyo is very large (7.348) implying a significant positive association, and that for older Tokyo women is extremely negative (–5.648). The reverse is true for the women from Boston. If you use the **Column percent** option in **Xtab** to print column percents for *CENTER$* by *AGE*, you will see that among the "Under 50" women, more than 50% of the women are from Tokyo (52.1), while only 23% are from Boston. In the "70 & Over" age group, 14% are from Tokyo and 55% from Boston.

The "Alive" estimate for Tokyo shows a strong positive association (3.207) with survival in Tokyo. The relationship in Boston is negative (–1.959). In this study, the overall survival rate is 72.5%. In Tokyo, 79.3% of the women survived, while in Boston 67.6% survived. There is a negative association for having a malignant tumor with minimal inflammation in Tokyo (–3.862). The same relationship is strongly positive in Glamorgan (3.199). Also see the discussion of multiplicative effects in ❷ in Example 15.2.

❼ *Model ln(MLE)*. The natural log of the maximum likelihood estimate.

❽ *The 3 most outlandish cells.* Cells that depart from the current model are identified here in a stepwise manner. The first cell has the largest Freeman-Tukey deviate (these deviates are similar to z-scores when the data are from a Poisson distrubution). It is treated as a structural zero (see Example 15.4), the model is fit to the remaining cells, and the cell with the largest Freeman-Tukey deviate is identified. This process continues step by step, each time including one more cell as a structural zero and refitting the model.

For the current model, the observations in the cell corresponding to the youngest non-survivors from Tokyo with benign tumors and minimal inflammation (Tokyo, Under 50, Dead, MinBengn) differs the most from its expected value. There are seven women in the cell and the expected value is 15.9 women. The next most unusual cell is 2,3,2,3 (Boston, 70 & Over, Alive, MaxMalig), and so on. See Example 15.4 for information on a strategy for outlier cells.

Shortcut notation for specifying the model

Use MODEL to specify both the frequency table, and the terms (or effects) in the model to fit. To define model terms, you can use the shortcut notation:

A .. D	Include all variables from A to D (if stored consecutively in the data file); that is, $A+B+C+D$
A # B	Include lower-order effects with the interaction term, that is, $A + B + A*B$
A..D^i or (A+B+C+D)^i	Include all ith and lower-order terms
−(...)	Remove terms (...) from preceding specification

Example 15.2 specifies the same model as that in Example 15.1, using the # notation to include the first-order effects arising from each interaction:

```
MODEL center$*age*survive$*tumor$ = age # center$,
                              + survive$ # center$,
                                  + tumor$ # center$
```

Example 15.4 demonstrates an even shorter way to specify the terms:

```
                = (age + survive$ + tumor$) # center$
```

Example 15.3 uses the ^2 notation to indicate a model that includes all second-order terms (two-way interactions) and their corresponding first-order effects; and follow this with a minus sign to exclude a specific interaction (*AGE * TUMOR$*):

```
MODEL center$*age*survive$*tumor$ = tumor$ .. center$^2,
                                  - age*tumor$
```

For complicated models, this notation can make model specification much shorter. For example, here is a model with all three-way and four-way terms (15 terms)!

```
A..E^4 - A..E^2
```

Extended results

You can control what report panels appear in the output by globally setting output length to **Short**, **Medium**, or **Long** in the **Edit➠Options** dialog box. You can also use the PRINT command in LOGLIN to request reports individually. You can specify individual panels by specifying the particular option. For example, to request all short panels plus the likelihood ratio deviate for each cell, type:

```
PRINT SHORT / LRDEV
```

Short. Short output panels are:

OBSFREQ	Observed frequency for each cell
CHISQ	Pearson and likelihood ratio chi-square statistics
RATIO	Lambda divided by the standard error of lambda
MLE	Log of the model's maximized likelihood value

plus a report of the three most outlandish cells.

Medium. Medium results include all of the above, plus the following:

EXPECT	Expected frequency for each cell (current model)
STAND	Standardized deviations
ELAMBDA	Multiplicative effects (EXP(lambda))
TERM	Test each term by removing it from the model
HTERM	Test each term by removing it and its higher-order interactions from the model

and the five most outlandish cells.

LONG. Long results add the following:

PARAM	Coefficients of design variables
COVA	Covariance matrix of the parameters
CORR	Correlation matrix of the parameters
LAMBDA	Additive effect of each level for each term
SELAMBDA	Standard errors of the lambdas
DEVIATES	Observed-expected frequency for each cell
PEARSON	Contribution to Pearson chi-square from each cell
LRDEV	Likelihood ratio deviate for each cell
FTDEV	Freeman-Tukey deviate for each cell
LOGLIKE	Contribution to model's log-likelihood from each cell

and the 10 most outlandish cells.

As a PRINT option, you can also specify CELLS=*n*, where *n* is the number of outlandish cells to identify.

Estimate options

Use ESTIMATE to specify computational controls:

```
ESTIMATE / CONV=n  LCONV=n  TOL=n  ITER=n  HALF=n  DELTA=n
```

CONV=*n*	Parameter convergence criteria. Default=0.0001
LCONV=*n*	Likelihood convergence criteria. Default=0.000001
TOL=*n*	Tolerance limit. Default=0.001
ITER=*n*	Maximum number of iterations. Default=10
HALF=*n*	Maximum number of step halvings. Default=10
DELTA=*n*	Constant value added to observed frequency in each cell. Default=0.0

Saving results

You can save the results of your analysis in a SYSTAT data file for later analysis. For example, if you plan to explore fitting several models to a multiway table or marginal subtables and have tens of thousands of cases, you can save the cell counts and initiate later analyses from them. Or you may want to save deviates or contributions to the model Pearson or likelihood ratio chi-square. Use the ESTIMATES option to do this. One record is generated for each cell in the table. Alternatively, you may want to save one record for each parameter in the model. For this, use LAMBDAS. For example:

```
SAVE filename / ESTIMATES or
SAVE filename / LAMBDAS
```

ESTIMATES	For each cell in the table, save the observed and expected frequencies and their differences, standardized and Freeman-Tukey deviates, the contribution to the Pearson and likelihood-ratio chi-square statistics, the contribution to the log-likelihood, and the cell indices.
LAMBDAS	For each level of each term in the model, save the estimate of lambda, the standard error of lambda, the ratio of lambda to its standard error: the multiplicative effect (EXP(lambda)), and the indices of the table factors.

15.2
Medium
output:
extended
results

This example continues the analysis in Example 15.1, repeating the same model, but changing the PRINT (output length) setting to request medium-length results:

continuing from Example 15.1
```
PRINT MEDIUM
MODEL center$*age*survive$*tumor$ = age # center$,
                          + survive$ # center$,
                          + tumor$ # center$

ESTIMATE / DELTA=0.5
```

❶

```
***  We omit the panel of Observed Frequencies, the Pearson and LR ChiSquare
     statistics, and Expected Values, shown in Example 15.1.              ***

Standardized Deviates = (Obs-Exp)/sqrt(Exp)
==================================================================
CENTER$    AGE        SURVIVE$                    TUMOR$
                                 MinMalig   MinBengn   MaxMalig   MaxBengn
--------+---------+---------+----------------------------------------------
Tokyo      Under 50   Dead        0.410     -2.237     -1.282      0.262
                      Alive      -0.392      1.464     -0.361     -0.074

           50 to 69   Dead        1.085     -1.048      2.034     -0.044
                      Alive      -0.519      0.065     -0.754     -0.876

           70 & Over  Dead        0.774      0.414     -0.109     -0.619
                      Alive      -1.551     -0.843      0.507     -0.315
--------+---------+---------+----------------------------------------------
Boston     Under 50   Dead        0.241     -1.471      2.403     -0.836
                      Alive       0.018     -0.077     -0.318     -1.186

           50 to 69   Dead       -0.918     -0.933     -0.798      0.486
                      Alive      -0.897      1.202      0.153      0.084

           70 & Over  Dead        0.864      0.760      0.062     -0.932
                      Alive       0.384     -0.777     -1.999     -0.565
--------+---------+---------+----------------------------------------------
Glamorgn   Under 50   Dead        2.196     -0.981     -0.255     -0.959
                      Alive      -0.892     -0.374      0.195     -0.695

           50 to 69   Dead       -0.004     -0.832     -0.977     -1.177
                      Alive      -0.568      1.089     -0.373      0.592

           70 & Over  Dead       -1.093      0.376      0.633     -0.743
                      Alive       0.002     -0.567     -0.227     -0.171
--------+---------+---------+----------------------------------------------
*** We omit the panel of parameters divided by their standard errors, shown in Example 15.1.
                                    ***
```

❷

```
Multiplicative Effects = exp(Lambda)
====================================

    THETA
    ----------
     6.209
    ----------

            CENTER$
   Tokyo     Boston      Glamorgn
   -------------------------------------
    1.050     1.001       0.951
   -------------------------------------


             AGE
  Under 50   50 to 69    70 & Over
  -------------------------------------
    1.156     1.559       0.555
```

```
----------------------------------------
      SURVIVE$
  Dead        Alive
----------------------------------------
     0.634       1.578
----------------------------------------


                  TUMOR$
  MinMalig   MinBengn   MaxMalig   MaxBengn
----------------------------------------------
     1.616      2.748      0.865      0.260
----------------------------------------------


CENTER$ |                AGE
        |   Under 50      50 to 69      70 & Over
--------+-------------------------------------------
Tokyo   |     1.760         1.044         0.544
Boston  |     0.635         0.958         1.644
Glamorgn|     0.895         1.000         1.118
--------+-------------------------------------------

CENTER$ |       SURVIVE$
        |   Dead        Alive
--------+-----------------------------
Tokyo   |     0.835       1.198
Boston  |     1.113       0.899
Glamorgn|     1.077       0.929
--------+-----------------------------

CENTER$ |                 TUMOR$
        |   MinMalig   MinBengn   MaxMalig   MaxBengn
--------+------------------------------------------------
Tokyo   |     0.692      0.826      1.238      1.412
Boston  |     1.045      1.370      0.837      0.834
Glamorgn|     1.382      0.884      0.965      0.849
--------+------------------------------------------------
 Model ln(MLE):  -160.563
```

❸

Term tested	The model without the term				Removal of term from model		
	ln(MLE)	Chi-Sq	df	p-value	Chi-Sq	df	p-value
CENTER$. . . .	-160.799	56.31	53	0.3523	0.47	2	0.7894
AGE.	-216.120	166.95	53	0.0000	111.11	2	0.0000
SURVIVE$ . . .	-234.265	203.24	52	0.0000	147.41	1	0.0000
TUMOR$	-344.471	423.65	54	0.0000	367.82	3	0.0000

❹

Term tested hierarchically	The model without the term				Removal of term from model		
	ln(MLE)	Chi-Sq	df	p-value	Chi-Sq	df	p-value
CENTER$. . . .	-224.289	183.29	65	0.0000	127.45	14	0.0000
AGE.	-246.779	228.26	57	0.0000	172.43	6	0.0000
SURVIVE$ . . .	-242.434	219.57	54	0.0000	163.74	3	0.0000
TUMOR$	-363.341	461.39	60	0.0000	405.56	9	0.0000

The 5 most outlandish cells (based on FTD, stepwise):

				CENTER$			
					AGE		
						SURVIVE$	
ln(MLE)	LR_ChiSq	p-value	Frequency				TUMOR$
-154.685	11.755	0.001	7	1	1	1	2
-150.685	8.001	0.005	1	2	3	2	3
-145.024	11.321	0.001	16	3	1	1	1
-140.740	8.569	0.003	6	2	1	1	3
-136.662	8.157	0.004	11	1	2	1	3

❶ *Standardized Deviates.* The tests in **❸** in Example 15.1 provide an overall indication of how close the expected values are to the cell counts. Just as you study residuals for each case in multiple regression, you can use deviates to compare the observed and expected values for each cell. A standardized deviate is the square root of each cell's contribution to the Pearson chi-square statistic—that is, (the observed frequency minus the expected frequency) divided by the square root of the expected frequency. These values are similar to z-scores. For the second cell in the first row, the expected value under your model is considerably larger than the observed count (its deviate is -2.237; the observed count 7; and the expected count 15.9). In Example 15.1, this cell was identified as the most "outlandish" cell using Freeman-Tukey deviates.

Note that LOGLIN produces five types of deviates or residuals: standardized, the observed-expected frequency, the likelihood ratio deviate, the Freeman-Tukey deviate, and the Pearson deviate.

❷ *Multiplicative Effects = EXP(Lambda)*. Estimates of the multiplicative parameters $\hat{\beta}$, where $\hat{\beta} = \mathrm{EXP}(\hat{\lambda})$. Look for values that depart markedly from 1.0. Very large values indicate an increased probability for that combination of indices and, conversely, a value considerably less than 1.0, an unlikely combination. A test of the hypothesis that $\beta=1.0$ is the same as that for $\lambda=0$; so use the values of λ / S.E. in ❻, Example 15.1, to test the values in this panel. For the CENTER$ by AGE interaction, the most likely combination is "Under 50" women from Tokyo ($e^{\lambda}=1.76$); the least likely combination is "70 & Over" from Tokyo ($e^{\lambda}=0.544$).

❸ *Term tested.* The PRINT option TERM produces this panel. One at a time, LOGLIN removes each first-order effect and each interaction term from the model. For each smaller model, LOGLIN provides:

– A likelihood ratio chi-square for testing the fit of the model.
– The difference in the chi-square statistics between the smaller model and the full model. (See Example 15.3 for more discussion regarding the additive property of the likelihood ratio chi-square.)

The likelihood ratio chi-square for the full model is 55.833 (See ❸, Example 15.1). For a model that omits AGE, the likelihood ratio chi-square is 166.95. This smaller model does not fit the observed frequencies (p value < 0.00005). To see if the removal of this term results in a significant decrease in the fit, look at the difference in the statistics: $166.95 - 55.833=111.117$, p value < 0.00005. From the second line in this panel, it appears that a model without the first-order term for CENTER$ does fit (p value $= 0.3523$). However, from the tests in the panel on the right, each of the second-order effects with CENTER$ improves the fit significantly.

❹ *Term tested hierarchically.* The PRINT option HTERM produces this panel. These tests are similar to those in ❸ except that only hierarchical models are tested—if a lower-order effect is removed, so are the higher-order effects that include it. For example, in the first line, when *CENTER$* is removed, the three interactions with *CENTER$* are also removed. Interaction terms are omitted when they are identical to results in ❸.

15.3 Screening effects

The likelihood ratio chi-square is additive under partitioning for nested models. Two models are **nested** if all the effects of the first are a subset of the second. The likelihood ratio chi-square is **additive** because the statistic for the second model can be subtracted from that for the first. The difference provides a test of the additional effects—that is, the difference in the two statistics has an asymptotic chi-square distribution with degrees of freedom equal to the difference between those for the two model chi-squares (or the difference between the number of effects in the two models). This property does not hold for the Pearson chi-square. The additive property for the likelihood ratio chi-square is useful for screening effects to include in a model.

In this example, you pretend that no models have been fit to the cancer data (that is, you have not seen Example 15.1 and Example 15.2). As a place to start, first fit a model with all second-order interactions finding that it fits. Then fit models nested within the first by using results from the HTERM (terms tested hierarchically) panel to guide your selection of terms to be removed.

Here's a summary of your instructions: you study the output generated from the first MODEL and ESTIMATE statements and decide to remove *AGE* by *TUMOR$*. After seeing the results for this smaller model, you decide to remove *AGE* by *SURVIVE$*, too.

```
LOGLIN
   USE cancer
   FREQ = number
   PRINT NONE / CHI  HTERM
   MODEL center$*age*survive$*tumor$ =,
                               tumor$..center$^2
   ESTIMATE / DELTA=0.5

   MODEL center$*age*survive$*tumor$ =,
                               tumor$..center$^2,
                                 - age*tumor$
```

```
ESTIMATE / DELTA=0.5
MODEL center$*age*survive$*tumor$ =,
                              tumor$..center$^2,
                            - age*tumor$,
                            - age*survive$

ESTIMATE / DELTA=0.5
```

All 2-way interactions

❶

```
Pearson ChiSquare  40.1650  df  40  Probability  0.46294
     LR ChiSquare  39.9208  df  40  Probability  0.47378
    Raftery's BIC -225.6219
    Dissimilarity    7.6426
```

Term tested hierarchically	The model without the term ln(MLE)	Chi-Sq	df	p-value	Removal of term from model Chi-Sq	df	p-value
TUMOR$	-361.233	457.17	58	0.0000	417.25	18	0.0000
SURVIVE$ . . .	-241.675	218.06	48	0.0000	178.14	8	0.0000
AGE.	-241.668	218.04	54	0.0000	178.12	14	0.0000
CENTER$. . . .	-213.996	162.70	54	0.0000	122.78	14	0.0000
SURVIVE$ * TUMOR$ . . .	-157.695	50.10	43	0.2125	10.18	3	0.0171
AGE * TUMOR$ . . .	-153.343	41.39	46	0.6654	1.47	6	0.9613
AGE * SURVIVE$ . .	-154.693	44.09	42	0.3831	4.17	2	0.1241
TUMOR$ * CENTER$ . . .	-169.724	74.15	46	0.0053	34.23	6	0.0000
SURVIVE$ * CENTER$ . .	-156.501	47.71	42	0.2518	7.79	2	0.0204
CENTER$ * AGE.	-186.011	106.73	44	0.0000	66.81	4	0.0000

Remove age*tumor

❷

```
Pearson ChiSquare  41.8276  df  46  Probability  0.64758
     LR ChiSquare  41.3934  df  46  Probability  0.66536
    Raftery's BIC -263.9807
    Dissimilarity    7.8682
```

Term tested hierarchically	The model without the term ln(MLE)	Chi-Sq	df	p-value	Removal of term from model Chi-Sq	df	p-value
TUMOR$	-361.233	457.17	58	0.0000	415.78	12	0.0000
SURVIVE$ . . .	-242.434	219.57	54	0.0000	178.18	8	0.0000
AGE.	-241.668	218.04	54	0.0000	176.65	8	0.0000
CENTER$. . . .	-215.687	166.08	60	0.0000	124.69	14	0.0000
SURVIVE$ * TUMOR$ . . .	-158.454	51.61	49	0.3719	10.22	3	0.0168
AGE * SURVIVE$ . .	-155.452	45.61	48	0.5713	4.22	2	0.1214
TUMOR$ * CENTER$ . . .	-171.415	77.54	52	0.0124	36.14	6	0.0000
SURVIVE$ * CENTER$ . .	-157.291	49.29	48	0.4214	7.90	2	0.0193
CENTER$ * AGE.	-187.702	110.11	50	0.0000	68.72	4	0.0000

Remove age*tumor$ and age*survive$ age*survive$

❸

```
Pearson ChiSquare  45.3579  df  48  Probability  0.58174
     LR ChiSquare  45.6113  df  48  Probability  0.57126
    Raftery's BIC -273.0400
    Dissimilarity    8.4720
```

Term tested hierarchically	The model without the term ln(MLE)	Chi-Sq	df	p-value	Removal of term from model Chi-Sq	df	p-value
TUMOR$	-363.341	461.39	60	0.0000	415.78	12	0.0000
SURVIVE$ . . .	-242.434	219.57	54	0.0000	173.96	6	0.0000
AGE.	-241.668	218.04	54	0.0000	172.43	6	0.0000
CENTER$. . . .	-219.546	173.80	62	0.0000	128.19	14	0.0000
SURVIVE$ * TUMOR$ . . .	-160.563	55.83	51	0.2981	10.22	3	0.0168
CENTER$ * TUMOR$ . . .	-173.524	81.75	54	0.0087	36.14	6	0.0000
SURVIVE$ * CENTER$ . .	-161.264	57.23	50	0.2245	11.62	2	0.0030
CENTER$ * AGE.	-191.561	117.83	52	0.0000	72.22	4	0.0000

The highlighted numbers below correspond to those in the output:

❶ The likelihood ratio chi-square for the model that includes all two-way interactions is 39.9 (*p* value = 0.4738). If the *AGE* by *TUMOR$* interaction is removed, the chi-square for the smaller model is 41.39 (*p* value = 0.6654). Does the removal of this interaction cause a significant change? No, chi-square = 1.47 (*p* value = 0.9613). This chi-square is computed as 41.39 minus 39.92 with 46 minus 40 degrees of freedom. The removal of this interaction results in the least change, so you remove it first. Notice also that the estimate of the maximized likelihood function is largest when this second-order effect is removed (−153.343).

❷ The model chi-square for this second model is the same as that in ❶ (41.3934). Here, if *AGE* by *SURVIVE$* is removed, the new model fits ($\chi^2 = 45.61$, *p* value = 0.5713) and the change between the model minus one interaction and that minus two interactions is insignificant (*p* value = 0.1214).

❸ If *SURVIVE$* by *TUMOR$* is removed from the current model with four interactions, the new model fits ($\chi^2 = 55.83$, *p* value = 0.2981). This model with these second-order effects is the same one analyzed in Example 15.1 and Example 15.2, so you stop removing terms here. Looking at the HTERM panel for it (❹ in Example 15.2), you see that a model without *CENTER$* by *SURVIVE$* has a marginal fit ($\chi^2 = 66.75$, *p* value = 0.0975) and the χ^2 for the difference is significant ($\chi^2 = 10.89$, *p* value = 0.0043). Although the goal is parsimony and technically a model with only two interactions does fit, you opt for the model that also includes *CENTER$* by *SURVIVE$* because it is a significant improvement over the very smallest model.

15.4 Structural zeros and tests of quasi-independence

A cell is declared to be a **structural zero** when the probability is zero that there are counts in the cell. Notice that such zero frequencies do not arise because of small samples but because the cells are empty naturally (a male hysterectomy patient) or by design (the diagonal of a two-way table comparing father's (rows) and son's (columns) occupations is not of interest when studying changes or mobility).

When fitting a model, LOGLIN excludes cells identified as structural zeros, and then, as in a regression analysis with zero weight cases, it can compute expected values, deviates, and so on, for all cells including the structural zero cells.

You might consider identifying cells as structural zeros when:

— It is meaningful to the study at hand to exclude some cells—for example, the diagonal of a two-way table crossing the occupations of fathers and sons.
— You want to determine whether an interaction term is necessary only because there are one or two aberrant cells. That is, after you select the "best" model, fit a second model with fewer effects and identify the outlier cells (the most outlandish cells) for the smaller model. Then refit the "best" model declaring the outlier cells to be structural zeros. If the additional interactions are no longer necessary, you might report the smaller model, adding a sentence describing how the unusual cell(s) depart from the model.

This example demonstrates the latter, first identifying outliers, and then declaring them to be structural zeros. You wonder if any of the interactions in the Example 15.1 model are necessary only because of a few unusual cells. To identify the unusual cells, first pull back from your "ideal" model and fit a model with main effects only, asking for the four most unusual cells. (Why four cells? Because 5% of 72 cells is 3.6 or roughly 4.)

```
USE cancer
FREQ = number
ORDER center$ survive$ tumor$ / SORT=NONE
MODEL center$*age*survive$*tumor$ = tumor$ .. center$
PRINT / CELLS=4
ESTIMATE / DELTA=0.5
```

Of course this model doesn't fit, but here are selections from the output:

```
Pearson ChiSquare 181.3892  df  63  Probability  0.00000
      LR ChiSquare 174.3458  df  63  Probability  0.00000
Raftery's BIC -243.8839
Dissimilarity    19.3853


The  4 most outlandish cells (based on FTD, stepwise):
================================================================
                                        CENTER$
                                        |  AGE
                                        |  |  SURVIVE$
                                        |  |  |  TUMOR$
   ln(MLE)  LR_ChiSq  p-value Frequency |  |  |  |
  --------  --------  ------- --------- -  -  -  -
  -203.261   33.118    0.000     68     1  1  2  2
  -195.262   15.997    0.000      1     1  3  2  1
  -183.471   23.582    0.000     25     1  1  2  3
  -176.345   14.253    0.000      6     1  3  2  2
```

Next fit your "ideal" model, identifying these four cells as structural zeros and also requesting PRINT / HTERM to test the need for each interaction term.

Identifying cells as structural zeros. Use ZERO CELL to specify one or more cells for treatment as structural zeros. Specify the indicies of each cell in the order the factor appears in the table. Above, the most unusual cell is identified as 1,1,2,2 (Tokyo, Under 50, Alive, MinBengn) or the youngest Tokyo survivors with benign tumors with mimimal inflammation. In fact, all four unusual cells are survivors from Tokyo; two are from the youngest age group and two from the oldest. Declare all four cells as structural zeros by typing:

```
ZERO CELL=1 1 2 2    CELL=1 3 2 1,
      CELL=1 1 2 3    CELL=1 3 2 2
```

Each new ZERO statement clears all cells previously identified as structural zeros.

As an alternative, arrange your data so that the frequency of each structural zero cell is 0, then specify:

```
ZERO EMPTY
```

SYSTAT looks for the zero values before DELTA, so you can use both options.

Removing strata. If you want to select a layer or level of a factor, use 0's for the other factors. For example, to declare the fourth level of *TUMOR$* as structural zeros with commands, type:

```
ZERO CELL=0 0 0 4    or    ZERO CELL=0,0,0,4
```

Alternatively, you can replace the 0's with blanks or periods:

```
ZERO CELL= , , ,4    or    ZERO CELL=. . .,4
```

Defining
four cells
as structural
zeros

Continuing from the analysis of main effects only, now specify your original model with its three second-order effects:

```
MODEL center$*age*survive$*tumor$ = ,
            (age + survive$ + tumor$) # center$
ZERO CELL=1 1 2 2    CELL=1 3 2 1,
    CELL=1 1 2 3    CELL=1 3 2 2
PRINT / HTERMS
ESTIMATE / DELTA=0.5
```

Here are selections from the output. Notice that asterisks mark the structural zero cells.

```
Number of cells (product of levels):   72
       Number of structural zero cells:    4
                      Total count:  664

Observed Frequencies
====================
CENTER$   AGE       SURVIVE$ |                    TUMOR$
                             | MinMalig   MinBengn   MaxMalig   MaxBengn
--------+---------+--------+-------------------------------------------
Tokyo     Under 50  Dead    |      9          7          4          3
                    Alive   |     26        *68        *25          9
                            +
          50 to 69  Dead    |      9          9         11          2
                    Alive   |     20         46         18          5
                            +
          70 & Over Dead    |      2          3          1          0
                    Alive   |     *1         *6          5          1
--------+---------+--------+-------------------------------------------
Boston    Under 50  Dead    |      6          7          6          0
                    Alive   |     11         24          4          0
```

*** The rest of the table is omitted because it is the same as Example 15.1 ***

```
         *   indicates structural zero cells

Pearson ChiSquare  46.8417  df  47  Probability  0.47906
     LR ChiSquare  44.8815  df  47  Probability  0.56072
  Raftery's BIC -260.5378
  Dissimilarity  10.1680
```

Term tested hierarchically	The model without the term ln(MLE)	Chi-Sq	df	p-value	Removal of term from model Chi-Sq	df	p-value
AGE.	-190.460	132.87	53	0.0000	87.98	6	0.0000
SURVIVE$ . . .	-206.152	164.25	50	0.0000	119.37	3	0.0000
TUMOR$	-326.389	404.72	56	0.0000	359.84	9	0.0000
CENTER$. . . .	-177.829	107.60	61	0.0002	62.72	14	0.0000
CENTER$ * AGE.	-158.900	69.75	51	0.0416	24.86	4	0.0001
CENTER$ * SURVIVE$ . .	-149.166	50.28	49	0.4226	5.40	2	0.0674
CENTER$ * TUMOR$ . . .	-162.289	76.52	53	0.0189	31.64	6	0.0000

The model has a nonsignificant test-of-fit and so does a model without the *CENTER\$* by *SURVIVAL\$* interaction ($\chi^2 = 50.28$, p value = 0.4226).

Eliminating only the young women

Two of the extreme cells are from the youngest age group. What happens to the *CENTER\$* by *SURVIVE\$* effect if only these cells are defined as structural zeros? HTERM remains in effect.

```
MODEL center$*age*survive$*tumor$ =,
             (age + survive$ + tumor$) # center$
ZERO CELL=1 1 2 2   CELL=1 1 2 3
ESTIMATE / DELTA=0.5
```

```
Number of cells (product of levels):  72
    Number of structural zero cells:   2
                    Total count:  671

Pearson ChiSquare  50.2610  df  49  Probability  0.42326
     LR ChiSquare  49.1153  df  49  Probability  0.46850
    Raftery's BIC  -269.8144
    Dissimilarity  10.6372

Term tested        The model without the term      Removal of term from model
hierarchically     ln(MLE)   Chi-Sq   df  p-value    Chi-Sq    df   p-value
--------------     -------   ------   ---  -------    --------  ---  -------
AGE. . .  . . .    -221.256  188.37   55  0.0000     139.25    6    0.0000
SURVIVE$ . . .     -210.369  166.60   52  0.0000     117.48    3    0.0000
TUMOR$ . . . .     -331.132  408.12   58  0.0000     359.01    9    0.0000
CENTER$. . . .     -192.179  130.22   63  0.0000      81.10   14    0.0000
CENTER$
* AGE. . . . .     -172.356   90.57   53  0.0010      41.45    4    0.0000
CENTER$
* SURVIVE$ . .     -153.888   53.63   51  0.3737       4.52    2    0.1045
CENTER$
* TUMOR$ . . .     -169.047   83.95   55  0.0072      34.84    6    0.0000
```

When the two cells for the *young* women from Tokyo are excluded from the model estimation, the *CENTER$* by *SURVIVE$* effect is not needed (X^2 = 53.63, *p* value = 0.3737).

Eliminating the older women

Here you define the two cells for the Tokyo women from the oldest age group as structural zeros.

```
MODEL center$*age*survive$*tumor$ =,
            (age + survive$ + tumor$) # center$
ZERO CELL=1 3 2 1   CELL=1 3 2 2
ESTIMATE / DELTA=0.5
```

```
Number of cells (product of levels):  72
    Number of structural zero cells:   2
                    Total count:  757

Pearson ChiSquare  53.4348  df  49  Probability  0.30782
     LR ChiSquare  50.9824  df  49  Probability  0.39558
    Raftery's BIC  -273.8564
    Dissimilarity   9.4583

Term tested        The model without the term      Removal of term from model
hierarchically     ln(MLE)   Chi-Sq   df  p-value    Chi-Sq    df   p-value
--------------     -------   ------   ---  -------    --------  ---  -------
AGE. . . . . .     -203.305  147.41   55  0.0000      96.42    6    0.0000
SURVIVE$ . . .     -238.968  218.73   52  0.0000     167.75    3    0.0000
TUMOR$ . . . .     -358.521  457.84   58  0.0000     406.86    9    0.0000
CENTER$. . . .     -209.549  159.89   63  0.0000     108.91   14    0.0000
CENTER$
* AGE. . . . .     -177.799   96.39   53  0.0003      45.41    4    0.0000
CENTER$
* SURVIVE$ . .     -161.382   63.56   51  0.1114      12.58    2    0.0019
CENTER$
* TUMOR$ . . .     -171.123   83.04   55  0.0086      32.06    6    0.0000
```

When the two cells for the women from the older age group are treated as structural zeros, the case for removing the *CENTER$* by *SURVIVE$* effect is much weaker than when the cells for the younger women are structural zeros. Here, the inclusion of the effect results in a significant improvement in the fit of the model (X^2 = 12.58, *p* value = 0.0019).

Conclusion. The structural zero feature allowed you to quickly focus on two of the 72 cells in your multiway table: the Under 50 survivors from Tokyo, especially those with benign tumors with minimal inflammation. The overall survival rate for the 764 women is 72.5%; that for Tokyo, 79.3%; and that for the most unusual cell, 90.67%. See Example 2.6. Half of the Tokyo women under age 50 have "MinBengn" tumors (75 out of 151) and almost 10% of the 764 women (spread across 72 cells) are concentrated here. Possibly the protocol for study entry (including definition of a "tumor") was executed differently at this center than at the others.

15.5 Requesting a table— no analysis

If you want only a frequency table and no analysis, use TABULATE. Simply specify the table factors in the same order you want to view them from left to right. In other words, the last variable defines the columns of the table and cross-classifications of the preceding variables the rows.

To produce only the table displayed in ❷ of Example 15.1, specify:

```
TABULATE center$*age*survive$*tumor$
```

Remember to use **Data➠Frequency** if the input is cell counts. You can also use **Data➠Label** (or the LABEL command, shown in Example 15.1).

References

Agresti, A. 1990. *Categorical data analysis*. New York: Wiley-Interscience.

Agresti, A. 1984. *Analysis of ordinal categorical data*. New York: Wiley-Interscience.

Bishop, Y.M.M., Fienberg, S.E., and Holland, P.W. 1975. *Discrete multivariate analysis: theory and practice*. Cambridge, Mass.: McGraw-Hill.

Fienberg, S.E. 1980. *The analysis of cross-classified categorical data*, 2nd ed. Cambridge, Mass.: MIT Press.

Goodman, L.A. 1978. *Analyzing qualitative/categorical data: Log-linear models and latent structure analysis*. Cambridge, Mass.: Abt Books.

Haberman, S.J. 1978. *Analysis of qualitative data, Vol. 1: Introductory topics*. New York: Academic Press.

Knoke, D., and P.S. Burke. 1980. *Log-linear models.* Newbury Park: Sage.

Morrison, D.F. 1976. *Multivariate statistical methods.* New York: McGraw-Hill.

Factor Analysis

Leland Wilkinson and Herb Stenson

Factor Analysis provides principal components analysis (PCA) and common factor analysis (MLA for maximum likelihood and IPA for iterated principal axis). SYSTAT has options to rotate, sort, plot, and save factor loadings. With the PCA method, you can also save the scores and coefficients. Orthogonal methods of rotation include varimax, equamax, quartimax, and orthomax. A direct oblimin method is also available for oblique rotation. Users can explore other rotations by interactively rotating a 3-D *Quick Graph* plot of the factor loadings. Various inferential statistics (for example, confidence intervals, standard errors, and chi-square tests) are provided depending on the nature of the analysis that is run.

Before factoring, Factor Analysis reads a correlation or covariance matrix or computes one from a rectangular SYSTAT data file. When data values are missing, SYSTAT can compute correlations or covariances using only those cases with all values present (*listwise deletion*), or it can compute each statistic using all cases with both values present (*pairwise deletion*).

Factor Analysis

Overview

Principal components (PCA) and common factor (MLA for maximum likelihood and IPA for iterated principal axis) analyses are methods of decomposing a correlation or covariance matrix. Although principal components and common factor analyses are based on different mathematical models, they can be used on the same data and both usually produce similar results. Factor analysis is often used in exploratory data analysis to:

- Study the correlations of a large number of variables by grouping the variables in "factors" so that variables within each factor are more highly correlated with variables in that factor than with variables in other factors.
- Interpret each factor according to the meaning of the variables.
- Summarize many variables by a few factors. The scores from the factors can be used as input data for t tests, regression, ANOVA, discriminant analysis, and so on.

Often the users of factor analysis are overwhelmed by the gap between theory and practice. In this chapter, we try to offer practical hints. It is important to realize that you may need to make several passes through the procedure, changing options each time, until the results give you the necessary information for your problem.

Here is an example of how factor analysis can help you study correlations. This example uses 12 items from a 43-item questionnaire developed by Murray Jarvik, M.D., and cited in the 1985 *BMDP Statistical Software Manual*. The questionnaire was administered to subjects in treatment to help them quit smoking. The "smoking" items are queries about desire. For example, "After a good meal, how much do you want a cigarette?" The other questions relate to the psychological and physical state of the subject.

A correlation matrix for 12 of the items looks like this:

	Concentr	Annoy	Smoking1	Sleepy	Smoking2	Tense	Smoking3	Alert	Irritabl	Tired	Content	Smoking4
Concentr	1.000											
Annoy	0.562	1.000										
Smoking1	0.086	0.144	1.000									
Sleepy	0.200	0.360	0.140	1.000								
Smoking2	0.579	0.119	0.785	0.211	1.000							
Tense	0.041	0.705	0.222	0.273	0.301	1.000						
Smoking3	0.802	0.060	0.810	0.126	0.816	0.120	1.000					
Alert	0.592	0.578	0.101	0.606	0.223	0.594	0.039	1.000				
Irritabl	0.595	0.796	0.189	0.337	0.221	0.725	0.108	0.605	1.000			
Tired	0.512	0.413	0.199	0.798	0.274	0.364	0.139	0.698	0.428	1.000		
Content	0.492	0.739	0.239	0.240	0.235	0.711	0.100	0.605	0.697	0.394	1.000	
Smoking4	0.228	0.122	0.775	0.277	0.813	0.214	0.845	0.201	0.156	0.271	0.171	1.000

Imagine trying to study correlations for all 43 items! By using the loadings from one default run of Factor Analysis with an orthogonal rotation, you can reorder the questions:

	Smoking3	Smoking4	Smoking1	Smoking2	Annoy	Irritabl	Content	Tense	Concentr	Sleepy	Tired	Alert
Smoking3	1.00											
Smoking4	0.85	1.00										
Smoking1	0.81	0.78	1.00									
Smoking2	0.82	0.81	0.79	1.00								
Annoy	0.06	0.12	0.14	0.12	1.00							
Irritabl	0.11	0.16	0.19	0.22	0.80	1.00						
Content	0.10	0.17	0.24	0.24	0.74	0.70	1.00					
Tense	0.12	0.21	0.22	0.30	0.71	0.73	0.71	1.00				
Concentr	0.04	0.23	0.09	0.20	0.56	0.60	0.49	0.58	1.00			
Sleepy	0.13	0.28	0.14	0.21	0.36	0.34	0.24	0.27	0.46	1.00		
Tired	0.14	0.27	0.20	0.27	0.41	0.43	0.34	0.36	0.51	0.80	1.00	
Alert	0.04	0.20	0.10	0.22	0.58	0.61	0.61	0.59	0.80	0.61	0.70	1.00

Now it is easy to see that the four smoking items are more related to one another than to the other questions; and that the remaining items fall into two groups—except that *ALERT* and *CONCENTR* (concentration) overlap somewhat. Factor Analysis can compute a score for each group of variables (or factor) that is a linear combination of the variables. For example, the score for the first factor is a measure of the "desire to smoke." In the example, the three scores for each subject incorporate almost as much information as the original 12 variables. These scores can be used in further analyses along with other data collected on the subjects. Incidentally, from the results for the complete questionnaire, the researchers found that an additional question about the desire to smoke did not correlate with the others. They looked at the wording on this item and found it differed from the others. In their final analysis, the item was not used to construct a "desire to smoke" score.

Getting started   For factor analysis, use **Stats⟶Factor Analysis**:

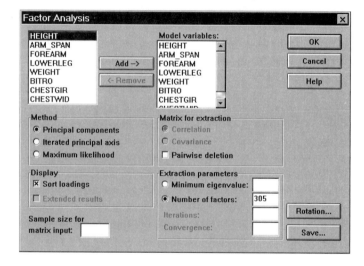

For a discussion about rotating factor loadings, see "Rotation" on p. 549. The **Rotation Parameters** dialog box appears below:

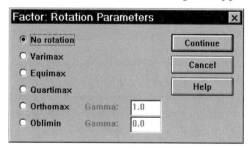

For a PCA analysis, you can save factor scores, loadings, or coefficients; for MLA and IPA, you can save only factor loadings. See the section about saving below and Example 16.7. The **Save** dialog box appears below:

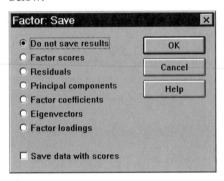

Using commands

With commands:

```
ESTIMATE / METHOD=PCA or IPA or MLA,
           LIST or PAIR, N=n, CORR or COVA,
           NUMBER=n, EIGEN=n, ITER=n, CONV=n, SORT,
           ROTATE=VAR or QUART or EQUA or ORTH or OBLIM
           GAMMA=n (with OBLIMIN or ORTHOMAX only)
```

Method

Factor Analysis provides three methods of factor extraction: **Principal components** (the default), **Iterated principal axis**, and **Maximum likelihood**. For more information, see Example 16.1, Example 16.2, and Example 16.3.

Display

Sort loadings sorts the factor loadings from largest to smallest and group loading > 0.5 together within each component. See Example 16.1.

Extended results

Factor Analysis offers three categories of output: short (the default), medium, and long. Each has specific output panels associated with it. To change the output length, use **Edit➠Options** and set **Length=Short, Medium,** or **Long**. The output in Example 16.1 illustrates the features printed by default. With commands:

```
PRINT SHORT or MEDIUM or LONG
```

Short

For **Short**, the default, panels are:

- Latent roots or eigenvalues (not MLA)
- Initial and final communality estimates (not PCA)
- Component loadings (PCA) or factor pattern (MLA, IPA)
- Variance explained by components (PCA) or factors (MLA, IPA)
- Percentage of total variance explained
- Change in uniqueness and log likelihood at each iteration (MLA only)
- Canonical correlations (MLA only)

When a rotation is requested:
- Rotated loadings (PCA) or pattern (MLA, IPA) matrix
- Variance explained by rotated components
- Percentage of total variance explained
- Correlations among oblique components or factors (**Oblimin** only)

Medium

By specifying **Medium**, you get the panels listed for **Short**, plus:

- The matrix to factor
- Chi-square test that all eigenvalues are equal (PCA only)
- Chi-square test that last k eigenvalues are equal (PCA only)
- Differences of original correlations or covariances minus fitted values

Covariance matrix input (not MLA or IPA):
- Asymptotic 95% confidence limits for the eigenvalues
- Estimates of the population eigenvalues with standard errors

Long

With **Long**, you get the panels listed for **Short** and **Medium**, plus:

- Latent vectors (eigenvectors) with standard errors (not MLA)
- Chi-square test that the number of factors is k (MLA only)

*With an **Oblimin** rotation:*
- Direct and indirect contribution of factors to variances
- Rotated structure matrix

Matrix for extraction

You can choose to factor the Correlation or Covariance matrix. Most frequently the correlation matrix is used. See Example 16.6 for the use of a covariance matrix.

Missing data

Ordinarily, Factor Analysis and other multivariate procedures delete all cases having missing values on any variable selected for analysis. This is **Listwise deletion.** For data with many missing values, you may end up with too few complete cases for analysis. Select **Pairwise deletion** if you want covariances or correlations computed separately for each pair of variables selected for analysis. Pairwise deletion takes more time than the standard listwise deletion because all possible pairs of variances and covariances are computed. The same option is offered in **Stats⟶ Correlation**, should you decide to create a symmetric matrix for use in Factor analysis that way. Also notice that Correlation provides an EM algorithm for estimating correlation or covariance matrices when data are missing.

Be careful. When you use **Pairwise deletion**, you can end up with negative eigenvalues for principal components or be unable to compute common factors at all. With either method, it is desirable that the pattern of missing data be random. Otherwise, the factor structure you compute will be influenced systematically by the pattern of how values are missing. With commands:

```
ESTIMATE / PAIR or LIST
```

Extraction parameters

The default number of factors selected by the program or indicated by tests is often larger than needed. Use **Minimum eigenvalue** (not available with MLA) or **Number of factors** to limit the number of factors computed. For the former, type the smallest eigenvalue to retain. The default is 1.0 for PCA and IPA. Incidentally, if you specify 0, Factor Analysis ignores components with negative eigenvalues (which can occur with pairwise deletion). **Number of factors** lets you limit the number of factors directly. If you use both options, Factor Analysis uses whichever criterion results in the smaller number of components. With commands:

```
ESTIMATE / NUMBER=n  EIGEN=n
```

For the MLA and IPA methods, use **Iterations** to set the number of iterations and **Convergence** to set the convergence criterion. The default for the former is 25; for the latter, 0.001.

Saving scores, loadings, and coefficients

To save factor scores, loadings, or coefficients in a SYSTAT file:

    SAVE filename / options

For the MLA and IPA methods, you can save only loadings. For the PCA method, select from these options:

Do not save results	Results are not saved.
Factor scores	Standardized factor scores (PCA only).
Residuals	Residuals for each case. For **Correlation**, the residual is the actual z-score minus the predicted z-score using the factor scores times the loadings to get the predicted scores. For **Covariance**, the residuals are from unstandardized predictions. With an orthogonal rotation, Q and $PROB$ are also saved. Q is the sum of the squared residuals, and $PROB$ is its probability.
Principal components	Unstandardized principal components scores with mean 0 and variance equal to the eigenvalue for the factor (only for PCA without rotation).
Factor coefficients	Coefficients that produce standardized scores. With Correlation, multiply the coefficients by the standardized variables; with Covariance, use the original variables.
Eigenvectors	Eigenvectors (only for PCA without a rotation). Use to produce unstandardized scores.
Factor loadings	Factor loadings.
Save data with scores	Data. Use with options for scores (not loadings, coefficients, or other similar options).

If you save scores, the variables in the file are labeled *FACTOR(1)*, *FACTOR(2)*, and so on. (If you want to change these names, open the file into the Data Editor Worksheet and type your names in the top row.) Any observations with missing values on any of the input variables will have missing values for all scores. The scores are normalized to have zero mean and, if the correlation matrix is used, unit variance. If you use the covariance matrix and perform no rotations, SYSTAT does not standardize the component scores. The sum of their variances is the same as for the original data.

If you want to use the score coefficients to get component scores for new data, multiply the coefficients by the standardized data. SYSTAT does this when it saves scores. Another way to do cross-validation is to assign a zero weight to those cases not used in the factoring and to assign a unit weight to those cases used. The zero-weight cases are not used in the factoring, but scores are computed for them.

When **Factor scores** or **Principal components** is requested *T2* and *PROB* are also saved. The former is the **Hotelling** T^2 statistic that squares the standardized distance from each case to the centroid of the factor space (that is, the sum of the squared, standardized factor scores). *PROB* is the upper-tail probability of *T2*. Use this statistic to identify outliers within the factor space. *T2* is not computed with an oblique rotation.

Extracting Factors

Factor analysis involves several steps:

- First, the correlation or covariance matrix is computed from the usual cases-by-variables data file or it is input as a matrix.
- Second, the factor loadings are estimated. This is called initial factor extraction. Extraction methods are described in this section.
- Third, the factors are rotated to make the loadings more interpretable—that is, rotation methods make the loadings for each factor either large or small, not in-between. These methods are described in the next section.

In addition, for principal components, factor scores can be computed for each case (see Example 16.7). Ideally, a few factor scores can be used in later analyses in place of a large unwieldy set of variables. Under certain circumstances, these few factor scores have less error and are more reliable measures than the original variables.

Factor Analysis provides three methods of factor extraction:

Principal components	Principal components analysis (PCA); the default
Iterated principal axis	Common factor analysis (IPA); an iterative method that finds common factors by starting with the principal components solution and iteratively solving for communalities
Maximum likelihood	Maximum likelihood analysis (MLA) that iteratively finds communalities and common factors

With commands:

```
ESTIMATE / METHOD=PCA or IPA or MLA
```

Although principal components and common factor analysis methods are based on different mathematical models, they usually produce similar results for the same data from a real world application. Factor analysis purists may not agree with our grouping principal components with common factor analysis; but we do so here because, for a real problem, you may want to explore features from each method.

Principal components are weighted linear combinations of the observed variables. For example, a size component might be:

size = 0.096*height + 0.114*weight + 0.083*age

The component has the form:

component = linear combination of the observed variables

Factor analysis turns this relation around:

observed variable = linear combination of unobserved factors + error

More specifically, the first principal component is the linear combination of the variables that contributes the maximum to the total *variance*; the second component is uncorrelated with the first and contributes a maximum to the residual variance; and so on, until the total variance is accounted for. Ideally, a few components may account for a large percentage of the total variance.

In contrast to maximizing the variance, the "classical factor analysis" model aims to best *reproduce the correlations*. The model is:

$$z_j = a_{j1}F_1 + a_{j2}F_2 \ldots + a_{jm}F_m + U_j$$

where

z_j = the jth standardized variable
m = the number of factors common to all the variables
U_j = the factor unique to variable z_j
a_{ji} = factor loadings

The number of factors, *m*, and the contribution of the unique factors, U_j, should be small, and the factor loadings, a_j, should be either very large or very small, so each variable is associated with a small number of factors. Each factor is interpreted according to the high loadings associated with it.

The data. To illustrate the three methods of factor extraction, we borrow data from Harman (1967), who borrowed them from a 1937 unpublished thesis by Mullen. This classic data set is widely used in the literature. For example, Jackson (1991) reports loadings for the PCA, MLA, and IPA methods. The data are measurements recorded for 305 girls: height, arm span, length of forearm, length of lower leg, weight, bitrochanteric diameter (the upper thigh), chest girth, and chest width.

Because the units of these measurements differ, we analyze a correlation matrix:

	Height	Arm_Span	Forearm	Lowerleg	Weight	Bitro	Chestgir	Chestwid
Height	1.000							
Arm_Span	0.846	1.000						
Forearm	0.805	0.881	1.000					
Lowerleg	0.859	0.826	0.801	1.000				
Weight	0.473	0.376	0.380	0.436	1.000			
Bitro	0.398	0.326	0.319	0.329	0.762	1.000		
Chestgir	0.301	0.277	0.237	0.327	0.730	0.583	1.000	
Chestwid	0.382	0.415	0.345	0.365	0.629	0.577	0.539	1.000

Note: *The examples in this section use a correlation matrix as input. SYSTAT also accepts the usual cases-by-variables data file (Example 16.7) and covariance matrix input (Example 16.6).*

The examples in this section define statistics and describe Factor Analysis options. Information interpreting a specific output panel is presented with the first output that generates the panel. If you start reading a later example, you may need to refer back to earlier examples.

16.1 Principal components: PCA

Principal components (PCA, the default method) is a good way to begin a factor analysis (and possibly the only method you may need). If one variable is a linear combination of the others, the program will not stop (MLA and IPA both require a nonsingular correlation or covariance matrix); also, the PCA output can provide indications that:

- One or more variables have little relation to the others and, therefore, are not suited for factor analysis—so in your next run, you might consider omitting them.
- The final number of factors may be three or four and not double or triple this number.

For this example, you analyze the correlation matrix of physical measurements for 305 girls described above. The correlation matrix is stored in the *GIRLS* file. When you use **File⟶Open⟶Data** to read your data file, SYSTAT knows that the file contains a correlation matrix, so no special instructions are needed to read the matrix. On the **Stats⟶Factor Analysis** dialog box, start by identifying the model variables you want to analyze because principal components is the default method. With commands:

```
FACTOR
    USE girls
    MODEL height .. chestwid
    ESTIMATE / METHOD=PCA  N=305  SORT  ROTATE=VARIMAX
```

Notice the shortcut notation (..) for listing consecutive variables in a file.

Here, n, the sample size originally used to compute the correlation matrix, is also specified (this option is not used for cases-by-variables input). If you use **Edit➡Options** and set **Length=Long**, n is used to compute inferential statistics; otherwise, it is not needed. Specify **Sort loadings** to sort factor loadings from largest to smallest and position loadings larger than 0.5 together within each component.

You also request that the loadings be rotated, but the discussion of this output and rotation features can be found in the next section.

❶ Latent Roots (Eigenvalues)

	1	2	3	4	5
	4.673	1.771	0.481	0.421	0.233
	6	7	8		
	0.187	0.137	0.096		

❷ Component loadings

	1	2
HEIGHT	0.859	0.372
ARM_SPAN	0.842	0.441
LOWERLEG	0.840	0.395
FOREARM	0.813	0.459
WEIGHT	0.758	-0.525
BITRO	0.674	-0.533
CHESTWID	0.671	-0.418
CHESTGIR	0.617	-0.580

❸ Variance Explained by Components

	1	2
	4.673	1.771

Percent of Total Variance Explained

	1	2
	58.411	22.137

❹ Rotated Loading Matrix (Varimax, Gamma = 1.0000)

	1	2
ARM_SPAN	0.930	0.195
FOREARM	0.919	0.164
HEIGHT	0.900	0.260
LOWERLEG	0.899	0.229
WEIGHT	0.251	0.887
BITRO	0.181	0.840
CHESTGIR	0.107	0.840
CHESTWID	0.251	0.750

```
"Variance" Explained by Rotated Components
                    1          2
                  3.497      2.947
Percent of Total Variance Explained
                    1          2
                  43.717     36.832
```

Scree Plot

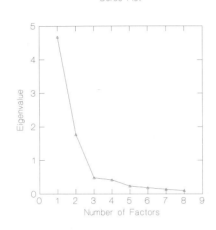

Factor Loadings Plot

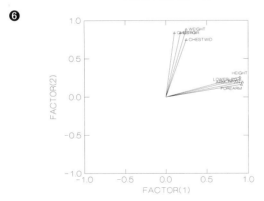

The highlighted numbers below correspond to those in the output:

❶ *Eigenvalues.* You did not specify how many factors you want. For PCA, the assumption is to compute as many factors as there are eigenvalues greater than 1.0—so in this run, you study results for two factors. After examining the output, you may want to use **Minimum eigenvalue** to specify a larger value; or, very rarely, a lower limit. See ❸ and also view a plot of these values in ❺.

❷ *Unrotated loadings.* Unrotated loadings (and orthogonally rotated loadings) are correlations of the variables with the principal components (factors). They are also the eigenvectors of the correlation matrix multiplied by the square roots of the corresponding eigenvalues. Usually these loadings are not useful for interpreting the factors. For some industrial applications, researchers prefer to examine the eigenvectors alone. The eigenvectors (and also the standard error for each element) are available by using **Edit➠Options** and setting **Length=Long**. See Example 16.6.

❸ The *Variance explained* for each component is the eigenvalue for the factor. The first factor accounts for 58.4% of the variance; the second, 22.1%. The *Total Variance* is the sum of the diagonal elements of the correlation (or covariance) matrix. By summing the *Percent of Total Variance Explained* for the two factors (58.411+22.137=80.548), you can say that more than 80% of the variance of all eight variables is explained by the first two factors.

❹ *Rotated loadings.* Because you selected **Sort loadings**, the rows of this display have been sorted, placing the loadings > 0.5 for Factor 1 first, and so on. These are the coefficients of the factors after rotation, so notice that large values in ❷ are larger here and the small values in ❷ are smaller. The sums of squares of these coefficients (for each factor or column) are printed below under the heading *Variance Explained by Rotated Components*; and together the two rotated factors explain more than 80% of the variance. Factor Analysis offers five types of rotation. Here, by default, the orthogonal Varimax method is used. Rotation is discussed in the next section.

To interpret each factor, look for variables with high loadings. The four variables that load highly on Factor 1 can be said to measure "lankiness"; while the four that load highly on Factor 2, "stockiness." Other data sets may include variables that do not load highly on any specific factor.

❺ *Factor Scree Plot.* In this *Quick Graph*, the eigenvalues listed in ❶ are plotted against their order (or associated component). Use this display to identify large values that separate well from smaller eigenvalues. This can help to identify a useful number of factors to retain. Scree is the rubble at the bottom of a cliff; so the large retained roots are the cliff, and the deleted ones are the rubble. To omit *Quick Graphs*, specify GRAPH=NONE before ESTIMATE.

❻ *Factor Loadings Plot.* The points in this plot are variables and the coordinates are the loadings from ❹. This plot is discussed in the introduction to the next section.

Signs of component loadings

The signs of loadings within components are arbitrary. If a component (or factor) has more negative than positive loadings, you can change minus signs to plus and plus to minus. SYSTAT does this automatically for components that have more negative than positive loadings, and thus will occasionally produce components or factors that have different signs from those in other computer programs. This occasionally confuses users. In mathematical terms, $Ax = \lambda x$ and $-Ax = -\lambda x$ are equivalent.

16.2 Maximum likelihood: MLA

This example uses maximum likelihood for initial factor extraction and 2 as the **Number of factors**. Other options remain as in Example 16.1.

continuing from Example 16.1

```
ESTIMATE / METHOD=MLA   N=305   NUMBER=2   SORT,
              ROTATE=VARIMAX
```

❶ Initial Communality Estimates

1	2	3	4	5
0.816	0.849	0.801	0.788	0.749

6	7	8
0.604	0.562	0.478

❷ Iterative Maximum Likelihood Factor Analysis: Convergence = 0.001000

Iteration Number	Maximum Change in Sqrt(Uniqueness)	Negative Log of Likelihood
1	.722640	.384050
2	.243793	.273332
3	.051182	.253671
4	.010359	.253162
5	.000493	.253162

Final Communality Estimates

1	2	3	4	5
0.830	0.893	0.834	0.801	0.911

6	7	8
0.636	0.584	0.463

Canonical Correlations

1	2
0.982	0.949

❸ Factor Pattern

1	2

```
       HEIGHT              0.880        0.237
     ARM_SPAN              0.874        0.360
     LOWERLEG              0.855        0.263
      FOREARM              0.846        0.344
       WEIGHT              0.705       -0.644
        BITRO              0.589       -0.538
     CHESTWID              0.574       -0.365
     CHESTGIR              0.526       -0.554
```

④ Variance Explained by Factors

```
                       1             2

                     4.434         1.518
```

Percent of Total Variance Explained

```
                       1             2

                    55.422        18.974
```

⑤ Rotated Pattern Matrix (Varimax, Gamma =   1.0000)

```
                       1             2

     ARM_SPAN         0.926         0.187
      FOREARM         0.894         0.185
       HEIGHT         0.863         0.293
     LOWERLEG         0.857         0.258
       WEIGHT         0.227         0.927
        BITRO         0.189         0.775
     CHESTGIR         0.129         0.753
     CHESTWID         0.273         0.623
```

"Variance" Explained by Rotated Factors

```
                       1             2

                     3.315         2.637
```

Percent of Total Variance Explained

```
                       1             2

                    41.433        32.963
```

Percent of Common Variance Explained

```
                       1             2

                    55.693        44.307
```

Factor Loadings Plot

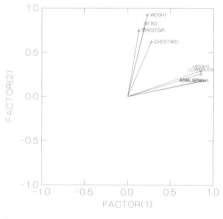

The highlighted numbers below correspond to those in the output:

❶ *Initial Communality Estimates.* The communality of a variable is its theoretical squared multiple correlation with the factors extracted. For MLA (and IPA), the assumption for the initial communalities is the observed squared multiple correlation with all the other variables.

❷ Convergence is reached rapidly in five iterations. The communalities are obtained from two factors. The *Canonical Correlations* are the largest multiple correlations for successive orthogonal linear combination of factors with successive orthogonal linear combination of variables. These values are comfortably high. If, for other data, some of the factors have values that are much lower, you might want to request fewer factors.

❸ *Factor Pattern.* These are the unrotated loadings similar to ❷ in Example 16.1 and are more interesting after they are rotated.

❹ As with the PCA analysis, both factors contribute to explaining the variance of the variables.

❺ An orthogonal rotation of these MLA factors results in two clearly defined factors as was the case for the PCA analysis. **Common Variance** is the sum of the communalities. If **A** is the unrotated MLA factor pattern matrix, common variance is the trace of **A'A**.

Number of factors

In this example, **Number of factors** is used to specify the number of factors to extract. If you were to omit it and rerun the example, SYSTAT adds this report following ❶:

```
The Maximum Number of Factors for Your Data is 4
```

SYSTAT will also report this message if you request more than four factors for these data. This result is due to a theorem by Lederman and indicates that the degrees of freedom allow estimates of loadings and communalities for only four factors.

If you use **Edit➡Options** and set **Length=Long**, SYSTAT would report:

```
Chi-square Test that the Number of Factors is 4
CSQ = 4.3187 P = 0.1154 DF = 2.00
```

The results of this chi-square test indicate that you do not reject the hypothesis that there are four factors (*p* value > 0.05). Technically, the hypothesis is that, "no more than four factors are required." This, of course, does not negate two as the right number. For the *GIRLS* data, here are rotated loadings for four factors:

```
Rotated Pattern Matrix (Varimax, Gamma = 1.000)

                    1          2          3          4
ARM_SPAN          0.937      0.198     -0.283      0.047
LOWERLEG          0.886      0.214      0.188      0.136
HEIGHT            0.878      0.282      0.113     -0.008
FOREARM           0.873      0.196     -0.085     -0.006
WEIGHT            0.241      0.883      0.108      0.108
BITRO             0.182      0.823      0.016     -0.078
CHESTGIR          0.113      0.732     -0.005      0.522
CHESTWID          0.260      0.646     -0.140      0.082
```

The loadings for the last two factors do not make sense. Possibly, the fourth factor has one variable, *CHESTGIR*; but it still has a healthier loading on Factor 2. This test is based on an assumption of multivariate normality (as is MLA itself). If not true, then the test is invalid.

Saving loadings

If you select MLA, you can save factor loadings but not the scores or coefficients (the scores and coefficients cannot be uniquely determined).

16.3 Iterated principal axis: IPA

This example continues with the *GIRLS* data, this time using the IPA (iterated principal axis) method to extract factors.

continuing from the previous example
```
ESTIMATE / METHOD=IPA  SORT  ROTATE=VARIMAX
```

```
        *** We omit the Initial Communality Estimates. See Example 16.2. ***
❶ Iterative Principal Axis Factor Analysis: Convergence = 0.001000

    Iteration   Maximum Change in
     Number     Sqrt(Communality)
        1           .308775
        2           .039358
        3           .017077
        4           .008751
        5           .004934
        6           .002923
        7           .001776
        8           .001093
        9           .000677

❷ Final Communality Estimates

                    1          2          3          4          5
                  0.838      0.889      0.821      0.808      0.888

                    6          7          8
                  0.640      0.583      0.492

❸ Latent Roots (Eigenvalues)
```

	1	2	3	4	5
	4.449	1.510	0.102	0.055	0.015
	6	7	8		
	-0.037	-0.060	-0.074		

Factor Pattern

	1	2
HEIGHT	0.856	0.324
ARM_SPAN	0.848	0.411
LOWERLEG	0.831	0.342
FOREARM	0.808	0.409
WEIGHT	0.750	-0.571
BITRO	0.631	-0.492
CHESTWID	0.607	-0.351
CHESTGIR	0.569	-0.510

Variance Explained by Factors

	1	2
	4.449	1.510

Percent of Total Variance Explained

	1	2
	55.611	18.875

Rotated Pattern Matrix (Varimax, Gamma =   1.0000)

	1	2
ARM_SPAN	0.920	0.204
FOREARM	0.887	0.182
HEIGHT	0.872	0.278
LOWERLEG	0.864	0.248
WEIGHT	0.233	0.913
BITRO	0.188	0.778
CHESTGIR	0.129	0.753
CHESTWID	0.258	0.652

"Variance" Explained by Rotated Factors

	1	2
	3.315	2.644

Percent of Total Variance Explained

	1	2
	41.438	33.049

Percent of Common Variance Explained

	1	2
	55.631	44.369

*** We omit the factor scree plot. It is similar to that in Example 16.1. ***
*** We omit the factor loading plot. It is displayed in the section on Rotation. ***

The highlighted numbers below correspond to those in the output:

❶ Convergence is achieved after nine iterations.

❷ *Final Communality Estimates.* Before the first iteration, the communality of a variable is its multiple correlation squared with the remaining variables. At each iteration, communalities are estimated from the loadings matrix, **A**, by finding the trace of **A'A**, where the number of columns in **A** is the number of factors. Iterations continue until the largest change in any communality is less than that specified with **Convergence**.

❸ The diagonal of the correlation (or covariance) matrix is replaced by the final estimates of communalities, and eigenvalues are computed.

Saving
loadings

If you select IPA, you can save factor loadings but not the scores or coefficients (the scores and coefficients cannot be uniquely determined).

Rotation

Usually the initial factor extraction does not give interpretable factors. One of the purposes of rotation is to obtain factors that can be named and interpreted. That is, if you can make the large loadings larger than before and the smaller loadings smaller, then each variable is associated with a minimal number of factors. Hopefully, the variables that load strongly together on a particular factor will have a clear meaning with respect to the subject area at hand.

It helps to study plots of loadings for one factor against those for another. Ideally, you want to see clusters of loadings at extreme values for each factor: like what A and C are for Factor 1, and B and D are for Factor 2 in the left plot, and not like E and F in the middle plot.

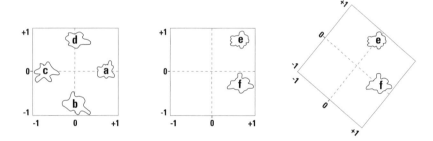

In the middle plot, the loadings in groups E and F are sizeable for *both* Factors 1 and 2. However, if you lift the plot axes away from E and F, rotating them 45 degrees, and then set them down as on the right, you achieve the desired effect. Sounds easy for two factors. For three factors, imagine that the loadings are balls floating in a room and that you rotate the floor and walls so that each loading is as close to the floor or a wall as it can be. This concept generalizes to more dimensions.

Researchers let the computer do the rotation automatically. There are many criteria for achieving a *simple structure* among component loadings, although Thurstone's are most widely cited. For p variables and m components:

– Each component should have at least m near-zero loadings.
– Few components should have non-zero loadings on the same variable.

Factor Analysis provides five methods of rotating loadings:

Varimax   Varimax rotation.

Equamax   Equamax rotation.

Quartimax   Quartimax rotation.

Orthomax   Orthomax rotation. Default **Gamma** is 1.

Oblimin   Direct oblimin with optional **Gamma**. Default **Gamma** is 0.

Plus **Gamma**=n, a parameter for **Orthomax** and **Oblimin**.

The first four are orthogonal rotations; Oblimin is an oblique rotation. This means that the resulting factors may be correlated. Orthomax with default Gamma 1 produces a varimax rotation and Orthomax with Gamma 0 produces a quartimax rotation. Large negative values of gamma produce loadings similar to principal components loadings. In general, smaller values of gamma tend to maximize the variance of the rotated loadings across rows, as for quartimax rotation. Larger values of gamma tend to maximize the variance down columns, as for varimax rotation. Specifying gamma as negative for Oblimin restricts the amount correlation among factors so that with large negative values of gamma, the results look similar to Varimax. Increasing gamma positively from 0 results in higher correlations among factors. When gamma gets in the vicinity of 1.5 to 1.8, perfect collinearly (all factors the same) may result. See Clarkson and Jennrich (1988). Notice that **Gamma** need not be an integer. With commands:

```
ESTIMATE / ROTATE=OBLIMIN or ORTHOMAX or EQUAMAX or
                 QUARTIMAX or VARIMAX,  GAMMA=n
```

Rotating Quick Graphs

You can rotate the 3-D *Quick Graph* Factor Loadings Plot. See if you can surpass the automated methods. Rotate the loadings the same way you rotate any 3-D SYSTAT display.

16.4 Components for the GIRLS data

Let's compare the unrotated and orthogonally rotated loadings from Example 16.1 with those from an oblique rotation. Before showing how to instruct Factor Analysis to do this, let's look at pictures of the results:

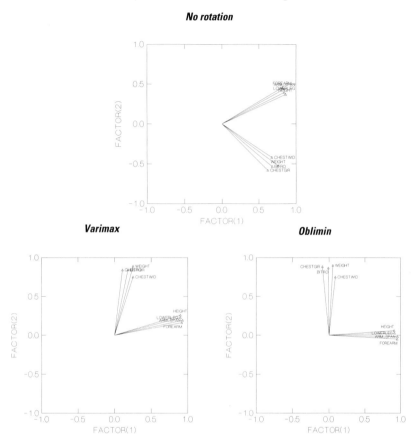

No rotation

Varimax

Oblimin

While the unrotated factor loadings form two distinct clusters, they both have strong positive loadings for Factor 1. The "lanky" variables have moderate positive loadings on Factor 2 while the "stocky" variables have negative loadings on Factor 2. With the Varimax rotation, the "lanky" variables load highly on Factor 1 with small loadings on Factor 2; the "stocky" variables load highly on Factor 2. The Oblimin rotation does a much better job of centering each cluster at 0 on its minor factor.

continuing from Example 16.1, *replace* `ROTATE=VARIMAX` *with* `ROTATE=OBLIMIN`

```
*** We omit the output panels as displayed in
       ❶, ❷ and ❸ of Example 16.1              ***

Rotated Pattern Matrix (Oblimin, Gamma = 0.0000)

                1          2

ARM_SPAN     0.957     -0.017
FOREARM      0.953     -0.048
LOWERLEG     0.916      0.028
HEIGHT       0.909      0.060
WEIGHT       0.054      0.897
CHESTGIR    -0.090      0.882
BITRO       -0.011      0.864
CHESTWID     0.088      0.749

"Variance" Explained by Rotated Components

                1          2

             3.527      2.917

Percent of Total Variance Explained

                1          2

            44.091     36.457

Correlations among Oblique Factors or Components

                1          2

        1   1.000
        2   0.431      1.000
```

Extended results

If you use **Edit➡Options** and set **Length=Long**, you get the following additional output:

```
Direct and Indirect Contributions of Factors To Variance

                1          2

        1   3.509
        2   0.019      2.898

Rotated Structure Matrix

                1          2

ARM_SPAN     0.935      0.452
FOREARM      0.950      0.396
LOWERLEG     0.928      0.423
HEIGHT       0.933      0.363
WEIGHT       0.441      0.921
CHESTGIR     0.362      0.860
BITRO        0.410      0.787
CHESTWID     0.290      0.843
```

The values in the *Direct and Indirect Contributions of Factors to Variance* are useful for determining if part of a factor's contribution to *"Variance" Explained* is due to its correlation with another factor. Notice that

$$3.509 + 0.019 = 3.528 \text{ (or 3.527)}$$

is the *"Variance" Explained* for Factor 1, and

$$2.898 + 0.019 = 2.917$$

is the *"Variance" Explained* for Factor 2 (differences in the last digit are due to rounding error).

Think of the values in the *Rotated Structure Matrix* as correlations of the variable with the factors.

16.5 Factors for the GIRLS data

Here are rotated loadings from the MLA and IPA analyses (Example 16.2 and Example 16.3):

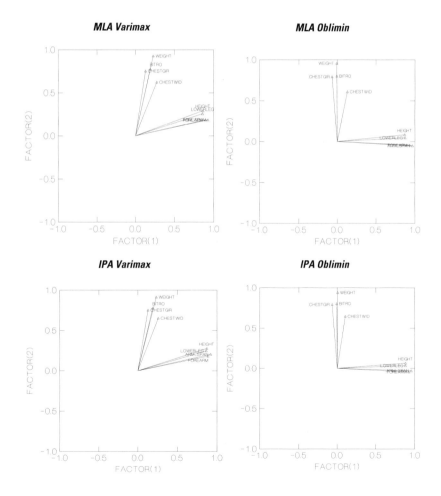

To request these loadings, modify the instructions in Example 16.2 and Example 16.3 by substituting **Oblimin** rotation for **Varimax**. Also use **Edit▸Options** and set **Length=Long**. Here is the text output that results:

An oblique rotation for an MLA extraction

```
*** We omit the output panels ❶, ❷,❸ and ❹ as
      displayed in Example 16.2                        ***

Rotated Pattern Matrix (Oblimin,  Gamma =    0.0000)

                              1          2

    ARM_SPAN             0.968     -0.050
     FOREARM             0.933     -0.044
    LOWERLEG             0.872      0.046
      HEIGHT             0.869      0.083
      WEIGHT            -0.007      0.958
       BITRO            -0.006      0.801
    CHESTGIR            -0.066      0.793
    CHESTWID             0.129      0.610

"Variance" Explained by Rotated Factors

                              1          2

                          3.361      2.591

Percent of Total Variance Explained

                              1          2

                         42.009     32.387

Percent of Common Variance Explained

                              1          2

                         56.467     43.533

Correlations among Oblique Factors or Components

                              1          2

            1         1.000
            2         0.473      1.000
```

An oblique rotation for an IPA extraction

```
***  We omit the output panels ❶, ❷ and ❸ as
       displayed in Example 16.3                       ***

Rotated Pattern Matrix (Oblimin,  Gamma =    0.0000)

                              1          2

    ARM_SPAN             0.956     -0.029
     FOREARM             0.926     -0.045
      HEIGHT             0.883      0.065
    LOWERLEG             0.882      0.034
      WEIGHT             0.005      0.940
       BITRO            -0.007      0.803
    CHESTGIR            -0.065      0.793
    CHESTWID             0.104      0.646

Variance Explained by Rotated Factors

                              1          2

                          3.360      2.599

Percent of Total Variance Explained

                              1          2

                         42.002     32.484


Percent of Common Variance Explained
```

	1	2
	56.389	43.611

Correlations among Oblique Factors or Components

	1	2
1	1.000	
2	0.472	1.000

Extended results

When you use **Edit➧Options** and set **Length=Long**, you get the following additional output:

MLA

Direct and Indirect Contributions of
Factors To Variance

	1	2
1	3.343	
2	0.018	2.573

Rotated Structure Matrix

	1	2
ARM_SPAN	0.908	0.494
FOREARM	0.944	0.407
LOWERLEG	0.894	0.459
HEIGHT	0.912	0.398
WEIGHT	0.446	0.954
BITRO	0.372	0.798
CHESTGIR	0.417	0.671
CHESTWID	0.309	0.762

IPA

Direct and Indirect Contributions of
Factors To Variance

	1	2
1	3.345	
2	0.016	2.583

Rotated Structure Matrix

	1	2
ARM_SPAN	0.914	0.481
FOREARM	0.942	0.422
HEIGHT	0.898	0.450
LOWERLEG	0.905	0.392
WEIGHT	0.448	0.942
BITRO	0.372	0.800
CHESTGIR	0.409	0.695
CHESTWID	0.308	0.762

More Examples

The input for the earlier examples was a correlation matrix. In these examples, you input a covariance matrix and the usual cases-by-variables rectangular data file.

16.6 Starting from a covariance matrix

Jackson (1991) describes a project in which the maximum thrust of ballistic missiles was measured. For a specific measure called "total impulse," it is necessary to calculate the area under a curve. Originally a planimeter was used to obtain the area, and later an electronic device performed the integration directly but unreliably in its early usage. As data, two strain gauges were attached to each of 40 Nike rockets and both types of measurements were recorded in parallel (making four measurements per rocket). The covariance matrix of the measures is stored in the *MISSLES* file:

	Integra1	Planmtr1	Integra2	Planmtr2
Integra1	102.740			
Planmtr1	88.670	142.740		
Integra2	67.040	86.560	84.570	
Planmtr2	54.060	80.030	69.420	99.060

To illustrate features associated with covariance matrix input (asymptotic 95% confidence limits for the eigenvalues, estimates of the population eigenvalues with standard errors, and latent vectors (eigenvectors or characteristic vectors) with standard errors), use **Edit➧Options** and set **Length=Long**. Next, use **Stats➧Factor Analysis**, then select **Principle components** as the method of factor analysis. Move *INTEGRA1*, *PLANMTR1*, *INTEGRA2*, and *PLANMTR2* to the **Model Variables** list. Select **Covariance** and **Sort loadings**. In the **Sample size for matrix input** text box, type 40.

```
FACTOR
    USE missles
    MODEL integra1 planmtr1 integra2 planmtr2
    PRINT = LONG
    ESTIMATE / METHOD=PCA  COVA  N=40  SORT
```

```
Latent Roots (Eigenvalues)

                            1           2           3           4

                        335.335      48.034      29.330      16.410

Asymptotic 95% Confidence Limits for the Eigenvalues,  N =      40

      Upper Limits:

                            1           2           3           4

                        596.960      85.510      52.214      29.212

      Lower Limits:

                            1           2           3           4

                        233.153      33.398      20.393      11.409

Unbiased Estimates of Population Eigenvalues

                            1           2           3           4

                        332.699      46.930      31.086      18.395

Unbiased Estimates of Standard Errors of Eigenvalues

                            1           2           3           4

                         74.946      10.177       5.735       3.253
```

❶
```
Chi-Square Test that all Eigenvalues are Equal, N =      40

     CSQ =    110.6871      P =  0.0000      DF =        9.00
```

❷
```
Latent Vectors (Eigenvectors)

                            1           2           3           4

      PLANMTR1          0.468       0.621       0.572       0.261
      INTEGRA1          0.608       0.179      -0.759       0.147
      INTEGRA2          0.459      -0.139       0.168      -0.861
      PLANMTR2          0.448      -0.750       0.262       0.410


Standard Error for Each Eigenvector Element

                            1           2           3           4

      PLANMTR1          0.053       0.188       0.211       0.177
      INTEGRA1          0.041       0.246       0.076       0.207
      INTEGRA2          0.034       0.136       0.237       0.052
      PLANMTR2          0.056       0.106       0.263       0.128

Component Loadings

                            1           2           3           4

      PLANMTR1         11.132       1.239      -4.113       0.597
      INTEGRA1          8.573       4.307       3.095       1.056
      INTEGRA2          8.405      -0.962       0.908      -3.489
      PLANMTR2          8.202      -5.198       1.416       1.662

Variance Explained by Components

                            1           2           3           4

                        335.335      48.034      29.330      16.410

Percent of Total Variance Explained

                            1           2           3           4

                         78.147      11.194       6.835       3.824

Differences: Original Minus Fitted Correlations or Covariances
```

	PLANMTR1	INTEGRA1	INTEGRA2	PLANMTR2
PLANMTR1	-0.000			
INTEGRA1	-0.000	-0.000		
INTEGRA2	-0.000	-0.000	-0.000	
PLANMTR2	-0.000	-0.000	-0.000	0.000

❸

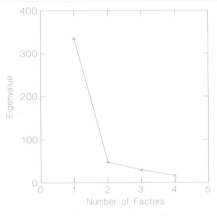

Scree Plot

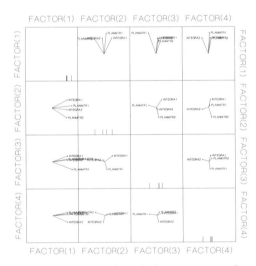

Factor Loadings Plot

The highlighted numbers below correspond to those in the output:

❶ *Chi-Square Test that all eigenvalues are equal.* The null hypothesis here is that all four eigenvalues are equal against an alternative hypothesis that at least one root is different. The results here indicate that you reject the null hypothesis ($p < 0.00005$).

❷ *Latent Eigenvectors.* The first eigenvectors has fairly similar coefficients. The second represents gauge differences because the signs are different for each. The last two are less clear.

❸ When there are four or more factors, the *Quick Graph* of the loadings is a SPLOM. The first component represents 78% of the variability of the product, so plots of loadings for Factors 2 through 4 convey little information (notice that values in the stripe displays along the diagonal concentrate around 0, while those for Factor 1 fall to the right).

16.7 Starting from a rectangular file

Begin this analysis from the *OURWORLD* cases-by-variables data file. Each case contains information for one of 57 countries. You will study the interrelations among a subset of 13 variables including economic measures (gross domestic product per capita and U.S. dollars spent per person on education, health, and the military), birth and death rates, population estimates for 1983, 1986, and 1990 plus predictions for 2020, and the percentages of the population who can read and who live in cities.

You request principal components extraction with an oblique rotation. As a first step, SYSTAT computes the correlation matrix. Correlations measure linear relations. However, plots of the economic measures and population values as recorded indicate a lack of linearity, so you use base 10 logarithms to transform six variables, and you use square roots to transform two others.

```
FACTOR
    USE ourworld
    LET (gdp_cap, gnp_86, pop_1983, pop_1986, pop_1990,
        pop_2020) = L10(@)
    LET (mil,educ) = SQR(@)
    MODEL urban birth_rt death_rt gdp_cap gnp_86 mil,
          educ b_to_d literacy pop_1983 pop_1986,
          pop_1990 pop_2020
    PRINT=MEDIUM
    SAVE pcascore / SCORES
    ESTIMATE / METHOD=PCA SORT ROTATE=OBLIMIN
```

```
Matrix to be Factored
               URBAN BIRTH_RT DEATH_RT  GDP_CAP   GNP_86      MIL     EDUC

URBAN          1.000
BIRTH_RT      -0.800   1.000
DEATH_RT      -0.513   0.511    1.000
GDP_CAP        0.764  -0.919   -0.401    1.000
GNP_86         0.775  -0.879   -0.452    0.974    1.000
MIL            0.645  -0.755   -0.148    0.866    0.851    1.000
EDUC           0.624  -0.753   -0.215    0.900    0.921    0.887    1.000
B_TO_D        -0.307   0.511   -0.434   -0.529   -0.441   -0.618   -0.525
LITERACY       0.800  -0.930   -0.660    0.834    0.840    0.642    0.687
POP_1983       0.213  -0.084    0.015    0.058    0.009    0.221   -0.006
POP_1986       0.190  -0.052    0.029    0.025   -0.021    0.194   -0.031
POP_1990       0.170  -0.025    0.028   -0.002   -0.045    0.173   -0.051
POP_2020       0.005   0.188    0.074   -0.212   -0.248   -0.034   -0.255

               B_TO_D LITERACY POP_1983 POP_1986 POP_1990 POP_2020

B_TO_D         1.000
LITERACY      -0.274   1.000
POP_1983      -0.153  -0.005    1.000
POP_1986      -0.136  -0.033    0.998    1.000
POP_1990      -0.107  -0.053    0.997    0.999    1.000
POP_2020       0.062  -0.236    0.953    0.960    0.967    1.000

Number of observations: 49
```

❶ Latent Roots (Eigenvalues)

```
                    1         2         3         4         5

                 6.395     4.017     1.656     0.433     0.239

                    6         7         8         9        10

                 0.097     0.081     0.040     0.025     0.011

                   11        12        13

                 0.005     0.001     0.000
```

Empirical upper bound for the first Eigenvalue =   7.4817.

Chi-Square Test that all Eigenvalues are Equal, N = 49
      CSQ =   1542.2903   P = 0.0000   DF =   78.00

Chi-Square Test that the Last 10 Eigenvalues Are Equal
      CSQ =   636.4350   P = 0.0000   DF =   59.89

Component loadings

```
                    1         2         3

GDP_CAP          0.977    -0.037    -0.061
GNP_86           0.970    -0.085     0.004
BIRTH_RT        -0.951     0.014    -0.077
LITERACY         0.897    -0.101     0.300
EDUC             0.893    -0.086    -0.230
MIL              0.877     0.150    -0.291
URBAN            0.839     0.143     0.230
B_TO_D          -0.517    -0.123     0.776
POP_1990         0.038     0.997     0.039
POP_1986         0.064     0.997     0.025
POP_1983         0.095     0.994     0.025
POP_2020        -0.180     0.975     0.100
DEATH_RT        -0.453     0.082    -0.866
```

Variance Explained by Components

```
                    1         2         3

                 6.395     4.017     1.656
```

Percent of Total Variance Explained

```
                    1         2         3

                49.192    30.896    12.736
```

❷ Rotated Pattern Matrix (OBLIMIN,Gamma =   0.0)

```
                    1         2         3

GDP_CAP          0.978    -0.040     0.052
GNP_86           0.971    -0.082    -0.015
BIRTH_RT        -0.951     0.004     0.084
EDUC             0.896    -0.105     0.219
```

```
         LITERACY          0.896      -0.070      -0.311
         MIL               0.878       0.124       0.292
         URBAN             0.835       0.166      -0.228
         B_TO_D           -0.522      -0.050      -0.779
         POP_1990          0.024       0.998       0.009
         POP_1986          0.049       0.996       0.023
         POP_1983          0.080       0.993       0.024
         POP_2020         -0.194       0.981      -0.051
         DEATH_RT         -0.446      -0.001       0.873
```

"Variance" Explained by Rotated Components

```
                           1           2           3

                         6.395       4.006       1.667
```

❸ Percent of Total Variance Explained

```
                           1           2           3

                        49.190      30.813      12.823
```

Correlations among Oblique Factors or Components

```
                           1           2           3

              1         1.000
              2         0.013       1.000
              3        -0.002       0.045       1.000
```

Scree Plot

❹

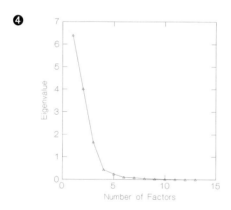

Factor Loadings Plot

❺

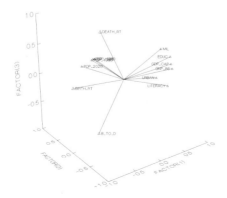

```
        *** We omit "Differneces: Original Minus Fitted Correlations or Covariance" ***
❻  Coefficients for Standardized Factor Scores

                              1            2            3

       GDP_CAP            0.153       -0.009        0.034
       GNP_86             0.152       -0.019       -0.006
       BIRTH_RT          -0.148       -0.001        0.048
       EDUC               0.141       -0.026        0.135
       LITERACY           0.139       -0.014       -0.184
       MIL                0.138        0.031        0.177
       URBAN              0.130        0.044       -0.136
       B_TO_D            -0.084       -0.009       -0.469
       POP_1990           0.005        0.249       -0.000
       POP_1986           0.009        0.249        0.008
       POP_1983           0.014        0.248        0.008
       POP_2020          -0.029        0.245       -0.037
       DEATH_RT          -0.067       -0.006        0.523

   Standardized scores have been saved.
```

The highlighted numbers below correspond to those in the output:

❶ By default, SYSTAT extracts three factors because three eigenvalues are greater than 1.0.

❷ Seven or eight variables have high loadings on Factor 1. The eighth, *B_TO_D* (a ratio of birth-to-death rate) has a higher loading on Factor 3. With the exception of *BIRTH_RT*, the other variables are economic measures, so let's identify this as the "economic" factor. Clearly, the second factor can be named "population," and the third, less clearly, "death rates."

❸ The economic and population factors account for 80% (49.19 + 30.81) of the total variance, so a plot of the scores for these factors should be useful for characterizing differences among the countries.

❹ The eigenvalues for the first two factors are sizeable, while that for the third is less indicative of a strong factor.

❺ For analyses with three factors, SYSTAT draws a 3-D *Quick Graph* of the loadings. Use the pop-up graph tool to rotate it.

❻ Because you requested that the factor scores be saved, SYSTAT prints the coefficients used to compute them. These coefficients are for the standardized variables.

Revisiting the correlation matrix

Here is a correlation matrix from **Stats**➟**Correlation** for the variables in this example. You ordered them using their order in the sorted **Rotated Pattern Matrix**. Use an editor to insert the dotted line.

```
Pearson correlation matrix

            GDP_CAP  GNP_86 BIRTH_RT    EDUC LITERACY     MIL   URBAN
 GDP_CAP     1.000
 GNP_86      0.974   1.000
 BIRTH_RT   -0.919  -0.879   1.000
 EDUC        0.900   0.921  -0.753   1.000
 LITERACY    0.834   0.840  -0.930   0.687   1.000
 MIL         0.866   0.851  -0.755   0.887   0.642   1.000
 URBAN       0.764   0.775  -0.800   0.624   0.800   0.645   1.000
            ---------------------------------------------------------
 POP_1990   -0.002  -0.045  -0.025  -0.051  -0.053   0.173   0.170
 POP_1986    0.025  -0.021  -0.052  -0.031  -0.033   0.194   0.190
 POP_1983    0.058   0.009  -0.084  -0.006  -0.005   0.221   0.213
 POP_2020   -0.212  -0.248   0.188  -0.255  -0.236  -0.034   0.005
 B_TO_D     -0.529  -0.441   0.511  -0.525  -0.274  -0.618  -0.307
 DEATH_RT   -0.401  -0.452   0.511  -0.215  -0.660  -0.148  -0.513

            POP_1990 POP_1986 POP_1983 POP_2020   B_TO_D DEATH_RT
 POP_1990    1.000
 POP_1986    0.999   1.000
 POP_1983    0.997   0.998   1.000
 POP_2020    0.967   0.960   0.953   1.000
            ---------------------------------------------------------
 B_TO_D     -0.107  -0.136  -0.153   0.062   1.000
 DEATH_RT    0.028   0.029   0.015   0.074  -0.434   1.000
```

The top triangle of the matrix shows the correlations of the variables within the "economic" factor. BIRTH_RT has strong negative correlations with the other variables. Correlations of the population variables with the economic variables are displayed in the four rows below the top triangle, and correlations for variables within the population factor are displayed in the top triangle of the bottom panel. The correlation between the variables in Factor 3 (B_TO_D and DEATH_RT) is −0.434 and is smaller than any of the other within-factor correlations.

Factor scores

Look at the scores just stored in PCASCORE. First, merge the name of each country and the grouping variable GROUP$ with the scores. The values of GROUP$ identify each country as *Europe, Islamic,* or *New World.* Next, plot Factor 2 against Factor 1 (labeling points with country names) and Factor 3 against Factor 1 (labeling points with the first letter of their group membership). Finally, use SPLOMs to display the scores, adding 75% confidence ellipses for each subgroup in the plots and normal curves for the univariate distributions. Repeat the latter using kernel density estimators.

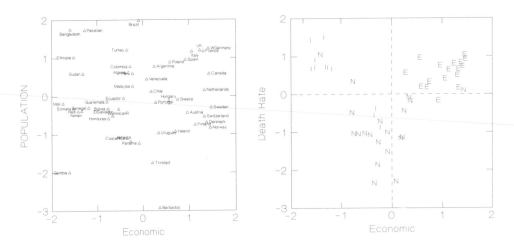

High loadings on the "economic" factor show countries that are strong economically (Germany, Canada, Netherlands, Sweden, Switzerland, Denmark, and Norway) relative to those with low loadings (Bangladesh, Ethiopia, Mali, and Gambia). Not surprisingly, the population factor identifies Barbados as the smallest and Bangladesh, Pakistan, and Brazil as largest. The questionable third factor (death rate) does help to separate the New World countries from the others.

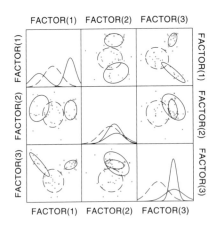
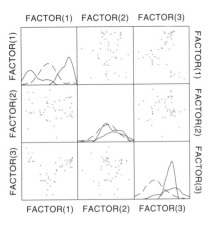

In each SPLOM, the dashed lines marking curves, ellipses, and kernel contours identify New World countries. The kernel contours in the plot of Factor 3 against Factor 1 (bottom left in the right SPLOM) identify a pocket of Islamic countries within the New World group.

More about Factor Analysis

Although principal components and common factor analysis methods are based on different mathematical models, they usually produce similar results for the same data. If you understand the component model, you are on the way toward understanding the factor model, so let's begin with the former.

A principal component

What is a principal component? The simplest way to see is through real data. The following data, stored in the *GRE* data file, consist of Graduate Record Examination verbal and quantitative scores. These scores are from 25 applicants to a graduate psychology department.

VERBAL	QUANT	VERBAL	QUANT
590	530	520	530
620	620	660	650
640	620	750	710
650	550	630	640
620	610	570	660
610	660	600	650
560	570	570	570
610	730	600	550
600	650	690	540
740	790	770	670
560	580	610	660
680	710	600	640
600	540		

Now, you could decide to use **Stats**➡**General Linear Model** to predict verbal scores from quantitative; or you could decide to predict quantitative from verbal by the same method. The data don't suggest which is a dependent variable; either will do. What if you aren't interested in predicting either one separately but instead want to know how both variables work together jointly? This is what a principal component does. Karl Pearson, who developed principal components analysis in 1901, described a component as a "line of closest fit to systems of points in space." In short, the regression line indicates best *prediction* and the component line indicates best *association*.

The following figure shows the regression and component lines for the *GRE* data. The regression of *y* on *x* is the line with the smallest slope. The regression of *x* on *y* is the line with the largest slope. The component line is between the other two. Interestingly, when most people are asked to draw a line relating two variables in a scatterplot, they tend to approximate the component line. It takes many explanations to get them to realize that this is not the best line for predicting the vertical axis variable (y) or the horizontal axis variable (x).

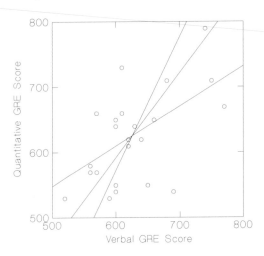

Notice that the slope of the component line is approximately 1, which means that the two variables are weighted almost equally (assuming the axis scales are the same). You could make a new variable called *GRE* that is the sum of the two tests:

GRE = VERBAL + QUANTITATIVE

This new variable could summarize, albeit crudely, the information in the other two. If the points clustered almost perfectly around the component line, then the new component variable could summarize both variables almost perfectly.

Multiple principal components

The goal of principal components analysis is to summarize a multivariate data set as accurately as possible using a few components. So far, you have seen only one component. It is possible, however, to draw a second component perpendicular to the first. The first component will summarize as much of the joint variation as possible. The second will summarize what's left. If you do this with the *GRE* data, of course, you will have as many components as original variables—not much of a saving. You usually seek fewer components than variables, so that the variation left over is negligible.

Component coefficients

In the above equation for computing the first principal component on the test data, you made both coefficients equal. In fact, when you run the sample covariance matrix using **Stats▸Factor Analysis**, the coefficients are as follows:

$$GRE = 0.008*VERBAL + 0.01*QUANTITATIVE$$

They are nearly equal. Their magnitude is considerably less than 1 because principal components are usually scaled to conserve variance. That is, after you compute the components with these coefficients, the total variance on the components is the same as the total variance on the original variables.

Component loadings

Most researchers want to know the relation between the original variables and the components. Some components may be nearly identical to an original variable; in other words, their coefficients may be nearly 0 for all variables except one. Other components may be a more even amalgam of several original variables.

Component loadings are the covariances of the original variables with the components. In the example, these loadings are 51.085 for *VERBAL* and 62.880 for *QUANTITATIVE*. You may have noticed that these are proportional to the coefficients; they are simply scaled differently. If you square each of these loadings and add them up separately for each component, you will have the variance accounted for by each component.

Correlations or covariances

Most researchers prefer to analyze the correlation rather than covariance structure among their variables. Sample correlations are simply covariances of sample standardized variables. Thus, if your variables are measured on very different scales or if you feel the standard deviations of your variables are not theoretically significant, you will want to work with correlations instead of covariances. In the test example, working with correlations yields loadings of 0.879 for each variable instead of 51.085 and 62.880. When you factor the correlation instead of the covariance matrix, then the loadings are the correlations of each component with each original variable.

For the test data, loadings of 0.879 mean that if you created a *GRE* component by standardizing *VERBAL* and *QUANTITATIVE* and adding them together weighted by the coefficients, you would find the correlation between these component scores and the original *VERBAL* scores to be 0.879. The same would be true for *QUANTITATIVE*.

Rotation

Components are uniquely defined mathematically. They are not laws of nature, however. Components will not necessarily be more theoretically meaningful than any other linear combination of your variables.

SYSTAT offers several methods for approximating these conditions. The most popular is the default Varimax rotation. You won't rotate the test data because rotating components based on fewer than three variables is pointless.

Factor analysis

You have seen how principal components analysis is a method for computing new variables that summarize variation in a space parsimoniously. For the test variables, the equation for computing the first component was:

$$GRE = 0.006 * VERBAL + 0.01 * QUANTITATIVE$$

This component equation is linear, of the form:

component = linear combination of {observed variables}

Factor analysts turn this equation around:

observed variable = linear combination of {factors} + error

This model was presented by Spearman near the turn of the century in the context of a single intelligence factor and extended to multiple mental measurement factors by Thurstone several decades later. Notice that the factor model makes observed variables a function of unobserved factors. Even though this looks like a linear regression model, none of the graphical and analytical techniques used for regression can be applied to the factor model because there is no unique, observable set of factor scores or residuals to examine.

Factor analysts are less interested in prediction than in decomposing a covariance matrix. This is why the fundamental equation of factor analysis is not the above linear model, but rather its *quadratic form*:

observed covariances = factor covariances + error covariances

The covariances in this equation are usually expressed in matrix form, so that the model decomposes an observed covariance matrix into a hypothetical factor covariance matrix plus a hypothetical error covariance matrix. The diagonals of these two hypothetical matrices are known, respectively, as *communalities* and *specificities*.

In ordinary language, then, the factor model expresses variation within and relations among observed variables as partly common variation among factors and partly specific variation among random errors.

Estimating factors

Factors must be estimated iteratively in a computer. There are several methods available. The most popular approach, used in SYSTAT, is to modify the diagonal of the observed covariance matrix and calculate factors the same way components are computed. This procedure is repeated until the communalities reproduced by the factor covariances are indistinguishable from the diagonal of the modified matrix.

If you're interested in confirmatory factor models, path models, and causal models, see Chapter 18.

Principal components versus factor analysis

Factor Analysis performs both principal components and common factor analysis. Some view principal components analysis as a method of factor analysis, though there is a theoretical distinction between the two. Principal components are weighted linear composites of observed variables. Common factors are unobserved variables that are hypothesized to account for the intercorrelations among observed variables.

One significant practical difference is that common factor scores are indeterminate, whereas principal component scores are not. There are no sufficient estimators of scores for subjects on common factors (rotated or unrotated, maximum likelihood or otherwise). Some computer programs provide regression estimates of factor scores, but these are not estimates in the usual statistical sense. This problem arises not because factors can be arbitrarily rotated (so can principal components), but because the common factor model is based on more unobserved parameters than observed data points, an unusual circumstance in statistics.

In recent years, maximum likelihood factor analysis algorithms have been devised to estimate common factors. The implementation of these algorithms in popular computer packages has led some users to believe that the factor indeterminacy problem does not exist for maximum likelihood factor estimates. It does.

Mathematicians and psychometricians have known about the factor indeterminacy problem for decades. For a historical review of the issues, see Steiger (1979), and for a general review, see Rozeboom (1982). For further information on principal components, consult Harman (1976), Mulaik (1978), Gnanadesikan (1977), or Mardia, Kent, and Bibby (1979).

Because of the indeterminacy problem, Factor Analysis computes subjects' scores only for the principal components model where subjects' scores are a simple linear transformation of scores on factored variables. Factor Analysis does not save scores from a common factor model.

Applications and caveats

You may want to analyze *OURWORLD* data in Example 16.7 using the factor model instead of the component model. The results are quite similar. While there is not room here to discuss more statistical issues, you should realize that there are several myths about factors versus components:

Myth: The factor model allows hypothesis testing; the component model doesn't. **Fact**: Morrison (1967) and others present a full range of formal statistical tests for components.

Myth: Factor loadings are real; principal component loadings are approximations. **Fact**: This statement is too ambiguous to have any meaning. It is easy to define things so that factors are approximations of components.

Myth: Factor analysis is more likely to uncover lawful structure in your data; principal components are more contaminated by error. **Fact**: Again, this statement is ambiguous. With further definition, it can be shown to be true for some data, false for other. It is true that, in general, factor solutions will have lower dimensionality than corresponding component solutions. This can be an advantage when searching for simple structure among noisy variables, as long as you compare the result to a principal components solution to avoid being fooled by the sort of degeneracies illustrated above.

Summary

Computation

Provisional methods are used for computing covariance or correlation matrices (see Chapter 9 for references). Components are computed by using a Householder tridiagonalization and implicit QL iterations (see Chapter 8, Chapter 6, and Chapter 12 for references). Rotations are computed with a variant of Kaiser's iterative algorithm, described in Mulaik (1972).

References

Afifi, A.A., and V. Clark. 1984. *Computer-aided multivariate analysis.* Belmont, Calif.: Lifetime Learning Publications.

Clarkson, D.B. and Jennrich, R.I. 1988. Quartic rotation criteria and algorithms, *Psychometrika*, 53: 251–259.

Dixon, W.J. et al. 1985. *BMDP statistical software manual.* Berkeley: University of California Press.

Gnanadesikan, R. 1977. *Methods for statistical data analysis of multivariate observations.* New York: John Wiley & Sons, Inc.

Harman, H.H. 1976. *Modern factor analysis*, 3rd ed. Chicago: University of Chicago Press.

Jackson, J.E. 1991. A *user's guide to principal components.* New York: John Wiley & Sons, Inc.

Jennrich, R.I., and S.M. Robinson. 1969. A newton-raphson algorithm for maximum likelihood factor analysis. *Psychometrika*, 34: 111-123.

Mardia, K.V., Kent, J.T., and Bibby, J.M. 1979. *Multivariate analysis.* London: Academic Press.

Morrison, D.F. 1976. *Multivariate statistical methods*, 2nd ed. New York: McGraw-Hill.

Mulaik, S.A. 1972. *The foundations of factor analysis.* New York: McGraw-Hill.

Rozeboom, W.W. 1982. The determinacy of common factors in large item domains. *Psychometrika*, 47: 281-295.

Steiger, J.H. 1979. Factor indeterminacy in the 1930's and 1970's: some interesting parallels. *Psychometrika*, 44: 157-167.

Multidimensional Scaling

Leland Wilkinson

Multidimensional scaling (MDS) offers nonmetric
multidimensional scaling of a similarity or dissimilarity matrix in
one to five dimensions. MDS is a powerful data reduction
procedure that can be used on a direct similarity or dissimilarity
matrix or on one derived from rectangular data with Correlations.
SYSTAT provides three MDS loss functions (Kruskal, Guttman,
and Young) that produce results comparable to those from three of
the major MDS packages (KYST, SSA, and ALSCAL). All three
methods perform a similar function: to compute coordinates for a
set of points in a space such that the distances between pairs of
these points fit as closely as possible to measured dissimilarities
between a corresponding set of objects.

The family of procedures called *principal components* or *factor
analysis* is related to multidimensional scaling in function, but
multidimensional scaling differs from this family in important
respects. Usually, but not necessarily, multidimensional scaling
can fit an appropriate model in fewer dimensions than can these
other procedures. Furthermore, if it is implausible to assume a
linear relationship between distances and dissimilarities,
multidimensional scaling provides a simple dimensional model.
For more information, see Borg and Lingoes (1987), Borg (1981),
Carroll and Arabie (1980), Davison (1983), Green and Rao
(1972), Kruskal and Wish (1978), Schiffman, Reynolds, and
Young (1981), and Shepard, Romney, and Nerlove (1972).

MDS also computes the INDSCAL (individual differences multidimensional scaling) model (Carroll and Chang, 1970; Carroll and Wish, 1974). The INDSCAL model fits dissimilarity/similarity matrices for multiple subjects into one common space, with jointly estimated weight parameters for each subject. MDS can fit the INDSCAL model using any of the three loss functions, although we recommend using Kruskal's STRESS for this purpose.

Finally, MDS can fit the nonmetric unfolding model (Coombs, 1964). This allows you to analyze rank order preference data.

Overview

Loss functions

MDS scales similarity or dissimilarity matrices using three loss functions:

KRUSKAL   Kruskal's STRESS formula 1 scaling method (Kruskal, 1964); the default

GUTTMAN   Guttman's coefficient of alienation scaling method (Guttman, 1954)

YOUNG   Young's SSTRESS scaling method, which allows you to scale using the loss function featured in ALSCAL (Takane, Young and de Leeuw, 1977)

Use the LOSS option of the ESTIMATE command to specify your function:

    ESTIMATE / LOSS = GUTTMAN *or* KRUSKAL *or* YOUNG

Iterations with Kruskal's method are faster but usually take longer to converge to a minimum value than those with the Guttman method. The procedure used in the latter has been found in simulations to be less susceptible to local minima than that used in the Kruskal method (Lingoes and Roskam, 1973). We do not recommend Young's SSTRESS loss function. Because it weights squares of distances, large distances have more influence than smaller ones. Weinberg and Menil (1993) summarized why this is a problem: "…error variances of dissimilarities tend to be positively correlated with their means. If this is the case, large distances should be, if anything, *down*-weighted relative to small distances."

Note: *Using these loss functions does not guarantee that you will get exactly the same results as other MDS programs. You may see minor differences in scaling of coordinates, stress values at convergence, or translation and rotation of axes.*

Getting started MDS analyses are performed on a SYSTAT data file that contains an SSCP, covariance, correlation, or dissimilarity matrix. When you open the data file, MDS automatically recognizes its type. MDS ignores missing values in calculating its loss function (see "Missing data" on p. 602).

MDS analysis is available only by using SYSTAT commands. You can either enter MDS commands at the command prompt in the main window; submit MDS commands from the Command Editor; or use the menus to select **Stats➧Mutidimensional Scaling**, and enter and submit MDS commands in the MDS window.

You can obtain different results by specifying ESTIMATE and selecting one of the following options: LOSS, DIMENSION, R, ITERATIONS, REGRESSION, WEIGHT, SPLIT, CONVERGE.

- For Kruskal or Young analyses, specify REGRESSION=MONTONIC or REGRESSION=LINEAR.
- For an individual differences or unfolding model, use SPLIT=MATRIX or SPLIT=ROWS.
- For an individual differences model, use WEIGHT.
- To input your own starting configuration, use CONFIGURATION.

To save distances, see "Saving distances" on p. 599.

Two-Way Scaling

17.1 Kruskal method

The data in the *ROTHKOPF* data file, shown below, are adapted from an experiment by Rothkopf (1957). They were originally obtained from 598 subjects who judged whether or not pairs of Morse code signals presented in succession were the same. Morse code signals for letters and digits were used in the experiment, and all pairs were tested in each of two possible sequences. For multi-dimensional scaling, the data for letter signals have been averaged across sequence, and the diagonal (pairs of the same signal) has been omitted. The data in this form were first scaled by Shepard.

```
CODE$ A   B   C   D   E   F   G   H   I   J   K   L   M   N   O   P   Q   R   S   T   U   V   W   X   Y   Z
.-     .
-...   4   .
-.-.   5  37   .
-..   10  46  17   .
.      4   9   9   6   .
..-.   9  39  31  21   2   .
--.    9  17  20  39   2  12   .
....   8  33  15  30   6  30   7   .
..    55   6   9  11  13   6   5  11   .
.---   6  14  28  11   1  28  20   7   3   .
-.-   13  29  31  77   3  16  29  10   5  24   .
.-..   2  54  39  50   8  37  14  27  12  30  30   .
--    24   9   9  11   5  12  21   6  10   9  16   7   .
-.    32   7   8  18   6   9  11  12  21   3  14   5  60   .
---    6   9  14   7   5   9  69   7   4  30  28   9   7   6   .
.--.   5  22  42  19   3  39  37  13   3  70  14  41   7   7  29   .
--.-   8  22  36  10   4  13  16   6   3  37  27  31  11   5  28  47   .
.-.   24  15  20  34   7  34  23  16  13  11  21  30  17  20  11  26   9   .
...   20  21   9  29   9  20   5  48  25   2   8  11   6  14   4   7   2  17   .
-      9   6   3   5  56   2   4   5  15   6   8   6   7   7   5   7   3   3   8   .
..-   25  23   9  24   3  26  13  35  15   8  33  24  12  14   8  16   9  31  53   7   .
...-   9  25  17  18   6  28  10  49   5  10  21  31   4   2  11  18  12  20  17   5  44   .
.--   13  15  22  24   5  30  28  12   6  17  31  19  18   9  25  19  18  61  12   4  26  18   .
-..-   9  74  38  29   4  23  16  19   1  28  56  36   9   6  29  25  49  12  11   2  14  37  21   .
-.--   8  26  72  15   5  26  22  11   3  31  14  19  11   6  20  35  51   8   6   3   7  24  23  46   .
--..   3  44  41  25   3  17  28  10   7  25  19  55   9   6  21  44  67  13   5   4  10  10  17  31  32   .
```

The commands for this example are:

```
MDS
    USE ROTHKPF1
    MODEL a .. z
    ESTIMATE / LOSS=KRUSKAL
```

Use the shortcut notation (..) in MODEL for listing consecutive variables in the file (otherwise simply list each variable name separated by a space).

The program begins by generating an initial configuration of points whose interpoint distances are a linear function of the input data. For this estimation, MDS uses a metric multidimensional scaling. To do this, missing values in the input dissimilarities matrix are replaced by mean values for the whole matrix. Then the values are converted to distances by adding a constant.

```
Monotonic Multidimensional Scaling
The data are analyzed as similarities
Minimizing Kruskal STRESS (form 1) in 2 dimensions
Iteration        STRESS
---------        ------
     0          0.263538
     1          0.237909
     2          0.218821
     3          0.202184
     4          0.190513
     5          0.184340
     6          0.181176
     7          0.179394
     8          0.178271
Stress of final configuration is: 0.17827
Proportion of variance (RSQ) is: 0.84502
Coordinates in 2 dimensions
Variable              Dimension
--------              ---------
                         1     2
     A               -1.21   -.31
     B                 .59   -.45
     C                 .67    .05
     D                 .06   -.44
     E               -1.54    .89
     F                 .48   -.57
     G                 .22    .65
     H                 .03  -1.05
     I               -1.45   -.38
     J                 .78    .77
     K                 .22    .02
     L                 .60   -.27
     M                -.62    .76
     N               -1.15   -.04
     O                 .47   1.02
     P                 .63    .31
     Q                 .90    .56
     R                -.28   -.34
     S                -.66  -1.04
     T               -1.47    .95
     U                -.31   -.75
     V                 .37   -.87
     W                 .04    .13
     X                 .83   -.15
     Y                 .87    .38
     Z                 .94    .18
```

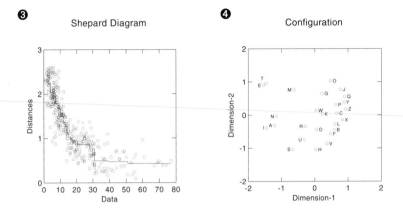

❸ Shepard Diagram ❹ Configuration

The highlighted numbers below correspond to those in the output:

❶ The solution required eight iterations. *Stress* is the Kruskal goodness-of-fit statistic that MDS tries to minimize. It consists of the square root of the normalized squared discrepancies between interpoint distances in the MDS plot and the smoothed distances predicted from the dissimilarities. Stress varies between 0 and 1, with values near 0 indicating better fit. It is printed for each iteration, which is one movement of all of the points in the plot toward a better solution. Make sure that iterations proceed smoothly to a minimum. This is true for the examples in this chapter. If you find that the stress values increase or decrease in uneven steps, you should be suspicious.

❷ SYSTAT prints the coordinates of the solution and then plots them in ❹ for every pair of dimensions. The plot of points is the solution you seek.

❸ *Shepard Diagram.* This plot is a scatterplot of distances between points in the MDS plot against the observed dissimilarities or similarities. In monotonic scaling, the regression function has steps at various points. For most solutions, the function in this plot should be relatively smooth (without large steps). If the function looks like one or two large steps, you should consider setting REGRESSION to LOG or LINEAR under ESTIMATE (see "Regression function" on p. 581).

❹ The points should be scattered fairly evenly through the space. If you are scaling in more than two dimensions, you should examine plots of pairs of axes or rotate the solution in three dimensions. The orientation of axes is arbitrary—remember, you are scaling distances, not axes. Feel free to reverse axes or rotate the solution. MDS rotates the solution to the largest dimensions of variation, but these don't necessarily mean anything for your data.

The solution has been rotated to principal axes (that is, the major variation is on the first dimension). This rotation is not performed unless the scaling is in Euclidean space, as in the present example.

You can interpret the axes as in principal components or factor analysis. More often, however, you should look for clusters of objects or regular patterns among the objects, such as circles, curved manifolds, and other structures.

The next figure was produced by adding the IDVAR command before ESTIMATE:

```
IDVAR=code$
```

The variable *CODE$* contains the Morse Codes. The two-dimensional solution clearly distinguishes short signals from long and dots from dashes. Dashes tend to appear in the upper right and dots in the lower left. Long codes tend to appear in the lower right and short in the upper left.

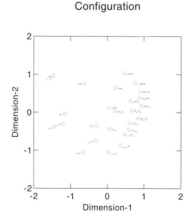

Configuration

Regression function

If you use the Kruskal or Young loss function, you can use the REGRESSION option on ESTIMATE to fit a MONOTONIC, LINEAR, or LOG function of distances onto input dissimilarities. The standard option is MONOTONIC multidimensional scaling. To avoid degenerate solutions, however, log or linear scaling is sometimes handy. Log scaling is recommended for this purpose because it allows a smooth curvilinear relation between dissimilarities and distances. The commands are:

```
ESTIMATE / REGRESS=MONOTONIC   or   REGRESS=LINEAR
                               or   REGRESS=LOG
```

17.2 Guttman loss function

To illustrate the Guttman loss function, this example uses judged similarities among 14 spectral colors (from Ekman, 1954). Nanometer wave lengths (*W434*, …, *W674*) are used to name the variables for each color. Blue-violets are in the 400's; reds, in the 600's. The judgments are averaged across 31 subjects; the larger the number for a pair of colors, the more similar the two colors are. The file (*EKMAN*) has no diagonal elements, and its type is SIMILARITY.

W434	W445	W465	W472	W490	W504	W537	W555	W584	W600	W610	W628	W651	W674
86													
42	50												
42	44	81											
18	22	47	54										
6	9	17	25	61									
7	7	10	10	31	62								
4	7	8	9	26	45	73							
2	2	2	2	7	14	22	33						
7	4	1	1	2	8	14	19	58					
9	7	2	0	2	2	5	4	37	74				
12	11	1	1	1	2	2	3	27	50	76			
13	13	5	2	2	2	2	2	20	41	62	85		
16	14	3	4	0	1	0	2	23	28	55	68	76	

The Guttman method is used to scale these judgments in two dimensions to see if the data fit a perceptual color wheel. The Kruskal loss function will give you a similar result.

```
MDS
    USE ekman
    MODEL w434 .. w674
    ESTIMATE / LOSS=GUTTMAN
```

❶

```
Monotonic Multidimensional Scaling

The data are analyzed as similarities

Minimizing Guttman/Lingoes Coefficient of Alienation in 2 dimensions

Iteration   Alienation
---------   ----------
      0       0.070825
      1       0.042070
      2       0.037767
      3       0.036155
      4       0.035069
Alienation of final configuration is: 0.03507
Proportion of variance (RSQ) is: 0.99623
```

```
Coordinates in 2 dimensions

Variable              Dimension
--------              --------
                        1      2
    W434               .31   -.91
    W445               .40   -.84
    W465               .89   -.57
    W472               .95   -.48
    W490               .98    .11
    W504               .81    .64
    W537               .55    .89
    W555               .33    .97
    W584              -.54    .73
    W600              -.83    .38
    W610             -1.01    .06
    W628             -1.01   -.18
    W651              -.94   -.33
    W674              -.90   -.47
```

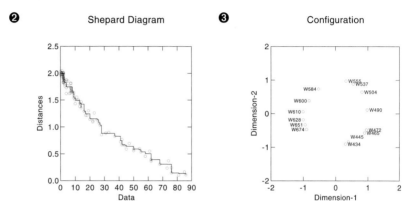

❷   Shepard Diagram   ❸   Configuration

The highlighted numbers below correspond to those in the output:

❶ The fit of configuration distances to original data is extremely close, as evidenced by the low coefficient of alienation and clean Shepard diagram.

❷ *Shepard Diagram.* This is the default display. See Example 17.1 for its definition.

❸ The resulting configuration is almost circular, denoting a "circumplex" by Guttman (1954). There is a large gap at the bottom of the figure, however, because the perceptual color between deep red and dark purple is not a spectral color.

Three-Way Scaling

**17.3
Individual
differences
multidimen-
sional scaling**

The data in the *COLAS* data file are taken from Schiffman, Reynolds, and Young (1981). They are judgments by 10 subjects of the dissimilarity (0–100) between pairs of colas. The example will fit the INDSCAL model (INDividual differences SCALing) to these data, seeking a common group space for the 10 different colas and a parallel weight space for the 10 different judges.

The data in this file have an unusual structure. The file consists of 10 dissimilarity matrices stacked on top of each other like this:

```
Case number DIE  RC YUK PEP SHA COK DIE TAB PEP DIE
          1   0   .   .   .   .   .   .   .   .   .
          2  16   0   .   .   .   .   .   .   .   .
          3  81  47   0   .   .   .   .   .   .   .
          4  56  32  71   0   .   .   .   .   .   .
          5  87  68  44  71   0   .   .   .   .   .
          6  60  35  21  98  34   0   .   .   .   .
          7  84  94  98  57  99  99   0   .   .   .
          8  50  87  79  73  19  92  45   0   .   .
          9  99  25  53  98  52  17  99  84   0   .
         10  16  92  90  83  79  44  24  18  98   0
         11   0   .   .   .   .   .   .   .   .   .
         12   9   0   .   .   .   .   .   .   .   .
         13  90  70   0   .   .   .   .   .   .   .
         14  87  65   6   0   .   .   .   .   .   .
         15  87  77  83  83   0   .   .   .   .   .
         16  33  79  25  89  39   0   .   .   .   .
         17  86  86  99  22  90  40   0   .   .   .
         18  81  30  57  88  69  39  97   0   .   .
         19  74  20  94  78   5  81  92  88   0   .
         20  23  26  72  94   2  76  81  20   5   0
         21   0   .   .   .   .   .   .   .   .   .
         22  49   0   .   .   .   .   .   .   .   .
         23  96  96   0   .   .   .   .   .   .   .
         24  97  92  94   0   .   .   .   .   .   .
         25  68  12  90  93   0   .   .   .   .   .
         26  77  44  88  90  26   0   .   .   .   .
         27  97  93  94  25  93  49   0   .   .   .
         28  54  76  92  94  20  24  93   0   .   .
         29  47  48  92  94  35  18  94  23   0   .
         30  21  47  90  92  68  67  87  55  15   0
         31   0   .   .   .   .   .   .   .   .   .
         32  23   0   .   .   .   .   .   .   .   .
         33  99  51   0   .   .   .   .   .   .   .
         34  99  23  78   0   .   .   .   .   .   .
         35  90  16  22  49   0   .   .   .   .   .
         36  74  55  50  99  13   0   .   .   .   .
         37  14  88  77  75  50  70   0   .   .   .
         38  25  95  48  99  99  79  99   0   .   .
         39  60  36  69  24  21  53  99  99   0   .
         40   .  89  72  81  77  71  74  51  71   0
        *** Cases 41-90 not shown ***
         91   0   .   .   .   .   .   .   .   .   .
         92  69   0   .   .   .   .   .   .   .   .
         93  63  58   0   .   .   .   .   .   .   .
         94  76  85  79   0   .   .   .   .   .   .
         95  52  14  51  81   0   .   .   .   .   .
         96  61  39  35  83  36   0   .   .   .   .
         97  80  90  93   6  78  85   0   .   .   .
         98  28  87  83  94  64  44  90   0   .   .
         99  80  20  92  98  51  23  80  33   0   .
        100  78  28  40  99  36  71  82  62  13   0
```

The example uses the recommended LOSS set to KRUSKAL for the individual differences model. The WEIGHT, SPLIT and DIM options are also used:

WEIGHT   Add weights for each dimension and each matrix (subject) into the calculation of separate distances which are used in the minimization.

SPLIT=ROW   Split calculation of the loss function by rows of the
MATRIX   matrix or by matrices.

DIM=*n*   Specify the number of dimensions (1 through 5) in which to scale your points. Default=2.

Use the ESTIMATE command to specify these options:

```
ESTIMATE / WEIGHT  LOSS=method  DIM=n,
            SPLIT=MATRIX
```

For this example, specify:

```
MDS
    USE colas
    MODEL dietpeps .. dietrite
    ESTIMATE / LOSS=KRUSKAL  WEIGHT  SPLIT=MATRIX
                DIM=3
```

```
Monotonic Multidimensional Scaling

The data are analyzed as dissimilarities
There are 10 replicated data matrices
Dimensions are weighted separately for each matrix
Fitting is split between data matrices

Minimizing Kruskal STRESS (form 1) in 3 dimensions

Iteration     STRESS
---------     ------
    0        0.220898
    1        0.184421
    0        0.221307
    1        0.184507

Stress of final configuration is: 0.18451
Proportion of variance (RSQ) is: 0.53501

Coordinates in 3 dimensions

Variable          Dimension
--------          ---------

                  1      2     3
DIETPEPS        -.61    .20    .78
RC               .52    .05    .76
YUKON            .42   -.09   -.87
PEPPER           .27  -1.27    .06
SHASTA           .80    .02   -.14
COKE             .39    .84   -.35
DIETPEPR        -.75   -.84   -.17
TAB             -.79    .44   -.61
PEPSI            .57    .22    .38
DIETRITE        -.82    .43    .17
```

```
Matrix Weights

Matrix   Stress   RSQ     Dimension
------   ------   ---     ---------
                          1     2     3
  1      .188    .548    .70   .43   .53
  2      .200    .416    .45   .47   .72
  3      .196    .468    .35   .52   .74
  4      .171    .564    .59   .49   .61
  5      .178    .594    .70   .37   .56
  6      .172    .621    .70   .37   .57
  7      .181    .552    .42   .58   .66
  8      .180    .560    .48   .60   .61
  9      .163    .625    .56   .50   .63
 10      .212    .402    .44   .61   .62
```

Shepard Diagram

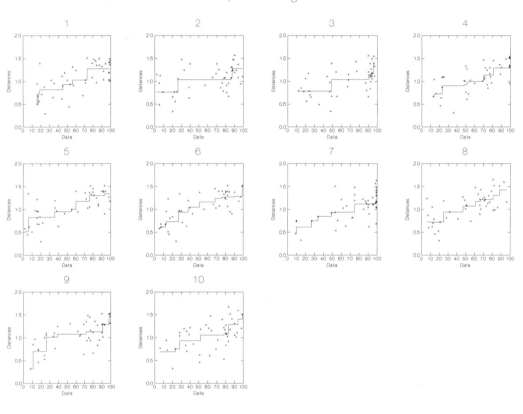

Configuration

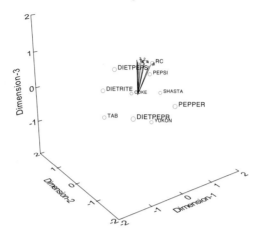

The WEIGHT option tells SYSTAT to weight each matrix separately. Without this option, all matrices would be weighted equally, and you would have a single pooled solution. You want to use weighting so that you can see which subjects favor one dimension over the others in their judgments. The MATRIX option of SPLIT tells SYSTAT to compute separate (monotonic) regression functions for each subject (matrix). Finally, scale the result in three dimensions, as did Schiffman, et al. (1981).

The solution required four iterations. Notice that the second two iterations appear to be a restart. That is exactly what they are. Because the fourth matrix has a missing value, SYSTAT uses the EM algorithm to reestimate this value, compute a new metric solution, and iterate two more times until convergence. This extra set of iterations did not do much for you in this example because the stress is insignificantly higher than it would have been had you stopped at only two iterations. With many missing values, however, the EM algorithm will improve MDS solutions substantially.

For the INDSCAL model, you have a set of coordinates for the colas and one for the subjects. In the three-dimensional graph of the coordinates, the colas are represented by little cubes and the subjects by vectors. In addition, for each subject, you have a contribution to overall stress and a separate squared correlation (RSQ) between the predicted and obtained distances in the configuration. Notice that Subject 10 is fit worst (STRESS=0.212) and Subject 9 best (STRESS=0.163). Furthermore, Subjects 1, 5, and 6 have a high loading on the first dimension, indicating that they place a higher emphasis on diet/nondiet differences than on cherry cola/cola differences. Subjects 7, 8, and 10, on the other hand, emphasize the second dimension more.

Unfolding

**17.4
Nonmetric
unfolding**

The *COLRPREF* data set contains color preferences among 15 SYSTAT employees for five primary colors. This example uses the MDS unfolding model to scale the people and the colors in two dimensions such that each person's coordinate is near his or her favorite color's coordinate and far from his or her least favorite color coordinate. For this example, use ROWS to specify the number of rows for a rectangular matrix and SHAPE to specify the type of matrix input to use. When you enter these data for the first time, you must remember to specify their type as DISSIMILARITY so that small numbers are understood as meaning *most similar* (preferred).

RED	ORANGE	YELLOW	GREEN	BLUE	NAME$
3	5	4	1	2	Patrick
1	4	3	5	2	Laszlo
3	5	1	4	2	Mary
1	3	5	4	2	Jenna
5	3	2	4	1	Julie
3	2	5	1	4	Steve
3	4	5	2	1	Phil
2	4	3	5	1	Mike
4	5	3	1	2	Keith
2	5	4	3	1	Kathy
1	5	2	4	3	Leah
1	5	4	2	3	Stephanie
1	4	5	2	3	Lisa
2	5	3	4	1	Mark
1	2	3	4	5	John

To scale these with the unfolding model, specify:

```
MDS
    USE colrpref
    MODEL red .. blue / SHAPE=RECT
    IDVAR=name$
    ESTIMATE / SPLIT=ROWS
```

Notice that you are using the Kruskal loss function as the default. The output is shown below:

```
Monotonic Multidimensional Scaling

The data are analyzed as dissimilarities
The data are rectangular (lower corner matrix)
Fitting is split between rows of data matrix

Minimizing Kruskal STRESS (form 1) in 2 dimensions

Iteration     STRESS
---------     ------
    0        0.148373
    1        0.135422
    2        0.125152
    3        0.117256
    4        0.111130
    5        0.106394
    6        0.102623
    7        0.099540
    8        0.096883
    9        0.094498
    0        0.107456
    1        0.100497
    2        0.096037
    3        0.092747
    4        0.090086
Stress of final configuration is: 0.09009

Proportion of variance (RSQ) is: 0.94001

Coordinates in 2 dimensions

Variable           Dimension
--------           ---------
                     1     2
RED                 .25  -.49
ORANGE              .53 -1.70
YELLOW            -1.31  -.56
GREEN              1.39   .26
BLUE               -.55   .79
Patrick             .56   .78
Laszlo             -.73  -.13
Mary              -1.01   .11
Jenna               .19  -.25
Julie              -.70  -.22
Steve              1.18  -.76
Phil                .61   .61
Mike               -.80  -.02
Keith               .27   .76
Kathy               .05   .76
Leah               -.72   .00
Stephanie           .50   .58
Lisa                .78   .21
Mark               -.57   .50
John                .06 -1.24

Row Fit Measures

   Row      Stress   RSQ
   ---      ------   ---
Patrick      .000  1.000
Laszlo       .068   .970
Mary         .004  1.000
Jenna        .048   .983
Julie        .272   .508
Steve        .033   .993
Phil         .061   .972
Mike         .083   .958
Keith        .172   .774
Kathy        .000  1.000
Leah         .067   .971
Stephanie    .029   .994
Lisa         .055   .981
Mark         .000  1.000
John         .025   .996
```

Shepard Diagram

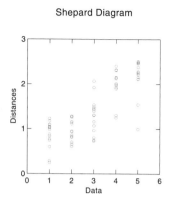

Configuration

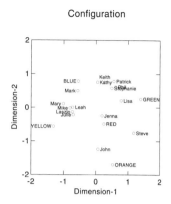

The subjects are labeled as the *row* variables.

You use the SHAPE=RECT option on MODEL to specify the matrix input as rectangular format.

Also use the ROWS=*n* option on MODEL to specify the number of rows for a rectangular matrix. The default is the number of columns (that is, the number of variables in the MODEL statement). With commands:

```
MODEL varlist / SHAPE=RECT  ROWS=n
```

17.5 A test example

The nonmetric unfolding model has often presented problems to MDS programs because so much data are missing. If you think of the unfolding matrix as the lower corner matrix in a larger triangular matrix of subjects + objects, you can visualize how much data (namely all the subject-object comparisons) are missing. Since SYSTAT uses the EM algorithm for missing values, unfolding models do not degenerate as frequently. SYSTAT does a complete MDS using all available data and then estimates missing dissimilarities/similarities using the distances in the solution. These estimated values are then used to get a starting configuration for another complete iteration cycle. This process continues until there are no changes between EM cycles.

The following example, from Borg and Lingoes (1987) adapted from Green and Carmone (1970), shows how this works. This unfolding data set contains dissimilarities only between the points delineating *A* and *M*, and these dissimilarities are treated only as rank orders. Borg and Lingoes discuss the problems in fitting an unfolding model to these data.

	A1	A2	A3	A4	A5	A6	A7	A8	A9	A10	A11	A12	A13	A14	A15	A16
M1	8	8	9	9	9	10	11	10	9	8	7	7	6	9	9	8
M2	8	8	8	8	9	9	10	9	8	7	7	6	5	8	8	8
M3	7	7	8	8	8	9	9	8	8	7	6	5	4	8	7	7
M4	7	7	7	7	8	8	9	8	7	6	5	5	4	7	7	6
M5	6	6	7	7	7	7	8	7	6	6	5	4	3	6	6	6
M6	6	6	6	6	7	7	7	6	6	5	4	3	3	6	6	5
M7	6	6	6	6	6	6	7	6	5	4	4	3	2	5	5	5
M8	7	7	7	7	7	7	8	7	6	5	5	4	3	6	6	6
M9	8	8	8	8	8	8	9	8	7	6	6	5	4	7	7	7
M10	9	9	9	9	9	9	10	9	8	7	7	6	5	8	8	8
M11	9	9	9	9	9	9	10	9	8	7	7	6	5	9	8	8
M12	9	9	9	9	9	9	10	9	8	7	7	6	5	9	8	8
M13	10	10	10	10	9	10	10	9	8	8	7	6	6	9	9	8
M14	10	10	10	10	10	10	10	9	9	8	7	6	6	9	9	8
M15	10	10	10	10	10	10	11	10	9	8	8	7	6	10	9	9
M16	11	10	10	10	11	11	11	10	10	9	8	7	7	10	10	9
M17	11	11	11	11	11	11	12	11	10	9	9	8	7	10	10	10
M18	11	11	11	11	12	12	12	11	11	10	9	8	8	11	11	10
M19	11	11	12	12	12	12	13	12	11	10	10	9	8	11	11	11

To scale these with the unfolding model, specify:

```
MDS
    USE am
    MODEL / SHAPE=RECT
    ESTIMATE / LOSS=GUTTMAN  SPLIT=ROWS
```

Notice that the example uses the Guttman loss function, but the others provide similar results. The output is shown below:

```
Monotonic Multidimensional Scaling
The data are analyzed as dissimilarities
The data are rectangular (lower corner matrix)
Fitting is split between rows of data matrix
Minimizing Guttman/Lingoes Coefficient of
Alienation in 2 dimensions

Iteration  Alienation
---------  ----------
    0       0.076135
    1       0.037826
    2       0.023540
    3       0.017736
    4       0.013277
    5       0.009962
Alienation of final configuration is: 0.00996
Proportion of variance (RSQ) is: 0.99925

Coordinates in 2 dimensions
Variable          Dimension
--------          ---------

                     1     2
A1                 -.94 -1.02
A2                 -.89  -.98
A3                -1.09  -.41
A4                -1.07  -.40
A5                -1.19   .15
A6                -1.23   .34
A7                -1.54   .67
A8                -1.00   .55
A9                 -.69   .47
A10                -.31   .36
A11                 .01   .10
A12                 .10   .10
A13                 .13   .09
A14                -.85   .09
A15                -.74   .14
A16                -.57   .13
Row    1            .74 -1.08
Row    2            .43  -.52
Row    3            .20  -.56
Row    4            .01  -.43
Row    5           -.15  -.33
Row    6           -.21  -.18
Row    7           -.17   .12
Row    8           -.06   .22
Row    9            .18   .27
Row   10            .56   .24
Row   11            .59   .22
Row   12            .59   .22
Row   13            .83   .87
Row   14            .89   .66
Row   15           1.04   .21
Row   16           1.24   .16
Row   17           1.50   .23
Row   18           1.70  -.21
Row   19           1.94  -.49
Row Fit Measures
    Row      Stress    RSQ
    ---      ------    ---
Row    1      .000    1.000
Row    2      .000    1.000
Row    3      .000    1.000
Row    4      .000    1.000
Row    5      .027     .993
Row    6      .022     .996
Row    7      .024     .997
Row    8      .016     .999
Row    9      .000    1.000
Row   10      .000    1.000
Row   11      .000    1.000
Row   12      .000    1.000
Row   13      .002    1.000
Row   14      .000    1.000
Row   15      .000    1.000
Row   16      .000    1.000
Row   17      .000    1.000
Row   18      .000    1.000
Row   19      .000    1.000
```

Shepard Diagram

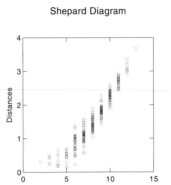

Configuration

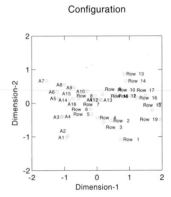

Power Scaling

**17.6
Power scaling
ratio data**

Because similarities or dissimilarities are often collected as rank order data, the nonmetric MDS model has to work "backwards" in order to solve for a configuration fitting the data. As J.D. Carroll has pointed out, the MDS model should really express observed data as a function of distances between points in a configuration rather than the other way around. If your data are direct or derived distances, however, you should try setting REGRESSION=POWER with the LOSS=FUNCTION. This way, you can fit a Stevens power function to the data using distances between points in the configuration. The results may not always differ much from nonmetric or linear or log MDS, but SYSTAT will also tell you the exponent of the power function in the Shepard diagram. Notice with this model that the *Data* and *Distances* are transposed in the Shepard diagram because loss is being computed from errors in the data rather than the distances. SYSTAT calls the loss for the power model PSTRESS to distinguish it from Kruskal's STRESS. In PSTRESS, you use DATA and its DHAT instead of DIST and its DHAT to compute the loss.

The *HELM* data set contains highly accurate estimates of distance between color pairs by one experimental subject (CB). These are from Helm (1959) and reprinted by Borg and Lingoes (1987).

	A	C	E	G	I	K	M	O	Q	S
A	0	.	.	.	.	.	.	.	.	.
C	7	0	.	.	.	.	.	.	.	.
E	13	5	0	.	.	.	.	.	.	.
G	14	8	5	0	.	.	.	.	.	.
I	14	10	7	4	0	.	.	.	.	.
K	13	12	10	6	4	0	.	.	.	.
M	11	14	11	10	7	4	0	.	.	.
O	9	14	14	11	10	7	5	0	.	.
Q	6	12	15	12	12	10	7	5	0	.
S	4	9	14	13	11	11	9	6	4	0

To scale these with power model, specify:

```
MDS
    USE helm
    MODEL a .. s
    ESTIMATE / REGRESS=POWER
```

The output is shown below:

```
Power regression function, where Dissimilarities=a*Distances^p

 The data are analyzed as dissimilarities

 Minimizing PSTRESS (STRESS with DIST and DATA exchanged) in 2 dimensions

 Iteration    PSTRESS
 ---------    -------
     0       0.142062
     1       0.131424
     2       0.127134
     3       0.125207

 Stress of final configuration is: 0.12521
 Estimated exponent for power regression is: 0.85154
 Proportion of variance (RSQ) is: 0.91039

 Coordinates in 2 dimensions

 Variable         Dimension
 --------         ---------
                    1      2
     A           -.83   -.79
     C            .40  -1.09
     E           1.13   -.50
     G            .98    .10
     I            .79    .48
     K            .33    .68
     M           -.21    .80
     O           -.73    .58
     Q          -1.00    .05
     S           -.87   -.32
```

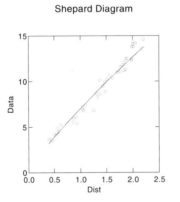

Shepard Diagram

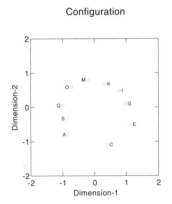

Configuration

SYSTAT estimated the power exponent for the function, fitting distances to dissimilarities as 0.85. Color and many other visual judgments show similar power exponents less than 1.0.

Other Features

You can use the following features to control your analysis.

The distance metric

Use R, an option on ESTIMATE, to specify the exponent (r) in a general power metric. MDS can use a power (Minkowski) metric in its calculations of distances between points in the configuration:

$$d_{jk} = \left[\sum_{i=1}^{p} |x_{ij} - x_{ik}| \right]^{\frac{1}{r}}$$

In this equation, p is the number of dimensions. For ordinary Euclidean distance, $r=2$. This is the default value.

If you specify $r=1$, the distance metric is called "city block distance" because distances between points in the scaling configuration are measured along "streets" parallel to the reference axes. For values other than 1 or 2, computation is slower because logarithms and exponentials are used.

```
ESTIMATE / R=n
```

Controlling convergence

There are several methods for controlling the number of iterations needed to produce a satisfactory solution:

ITER=n Limit for the number of iterations. Default=50.

CONV=n Terminate iterations when the maximum absolute difference between any coordinate in the solution at iteration i versus iteration i-1 is less than n. Because the configuration is standardized to unit variance on every iteration, iterations stop when no coordinate moves more than 0.005 (or n) units from its value on the previous iteration. This is the same type of convergence criterion used in NONLIN and other estimation problems, where change in parameter values, rather than loss, is of concern.

Most MDS programs terminate when stress reaches a predetermined value or changes by less than a small amount. These programs can terminate prematurely, however, because comparable stress values can result from different configurations. The SYSTAT convergence criterion allows you to stop iterating when the configuration ceases to change. The default value is 0.005.

With commands:

```
ESTIMATE / ITER=n  CONVERGE=n
```

Configuration

If you have problems with degenerate solutions, you can specify your own starting configuration for the points:

```
CONFIGURATION [matrix; ... ] or CONFIGURATION=LAST
```

When you type a matrix, SYSTAT reads as many numbers in each row as you specify (the same way as for hypothesis matrices in general linear modeling or in the Matrix procedure. It reads as many rows as there are points to scale. After you type your starting configuration, use MDS to define your analysis. Check the configuration in your output to be sure you entered it correctly. The LAST argument allows you to reuse the configuration from the previous scaling.

Confirmatory scaling

You can specify a configuration for confirmatory analysis. Enter a hypothesized configuration and let the program iterate only once (specify 1 for ITER). Then look at the stress.

Saving distances

To save the matrix of distances between points in the final scaled configuration or the observed and fitted distances, use SAVE with one of the following options:

DIST   Matrix of distances between points in the final scaled configuration. This is the default.

CONFIG   Final configuration.

RESID   Data (DATA), distances (DIST), estimated distances (DHAT), the residuals (RESIDUAL), and the ROW and COLUMN number of the original distance in a rectangular SYSTAT file (each entry from the original matrix is now a case).

```
SAVE filename / CONFIG  or  DIST  or  RESID
```

For RESID, MDS displays the root mean squared residuals for each point in its output. Because STRESS is a function of the sum of squared residuals, the root mean squared residuals are a measure of the influence of each point on the STRESS statistic. This can help you identify ill-fitting points.

More about Multidimensional Scaling

Multidimensional scaling (MDS) is a procedure for fitting a set of points in a space such that the distances between points correspond as closely as possible to a given set of dissimilarities between a set of objects. Dissimilarities may be measured directly, as in psychological judgments, or derived indirectly, as in correlation matrices computed on rectangular data.

Assumptions

Because MDS, like cluster analysis, operates directly on dissimilarities, no statistical distribution assumptions are necessary. There are, however, other important assumptions. First, multidimensional scaling is a spatial model. To fit points in the kinds of spaces that MDS covers, you assume that your data satisfy *metric* conditions:

- The distance from an object to itself is 0.
- The distance from object A to object B is the same as that from B to A.
- The distance from object A to C is less than or equal to the distance from A to B plus B to C. This is sometimes called the **triangle inequality**.

You may think these conditions are obvious, but there are numerous counter-examples in psychological perception and elsewhere. For example, commuters often view the distance from home to the city as closer than the distance from the city to home because of traffic patterns, terrain, and psychological expectations related to time of day. Framing or context effects can also disrupt the metric axioms, as Amos Tversky has shown. For example, Miami is similar to Havana. Havana is similar to Moscow. Is Miami similar to Moscow? If your data (objects) are not consistent with these three axioms, do not use MDS.

Second, there are ways of deriving distances from rectangular data that do not satisfy the metric axioms. The ones available in Correlations do, but if you are thinking of using some other derived measure of similarity, check it carefully.

Finally, it is assumed that all of your objects will fit in the same metric space. It is best if they diffuse somewhat evenly through this space as well. Don't expect to get interpretable results for 25 nearly indistinguishable objects and one that is radically different.

Collecting dissimilarity data

You can collect dissimilarities directly or compute them indirectly.

Direct methods

Examples of direct dissimilarities are:

Distances. Take distances between objects (for example, cities) directly off a map. If the scale is local, MDS will reproduce the map nicely. If the scale is global, you will need three dimensions for an MDS fit. Two- or three-dimensional spatial distances can be measured directly. Direct measures of social distance might include spatial propinquity or the number of times or amount of time one individual interacts with another.

Judgments. Ask subjects to give a numerical rating of the dissimilarity (for example, 0 to 10) between all pairs of objects.

Clusters. Ask people to sort objects into piles; or examine naturally occurring aggregates, such as paragraphs, communities, and associations. Record 0 if two objects occur in the same group, 1 if they do not. Sum these counts over replications or judges.

Triads. Ask subjects to compare three objects at a time and report which two are most similar (or which is odd one out). Do this over all possible triads of objects. To compute dissimilarities, sum over all triads, as for the clustering method. There are usually many more triads than pairs of objects, so this method is more tedious; however, it allows you to assess independently possible violations of the triangle inequality.

Indirect methods

Indirect dissimilarities are computed over a rectangular matrix whose columns are objects and rows are attributes. You can transpose this matrix if you want to scale rows instead. Possible indirect dissimilarities include:

Computed Euclidean distances. These are the square root of the sum of squared discrepancies between columns of the rectangular matrix.

Negatives of correlations. For standardized data (mean of 0 and standard deviation of 1), Pearson correlations are proportional to Euclidean distances. For unstandardized data, Pearson correlations are comparable to computing Euclidean distances after standardizing. MDS automatically negates correlations if you do not. Other types of correlations—for example, Spearman and gamma—are analogous to standardized distances, but only approximately. Also, be aware that large negative correlations will be treated as large distances and large positive correlations as small distances. Make sure that all variables are scored in the same direction before computing correlations. If you find that a whole row of a correlation matrix is negative, reverse the variable by multiplying by –1, and recompute the correlations.

Counts of discrepancies. Counting discrepancies between columns or using some of the binary association measures in Correlations is closely related to computing the Euclidean distance. These methods are also related to the clustering distance calculations mentioned above for direct distances.

Missing data

Missing values in a similarity/dissimilarity matrix are ignored in the computation of the loss function that determines how points in the configuration are moved. For information on how this function is computed, see the discussion of algorithms in "Computation" below.

If you compute a similarity matrix with Correlations for input to MDS, the matrix will have no missing values unless all of your cases in the raw data have a constant or missing value on one or more variables.

Summary

Computation

This section summarizes algorithms separately for the Kruskal and Guttman methods. The algorithms in these options substantially follow those of Kruskal (1964ab) and Guttman (1968). MDS output should agree with other nonmetric multidimensional scaling except for rotation, dilation, and translation of the configuration. Secondary documentation can be found in Schiffman, Reynolds, and Young (1981) and the other multidimensional scaling references. The summary assumes that dissimilarities are input. If similarities are input, MDS inverts them.

Kruskal method

The program begins by generating a configuration of points whose interpoint distances are a linear function of the input data. For this estimation, MDS uses a metric multidimensional scaling. Missing values in the input dissimilarities matrix are replaced by mean values for the whole matrix. Then the values are converted to distances by adding a constant. A scalar products matrix B is then calculated following the procedures described in Torgerson (1958). The initial configuration matrix X in p dimensions is computed from the first p eigenvectors of B using the Young-Householder procedure (Torgerson, 1958)

After an initial configuration is computed by the metric method, nonmetric optimization begins (there are no metric pre-iterations). At the beginning of each iteration, the configuration is normalized to have zero centroid and unit dispersion. Next, Kruskal's DHAT (fitted) distance values are computed by a monotonic regression of distances onto data. Tied data values are ordered according to their corresponding distances in the configuration.

Stress (formula 1) is calculated from fitted distances, observed distances, and input data values. If the stress is less than 0.001 or has decreased in the last five iterations less than 0.001 per iteration, or the number of iterations equals the number specified by the user (default is 50), iterations terminate (that is, go to the next paragraph). Otherwise, the negative gradient is computed for each point in the configuration by taking the partial derivatives of stress with respect to each dimension. Points in the configuration are moved along their gradients with a step size chosen as a function of the rate of descent; the steeper the descent, the smaller the step size. This completes an iteration.

After the last iteration, the configuration is shifted so that the origin lies in the centroid. Thus, the point coordinates sum to 0 on each dimension. Moreover, the configuration is normalized to unit size so that the sum of squares of its coordinates is 1. If the Minkowski constant is 2 (Euclidean scaling, which is the standard option), the final configuration is rotated to its principal axis.

Guttman method The initial configuration for the Guttman option is computed according to Lingoes and Roskam (1973). Principal components are computed on a matrix **C**,

$$c_{ij} = 1 - \frac{r_{ij}}{\frac{n(n-1)}{2}}$$

where r_{ij} are the ranks of the input dissimilarities (smallest rank corresponding to smallest dissimilarity), and n is the number of points. The diagonal elements of **C** are

$$c_{ij} = 1 - \Sigma r_{ij}$$

where the sum is taken over the entire row of the dissimilarity matrix.

For the iteration stage, the initial configuration is normalized as in the Kruskal method. Then rank images corresponding to each distance in the configuration are computed by permuting the configuration distances so that they mirror the rank order of the original input dissimilarities. Ties in the data are handled as in the Kruskal method. These rank images are used to compute the Guttman/Lingoes coefficient of alienation. Iterations are terminated if this coefficient becomes arbitrarily small, if the number of iterations exceeds the maximum, or if the change in its value becomes small. Otherwise, the points in the configuration are moved five times using the same rank images but different interpoint distances each time to compute a new negative gradient. These five cycles within each iteration are what lengthens the calculations in the Guttman method. This completes an iteration.

The final configuration is rotated and scaled as with the Kruskal method. Guttman/Lingoes programs normalize the extreme values of the configuration to unity and thus do not plot the configuration with a zero centroid, so MDS output corresponds to their output within rigid motion and configuration size.

References

Borg, I., and Lingoes, J. 1987. *Multidimensional similarity structure analysis*. New York: Springer Verlag.

Borg, I., and Lingoes, J. 1981. *Multidimensional data representations: When and why?* Ann Arbor: Mathesis Press.

Carroll, J.D. and Arabie, P. 1980. Multidimensional scaling. M.R. Rosenzweig and L.W. Porter, eds., *Annual Review of Pyschology*, 31: 607–649.

Carroll, J.D., and Chang, J.J. 1970. Analysis of individual differences in multidimensional scaling via an N-way generalization of Eckart-Young decomposition. *Psychometrika*, 35: 283-319.

Carroll, J.D., and Wish, M. 1974. Models and methods for three-way multidimensional scaling. D.H. Krantz, R.C. Atkinson, R.D. Luce, and P. Suppes, eds., *Contemporary Developments in Mathematical Psychology, Vol. II: Measurement, Psychophysics, and Neural Information Processing*. San Francisco: W.H. Freeman and Company.

Coombs, C.H. 1964. *A theory of data*. New York: John Wiley & Sons, Inc.

Davison, M.L. 1983. *Multidimensional scaling*. New York: John Wiley & Sons, Inc.

Ekman, G. 1954. Dimensions of color vision. *Journal of Psychology*, 38: 467-474.

Green, P.E., and Carmone, F.J. 1970. *Multidimensional scaling and related techniques*. Boston: Allyn and Bacon.

Green, P.E., and Rao, V.R. 1972. *Applied multidimensional scaling*. New York: Holt, Rinehart, and Winston.

Guttman, L. 1954. A new approach to factor analysis: The radex. P.F. Lazarsfeld, ed. *Mathematical Thinking in the Social Sciences*. New York: Free Press.

Guttman, L. 1968. A general nonmetric technique for finding the smallest coordinate space for a configuration of points. *Psychometrika*, 33: 469-506.

Helm, C.E. 1959. A multidimensional ratio scaling analysis of color relations. *Technical Report*, Princeton University and Educational Testing Service, June 1959.

Kruskal, J.B., and Wish, M. 1978. *Multidimensional scaling*. Beverly Hills, Calif.: Sage Publications.

Kruskal, J.B. 1964. Multidimensional scaling by optimizing goodness of fit to a nonmetric hypothesis. *Psychometrika*, 29: 1-27.

Kruskal, J.B. 1964. Nonmetric multidimensional scaling: A numerical method. *Psychometrika*, 29: 115-129.

Lingoes, J.C., and Roskam, E.E. 1973. A mathematical and empirical study of two multidimensional scaling algorithms. *Psychometrika Monograph Supplement*, 19.

Rothkopf, E.Z. 1957. A measure of stimulus similarity and errors in some paired-associate learning tasks. *Journal of Experimental Psychology*, 53: 94-101.

Schiffman, S.S., Reynolds, M.L., and Young, F.W. 1981. *Introduction to multidimensional scaling: Theory, methods, and applications*. New York: Academic Press.

Shepard, R.N. 1963. Analysis of proximities as a study of information processing in man. *Human Factors,* 5: 33-48.

Shepard, R.N., Romney, A.K., and Nerlove, S., eds. 1972. *Multidimensional scaling: Theory and application in the behavioral sciences.* New York: Academic Press.

Takane, Y., Young, F.W., and de Leeuw, J. 1977. Nonmetric individual differences scaling: An alternating least squares method with optimal scaling features. *Psychometrika*, 42: 3-27.

Torgerson, W.S. 1958. *Theory and methods of scaling*. New York: John Wiley & Sons, Inc.

Weinberg, S.L., and Menil, V.C. 1993. The recovery of structure in linear and ordinal data: INDSCAL and ALSCAL. *Multivariate Behavioral Research*, 28(2): 215-233.

18

Path Analysis: RAMONA

Michael W. Browne and Gerhard Mels

RAMONA implements the McArdle and McDonald Reticular Action Model (RAM) for path analysis with manifest and latent variables. Input to the program is coded directly from a path diagram without reference to any matrices. In fact, the use of RAMONA does not require knowledge of matrix algebra. We assume only that you know how to draw a path diagram.

RAMONA stands for **RAM O**r **N**ear **A**pproximation. The deviation from RAM is minor—no distinction is made between residual variables and other latent variables. As in RAM, only two parameter matrices are involved in the model. One represents single-headed arrows in the path diagram (path coefficients) and the other represents double-headed arrows (covariance relationships).

RAMONA can correctly fit path analysis models to correlation matrices and avoid the errors associated with treating a correlation matrix as if it were a covariance matrix (Cudeck, 1989). Furthermore, you can require that both exogenous and endogenous latent variable variances have unit variances. Consequently, estimates of standardized path coefficients, *with the associated standard errors*, can be obtained, and difficulties associated with the interpretation of unstandardized path coefficients (Bollen, 1989) can be avoided.

Overview

Examples

More about RAMONA

Note: *RAMONA's command language has been influenced by Steiger's (1985) use of ASCII symbols to represent arrows in a path diagram and by McArdle's use of parameter lists to summarize path diagrams.*

Path Analysis: RAMONA

Overview

The RAMONA procedure has the following commands:

MANIFEST	Specify the manifest variables in the model.
LATENT	Specify the latent variables in the model.
MODEL	Specify the path analysis model. Use a <- symbol to denote each dependence relationship, and use <-> to denote each covariance relationship.
ESTIMATE	Specify the type of matrix to be analyzed as covariance (TYPE=COVA, the default) or correlation (TYPE=CORR). Specify the METHOD of estimation (MWL, GLS, OLS, ADFG, ADFU).
	Select more features to set model limits and constraints: START, NCASES, ITER, CONVERGENCE, CONFI, RESTART

Getting started   RAMONA analysis is available only by using SYSTAT commands. You can submit RAMONA commands at the command prompt in the Main window, submit commands from the Command Editor, or use **Stats**➧ **Path Analysis (RAMONA)** and submit commands in the **Ramona** window. It is not necessary to type RAMONA in the **Ramona** window.

First, specify your data:

```
USE filename
```

Then continue as follows:

```
MANIFEST varlist
LATENT varlist
MODEL depvar1 <-  explanvar1(i,n1),
                  explanvar2(j,n2) ...
        e1 <-> e2, e3(k,n3)...
```

where i, j, and k are integer parameter numbers used to fix or constrain parameters and n1, n2, and n3 are the starting values.

```
ESTIMATE / options
```

where options include TYPE, METHOD, START, NCASES, ITER, CONVG, RESTART, and CONFI.

 To display the command prompt in the Main window, use **Edit➡Options** and select **Command Prompt**.

The path diagram

The input file for RAMONA is coded directly from a path diagram. We first briefly review the main characteristics of path diagrams. More information can be found in texts dealing with structural equation modeling (Bollen, 1989; Everitt, 1984; McDonald, 1985).

Look at the path diagram in Figure 1 on p. 611. This is a model, adapted from Jöreskog (1977), for a study of the stability of attitudes over time conducted by Wheaton, Muthén, Alwin, and Summers (1977). Attitude scales measuring anomia (*ANOMIA*) and powerlessness (*POWRLS*) were regarded as indicators of the latent variable alienation (*ALNTN*) and administered to 932 persons in 1967 and 1971. A socioeconomic index (*SEI*) and years of school completed (*EDUCTN*) were regarded as indicators of the latent variable socioeconomic status (*SES*).

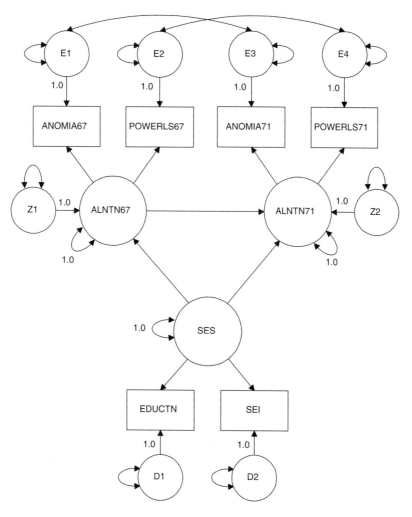

Figure 1

In Figure 1, a manifest (observed) variable is represented by a square or rectangular box:

while a circle or ellipse signifies a latent (unobservable) variable:

A **dependence path** is represented by a single-headed arrow emitted by the *explanatory* variable and received by the *dependent* variable:

while a **covariance path** is represented by a double-headed arrow:

In many diagrams, **variance paths** are omitted. Because variances form an essential part of a model and must be specified for RAMONA, we represent them here explicitly by curved double-headed arrows (McArdle, 1988) with both heads touching the same circle or square:

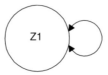

If a path coefficient, variance, or covariance is fixed (at a nonzero value), we attach the value to the single- or double-headed arrow:

A variable that acts as an explanatory variable in all of its dependence relationships (emits single-headed arrows but does not receive any) is **exogenous** (outside the system):

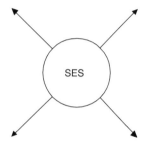

A variable that acts as a dependent variable in at least one dependence relationship (receives at least one single-headed arrow) is **endogenous** (inside the system), whether or not it ever acts as an explanatory variable (emits any arrows):

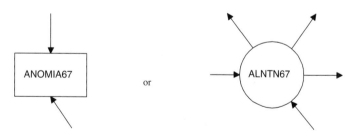

A parameter in RAMONA is associated with each dependence path and covariance path between two exogenous variables. Covariance paths are permitted only between exogenous variables. For example, the following covariance paths are permissible:

Permissible

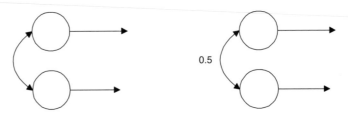

Variances and covariances of endogenous variables are implied by the corresponding explanatory variables and have no associated parameters in the model. Thus, an endogenous variable may not have a covariance path with any other variable. The covariance is a function of path coefficients and variances or covariances of exogenous variables and is not represented by a parameter in the model. The following covariance paths, for example, are not permissible:

Not permissible

Also, an endogenous variable does not have a free parameter representing its variance. Its variance is a *function* of the path coefficients and variances of its explanatory variables. Therefore, it may not have an associated double-headed arrow with no fixed value:

Not permissible

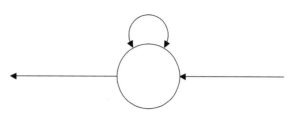

Exogenous variables alone may have free parameters representing their variances:

Permissible

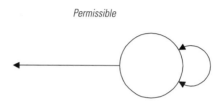

We do, however, allow *fixed* variances for both endogenous and exogenous variables. These two types of fixed variances are interpreted differently in the program:

- A fixed variance for an endogenous variable is treated as a nonlinear equality constraint on the parameters in the model:

Constraint

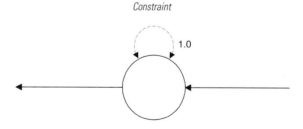

The fixed implied variance is represented by a dotted two-headed arrow instead of a solid two-headed arrow because it is a nonlinear constraint on several other parameters in the model and does not have a single fixed parameter associated with it.

- A fixed variance for an exogenous variable is treated as a model parameter with a fixed value:

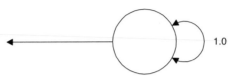

Every latent variable must emit at least one arrow. No latent variable can receive arrows without emitting any:

The scale of every latent variable (exogenous or endogenous) should be fixed to avoid indeterminate parameter values. Some ways for accomplishing this are:

- To fix one of the path coefficients, associated with an emitted arrow, to a nonzero value (usually 1.0):

- To fix both the variance and path coefficient of an associated error term, if the latent variable is endogenous (for example, Jöreskog and Goldberger, 1975):

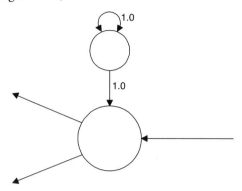

- To fix the variance of the latent variable:

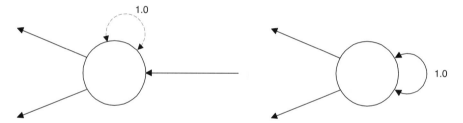

If a latent variable is endogenous and the third method is used, RAMONA fixes the implied variance by means of equality constraints. Programs that do not have this facility require the user to employ the first or second method to determine the scales of endogenous latent variables.

Consider *ALNTN67* in Figure 1. This latent variable is endogenous (it receives arrows from *SES* and *Z1*). It also emits arrows to *ANOMIA67* and *POWRLS67*. Consequently, it is necessary to fix either the variance of *ALNTN67*, the path coefficient from *ALNTN67* to *ANOMIA67*, the path coefficient from *ALNTN67* to *POWRLS67*, or the variance of *Z1*. It is conventional to use 1.0 as the fixed value. Our preference is to use the third method and fix the variance of *ALNTN67* rather than use the first or second method because we find standardized path coefficients easier to interpret (Bollen, 1989). The first two methods result in latent variables with nonunit variances. RAMONA does, however, allow the use of these methods.

The model shown in Figure 1 is equivalent to Jöreskog's (1977) model but makes use of different identification conditions. We apply nonlinear equality constraints to fix the variances of the endogenous variables *ALNTN67* and *ALNTN71*, but treat the path coefficients from *ALNTN67* to *ANOMIA67* and from *ALNTN71* to *ANOMIA71* as free parameters. Jöreskog fixed the path coefficients from *ALNTN67* to *ANONMIA67* and from *ALNTN71* to *ANOMIA71* and did not apply any nonlinear equality constraints.

An error term is an exogenous latent variable that emits only one single-headed arrow and shares double-headed arrows only with other error terms. In Figure 1, the variables *E1*, *E2*, *E3*, *E4*, *D1*, *D2*, *Z1*, and *Z2* are error terms. RAMONA treats error terms in exactly the same manner as other latent variables.

Examples

In this section, we present four examples:

- Example 18.1 treats the model specified in Figure 1.
- Example 18.2 illustrates the use of a restart file.
- Example 18.3 shows how asymptotically distribution free estimates can be obtained if new data are entered using a SYSTAT cases-by-variables data file.
- Example 18.4 demonstrates how RAMONA produces correct standard errors for maximum likelihood estimates when a correlation matrix is input.

18.1 Stability of alienation

In this first example, we specify the model of Figure 1. The covariance matrix of the six manifest variables is shown below. These covariances and variances were computed from a sample of 932 respondents and are stored in the *EX1* data file.

	ANOMIA67	POWRLS67	ANOMIA71	POWRLS71	EDUCTN	SEI
ANOMIA67	11.834					
POWRLS67	6.947	9.364				
ANOMIA71	6.819	5.091	12.532			
POWRLS71	4.783	5.028	7.495	9.986		
EDUCTN	-3.839	-3.889	-3.841	-3.625	9.610	
SEI	-21.899	-18.831	-21.748	-18.755	35.522	450.288

The role of the manifest and latent variables is clear from the MODEL statement below. Manifest variables are in the SYSTAT file (latent variables are not). We define the syntax for the MODEL statement after describing the output for this example.

We use the default maximum Wishart likelihood method (METHOD=MWL) to analyze the correlation matrix. Our analysis differs from Jöreskog's analysis in that the model is treated as a correlation structure rather than a covariance structure. The display correlation option of ESTIMATE (TYPE=CORR) identifies that the input is a correlation matrix, and NCASES=932 denotes the sample size used to compute it.

With commands:

```
RAMONA
  USE ex1
  MODEL anomia67 <-  alntn67(*,*) e1(0,1.0),
        powrls67 <-  alntn67(*,*) e2(0,1.0),
        anomia71 <-  alntn71(*,*) e3(0,1.0),
        powrls71 <-  alntn71(*,*) e4(0,1.0),
          eductn <-  ses(*,*) d1(0,1.0),
             sei <-  ses(*,*) d2(0,1.0),
          alntn67 <- ses(*,*) z1(0,1.0),
          alntn71 <- alntn67(*,*) ses(*,*) z2(0,1.0),
             ses <-> ses(0,1.0),
              e1 <-> e1(*,*) e3(*,*),
              e2 <-> e2(*,*) e4(*,*),
              e3 <-> e3(*,*),
              e4 <-> e4(*,*),
              d1 <-> d1(*,*),
              d2 <-> d2(*,*),
              z1 <-> z1(*,*),
              z2 <-> z2(*,*),
         alntn71 <-> alntn71(0,1.0),
         alntn67 <-> alntn67(0,1.0)
  PRINT = MEDIUM
  ESTIMATE / TYPE=CORR  NCASES=932
```

If you were to specify explicitly the default values of the options for ESTIMATE, the last statement would read:

```
ESTIMATE / TYPE=CORR  METHOD=MWL  START=ROUGH,
           CONVG=0.0001 ITER=500
```

```
Variables in the SYSTAT covariance file are:
ANOMIA67     POWRLS67     ANOMIA71     POWRLS71     EDUCATN     SEI

There are 6 manifest variables in the model. They are:
    ANOMIA67 POWRLS67 ANOMIA71 POWRLS71 EDUCTN SEI


There are 11 latent variables in the model. They are:
    ALNTN67 E1 E2 ALNTN71 E3 E4 SES D1 D2 Z1 Z2


RAMONA options in effect are:
    Display               Corr
    Method                MWL
    Start                 Rough
    Convg                 0.000100
    Maximum iterations    100
    Number of cases       932
    Restart               No
    Confidence Interval   90

Number of manifest variables             =    6
Total number of variables in the system  =   23.
Reading covariance matrix...

                  Details of Iterations
```

❶

Iter	Method	Discr. Funct.	Max.R.Cos.	Max.Const.	NRP	NBD
0	OLS	2.990254		0.000000		
1(0)	OLS	9363.179841	0.999315	87.020340	0	0
1(1)	OLS	67.826312	0.974346	9.357014	0	0
1(2)	OLS	1.861094	0.657239	1.221196	0	0
2(0)	OLS	0.863526	0.644690	0.787367	0	0
3(0)	OLS	0.020374	0.512199	0.131453	0	0
4(0)	OLS	0.001137	0.301991	0.004030	0	0
5(0)	OLS	0.001007	0.001247	0.000027	0	0
5(0)	MWL	0.005313	0.034276	0.000027	0	0
6(0)	MWL	0.005095	0.009493	0.000065	0	0
7(0)	MWL	0.005090	0.000712	0.000003	0	0
8(0)	MWL	0.005090	0.000172	0.000000	0	0
9(0)	MWL	0.005090	0.000014	0.000000	0	0
10(0)	MWL	0.005090	0.000003	0.000000	0	0

Iterative procedure complete.

Convergence limit for residual cosines = 0.000100 on 2 consecutive
iterations.

Convergence limit for variance constraint violations = 5.00000E-07
Value of the maximum variance constraint violation = 1.29230E-11

❷ Sample Correlation Matrix :

	ANOMIA67	POWRLS67	ANOMIA71	POWRLS71	EDUCTN
ANOMIA67	1.000				
POWRLS67	0.660	1.000			
ANOMIA71	0.560	0.470	1.000		
POWRLS71	0.440	0.520	0.670	1.000	
EDUCTN	-0.360	-0.410	-0.350	-0.370	1.000
SEI	-0.300	-0.290	-0.290	-0.280	0.540

	SEI
SEI	1.000

Number of cases = 932.

Reproduced Correlation Matrix :

	ANOMIA67	POWRLS67	ANOMIA71	POWRLS71	EDUCTN
ANOMIA67	1.000				
POWRLS67	0.660	1.000			
ANOMIA71	0.560	0.469	1.000		
POWRLS71	0.441	0.520	0.670	1.000	
EDUCTN	-0.367	-0.404	-0.357	-0.369	1.000
SEI	-0.280	-0.308	-0.272	-0.281	0.540

	SEI
SEI	1.000

Residual Matrix (correlations) :

	ANOMIA67	POWRLS67	ANOMIA71	POWRLS71	EDUCTN
ANOMIA67	-0.000				
POWRLS67	0.000	-0.000			
ANOMIA71	-0.000	0.001	-0.000		
POWRLS71	-0.001	0.000	-0.000	-0.000	
EDUCTN	0.007	-0.006	0.007	-0.001	-0.000
SEI	-0.020	0.018	-0.017	0.001	0.000

	SEI
SEI	-0.000

Value of the maximum absolute residual = 0.020.

ML Estimates of Free Parameters in Dependence Relationships

❸

	Path	Param #	Point Estimate	90.00% Conf. Int. Lower	Upper	Standard Error	T Value
ANOMIA67	<- ALNTN67	1	0.774	0.733	0.816	0.025	30.73
POWRLS67	<- ALNTN67	2	0.852	0.810	0.894	0.026	33.06
ANOMIA71	<- ALNTN71	3	0.805	0.763	0.848	0.026	31.03
POWRLS71	<- ALNTN71	4	0.832	0.788	0.876	0.027	31.19
EDUCTN	<- SES	5	0.842	0.789	0.894	0.032	26.44
SEI	<- SES	6	0.642	0.592	0.691	0.030	21.30
ALNTN67	<- SES	7	-0.563	-0.620	-0.506	0.035	-16.26
ALNTN71	<- ALNTN67	8	0.567	0.500	0.634	0.041	13.88
ALNTN71	<- SES	9	-0.207	-0.281	-0.133	0.045	-4.60

❹ Scaled Standard Deviations (nuisance parameters)

Variable	Estimate
ANOMIA67	1.000
POWRLS67	1.000
ANOMIA71	1.000
POWRLS71	1.000
EDUCTN	1.000
SEI	1.000

Values of Fixed Parameters in Dependence Relationships

Path		Value
ANOMIA67	<- E1	1.000
POWRLS67	<- E2	1.000
ANOMIA71	<- E3	1.000
POWRLS71	<- E4	1.000
EDUCTN	<- D1	1.000
SEI	<- D2	1.000
ALNTN67	<- Z1	1.000
ALNTN71	<- Z2	1.000

❺ ML estimates of free parameters in variance/covariance relationships

Path		Param #	Point Estimate	90.00% Conf. Int. Lower	Upper	Standard Error	T Value
E1	<-> E1	10	0.400	0.341	0.470	0.039	10.25
E1	<-> E3	11	0.133	0.091	0.175	0.026	5.22
E2	<-> E2	12	0.274	0.211	0.357	0.044	6.24
E2	<-> E4	13	0.035	-0.009	0.080	0.027	1.30
E3	<-> E3	14	0.351	0.289	0.427	0.042	8.40
E4	<-> E4	15	0.308	0.243	0.390	0.044	6.94
D1	<-> D1	16	0.292	0.216	0.395	0.054	5.44
D2	<-> D2	17	0.588	0.528	0.656	0.039	15.22
Z1	<-> Z1	18	0.683	0.616	0.743	0.039	17.52
Z2	<-> Z2	19	0.503	0.448	0.557	0.033	15.08

Values of Fixed Parameters in Variance/Covariance Relationships

Path		Value
SES	<-> SES	1.000

Equality Constraints on Variances

❻

Constraint		Value	Lagrange Multiplier	Standard Error
ALNTN71	<-> ALNTN71	1.0000	-0.000	0.000
ALNTN67	<-> ALNTN67	1.0000	-0.000	0.000
ANOMIA67	<-> ANOMIA67	1.0000	0.000	0.000
POWRLS67	<-> POWRLS67	1.0000	0.000	0.000
ANOMIA71	<-> ANOMIA71	1.0000	0.000	-0.000
POWRLS71	<-> POWRLS71	1.0000	-0.000	0.000
EDUCTN	<-> EDUCTN	1.0000	0.000	-0.000
SEI	<-> SEI	1.0000	-0.000	0.000

Maximum Likelihood Discrepancy Function

❼ Measures of fit of the model

Sample Discrepancy Function Value   : 0.005 (5.090285E-03)

Population discrepancy function value, Fo
Bias adjusted point estimate   : 0.001
90.000 percent confidence interval   :(0.0,0.011)

Root mean square error of approximation
Steiger-Lind : RMSEA = SQRT(Fo/DF)
Point estimate   : 0.014
90.000 percent confidence interval   :(0.0,0.053)

Expected cross-validation index
Point estimate (modified AIC)   : 0.042
90.000 percent confidence interval   :(0.041,0.052)
CVI (modified AIC) for the saturated model   : 0.045

Test statistic: : 4.739
Exceedance probabilities:-
Ho: perfect fit (RMSEA = 0.0)   : 0.315
Ho: close fit   (RMSEA <=   0.050)   : 0.929

Multiplier for obtaining test statistic =   931.000
Degrees of freedom   =   4
Effective number of parameters   =   17

The highlighted numbers below correspond to those in the output:

❶ Details of the iteration process: *Iter*, the number of the iteration. The number of the step halving step, carried out to yield a reduction in the discrepancy function plus a penalty for constraint violations, is given in parentheses next to the iteration number. *Method*, the method of estimation. *Discr. Funct.*, the discrepancy function value. *Max. R. Cos.*, the absolute value of the maximum residual cosine used to indicate convergence. *Max. Const.*, the absolute value of the maximum violated variance constraint. *NRP*, the number of apparently redundant parameters (number of zero pivots of the coefficient matrix of the normal equations). *NBD*, the number of active bounds on parameter values.

The values of *NRP* and *NBD* can change from iteration to iteration. If *NRP* has a constant nonzero value for several iterations prior to convergence, this suggests that the model could be overparameterized. The value of *NBD* indicates the number of variance or correlation estimates on bounds at any iteration.

If the usual SYSTAT cases-by-variables file is used as input, then kurtosis estimates are printed before the iteration details (see Example 18.3). These can be used to judge the appropriateness of normality assumptions. They can also be used to apply corrections manually to test statistics and standard errors if the user is willing to accept that the assumption of an elliptical distribution is appropriate for the data (Shapiro and Browne, 1987).

❷ The sample correlation (covariance) matrix, the correlation (covariance) matrix reproduced by the model and the matrix of residuals. The residual matrix is the difference between the sample correlation (covariance) matrix and the reproduced correlation (covariance) matrix. If the input is a correlation matrix (TYPE=CORR), the residual matrix will have null diagonal elements.

❸ Estimates of the *free* path coefficients and the values of all fixed path coefficients involved in the model. The following values are reported:
  - *Path*.
  - *Param #*: the number of the parameter. This number need not be the same as the number in the input file. (It is the number assigned to the parameter name in the asymptotic covariance matrix of estimators given subsequently.)
  - *Point Estimate*: the estimate of the path coefficient.

- *90.00% Conf. Int.*: a 90% confidence interval for the path coefficient (the default). If you want to alter the confidence level, specify, for example, CONFI=0.95.
- *Standard Error*: an estimate of the standard error of the estimator.
- *T value*: the value of the *t* statistic (ratio of estimate to standard error).

❹ *Scaled Standard Deviations*: the ratios of standard deviations estimated under the model to sample standard deviations.

❺ Estimates of the *free* variances and covariances (correlations) and values of the *fixed* variance parameters. A table similar to that used to present estimates of path coefficients is printed for estimates of variances, covariances, and correlations.

❻ If applicable, information about equality constraints on endogenous variable variances is presented:
- *Constraint*: the variance path that is constrained.
- *Value*: the value of the endogenous variable variance at convergence.
- *Lagrange Multiplier*: the value of the Lagrange multiplier at convergence.
- *Standard Error*: an estimate of the standard error of the Lagrange multiplier.

In most applications, the constraints on endogenous variable variances serve as identification conditions and all Lagrange multipliers and standard errors are 0.

If the input is a correlation matrix, the scaled standard deviations (nuisance parameters) are reported with:
- The name of the manifest variable.
- The ratio of the standard deviation reproduced from the model to the sample standard deviation.

❼ Measures of fit of the model (see "More about RAMONA" on p. 656):

- – The sample discrepancy function value.
- – Bias adjusted estimate of the population discrepancy function value.
- – 90% confidence interval for the population discrepancy function value.
- – The point estimate of the Steiger-Lind root mean square error of approximation (RMSEA).
- – The 90% confidence interval for the RMSEA.
- – The point estimate of the expected cross-validation index (ECVI) for the model. This point estimate is equivalent to the Akaike Information Criterion (Akaike, 1973) when the method is specified as MWL.
- – 90% confidence interval for the modified ECVI.
- – The modified ECVI for the saturated model. The chi-square test statistic with its degrees of freedom and exceedance probabilities.
- – The chi-square test statistic with its degrees of freedom and the exceedance probabilities for the null hypotheses of perfect fit and of close fit.

If you choose **Edit➠Options** and select **Long** from the **Output Results** drop-down list (PRINT=LONG), an estimate of the asymptotic correlation matrix of parameter estimators is printed (see "Print features" on p. 632 for more details). Its rows and columns are headed by *PARAM1, PARAM2,...*. These headings correspond to the parameter numbers provided in the tables of path coefficient and variance/covariance estimates:

```
Large sample correlation matrix of the estimators:

              PARAM1      PARAM2      PARAM3      PARAM4      PARAM5
PARAM1        1.000
PARAM2       -0.604       1.000
PARAM3        0.497      -0.402       1.000
PARAM4       -0.372       0.431      -0.650       1.000
PARAM5        0.016       0.012       0.013       0.011       1.000
PARAM6        0.026       0.019       0.020       0.018      -0.503
PARAM7       -0.155       0.107      -0.133       0.033       0.294
PARAM8        0.061       0.002       0.013       0.099      -0.177
PARAM9        0.002      -0.042      -0.010       0.063       0.172
PARAM10       0.155      -0.061      -0.002      -0.274      -0.210
PARAM11       0.124      -0.085      -0.030      -0.043      -0.085
PARAM12      -0.107      -0.002       0.042      -0.137      -0.207
PARAM13      -0.110      -0.150      -0.080      -0.041      -0.016
PARAM14       0.133      -0.013       0.010      -0.151      -0.072
PARAM15      -0.033      -0.099      -0.063      -0.015      -0.099
PARAM16      -0.294      -0.177      -0.172      -0.034      -0.041
PARAM17       0.239       0.081       0.112      -0.055      -0.067
PARAM18       1.000       0.059       0.016      -0.154      -0.187
PARAM19       0.167      -0.511       0.071      -0.259      -0.254

              PARAM6      PARAM7      PARAM8      PARAM9      PARAM10
PARAM6        1.000
PARAM7       -0.239       1.000
PARAM8       -0.081       0.059       1.000
PARAM9       -0.112       0.016       0.809       1.000
PARAM10      -0.169      -0.082      -0.064      -0.037       1.000
PARAM11      -0.045      -0.085      -0.032      -0.018       0.669
PARAM12      -0.021      -0.087      -0.047      -0.027      -0.604
PARAM13      -0.050      -0.012      -0.009      -0.005      -0.511
PARAM14      -0.234      -0.179      -0.050      -0.029       0.497
PARAM15      -0.161      -0.218      -0.044      -0.025      -0.372
PARAM16      -0.032      -0.034      -0.179      -0.074       0.016
PARAM17      -0.052      -0.056      -0.206      -0.290       0.026
PARAM18      -0.145      -0.142      -0.182      -0.106       0.155
PARAM19      -0.279      -0.255      -0.137      -0.080       0.136

              PARAM11     PARAM12     PARAM13     PARAM14     PARAM15
PARAM11       1.000
PARAM12      -0.527       1.000
PARAM13      -0.624       0.644       1.000
PARAM14       0.679      -0.402      -0.574       1.000
PARAM15      -0.513       0.431       0.669      -0.650       1.000
PARAM16       0.008       0.012       0.002       0.013       0.011
PARAM17       0.013       0.019       0.004       0.020       0.018
PARAM18       0.124      -0.107      -0.110       0.133      -0.033
PARAM19       0.131       0.037       0.111       0.067       0.068

              PARAM16     PARAM17     PARAM18     PARAM19
PARAM16       1.000
PARAM17      -0.503       1.000
PARAM18      -0.294       0.239       1.000
PARAM19      -0.019       0.082       0.167       1.000
```

Defining the model

MODEL defines the paths or relationships in the diagram. Describe the relationship for each arrow:

> MODEL   *1st relationship,*
> *2nd relationship*
> ⋮

The first six arrows in the Example 18.1 model statement define arrows going to the *manifest* variables. SYSTAT checks each variable name in the MODEL statement to see if it is in the input file. (If it is in the file, SYSTAT considers it *manifest*; if not, it is considered *latent*). To help organize the specification, you can use MANIFEST and LATENT to identify the role of each variable. These options are not necessary, however.

Manifest variables. Use MANIFEST to identify the manifest variables (enclosed in rectangles) in the path diagram. For example,

```
MANIFEST = anomia67 powrls67 anomia71 powrls71,
           eductn sei
```

Latent variables. Use LATENT to identify the latent variables (enclosed in circles) in the path diagram. Decide upon descriptive names including errors. A systematic way of organizing names is to let the endogenous latent variables be followed by the exogenous latent variables and to include the error terms last. It is not, however, essential to do this.

Inspection of the path diagram in Figure 1 shows that the latent variables (indicated by circular symbols) are *ALNTN67, ALNTN71, SES, E1, E2, E3, E4, D1, D2, Z1*, and *Z2*. For example,

```
LATENT = alntn67 alntn71 ses e1 e2 e3 e4 d1 d2 z1 z2
```

specifies the latent variables.

Defining paths

The relationships in the MODEL statement (arrows in the path diagram) are of two types:

– Dependence relationships
– Covariance relationships

Dependence relationships

A dependence relationship is indicated by the symbol <-, which relates directly to a single-headed arrow in the path diagram. To code a dependence path, enter the descriptive name of the dependent variable followed by the symbol <-. Then name the explanatory variable, including the parameter number and the starting value for the parameter involved within parentheses. For example,

```
dependent <- explanatory (1, 0.6)
```

The parameter number is an integer employed to indicate fixed parameters or parameters whose values are constrained to be equal. A fixed parameter must have a parameter number of 0. Any free parameters whose values are required to be equal are assigned the same parameter number. A free parameter that is not constrained to equality with any other parameter may be assigned the symbol * instead of a parameter number. Its parameter number is assigned within the program.

The starting value is a real number and is used to initialize the iterative process. Some rules for choosing starting values are given by Bollen (1989). If you have difficulty in deciding on a starting value, you can replace it with a *. The program then chooses a very rough starting value. If a parameter is fixed with a 0 as parameter number, then the fixed value must replace the starting value. It is not permissible to use a * instead of the fixed value.

Inspection of Figure 1 shows that the endogenous manifest variable *POWRLS67* receives single-headed arrows from the latent variable *ALNTN67* and the measurement error *Z1*. These dependence relationships can be coded as:

```
powrls67 <- alntn67(*,*),
powrls67 <- e2(0,1.0)
```

In the first path, the parameter is free and not constrained to equality with any other parameter. The parameter number is replaced by a *. No starting value is specified and it is replaced by a *. The parameter in the second path is fixed at 1.0 so that the parameter number is 0 and the parameter value is 1.0.

The default is (*,*), so it is not necessary to type it:

```
powrls67 <- alntn67,
powrls67 <- e2(0,1.0)
```

It is not necessary to have a different statement for each path. Several paths with the same dependent (receiving) variable can be combined into one statement. Since the same endogenous variable, *POWRLS67*, is involved in two dependence relationships, the two paths can be coded in a single statement as:

```
powrls67 <- alntn67 e2(0,1.0)
```

If the statement continues to a second line, place a comma at the end of the first line.

Constraining parameters. If you want to constrain two or more free parameters to be equal, the parameters are assigned the same nonzero positive integer for the parameter number. Suppose you want to constrain the path coefficient from *SES* to *ALNTN67* and that from *SES* to *ALNTN71* to be equal. You can specify:

```
alntn67 <- ses(7,*) z1(0,1.0),
alntn71 <- alntn67 ses(7,*) z2(0,1.0)
```

Providing starting values. You can provide starting values for free parameters. Suppose that it is known from a previous run that the path coefficient of *ALNTN67* to *ALNTN71* is approximately 0.6. In this case, you can specify the following:

```
alntn71 <- alntn67(*,0.6) ses(7,*) z2(0,1.0)
```

When specifying dependence relationships, bear in mind that:

- Dependence relationships can be specified in any order.
- A statement can specify several dependence paths involving the same dependent variable.
- Specified path numbers need not be sequential; for example, 5, 3, 9 can be used. Sequential path numbers will be reassigned by the program.

Covariance relationships

A variance or a covariance relationship is indicated by the symbol <->, which relates directly to the double-headed arrow in the path diagram. To specify a covariance path, enter the name of one of the variables in the path followed by the symbol <->. Then enter the name of the other variable, and include the path number and the starting value within parentheses. Unlike the dependence relationship, it does not matter which variable is given first.

The same guidelines regarding the numbers and starting values of the parameters we provided in "Dependence relationships" on p. 627 are applicable here. You can replace the number and/or the starting value of a free parameter with the symbol *. In this case, they are provided by the program. In the case of a fixed parameter, however, you must specify 0 as the number of the parameter and the fixed value of the parameter.

Inspection of Figure 1 shows that double-headed arrows are employed from the measurement error *E1* to itself to specify a variance and to *E3* to specify a covariance. These relationships are specified in the statement:

```
e1 <-> e1(*,*) e3(*,*) or
e1 <-> e1 e3
```

Covariance paths can be constrained to be equal in the same manner as dependence paths. Suppose you want to specify that the variances of the measurement errors *E1*, *E2*, and *E3* must be equal:

```
e1 <-> e1 (10,*) e3,
e2 <-> e2 (10,*),
e3 <-> e3 (10,*)
```

You can again provide starting values for free parameters:

```
e3 <-> e3(*,0.32)
```

As mentioned previously, variances of both exogenous and endogenous variables can be required to have fixed values. Thus, both

```
ses <-> ses(0,1.0)
```

and

```
altntn67 <-> altntn67(0,1.0)
```

are acceptable. They are, however, treated differently within the program. The exogenous latent variable, *SES*, has a parameter associated with its variance and it is set equal to 1.0. There is no parameter representing the variance of the endogenous latent variable, *ALNTN67*. This variance is a function of the path coefficient, **ALNTN67<-SES**, the variance of *SES*, and the variance of *Z1*. It is constrained to have a value of 1.0 by RAMONA.

When specifying covariance relationships, bear in mind that:

- Covariance paths can be specified in any order.
- Several covariance paths per statement can be specified. For example, the variance of an exogenous variable as well as its covariances with other exogenous variables can be specified in the same statement.
- Dependence paths and covariance paths must be specified in separate substatements. The dependence path subparagraph must precede the covariance path subparagraph.
- If every manifest endogenous variable has a corresponding measurement error with an unconstrained variance (see the model in

Figure 1), the coding of these variances can be omitted. When all error path coefficients are fixed, and no error variance paths are input for the measurement errors, the program will automatically provide the error variance paths.

— If there are exogenous manifest variables and if all of their variances and covariances are present in the system and are unrestricted, the coding of these variance and covariance paths can be omitted. When no variance and covariance paths for exogenous manifest variables are input, the program will automatically provide them.

Estimate options

ESTIMATE initiates the computation and provides many options:

TYPE		Specifies whether a covariance or correlation matrix is analyzed.
	= COVA	Covariance matrix. If the input matrix is a correlation matrix (has unit diagonal elements), the analysis is performed, but RAMONA prints a warning in the output. This is the default.
	= CORR	Correlation matrix. If a covariance matrix is input, RAMONA rescales it to be a correlation matrix.
METHOD		Specifies the method of estimation. (See "More about RAMONA" on p. 656 for details on the discrepancy functions.)
	= MWL	Maximum Wishart likelihood. This is the default.
	= GLS	Generalized least squares assuming a Wishart distribution for S.
	= OLS	Ordinary least squares. With OLS, no measures of fit and no standard errors of estimators are printed.
	= ADFG	Asymptotically distribution free estimate. ADFG uses a biased but Gramian (non-negative definite) estimate of the asymptotic covariance matrix Γ, of the elements of the sample covariance matrix.
	= ADFU	Asymptotically distribution free estimate that uses an unbiased estimate of Γ.

When specifying ADFG or ADFU, a cases-by-variables input file must be used.

START	Affects how starting values are scaled.
= ROUGH	Rescale starting values to satisfy the specified variance constraints and to yield $\text{Diag}[\hat{\Sigma}] = \text{Diag}[S]$. RAMONA applies OLS initially. After partial convergence, RAMONA switches to the procedure specified by METHOD. If you require MWL estimates and supply poor starting values or if you use the * alternative for the starting value, use ROUGH. It is also advisable to use ROUGH with ADFG and ADFU if starting values are poor because the time taken per iteration is less for GLS than for ADFG and ADFU. This is the default.
= CLOSE	Do not rescale starting values and RAMONA employs the estimation procedure specified with METHOD from the beginning of the iterative procedure. CLOSE should always be used with OLS.
	The MWL procedure may yield an indefinite reproduced covariance matrix during initial iterations if starting values are poor.
NCASES=n	Number of cases used to compute the matrix. NCASES should exceed the number of p manifest variables if METHOD is MWL or GLS and must exceed $\frac{1}{2}p(p+1)$ if METHOD is ADFG or ADFU. The default is 500.
ITER=n	Maximum number of iterations allowed for the iterative procedure.
CONVG=n	Limit for the residual cosine employed as a convergence criterion. The default is 0.0001.
CONFI=n	Confidence interval range.
RESTART	Save the commands for the current run using RAMONA's estimates of the parameters inserted. Use with the BATCH feature of OUTPUT.

Print features

The **Output Results** option in the **Options** dialog box offers **Short**, **Medium**, and **Long**. Each has specific report panels associated with it.

Short	The sample covariance (correlation) matrix; a table consisting of path coefficient estimates, 90% confidence intervals (see "More about RAMONA" on p. 656), standard errors and t statistics (estimate divided by standard

error); a table consisting of variance and covariance or correlation estimates, 90% confidence intervals, standard errors and t statistics; measures of t of the model.

Medium   The panels listed for **Short**, plus details of the iterative procedure; the reproduced covariance or correlation matrix; the matrix of residuals; information about equality constraints on variances (if applicable). This is the default.

Long   The panels listed for **Medium**, plus the asymptotic correlation matrix of the estimators.

With commands, type, for example, PRINT=MEDIUM.

18.2 Peer influence on ambition

This example is based on Jöreskog's (1977) path analysis model for Duncan, Haller, and Portes (1971) data on peer influences on ambition. It illustrates a situation where some manifest variables are exogenous. It also illustrates the use of a restart file for creating a data file for a second run where some modifications have been made (see "Using the RESTART file" on p. 638).

The example consists of two runs. Jöreskog's original model is used for the first run. The model is treated as a covariance structure—this is inappropriate because a correlation matrix is used as input. In the second run, we use a restart file that treats the model as a correlation structure.

In Figure 2, the six manifest exogenous variables are:

RPARASP	respondent's parental aspiration
RESOCIEC	respondent's socioeconomic status
REINTGCE	respondent's intelligence
BFINTGCE	best friend's intelligence
BFSOCIEC	best friend's socioeconomic status
BFPARASP	best friend's parental aspiration

The four endogenous variables are:

REOCCASP	respondent's occupational aspiration
BFEDASP	best friend's educational aspiration
REEDASP	respondent's educational aspiration
BFOCCASP	best friend's occupational aspiration

The latent endogenous variables are:

REAMBITN	respondent's ambition
BFAMBITN	best friend's ambition

And the exogenous error variables are *E1*, *E4*, *E2*, *Z1*, *E3*, and *Z2*.

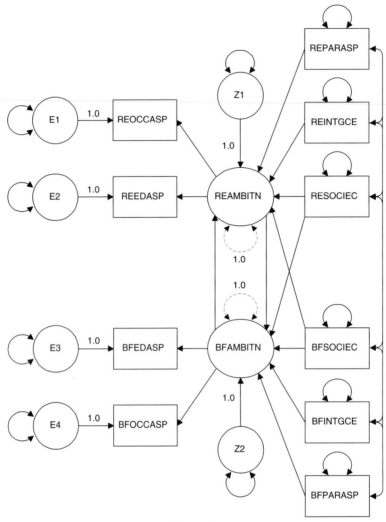

Figure 2

The correlation matrix for the manifest variables is stored in the file *EX2.CMD*. The **RESTART** option of **ESTIMATE** creates a restart command file, *EX2B.CMD*, that is submitted as input in the second run. **RESTART** tells RAMONA to take the estimated parameter values and insert them as starting values in the **MODEL** statement. Note that we must also type **OUTPUT BATCH**=*filename* to do this. Before the second run, we modify

EX2B.CMD to treat the model as a correlation structure. Following is the input file for the first run:

```
RAMONA
    USE ex2
    MANIFEST = reintgce reparasp resociec reoccasp,
               reedasp bfintgce bfparasp bfsociec,
               bfoccasp bfedasp
    LATENT = reambitn bfambitn e1 e2 e3 e4 z1 z2
    MODEL reoccasp <-  reambitn(0,1.0) e1(0,1.0),
          reedasp <-  reambitn e2(0,1.0),
          bfedasp <-  bfambitn e3(0,1.0),
          bfoccasp <- bfambitn(0,1.0) e4(0,1.0),
          reambitn <- bfambitn z1(0,1.0) reparasp,
          reambitn <- reintgce resociec bfsociec,
          bfambitn <- reambitn z2(0,1.0) resociec,
          bfambitn <- bfsociec bfintgce bfparasp,
          reparasp <-> reparasp reintgce resociec,
          reparasp <-> bfsociec bfintgce bfparasp,
          reintgce <-> reintgce resociec bfsociec,
          reintgce <-> bfintgce bfparasp,
          resociec <-> resociec bfsociec bfintgce,
          resociec <-> bfparasp,
          bfsociec <-> bfsociec bfintgce bfparasp,
          bfintgce <-> bfintgce bfparasp,
          bfparasp <-> bfparasp,
                e1 <-> e1,
                e2 <-> e2,
                e3 <-> e3,
                e4 <-> e4,
                z1 <-> z1,
                z2 <-> z2
    PRINT = MEDIUM
    OUTPUT BATCH = 'ex2b.cmd' / PROGRAM
    ESTIMATE / TYPE=COVA  NCASES=329  RESTART
```

You would specify the default values of other options for **ESTIMATE** as:

```
    ESTIMATE / TYPE=COVA  METHOD=MWL  START=ROUGH  ITER=500,
              CONVG=0.0001  NCASES  RESTART
```

Following Jöreskog's model, the path coefficients REOCCASP <- REAMBITN and BFOCCASP <- BFAMBITN are set equal to 1 for identification purposes.

```
Variables in the SYSTAT Correlation file are:
    REINTGCE    REPARASP    RESOCIEC    REOCCASP    REEDASP    BFINTGCE
    BFPARASP    BFSOCIEC    BFOCCASP    BFEDASP

There are 10 manifest variables in the model. They are:
    REINTGCE REPARASP RESOCIEC REOCCASP REEDASP BFINTGCE BFPARASP
    BFSOCIEC BFOCCASP BFEDASP

There are 8 latent variables in the model. They are:
    REAMBITN E1 E2 BFAMBITN E3 E4 Z1 Z2

RAMONA options in effect are:
    Display              Covar
    Method               MWL
    Start                Rough
    Convg                0.000100
    Maximum iterations   100
    Number of cases      329
    Restart              Yes
    Confidence Interval  90

Number of manifest variables        =   10
Total number of variables in the system  =   18.


***WARNING***:
A correlation matrix was provided although TYPE=COVA. Fit measures and
standard errors may be inappropriate

  Reading correlation matrix...

                      Details of Iterations
    Iter   Method  Discr. Funct.  Max.R.Cos.   Max.Const.   NRP  NBD
   ------  ------  -------------  ------------  ------------ ---------
       0    OLS      1.500570
     1(0)   OLS      0.325498       0.720392                  0    0
     2(0)   OLS      0.023128       0.191263                  0    0
     3(0)   OLS      0.019538       0.007112                  0    0
     3(0)   MWL      0.085416       0.059603                  0    0
     4(0)   MWL      0.082172       0.016527                  0    0
     5(0)   MWL      0.082003       0.003878                  0    0
     6(0)   MWL      0.081991       0.001141                  0    0
     7(0)   MWL      0.081990       0.000260                  0    0
     8(0)   MWL      0.081990       0.000081                  0    0
     9(0)   MWL      0.081990       0.000018                  0    0

Iterative procedure complete.


Convergence limit for residual cosines = 0.000100 on 2 consecutive
iterations.

Sample Covariance Matrix :

              REINTGCE   REPARASP   RESOCIEC   REOCCASP   REEDASP
  REINTGCE     1.000
  REPARASP     0.184      1.000
  RESOCIEC     0.222      0.049      1.000
  REOCCASP     0.410      0.214      0.324      1.000
  REEDASP      0.404      0.274      0.405      0.625      1.000
  BFINTGCE     0.336      0.078      0.230      0.299      0.286
  BFPARASP     0.102      0.115      0.093      0.076      0.070
  BFSOCIEC     0.186      0.019      0.271      0.293      0.241
  BFOCCASP     0.260      0.084      0.279      0.422      0.328
  BFEDASP      0.290      0.112      0.305      0.327      0.367

              BFINTGCE   BFPARASP   BFSOCIEC   BFOCCASP   BFEDASP
  BFINTGCE     1.000
  BFPARASP     0.209      1.000
  BFSOCIEC     0.295     -0.044      1.000
  BFOCCASP     0.501      0.199      0.361      1.000
  BFEDASP      0.519      0.278      0.410      0.640      1.000

Number of cases = 329.


Reproduced Covariance Matrix :

              REINTGCE   REPARASP   RESOCIEC   REOCCASP   REEDASP
  REINTGCE     1.000
  REPARASP     0.184      1.000
  RESOCIEC     0.222      0.049      1.000
  REOCCASP     0.393      0.239      0.357      0.999
  REEDASP      0.417      0.254      0.379      0.623      0.999
  BFINTGCE     0.336      0.078      0.230      0.258      0.274
```

```
        BFPARASP    0.102      0.115      0.093      0.103      0.110
        BFSOCIEC    0.186      0.019      0.271      0.255      0.270
        BFOCCASP    0.255      0.095      0.282      0.330      0.351
        BFEDASP     0.273      0.102      0.303      0.354      0.376

                  BFINTGCE   BFPARASP   BFSOCIEC   BFOCCASP   BFEDASP
        BFINTGCE    1.000
        BFPARASP    0.209      1.000
        BFSOCIEC    0.295     -0.044      1.000
        BFOCCASP    0.489      0.237      0.374      0.999
        BFEDASP     0.525      0.254      0.401      0.639      0.999

Residual Matrix (covariances) :

                  REINTGCE   REPARASP   RESOCIEC   REOCCASP   REEDASP
        REINTGCE    0.0
        REPARASP    0.0        0.0
        RESOCIEC    0.0        0.000      0.0
        REOCCASP    0.018     -0.026     -0.033      0.001
        REEDASP    -0.013      0.020      0.026      0.001      0.001
        BFINTGCE    0.0        0.0        0.0        0.042      0.013
        BFPARASP    0.0        0.0        0.0       -0.027     -0.039
        BFSOCIEC    0.0        0.0        0.0        0.038     -0.030
        BFOCCASP    0.005     -0.011     -0.004      0.091     -0.023
        BFEDASP     0.017      0.010      0.003     -0.027     -0.009

                  BFINTGCE   BFPARASP   BFSOCIEC   BFOCCASP   BFEDASP
        BFINTGCE    0.0
        BFPARASP    0.0        0.0
        BFSOCIEC    0.0        0.0        0.0
        BFOCCASP    0.011     -0.038     -0.013      0.001
        BFEDASP    -0.006      0.024      0.009      0.001      0.001

Value of the maximum absolute residual =        0.091.

        ML Estimates of Free Parameters in Dependence Relationships

                                      Point    90.00% Conf. Int.  Standard     T
                 Path        Param #  Estimate   Lower    Upper     Error    Value
        -----------------------    -------  --------  -------  -------   -------  -----
        REEDASP   <- REAMBITN     1      1.062    0.914    1.210     0.090   11.80
        BFEDASP   <- BFAMBITN     2      1.073    0.940    1.206     0.081   13.23
        REAMBITN  <- BFAMBITN     3      0.174    0.032    0.316     0.086    2.02
        REAMBITN  <- REPARASP     4      0.164    0.100    0.228     0.039    4.23
        REAMBITN  <- REINTGCE     5      0.255    0.185    0.324     0.043    5.99
        REAMBITN  <- RESOCIEC     6      0.222    0.151    0.294     0.043    5.11
        REAMBITN  <- BFSOCIEC     7      0.079    0.001    0.156     0.047    1.68
        BFAMBITN  <- REAMBITN     8      0.185    0.054    0.317     0.080    2.33
        BFAMBITN  <- RESOCIEC     9      0.067   -0.004    0.138     0.043    1.55
        BFAMBITN  <- BFSOCIEC    10      0.218    0.151    0.284     0.040    5.38
        BFAMBITN  <- BFINTGCE    11      0.330    0.262    0.398     0.041    7.97
        BFAMBITN  <- BFPARASP    12      0.152    0.092    0.212     0.036    4.18

            Values of Fixed Parameters in Dependence Relationships

                       Path                    Value
              -----------------------    ------------
              REOCCASP    <- REAMBITN     1.000
              REOCCASP    <- E1           1.000
              REEDASP     <- E2           1.000
              BFEDASP     <- E3           1.000
              BFOCCASP    <- BFAMBITN     1.000
              BFOCCASP    <- E4           1.000
              REAMBITN    <- Z1           1.000
              BFAMBITN    <- Z2           1.000

        ML estimates of free parameters in variance/covariance relationships

                                      Point    90.00% Conf. Int.  Standard     T
                 Path        Param #  Estimate   Lower    Upper     Error    Value
        -----------------------    -------  --------  -------  -------   -------  -----
        REPARASP  <-> REPARASP    13     1.000    0.879    1.137     0.078   12.81
        REPARASP  <-> REINTGCE    14     0.184    0.092    0.276     0.056    3.28
        REPARASP  <-> RESOCIEC    15     0.049   -0.042    0.140     0.055    0.88
        REPARASP  <-> BFSOCIEC    16     0.019   -0.072    0.109     0.055    0.34
        REPARASP  <-> BFINTGCE    17     0.078   -0.013    0.169     0.055    1.41
        REPARASP  <-> BFPARASP    18     0.115    0.023    0.206     0.056    2.06
        REINTGCE  <-> REINTGCE    19     1.000    0.879    1.137     0.078   12.81
        REINTGCE  <-> RESOCIEC    20     0.222    0.129    0.315     0.057    3.93
        REINTGCE  <-> BFSOCIEC    21     0.186    0.094    0.278     0.056    3.31
        REINTGCE  <-> BFINTGCE    22     0.336    0.240    0.431     0.058    5.76
        REINTGCE  <-> BFPARASP    23     0.102    0.011    0.193     0.056    1.84
        RESOCIEC  <-> RESOCIEC    24     1.000    0.879    1.137     0.078   12.81
        RESOCIEC  <-> BFSOCIEC    25     0.271    0.177    0.365     0.057    4.73
        RESOCIEC  <-> BFINTGCE    26     0.230    0.137    0.323     0.057    4.06
        RESOCIEC  <-> BFPARASP    27     0.093    0.002    0.184     0.055    1.68
```

```
BFSOCIEC   <-> BFSOCIEC   28    1.000    0.879    1.137    0.078  12.81
BFSOCIEC   <-> BFINTGCE   29    0.295    0.200    0.390    0.058   5.12
BFSOCIEC   <-> BFPARASP   30   -0.044   -0.135    0.047    0.055  -0.79
BFINTGCE   <-> BFINTGCE   31    1.000    0.879    1.137    0.078  12.81
BFINTGCE   <-> BFPARASP   32    0.209    0.116    0.301    0.056   3.70
BFPARASP   <-> BFPARASP   33    1.000    0.879    1.137    0.078  12.81
E1         <-> E1         34    0.412    0.336    0.506    0.051   8.07
E2         <-> E2         35    0.337    0.262    0.434    0.052   6.50
E3         <-> E3         36    0.313    0.246    0.399    0.046   6.84
E4         <-> E4         37    0.404    0.335    0.487    0.046   8.75
Z1         <-> Z1         38    0.281    0.214    0.370    0.047   6.03
Z2         <-> Z2         39    0.229    0.173    0.303    0.039   5.86

Maximum Likelihood Discrepancy Function

Measures of fit of the model
----------------------------
Sample Discrepancy Function Value                 : 0.082  (8.199040E-02)

Population discrepancy function value, Fo
Bias adjusted point estimate                      : 0.033
90.000 percent confidence interval                :(0.001,0.089)

Root mean square error of approximation
Steiger-Lind : RMSEA = SQRT(Fo/DF)
Point estimate                                    : 0.046
90.000 percent confidence interval                :(0.008,0.075)

Expected cross-validation index
Point estimate (modified AIC)                     : 0.320
90.000 percent confidence interval                :(0.288,0.376)
CVI (modified AIC) for the saturated model        : 0.335

Test statistic:                                   : 26.893
Exceedance probabilities:-
Ho: perfect fit (RMSEA = 0.0)                      : 0.043
Ho: close fit   (RMSEA <=     0.050)               : 0.560

Multiplier for obtaining test statistic  =    328.000
Degrees of freedom                       =  16
Effective number of parameters           =  39
```

Using the RESTART file

A restart file was created during the first run to form an input file that specifies the model represented in Figure 2 (see p. 634). Now type the following modifications into the *EX2B* restart file and save the file:

1. TYPE=COV is replaced by TYPE=CORR
2. START=ROUGH is replaced by START=CLOSE
3. reoccasp <- reambitn(0,1.0) is replaced by reoccasp <- reambitn(*,1.0), freeing a fixed path coefficient
4. bfoccasp <- bfambitn(0,1.0) is replaced by bfoccasp <- bfambitn(*,1.0), freeing a fixed path coefficient
5. reambitn <-> reambitn(0,1.0) is added, imposing a variance constraint on an endogenous latent variable
6. bfambitn <-> bfambitn(0,1.0) is added, imposing a variance constraint on an endogenous latent variable

This is what the modified restart file looks like:

```
RAMONA
 USE ex2
 MODEL reoccasp <-   reambitn(*,1.0) e1(0,1.0),
         reedasp <-   reambitn(1,1.062) e2(0,1.0),
         bfedasp <-   bfambitn(2,1.073) e3(0,1.0),
        bfoccasp <-   bfambitn(*,1.0) e4(0,1.0),
        reambitn <-   bfambitn(3,0.174) z1(0,1.0),
                      reparasp(4,0.164) reintgce(5,0.255),
                      resociec(6,0.222) bfsociec(7,0.079),
        bfambitn <-   reambitn(8,0.185) z2(0,1.0),
                      resociec(9,0.668),
                      bfsociec(10,0.218),
                      bfintgce(11,0.330),
                      bfparasp(12,0.152),
        reparasp <-> reparasp(13,1.0,),
                      reintgce(14,0.184),
                      resociec(15,0.049),
                      bfsociec(16,0.019),
                      bfintgce(17,0.078),
                      bfparasp(18,0.115),
        reintgce <-> reintgce(19,1.000),
                      resociec(20,0.222),
                      bfsociec(21,0.186),
                      bfintgce(22,0.336),
                      bfparasp(23,0.102),
        resociec <-> resociec(24,1.0),
                      bfsociec(25,0.271),
                      bfintgce(26,0.230),
                      bfparasp(27,0.093),
        bfsociec <-> bfsociec(28,1.0),
                      bfintgce(29,0.29),
                      bfparasp(30,-0.044),
        bfintgce <-> bfintgce(31,1.0),
                      bfparasp(32,0.209),
        bfparasp <-> bfparasp(33,1.0),
              e1 <-> e1(34,0.412),
              e2 <-> e2(35,0.337),
              e3 <-> e3(36,0.313),
              e4 <-> e4(37,0.404),
              z1 <-> z1(38,0.281),
              z2 <-> z2(39,0.229),
        reambitn <-> reambitn(0,1.0),
        bfambitn <-> bfambitn(0,1.0)
 PRINT = MEDIUM
 ESTIMATE / TYPE=CORR  START=CLOSE  NCASES=329
```

Modifications are underlined. Note that we rounded some parameter values to shorten the commands.

Now execute this modified file (after you have edited it and saved it using FEDIT or another text editor):

```
SUBMIT ex2b
```

```
There are 10 manifest variables in the model. They are:
      REINTGCE REPARASP RESOCIEC REOCCASP REEDASP BFINTGCE BFPARASP
      BFSOCIEC BFOCCASP BFEDASP


There are 8 latent variables in the model. They are:
      REAMBITN E1 E2 BFAMBITN E3 E4 Z1 Z2


RAMONA options in effect are:
    Display              Corr
    Method               MWL
    Start                Close
    Convg                0.000100
    Maximum iterations   100
    Number of cases      329
    Restart              No
    Confidence Interval  90

Number of manifest variables          =    10
Total number of variables in the system =  28.
Reading correlation matrix...

                    Details of Iterations
   Iter    Method  Discr. Funct.  Max.R.Cos.   Max.Const.   NRP  NBD
  -------- ------- -------------- ------------ ------------- ---------
       0    MWL      1.009299                    0.000000
     1(0)   MWL      0.155441      0.435343      0.117338     0    0
     2(0)   MWL      0.084226      0.149814      0.018456     0    0
     3(0)   MWL      0.081995      0.005204      0.000551     0    0
     4(0)   MWL      0.081990      0.000315      0.000001     0    0
     5(0)   MWL      0.081990      0.000083      0.000000     0    0
     6(0)   MWL      0.081990      0.000020      0.000000     0    0

Iterative procedure complete.


Convergence limit for residual cosines = 0.000100 on 2 consecutive
iterations.

Convergence limit for variance constraint violations =  5.00000E-07
Value of the maximum variance constraint violation =  9.93056E-10


Sample Correlation Matrix :
                REINTGCE    REPARASP    RESOCIEC    REOCCASP    REEDASP
   REINTGCE      1.000
   REPARASP      0.184       1.000
   RESOCIEC      0.222       0.049       1.000
   REOCCASP      0.410       0.214       0.324       1.000
   REEDASP       0.404       0.274       0.405       0.625       1.000
   BFINTGCE      0.336       0.078       0.230       0.299       0.286
   BFPARASP      0.102       0.115       0.093       0.076       0.070
   BFSOCIEC      0.186       0.019       0.271       0.293       0.241
   BFOCCASP      0.260       0.084       0.279       0.422       0.328
   BFEDASP       0.290       0.112       0.305       0.327       0.367

                BFINTGCE    BFPARASP    BFSOCIEC    BFOCCASP    BFEDASP
   BFINTGCE      1.000
   BFPARASP      0.209       1.000
   BFSOCIEC      0.295      -0.044       1.000
   BFOCCASP      0.501       0.199       0.361       1.000
   BFEDASP       0.519       0.278       0.410       0.640       1.000

Number of cases = 329.
```

```
Reproduced Correlation Matrix :
                REINTGCE   REPARASP   RESOCIEC   REOCCASP   REEDASP
REINTGCE         1.000
REPARASP         0.184      1.000
RESOCIEC         0.222      0.049      1.000
REOCCASP         0.393      0.240      0.357      1.000
REEDASP          0.417      0.254      0.379      0.624      1.000
BFINTGCE         0.336      0.078      0.230      0.258      0.274
BFPARASP         0.102      0.115      0.093      0.103      0.110
BFSOCIEC         0.186      0.019      0.271      0.255      0.270
BFOCCASP         0.255      0.095      0.282      0.330      0.351
BFEDASP          0.273      0.102      0.303      0.355      0.376

                BFINTGCE   BFPARASP   BFSOCIEC   BFOCCASP   BFEDASP
BFINTGCE         1.000
BFPARASP         0.209      1.000
BFSOCIEC         0.295     -0.044      1.000
BFOCCASP         0.489      0.237      0.374      1.000
BFEDASP          0.525      0.254      0.401      0.640      1.000

Residual Matrix (correlations) :

                REINTGCE   REPARASP   RESOCIEC   REOCCASP   REEDASP
REINTGCE         0.0
REPARASP         0.0        0.0
RESOCIEC         0.0        0.000      0.0
REOCCASP         0.017     -0.026     -0.033     -0.000
REEDASP         -0.013      0.020      0.025      0.001     -0.000
BFINTGCE         0.0        0.0       -0.000      0.042      0.012
BFPARASP        -0.000      0.0        0.0       -0.027     -0.039
BFSOCIEC         0.0       -0.000      0.0        0.038     -0.030
BFOCCASP         0.005     -0.011     -0.004      0.091     -0.023
BFEDASP          0.017      0.010      0.002     -0.028     -0.010

                BFINTGCE   BFPARASP   BFSOCIEC   BFOCCASP   BFEDASP
BFINTGCE         0.0
BFPARASP         0.0        0.0
BFSOCIEC         0.0       -0.000      0.0
BFOCCASP         0.011     -0.038     -0.013     -0.000
BFEDASP         -0.006      0.024      0.009      0.001     -0.000

Value of the maximum absolute residual =      0.091.
```

ML Estimates of Free Parameters in Dependence Relationships

	Path	Param #	Point Estimate	90.00% Conf. Int. Lower	Upper	Standard Error	T Value
REOCCASP	<- REAMBITN	1	0.766	0.710	0.823	0.034	22.22
REEDASP	<- REAMBITN	2	0.814	0.759	0.868	0.033	24.52
BFEDASP	<- BFAMBITN	3	0.828	0.781	0.876	0.029	28.49
BFOCCASP	<- BFAMBITN	4	0.772	0.721	0.823	0.031	24.75
REAMBITN	<- BFAMBITN	5	0.175	0.034	0.317	0.086	2.04
REAMBITN	<- REPARASP	6	0.214	0.133	0.294	0.049	4.36
REAMBITN	<- REINTGCE	7	0.332	0.248	0.417	0.051	6.47
REAMBITN	<- RESOCIEC	8	0.290	0.201	0.378	0.054	5.39
REAMBITN	<- BFSOCIEC	9	0.103	0.002	0.204	0.061	1.69
BFAMBITN	<- REAMBITN	10	0.184	0.055	0.313	0.078	2.35
BFAMBITN	<- RESOCIEC	11	0.087	-0.005	0.178	0.056	1.55
BFAMBITN	<- BFSOCIEC	12	0.282	0.200	0.365	0.050	5.62
BFAMBITN	<- BFINTGCE	13	0.428	0.349	0.506	0.048	9.00
BFAMBITN	<- BFPARASP	14	0.197	0.121	0.273	0.046	4.27

```
Scaled Standard Deviations (nuisance parameters)

        Variable    Estimate
        --------    --------
        REOCCASP     1.000
        REEDASP      1.000
        BFOCCASP     1.000
        BFEDASP      1.000
        REPARASP     1.000
        BFINTGCE     1.000
        BFPARASP     1.000
        BFSOCIEC     1.000
        RESOCIEC     1.000
        REINTGCE     1.000
```

Values of Fixed Parameters in Dependence Relationships

Path		Value
REOCCASP	<- E1	1.000
REEDASP	<- E2	1.000
BFEDASP	<- E3	1.000
BFOCCASP	<- E4	1.000
REAMBITN	<- Z1	1.000
BFAMBITN	<- Z2	1.000

ML estimates of free parameters in variance/covariance relationships

Path		Param #	Point Estimate	90.00% Conf. Int. Lower	Upper	Standard Error	T Value
REPARASP	<-> REINTGCE	15	0.184	0.095	0.270	0.053	3.45
REPARASP	<-> RESOCIEC	16	0.049	-0.042	0.139	0.055	0.89
REPARASP	<-> BFSOCIEC	17	0.019	-0.072	0.109	0.055	0.34
REPARASP	<-> BFINTGCE	18	0.078	-0.012	0.168	0.055	1.42
REPARASP	<-> BFPARASP	19	0.115	0.024	0.203	0.054	2.10
REINTGCE	<-> RESOCIEC	20	0.222	0.134	0.306	0.052	4.23
REINTGCE	<-> BFSOCIEC	21	0.186	0.097	0.272	0.053	3.49
REINTGCE	<-> BFINTGCE	22	0.336	0.253	0.414	0.049	6.85
REINTGCE	<-> BFPARASP	23	0.102	0.012	0.191	0.055	1.87
RESOCIEC	<-> BFSOCIEC	24	0.271	0.185	0.353	0.051	5.29
RESOCIEC	<-> BFINTGCE	25	0.230	0.143	0.314	0.052	4.40
RESOCIEC	<-> BFPARASP	26	0.093	0.003	0.182	0.055	1.70
BFSOCIEC	<-> BFINTGCE	27	0.295	0.210	0.376	0.050	5.85
BFSOCIEC	<-> BFPARASP	28	-0.044	-0.134	0.047	0.055	-0.79
BFINTGCE	<-> BFPARASP	29	0.209	0.120	0.294	0.053	3.95
E1	<-> E1	30	0.413	0.334	0.509	0.053	7.80
E2	<-> E2	31	0.338	0.259	0.439	0.054	6.25
E3	<-> E3	32	0.314	0.244	0.404	0.048	6.51
E4	<-> E4	33	0.404	0.332	0.492	0.048	8.39
Z1	<-> Z1	34	0.479	0.390	0.570	0.055	8.64
Z2	<-> Z2	35	0.384	0.305	0.470	0.051	7.59

Values of Fixed Parameters in Variance/Covariance Relationships

Path		Value
REPARASP	<-> REPARASP	1.000
REINTGCE	<-> REINTGCE	1.000
RESOCIEC	<-> RESOCIEC	1.000
BFSOCIEC	<-> BFSOCIEC	1.000
BFINTGCE	<-> BFINTGCE	1.000
BFPARASP	<-> BFPARASP	1.000

Equality Constraints on Variances

Constraint		Value	Lagrange Multiplier	Standard Error
REAMBITN	<-> REAMBITN	1.0000	0.000	-0.000
BFAMBITN	<-> BFAMBITN	1.0000	0.000	0.000
REOCCASP	<-> REOCCASP	1.0000	0.000	-0.000
REEDASP	<-> REEDASP	1.0000	-0.000	0.000
BFOCCASP	<-> BFOCCASP	1.0000	-0.000	-0.000
BFEDASP	<-> BFEDASP	1.0000	0.000	0.000

Maximum Likelihood Discrepancy Function

Measures of fit of the model

Sample Discrepancy Function Value   : 0.082   (8.199040E-02)

Population discrepancy function value, Fo
Bias adjusted point estimate   : 0.033
90.000 percent confidence interval   :(0.001,0.089)

Root mean square error of approximation
Steiger-Lind : RMSEA = SQRT(Fo/DF)
Point estimate   : 0.046
90.000 percent confidence interval   :(0.008,0.075)

Expected cross-validation index
Point estimate (modified AIC)   : 0.320
90.000 percent confidence interval   :(0.288,0.376)
CVI (modified AIC) for the saturated model   : 0.335

Test statistic: : 26.893
Exceedance probabilities:-
Ho: perfect fit (RMSEA = 0.0)   : 0.043
Ho: close fit   (RMSEA <=   0.050)   : 0.560

Multiplier for obtaining test statistic   =   328.000
Degrees of freedom   = 16
Effective number of parameters   = 39

Note that the START setting, ROUGH, has been changed to CLOSE (under ESTIMATE) because a restart file is used.

The discrepancy function values and measures of fit of the model are the same in both runs, but the maximum likelihood estimates differ because of different identification conditions. The standard errors in the second run differ (those in the first run were incorrect). An appropriate warning has been output by RAMONA. Notice in the last run that the Lagrange multipliers and the corresponding standard errors are 0 because all equality constraints on endogenous variable variances act as identification conditions, not constraints on the model. This is the case in most, but not all, practical applications.

18.3 Job satisfaction among nurses

This example (Mels and Koorts, 1989) illustrates how RAMONA uses the usual cases-by-variables SYSTAT data file. Asymptotically distribution free estimates are obtained.

A questionnaire concerned with job satisfaction was completed by 213 nurses. There are 10 manifest variables that serve as indicators of 4 latent variables: job security (*JOBSEC*), attitude toward training (*TRAING*), opportunities for promotion (*PROMOT*), and relations with superiors (*RELSUP*). Figure 3 (see p. 644) shows a model to account for causal relationships between the three latent variables.

Following are the data for the first and last five cases:

CASE	UNFAIR	DCHARGE	UNEMP	ITRAIN	STRAIN	ETRAIN	IPROMOT	OPROMOT	ISUP	PROPSUP
1	2.0	5.0	5.0	1.0	2.0	4.0	3.0	2.0	2.0	1.0
2	5.0	4.0	4.0	3.0	2.0	2.0	2.0	2.0	4.0	3.0
3	5.0	5.0	5.0	4.0	4.0	4.0	3.0	3.0	5.0	5.0
4	3.0	5.0	3.0	2.0	4.0	2.0	1.0	3.0	3.0	4.0
5	5.0	5.0	5.0	3.0	1.0	4.0	4.0	3.0	5.0	5.0

*** *we omit cases 6-208* ***

CASE	UNFAIR	DCHARGE	UNEMP	ITRAIN	STRAIN	ETRAIN	IPROMOT	OPROMOT	ISUP	PROPSUP
209	5.0	5.0	5.0	5.0	5.0	5.0	4.0	4.0	5.0	5.0
210	5.0	5.0	5.0	1.0	5.0	4.0	4.0	3.0	5.0	3.0
211	4.0	5.0	5.0	4.0	2.0	3.0	4.0	4.0	3.0	3.0
212	4.0	5.0	5.0	4.0	5.0	5.0	4.0	4.0	3.0	3.0
213	3.0	4.0	2.0	5.0	5.0	5.0	4.0	4.0	2.0	1.0

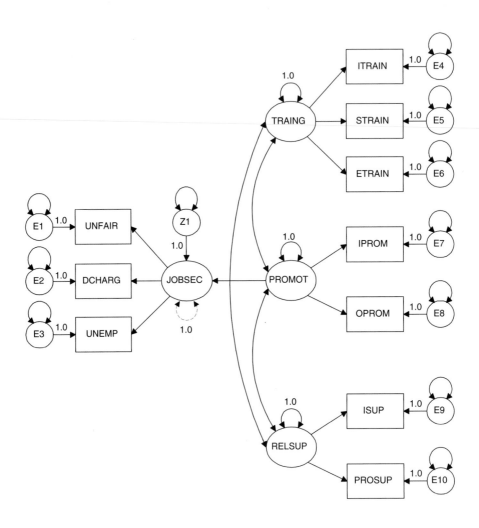

Figure 3

Following is the input file:

```
RAMONA
  USE ex3
  MANIFEST = unfair dcharg unemp itrain strain etrain,
             ipromot opromot isup prosup
  LATENT = jobsec traing promot relsup e1 e2 e3 e4 e5,
           e6 e7 e8 e9 e10 z1
  MODEL unfair <-  jobsec e1(0,1.0),
        dcharg <-  jobsec e2(0,1.0),
         unemp <-  jobsec e3(0,1.0),
        itrain <-  traing e4(0,1.0),
        strain <-  traing e5(0,1.0),
        etrain <-  traing e6(0,1.0),
       ipromot <-  promot e7(0,1.0),
       opromot <-  promot e8(0,1.0),
          isup <-  relsup e9(0,1.0),
        prosup <-  relsup e10(0,1.0),
        jobsec <-  traing promot relsup z1(0,1.0),
        traing <-> traing (0,1.0),
        promot <-> promot (0,1.0),
        relsup <-> relsup (0,1.0),
        traing <-> promot,
        traing <-> relsup,
        promot <-> relsup,
            e1 <-> e1,
            e2 <-> e2,
            e3 <-> e3,
            e4 <-> e4,
            e5 <-> e5,
            e6 <-> e6,
            e7 <-> e7,
            e8 <-> e8,
            e9 <-> e9,
           e10 <-> e10,
            z1 <-> z1,
        jobsec <-> jobsec(0,1.0)
  PRINT = MEDIUM
  ESTIMATE / TYPE=CORR  METHOD=ADFU
```

The output for this example includes kurtosis coefficients (these are not available with correlation or covariance matrix input).

```
Variables in the SYSTAT Rectangular file are:
   UNFAIR      DCHARG      UNEMP        ITRAIN       STRAIN       ETRAIN
   IPROMOT     OPROMOT     ISUP         PROSUP

There are 10 manifest variables in the model. They are:
     UNFAIR DCHARG UNEMP ITRAIN STRAIN ETRAIN IPROMOT OPROMOT
     ISUP PROSUP
There are 15 latent variables in the model. They are:
     JOBSEC E1 E2 E3 TRAING E4 E5 E6 PROMOT E7 E8 RELSUP E9
     E10 Z1

RAMONA options in effect are:
   Display              Corr
   Method               ADFU
   Start                Rough
   Convg                0.000100
   Maximum iterations   100
   Number of cases      determined when data are read
   Restart              No
   Confidence Interval  90

Number of manifest variables          =     10
Total number of variables in the system  =   35.
Computing mean vector...
Computing covariance matrix and fourth order moments...
Computing ADF weight matrix...

          Overall kurtosis =        19.754
               Normalised =         9.305
                 Relative =         1.165

                       Individual
             Variable   kurtoses    Normalised    Relative
             UNFAIR       1.395        4.155        1.465
             DCHARG       1.866        5.560        1.622
             UNEMP        0.181        0.540        1.060
             ITRAIN      -0.560       -1.669        0.813
             STRAIN      -1.102       -3.282        0.633
             ETRAIN      -0.730       -2.174        0.757
             IPROMOT     -1.006       -2.997        0.665
             OPROMOT     -0.757       -2.256        0.748
             ISUP        -0.945       -2.815        0.685
             PROSUP      -0.547       -1.628        0.818

Smallest relative pivot of covariance matrix of sample
covariances =        0.149.

                    Details of Iterations
  Iter    Method   Discr. Funct.  Max.R.Cos.   Max.Const.   NRP  NBD
 -------- ------   -------------  ----------   ----------   ---- ----
     0    OLS       1.254639                    0.000000
   1(0)   OLS       0.398537       0.556472     0.405283     0    0
   2(0)   OLS       0.079200       0.115359     0.045912     0    0
   3(0)   OLS       0.075227       0.010971     0.000398     0    0
   4(0)   OLS       0.075196       0.002148     0.000018     0    0
   4(0)   ADFU      0.393299       0.361351     0.000018     0    0
   5(0)   ADFU      0.190011       0.084716     0.039737     0    0
   6(0)   ADFU      0.184936       0.019973     0.004648     0    0
   7(0)   ADFU      0.184639       0.003195     0.000205     0    0
   8(0)   ADFU      0.184609       0.001973     0.000061     0    0
   9(0)   ADFU      0.184606       0.000414     0.000002     0    0
  10(0)   ADFU      0.184605       0.000219     0.000001     0    0
  11(0)   ADFU      0.184605       0.000049     0.000000     0    0
  12(0)   ADFU      0.184605       0.000025     0.000000     0    0

Iterative procedure complete.

Convergence limit for residual cosines = 0.000100 on 2 consecutive
iterations.

Convergence limit for variance constraint violations =  5.00000E-07
Value of the maximum variance constraint violation =  1.13880E-08

Sample Correlation Matrix :

                 UNFAIR     DCHARG     UNEMP      ITRAIN     STRAIN
     UNFAIR      1.000
     DCHARG      0.438      1.000
     UNEMP       0.249      0.455      1.000
     ITRAIN      0.150      0.110      0.056      1.000
     STRAIN      0.173      0.209      0.028      0.543      1.000
     ETRAIN      0.184      0.168     -0.006      0.544      0.694
     IPROMOT     0.134      0.210      0.169      0.082      0.240
     OPROMOT     0.099      0.179      0.159      0.115      0.184
     ISUP        0.154      0.177      0.140      0.284      0.456
     PROSUP      0.213      0.212      0.038      0.263      0.337
```

	ETRAIN	IPROMOT	OPROMOT	ISUP	PROSUP
ETRAIN	1.000				
IPROMOT	0.237	1.000			
OPROMOT	0.208	0.683	1.000		
ISUP	0.348	0.389	0.319	1.000	
PROSUP	0.262	0.263	0.185	0.475	1.000

Number of cases = 213.

Reproduced Correlation Matrix :

	UNFAIR	DCHARG	UNEMP	ITRAIN	STRAIN
UNFAIR	1.000				
DCHARG	0.481	1.000			
UNEMP	0.382	0.602	1.000		
ITRAIN	0.081	0.128	0.102	1.000	
STRAIN	0.093	0.146	0.116	0.638	1.000
ETRAIN	0.089	0.140	0.111	0.609	0.695
IPROMOT	0.140	0.221	0.176	0.171	0.195
OPROMOT	0.121	0.192	0.152	0.148	0.169
ISUP	0.124	0.196	0.156	0.364	0.415
PROSUP	0.098	0.154	0.122	0.286	0.326

	ETRAIN	IPROMOT	OPROMOT	ISUP	PROSUP
ETRAIN	1.000				
IPROMOT	0.186	1.000			
OPROMOT	0.161	0.743	1.000		
ISUP	0.396	0.377	0.327	1.000	
PROSUP	0.311	0.296	0.257	0.560	1.000

Residual Matrix (correlations) :

	UNFAIR	DCHARG	UNEMP	ITRAIN	STRAIN
UNFAIR	-0.000				
DCHARG	-0.043	-0.000			
UNEMP	-0.133	-0.148	-0.000		
ITRAIN	0.068	-0.018	-0.045	-0.000	
STRAIN	0.080	0.062	-0.088	-0.095	-0.000
ETRAIN	0.095	0.028	-0.117	-0.065	-0.000
IPROMOT	-0.007	-0.011	-0.007	-0.089	0.045
OPROMOT	-0.023	-0.013	0.007	-0.033	0.016
ISUP	0.030	-0.020	-0.016	-0.080	0.042
PROSUP	0.115	0.057	-0.084	-0.023	0.012

	ETRAIN	IPROMOT	OPROMOT	ISUP	PROSUP
ETRAIN	-0.000				
IPROMOT	0.051	-0.000			
OPROMOT	0.047	-0.060	-0.000		
ISUP	-0.047	0.011	-0.008	-0.000	
PROSUP	-0.049	-0.034	-0.072	-0.085	-0.000

Value of the maximum absolute residual =   0.148.

ADFU Estimates of Free Parameters in Dependence Relationships

	Path	Param #	Point Estimate	90.00% Conf. Int. Lower	Upper	Standard Error	T Value
UNFAIR	<- JOBSEC	1	0.552	0.451	0.653	0.061	9.01
DCHARG	<- JOBSEC	2	0.871	0.770	0.972	0.061	14.22
UNEMP	<- JOBSEC	3	0.692	0.592	0.791	0.061	11.42
ITRAIN	<- TRAING	4	0.748	0.670	0.826	0.047	15.78
STRAIN	<- TRAING	5	0.853	0.808	0.899	0.028	30.81
ETRAIN	<- TRAING	6	0.814	0.756	0.873	0.035	23.04
IPROMOT	<- PROMOT	7	0.926	0.842	1.011	0.052	17.98
OPROMOT	<- PROMOT	8	0.802	0.714	0.891	0.054	14.96
ISUP	<- RELSUP	9	0.844	0.752	0.937	0.056	14.97
PROSUP	<- RELSUP	10	0.663	0.568	0.758	0.058	11.48
JOBSEC	<- TRAING	11	0.074	-0.129	0.277	0.123	0.60
JOBSEC	<- PROMOT	12	0.192	0.075	0.310	0.071	2.70
JOBSEC	<- RELSUP	13	0.132	-0.081	0.345	0.130	1.02

Scaled Standard Deviations (nuisance parameters)

Variable	Estimate
UNFAIR	1.008
DCHARG	0.962
UNEMP	0.974
ITRAIN	1.000
STRAIN	1.002
ETRAIN	0.983
IPROMOT	0.989
OPROMOT	1.001
ISUP	0.998
PROSUP	0.970

```
      Values of Fixed Parameters in Dependence Relationships

                    Path                  Value
          ----------------------   -------------
          UNFAIR    <- E1              1.000
          DCHARG    <- E2              1.000
          UNEMP     <- E3              1.000
          ITRAIN    <- E4              1.000
          STRAIN    <- E5              1.000
          ETRAIN    <- E6              1.000
          IPROMOT   <- E7              1.000
          OPROMOT   <- E8              1.000
          ISUP      <- E9              1.000
          PROSUP    <- E10             1.000
          JOBSEC    <- Z1              1.000

ADFU estimates of free parameters in variance/covariance relationships

                                   Point   90.00% Conf. Int.   Standard    T
               Path        Param #  Estimate   Lower   Upper      Error   Value
          ----------------------   -------  -------  ------- -------   -------  -----
TRAING    <-> PROMOT        14     0.246    0.120    0.364    0.075    3.30
TRAING    <-> RELSUP        15     0.576    0.452    0.677    0.069    8.40
PROMOT    <-> RELSUP        16     0.482    0.354    0.593    0.073    6.62
E1        <-> E1            17     0.695    0.593    0.816    0.068   10.28
E2        <-> E2            18     0.242    0.117    0.499    0.107    2.26
E3        <-> E3            19     0.522    0.400    0.679    0.084    6.22
E4        <-> E4            20     0.440    0.338    0.574    0.071    6.21
E5        <-> E5            21     0.272    0.204    0.362    0.047    5.75
E6        <-> E6            22     0.337    0.254    0.446    0.058    5.85
E7        <-> E7            23     0.142    0.047    0.429    0.095    1.48
E8        <-> E8            24     0.356    0.239    0.530    0.086    4.14
E9        <-> E9            25     0.287    0.166    0.495    0.095    3.01
E10       <-> E10           26     0.560    0.448    0.702    0.077    7.31
Z1        <-> Z1            27     0.898    0.818    0.945    0.037   24.06

Values of Fixed Parameters in Variance/Covariance Relationships

             Path                  Value
       ----------------------   -------------
TRAING    <-> TRAING             1.000
PROMOT    <-> PROMOT             1.000
RELSUP    <-> RELSUP             1.000

                   Equality Constraints on Variances

                                          Lagrange           Standard
            Constraint            Value    Multiplier          Error
       ----------------------   -----   ----------         --------
JOBSEC    <-> JOBSEC           1.0000     0.000            -0.000
UNFAIR    <-> UNFAIR           1.0000     0.000            -0.000
DCHARG    <-> DCHARG           1.0000    -0.000            -0.000
UNEMP     <-> UNEMP            1.0000    -0.000            -0.000
ITRAIN    <-> ITRAIN           1.0000    -0.000             0.000
STRAIN    <-> STRAIN           1.0000     0.000             0.000
ETRAIN    <-> ETRAIN           1.0000     0.000            -0.000
IPROMOT   <-> IPROMOT          1.0000    -0.000            -0.000
OPROMOT   <-> OPROMOT          1.0000    -0.000             0.000
ISUP      <-> ISUP             1.0000    -0.000             0.000
PROSUP    <-> PROSUP           1.0000    -0.000            -0.000

ADFU Discrepancy Function

 Measures of fit of the model
 ----------------------------
 Sample Discrepancy Function Value             : 0.185   (1.846051E-01)

 Population discrepancy function value, Fo
 Bias adjusted point estimate                  : 0.048
 90.000 percent confidence interval            :(0.0,0.144)

 Root mean square error of approximation
 Steiger-Lind : RMSEA = SQRT(Fo/DF)
 Point estimate                                : 0.041
 90.000 percent confidence interval            :(0.0,0.071)

 Expected cross-validation index
 Point estimate (modified AIC)                 : 0.430
 90.000 percent confidence interval            :(0.382,0.526)
 CVI (modified AIC) for the saturated model    : 0.519

 Test statistic:                               : 39.136
 Exceedance probabilities:-
 Ho: perfect fit (RMSEA = 0.0)                 : 0.099
 Ho: close fit   (RMSEA <=      0.050)         : 0.662

 Multiplier for obtaining test statistic  =    212.000
 Degrees of freedom                       =  29
 Effective number of parameters           =  26
```

18.4
Ability tests
for children

Lawley and Maxwell (1971) gave correct standard errors for maximum
likelihood parameter estimates in a restricted factor analysis model for a
correlation matrix. This example shows how RAMONA can produce
these correct standard errors. The method used for calculating the
standard errors differs from that of Lawley and Maxwell: RAMONA
makes use of constrained optimization and Lawley and Maxwell obtained
their formula by applying the delta method to standardized estimates. It
can be shown, however, that the two methods are equivalent and give the
same results. Lawley and Maxwell made use of a sample correlation
matrix between nine ability tests administered to 72 children.

Analyzing the
covariance
structure

We analyze the relationships in Figure 4 (see p. 650) using the correlation
matrix. The difference between the two runs is that we first treat the
model (inappropriately) as a covariance structure and then as a
correlation structure. We specify TYPE as COVA in the first run and CORR
in the second. Following is the input file for the first run:

```
RAMONA
  USE ex4a
  MANIFEST = y1 y2 y3 y4 y5 y6 y7 y8 y9
  LATENT = visual verbal speed e1 e2 e3 e4 e5 e6,
           e7 e8 e9
  MODEL y1 <-  visual e1(0,1.0),
        y2 <-  visual e2(0,1.0),
        y3 <-  visual e3(0,1.0),
        y4 <-  verbal e4(0,1.0),
        y5 <-  verbal e5(0,1.0),
        y6 <-  verbal e6(0,1.0),
        y7 <-  speed e7(0,1.0),
        y8 <-  speed e8 (0,1.0),
        y9 <-  visual speed e9(0,1.0),
    visual <-> visual(0,1.0),
    verbal <-> verbal(0,1.0),
     speed <-> speed(0,1.0),
    visual <-> verbal,
    visual <-> speed,
    verbal <-> speed
  PRINT = MEDIUM
  ESTIMATE / TYPE=COVA   NCASES=72
```

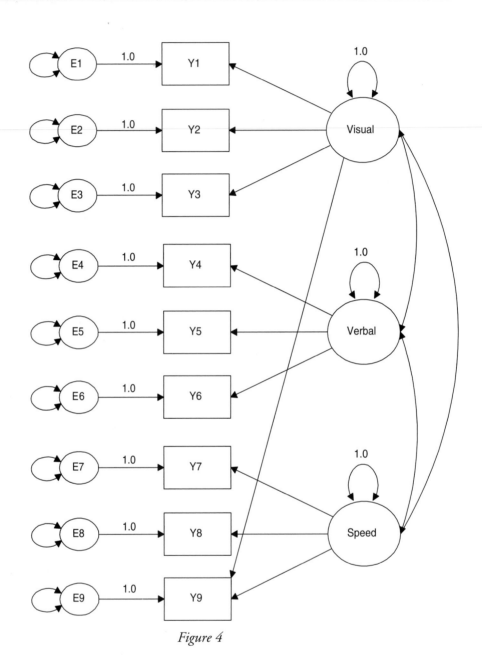

Figure 4

```
Variables in the SYSTAT Correlation file are:
  Y1          Y2            Y3           Y4          Y5         Y6
  Y7          Y8            Y9

There are 9 manifest variables in the model. They are:
      Y1 Y2 Y3 Y4 Y5 Y6 Y7 Y8 Y9


There are 12 latent variables in the model. They are:
      VISUAL E1 E2 E3 VERBAL E4 E5 E6 SPEED E7 E8 E9

RAMONA options in effect are:
      Display              Covar
      Method               MWL
      Start                Rough
      Convg                0.000100
      Maximum iterations   100
      Number of cases      72
      Restart              No
      Confidence Interval  90

Variance paths for errors were omitted from the job specification
and have been added by RAMONA.

Number of manifest variables          =    9
Total number of variables in the system  =   21.

***WARNING***:
A correlation matrix was provided although TYPE=COVA. Fit measures and
standard errors may be inappropriate

Reading correlation matrix...

                       Details of Iterations
   Iter    Method  Discr. Funct.  Max.R.Cos.   Max.Const.   NRP  NBD
  --------  ------  -------------  ------------  ------------  ---------
       0     OLS      1.013354
     1(0)    OLS      0.437034      0.649686                    0    0
     2(0)    OLS      0.143538      0.092248                    0    0
     3(0)    OLS      0.135197      0.053602                    0    0
     4(0)    OLS      0.134714      0.004511                    0    0
     4(0)    MWL      0.472377      0.164664                    0    0
     5(0)    MWL      0.425693      0.031463                    0    0
     6(0)    MWL      0.421825      0.019794                    0    0
     7(0)    MWL      0.421170      0.006232                    0    0
     8(0)    MWL      0.421041      0.005613                    0    0
     9(0)    MWL      0.421014      0.001271                    0    0
    10(0)    MWL      0.421008      0.001616                    0    0
    11(0)    MWL      0.421006      0.000284                    0    0
    12(0)    MWL      0.421006      0.000478                    0    0
    13(0)    MWL      0.421006      0.000085                    0    0
    14(0)    MWL      0.421006      0.000144                    0    0
    15(0)    MWL      0.421006      0.000028                    0    0
    16(0)    MWL      0.421006      0.000044                    0    0

Iterative procedure complete.


Convergence limit for residual cosines = 0.000100 on 2 consecutive
iterations.

Sample Covariance Matrix :
              Y1           Y2           Y3           Y4           Y5
  Y1        1.000
  Y2        0.245        1.000
  Y3        0.418        0.362        1.000
  Y4        0.282        0.217        0.425        1.000
  Y5        0.257        0.125        0.304        0.784        1.000
  Y6        0.239        0.131        0.330        0.743        0.730
  Y7        0.122        0.149        0.265        0.185        0.221
  Y8        0.253        0.183        0.329        0.021        0.139
  Y9        0.583        0.147        0.455        0.381        0.400

              Y6           Y7           Y8           Y9
  Y6        1.000
  Y7        0.118        1.000
  Y8       -0.027        0.601        1.000
  Y9        0.235        0.385        0.462        1.000

Number of cases = 72.
```

Reproduced Covariance Matrix :

	Y1	Y2	Y3	Y4	Y5
Y1	1.000				
Y2	0.232	1.000			
Y3	0.448	0.225	1.000		
Y4	0.341	0.171	0.330	1.000	
Y5	0.325	0.163	0.315	0.788	1.000
Y6	0.309	0.155	0.300	0.748	0.715
Y7	0.210	0.105	0.203	0.052	0.050
Y8	0.298	0.149	0.289	0.074	0.070
Y9	0.517	0.260	0.501	0.351	0.336

	Y6	Y7	Y8	Y9
Y6	1.000			
Y7	0.047	1.000		
Y8	0.067	0.601	1.000	
Y9	0.319	0.331	0.471	1.000

Residual Matrix (covariances) :

	Y1	Y2	Y3	Y4	Y5
Y1	-0.000				
Y2	0.013	-0.000			
Y3	-0.030	0.137	-0.000		
Y4	-0.059	0.046	0.095	-0.000	
Y5	-0.068	-0.038	-0.011	-0.004	-0.000
Y6	-0.070	-0.024	0.030	-0.005	0.015
Y7	-0.088	0.044	0.062	0.133	0.171
Y8	-0.045	0.034	0.040	-0.053	0.069
Y9	0.066	-0.113	-0.046	0.030	0.064

	Y6	Y7	Y8	Y9
Y6	-0.000			
Y7	0.071	-0.000		
Y8	-0.094	-0.000	-0.000	
Y9	-0.084	0.054	-0.009	-0.000

Value of the maximum absolute residual = 0.171.

ML Estimates of Free Parameters in Dependence Relationships

	Path	Param #	Point Estimate	90.00% Conf. Int. Lower	Upper	Standard Error	T Value
Y1	<- VISUAL	1	0.679	0.483	0.876	0.119	5.70
Y2	<- VISUAL	2	0.341	0.128	0.554	0.130	2.63
Y3	<- VISUAL	3	0.659	0.462	0.856	0.120	5.50
Y4	<- VERBAL	4	0.908	0.751	1.065	0.095	9.51
Y5	<- VERBAL	5	0.867	0.707	1.028	0.098	8.87
Y6	<- VERBAL	6	0.824	0.659	0.989	0.100	8.23
Y7	<- SPEED	7	0.651	0.435	0.866	0.131	4.97
Y8	<- SPEED	8	0.924	0.691	1.158	0.142	6.51
Y9	<- VISUAL	9	0.670	0.449	0.892	0.135	4.98
Y9	<- SPEED	10	0.192	-0.023	0.406	0.130	1.47

Values of Fixed Parameters in Dependence Relationships

	Path	Value
Y1	<- E1	1.000
Y2	<- E2	1.000
Y3	<- E3	1.000
Y4	<- E4	1.000
Y5	<- E5	1.000
Y6	<- E6	1.000
Y7	<- E7	1.000
Y8	<- E8	1.000
Y9	<- E9	1.000

ML estimates of free parameters in variance/covariance relationships

	Path	Param #	Point Estimate	90.00% Conf. Int. Lower	Upper	Standard Error	T Value
VISUAL	<-> VERBAL	11	0.552	0.369	0.735	0.111	4.97
VISUAL	<-> SPEED	12	0.474	0.239	0.708	0.143	3.32
VERBAL	<-> SPEED	13	0.088	-0.131	0.307	0.133	0.66
E1	<-> E1	14	0.538	0.373	0.777	0.120	4.49
E2	<-> E2	15	0.884	0.664	1.177	0.154	5.75
E3	<-> E3	16	0.566	0.398	0.806	0.122	4.65
E4	<-> E4	17	0.175	0.100	0.308	0.060	2.92
E5	<-> E5	18	0.248	0.162	0.378	0.064	3.88
E6	<-> E6	19	0.321	0.224	0.459	0.070	4.59
E7	<-> E7	20	0.577	0.387	0.859	0.140	4.13
E8	<-> E8	21	0.146	0.014	1.473	0.205	0.71
E9	<-> E9	22	0.392	0.255	0.604	0.103	3.81

```
Values of Fixed Parameters in Variance/Covariance Relationships
            Path                      Value
----------------------------  ------------
VISUAL     <-> VISUAL              1.000
VERBAL     <-> VERBAL              1.000
SPEED      <-> SPEED               1.000

Maximum Likelihood Discrepancy Function

 Measures of fit of the model
 ----------------------------
 Sample Discrepancy Function Value              : 0.421  (4.210057E-01)

 Population discrepancy function value, Fo
 Bias adjusted point estimate                   : 0.097
 90.000 percent confidence interval             :(0.0,0.354)

 Root mean square error of approximation
 Steiger-Lind : RMSEA = SQRT(Fo/DF)
 Point estimate                                 : 0.065
 90.000 percent confidence interval             :(0.0,0.124)

 Expected cross-validation index
 Point estimate (modified AIC)                  : 1.041
 90.000 percent confidence interval             :(0.944,1.298)
 CVI (modified AIC) for the saturated model     : 1.268

 Test statistic:                                : 29.891
 Exceedance probabilities:-
 Ho: perfect fit (RMSEA = 0.0)                  : 0.153
 Ho: close fit   (RMSEA <=       0.050)         : 0.330

 Multiplier for obtaining test statistic  =     71.000
 Degrees of freedom                        = 23
 Effective number of parameters            = 22
```

Analyzing the correlation structure

The maximum likelihood estimates and measures of t from the two jobs are the same; the standard errors differ. Those from the first job agree with the incorrect standard errors in Lawley and Maxwell; those from the second job agree with Lawley and Maxwell's correct standard errors. Comparison of iteration times in the two jobs shows that the introduction of additional (nuisance) parameters and Lagrange multipliers (TYPE=CORR) results in substantially slower iteration times. The second run differs from the first only in that we specified TYPE=CORR instead of TYPE=COVA. With commands:

```
RAMONA
  USE ex4b
  MANIFEST = y1 y2 y3 y4 y5 y6 y7 y8 y9
  LATENT = visual verbal speed e1 e2 e3 e4 e5,
           e6 e7 e8 e9
  MODEL y1 <-  visual e1(0,1.0),
        y2 <-  visual e2(0,1.0),
        y3 <-  visual e3(0,1.0),
        y4 <-  verbal e4(0,1.0),
        y5 <-  verbal e5(0,1.0),
        y6 <-  verbal e6(0,1.0),
        y7 <-  speed e7(0,1.0),
        y8 <-  speed e8(0,1.0),
```

```
      y9 <-  visual speed e9(0,1.0),
   visual <-> visual(0,1.0),
   verbal <-> verbal(0,1.0),
    speed <-> speed(0,1.0),
   visual <-> verbal,
   visual <-> speed,
   verbal <-> speed
PRINT = MEDIUM
ESTIMATE / TYPE=CORR  NCASES=72
```

```
Variables in the SYSTAT Correlation file are:
Y1        Y2        Y3        Y4        Y5        Y6        Y7        Y8

There are 9 manifest variables in the model. They are:
    Y1 Y2 Y3 Y4 Y5 Y6 Y7 Y8 Y9

There are 12 latent variables in the model. They are:
    VISUAL E1 E2 E3 VERBAL E4 E5 E6 SPEED E7 E8 E9

RAMONA options in effect are:
    Display              Corr
    Method               MWL
    Start                Rough
    Convg                0.000100
    Maximum iterations   100
    Number of cases      72
    Restart              No
    Confidence Interval  90

Variance paths for errors were omitted from the job specification
and have been added by RAMONA.

Number of manifest variables            =    9
Total number of variables in the system =   30.
Reading correlation matrix...

                     Details of Iterations
  Iter    Method  Discr. Funct.  Max.R.Cos.    Max.Const.    NRP   NBD
 -------  ------  -------------  ------------  ------------  ----- -----
     0    OLS      1.013354                     0.0
    1(0)  OLS      0.437034       0.649686      0.192907      0     0
    2(0)  OLS      0.143538       0.092248      0.017916      0     0
    3(0)  OLS      0.135197       0.053602      0.006726      0     0
    4(0)  OLS      0.134714       0.004511      0.000055      0     0
    4(0)  MWL      0.472377       0.164664      0.000055      0     0
    5(0)  MWL      0.425693       0.031463      0.003106      0     0
    6(0)  MWL      0.421825       0.019794      0.001177      0     0
    7(0)  MWL      0.421170       0.006232      0.000072      0     0
    8(0)  MWL      0.421041       0.005613      0.000050      0     0
    9(0)  MWL      0.421014       0.001271      0.000003      0     0
   10(0)  MWL      0.421008       0.001616      0.000003      0     0
   11(0)  MWL      0.421006       0.000284      0.000000      0     0
   12(0)  MWL      0.421006       0.000478      0.000000      0     0
   13(0)  MWL      0.421006       0.000085      0.000000      0     0
   14(0)  MWL      0.421006       0.000144      0.000000      0     0
   15(0)  MWL      0.421006       0.000028      0.000000      0     0
   16(0)  MWL      0.421006       0.000044      0.000000      0     0

Iterative procedure complete.

Convergence limit for residual cosines = 0.000100 on 2 consecutive
iterations.

Convergence limit for variance constraint violations =  5.00000E-07
Value of the maximum variance constraint violation =  2.14295E-09
```

*** *the Sample Correlation Matrix, Reproduced Correlation Matrix and Residual* ***
Matrix are the same as those for the analysis using covariances, so we omit them

```
             ML Estimates of Free Parameters in Dependence Relationships
                                        Point    90.00% Conf. Int.  Standard     T
              Path         Param #    Estimate   Lower    Upper      Error    Value
--------------------------------------------------------------------------------------
Y1     <- VISUAL      1        0.679    0.537    0.822      0.086     7.87
Y2     <- VISUAL      2        0.341    0.143    0.539      0.121     2.83
Y3     <- VISUAL      3        0.659    0.513    0.804      0.089     7.44
Y4     <- VERBAL      4        0.908    0.850    0.967      0.036    25.52
Y5     <- VERBAL      5        0.867    0.801    0.934      0.041    21.41
Y6     <- VERBAL      6        0.824    0.747    0.901      0.047    17.66
Y7     <- SPEED       7        0.651    0.480    0.821      0.103     6.29
Y8     <- SPEED       8        0.924    0.741    1.108      0.111     8.30
Y9     <- VISUAL      9        0.670    0.485    0.856      0.113     5.96
Y9     <- SPEED      10        0.192   -0.021    0.404      0.129     1.48

Scaled Standard Deviations (nuisance parameters)
              Variable     Estimate
              ------------ ------------
              Y1           1.000
              Y2           1.000
              Y3           1.000
              Y4           1.000
              Y5           1.000
              Y6           1.000
              Y7           1.000
              Y8           1.000
              Y9           1.000

          Values of Fixed Parameters in Dependence Relationships
                        Path                    Value
              ------------------------------  -------------
              Y1         <- E1                 1.000
              Y2         <- E2                 1.000
              Y3         <- E3                 1.000
              Y4         <- E4                 1.000
              Y5         <- E5                 1.000
              Y6         <- E6                 1.000
              Y7         <- E7                 1.000
              Y8         <- E8                 1.000
              Y9         <- E9                 1.000

    ML estimates of free parameters in variance/covariance relationships
                                        Point    90.00% Conf. Int.  Standard     T
              Path         Param #    Estimate   Lower    Upper      Error    Value
--------------------------------------------------------------------------------------
VISUAL   <-> VERBAL     11        0.552    0.344    0.708      0.111     4.97
VISUAL   <-> SPEED      12        0.474    0.210    0.674      0.143     3.32
VERBAL   <-> SPEED      13        0.088   -0.132    0.299      0.133     0.66
E1       <-> E1         14        0.538    0.376    0.771      0.117     4.59
E2       <-> E2         15        0.884    0.758    1.030      0.082    10.74
E3       <-> E3         16        0.566    0.403    0.794      0.117     4.85
E4       <-> E4         17        0.175    0.096    0.322      0.065     2.72
E5       <-> E5         18        0.248    0.155    0.395      0.070     3.52
E6       <-> E6         19        0.321    0.216    0.476      0.077     4.17
E7       <-> E7         20        0.577    0.393    0.847      0.135     4.29
E8       <-> E8         21        0.146    0.014    1.491      0.206     0.71
E9       <-> E9         22        0.392    0.250    0.615      0.107     3.66

   Values of Fixed Parameters in Variance/Covariance Relationships

              Path                    Value
   ------------------------------  -------------
VISUAL   <-> VISUAL                 1.000
VERBAL   <-> VERBAL                 1.000
SPEED    <-> SPEED                  1.000

                 Equality Constraints on Variances
                                              Lagrange           Standard
              Constraint            Value    Multiplier           Error
   ------------------------------  -------   ----------          --------
Y1       <-> Y1       1.0000        0.000              -0.000
Y2       <-> Y2       1.0000       -0.000              -0.000
Y3       <-> Y3       1.0000        0.000               0.000
Y4       <-> Y4       1.0000        0.000               0.000
Y5       <-> Y5       1.0000        0.000              -0.000
Y6       <-> Y6       1.0000       -0.000              -0.000
Y7       <-> Y7       1.0000        0.000              -0.000
Y8       <-> Y8       1.0000       -0.000              -0.000
Y9       <-> Y9       1.0000       -0.000               0.000
```

*** *Results for the maximum likelihood discrepancy function are the*
    same as those for the analysis using covariances, so we omit these.   ***

More about **RAMONA**

RAMONA's model

Let v_1 be a $p \times 1$ vector of manifest variables, v_2 be an $m \times 1$ vector of latent variables, and let

$$v = \begin{bmatrix} v_1 \\ v_2 \end{bmatrix} \tag{1}$$

be the $t \times 1$ vector ($t = p + m$) representing all variables in the system, manifest and latent. Suppose that B is a $t \times t$ matrix of path coefficients. The path coefficient corresponding to the directed arrow from the jth element, v_j, of v to the ith element, v_i, will appear in the ith row and jth column of B. Let v_x be a $t \times 1$ vector formed from v by replacing all elements corresponding to non-null rows of B by zeroes. Thus, v_x consists of exogenous variables with endogenous variables replaced by zeroes. The system of directed paths represented in the path diagram is then given by:

$$v = Bv + v_x \tag{2}$$

The formulation of the model given in (1) differs only slightly from that of RAM (McArdle and McDonald, 1984). All non-null elements of v_x are also elements of v. Also, the non-null elements of v_x can, in some situations, be common factors rather than residuals. Let

$$\Phi = \mathrm{Cov}(v_x, v_x')$$

be the $t \times t$ covariance matrix of v_x. Thus, the nonzero elements of Φ are parameters associated with two-headed arrows in the path diagram. Null rows and columns of Φ will be associated with endogenous variables in v.

Let $\Upsilon = \mathrm{Cov}(v, v')$. It follows from (2) that (McArdle and McDonald)

$$\Upsilon = (I-B)^{-1} \Phi (I-B')^{-1} \tag{3}$$

The manifest variable covariance matrix $\Sigma = \mathrm{Cov}(v_1, v_1')$ is the first $p \times p$ submatrix of Υ (see (1)). Specified values may be assigned to exogenous variable covariances by applying constraints to appropriate diagonal elements of Υ.

The structural model employed by RAMONA is given in (3). Both $\boldsymbol{B}$ and Φ are large matrices with most of their elements equal to 0. Their nonzero elements alone are stored in RAMONA. Sparse matrix methods are used in the computation of $(\boldsymbol{I}-\boldsymbol{B})^{-1}$ and $\boldsymbol{\Upsilon}$. Details can be found in Mels (1988).

The covariance structure in (3) differs from a formulation of Bentler and Weeks (1980) in that there is a single matrix, $\boldsymbol{B}$, for path coefficients instead of two.

Structural equation models are often fitted to sample correlation matrices. There are many published studies where this has been done incorrectly (Cudeck, 1989). RAMONA fits a correlation structure by introducing a duplicate standardized variable, $\boldsymbol{v}_i^*$, with unit variance to correspond to each manifest variable $\boldsymbol{v}_i$, $i \le p$, and then taking

$$\boldsymbol{v}_i = \sigma_i \boldsymbol{v}_i^* \quad i \le p$$

where σ_i stands for the standard deviation of $\boldsymbol{v}_i$. The duplicate variables are treated in the same way as latent variables—with variances constrained to unity if they are endogenous and fixed at unity if they are exogenous. Also, the standard deviation, σ_i, is treated in the same way as a path coefficient. This procedure is equivalent to expressing the manifest variable covariance matrix in the form

$$\Sigma = D_\sigma P D_\sigma$$

where D_σ is a diagonal matrix with the σ_i, $i \le p$, as diagonal elements, and $\boldsymbol{P}$ is the manifest variable correlation matrix, which is treated as the covariance matrix of the standardized duplicate variables $\boldsymbol{v}_i^*$, $i \le p$. Fitting the model to a sample correlation matrix instead of a sample covariance matrix results in the estimates $\hat{\sigma}_i$ being replaced by $\hat{\sigma}_i / s_i$, where s_i is a sample standard deviation. These quantities are referred to as *Scaled Standard Deviations (nuisance parameters)* in the output. Other parameter estimates are not affected.

This approach involves the introduction of p additional parameters, σ_i, and p additional constraints on the variances of the $\boldsymbol{v}_i^*$. The number of degrees of freedom is not affected (unless some parameters or constraints are redundant), but computation time is increased because of the additional parameters and additional constraints.

Some details of the estimation procedure

Let γ be the parameter vector and $\Sigma = \Sigma(\gamma)$ the covariance structure. Parameter estimates are obtained by minimizing a discrepancy function, $F(S, \Sigma(\gamma))$, specified using METHOD. Alternatives are:

MWL   Maximum Wishart likelihood.

$$F(S, \Sigma) = \ln|\Sigma| - \ln|S| + \mathrm{tr}[S\,\Sigma^{-1}] - p$$

GLS   Generalized least squares assuming a Wishart distribution for S.

$$F(S, \Sigma) = \tfrac{1}{2}\,\mathrm{tr}[S^{-1}(S - \Sigma)]^2$$

OLS   Ordinary least squares.

$$F(S, \Sigma) = \tfrac{1}{2}\,\mathrm{tr}[(S - \Sigma)]^2$$

ADFU, ADFG   Asymptotically distribution free methods.

$$F(S, \Sigma) = (s - \sigma)'\,\hat{\Gamma}^{-1}(s - \sigma)$$

where s and σ are column vectors with $p\,(p+1)/2$ elements formed from the distinct elements of S and Σ, respectively, and $\hat{\Gamma}$ is an estimate of the asymptotic covariance matrix of sample covariances. For ADFU, $\hat{\Gamma}$ is unbiased (Browne, 1982) but need not be positive definite. If $\hat{\Gamma}$ is indefinite, the program moves automatically from ADFU to ADFG. With ADFG, $\hat{\Gamma}$ is biased but Gramian (Browne, 1982).

An iterative Gauss-Newton computing procedure with constraints (Browne and Du Toit, 1992) is used to obtain parameter estimates. With MWL, the weight matrix is respecified on each iteration. The procedure is then equivalent to the Aitchison and Silvey (1960) adaptation of the Fisher scoring method to deal with equality constraints.

Some computer programs can yield negative estimates of variances. This does not happen with RAMONA. Bounds are imposed to ensure that variance estimates are non-negative and that all correlation estimates lie between -1 and $+1$. The imposition of these bounds can result in the convergence of RAMONA in situations where programs that do not impose them fail to converge. In some cases, a program that allows negative variance estimates and does converge will yield a smaller discrepancy function value than RAMONA.

Iteration is continued until the largest absolute residual cosine (Browne, 1982) falls below a tolerance, specified in CONVG, on two consecutive iterations.

Confidence intervals

Approximate 90% confidence intervals are given for parameter estimates associated with dependence paths and with covariance paths. Confidence intervals for path coefficients and covariances (variances unrestricted) are provided under the assumption of a normal distribution for the estimator $\hat{\gamma}$ (Browne, 1974) and are symmetric about the parameter estimate. Confidence intervals for other parameters are nonsymmetric about the parameter estimate (Browne, 1974) and are obtained under the following assumptions:

- Correlation coefficients (covariances with both corresponding variances restricted to unity): a normal distribution is assumed for the z-transform, $\frac{1}{2}\ln[(1 + \hat{\gamma})/(1 - \hat{\gamma})]$, (Browne, 1974).
- Variances: a normal distribution is assumed for the natural logarithm, $\ln\hat{\gamma}$, (Browne, 1974).
- Error variances under a correlation structure (corresponding dependent variable variances are constrained to unity): a normal distribution is assumed for $-\ln(\hat{\gamma}^{-1} - 1)$ (Browne, 1974).

Measures of fit of a model

This section provides a brief description of the measures of fit output by RAMONA. Further information concerning these measures of fit can be found in Browne and Cudeck (1992).

Let $N = n + 1$ be the sample size; p, the number of manifest variables; and q, the number of free parameters in the model. Then the number of degrees of freedom is $d = \frac{1}{2} p(p + 1) - q$. The sample covariance matrix is denoted by S and the corresponding population covariance matrix by Σ_0.

The minimal sample discrepancy function value is

$$\hat{F} = \underset{\gamma}{\text{Min}} \ F\left(S, \sum(\gamma)\right)$$

and the corresponding minimal population discrepancy function value is

$$F = \underset{\gamma}{\text{Min}} \ F(\Sigma_0, \Sigma(\gamma))$$

Now F_0 is bounded below by 0 and takes on a value of 0 if and only if Σ_0 satisfies the structural model exactly. Therefore, we can regard F_0 as a measure of badness-of-fit of the model, $\Sigma(\gamma)$, to the population covariance matrix, Σ_0.

We assume that the test statistic $n\,\hat{F}$ has an approximate noncentral chi-square distribution with d degrees of freedom and a noncentrality parameter $\sigma = nF_0$. This will be true if the discrepancy function is correctly specified for the distribution of the data, F_0 is small enough, and N is large enough (Steiger, Shapiro, and Browne, 1985).

Then the expected value of $\hat{F}$ will be approximately $F_0 + d/n$, so that $\hat{F}$ is a biased estimator of F_0. As a less biased point estimator of F_0 we use:

$$\hat{F}_0 = \text{Max}\,\{\hat{F} - (d/n), 0\}$$

We also provide a 90% confidence interval on F_0 as suggested by Steiger and Lind (1980). Let $\Phi(x \mid \delta, d)$ be the cumulative distribution function of a noncentral chi-square distribution with noncentrality parameter δ and d degrees of freedom. Given $x = n \times \hat{F}$ and d, the lower limit, δ_L, of the 90% confidence interval on $n \times F_0$ is the solution for δ of the equation

$$\Phi(x \mid \delta, d) = 0.95$$

and the upper limit δ_U is the solution for δ of

$$\Phi(x \mid \delta, d) = 0.05$$

A 90% confidence interval on F_0 is then given by $(n^{-1}\delta_L; \; n^{-1}\delta_U)$.

Because F_0 cannot increase if additional parameters are added, it gives little guidance about when to stop adding parameters. It is preferable to use the root mean square error of approximation (Steiger and Lind, 1980):

$$\text{RMSEA} = \sqrt{\frac{\hat{F}_0}{d}}$$

as a measure of the fit per degree of freedom of the model. This population measure of badness-of-fit is also bounded below by 0 and will be 0 only if the model fits perfectly. It will decrease if the inclusion of additional parameters substantially reduces F_0 but will increase if the inclusion of additional parameters reduces F_0 only slightly. Consequently, it can give some guidance as to how many parameters to use. Practical experience has suggested that a value of the RMSEA of about 0.05 or less indicates a close fit of the model in relation to the degrees of freedom. A value of about 0.08 or less indicates a reasonable fit of the model in relation to the degrees of freedom.

A point estimate of the RMSEA is given by

$$\text{Estimate (RMSEA)} = \sqrt{\frac{\hat{F}_0}{d}}$$

and a 90% confidence interval by

$$\text{Interval Estimate (RMSEA)} = \left(\sqrt{\frac{\delta_L}{nd}}, \sqrt{\frac{\delta_U}{nd}} \right) \tag{4}$$

The RMSEA does not depend on sample size and therefore does not take into account the fact that it is unwise to fit a model with many parameters if N is small. A measure of fit that does this is the expected cross-validation index (ECVI). Consider two samples of size N—a calibration sample C and a validation sample V. Suppose that the model is fitted to the calibration sample yielding a reproduced covariance matrix $\hat{\Sigma}_C$. The discrepancy between $\hat{\Sigma}_C$ and the validation sample covariance matrix S_V is then measured with the discrepancy function yielding $F(S_V, \hat{\Sigma}_C)$ as a measure of stability under cross-validation. A difficulty with this approach is that two samples are required. One can avoid a second sample by estimating the expected value of $F(S_V, \hat{\Sigma}_C)$ from a single sample. Assume that the discrepancy function is correctly specified for the distribution of the data. Taking expectations over calibration samples and validation samples gives the expected cross-validation index:

$$\text{ECVI} = \underset{C\,V}{\xi\xi} F(Sv, \hat{\Sigma}_C) \approx F_0 + (d + 2q)/n \tag{5}$$

A point estimate of the ECVI is given by (Browne and Cudeck, 1990):

$$\text{Estimate (ECVI)} = \hat{F} + 2q/n \tag{6}$$

If METHOD is set to MWL, this point estimate of the ECVI is related by a linear transformation to the Akaike Information Criterion (Akaike, 1973) and will lead to the same conclusions.

The point estimate in (6) will decrease if an additional parameter reduces $\hat{F}$ sufficiently and increases otherwise. This will give some guidance as to the number of parameters to retain. However, the amount of reduction in $\hat{F}$ required before an increase in the point estimate occurs is affected by the sample size. If n is very large, increasing the number of parameters will tend to reduce the point estimate of the ECVI. One should also bear in mind that sampling variability affects the point estimates.

An approximate 90% confidence interval on the ECVI may be obtained from:

$$\text{Interval Estimate (ECVI)} = \left(\frac{\delta_L + d + 2q}{n} ; \frac{\delta_U + d + 2q}{n} \right) \quad (7)$$

It can happen that $(\hat{F} - d) < \delta_L$, so that the point estimate in (6) is smaller than the lower limit of the confidence interval in (7). In particular, this will be true if the (approximately unbiased) point estimate in (6) is less than the lower bound $(d + 2q)/n$ for the approximation to the ECVI given in (5).

For comparative purposes, RAMONA also provides the ECVI of the saturated model where no structure is imposed on Σ:

$$\text{ECVI (}\textit{Saturated Model}\text{)} = \frac{2 \times (d + q)}{n}$$

The test statistic $n \times \hat{F}$ is also output by RAMONA. We follow convention in providing the exceedance probability, $1 - \Phi(n\hat{F} \,|\, 0, d)$, for a test of the point hypothesis

$$H_0: F_0 = 0$$

$$(8)$$

which implies that the model holds exactly. Our opinion, however, is that this null hypothesis is implausible and that it does not much help to know whether or not the statistical test has been able to detect that it is false.

More relevant is the exceedance probability for an interval hypothesis of close fit, which we define by

$$H_0: \text{RMSEA} \le 0.05 \tag{9}$$

and which implies that $\delta \le \delta^* = n \times d \times 0.05^2$.

The exceedance probability output by RAMONA is given by

$$1 - \Phi(n\hat{F}|\delta^*,d) \ .$$

Note that the null hypothesis of perfect fit in (8) is not rejected at the 5% level if $\delta_L = 0$ or, equivalently, the lower limit of the confidence interval in (4) is 0. The null hypothesis of close fit in (9) is not rejected at the 5% level if the lower limit of the confidence interval in (4) is not greater than 0.05.

When METHOD is set to MWL, two sets of measures of fit are output. One is based on the maximum likelihood discrepancy function value

$$\hat{F} = \ln\left|\hat{\Sigma}\right| - \ln |S| + \text{tr}[S\hat{\Sigma}^{-1}] - p$$

and the other on the generalized least squares discrepancy function value

$$\hat{F} = \frac{1}{2}\text{tr}[\hat{\Sigma}^{-1}(S - \hat{\Sigma})]$$

When the model fits well, the differences between the two sets of fit measures should be small (Browne, 1974).

References

Aitchison, J., and Silvey, S.D. 1960. Maximum likelihood estimation procedures and associated tests of significance. *Journal of the Royal Statistical Society*, Series B, 22: 154-171.

Akaike, H. 1973. Information theory and an extension of the maximum likelihood principle. *Second International Symposium on Information Theory*, B.N. Petrov and F. Csaki, eds. Budapest: Akademiai Kiado.

Bentler, P.M., and Weeks, D.G. 1980. Linear structural equations with latent variables. *Psychometrika*, 45: 289-308.

Bollen, K.A. 1989. *Structural equations with latent variables.* New York: John Wiley & Sons, Inc.

Browne, M.W. 1974. Generalized least squares estimators in the analysis of covariance structures. *South African Statistical Journal,* 8: 1-24. (Reprinted in *Latent Variables in Socioeconomic Models,* D.J. Aigner and A.S. Goldberger, eds. 205-226. Amsterdam: North Holland.

Browne, M.W. 1982. Covariance structures. In *Topics in Applied Multivariate Analysis,* D.M. Hawkins, ed. 72-141. Cambridge: Cambridge University Press.

Browne, M.W., and Cudeck, R. 1990. Single sample cross-validation indices for covariance structures. *Multivariate Behavioral Research,* 24: 445-455.

Browne, M.W., and Cudeck, R. 1992. Alternative ways of assessing model fit. *Testing Structural Equation Models,* K.A. Bollen and J.S. Long, eds. Beverly Hills, Calif.: Sage.

Browne, M.W., and Du Toit, S.H.C. 1992. Automated fitting of nonstandard models. *Multivariate Behavioral Research.*

Cudeck, R. 1989. Analysis of correlation matrices using covariance structure models. *Psychological Bulletin,* 105: 317-327.

Duncan, O.D., Haller, A.O., and Portes, A. 1971. Peer influence on aspirations, a reinterpretation. *Causal Models in the Social Sciences,* H.M. Blalock, ed. 219-244. Aldine-Atherstone.

Everitt, B.S. 1984. *An introduction to latent variable models.* New York: Chapman and Hall.

Guttman, L. 1954. A new approach to factor analysis: The radex. *Mathematical Thinking in the Social Sciences,* P.F. Lazarsfeld, ed. 258-348. Glencoe: The Free Press.

Jöreskog, K.G. 1977. Structural equation models in the social sciences: Specification estimation and testing. *Applications of Statistics,* P.R. Krishnaiah, ed. 265-287. Amsterdam: North Holland.

Lawley, D.N., and Maxwell, A.E. 1971. *Factor analysis as a statistical method.* 2nd ed. New York: American Elsevier.

McArdle J.J. 1988. Dynamic but structural equation modeling of repeated measures data. *Handbook of Multivariate Experimental*

Psychology, J.R. Nesselroade and R.B. Cattell, eds. 2nd ed. 561-614. New York: Plenum.

McArdle, J.J., and McDonald, R.P. 1984. Some algebraic properties of the Reticular Action Model for moment structures. *British Journal of Mathematical and Statistical Psychology,* 37: 234-251.

McDonald, R.P. 1985. *Factor analysis and related methods.* Hillsdale: Erlbaum.

Mels, G. 1988. *A general system for path analysis with latent variables.* M. Sc. thesis, University of South Africa.

Mels, G., and Koorts, A.S. 1989. *Causal Models for various job aspects. SAIPA,* 24: 144-156.

Shapiro, A., and Browne, M.W. 1987. Analysis of covariance structures under elliptical distributions. *Journal of the American Statistical Association,* 82: 1092-1097

Steiger, J.H., and Lind, J. 1980. *Statistically based tests for the number of common factors.* Paper presented at the annual meeting of the Psychometric Society: Iowa City.

Steiger, J.H., Shapiro, A., and Browne, M.W. 1985. On the asymptotic distribution of sequential chi-square statistics. *Psychometrika,* 50: 253-264.

Wheaton, B., Muthén, B., Alwin, D.F., and Summers, G.F. 1977. Assessing reliability and stability in panel models. *Sociological Methodology 1977,* D.R. Heise, ed. 84-136. San Francisco: Jossey-Bass.

Acknowledgments

The development of this program was partially supported by the Institute of Statistical Research of the South African Human Sciences Research Council, the South African Foundation for Research Development, and the University of South Africa.

The authors are indebted to Professor S.H.C. du Toit and to Mrs. Yvette Seymore for a number of subroutines used in the program.

Time Series

Leland Wilkinson and Yuri Balasanov

Time Series implements a wide variety of time series models, including linear and nonlinear filtering, Fourier analysis, seasonal decomposition, nonseasonal and seasonal exponential smoothing, and the Box-Jenkins (1976) approach to nonseasonal and seasonal ARIMA. You can save results from transformations, smoothing, the deseasonalized series, and forecasts for use in other SYSTAT procedures.

Time Series

More about Time Series

ARIMA modeling and forecasting

Summary

Computation

Time Series

Overview

Time Series lets you interactively analyze time series data. The strategy is to:

- Plot the series using **T-plot, ACF, PACF** or **CCF**
- Transform the data to stabilize the variance across time or to make the series stationary using **Transform**
- smooth the series using moving averages, runnings medians, or general linear filters using **Smooth** or **LOWESS**
- Fit your model using **ARIMA**
- Examine the results by plotting the smoothed or forecasted results

You can save results from transformations, smoothing, the deseasonalized series, and forecasts for use in other SYSTAT procedures.

Getting started

To graph, transform, smooth, or model a time series, use **Stats**➠**Time Series**. Since **Time Series** has several dialog boxes, the boxes will be displayed as they are discussed.

Using commands

With commands:

```
SERIES
    USE filename
    TIME origin period first
    TPLOT var
    ACF var
    PACF var
    CCF var
    Transformations as needed (LOG, SQUARE, TREND, DIFFER,
    PCNTCHNG, INDEX, TAPER)
    SAVE filename
    SMOOTH
    EXPONENTIAL
    ADJSEASON
    ARIMA
    FOURIER
    CLEAR
    MISSING
```

Graphical Displays

Plotting data, autocorrelations, and partial autocorrelations is often one of the first steps in understanding time series data. **Stats▸Time Series** provides the following graphical displays:

T-plot Time series plots. Your variable is the dependent variable and the case is the independent variable. Use **Stats▸Time Series▸Time** to generate labels for time.

ACF Autocorrelations for lag 1 through lag k. For, say, lag j, the autocorrelation is the Pearson correlation between observations j time periods (lags) apart. That is, imagine writing the series in a column and then copying the series a second time. For lag 1, shift the second column down one time point and compute the correlation of each value with the previous time point's value: $(y_2, y_1; y_3, y_2; \ldots; y_n, y_{n-1})$. For lag 2, shift the series down two time points, and so on.

PACF Partial autocorrelations for lag 1 through k. Like the ACF for lag j, the partial correlation at lag j also measures the correlation among observations j time periods apart, except that all intervening lags are "partialed out."

CCF Cross-correlation plots. These plots help identify relations between two different series and any time delays to the relations.

For ACF, PACF, or CCF, plots use **Stats▸Time Series** and choose **ACF**, **PACF**, or **CCF**. These three dialog boxes are the same.

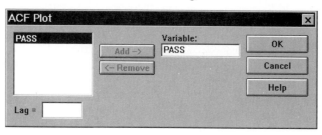

To generate labels for the cases in a **T-plot**, use **Stats⟶Time Series⟶Time**.

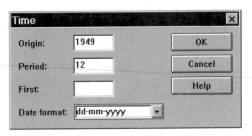

Specify the following:

Origin	Year of the first observation.
Period	Periodicity. For example, for monthly data, enter 12 as the period.
First	Period of the first observation. For example, if the period starts in March of that year, type 3.
Date format	Choose an appropriate date format from the drop-down list.

For quarterly data, use **Origin** to specify the year, **Period** to specify 4 quarters, and **First** to specify the first period of observation, say 4, for the fourth quarter.

The use of these plots continues through the analysis. By studying plots, you may identify a need to transform the data (thus meeting the assumption of constant variance over time) or to difference the series (removing a trend).

19.1
Plotting the time series

To illustrate these displays, we use monthly counts of international airline passengers during 1949–60. Box and Jenkins call the series G. Each of the 144 monthly counts is stored as a case in the SYSTAT file named *AIRLINE*.

Case plot with labels

T-plot provides a graphical view of the raw data. This can give you a general idea of the series, enabling you to detect a long-term trend, seasonal fluctuations, and gross outliers. Here we plot the *AIRLINE* passenger data. Use **Stats⟶Time Series⟶Time** and type 1949 in the **Origin** text box and 12 in the **Period** text box. Next, use **Stats⟶Time Series⟶T-plot** and select the variable *PASS*. With commands:

```
SERIES
    USE airline
    TIME 1949 12
    TPLOT pass
```

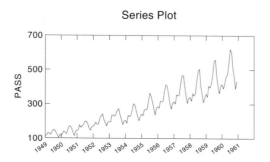

Series Plot

Notice that the counts tend to peak during the summer months each year and that the number of passengers tends to increase over time (a positive trend). Notice also that the spread or variance tends to increase over time. One way to deal with this problem is to log transform the data.

As another example, let's show the results for the logged series. Use **Data➧Transform➧Let** and use the **LOG** option to log transform the *PASS* variable. Then return to **Stats➧Time Series➧T-plot** and execute as before. With commands:

```
LOG pass
TPLOT pass
```

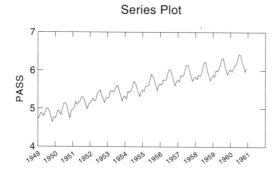

Series Plot

Compare this plot with the previous one—the variance across time now appears more stable, but there is still a positive upward trend over time.

19.2 Auto-correlations

Displays of autocorrelations help you to investigate the relation of each time point to previous time points. If the autocorrelation at lag 1 is high, then each value is highly correlated with the value at the previous time point. If the autocorrelation at lag 12 is high for data collected monthly, then each month is highly correlated with the same month a year before (for example, for monthly sales data, sales in December may be more related to those in previous Decembers than to those in November or January).

Use **Stats**➠**Time Series**➠**ACF** and use the **Lag** option to specify the number of lags for which autocorrelations are displayed. With commands:

continuing from Example 19.1
```
ACF pass
```

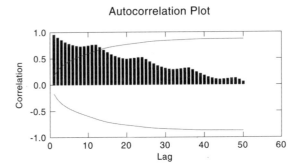

Autocorrelation Plot

Note that the logged values of *PASS* remain from the previous plot. The shading in the display indicates the size of the correlation at each lag (that is, like a bar chart). The correlation of each value with the previous value in time (lag 1) is close to 1.0; with values 12 months before (lag 12), it is around 0.75. The curved line marks approximate 95% confidence levels for the significance of each correlation. Notice the slow decay of these values. To most investigators, this indicates that the series should be differenced. Differencing is discussed in "Transforming Series" on p. 678.

19.3 Partial auto- correlations

Partial autocorrelation plots show the relationship of points in a series to preceding points after partialing out the influence of intervening points.

Use **Stats**➠**Time Series**➠**PACF** and use the **Lag** option to specify the number of lags for which partial autocorrelations are displayed. With commands:

continuing from Example 19.1
    PACF pass

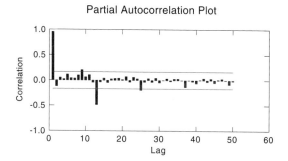

Partial Autocorrelation Plot

The first autocorrelation is the same as in the ACF plot. There are no previous autocorrelations, so it is not adjusted. The second-order autocorrelation was close to 0.90 in the ACF plot, but after adjusting for the first autocorrelation, it is reduced to –0.118.

19.4 Cross- correlations

Cross-correlation plots help to identify relations between two different series and any time delays to the relations. A correlation for a negative lag indicates the relation of the values in the first series to values in the second series. The correlation at lag 0 is the usual Pearson correlation. Similarly, correlations at positive lags relate values in the first series to subsequent values in the second series.

This example uses the *SPNDMONY* file, which contains two quarterly series, *SPENDING* (consumer expenditures) and *MONEY* (money stock) in billions of current dollars for the United States during the years 1952–1956. The first record (case) in the file contains the *SPENDING* and *MONEY* dollars for the first quarter of 1952; the second record, dollars for the second quarter of 1952, and so on (that is, if each case contains *SPENDING* and *MONEY* values for a quarter). These series are analyzed by Chatterjee and Price (1977).

After selecting the *SPNDMONY* file, use **Stats**➠**Time Series**➠**CCF** and select *SPENDING* and *MONEY* as variables and specify 15 as the **Lag** value. With commands:

```
SERIES
    USE spndmony
    CCF spending money / LAG=15
```

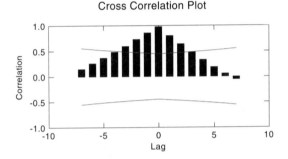

Cross Correlation Plot

There is strong correlation between the two series at lag 0, tapering off the further one goes in either direction. This is true of all cross-correlation functions between two trended series. Since both series are increasing, early values in both series tend to be small, and final values tend to be large. This produces a large positive correlation.

To better understand the relationship, if any, between the series, difference them to remove the common trend and then display a new CCF plot. (Fore more information, see "Transforming Series" on p. 678)

To difference both series, use **Stats**➠**Time Series**➠**Transform** and select *SPENDING*. From the **Type** drop-down list choose **Difference**. Type 15 in the **Lag** text box. Repeat these steps for *MONEY*. With commands:

```
    DIFFERENCE spending
    DIFFERENCE money
    CCF spending money / LAG=15
```

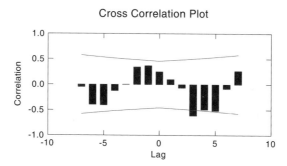

Cross Correlation Plot

This shows a significant negative correlation at only one time interval: +3 lags of the series. Since we selected *SPENDING* first, we see that consumer expenditures are negatively correlated with the money stock three quarters later. Thus, consumer spending may be a "leading indicator" of money stock.

Transforming Series

Use **Stats**➡**Time Series**➡**Transform** to transform each value in your series.

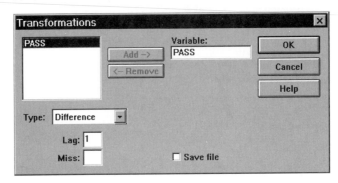

Choose a transformation from the **Type** drop-down list:

Mean
Subtract the mean from each value in the series.

Log
Replace the values in a series with their natural logarithms, and thus remove nonstationary variability, such as increasing variability over time.

Square
Square the values in a series. This is useful for producing periodograms and for normalizing variance across the series.

Trend
Remove linear trend from a series.

Difference
Replace each value by the difference between it and the previous value, thereby removing trend (nonstationarity in level over time). Using differences between each successive value is called lag 1. A **Lag** option allows seasonal differences (for example, for data collected monthly, request a **Lag** of 12).

Pcntchange
Replace each value by the difference from the previous value expressed as a percentage change—the difference in values divided by the previous value.

Index
Replace each value by the ratio of the value to the value of a base observation, which you can specify in the **Base**

text box. By default, SYSTAT uses the first observation in the series.

Taper   Smooth the series with the split-cosine-bell taper. Tapering weights the middle of a series more than the endpoints. Use it prior to a Fourier decomposition to reduce "leakage" between components. Type the proportion (P) of the series to be tapered in the **Proportion** text box. Choose a weight function that varies between a "boxcar" (P = 0) and a full cycle of a cosine wave from trough to trough (P = 1). For intermediate values of P, the weight function is flat in the center section and cosine tapered at either end. Default = 0.5

Transformations in **Time Series** are "in place." That is, the series is stored in the active work area and the transformed values are written over the old ones. The original file is not altered, however, because all the work is done in the memory of the computer.

You can pile up transformation commands in any order, as long as you do not encounter a mathematically undefined result. In that case, SYSTAT gives an error message and the variable is restored to its original value in the file.

19.5 Differencing

Let's replace the values of the series with the difference between each value and the previous value—first order (lag) differencing. Return to the *AIRLINE* passenger data, continuing from Example 19.3. Transform the *PASS* variable again by going to **Data**➡**Transform**➡**Let** (the data are now in log units).

Now, to difference the logged values, use **Stats**➡**Time Series**➡ **Transform** and specify the variable *PASS*. Then, select **Difference** from the **Type** drop-down list. With commands:

continuing from Example 19.1
```
DIFFERENCE pass
```

To look at graphical displays of the differenced series, return to **Stats**➡**Time Series**➡**T-plot** and select the variable *PASS*.

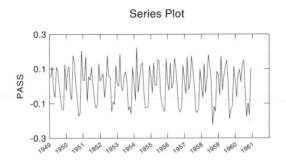

The strong upward trend seen in the earlier plots is not evident here. Notice also that the scale on this plot ranges from approximately –0.2 to +0.2, while on the plot in in Example 19.1, it ranges from 4.6 to 6.4.

For the autocorrelations of the differenced series, use **Stats**➠**Time Series**➠**ACF** and for the partial autocorrelations, use **Stats**➠**Time Series**➠**PACF** (Lag=15 is used for each plot):

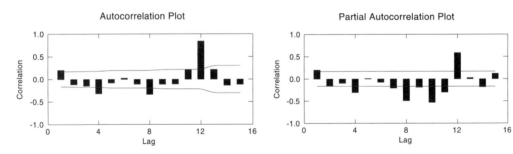

The very strong lag 12 ACF and PACF correlations with a decay of strong correlations for shorter lags suggest that the series is seasonal. (We suspected this after seeing the first plot of the data.) Differencing this monthly series by lag 12 can remove cycles from the series.

Order 12

Let's difference by order 12 and look at the plots. Let's summarize what has happened to the original data. First, the data were replaced by their log values. Next, the data were replaced by their first-order differences. Now we replace these differences with order 12 differences by going to **Stats**➠**Time Series**➠**Transform** and selecting **Difference** from the **Type** drop-down list. Type 12 in the **Lag** text box. With commands:

continuing from Example 19.1
```
DIFFERENCE pass / LAG=12
```
The autocorrelations and partial autocorrelations after differencing by order 12 are shown below:

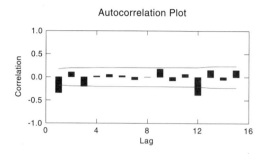

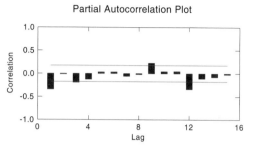

The ACF display has spikes at Lag 1 and Lag 12. We conclude that the number of airline passengers this month depends on the number last month and on the number one year ago during the same month.

Saving transformed series and other results

By default, **Time Series** works in working memory of the computer (RAM), never altering the data stored on disk. To save the results of a transformation (or the smoothed values of a series, the deseasonalized values, or forecasted residuals) to a SYSTAT file, use **Stats**➧**Time Series**➧**Transform** and click **Save file**.

Select **Save file** on the appropriate **Time Series** dialog box. With commands:

```
SAVE filename / SINGLE (or DOUBLE)
```

SYSTAT changes the name of the series to *TRANSF*. If you want to rename the series, open the file in the Worksheet and type in a new name.

Clearing the series from memory

Stats➧**Time Series**➧**Clear Series** clears the series transformation from memory and restores the original values of the series (the values that are still unchanged in the Worksheet). It is not possible to clear only the latest transformation (unless you are saving to files after each step)—

Clear Series undoes all the transformations. **Clear Series** does not affect any transformations or smoothings saved in SYSTAT files.

If you plot too many variables, you may run out of space in the active work area, or memory, of the computer. Use the **Graph** menu to plot fewer variables. To reclaim space in the work area, use **Clear Series**.

Missing data

Stats➠Time Series➠Missing Values enables you to choose the method for handling missing values embedded in series.

Interpolate	Interpolate missing values by using distance-weighted least squares (DWLS). DWLS interpolates by locally quadratic approximating curves that are weighted by the distance to each nonmissing point in the series. With this algorithm, all nonmissing values in the series contribute to the missing data estimates, and thus complex local features can be modeled by the interpolant. DWLS can also be found by going to Graph➠Plot➠Options➠Smoother.
Delete	Retain only the leading nonmissing values for analysis. In series that begin with one or more missing values, the series is deleted from the first missing value following one or more nonmissing values. This option enables you to forecast missing values from a nonmissing subsection of the series, for example. You can then insert these forecasts into the series and repeat the procedure later in the series if necessary.

Smoothing a Time Series

Sometimes, with a "noisy" time series, you simply want to view some sort of smoothed version of the series even though you have no idea what type of function generated the series. A variety of techniques can smooth, or filter, the noise from such a series. **Stats**➠**Time Series** provides two dialog boxes for smoothing—**Smooth** and **LOWESS**.

Smoothing

For smoothing, use **Stats**➠**Time Series**➠**Smooth**:

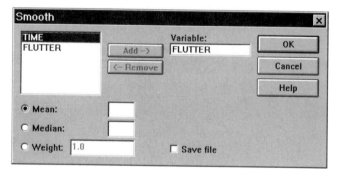

Smooth offers the following options:

Mean   Running means (moving averages). Specify the number of points in the **Mean** text box.

Median   Running medians. Specify the number of points in the **Median** text box.

Weight   General linear filters in which users can specify their own weights. **Smooth** transforms the weights before using them so that they sum to 1.0. **Weight** = 1, 2, 1 is the same as **Weight** = 0.25, 0.5, 0.25 or **Weight** = 3, 6, 3.

The following plot gives a typical "free decay record" from a "flutter test" of an aircraft wing (Bennett and Desmarais, 1975). It shows amplitude of vibration versus time in an aircraft component. Although the model for these data is known, we are going to try to recover a smooth series without using this information. The data are in the file *AIRCRAFT*. Use **Stats**➠**Time Series**➠**T-plot** and specify *FLUTTER* as the variable.

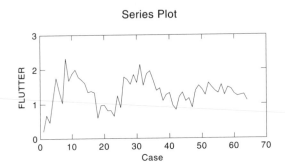

Series Plot

19.6 Moving averages

One of the simplest smoothers is a moving average. If a data point consists of a smooth component plus random error, then if we average several points surrounding a point, the errors should tend to cancel each other out. Two possible moving averages, three and four points wide, are shown below. The window shows which points are being averaged. The boldface shows which point in the series is replaced with the average.

Three-point window

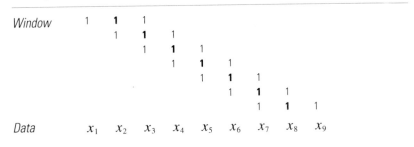

Four-point window

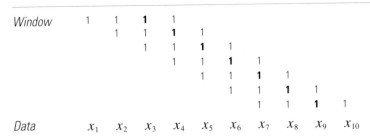

Notice that the four-point window does not have a point in the series at its center. Consequently, we replace the right point of the two in the middle with the average of the four points. This rule is followed for all even windows except two-point windows. Two-point windows can thus be used to shift asymmetrical smoothings back to the left.

If you prefer algebra, the following description shows how the three-point window smooths y into x.

$$x_1 = y_1$$

$$x_2 = \frac{y_1 + y_2 + y_3}{3}$$

$$x_3 = \frac{y_2 + y_3 + y_4}{3}$$

Notice also that the first and last points in the series are unchanged by the three-point window of moving averages. The four-point window leaves the first two and last two points unchanged.

A seven-point moving average and then a four-point moving average. Let's try a seven-point moving average on this series and smooth the resulting smoothed series with a four-point moving average. This should remove some of the jitters.

```
SERIES
    USE aircraft
    SMOOTH flutter / MEAN=7
```

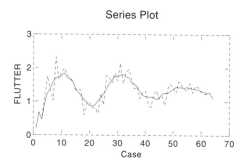

Series Plot

```
SMOOTH flutter / MEAN=4
```

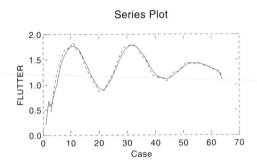

This is even smoother. We chose the lengths of the window by trial and error after looking at the data to see how much they "jitter" to the left and right of each point relative to the overall pattern of the series. You will do better if you know something about the function generating the data.

Weighted
running
smoothing

If you know something about filter design (see Bloomfield, 1976), you can construct a more general linear filter by going to **Stats**➠**Time Series**➠**Smooth** and using **Weight**. We have already done seven- and four-point moving averages with equal weights.

Our earlier smoothings used even weights of 1 for each member in the window since we did not specify otherwise. We could, however, set these weights to any real number (for example, 1, 2, 1). Some of you may recognize these as *Hanning* weights (Chambers, 1977; Velleman and Hoaglin, 1981). It is possible to show algebraically that weighting by (1, 2, 1) in a three-observation window is the same as smoothing twice with equal weights in a two-observation window. The DWLS smoothing method (available in **Graph**➠**Scatterplot**➠**Options**➠**Smoother**) is a form of weighting in which weights are determined by distance-weighted least squares.

Running
median
smoothers

Now let's look at another smoother: running medians. Sometimes it's handy to have a more robust filter when you suspect that the data do not contain Gaussian noise. You can choose this filter by going to **Stats**➠**Time Series**➠**Smooth** and selecting **Median**. It works like the **Mean** option, except that the values in the series are replaced by the median of the window instead of the mean.

Can you see why running mean and running median smoothers with a window of 2 are the same? In the next example, we use several running median smoothers and a weighted running smoother.

19.7
A 4253H
filter

We can use combinations of these smoothers to construct more complex nonlinear filters. The following sequence of smoothings comprises a nonlinear filter because it doesn't involve a simple weighted average of the values in a window (except for the final Hanning step). It uses a combination of running medians instead.

- Running median smoother, window 4
- Running median smoother, window 2
- Running median smoother, window 5
- Running median smoother, window 3
- Running means smoother, window 3, weights 1, 2, 1

```
SERIES
    USE aircraft
    SMOOTH flutter / MEDIAN=4
    SMOOTH flutter / MEDIAN=2
    SMOOTH flutter / MEDIAN=5
    SMOOTH flutter / MEDIAN=3
    SMOOTH flutter / WT=1,2,1
```

A *Quick Graph* follows each **Smooth** request. (To omit the display, type GRAPH=NONE, or use **Edit ➡ Options** and deselect **Statistical Quickgraphs**.) The display shown below follows the first request (MEDIAN=4):

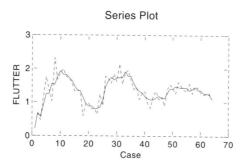

The final smooth (a running means smoother with weights) is shown below:

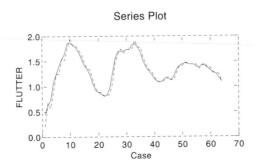

Series Plot

The previous smooth (MEDIAN=3) is marked by dashed lines. If you want a customized display of the smoother, see "Moving averages" on p. 684.

You can read about this filter (called 4253H) in Velleman and Hoaglin (1981). It is due to the work of Tukey (1977). It happens to be a generally effective compound smoother because it clears outliers out of the sequence in the early stages and polishes up the smooth later. Velleman and Hoaglin use this smoother twice on the same data by smoothing the data, smoothing the residuals from this smooth, and adding the two together. To save the smoothed values into a SYSTAT file with the last smoothing, use **Stats** ➡ **Time Series** ➡ **Smooth** and select **Save file**. You can then merge the files and compute residuals. In the final step, you can smooth the residuals.

LOWESS smoothing

Cleveland (1979) presented a method for smoothing values of Y paired with a set of ordered X values. Chambers et al. (1983) introduce this technique and present some clear examples. If you are not a statistician, and want a glimpse of some of the most exciting things professional statisticians are doing today, read the Chambers, et al., book and Velleman and Hoaglin (if you don't know about Tukey's work). Both are available in paperback.

Scatterplot smoothing enables you to look for a functional relation between Y and X without prejudging its shape (or its monotonicity). The method for finding smoothed values involves a locally weighted robust regression. SYSTAT implements Cleveland's LOWESS algorithm.

Use **Stats**➡**Time Series**➡**LOWESS** on equally spaced data values or on scatterplots of unequally spaced data values in **Graph** for smoothing in series. You can specify the **Tension** factor (called F by Cleveland). It is related to window width in running smoothers and determines the stiffness of the smooth. It varies between 0 and 1, with a default of 0.5.

Smoothing is a complex topic whose applications exceed space available here. Consult Velleman and Hoaglin (1981) or Bloomfield (1976) for more complete discussions.

**19.8
Using Tension
for more
detail**

Here is the *FLUTTER* variable smoothed by **Stats**➡**Time Series**➡ **LOWESS**. Use a **Tension** value of 0.18 to get more of the local detail.

```
SERIES
    USE aircraft
    SMOOTH flutter / LOWESS=.18
```

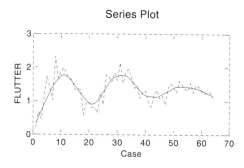

And the winner is…

The actual function used to generate the data in Example 19.6 and Example 19.7 is shown below:

$$Y(t) = 1 - e^{-0.03t} \cos(0.3t)$$

where $t = 1, 2, \ldots, 64$ (the index number of the series). We added normal (Gaussian) noise to this function in inverse proportion to the square root of t. We leave it to you engineers to design an optimal filter for the **Weight** option after looking at the noise distribution in the plot. The generating function on the data is shown below:

```
USE aircraft
BEGIN
PLOT flutter * time / HEI=1.5IN  WID=3.5IN,
              XMIN=0  XMAX=70  YMIN=0  YMAX=3,
              XLABEL='Time' YLABEL='Flutter',
              SYMB=1  SIZE=.75  FILL=1  COLOR=BLACK
FPLOT y=1-EXP(-0.03*t)*COS(.3*t) + (0.35) ; ,
              HEI=1.5IN  WID=3.5IN,
              XMIN=0  XMAX=70  YMIN=0  YMAX=3,
              XLAB=''  YLAB=''  AXES=NONE  SCALE=NONE
END
```

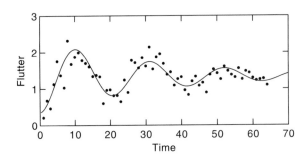

Is there a winner? The LOWESS smooth looks pretty good. Usually, for Gaussian data like these, it is hard to beat running means. Running medians and LOWESS do extremely well on non-Gaussian data, however, because they are less susceptible to outliers in the series. You will also find that exploratory smoothing requires a lot of fine tuning with window widths (tension) and weights.

Saving smoothed values

Use **Stats**⟹**Time Series** and use **Save file** on the **Smooth** or **LOWESS** dialog box to save the smoothed values in a SYSTAT file. The series is renamed *SMOOTH*.

Customizing a smooth over the data. Here, instead of SYSTAT's *Quick Graph*, we show PLOT commands for customizing your own display. We repeat the seven-point moving average and then a four-point moving average from Example 19.6, but we now save the smoothed values and merge them (side by side) with the data.

```
USE aircraft
SAVE junk
SMOOTH flutter / MEAN=7

SAVE avgseven
MERGE aircraft junk

BEGIN
PLOT flutter * time / HEI=1.5IN  WID=3.5IN,
                XMIN=0  XMAX=70  YMIN=0  YMAX=3,
                YLABEL='Flutter' XLABEL='Time',
                TITLE='Seven point moving average',
                LINE SYM=1 FILL=1
PLOT smooth * time / HEI=1.5IN  WID=3.5IN,
                XMIN=0  XMAX=70  YMIN=0  YMAX=3,
                SIZE=0  LINE  AXES=NONE  SCALE=NONE
END
```

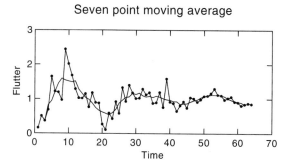

```
USE avgseven
SAVE junk
SMOOTH smooth / MEAN=4
```

```
SAVE avgfour
MERGE avgseven junk

BEGIN
PLOT flutter * t / HEI=1.5IN  WID=3.5IN,
                XMIN=0  XMAX=70  YMIN=0  YMAX=3,
                YLABEL='Flutter' XLABEL='Time',
                LINE SYM=1 FILL=1,
    TITLE='Four point smooth after 7 point smooth'
PLOT smooth * t / HEI=1.5IN  WID=3.5IN,
                XMIN=0  XMAX=70  YMIN=0  YMAX=3,
                SIZE=0  LINE  AXES=NONE  SCALE=NONE
END
```

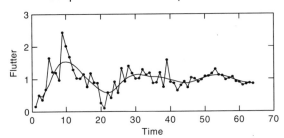

Four point smooth after 7 point smooth

Seasonal Decomposition and Adjustment

A time series can be viewed as a sum of individual components that may include a term for location (level or mean value), a trend component (long-term movements in the level of a series over time), a seasonal component, and an irregular component (the part unique to each time point). Use **Stats**➠**Time Series**➠**Transform**, and from the **Type** drop-down list use the **Mean** transformation to remove the mean (location) from a series, use **Trend** to remove a linear trend from a series, and use **Difference** to eliminate either a trend or a seasonal effect from a series. Each of these transformations changes the scale of the series but does not directly provide information about the form of the trend or the seasonal component.

Alternatively, you may want to adjust the values in a series for the seasonal component but leave the series in the same scale or unit. This enables you to interpret the value units in the same way as the original series and to compare values in the series after removing differences due to seasonality.

For example, sales data for many products are strongly seasonal. More suntan lotion is sold in the summer than in the winter. It is therefore difficult to compare suntan lotion sales from month to month without first taking seasonal differences into account.

Seasonal differences can be accounted for by determining a factor for each period of the cycle. Quarterly data may have a seasonal factor for each of the four quarters. Monthly data may have a seasonal factor for each of the 12 months.

Seasonal factors can take either of two forms: additive (fixed) or multiplicative (proportional). An additive seasonal factor is a fixed number of units above or below the general level of the series (for example, 10,000 more bottles of suntan lotion were sold in July than in the average month). In a multiplicative, or proportional, model, the seasonal factor is a percentage of the level of the series (for example, 200% more bottles of suntan lotion were sold in July than in the average month).

Additive seasonal effects are removed from a series by subtracting estimates of the appropriate seasonal factor from each point in the series. Multiplicative seasonal effects are removed by dividing each point by the appropriate seasonal factor. To computes either additive or multiplicative seasonal factors for a series and use them to adjust the original series, use **Stats**⟶**Time Series**⟶**Seasonal Adjustment**:

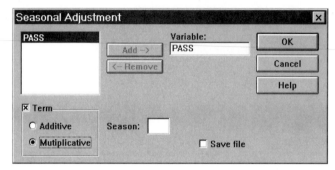

Season	Specifies periodicity. The default is 12.
Additive	Fits an additive model.
Multiplicative	Fits a multiplicative model.

19.9 Adjusting for a multiplicative seasonal factor

We use the same airline data from Box and Jenkins (1976) used in the beginning of this chapter. If you examine the plot there, you can see the strong periodicities. The size of the periodicities depends on the level of the series, so we know that the form of seasonality is multiplicative. Each year the number of passengers peaks during July and August, but there are also jagged spikes in the data that correspond, apparently, to holidays like Christmas and Easter.

Here we adjust the airline series for the multiplicative seasonal effect implied by the series plot. Use **Stats**⟶**Time Series**⟶**Seasonal Adjustment** and select the variable *PASS*. Then under **Term**, select **Multiplicative**. With commands:

```
SERIES
    USE airline
    TIME 1949 12
    ADJSEASON pass / MULTIPLICATIVE
```

```
Series originates at: 1949. Periodicity: 12. First Period: 1.
Adjust series for a seasonal periodicity of 12.
PASS copied from SYSTAT file into active work area
Seasonal indices for the series are:
      1:       91.077
      2:       88.133
      3:      100.825
      4:       97.321
      5:       98.305
      6:      111.296
      7:      122.636
      8:      121.652
      9:      105.997
     10:       92.200
     11:       80.397
     12:       90.164
Series is transformed.
```

Airline travel appears heaviest during the summer months, June (6) through September (9). The *Quick Graph* is shown below:

The plot shows that the trend and the irregular components remain, but the seasonal component has been removed from the series.

Saving deseasonalized values

Use Stats➠Time Series➠Seasonal Adjustment and select Save file to save the deseasonalized values in a SYSTAT file. For more information, see "Saving transformed series and other results" on p. 681.

Exponential Smoothing

Exponential smoothing forecasts future observations as weighted averages (a running smoother) of previous observations. For simple exponential smoothing, each forecast is the new estimate of location for the series. For models with trend and/or seasonal components, exponential smoothing smooths the location, trend, and seasonal components separately. For each component, you must specify a smoothing weight between 0 and 1. In practice, weights between 0.10 and 0.30 are most frequently used.

Stats➡**Time Series**➡**Exponential** allows you to specify a linear or percentage growth (also called exponential or multiplicative) trend or neither, and an additive or multiplicative seasonal component or neither. There is always a location component.

For exponential smoothing, use **Stats**➡**Time Series**➡**Exponential**:

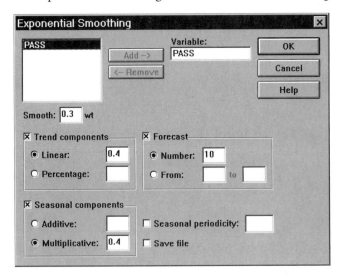

There are 9 possible models you can request by using the following:

Smooth=*n*	Smoothing weight. This weight usually varies between 0.1 and 0.3. The default is 0.2.
Linear=*n*	Linear model with weight *n*.
Percentage=*n*	Percentage growth model with weight *n*.
Additive=*n*	Additive seasonal component.
Multiplicative=*n*	Multiplicative seasonal component.

Forecast=*n*   Number or the range of new cases to predict. For example, **Forecast = 10** produces forecasts for 10 time points; **Forecast = 144 to 154** produces forecasts for time points 144 through 154.

Seasonal periodicity=*n*   Periodicity. The default is 12.

You can supply a weight for either a linear or percentage trend component. The weight is usually between 0.1 and 0.3. The default is 0.2. You can use any combination of linear and percentage options with the additive or multiplicative seasonal components options.

For either additive or multiplicative, you can supply a weight. Values usually range between 0.1 and 0.3. The default is 0.2. Be sure to specify seasonal periodicity if the periodicity of your series differs from the default values of 12.

Smoothing with a linear trend component and no seasonal component is Holt's method. Smoothing with both a linear trend and a multiplicative seasonal term is Winter's three-parameter model.

The exponential smoothing procedure obtains initial estimates of seasonal components in the same manner as **Stats⇒Time Series⇒ Seasonal Adjustment**. If there is a trend component, SYSTAT uses regression (after adjusting values for any seasonal effects) to estimate the initial values of the location and trend parameters. If there is neither a trend nor a seasonal component, the first value in the series is used as the initial estimate of location.

19.10 Modeling a linear trend and multiplicative seasonality

Earlier we looked at the *AIRLINE* data from Box and Jenkins. The plot of the series shows a strong increasing trend and what looks like multiplicative seasonality. We could try to forecast this series with a model having a linear trend and multiplicative seasonality.

Use **Stats⇒Time Series⇒Exponential** to select *PASS* and type 0.3 as the weight in the **Smooth** text box. Select **Trend components** and type 0.4 in the **Linear** text box. Select **Seasonal components** and type 0.4 in the **Multiplicative** text box. Finally, select **Forecast** and type 10 in the **Number** text box. With commands:

```
SERIES
    USE airline
    EXPONENTIAL pass / SMOOTH=.3  LINEAR=.4  MULT=.4,
                          FORECAST=10
```

The output begins with the model and initial parameter estimates:

```
Smooth location parameter with coefficient = 0.300
Linear trend with smoothing coefficient = 0.400
Multiplicative seasonality with smoothing coefficient = 0.400

Initial values

Seasonal indices for the series are:

    1:      91.077
    2:      88.133
    3:     100.825
    4:      97.321
    5:      98.305
    6:     111.296
    7:     122.636
    8:     121.652
    9:     105.997
   10:      92.200
   11:      80.397
   12:      90.164

Initial smoothed value =      88.263
Initial trend parameter =       2.645
```

The initial seasonal indices are the same as those obtained using
Stats➠**Time Series**➠**Seasonal Adjustment** and are interpreted and used
the same way. The initial smoothed value is a regression estimate of the
level of the seasonally adjusted series immediately before the first
observation in the sample. The initial trend parameter is the slope of the
regression of observations on observation number—the increase or
decrease from one observation to the next due to the overall trend. For a
percentage growth model, the trend parameter is the expected percentage
change from the previous to the current observation due to trend.

After the values are smoothed, SYSTAT prints the final estimates of the
seasonal, location, and trend parameters, plus the within-series forecast error:

```
Final values

Seasonal indices for the series are:

    1:      87.628
    2:      82.996
    3:      95.362
    4:      98.155
    5:     101.936
    6:     117.471
    7:     133.389
    8:     130.644
    9:     107.631
   10:      93.352
   11:      78.956
   12:      86.086

Final smoothed value =      497.921
Final trend parameter =       8.374
```

You can vary the smoothing coefficients and see if they reduce the standard error. First, use **Stats**➠**Time Series**➠**Clear Series** to clear the series. Then use **Stats**➠**Time Series**➠**Time**, identify *PASS* as the variable, and specify **Origin** as 1949 and **Period** as 12. Use **Stats**➠**Time Series**➠**Exponential**, type 0.2 in the **Linear** text box (under **Trend** components), 0.2 in the **Multiplicative** text box (under **Seasonal** components), and 10 in the **Number** text box (under **Forecast**). With commands:

```
CLEAR
TIME 1949 12
EXPONENTIAL / SMOOTH=.2  LINEAR=.2  MULT=.2,
             FORECAST=10
```

We get a smaller within-series forecast error. And finally, we get the out-of-series forecasts:

```
Within series MSE =      220.026, SE =      14.833

    Obs      Forecast

Jan, 1961    458.008
Feb, 1961    442.905
Mar, 1961    510.954
Apr, 1961    509.745
May, 1961    520.853
Jun, 1961    595.666
Jul, 1961    668.936
Aug, 1961    662.247
Sep, 1961    563.597
Oct, 1961    495.771
```

Following is a *Quick Graph* of the forecasts:

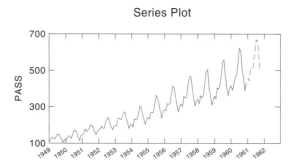

Series Plot

In-series forecasts

Sometimes it's best to develop a model on a portion of a series and see how well it predicts the remainder. There are 12 years of airline data for a total of 144 monthly observations. The following commands develop the smoothing model with the first 10 years of data (120 observations) and predict the final 2 years (observations 121–144):

```
CLEAR
EXPONENTIAL / SMOOTH=.3 LINEAR=.4  MULT=.4,
                 FORECAST=121 .. 144
```

Output from this procedure includes the following forecasts:

```
Within series MSE =      292.090, SE =      17.091

     Obs      Forecast

   Feb, 1959   354.228
   Mar, 1959   423.781
   Apr, 1959   426.328
   May, 1959   447.235
   Jun, 1959   530.144
   Jul, 1959   588.677
   Aug, 1959   580.174
   Sep, 1959   484.919
   Oct, 1959   420.917
   Nov, 1959   365.250
   Dec, 1959   407.409
   Jan, 1960   427.066
   Feb, 1960   418.752
   Mar, 1960   499.821
   Apr, 1960   501.697
   May, 1960   525.153
   Jun, 1960   621.184
   Jul, 1960   688.343
   Aug, 1960   677.034
   Sep, 1960   564.765
   Oct, 1960   489.287
   Nov, 1960   423.786
   Dec, 1960   471.840

   Forecast MSE =     1904.887 SE =       43.645
```

Note that the within-series standard error is not the same as in the previous run because it's now based on only the first 120 observations. The error for the actual forecasts (65.891) is much larger than that for the in-series forecasts (17.091).

For a thorough review of issues and developments in exponential smoothing models, see Gardner (1985). For an introduction to these models, see any introductory forecasting book, such as Makridakis, Wheelwright, and McGee (1983).

Saving forecasts

Use Stats⇒Time Series⇒Exponential and use Save file to save forecasts in a SYSTAT file. Both the forecasts and the residuals are saved. For more information, see "Saving transformed series and other results" on p. 681.

Box-Jenkins ARIMA Models

SYSTAT provides ARIMA (Auto Regressive Integrated Moving Average) models for time series. In Example 19.1, we display the *AIRLINE* data from Box and Jenkins. In this display, the cycles do not seem to be smooth functions of sine and cosine waves like the *NEWARK* temperature data in Example 19.1. Instead, there are jagged spikes in the data that correspond, apparently, to holidays such as Christmas and Easter.

The first thing to consider in modeling the *AIRLINE* passenger data is the increasing variance in the series over time. We logged the data and found that the variance stabilized. An upward trend remained, however, so we differenced the series. We now identify which ARIMA parameters we want to estimate by plotting the data in several ways. The parameters of the ARIMA model are:

	Name	*Description*
AR	**autoregressive**	Each point is a weighted function of a previous point plus random error.
I	**difference**	Each point's value is a constant difference from a previous point's value.
MA	**moving average**	Each point is a weighted function of a previous point's random error plus its own random error.

For seasonal ARIMA models, we need three additional parameters: Seasonal AR, Seasonal I, and Seasonal MA. Their definitions are the same as above, except that they apply to points that are not adjacent in a series. The *AIRLINE* data involve seasonal parameters, for example, because dependencies extend across years as well as months. In Example 19.12, we describe how to specify these parameters. First, we review some useful graphical displays.

19.11 Checking ACF and PACF displays

Let's start with the differencing parameter. There appears to be at least some differencing needed because the series drifts across time (overall level of passengers increases). ACF and PACF plots give us more detailed information on this. The first ACF and PACF plots from Example 19.12 and Example 19.13 are shown below; here we limit these lags to 15.

Autocorrelation Plot

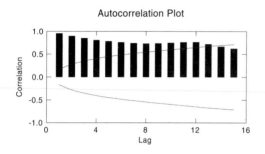

Partial Autocorrelation Plot

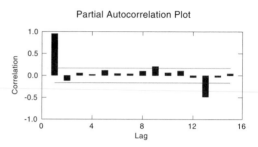

Notice that the autocorrelations are substantial and well outside two standard errors on the plot. There are two bulges in the ACF plot at Lag=1 and Lag=12, suggesting the nonseasonal (monthly) and seasonal (yearly) dependencies that we supposed. The PACF plot shows the same dependencies more distinctly. Here are the autocorrelations and partial autocorrelations of the differenced series from Example 19.5.

Autocorrelation Plot

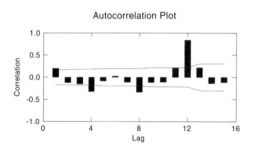

Partial Autocorrelation Plot

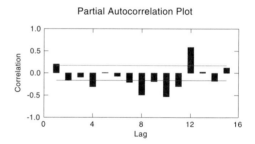

Now we have only 143 points in the series because the first point had no prior value to remove. It was therefore set to missing. The two plots show that the differencing has substantially removed the monthly changes in trend. We still have the seasonal (yearly) trend, however. Therefore, difference again and then replot. The autocorrelations and partial autocorrelations after differencing by order 12 are shown below. With commands:

```
DIFFERENCE / LAG=12
ACF / LAG=15
PACF / LAG=15
```

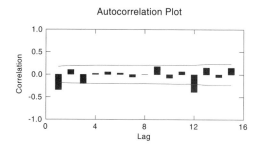

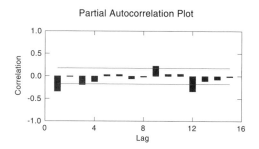

Most of the dependency seems to have been removed. Although there are some autocorrelations and partial autocorrelations outside two standard errors, we will not difference again. We will fit a model first because over-differencing can mask the effects of MA parameters. In fact, the pattern in this last plot suggests one regular and one seasonal MA parameter because there are ACF spikes (instead of bulges) at lags 1 and 13, and the PACF shows decay at lags 1 and 13. Consult the references previously cited for more information on how to read these plots for identification.

19.12
Fitting the
model

In SYSTAT, we use (P, Q) and (PS, QS) model notation for local and seasonal AR and MA orders respectively. For Auto Regressive Integrated Moving Average models, use **Stats**➧**Time Series**➧**ARIMA**.

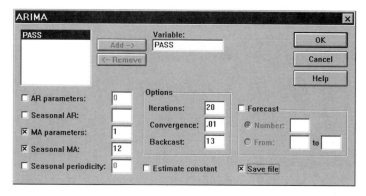

AR parameters=n	Number of AR parameters (P). The default is 0.
Seasonal AR=n	Number of seasonal AR parameters (PS).
MA parameters=n	Number of MA parameters (Q). The default is 0.
Seasonal MA=n	Number of seasonal MA parameters (QS).

Seasonal periodicity=*n*   Define the seasonal periodicity.
Estimate constant=*n*   Include a constant in the model.

With commands:

```
ARIMA var / P=n  Q=n  PS=n  QS=n  SEASON=n  CONSTANT
```

If you specify more than one AR (P) or MA (Q) parameter, SYSTAT automatically includes all parameters up to that order. For seasonal models, the default periodicity is 12. This periodicity applies to all seasonal AR and MA parameters. You can estimate a constant in your model by selecting **Estimate constant**. If you have differenced your data, this is usually unnecessary.

Here (continuing from Example 19.11) we fit a seasonal multiplicative ARIMA model with no autoregressive parameter, one difference parameter, one moving average parameter, no seasonal autoregressive parameter, one seasonal difference parameter, and one seasonal moving average parameter. Recall that we have already logged each value and differenced the series twice. Therefore, both difference parameters are done.

Note: *For each transformation or differencing operation, the results are written over the old ones in the **Time Series** active work area. The original file on disk is not altered, however.*

Now, use **Stats**➧**Time Series**➧**ARIMA** and identify *PASS* as the Variable. Type 1 in the **MA parameters** text box, 1 in the **Seasonal MA** text box, 12 in the **Seasonal periodicity** text box, and 13 in the **Backcast** text box. Next select **Save file**. After clicking **OK**, type a filename. With commands:

continue from Example 19.11
```
SAVE resid
ARIMA / Q=1  QS=1  SEASON=12  BACKCAST=13
```

Seasonal periodicity tells SYSTAT that the seasonal parameters have a period of 12 months. The **Backcast** option helps us compute a better estimate of the MA parameters. You can read more about it in the references, but it extends the series backwards (forecasting in reverse) to approximate a continuous function better. Although it slows down computation, you should use backcasting for seasonal models especially

and choose a length greater than the seasonal period. We didn't select
Estimate constant because the mean of the differenced logged series was
near 0. This is often true for differenced series.

```
Iteration   Sum of Squares   Parameter values
    0           .2392764D+00     .100   .100
    1           .1835532D+00     .345   .433
    2           .1764962D+00     .449   .633
    3           .1759952D+00     .416   .592
    4           .1758742D+00     .409   .613
    5         - .1758463D+00     .392   .614
    6           .1758443D+00     .396   .613
    7           .1758443D+00     .396   .613
    8           .1758443D+00     .396   .613
    9           .1758443D+00     .396   .613

Final value of MSE is        0.001

Index   Type    Estimate      A.S.E.       Lower  <95%> Upper
  1      MA       0.396        0.093        0.212        0.579
  2      SMA      0.613        0.074        0.467        0.760

Asymptotic correlation matrix of parameters

                              1              2

            1           1.000
            2          -0.171          1.000
```

With the **Save file** option, the residuals are saved in a SYSTAT file. The
original series is not altered. This means that you can check the adequacy
of the model (the third diagnosis stage of ARIMA modeling) by using the
various facilities of the **Stats** menu. You can also do normal probability
plots, stem-and-leaf plots, Kolmogorov-Smirnov tests, and other
statistical tests on residuals.

Let's focus on the question of serial dependence among the residuals.
First, open the file *RESID*. Next, use **Stats**➧**Time Series**➧**ACF** and select
RESIDUAL as the variable and type 15 in the **Lag** text box. With commands:

```
USE resid
  ACF / LAG=15
```

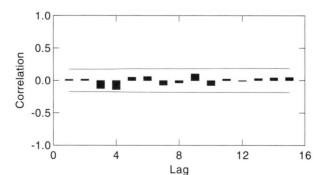

Autocorrelation Plot

Computational controls

To control the computation, use **Stats**➡**Time Series**➡**ARIMA** and use these items:

Iterations=*n*   Maximum number of iterations allowed to fit your model. Default is 20.

Convergence=*n* A number (*n*) that specifies how close the fitted values must be to the data values for the iterations to stop. The default is 0.01.

With commands, specify ITER=*n* and TOL=*n* as ARIMA command options.

Don't play around with convergence unless you are failing to get convergence of the estimates after many iterations. It is better to increase the number of iterations than to decrease the convergence criterion, since your estimates will be more precise. In any case, it cannot be set greater than a tenth. Sometimes models fail to converge after many iterations because you have misspecified them.

19.13 Forecasts

To forecast future values in a series (or for diagnosing the model, forecast values in the series itself) use **Stats**➡**Time Series**➡**ARIMA** and use the **Forecast** option.

Forecast   The number of new cases or the range of new cases to predict. For example, **Number = 10** produces forecasts for ten time points; **From = 144 to 154** produces forecasts for time points 144 through 154.

These features are options for the ARIMA command:

```
BACKCAST=n   FORECAST=n or FORECAST=n1 .. n2
```

You can backcast (forecast backwards—that is, estimate what "previous" cases were). Just specify the number of cases you want backcasted in the **Backcast** text box. This often improves MA and seasonal MA estimates. Choose a number for backcasting that is at least 10 or greater than your seasonal period.

We could have added forecasting by specifying 10 cases to be forecast:

continue from Example 19.12
```
ARIMA / Q=1  QS=1  SEASON=12  BACKCAST=13,
        FORECAST=10
```

SYSTAT forecasts the future values of the series:

```
                 Forecast values

Periods          Lower95      Forecast      Upper95

1961.01          418.862      450.296       484.090
1961.02          391.976      426.557       464.189
1961.03          438.329      482.099       530.240
1961.04          443.296      492.246       546.602
1961.05          453.832      508.378       569.480
1961.06          516.623      583.439       658.898
1961.07          587.307      668.338       760.549
1961.08          581.136      666.091       763.464
1961.09          484.248      558.844       644.931
1961.10          427.648      496.754       577.028
```

Series Plot

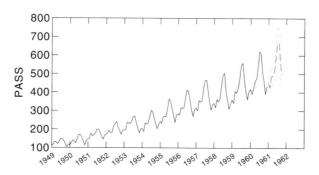

The "forecast origin" in this case is taken as the last point in the series. From there, the model computes and prints 10 new points with their upper and lower 95% asymptotic confidence intervals. SYSTAT automatically plots the forecasts.

Incidentally, the SYSTAT decision to put RESIDUAL in your active work area automatically after ARIMA was based on the need to always plot residuals after an analysis. Since plotting forecasts can wait until after you have correctly identified a model, the active work area was left free for further modeling steps.

You can also save the forecasts by going to **Stats**➡**Time Series**➡ **Exponential** and selecting **Save file**; then make your own customized plot with **Scatterplot** on the **Graph** menu. A plot of the original series is shown below.

```
SERIES
  USE airline
  LOG pass
  DIFFERENCE
  DIFFERENCE / LAG=12
  SAVE timefore
  ARIMA /Q=1 QS=1 SEASON=12 BACKCAST=13 FORECAST=10
  MERGE airline timefore
  LET year = 1949 + (CASE-1)/12
  SAVE airline2
  RUN

  BEGIN
  PLOT pass * year / XMIN=1948  XMAX=1963   YMIN=0,
                     YMAX=800  LINE  DASH=1  SIZE=0,
                     HEI=2IN  WID=4IN   INDENT,
                     YLAB='Passengers'  XTICK=5
  PLOT forecast * year / XMIN=1948  XMAX=1963  YMIN=0,
                     YMAX=800  LINE   DASH=11,
                     SIZE=0  HEI=2IN  WID=4IN,
                     INDENT  XLAB=' '  YLAB=' ',
                     SCALE=NONE  AXES=NONE

  END
```

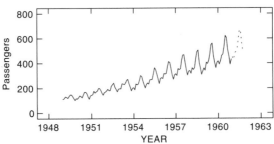

Saving forecasts

The forecasts and residuals are saved with the variable names *FORECAST* and *RESIDUAL*.

Fourier Analysis

The Fourier model decomposes a time series into a finite sum of trigonometric components—sine and cosine waves of different frequencies. If your data are cyclical at a particular frequency, such as monthly, then a few Fourier components might capture most of the nonrandom variation. See the discussion on Fourier analysis in "More about Time Series" on p. 713.

To decompose a time series into a finite sum of trigonometric components, use **Stats**➠**Time Series**➠**Fourier**:

Identify your variables. Optionally, you can type a number in the **Lag** text box. To save the real and imaginary components in a SYSTAT file, select **Save file**. With commands:

```
FOURIER var          or
FOURIER var1 var2
```

If you select two variables, SYSTAT assumes that you want the inverse transformation. The first variable selected is used as the real component and the second variable is used as the imaginary component.

Warning. The Fourier transform is an "in place" transformation. The magnitude of the transformation is written over the active work area where you stored the variable that you transformed. You can plot this magnitude with **Stats**➠**Time Series**➠**T-plot** or even smooth it. If you want to save the results of the transformation, select **Save file**.

Saving Fourier components

SYSTAT saves the real and imaginary components in a SYSTAT file. You can then manipulate these components. Real and imaginary components are saved instead of magnitude and phase because that allows you to do an inverse Fourier transform.

Inverse Fourier

Here is how to do an inverse transformation. Assume that you have saved the results of a direct transformation into a file *MYFOUR*. That file should contain two variables—*REAL* and *IMAG*—which are the two components of the transformation.

```
USE myfour
FOURIER real imag
```

Since you specify two variables, SYSTAT assumes that you want the inverse transformation, and that the first variable is the real component, and the second, the imaginary component. The work is done in the active work area, so the resulting real series is stored in the active work area occupied by *REAL* (or whatever you called the first variable corresponding to the real component).

Saving magnitude and phase

If you absolutely must have magnitude and phase in a SYSTAT file instead of the real and imaginary components, do the following transformations:

```
USE myfour
LET magnitude = SQR(real*real + imag*imag)
LET phase = ATN (imag/real)
```

19.14 Modeling temperature

Let's look at a typical Fourier application. The data in the *NEWARK* file are 64 average monthly temperatures in Newark, New Jersey, beginning in January, 1964. The data are from the U.S. government, cited in Chambers et al. (1983). Notice that their fluctuations look something like a sine wave, so we might expect that they could be modeled adequately by the sum of a relatively small number of trigonometric components. We have taken exactly 64 measurements to fulfill the **powers of** 2 rule.

```
SERIES
    USE newark
    TIME 1964,12
    TPLOT temp
```

Series Plot

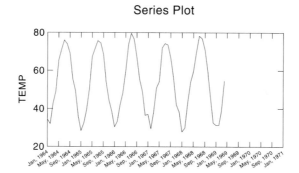

We remove the series mean and then do the decomposition:

```
MEAN temp
FOURIER temp / LAG=15
```

```
Fourier Components of     TEMP

Index Frequency      Real    Imaginary   Magnitude       Phase Periodogram

   1 0.00000        0.000      0.000       0.000         0.000      0.000
   2 0.01563       -0.763     -0.363       0.845        -2.697     11.416
   3 0.03125       -0.803     -0.177       0.822        -2.924     10.807
   4 0.04688       -1.587     -0.779       1.768        -2.685     50.016
   5 0.06250       -1.658     -1.817       2.460        -2.310     96.810
   6 0.07813       -6.248     -7.214       9.544        -2.285   1457.410
   7 0.09375        2.606      3.633       4.471         0.948    319.813
   8 0.10938        1.040      1.786       2.067         1.044     68.359
   9 0.12500        0.592      0.936       1.107         1.007     19.618
  10 0.14063        0.438      0.588       0.733         0.930      8.604
  11 0.15625       -0.127      1.135       1.142         1.682     20.859
  12 0.17188        0.067      0.715       0.718         1.477      8.252
  13 0.18750       -0.255      0.785       0.825         1.885     10.885
  14 0.20313        0.140      0.132       0.192         0.756      0.588
  15 0.21875       -0.071      0.291       0.299         1.811      1.432
```

We can get the original temperatures back by opening the file again or using **Stats**➠**Time Series**➠**Clear Series**. The *Quick Graph* now displays a **periodogram**—that is, the squared magnitude against frequencies.

Periodogram

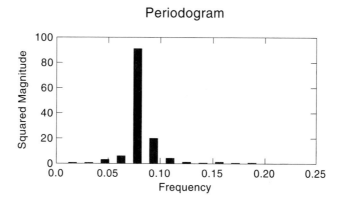

Notice that our hunch was largely correct. There is one primary peak at a relatively low frequency. This periodogram differs from that produced in earlier versions of SYSTAT. SYSTAT now uses

$N/$pi*squared magnitude

where N is the number of cases in the file.

Two final points follow. First, some analysts prefer to plot the logs of these values against frequency. We could do this in the following way:

```
SQUARE temp
LOG temp
TPLOT temp
```

Logging, by the way, looks noisier than the plot above but can reveal significant spikes that might be hidden in the raw periodogram.

The second point involves smoothing the periodogram. Often it is best to taper the series first before computing the periodogram. This makes the spikes more pronounced in the log-periodogram plot:

```
MEAN temp
TAPER temp
FOURIER temp
SQUARE temp
LOG temp
TPLOT temp
```

Since we didn't specify a value, Split-cosine-bell used its default, 0.5.

More about Time Series

Time series analysis can range from the purely exploratory to the confirmatory testing of formal models. A series encompasses both exploratory and confirmatory methods. Exploratory methods include smoothing and plotting. Among confirmatory models are two general approaches: time domain and frequency domain. In time domain models, we examine the behavior of variables over time directly. In frequency domain models, we examine frequency (periodic) components contributing to a time series.

Time domain (autoregressive, moving average, and trend) models represent a series as a function of previous points in the same series or as a systematic trend over time. Time domain models can fit complex patterns of time series with just a few parameters. Makridakis, Wheelwright, and McGee (1983), McCleary and Hay (1980), and Nelson (1973) introduce these models, while Box and Jenkins (1976) provide the primary reference for ARIMA models.

Frequency domain (spectral) models decompose a series into a sum of sinusoidal (wave form) elements. These models are particularly useful when a series arises from a relatively small set of cyclical functions. Bloomfield (1976) introduces these models.

In this section, we will discuss exploratory methods (smoothing), time domain models (ARIMA, seasonal decomposition, exponential smoothing), and frequency domain (Fourier) models.

Note: Note that some of the plots in this section are high-resolution plots produced using **Scatterplot** from the **Graph** menu.

ARIMA modeling and forecasting

The following data, in the *BIRTH* data file, show the United States birth rate (per 1000) for several decades during and following World War II. They were compiled from federal statistics, principally the U.S. census.

YEAR	RATE		YEAR	RATE
1943	22.7		1965	19.4
1944	21.2		1966	18.4
1945	20.4		1967	17.8
1946	24.1		1968	17.5
1947	26.6		1969	17.8
1948	24.9		1970	18.4
1949	24.5		1971	17.2
1950	24.1		1972	15.6
1951	24.9		1973	14.9
1952	25.1		1974	14.9
1953	25.1		1975	14.8
1954	25.3		1976	14.8
1955	25.0		1977	15.4
1956	25.2		1978	15.3
1957	25.3		1979	15.9
1958	24.5		1980	15.9
1959	24.3		1981	15.9
1960	23.7		1982	15.9
1961	23.3		1983	15.5
1962	22.4		1984	15.7
1963	21.7		1985	15.7
1964	21.0			

These data are a **time series** because they consist of values on a variable distributed across time. How can I use these data to forecast birth rates up to the year 2000? A popular statistical method for such a forecast is linear regression. Let's try it. The following chart plots birth rates against year with the least-squares line. The data points are connected so that you can see the series more clearly.

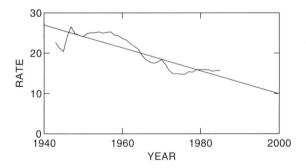

What's wrong with this forecasting method? You may want to read Chapter 8 if you haven't already done so. There, we discussed assumptions needed for estimating a model using least squares. We can legitimately fit a line to these data by least squares for the explicit purpose of getting predicted values on the line as close as possible, on average, to observed values in the data. In forecasting, however, we want to use a fitted model to extrapolate beyond the series. The fitted linear model is:

$$\text{RATE} = 579.342 - 0.285 \times \text{YEAR}$$

If we want our estimates of the slope and intercept in this model to be unbiased, we need to assume that the errors (e) in the population model are independent of each other and of *YEAR*. Does our data plot give us any indication of this?

On the contrary, it appears from the data that the randomness in this model is related to *YEAR*. Take any two adjacent years' data. On average, if there is an underprediction one year, there will be an underprediction the next. If there is overprediction one year, there is likely to be overprediction the next. These data clearly violate the assumption of independence in the errors.

Autocorrelation

There is a statistical index that reveals how correlated the residuals are. It is called the autocorrelation. The first-order autocorrelation is the ordinary Pearson correlation of a series of numbers with the same series shifted by one observation ($y_2, y_1; y_3, y_2; \ldots; y_n, y_{n-1}$). In our residuals from the linear model, this statistic is 0.953. If you remember about squaring correlation coefficients to reveal the proportion of variance, this means that over 89% of the variation in error from predicting one year's birth rate can be accounted for by the error in predicting the previous year's birth rate.

The second-order autocorrelation is produced by correlating the series ($y_3, y_1; y_4, y_2; \ldots; y_n, y_{n-2}$). Computing this statistic involves shifting the series down two years. As you may now infer, we can keep shifting and computing autocorrelations for as many years as there are in the series. There is a simple graphical way to display all of these autocorrelations. It looks like a bar graph of the autocorrelations sequenced by year, or index, in the series. The top bar is the first autocorrelation (0.953). The next highest bar is the second autocorrelation, and so on:

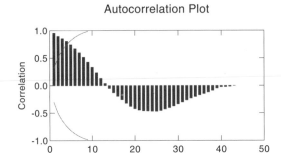

Autocorrelation Plot

This autocorrelation plot tells us about all the autocorrelations in the residuals from the linear model. As you can see, there is a strong dependence in the residuals. As we shift the series far enough back, the autocorrelations become negative, because the series crosses the prediction line and the residuals become negative. Over the entire series, there are three crossings and three corresponding shifts in sign among the autocorrelations.

Autoregressive models

We would have the same serial correlation problem if we refined our model to include a quadratic term:

$$\text{RATE} = \beta_0 + \beta_1 \text{ YEAR} + \beta_2 \text{ YEAR}^2 + \varepsilon$$

You can try this model with **Stats➠Linear Regression**, but you will find a large autocorrelation in the residuals even though the curve fits the data more closely. How can we construct a model that includes the autocorrelation structure itself?

The autoregressive model does this:

$$\text{RATE} = \beta_0 + \beta_1 \text{ RATE}i_{-1} + \varepsilon$$

Notice that this model expresses a year's birth rate as a function of the previous year's birth rate—not as a function of *YEAR*. Time becomes a sequencing variable, not a predictor.

To fit this, we fit an *AR(1)* model with the ARIMA procedure. Here is the result, with forecasts extending to the year 2000:

Series Plot

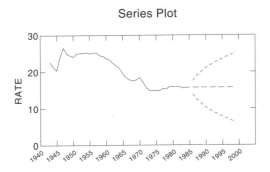

The forecasted values are represented by the dotted line. Unlike the regression model forecast, the autoregressive forecast begins at the last birth rate value and may drift back toward the mean of the series. This forecast behavior is typical of this particular model, which is often called a **random walk**.

Moving average models

There is another series model that can account for fluctuations across time. The **moving average model** looks like this:

$$y_i = \varepsilon_i - \beta_1 \varepsilon_{i-1}$$

This models a series as a cumulation of random shocks or disturbances. If this model represented someone's spending habits, for example, then whether the person went on a spending spree one day would depend on whether he or she went on one the day before. Unlike the autoregressive model, which represents an observation as a function of previous observations' *values*, the moving average model represents an observation as a function of the previous observations' *errors*. So that you can see the difference between the two, the following are examples of first-order autoregressive, or AR(1), and moving average, or MA(1), series:

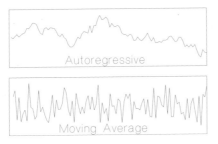

ARMA models

Autoregressive and moving average models can be mixed to make autoregressive moving average models. They can be mixed with different orders; an example is *AR(2)* plus *MA(1)*, which is often expressed as *ARMA(2,1)*. You will have to refer to a text on forecasting to see instances of these more complicated models. You could visually add the two sample series above, however, to see how an *ARMA(1,1)* model would look.

Identifying models

Before you can fit an *AR*, *MA*, or *ARMA* model, you need to identify which model is appropriate for your series. You can look at the series plot to find distinctive patterns, as in the figure contrasting *AR(1)* and *MA(1)* directly above. Real data seldom fit these ideal types as clearly, however. There are several powerful tools that distinguish these families of models. We have already seen one: the autocorrelation function plot (ACF). The partial autocorrelation function plot (PACF) provides additional information about serial correlation. To identify models, we use both of these plots.

Stationarity. Before doing these plots, however, you should be sure the series is stationary. This means:

— **The mean of the series is constant across time.** You can use the Trend transformation to remove linear trend from the series. This will not reduce quadratic or other curvilinear trend, however. A better method is to **Difference** the data. Use **Stats**➡**Time Series**➡**Transform** and choose **Difference** from the **Type** drop-down list. This transformation replaces values by the differences between each value and the previous value, thereby removing trend. For cyclical series, like monthly sales, seasonal differencing may be required before fitting a model (see below). Data that are drifting up or down across the series generally should be differenced.

— **The variance of the series is constant across time.** If the series variation is increasing around its mean level across time, try a **Log** transformation. If it is decreasing around its mean level across time (a rare occurrence), try a **Square** transformation. You should generally do this before differencing.

— **The autocorrelations of the series depend only on difference in time points and not on the time period itself.** If the first half of the ACF looks different from the second, try seasonal differencing after identifying a period on which the data are fluctuating. Monthly, quarterly, seasonal, and annual data often cycle this way.

ACF plots. The autocorrelation function plot displays the pattern of autocorrelations. We have seen in this section an ACF plot of the residuals from a linear fit to birth rate. The slow decay of the autocorrelations after the first indicates autoregressive behavior in the residuals.

PACF plots. The partial autocorrelation function plot displays autocorrelations, but each one below the first is conditioned on the previous autocorrelation. The PACF plot shows the relationship of points in a series to preceding points after partialing out the influence of intervening points. We examine them for effects that do not depend linearly on previous (smaller lag) autocorrelations.

Identification using ACF and PACF plots together. Let's summarize our identification strategy. First, make sure the series is stationary. If variance is nonconstant, transform it with log or square. Use **Stats▸Time Series▸Transform** and choose **Log** or **Square** from the **Type** drop-down list. If trend is present, remove it with differencing. Finally, if seasonality is present, remove it with seasonal differencing. Then examine ACF and PACF plots together. Below is a chart of possible types of patterns. Underneath each series is the ACF plot on the left and the PACF plot on the right. Several rows contain more than one possible plot. This is because coefficients in the model can be negative or positive and these plots show different combinations of signs.

Finally, remember that differencing can remove both trend and autoregressive effects. If an *AR(1)* model fits your data, as with our birth rate example, then differencing will produce only white noise and your ACF will look uniformly random. As a result, differencing is like constraining an autoregressive parameter to be exactly one.

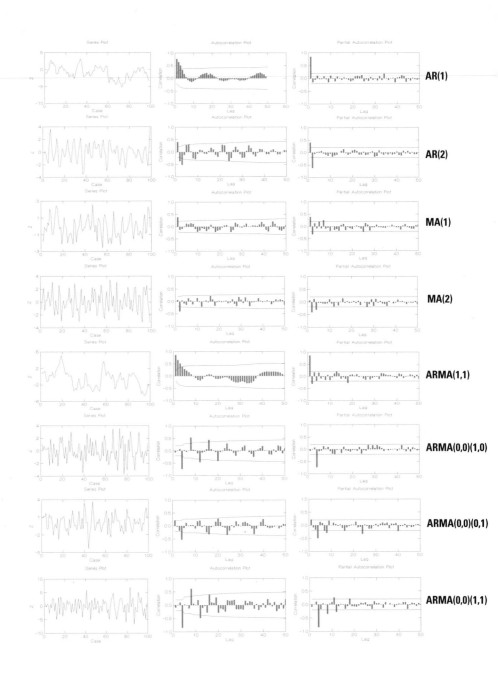

Estimating the ARIMA model

When you have identified the model as AR, MA, or a mixture, then you can fit it by specifying the AR order (P=n) and the MA order (Q=n). The "I" in ARIMA stands for "Integrated" and is a parameter that has to do with differencing. Any differencing you do while identifying the model will be included automatically in calculating your forecasts.

When you have estimated the model, pay attention to the standard errors of the parameters. If a parameter estimate is much smaller in absolute value than two standard errors away from 0, then it is probably unnecessary in the model. Refit the model without it. If you are uncertain about model identification, you can sometimes use this rule of thumb to compare two different models. The mean square error (*MSE*) of the model fit can also guide you. Generally, you are looking for a parsimonious model with small *MSE*.

Problems with forecast models

Forecasting is a vast field, and we cannot begin to explain even the basics in such a brief discussion. Makridakis, Wheelwright and McGee (1983) cover the topic fairly extensively. SYSTAT offers several methods for forecasting that you can use on these data. Exponential smoothing, for example, should provide similar forecasts to the ARIMA model. Keep in mind the following:

- **There is nothing like extrinsic knowledge.** We use forecasting methods at SYSTAT for budget planning. We always compare them to staff predictions of sales, however. In general, averaging staff predictions does better than the data-driven forecasting models. The reason is simple: staff know about external factors that are likely to affect sales. These are one-time events that are not easily included in models. Although we are not experts on the stock market, we would bet the same is true for investing. "Chartist" models that are based solely on the trends in stocks will not do as well, on average, as strategies based on knowledge of companies' economic performance and, in the illegal extreme, inside trading information.

- **Always examine your residuals.** The same reasons for using residual diagnostics in ordinary linear regression apply to nonlinear forecasting models. In both cases, you want to see independence, or *white noise*.

- **Don't extrapolate too far.** As in regression, predictions beyond the data are shaky. The farther you stray from the ends of the data, the less reliable are the predictions. The confidence limits on the forecasts will give you some flavor of this.

Box and Jenkins (1976) provide the primary reference for these procedures. Financial forecasters should consult Nelson (1973) and Vandaele (1983) for applied introductions. Social scientists should look at McCleary and Hay (1980) for applications to behavioral data.

Many treatments (including Box and Jenkins) outline the ARIMA modeling process in three stages: Identification, Estimation, and Diagnosis. This is the outline we have followed in this introduction. To identify models with SYSTAT, use **Stats➠Time Series** and use **Transform, T-plot, ACF,** and **PACF,** estimate them with **ARIMA,** and diagnose their adequacy with more plots. For more complex problems, you may have to use other procedures, also.

ARIMA—Auto Regressive Integrated Moving Average—models can fit many time series with remarkably few parameters. Sometimes, ARIMA and Fourier models can be used effectively on the same data. As with other modeling procedures, decisions about appropriateness of competing models must rest on theoretical grounds. Nevertheless, a researcher should lean toward ARIMA models when it is reasonable to assume that points in a process are primarily functions of previous points and their errors, rather than periodic signal plus noise.

Fourier analysis

If you believe your series is cyclical—such as astronomical or behavioral data—then you should consider Fourier analysis. The Fourier model decomposes a series into a finite sum of trigonometric components—sine and cosine waves of different frequencies. If your data are cyclical at a particular frequency, such as monthly, then a few Fourier components might be sufficient to capture most of the nonrandom variation.

Fourier analysis decomposes a time series just as a musical wave form can be decomposed into a fundamental wave plus harmonics. The French mathematician Fourier devised this decomposition around the beginning of the nineteenth century and applied it to heat transfer and other physical and mathematical problems. This transformation is of the general form:

$$f(t) = x_1 + x_2 sin(t) + x_3 cos(t) + x_4 sin(2t) + x_5 cos(2t) + \dots$$

The Fourier decomposition can be useful for designing a filter to smooth noise and for analyzing the spectral composition of a time series. The most frequent application involves constructing a periodogram which displays the squared amplitude (magnitude) of the trigonometric components versus their frequencies. Use **Stats**➠**Time Series**➠**Fourier** to construct these displays. For further details on Fourier analysis, consult Brigham (1974) or Bloomfield (1976).

Fourier transforms are time consuming to compute because they involve numerous trigonometric functions. Cooley and Tukey (1965) developed a fast algorithm for computing the transform on a discrete series that makes the spectral analysis of lengthy series practical. A variant of this Fast Fourier Transform algorithm is implemented in SYSTAT.

The discrete Fourier transform should be done on series with lengths (number of cases) that are powers of 2. If you do not have samples of 32, 64, 128, 256, and so on, you should pad your series with zeros up to the next power of 2. If you have a series called Series with only 102 cases, for example, you can use IF...THEN LET to add zeros to cases 103 through 128. If you do not pad the file in this way, the Fourier procedure finds the highest power of 2 less than the number of cases in the file and transforms only that number of cases. (In this example, it would have transformed only the first 64 cases.)

A useful graph to accompany Fourier analysis is the periodogram. This graph plots magnitude (or squared magnitude) against frequency. It reveals the relative contribution of different frequency wave forms to the overall shape of the series. If the periodogram contains one large spike, as in Example 19.14, then it means that the series can be fit well by a single sinusoidal wave form. The periodogram is itself like a series, so sometimes you may want to smooth it with one of the Series smoothers.

Fourier analysis is often used to construct a *filter*, which works like running smoothers. A filter allows variation of only a limited band of frequencies to pass through. A low-pass filter, for example, removes high frequency information. It is often used to remove noise in radio transmissions, recordings, and photographs. A high-pass filter, on the other hand, removes low frequency variation. It is used as one method for detecting edges in photographs. You can construct filters in SYSTAT by computing the Fourier transform, deleting real and imaginary components for low or high frequencies, and then using the inverse transform to produce a smoothed wave form.

Take a look at the monthly temperature data Example 19.14 to see how Fourier analysis identifies frequency components. If you reproduce a series from a few low frequency Fourier components, the resulting smooth will be similar to that achieved by a running window of an appropriate width. The Fourier method will constrain the smooth to be more regularly periodic, however, since the selected trigonometric components will completely determine the periodicity of the smooth.

Summary

Computation

The LOWESS algorithm for XY and scatterplot smoothing is documented in Cleveland (1979) and Cleveland (1981). All the smoothers are computed in single precision.

The Fast Fourier Transform is due to Gentleman and Sande (1966), and documented further in Bloomfield (1976). The Fourier routines are in single precision.

ARIMA models are estimated with a set of algorithms. Residuals and unconditional sums of squares for the seasonal multiplicative model are calculated by an algorithm in McLeod and Sales (1983). The sums of squares are minimized iteratively by a quasi-Newton method due to Fletcher (1972). A penalty function for inadmissible values of the parameters makes this procedure relatively robust when values are near the circumference of the unit circle. Standard errors for the parameter estimates are computed from the inverse of the numeric estimate of the Hessian matrix, following Fisher (1922). Forecasting is performed via the difference equations documented in Chapter 5 of Box and Jenkins (1976). Estimation is performed in double precision and forecasting is done in single precision.

References

Bloomfield, P. 1976. *Fourier analysis of time series: An introduction*. New York: John Wiley & Sons, Inc.

Box, G.E.P., and Jenkins, G.M. 1976. *Time series analysis: Forecasting and control*. Revised edition. Oakland, Calif.: Holden-Day, Inc.

Brigham, E.O. 1974. *The fast Fourier transform*. New York: Prentice-Hall.

Chambers, J.M., Cleveland, W.S., Kleiner, B., and Tukey, P. 1983. *Graphical methods for data analysis*. Belmont, Calif.: Wadsworth International Group.

Chatterjee and Price. 1977. *Regression analysis by example*. New York: John Wiley & Sons, Inc.

Cleveland, W.S. 1979. Robust locally weight regression and smoothing scatterplots. *Journal of the American Statistical Association,* 74: 829–836.

Cooley, J.W., and Tukey, J.W. 1965. An algorithm for the machine computation of complex Fourier series. *Mathematical Computation,* 19: 297–301.

Gardner, E.S. 1985. Exponential smoothing:the state of the art. *Journal of Forecasting,* 4: 1–28.

Makridakis, W., Wheelwright, S.C. and McGee, U.E. 1983. *Forecasting: Methods and applications.* 2nd ed. New York: John Wiley & Sons, Inc.

McCleary, R., and Hay, R.A. Jr. 1980. *Applied time series analysis for the social sciences.* Beverly Hills: Sage Publications.

Nelson, C.R. 1973. *Applied time series analysis for managerial forecasting.* San Francisco: Holden-Day, Inc.

Tukey, J.W. 1977. Exploratory data analysis. Reading: Addison-Wesley.

Vandaele, W. 1983. *Applied time series and Box-Jenkins models.* New York: Academic Press.

Velleman, P.F., and Hoaglin, D.C. 1981. *Applications, basics, and computing of exploratory data analysis.* Belmont: Duxbury Press.

Bibliography

Agresti, A. 1984. *Analysis of ordinal categorical data.* New York: Wiley-Interscience.

Akima, H. 1978. A method of bivariate interpolation and smooth surface fitting for irregularly distributed data points, *ACM Transactions on Mathematical Software,* 4: 148-159.

Anderberg, M.R. 1973. *Cluster analysis for applications.* New York: Academic Press.

Anderson, E. 1935. The irises of the Gaspe Peninsula, *Bulletin of the American Iris Society,* 59: 2-5.

Andrews, D.F. 1972. Plots of high-dimensional data, *Biometrics,* 28: 125-136.

Barnett, V., and Lewis, T. 1978. *Outliers in statistical data.* New York: John Wiley & Sons, Inc.

Beale, E.M.L., and Little, R.J.A. 1975. Missing values in multivariate analysis, *Journal of the Royal Statistical Society,* 37, Series B: 129-145.

Bebbington, A.C. 1975. A simple method of drawing a sample without replacement, *Applied Statistics,* 24: 136.

Bendel, R.B., and Afifi, A.A. 1977. Comparison of stopping rules in forward stepwise regression, *Journal of the American Statistical Association,* 72: 46-53.

Bennett, R.M., and Desmarais, R.N. 1976. Curve fitting of aeroelastic transient response data with exponential functions, *Flutter Testing Techniques.* Washington: NASA.

Berger, J.O. 1985. *Statistical decision theory and Bayesian analysis,* 2nd ed. New York: Springer-Verlag.

Bernhardson, C.S. 1975. Type I error rates when multiple comparison procedures follow a significant F test of ANOVA, *Biometrics,* 31: 229-232.

Bhat, M.V., and Haupt, A. 1976. An efficient clustering algorithm, *IEEE Transactions on Systems, Man, and Cybernetics*, 6: 61-64.

Bishop, Y.M.M., Fienberg, S.E., and Holland, P.W. 1975. *Discrete multivariate analysis: Theory and practice*. Cambridge, Mass.: MIT Press.

Borg, I. 1981. *Anwendungsorientierte multidimensionale skalierung*. Berlin: Springer-Verlag.

Box, G.E.P., and Cox, D.R. 1964. Analysis of transformations, *Journal of the Royal Statistical Society*, Series B, 26: 211- 252.

Box, G.E.P., and Muller, M.E. 1958. A note on the generation of random normal deviates, *Annals of Mathematical Statistics*, 29: 610-611.

Box, G.E.P., and Tiao, G.C. 1973. *Bayesian inference in statistical analysis*. Reading, Mass.: Addison-Wesley.

Brigham, E.O. 1974. *The fast Fourier transform*. New York: Prentice-Hall.

Brodlie, K.W. 1980. A review of methods for curve and function drawing, K.W. Brodlie, ed., *Mathematical Methods in Computer Graphics and Design*. London: Academic Press, Inc.

Brownlee, K.A. 1965. *Statistical theory and methodology in science and engineering*. New York: John Wiley & Sons, Inc.

Carmer, S.G., and Swanson, M.R. 1973. An evaluation of ten pairwise multiple comparison procedures by Monte Carlo methods, *Journal of the American Statistical Association*, 68: 66-74.

Chambers, J.M. 1977. *Computational methods for data analysis*. New York: John Wiley & Sons, Inc.

Chernoff, H. 1973. Using faces to represent points in k-dimensional space graphically, *Journal of the American Statistical Association*, 68: 361-368.

Chernoff, H., and Rizvi, M.H. 1975. Effect on classification error of random permutations of features in representing multivariate data by faces, *Journal of the American Statistical Association*, 70: 548-554.

Cleveland, W.S. 1981. LOWESS: A program for smoothing scatterplots by robust locally weighted regression, *The American Statistician*, 35: 54.

Cleveland, W.S. 1984. Graphical methods for data presentation: Full scale breaks, dot charts, and multi-based logging, *The American Statistician*, 38: 270-280.

Cleveland, W.S. and McGill, R. 1984. Graphical perception: theory, experimentation, and application to the development of graphical methods, *Journal of the American Statistical Association*, 79: 531-554.

Cleveland, W.S. and McGill, R. 1987. Graphical perception: The visual decoding of quantitative information on graphical displays of data. Unpublished paper. AT&T Bell Laboratories.

Cleveland, W.S., Harris, C.S., and McGill, R. 1982. Judgments of circle sizes on statistical maps, *Journal of the American Statistical Association*, 77: 541-547.

Cleveland, W.S., McGill, R., and McGill, M.E. 1988. The shape parameter of a two-variable graph, *Journal of the American Statistical Association*, in press.

Cook, R.D. 1977. Detection of influential observations in linear regression, *Technometrics*, 19: 15-18.

Cooley, J.W., and Tukey, J.W. 1965. An algorithm for the machine computation of complex Fourier series, *Mathematical Computation*, 19: 297-301.

Cormack, R.M. 1971. A review of classification, *Journal of the Royal Statistical Society*, Series A, 134: 321-367.

Croxton, F.E. and Struker, R.E. 1927. Bar charts versus circle diagrams, *Journal of the American Statistical Association*, 22: 473-482.

Dallal, G.E. and Wilkinson, L. 1986. An analytic approximation to the distribution of Lilliefor's test statistic for normality, *American Statistician*, 40: 294-296.

Daniel, C. 1959. The use of half-normal plots in interpreting factorial two level experiments, *Technometrics*, 1: 311-341.

Daniel, C., and Wood, F.S. 1971. *Fitting equations to data.* New York: John Wiley & Sons, Inc.

Dempster, A.P. 1969. *Elements of continuous multivariate analysis.* San Francisco: Addison-Wesley.

Dennis, J.E. Jr., and Schnabel, R.B. 1983. *Numerical methods for unconstrained optimization and nonlinear equations.* Englewood Cliffs, N.J.: Prentice-Hall, Inc.

Dixon, W.D. and Massey, F.J. Jr. 1969. *Introduction to statistical analysis,* 3rd. ed. New York: McGraw-Hill.

Eels, W.C. 1926. The relative merits of circles and bars for representing component parts, *Journal of the American Statistical Association,* 21: 119-132.

Einot, I., and Gabriel, K.R. 1975. A study of the powers of several methods of multiple comparisons, *Journal of the American Statistical Association,* 70: 574-583.

Everitt, B.S. 1980. *Cluster analysis,* 2nd ed. London: Heineman Education Books, Ltd.

Fienberg, S.E. 1979. Graphical methods in statistics, *The American Statistician,* 33: 165-177.

Fisher, R.A. 1922. On the mathematical foundations of theoretical statistics, *Philosophical Transactions of the Royal Society of London* (A), 222: 309-368.

Fletcher, R. 1972. *FORTRAN subroutines for minimization by quasi-Newton methods.* AERE R. 7125.

Freedman, D., Pisani, and Purves. 1980. *Statistics.* New York: W.W. Norton & Co.

Freni-Titulaer, L.W.J. and Louv, W.C. 1984. Comparisons of some graphical methods for exploratory multivariate data analysis, *The American Statistician,* 38: 184-188.

Gale, N. and Halperin, W.C. 1982. A case for better graphics: the unclassified choropleth map, *The American Statistician,* 36: 330-336.

Gentleman, W.M., and Sande, G. 1966. Fast Fourier transforms—for fun and profit. Fall Joint Computer Conference, *AFIPS Conference Proceedings,* 29: 563-578.

Giloh, H. and Sadat, J.W. 1982. Fluorescence microscopy: Reduced photobleaching of rhodamine and flourescein protein conjugates by n-propyl gallate, *Science,* 217: 1252-1255.

Grizzle, J.E., Starmer, C.F., and Koch, G.G. 1969. Analysis of categorical data by linear models, *Biometrics,* 25: 489-504.

Haberman, S.J. 1973. Log-linear fit for contingency tables: Algorithm AS 51, *Applied Statistics*, 21: 218-224.

Haberman, S.J. 1982. Analysis of dispersion of multinomial responses, *Journal of the American Statistical Association*, 77: 568-580.

Harris, J.E. 1987. Who should profit from cigarettes? *The New York Times*. Sunday, March 15, Section C: 3.

Hartigan, J.A., and Wong, M.A. 1979. A K-means clustering algorithm: Algorithm AS 136, *Applied Statistics*, 28: 126-130.

Hartigan, J.H. 1975b. *Clustering Algorithms*. New York: John Wiley & Sons, Inc.

Hershey, A.V. 1972. *A computer system for scientific typography*. Computer Graphics and Image Processing: 1, 373-385.

Hoaglin, D.C., Mosteller, F. and Tukey, J.W. 1983. *Understanding robust and exploratory data analysis*. New York: John Wiley & Sons, Inc.

Hubbard, R., and Allen, S.J. 1987. A cautionary note on the use of principal components analysis: Supportive empirical evidence, *Sociological Methods and Research,* 16: 301-308.

Huber, P.J. 1977. *Robust statistical procedures*. Philadelphia: SIAM.

Kritzer, H. 1979. Approaches to the analysis of complex contingency tables: A guide for the perplexed, *Sociological Methods and Research*, 7: 305-329.

Kruskal, W.H. 1982. Criteria for judging statistical graphics, *Utilitas Mathematica*, 21B: 283-310.

Launer, R.L., and Wilkinson, G.N. 1979. *Robustness in statistics*. New York: Academic Press.

Lenstra, J.K. 1974. Clustering a data array and the traveling salesman problem, *Operations Research*, 22: 413-414.

Lilliefors, H.W. 1967. On the Kolmogorov-Smirnov test for normality with mean and variance unknown, *Journal of the American Statistical Association*, 64: 399-402.

Lingoes, J.C. 1973. *The Guttman-Lingoes nonmetric program series*. Ann Arbor: Mathesis Press.

Lingoes, J.C., and Roskam, E.E. 1973. A mathematical and empirical study of two multidimensional scaling algorithms, *Psychometrika Monograph Supplement*, 19.

Long, L.H, ed. 1971. *The World Almanac and Book of Facts*. New York: Doubleday and Co., Inc.

Longley, J.W. 1967. An appraisal of least squares programs for the electronic computer from the point of view of the user, *Journal of the American Statistical Association*, 62: 819-831.

Lund, R.E., and Lund, J.R. 1983. Probabilities and upper quantiles for the studentized range, *Applied Statistics*, 32: 204-210.

Maindonald, J.H. 1984. *Statistical computation*. New York: John Wiley & Sons, Inc.

Marsaglia, G. 1961. Procedures for generating normal random variables, II, *Boeing Scientific Research Laboratories, Mathematical Note*, 243.

McCleary, R., and Hay, R.A., Jr. 1980. *Applied time series analysis for the social sciences*. Beverly Hills: Sage Publications.

McLeod, A.I., and Sales, P.R.H. 1983. An algorithm for approximate likelihood calculation of ARMA and seasonal ARMA models: Algorithm AS 191, *Applied Statistics*, 211-223.

Metzler, J., and Shepard, R.N. 1974. Transformational studies of the internal representation of three-dimensional objects, *Theories in cognitive psychology: The Loyola Symposium*, R. Solso, ed. Hillsdale, N.J.: Lawrence Erlbaum.

Michalske, T.A., and Bunker, B.C. 1987. The fracturing of glass, *Scientific American*, 257: 122-129.

Milliken, G.A., and Johnson, D.E. 1984. Analysis of messy data. *Designed Experiments*, Vol. 1. New York: Van Nostrand Reinhold Company.

Mosteller, F., and Tukey, J.W. 1977. *Data analysis and regression*. Reading, Mass.: Addison-Wesley, 1977.

Nelson, C.R. 1973. *Applied time series analysis for managerial forecasting*. San Francisco: Holden-Day, Inc.

Pomeranz, J. 1973. Exact cumulative distribution of the Kolmogorov-Smirnov statistic for small samples, *Collected Algorithms from CACM*. Algorithm 487.

Rosenbrock, H. 1960. An automatic method for finding the greatest or least value of a function, *Computer Journal*, 3: 175-184.

Roskam, E.E., and Lingoes, J.C. 1981. MINISSA. *Introduction to multidimensional scaling: Theory, methods, and applications*, S.S. Schiffman, M.L. Reynolds, and F.W. Young, eds. New York: Academic Press, 362-371.

Rudnick, J. and Gaspari, G. 1987. The shapes of random walks, *Science*, 237: 384-389.

Rummelhart, D.E. 1970. A multicomponent theory of the perception of briefly exposed visual displays, *Journal of Mathematical Psychology*, 7: 191-218.

Salsburg, D.S. 1985. The religion of statistics as practiced in medical journals, in *The American Statistician*, 39: 220-223.

SAS Institute Inc. *1986 SAS/GRAPH*. Cary, N.C.: SAS Institute Inc.

SAS Institute, Inc. 1982. *SAS user's guide: Statistics*. Cary, N.C.: SAS Institute Inc.

Scales, L.E. 1985. *Introduction to non-linear optimization*. London: MacMillan Publishers, Ltd.

Shepard, R.N. 1962. The analysis of proximities: Multidimensional scaling with an unknown distance function, *Psychometrika*, 27: 125-139.

Sibuya, M. 1962. On exponential and other random variable generators, *Annals of the Institute of Statistical Mathematics*, 13: 231-237.

Simon, A.L, ed. 1969. *Wines of the world*. New York: McGraw-Hill.

Slagel, J.R., Chang, C.L., and Heller, S.R. 1975. A clustering and data reorganizing algorithm, *IEEE Transactions on Systems, Man, and Cybernetics*, 5: 125-128.

Spicer, C.C. 1972. Calculation of power sums of deviations about the mean, *Applied Statistics*, 21: 226-227.

Svalastoga, K. 1959. *Prestige, class, and mobility*. London: Heineman Publishing.

Trumbo, B.E. 1981. A theory for coloring bivariate statistical maps, *The American Statistician*, 35: 220-226.

U.S. Bureau of the Census. 1986. *State and metropolitan area data book*. U.S. Government Printing Office.

Vandaele, W. 1983. *Applied time series and Box-Jenkins models.* New York: Academic Press.

Velicer, W.F. 1977. An empirical comparison of the similarity of principal component, image, and factor patterns, *Multivariate Behavioral Research,* 12: 3-22.

Velicer, W.F., Peacock, A.C., and Jackson, D.N. 1982. A comparison of component and factor patterns: A Monte Carlo approach, *Multivariate Behavioral Research,* 17: 371-388.

Wainer, H., and Francolini, C.M. 1980. An empirical inquiry concerning human understanding of two-variable color maps, *The American Statistician,* 34: 81-93.

Wainer, H., and Thissen, D. 1981. Graphical data analysis, *Annual Review of Psychology,* 32: 191-241.

Warner, B.G., Mathewes, R.W., and Clague, J.J. 1982. Ice-free conditions on the Queen Charlotte Islands, British Columbia, at the height of late Wisconsin glaciation, *Science,* 218: 675-677.

Weber, R. 1982. *EDP auditing: Conceptual foundations and practices.* New York: McGraw-Hill.

Wegman, E.J. 1986. Hyperdimensional data analysis using parallel coordinates, *George Mason University Center for Computational Statistics and Probability Technical Report,* No. 1.

Wichman, B.A., and Hill, I.D. 1982. An efficient and portable pseudo-random number generator: Algorithm AS 183, *Applied Statistics,* 311: 188-190.

Wilkinson, J.H., and Reinsch, C., eds. 1971. *Linear Algebra, Handbook for automatic computation,* vol. 2. New York: Springer Verlag.

Wilkinson, L. 1973. An assessment of the dimensionality of Moos' social climate scale, *American Journal of Community Psychology,* 1: 342-350.

Wilkinson, L. 1980. REGM: A multivariate general linear hypothesis program, *American Statistician,* 34: 182.

Wilkinson, L., and Dallal, G.E. 1977. Accuracy of sample moments calculations among widely used statistical programs, *The American Statistician,* 31: 128-131.

Index

Index

Index

Index

743

Index

Index

Index

Index

Index